The Sea Shanty Mandolin Tablature Songbook

A Collection of 52 Traditional Sea Songs & Shanties Arranged for Mandolin-Family Instruments Tuned To GDAE

Ben "Gitty" Baker

PUBLISHED BY HOBO MUSIC WORKS LLC · ROCHESTER, NEW HAMPSHIRE

Table of Contents

Table of Contents

Copyright Notice

About This Songbook

This is a collection of traditional songs of the sea: shanties, ballads and tunes either sung by sailors or about the sea, sailors and the sailing life. These songs come down from Ireland, Scotland, England and America, from the days when the huge sailing ships plied the oceans, carrying goods, hunting the whales and making war.

Arranged specifically for playing on mandolins, fiddles, Irish tenor banjos and related four-string instruments tuned to GDAE, these songs are chosen from amongst the older, well-known pieces that are assumed to be in the public domain... in other words, songs that have no active copyright.

For some works that have had many versions and arrangements over the years, some newer arrangements may still be copyrighted, and in such cases we have made every effort to present the oldest, most traditional and un-copyrighted form.

You Need an Instrument

To get started making music using this book, you will need a some form of stringed instrument tuned to GDAE. It can be a mandolin, or a 4-string tenor banjo, or a tenor guitar, Irish bouzouki, a fiddle or even a cigar box guitar. The choice is yours - any of these four-string instruments will work with the tablature in this book.

If you are adventurous, you might consider building your own instrument! There are free four-string cigar box guitar plans available over at **CigarBoxNation.com** and **CigarBoxGuitar.com**, which could be tuned to GDAE.

If you want to skip the building and get right to playing, you'll need to buy one built by someone else. There are a host of fairly inexpensive mandolins available in music stores and online, most of which would be fine for playing these songs. You may find that some of the more advanced Melody & Chords arrangements are easier to play on a longer-scale instrument.

Keys and Arrangements

All of the songs in this book are arranged in both the keys of C or G. These are the two most common keys for popular music, and also amongst the easiest to play and strum on the mandolin and other GDAE-tuned instruments.

For all of the songs in this book, multiple versions are presented, and you may wonder why this is. There are several reasons: vocal ranges, ease of playing, and playing skill practice.

- **Vocal Ranges** - different people are able to hit different ranges of notes when singing. A soprano can hit the highest notes, a bass singer can hit the low notes, and the rest of us usually fall somewhere in between. We have arranged all of these songs in two keys (C and G) because depending on the singer, one key may be easier than the other.

- **Ease of Playing** - you may find as you play your instrument more, that fingering the notes in one arrangement is easier for you than another. In this case, having the same song tabbed out in multiple keys is handy, since you can pick the one that feels best to you.
- **Playing Skill Practice** - playing the same song in multiple keys is good practice to help you become more familiar with your instrument. This is true both for picking out the notes that make up the melody of a song, and for strumming the chords. In time, you might begin to notice patterns. For example, if you look at a song tabbed out in both the key of C and the key of G, you will notice that every C chord in the former is replaced by a G chord in the latter. Likewise, every F is replaced by a C, every G is replaced by a D. This is not coincidence, and you'll see it hold true every time. The specific notes that make up the song also change following the same pattern. This changing of a song from one key to another is called transposing, and follows specific rules. How to transpose songs from one key to another could be the subject of a separate book. The more you play and practice and study, the more you may begin to get a feel for it.

How to Read & Play Tablature

Tablature (tab) is a visual method for showing you how to play songs on a stringed instrument. It is made up of horizontal lines, which represent the strings on the instrument you're playing. On these lines are placed numbers, which tell you what string to pluck, and which fret to push the string down on with your finger, to sound a particular note. When played in order with the right cadence and rhythm, these notes make up a song.

Tab also often includes letters to represent chords for rhythm playing, and words of the song as well. See the sample line of tab below.

Tablature is very powerful in this way, as it allows pretty much anyone to easily play the notes of a song. There is one thing though—you have to know "how the song goes" beforehand, to get the cadence and rhythm right. You can't really learn a new song entirely from tablature, since the tab doesn't tell you anything about rhythm or how long to hold each note. But if you already know the song, you're good to go!

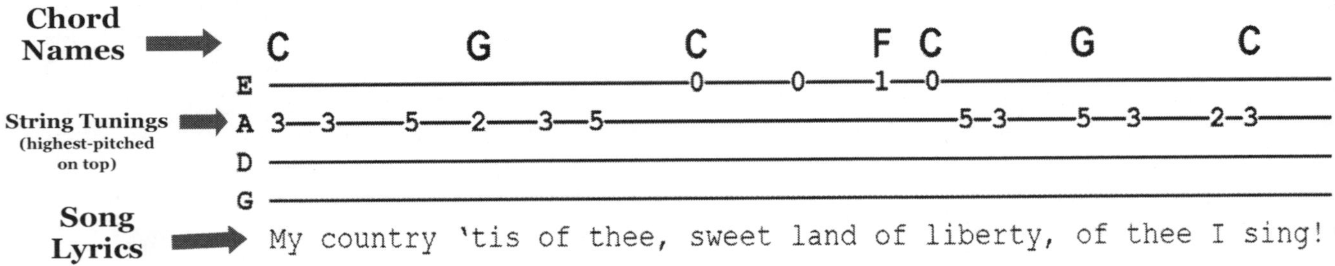

Take a look at the sample line of tab above. It is the first line from the old American patriotic song "My Country 'Tis of Thee".

The letters above the lines are chords that a rhythm player can strum along with the song. Underneath the lines are the lyrics/ words of the song.

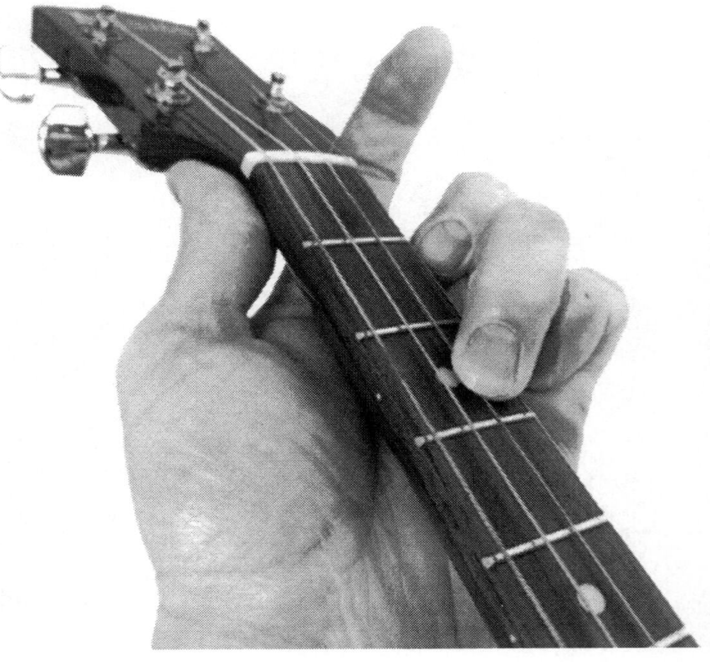

The four horizontal lines represent the strings of a 4-string GDAE-tuned instrument. The bold capital letters to the left of the lines show which string is which, and help you know what tuning the tablature is intended for.

It is important to realize that the top "E" line is the highest-pitched string on the instrument, which is actually on the bottom when you hold it in playing position. Why is this? Well, the quick answer is that it's just how tab (and standard musical notation) has always been done. Higher pitch means higher up on the lines. Conventional 6-string guitar tab is the same way. It can seem confusing, but it's just something you have to get used to.

So to walk our way through playing the first few notes from the line of tab on the previous page, you would do the following:

- Pluck the second string (A), using your middle or ring finger to fret it on the third fret, for the note corresponding to the word "My". You would use your middle finger on shorter-scale instruments like mandolins, and your ring finger for longer-scale instruments like tenor banjos and tenor guitars.
- Pluck the same note again for the first syllable of the word "country". You are playing a "C" note.
- Now use your ring or pinky finger to fret the same string (A) on the fifth fret for the second syllable of the word "country".
- Use your index/first finger to fret the A string at the second fret for "tis".
- Proceed in similar fashion until you hit the words "sweet" and "land". These notes requires you to pluck the high E string (the one all the way on the bottom when playing) open, or unfretted.
- Now fret that high E string on the first fret using your index/pointer finger, for the word "of," as shown in the photo above to the right.

You may have noticed that tablature also doesn't tell you what finger to use for fretting. For that matter, regular sheet music notation doesn't either. A general rule of thumb is: use the first (index) finger for frets one and two; the middle finger for fret three; the third (ring) finger for frets four and sometimes five, and the little finger (pinky) for frets five through seven. A lot of this comes down to what feels comfortable to you when playing. The scale length of your instrument also determines what reaches are feasible.

Some songs require you to move on up the neck a bit to hit the notes—almost always this is on the high E string. You can decide which fingers to use for these songs, whatever feels best to you, though usually the pinky is used. Only a few of the arrangements in this book go beyond the fifth fret, and only a couple go to the seventh and eighth.

More advanced "Melody & Chords" tablature arrangements will show multiple strings being plucked/fretted at the same time. These require you to use multiple fingers at a time to hit the notes, often using one finger to fret more than one string (known as barre-ing). Some of these arrangements require a good amount of skill and practice to master, but don't feel bad if you can't hit every note. The top note is almost always the melody line, and you can leave out one or more of the additional notes indicated beneath it as your playing level allows.

It will be up to you to figure out which fingers to use for fretting each string, but there are some general guidelines for how to make it easier.

Remember that any time you are strumming more than one string, you are actually playing a chord. For all of the Melody & Chords arrangements in this book, the additional notes I've added are based on the indicated chord for that portion of the song (or in some cases based on the next chord to come, as part of a transition). The chord forms included with each song will help give you an idea of what fingers to use.

In general, try to move your fingers as little as possible. Many times you can make a finger go from fretting one string at a particular location to fretting two (as a barre), without having to bring in another finger. This can be a big help in more complex arrangements.

Try to figure out ways to keep from moving your hand further up the neck when possible. Practice stretching that pinky out to hit higher notes on the high E string instead of moving your whole hand up.

There may be times when it makes sense to use a finger you wouldn't normally use to fret a particular string, based on the fingering that comes immediately after. Focus on figuring out what will allow the easiest and fastest transition between fingerings.

The numbers on the chord forms suggest what finger to use. 1 = Index, 2 = Middle, 3 = Ring, 4 = Pinky. A line connecting two circles with the same number indicates a barre.

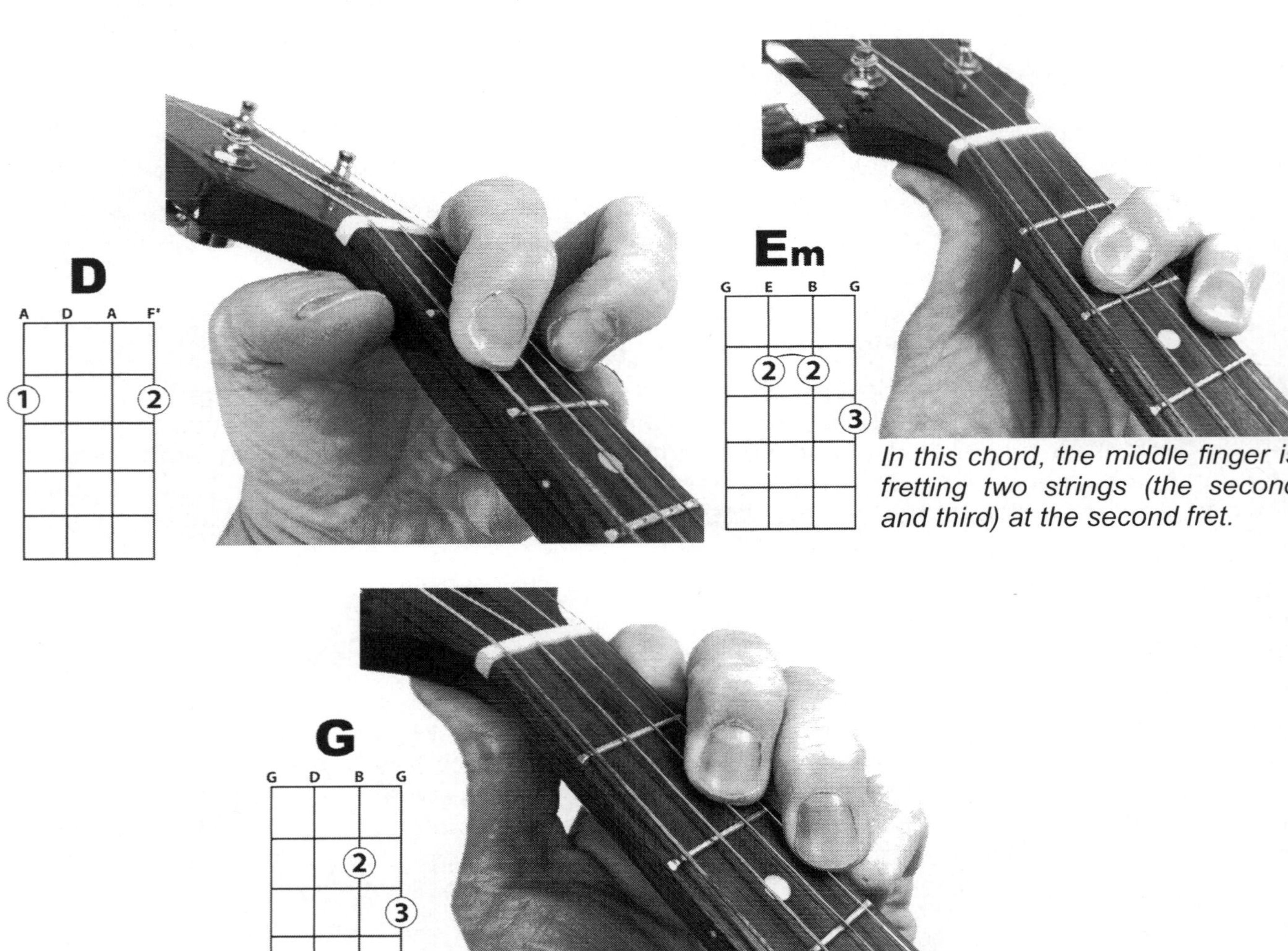

In this chord, the middle finger is fretting two strings (the second and third) at the second fret.

How to Play These Songs

Now that you hopefully have an idea of how to make sense of the tablature and chord forms, let's talk a little bit about how to play the songs in this book.

First, as mentioned above, the tablature doesn't tell you anything about how the song is "supposed to go" - in other words, it doesn't tell you anything about the rhythm. For that, you have to either already know the song, or find somewhere to listen to it. Fortunately this is easier than it's ever been, if you have any sort of Internet access... YouTube should have multiple versions, historic and modern, of pretty much every song in this book.

So that brings us to the first piece of advice for playing these songs: listen to a version or two on YouTube first. Try to find the more traditional/older versions if you can, rather than more modern remakes.

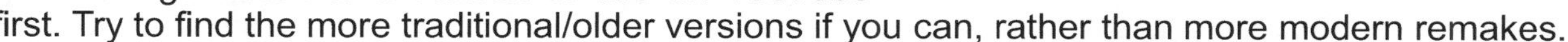

Once you have a good idea of how the song is supposed to go, then it's time to start playing it. There are three basic ways these songs can be played: pick the basic melody, strum the chords, or a combination of picking and strumming.

- **Picking the Melody** - this involves plucking the individual notes that make up the melody of the song, one at a time and in the right order, with the timing/rhythm that you have in your head based on how the song is supposed to go. This is the most basic and straightforward way to play a song, and is a good way to start when learning a new tune.
- **Strumming the Chords** - a lot of guitar players don't really worry too much about picking the melody itself, and instead focus on strumming the chord accompaniment. If you ever go to a jam session or campfire singalong, you are unlikely to see any players plucking out the notes of the melody while people sing. Rather, you'll see and hear them strumming the chords. This is sometimes called "playing rhythm", and covering how to do it could be the topic of at least a chapter if not an entire book. Getting the hang of "strumming along" to a song is a great skill to have.
- **Combination of Picking and Strumming** - the "Melody & Chords" arrangements in this book are an attempt to get you started with this method. If you look closely at songs where We give both "Basic Melody" and "Melody & Chords" arrangements, you will notice the latter ones usually just have one or two extra strings/notes added under the basic melody line. Plucking these extra strings helps "fill out" the sound and makes for a more complete performance. This form of playing can be further expanded as you progress rhythmically, to create a sort of hybrid strum/note-picking method. ***One thing to be aware of is that hitting every one of these notes perfectly can be tricky, especially on a mandolin where the frets and strings are so close together. Don't get frustrated if you can't play them exactly as shown - just use them as a suggestion of how you can strum some additional strings when playing to fill out the sound.***

There is one important thing to remember as you dive into this: if you're having fun, you are doing it right. Getting good at playing takes time and practice, and you have to be patient with yourself. It doesn't have to be perfect... you don't have to sound like Bill Monroe or David Grisman or Johnny Cash - you just need to sound like you. So take it easy, relax and have fun. Play the songs you know and like, and ignore the ones you don't. The only rules are the ones you set for yourself!

Mandolin / GDAE Chords

The following chord forms are some of the most commonly used for the GDAE tuning found on mandolins, Irish tenor banjos and other related instruments. Multiple versions of some of the chords are given—when playing a song, some fingerings of chords just seem to fit better sound-wise than others.

Also, a chord that is easily playable on a short-scale mandolin might be too hard to reach on a long-scale tenor guitar... and a chord that is comfortable on a longer-scale instrument might be too “tight” to be effective on a mandolin. For example, if you look at the first and second "F" chords shown on the next page, the first one is generally easier to play on a mandolin, and the second one (with or without the low G string fretted) is easier on longer-scale instruments.

You are free to use whatever versions you want, based on what sounds best to you -- and what your fingers can reach. If you are having trouble making a transition between two chords, practice making the change over and over. You don’t have to even strum, just practice getting your fingers to move back and forth between the two forms.

This develops “muscle memory” and will make it much easier to learn and play songs. Feel free to substitute one chord form for another in any song, if it is easier for you to play.

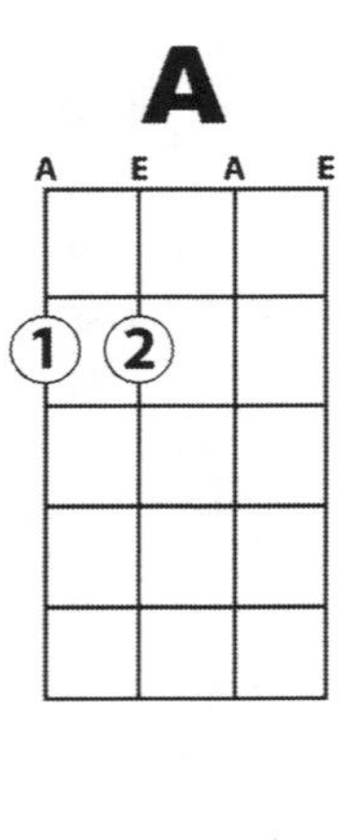

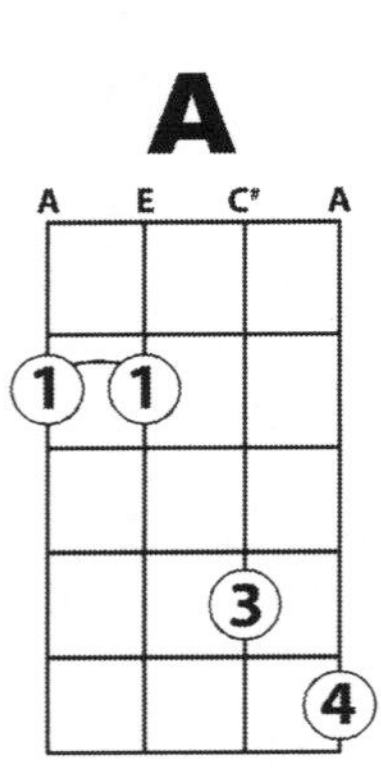

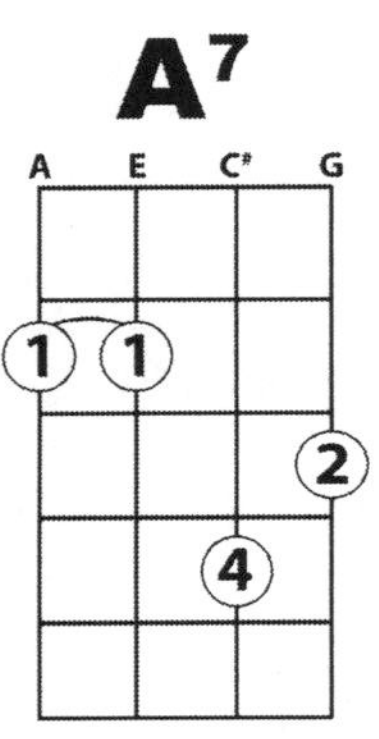

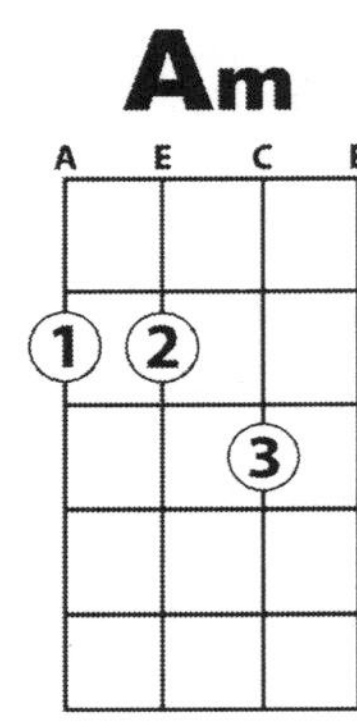

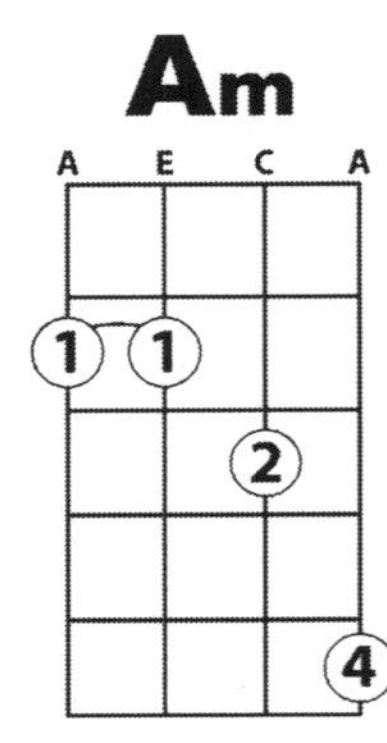

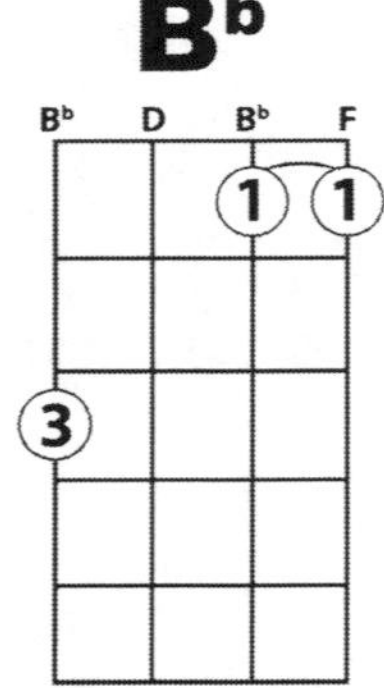

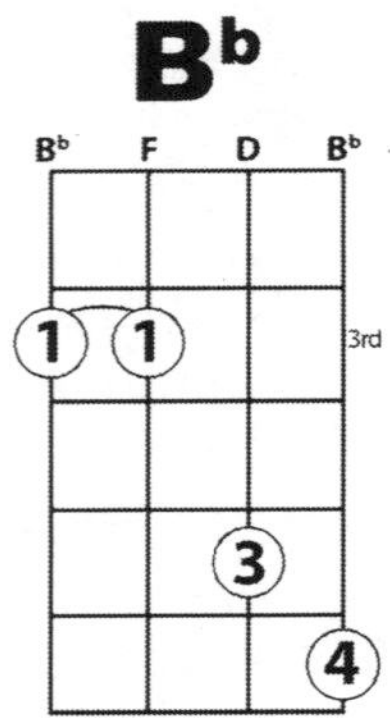

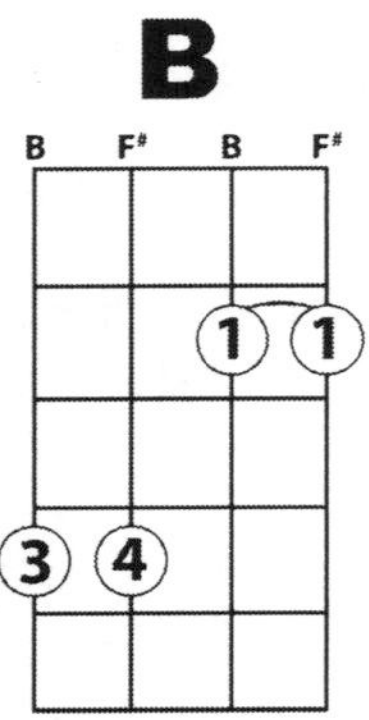

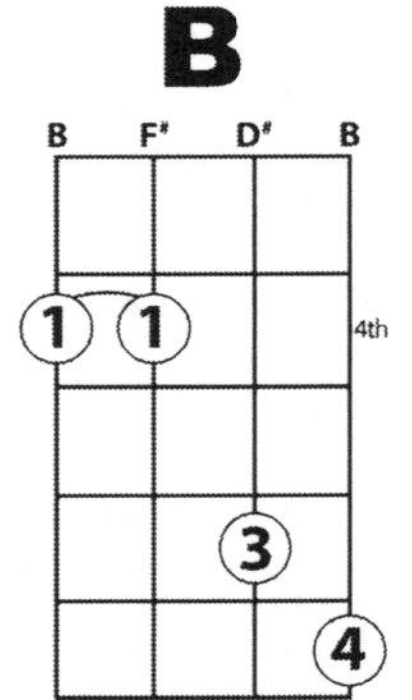

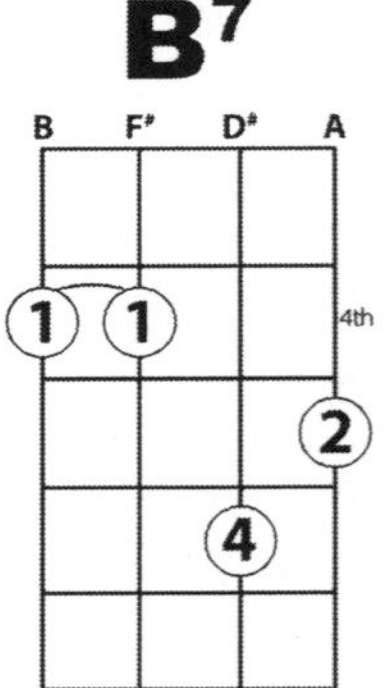

Mandolin / GDAE Chords (continued)

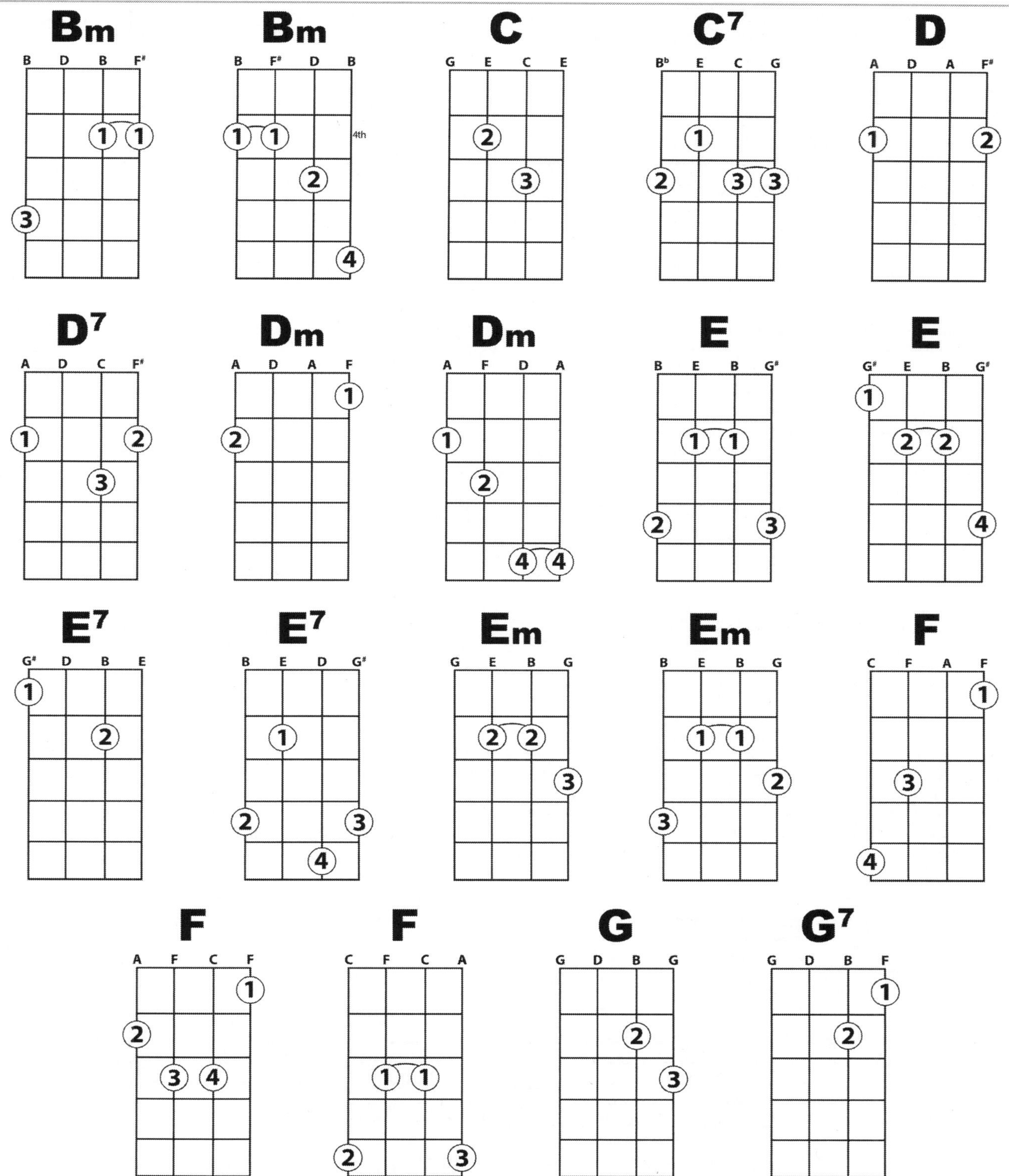

All For Me Grog

Basic Melody
Key of C (Low)

Words and Music
Traditional

This rollicking old drinking song tells the tale of a sailor who has sold all his possessions to buy booze. It has been recorded by most of the well-known Irish bands and singers over the years, including The Dubliners and The Clancy Brothers & Tommy Makem.

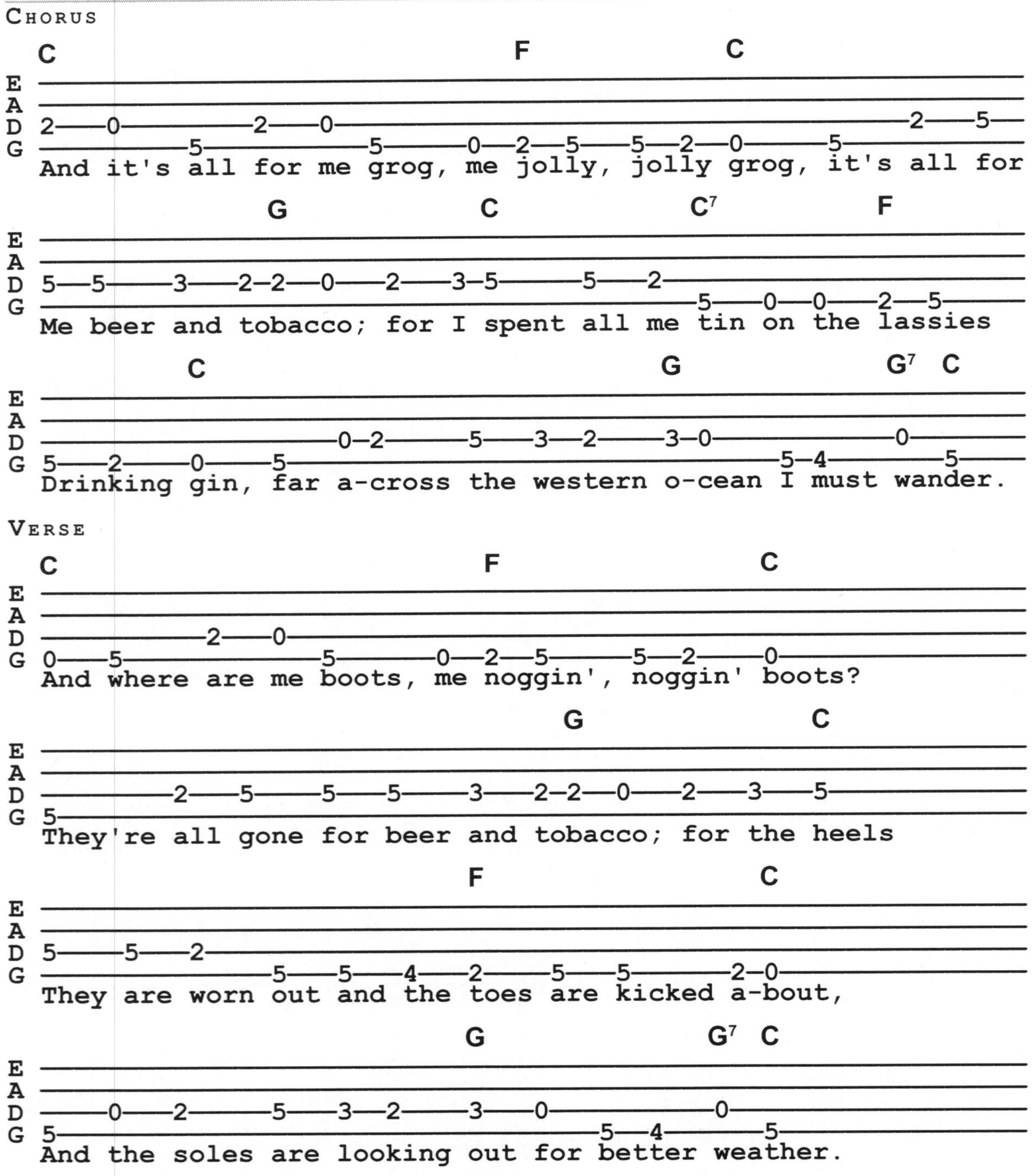

See Chord Forms and Additional Verses on Next Page

All For Me Grog (continued)

Chord Forms and Additional Verses

Chord Forms

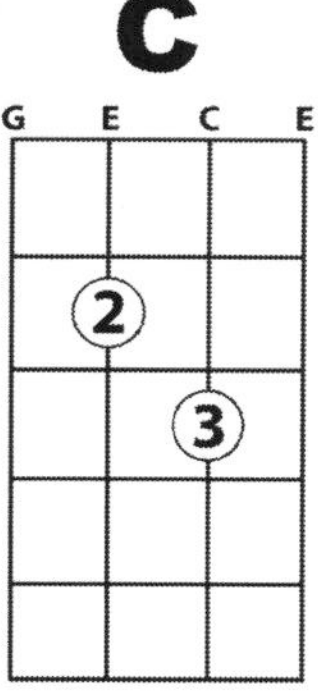

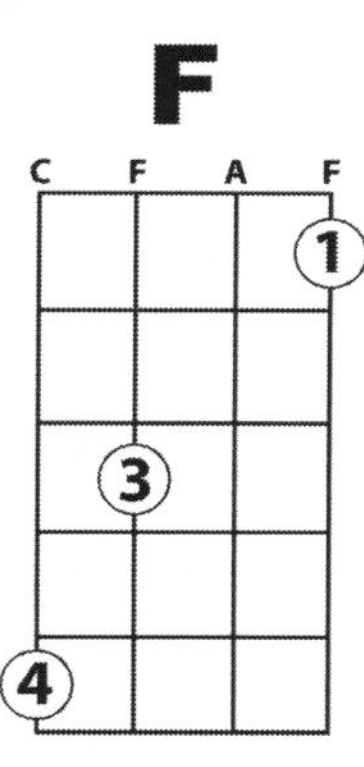

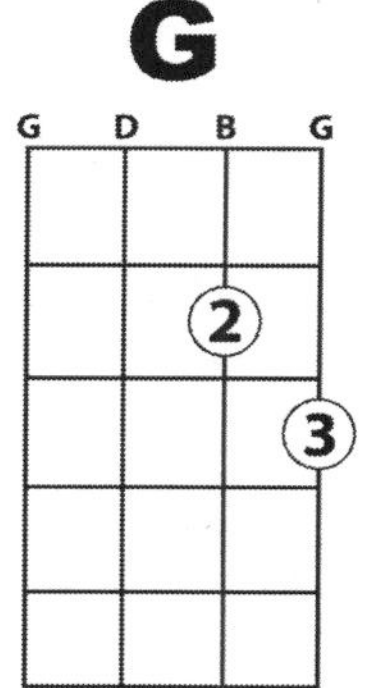

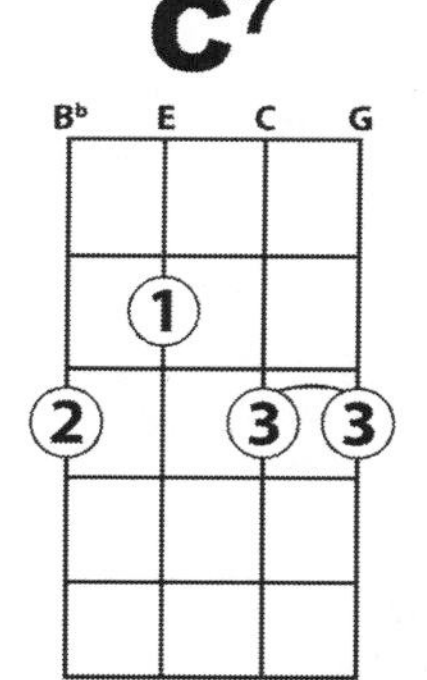

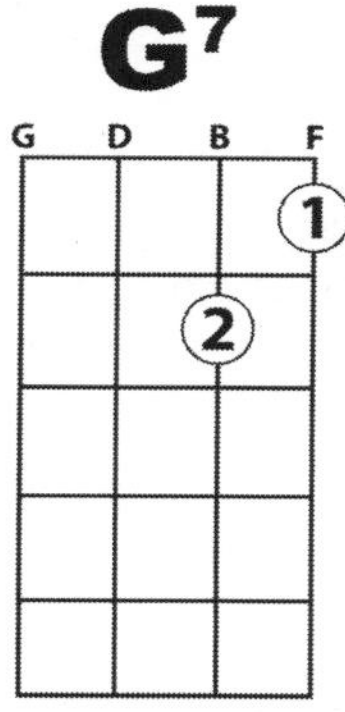

Additional Verses

Where is me shirt, me noggin', noggin' shirt?
It's all gone for beer and tobacco,
For the collar is all worn, and the sleeves they are all torn,
And the tails are looking out for better weather.

Now where is me bed, me noggin', noggin bed?
It's all gone for beer and tobacco;
For the sheets they were all worn,
And the mattress got all torn,
And the springs they're lookin' out for better weather!

I'm sick in the head and I haven't been to bed,
Since I came ashore with me plunder.
I've seen centipedes and snakes,
And I'm full of pains and aches,
And I think I'll make a path for way out yonder.

All For Me Grog (continued)

Basic Melody
Key of C (High)

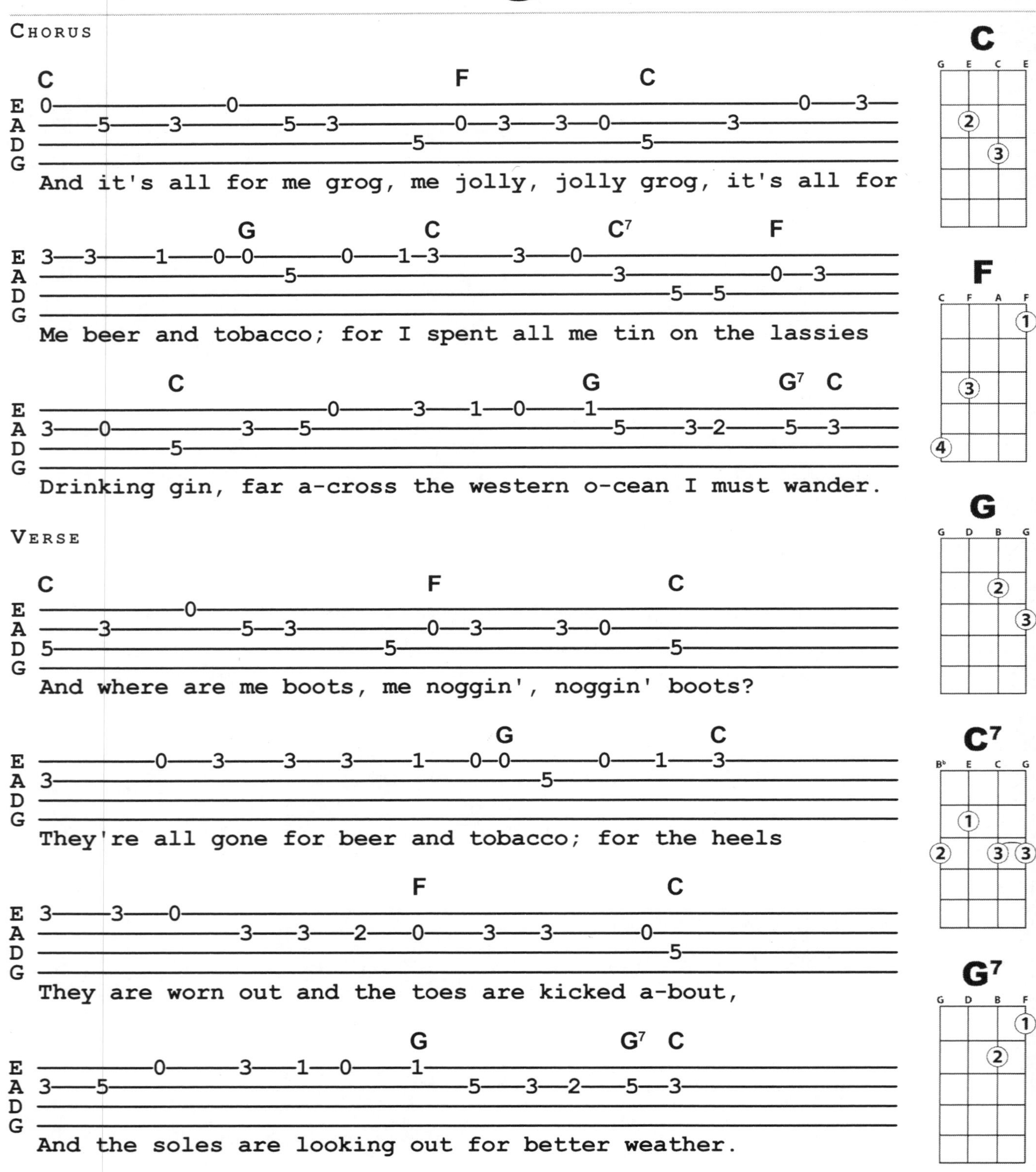

All For Me Grog (continued)

Melody & Chords
Key of C (High)

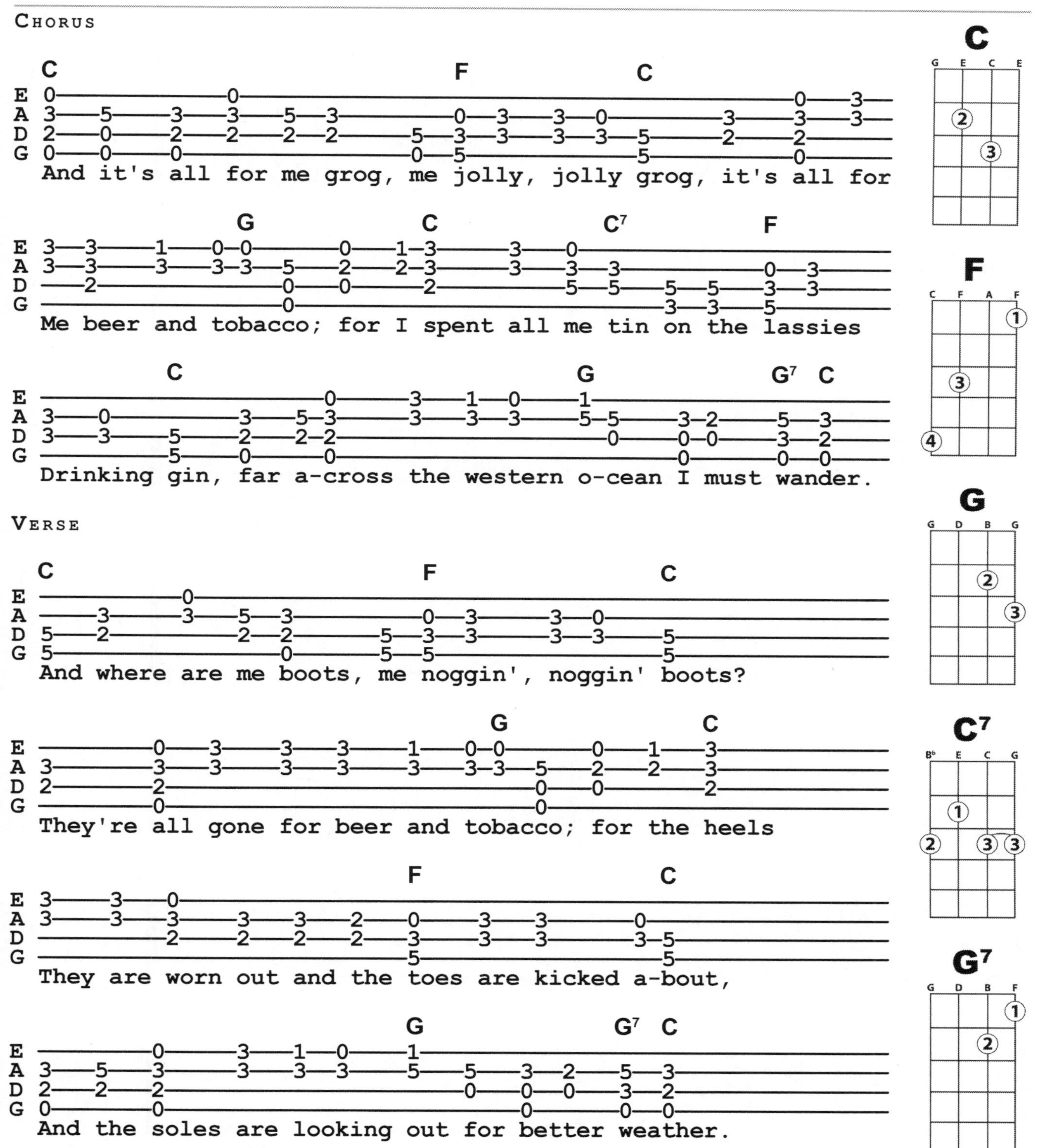

All For Me Grog (continued)

Basic Melody
Key of G

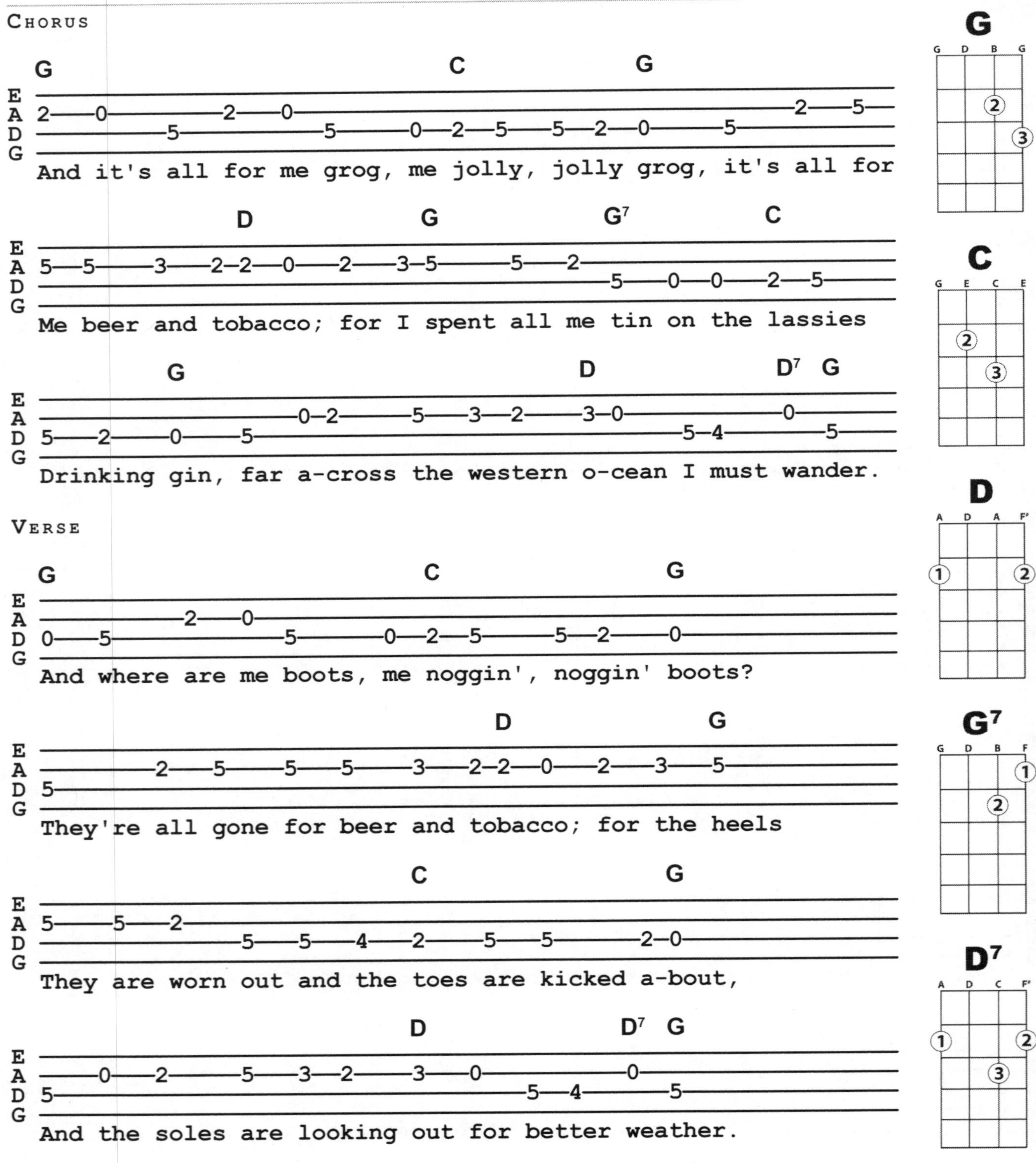

All For Me Grog (continued)

Melody & Chords

Key of G

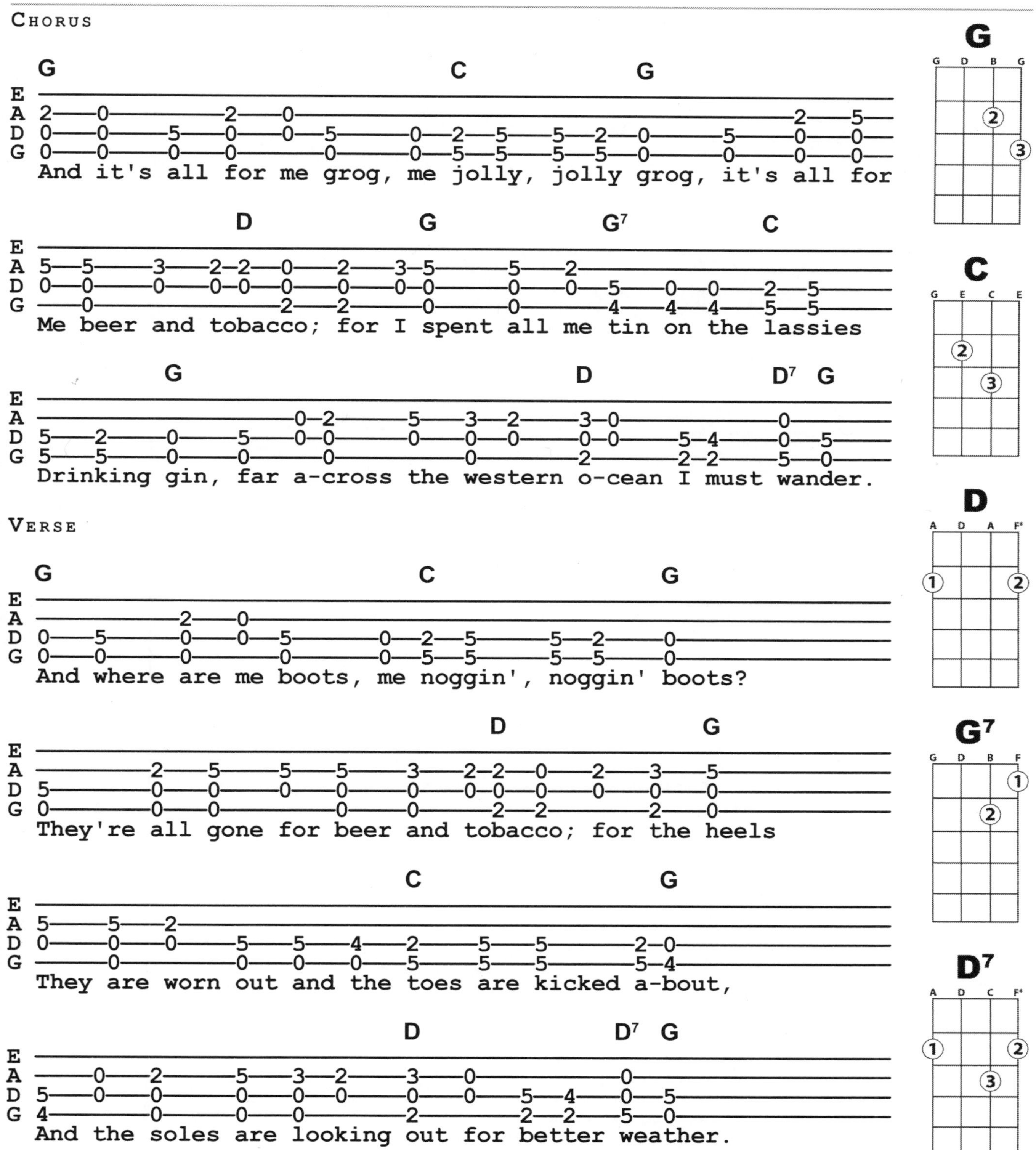

Anchors Aweigh

Basic Melody

Key of C

This well-known song serves as the fight song of the U. S. Naval Academy, as well as the march song of the U. S. Navy. The name of this song is often mistakenly written as "Anchors Away" which implies dropping a ship's anchor; actually, "Anchors Aweigh" refers to bringing the anchor in, which allows the ship to officially get under way.

Music by Charles Zimmermann

Lyrics by Alfred Hart Miles

```
   C           Am               C G       C
E --------------------------------------------------------
A ------------0---------0----3-5-------3-----------------
D --2-----5--------2----------------5--------------------
G 5------------------------------------------------------
  Anchors a-weigh, my boys, anchors a-weigh!

       F      C  F    G      Dm      D       G
E --------------------------------------------------------
A 0---3----0------0----2----3-------0--5-----3--2---------
D --------------5-------------------3-------------5--3--0-
G --------------------------------------------------------
  Farewell to college joys we sail at break of day-ay-ay-ay.

   C                 Am              C     G     C
E --------------------------------------------------------
A -------------------0--------0-----3------5-----3--------
D -------2---5---------------2-------------------5--------
G 5------------------------------------------------------
  Through our last night on shore, drink to the foam...

   F       C    F    G   Am    C                G           C
E -----------------------------0------------------------------
A 0--3--0-----------0---2---3---------------------5-----------3--
D -----------5-------------------------5---5---5-----5--5--5-----
G --------------------------------------------------------------
  Until we meet once more here's wishing you a happy voyage home!
```

Chord Forms

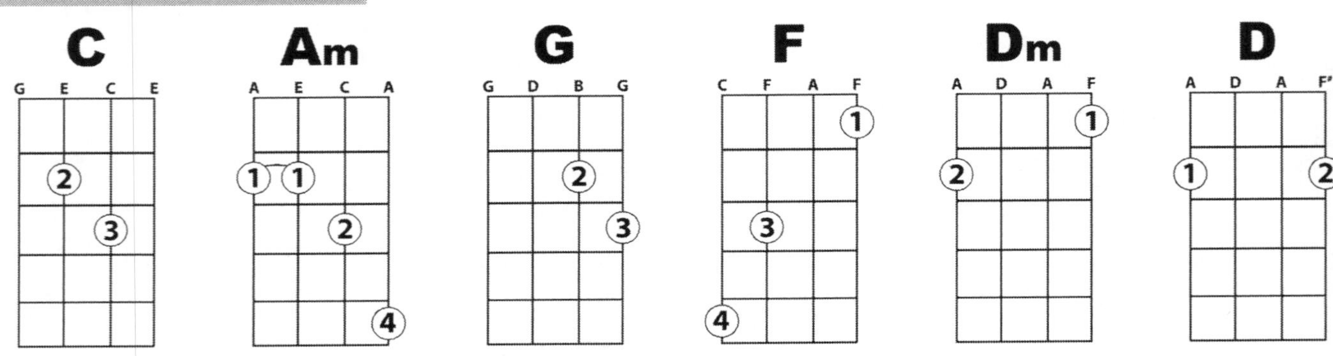

See Additional Verses on Next Page

Anchors Aweigh (continued)

Melody & Chords
Key of C

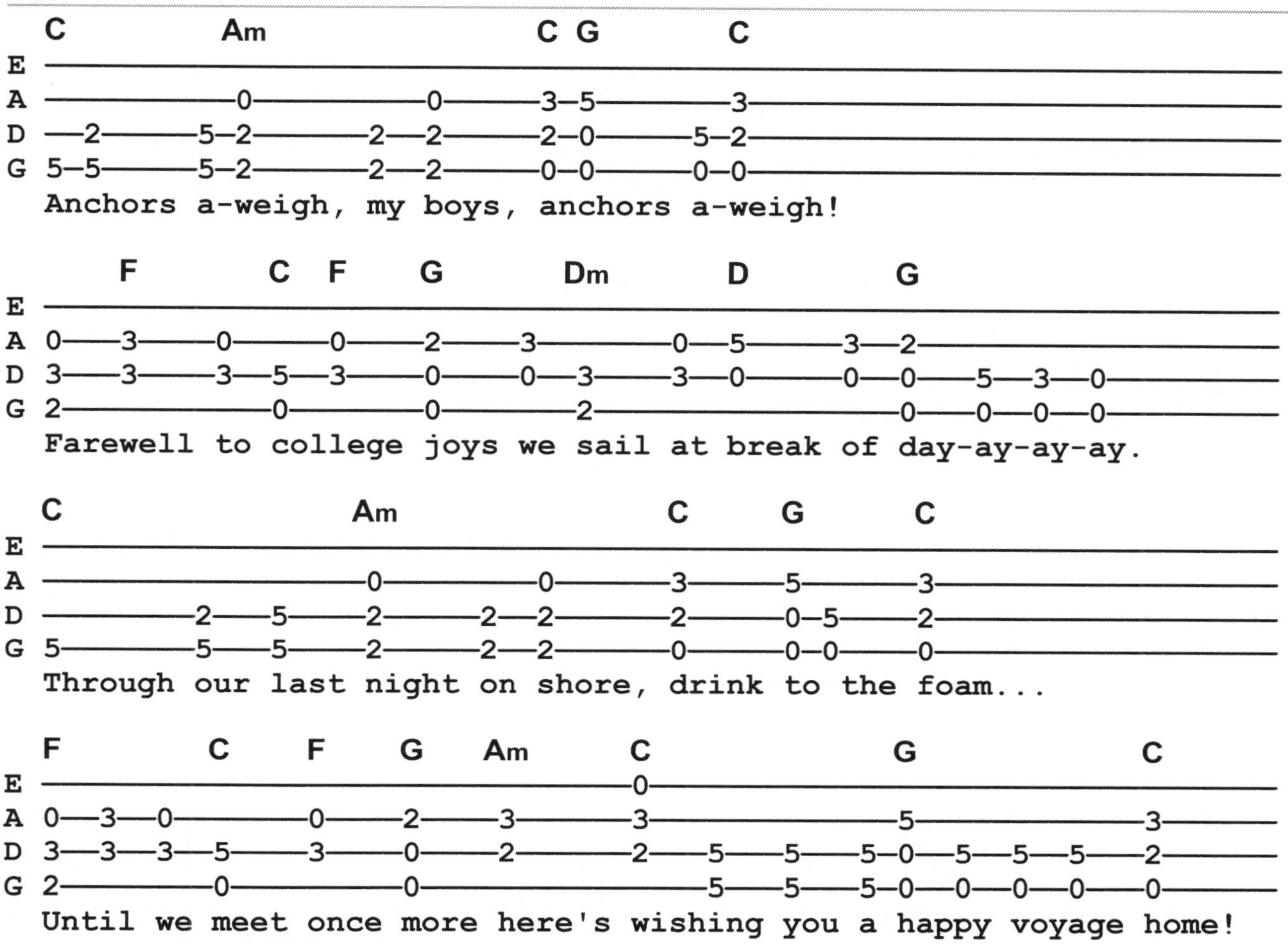

```
  C        Am                  C G        C
E ─────────────────────────────────────────────────────────────
A ──────────0─────────0─────3─5─────────3─────────────────────
D ─2──────5─2───────2──2────2─0──────5─2──────────────────────
G 5─5─────5─2───────2──2────0─0──────0─0──────────────────────
  Anchors a-weigh, my boys, anchors a-weigh!
```

```
     F        C  F    G      Dm      D       G
E ──────────────────────────────────────────────────────────────
A 0──3───0─────0───2────3────────0──5─────3──2──────────────────
D 3──3───3──5──3───0────0──3─────3──0─────0──0────5──3──0───────
G 2────────────0───0───────2─────────────────0────0──0──0───────
  Farewell to college joys we sail at break of day-ay-ay-ay.
```

```
  C                 Am              C     G      C
E ──────────────────────────────────────────────────────────────
A ──────────────────0───────0───────3─────5──────3──────────────
D ─────────2───5────2─────2──2──────2─────0──5───2──────────────
G 5────────5───5────2─────2──2──────0─────0──0───0──────────────
  Through our last night on shore, drink to the foam...
```

```
  F       C    F    G    Am     C                G           C
E ──────────────────────────────0───────────────────────────────
A 0──3──0──────0────2────3──────3────────────────5───────────3──
D 3──3──3──5───3────0────2──────2───5───5───5─0──5──5──5─────2──
G 2────────0────────0───────────────5───5───5─0──0──0──0─────0──
  Until we meet once more here's wishing you a happy voyage home!
```

Additional Verses

Blue of the mighty deep, gold of God's sun;
Let these colors be till all of time be done, done, done.
By Severn's shore we learn Navy's stern call:
Faith, courage, service true, with honor, over honor, over all.

Stand Navy down the field, sails set to the sky;
We'll never change our course, so Army you steer shy-y-y-y.
Roll up the score, Navy, anchors aweigh!
Sail Navy down the field, and sink the Army, sink the Army gray!

Get underway Navy, decks cleared for the fray;
We'll hoist true Navy blue, so Army down your gray-y-y-y;
Full speed ahead, Navy; Army heave to;
Furl black and gray and gold, and hoist the Navy, hoist the Navy blue!

See Chord Forms on Previous Page

Anchors Aweigh (continued)

Basic Melody
Key of G (Low)

```
  G             Em                    G D         G
E ------------------------------------------------------------
A -----------------------------------0------------------------
D ---------0-2----------2------5----------0-5-----------------
G 0-4-------------4-------------------------------------------
  Anchors a-weigh, my boys, anchors a-weigh!
```

```
    C       G  C    D     Am      A         D
E ------------------------------------------------------------
A -----------------------------------0------------------------
D 2--5---2--0--2---4---5-------2-----------5--4---0-----------
G ----------------------------5---------------------5--2------
  Farewell to college joys we sail at break of day-ay-ay-ay.
```

```
  G                Em                  G      D      G
E ------------------------------------------------------------
A ------------------------------------------0-----------------
D -------------0----2-------2-----5--------------0---5--------
G 0-------4-------------4-------------------------------------
  Through our last night on shore, drink to the foam...
```

```
  C       G    C    D   Em     G             D             G
E ------------------------------------------------------------
A ---------------------------2--------------0-----------------
D 2--5--2--0----2----4----5-------0---0---0------0--0--0---5--
G ------------------------------------------------------------
  Until we meet once more here's wishing you a happy voyage home!
```

Chord Forms

G

G D B G

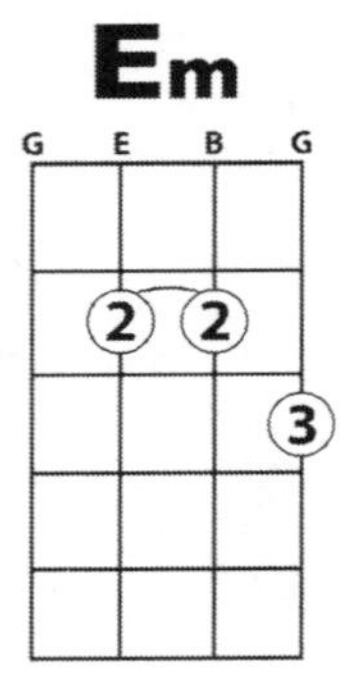

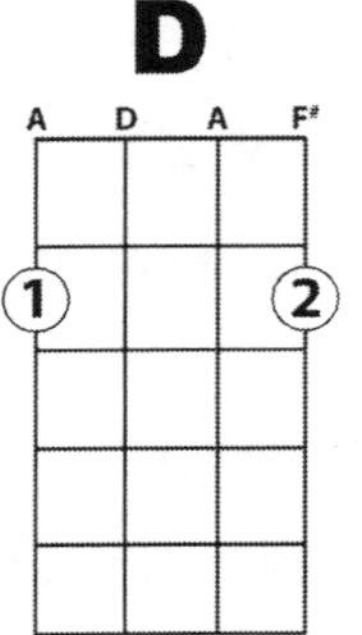

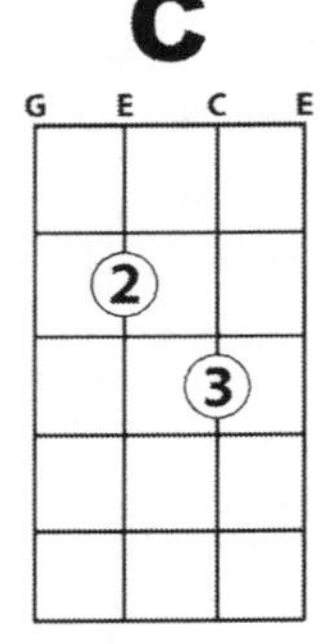

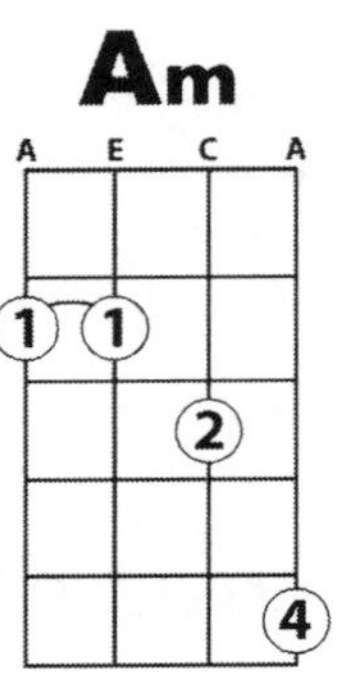

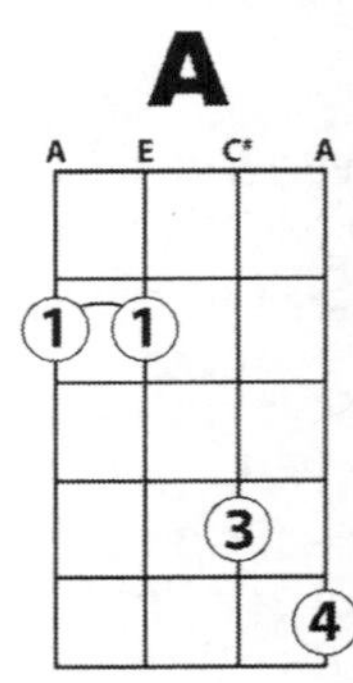

Anchors Aweigh (continued)

Melody & Chords
Key of G (Low)

```
    G          Em                      G D       G
E ----------------------------------------------------------------------
A ---------------------------------------0-------------------------------
D ---------0-2---------------2------5-0------0-5-------------------------
G 0-4------0-0---------4-4--------0-2------2-0---------------------------
  Anchors a-weigh, my boys, anchors a-weigh!
```

```
      C        G  C    D      Am      A          D
E ----------------------------------------------------------------------
A ------------------------------------0----------------------------------
D 2--5---2--0--2----4----5--------2--2-------5--4--0---------------------
G 0--5---5--0--0----2----2--5-----2--2-------2--2--2--5--2---------------
  Farewell to college joys we sail at break of day-ay-ay-ay.
```

```
  G               Em                G       D       G
E ----------------------------------------------------------------------
A -----------------------------------------0----------------------------
D ---------------0----2--------2-----5-----0--0--5----------------------
G 0--------4-----0----0-----4--4-----0-----2--2--0----------------------
  Through our last night on shore, drink to the foam...
```

```
  C       G    C    D    Em      G             D             G
E ----------------------------------------------------------------------
A ------------------------------2-------------0--------------------------
D 2--5--2--0----2----4----5-----0---0---0---0-0--0--0--0---5------------
G 5--5--5--0----0----2----4-----0---0---0---0-2--2--2--2---0------------
  Until we meet once more here's wishing you a happy voyage home!
```

Chord Forms

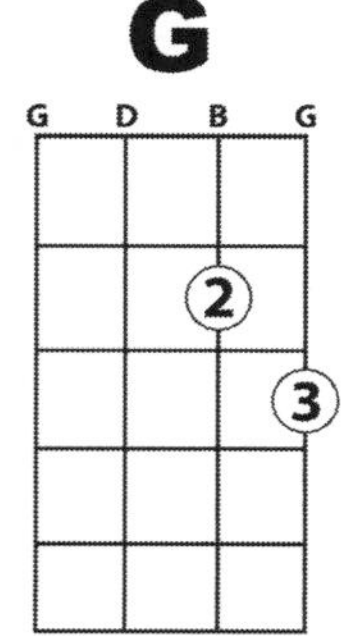

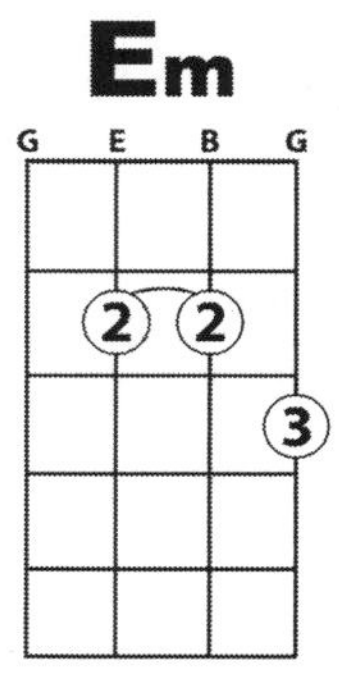

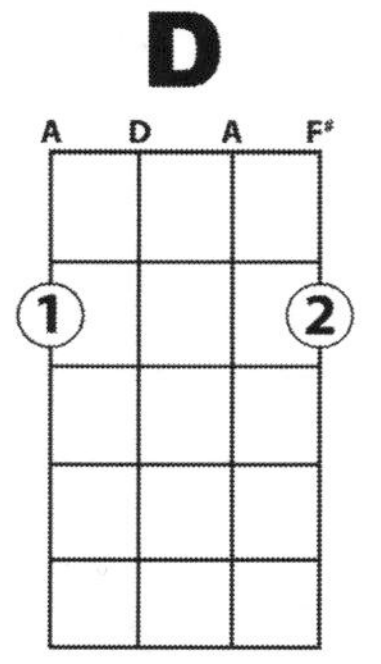

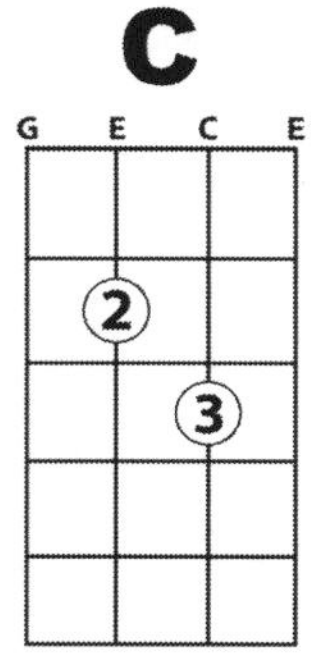

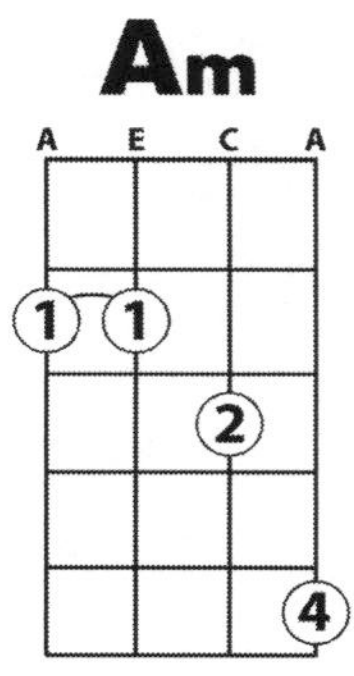

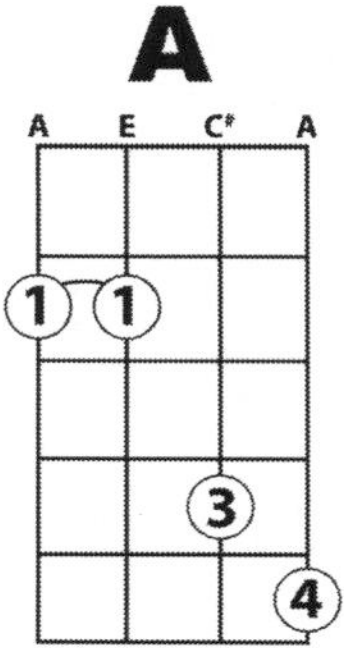

Anchors Aweigh (continued)

Basic Melody
Key of G (High)

```
   G            Em                    G D        G
E ──────────────0───────────0────────3─5─────────3──────────────────────────────
A ─2──────5──────────2───────────────────────5──────────────────────────────────
D 5─────────────────────────────────────────────────────────────────────────────
G ──────────────────────────────────────────────────────────────────────────────
  Anchors a-weigh, my boys, anchors a-weigh!

       C        G  C    D       Am       A        D
E 0────3─────0──────0────2────3──────────0──5───────3──2─────────────────────────
A ──────────────5───────────────────3─────────────────────────5──3──0────────────
D ───────────────────────────────────────────────────────────────────────────────
G ───────────────────────────────────────────────────────────────────────────────
  Farewell to college joys we sail at break of day-ay-ay-ay.

  G                    Em                 G      D      G
E ─────────────────────0─────────0────────3──────5──────3───────────────────────
A ──────────2──5──────────────2───────────────────────5─────────────────────────
D 5─────────────────────────────────────────────────────────────────────────────
G ──────────────────────────────────────────────────────────────────────────────
  Through our last night on shore, drink to the foam...

  C         G     C     D     Em      G              D              G
E 0──3──0─────────0─────2─────3───────7──────────────5──────────────3───────────
A ──────────5────────────────────────────5───5───5────5───5───5─────────────────
D ──────────────────────────────────────────────────────────────────────────────
G ──────────────────────────────────────────────────────────────────────────────
  Until we meet once more here's wishing you a happy voyage home!
```

Chord Forms

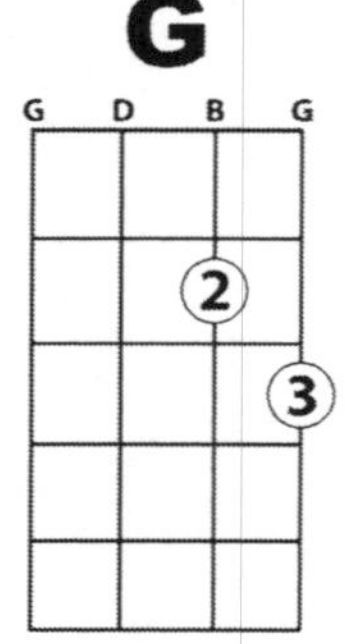

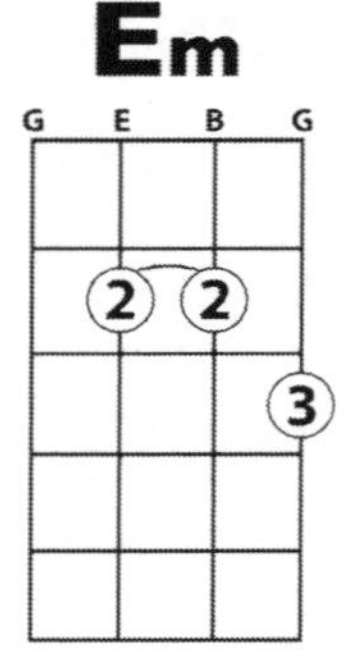

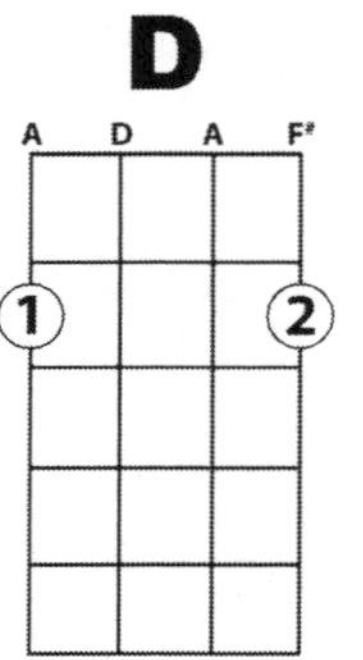

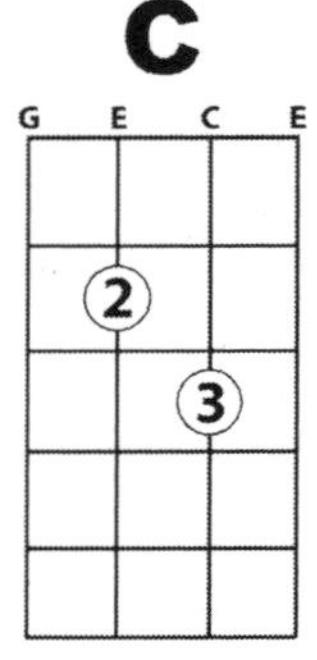

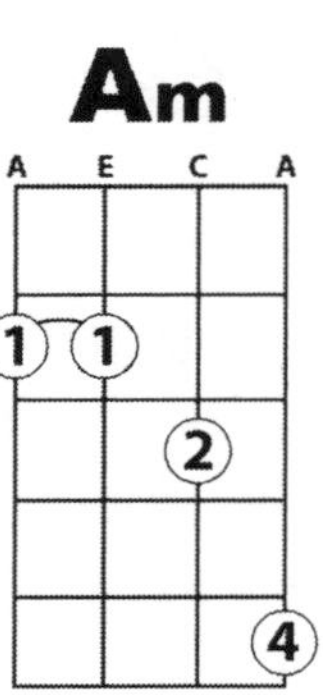

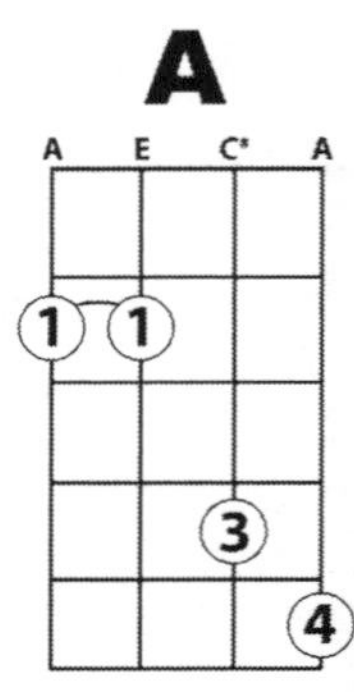

Anchors Aweigh (continued)

Melody & Chords
Key of G (High)

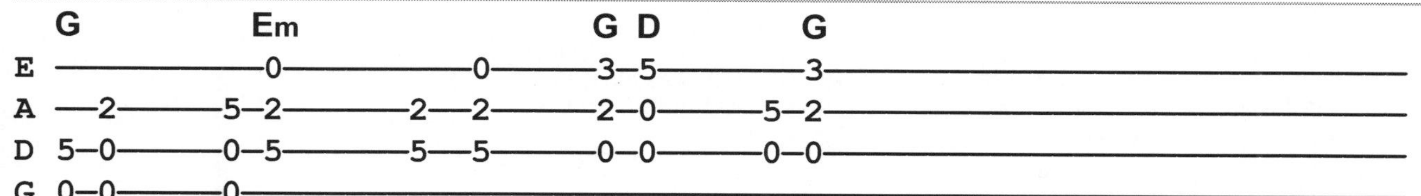

Anchors a-weigh, my boys, anchors a-weigh!

```
     C          G  C    D      Am      A        D
E 0——3——0———————0———2———3———————0—5——————3—2————————————————
A 2——3——3—5—3———0———0—3—————————3—4——————4—0——5—3—0————————
D 5——2——————0—2—0———————2———————————2——————2—0——0—0—0———————
G ——————————0———————————2———————————————————2——2—2—2————————
```

Farewell to college joys we sail at break of day-ay-ay-ay.

```
   G                Em           G      D       G
E ——————————————————0————————0———3——————5———————3———————————
A ————————2——5——————2————2—2—————2——————0—5—————2———————————
D 5———————0——0——————5————5—5—————0——————0—0—————0———————————
G 0———————0——0———————————————————0——————————————0———————————
```

Through our last night on shore, drink to the foam...

```
  C        G    C    D    Em      G            D            G
E 0—3—0—————————0————2————3———————7————————————5————————————3———
A 3—3—3—5———————3————0————2———————5——5——5——5—0——5——5——5——2———
D 2—————2—0——————————0————2———————5——5——5——5—0——0——0——0——0———
G —————————0————————————————————————————————————————————————0———
```

Until we meet once more here's wishing you a happy voyage home!

Chord Forms

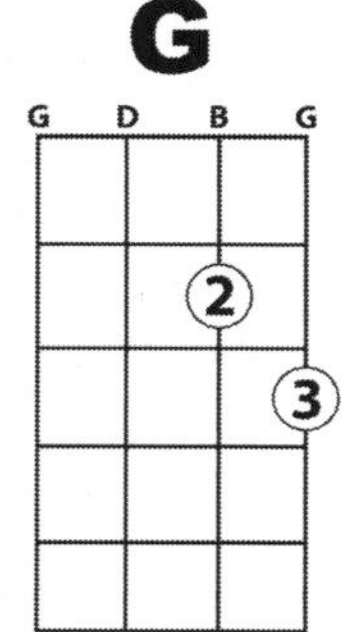

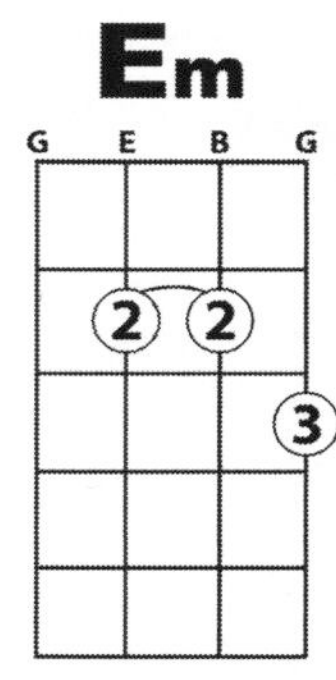

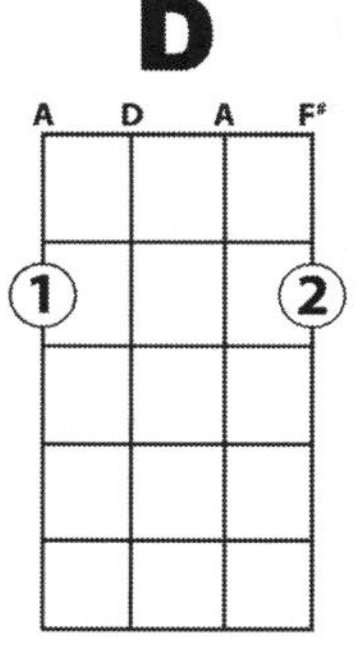

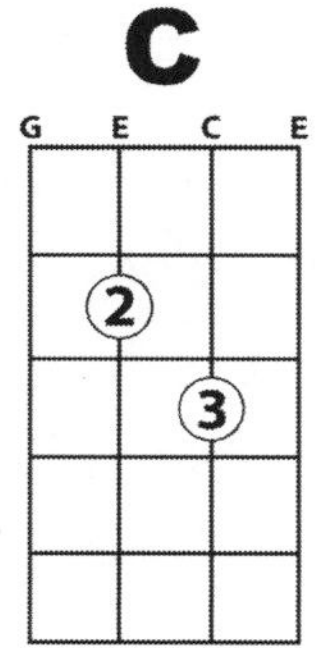

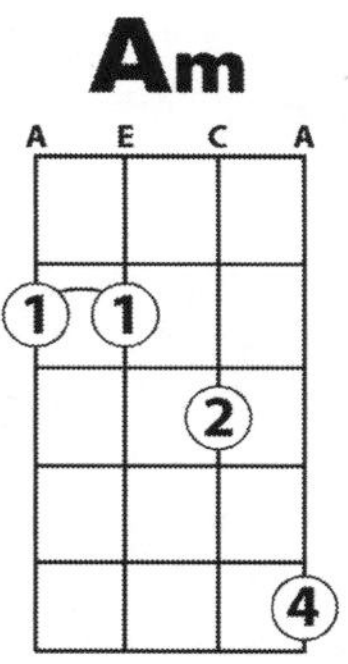

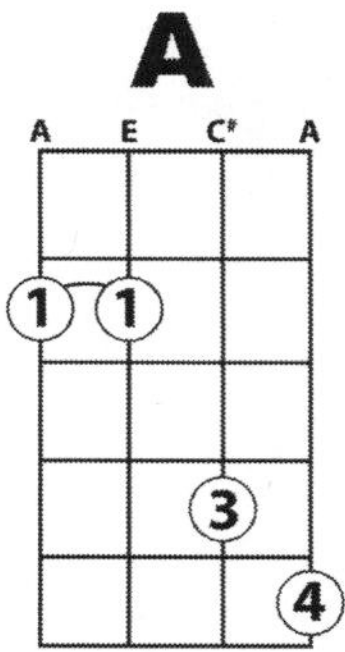

Aweigh Santy Anno

Basic Melody

Key of A Minor (Low)

Words and Music

Traditional

The exact origins of this old sea shanty are uncertain, and many versions of the verses have been sung (and recorded) over the years. It is thought to have originated in the mid 1800's around the time of the fighting between the United States and Mexico, with the Mexican general Antonio Lopez de Santa Anna being the namesake of the song. It has been recorded by many folk singers, including many Irish and Celtic groups such as the Clancy Brothers.

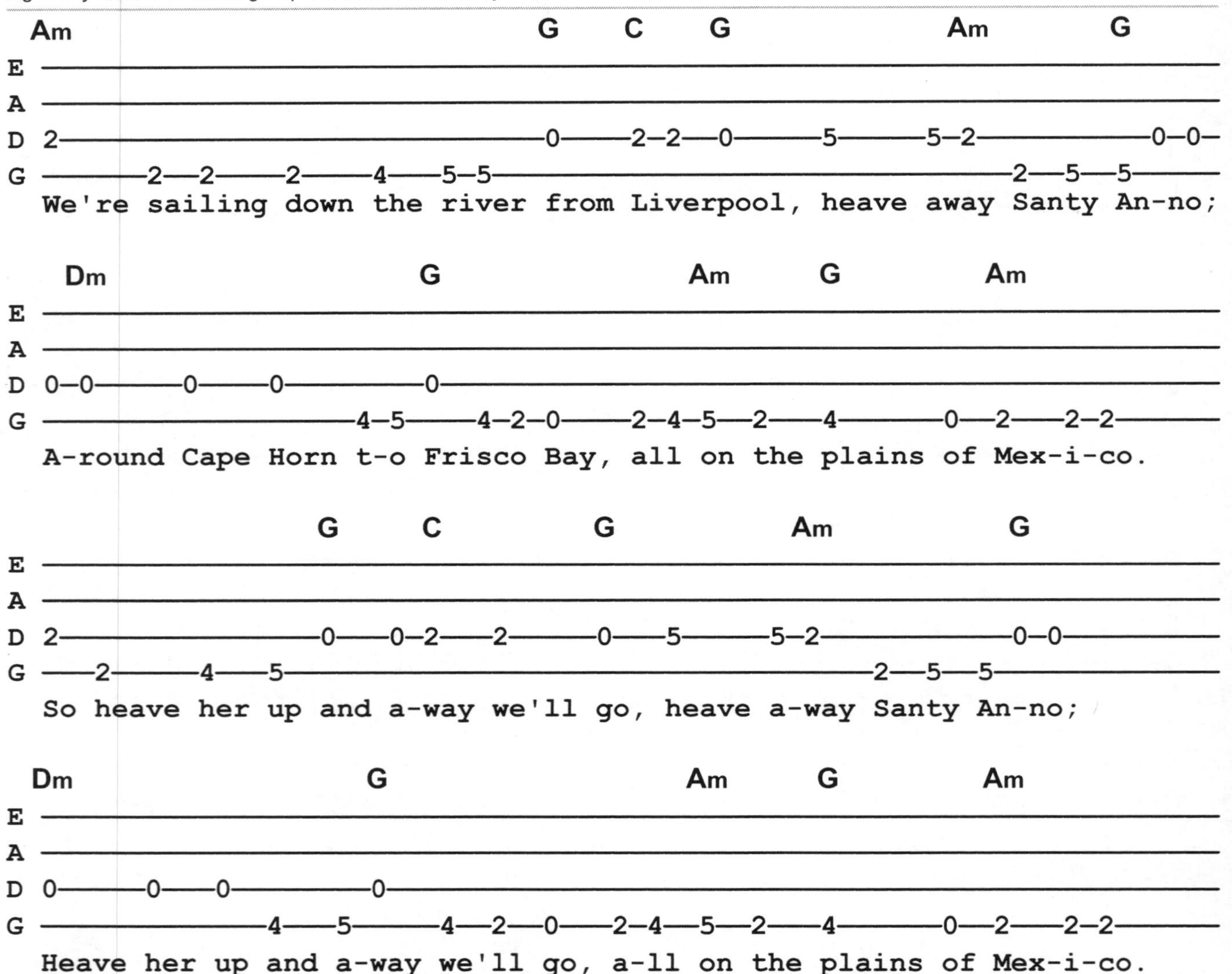

See Additional Verses on Next Page

Aweigh Santy Anno
(continued)

Chord Forms

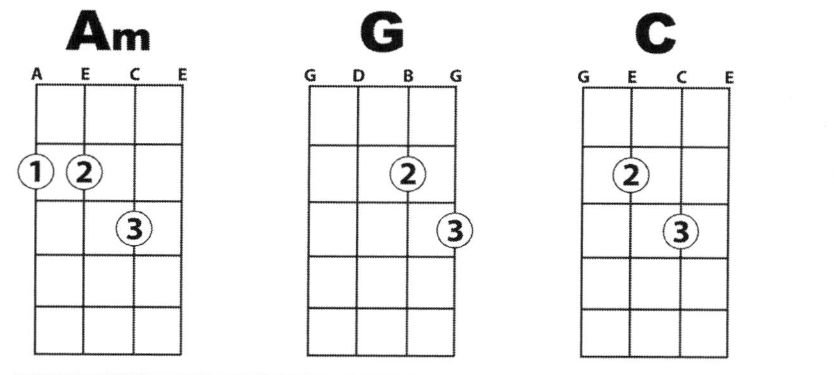

Additional Verses

She's a fast clipper ship and a bully good crew, heave away, Santy Anno;
A down-east Yankee for her captain, too, all on the plains of Mexico.
There's plenty of gold, so I've been told, heave away, Santy Anno;
There's plenty of gold, so I've been told, way out in Californ-i-o.

Back in the days of forty-nine, heave away, Santy Anno;
Those were the days of the good old times, all on the plains of Mexico.
When Zacharias Taylor gained the day, heave away, Santy Anno;
He made poor Santy run away, all on the plains of Mexico.

General Scott and Taylor, too, heave away, Santy Anno;
Made poor Santy meet his Waterloo, all on the plains of Mexico.
Santy Anno was a good old man, heave away, Santy Anno,
'Til he got into war with your Uncle Sam, all on the plains of Mexico.

When I leave this ship I will settle down, heave away, Santy Anno;
And marry a girl named Sally Brown, all on the plains of Mexico.
So heave her up and away we'll go, heave away, Santy Anno;
Heave her up and away we'll go, all on the plains of Mexico.

Aweigh Santy Anno
(continued)

Basic Melody

Key of A Minor (High)

```
  Am                                       G     C     G             Am        G
E 0────────────────────────────────────────────0─0─────────3──────3─0────────────────
A ───────0──0─────0─────2────3─3───5──────────────5─────────────────────0──3──3─5─5─
D ───────────────────────────────────────────────────────────────────────────────────
G ───────────────────────────────────────────────────────────────────────────────────
  We're sailing down the river from Liverpool, heave away Santy An-no;
```

```
    Dm                      G                 Am      G          Am
E ───────────────────────────────────────────────────────────────────────────
A 5─5──────5─────5─────2─3─5──2─0─────────0─2─3──0───2──────────0────0─0─────
D ──────────────────────────────────5───────────────────────5────────────────
G ───────────────────────────────────────────────────────────────────────────
  A-round Cape Horn t-o Frisco Bay, all on the plains of Mex-i-co.
```

```
                   G     C          G           Am          G
E ─────────────────────────0───0──────────3──────3─0─────────────────────
A ──0──────2───3───5───5───────────5─────────────────0──3──3─5─5─────────
D 2──────────────────────────────────────────────────────────────────────
G ───────────────────────────────────────────────────────────────────────
  So heave her up and a-way we'll go, heave a-way Santy An-no;
```

```
  Dm                  G                   Am      G          Am
E ───────────────────────────────────────────────────────────────────────────
A 5──────5───5──2────3─5───2──0─────────0─2──3──0───2──────────0────0─0──────
D ──────────────────────────────5─────────────────────────5──────────────────
G ───────────────────────────────────────────────────────────────────────────
  Heave her up and a-way we'll go, a-ll on the plains of Mex-i-co.
```

Chord Forms

Am

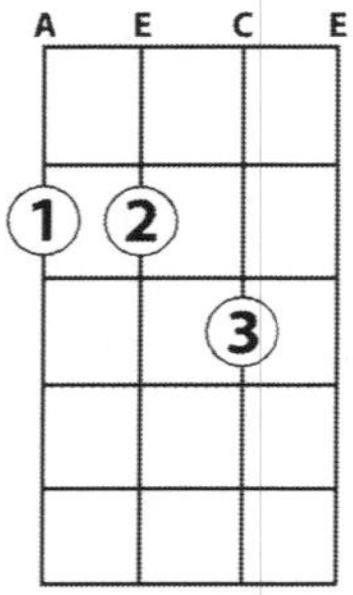

G

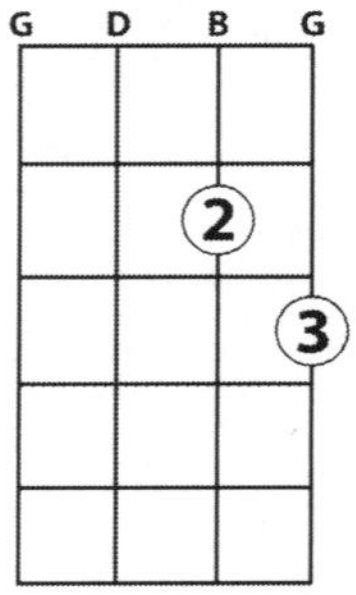

C

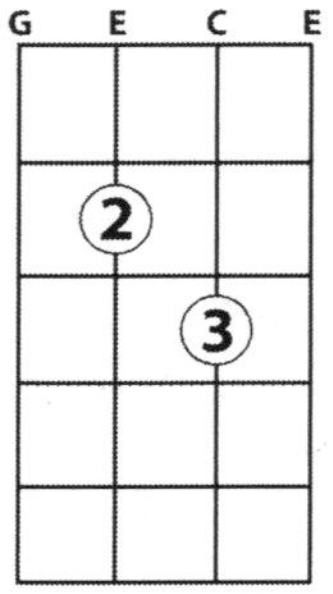

Dm

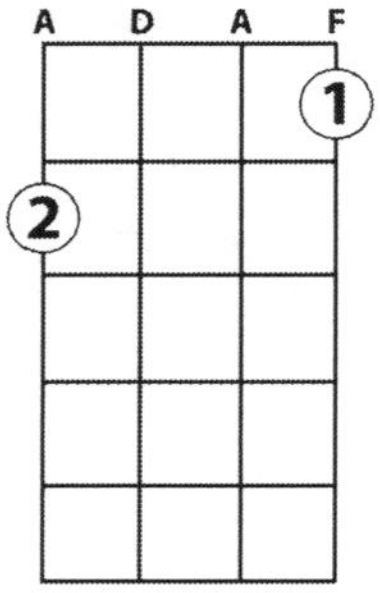

Aweigh Santy Anno
(continued)

Melody & Chords

Key of A Minor (High)

```
 Am                                      G     C     G           Am         G
E 0-----------------------------------------0-0---------3------3-0-------------
A 0-----0-0-----0-----2----3-3----5-----3-3--5-----2------2-0--0--3--3-5-5-
D 2-----2-2-----2-----2----2-2----0-----2----0---------------2--2--2--0-0-0-
G 2-----2-------2----------2------0----------0--------------------2-------0-
  We're sailing down the river from Liverpool, heave away Santy An-no;
```

```
  Dm                  G               Am      G        Am
E ------------------------------------------------------------------
A 5-5------5----5----2-3-5--2-0------0-2-3--0---2----------0---0-0---
D 0-3------3----3----3-3-0--0-0-5----0-0-2--2---0-------5--2---2-2---
G --2-----------2---------0----0-----------2------0-------0--2-----2---
  A-round Cape Horn t-o Frisco Bay, all on the plains of Mex-i-co.
```

```
                  G      C          G          Am          G
E ------------------------0---0-----------3------3-0-----------------
A ---0------2---3--5---5-3---3------5---2------2-0---0--3--3-5-5----
D 2--0------2---2--0---0-2---2------0---0----------2---2--2--2-0-0----
G 2--2----------2--0----------------0---------------2------------0----
  So heave her up and a-way we'll go, heave a-way Santy An-no;
```

```
 Dm                 G                 Am      G        Am
E ------------------------------------------------------------------
A 5------5---5--2---3-5---2--0--------0-2--3--0---2---------0---0-0---
D 3------3---3--3---3-0---0--0--5-----0-0--2--2---0------5--2---2-2---
G 2----------2----------0----0-------------2-------0-------0--2-----2---
  Heave her up and a-way we'll go, a-ll on the plains of Mex-i-co.
```

Chord Forms

Am

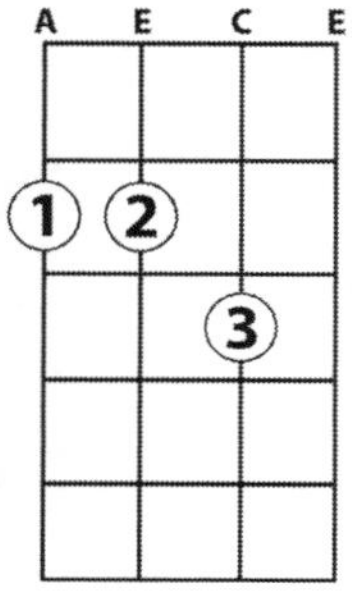

G

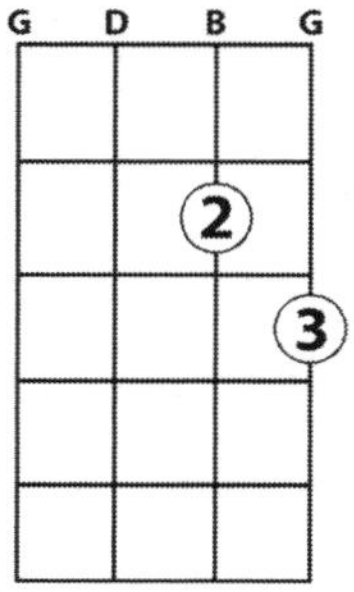

C

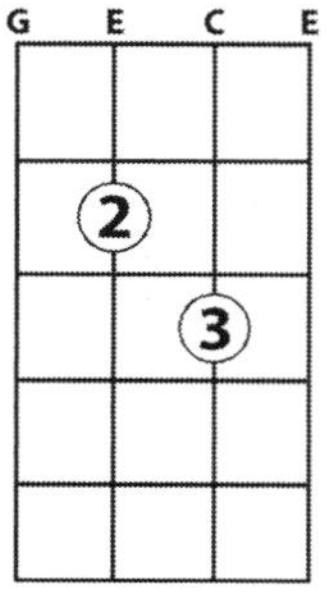

Dm

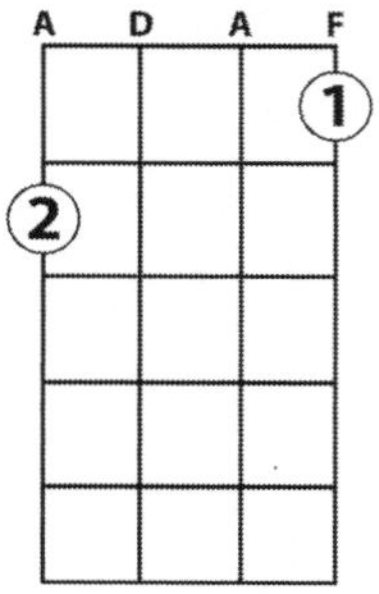

Aweigh Santy Anno
(continued)

Basic Melody

Key of E Minor

```
  Em                                        D    G    D             Em        D
E ---------------------------------------------------------------------------------
A 2-----------------------------------------0----2-2--0------5------5-2-----------0-0-
D ------------2--2-----2-----4----5-5-----------------------------------2--5--5------
G ---------------------------------------------------------------------------------
  We're sailing down the river from Liverpool, heave away Santy An-no;

    Am                     D                  Em      D        Em
E ---------------------------------------------------------------------------------
A 0-0------0-----0---------0------------------------------------------------------
D ---------------------4-5-----4-2-0-----2-4-5--2---4-------0--2---2-2-----------
G ---------------------------------------------------------------------------------
  A-round Cape Horn t-o Frisco Bay, all on the plains of Mex-i-co.

                    D     G         D          Em           D
E ---------------------------------------------------------------------------------
A ------------------0----0-2---2----0----5-----5-2-----------0-0-----------------
D ---2------4---5----------------------------------2---5---5----------------------
G 4--------------------------------------------------------------------------------
  So heave her up and a-way we'll go, heave a-way Santy An-no;

  Am                    D                   Em      D        Em
E ---------------------------------------------------------------------------------
A 0------0---0----------0---------------------------------------------------------
D -----------------4---5-----4--2--0---2-4--5--2---4-------0--2---2-2------------
G ---------------------------------------------------------------------------------
  Heave her up and a-way we'll go, a-ll on the plains of Mex-i-co.
```

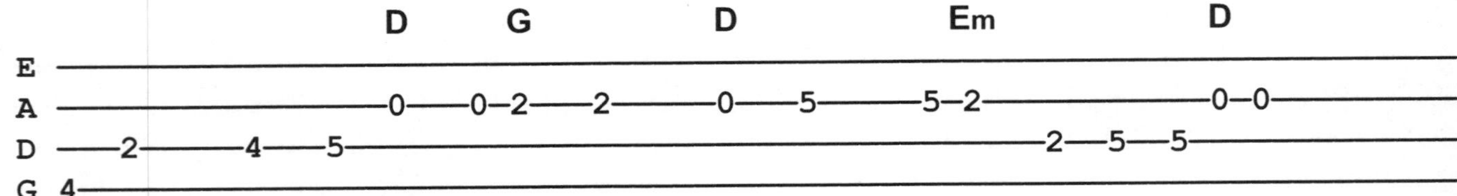

Chord Forms

Em

D

G

Am

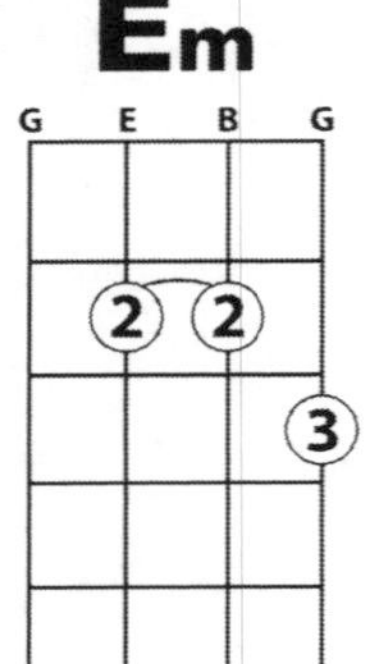

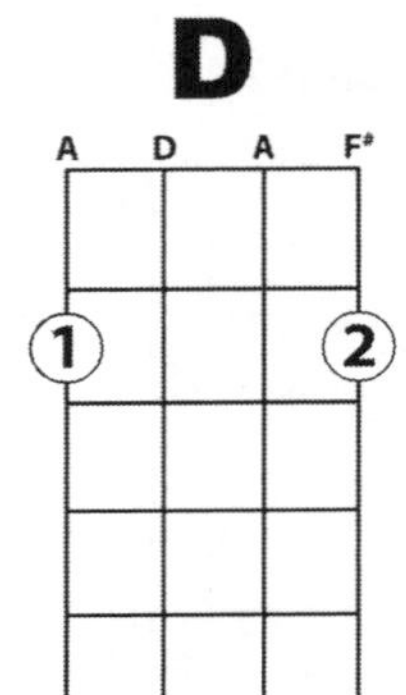

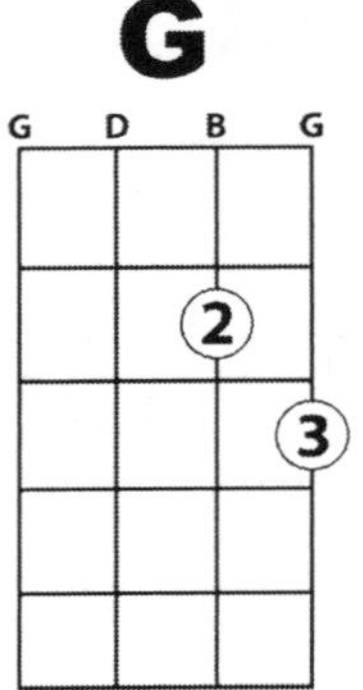

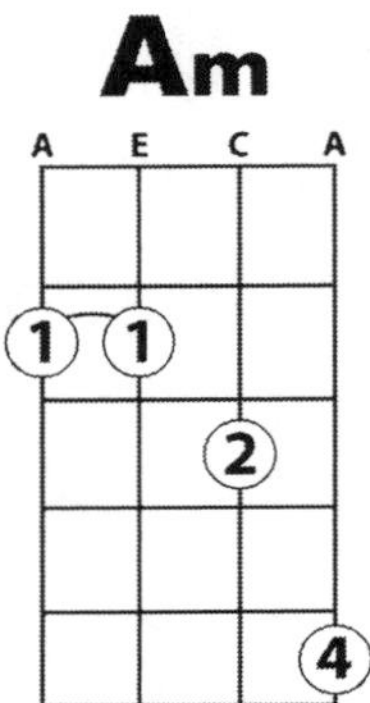

Aweigh Santy Anno
(continued)

Melody & Chords

Key of E Minor

```
  Em                                                      D       G       D               Em            D
E ------------------------------------------------------------------------------------------------------------
A 2-----------------------------------------------------0-------2--2--0-------5-------5-2-------------0--0-
D 2---------2--2-------2-------4-----5--5----0--------0--0--0-------0-------0--2---2---5---5--0--0-
G 4---------4--4-------4-------4-----4--4---------------0-------2-------2---------4---4---4---2----2-
  We're sailing down the river from Liverpool, heave away Santy An-no;
```

```
    Am                              D                         Em          D             Em
E ------------------------------------------------------------------------------------------------------------
A 0--0-------0-------0-------------0------------------------------------------------------------------------
D 0--2-------2-------2-------4-5-0--4-2-0---------2-4-5--2------4-----------0---2----2-2---------------
G --2----------------2-------2-2-2--2-2-2---------2-2-4--4------2-----------2---4----4-4---------------
  A-round Cape Horn t-o Frisco Bay, all on the plains of Mex-i-co.
```

```
                            D        G              D                 Em                  D
E ------------------------------------------------------------------------------------------------------------
A --------------------------0------0--2-----2---------0------5--------5--2-----------------0--0----------------
D ----2-----------4-----5---0------0--0-----0---------0------0--------0--2-----2----5---5--0--0----------------
G 4---4-----------4-----4---2-------------0-----0---------2------2------------4-----4----4---4-----2-----------
  So heave her up and a-way we'll go, heave a-way Santy An-no;
```

```
  Am                          D                           Em          D             Em
E ------------------------------------------------------------------------------------------------------------
A 0---------0-----0-----------0-----------------------------------------------------------------------------
D 2---------2-----2--4------5-0------4---2---0------2-4--5---2------4-----------0---2----2-2---------------
G 2---------------2--2------2-2------2---2---2------2-2--4---4------2-----------2---4----4-4---------------
  Heave her up and a-way we'll go, a-ll on the plains of Mex-i-co.
```

Chord Forms

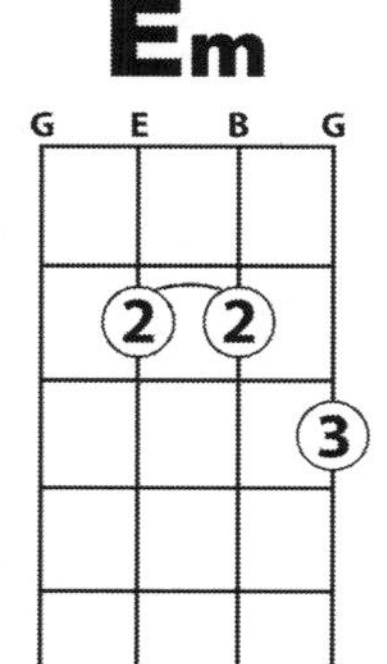

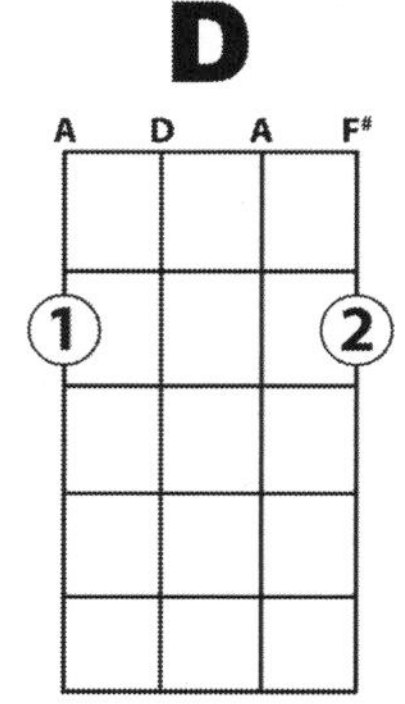

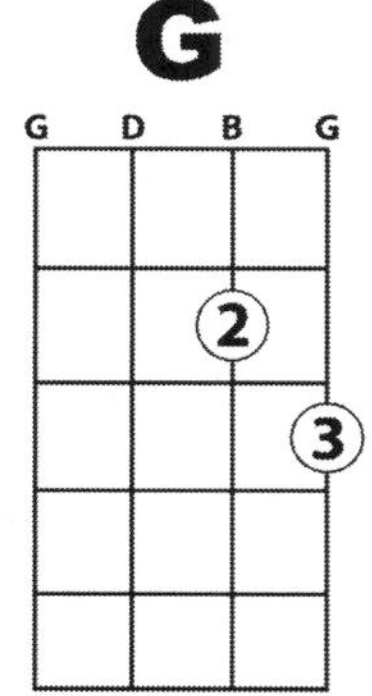

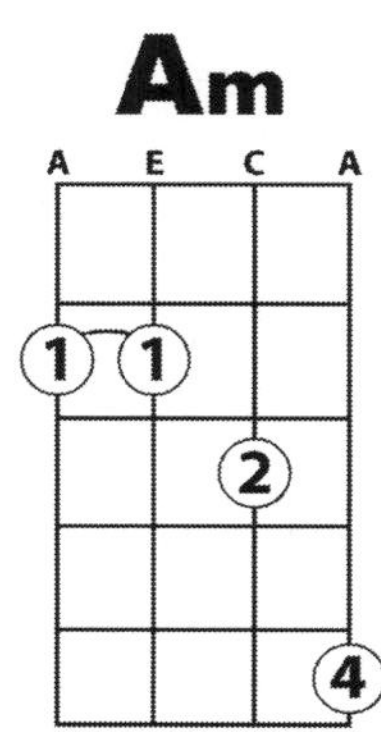

Blood Red Roses

Basic Melody
Key of C

Words and Music

Traditional

This is another great old sea shanty best belted out in full voice with friends. There is little agreement as to the meaning of the title phrase. Some have suggested it referred to "redcoat" British soldiers. Others have suggested it referred to the red blisters and callouses that would form on sailors' hands... and perhaps even the marks of a venereal disease. Usually sung a cappella, the chords indicated are just a suggestion of what could be played as accompaniment to this old song.

```
  C                                                        F
E ----------------------------------------------------------------------------------------------------
A -------------------------------------------0---1--------3---3-----1---------------------------------
D 5-----------0---2-------3---5--------------------5------------------------5-------------------------
G ----5-----------------------------------------------------------------------------------------------
  Our boots and clothes are all in pawn, go down you blood

      Am        F                        C
E ----------------------------------------------------------------------------------------------------
A 0---1--------3---3---------------------------------------------------------0------1-----------------
D ---------5----------------5---5----------------0---2---3---5---------------------------5------------
G ------------------------------------------5---------------------------------------------------------
  Red roses, go down. And it's mighty drafty 'round Cape Horn!

  F                               Am        C
E ----------------------------------------------------------------------------------------------------
A 3---3-----1------------0---1-----------3---3--------------------------------------------------------
D ----------------5---------------5-------------------------------------------------------------------
G ----------------------------------------------------------------------------------------------------
  Go down you blood red roses, go down.

  C                                    F                          Am        C
E 3---1----------0---1--------------------------------------------------------------------------------
A ---------5---------------5-----3---3-----1-----------0---1-----------3---3--------------------------
D ------------------------------------------------5-------------5-------------------------------------
G ----------------------------------------------------------------------------------------------------
  Oh, you pinks and posies; go down you blood red roses, go down.
```

Chord Forms

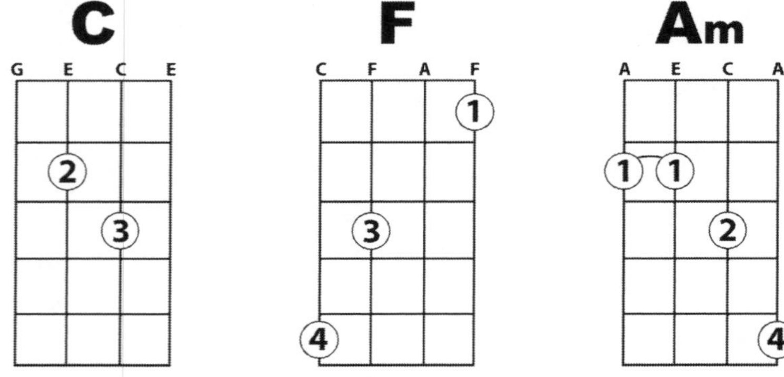

See Additional Verses on Next Page

Blood Red Roses (continued)

Melody & Chords

Key of C

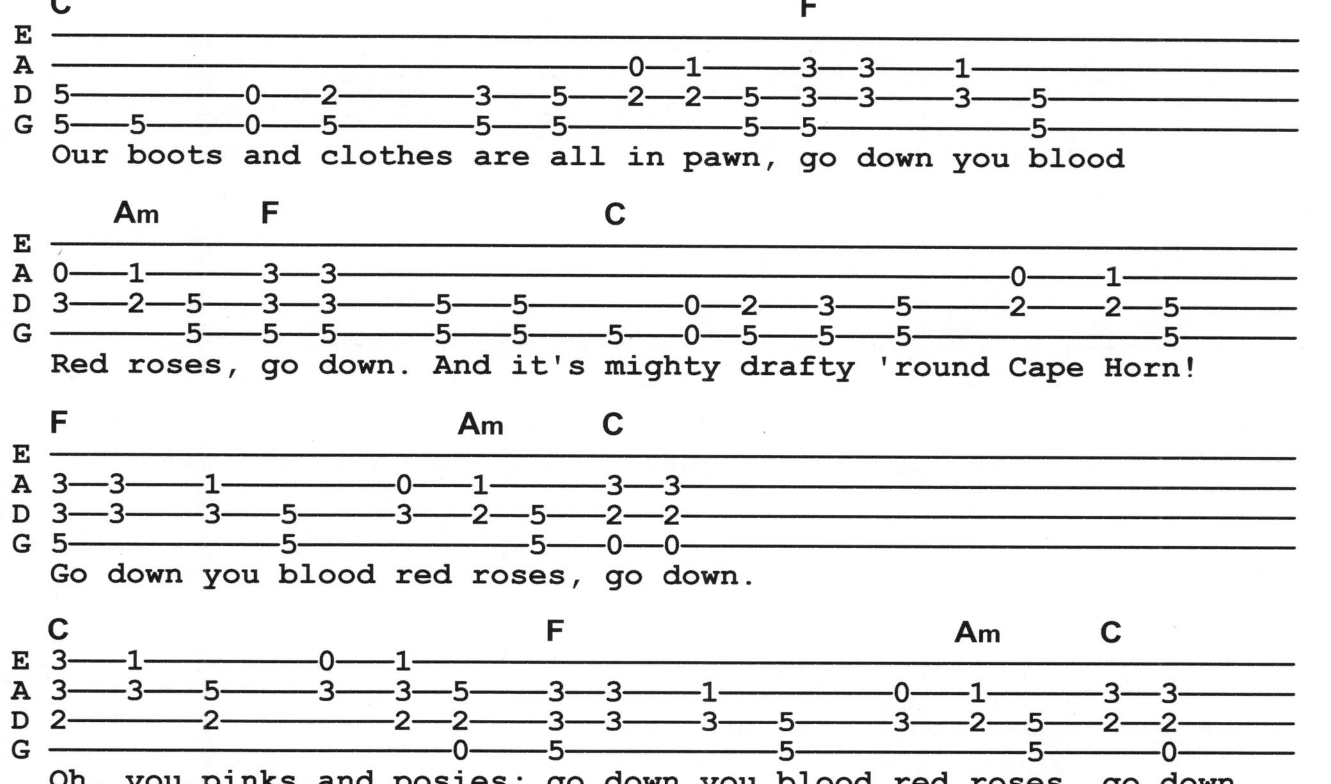

Chord Forms

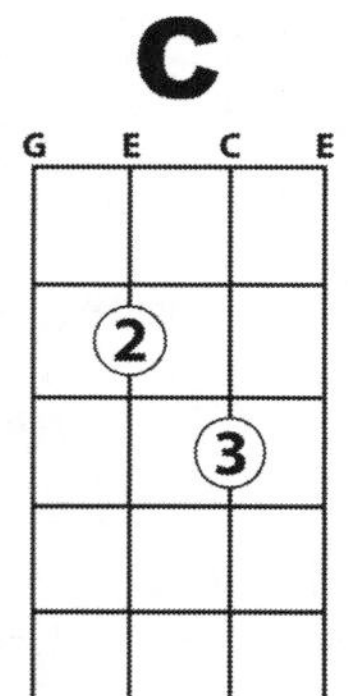

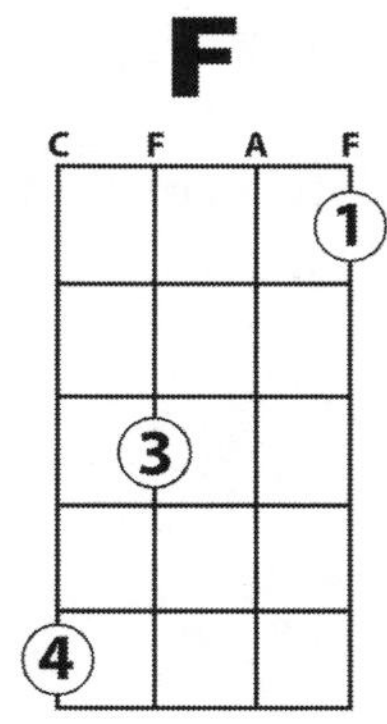

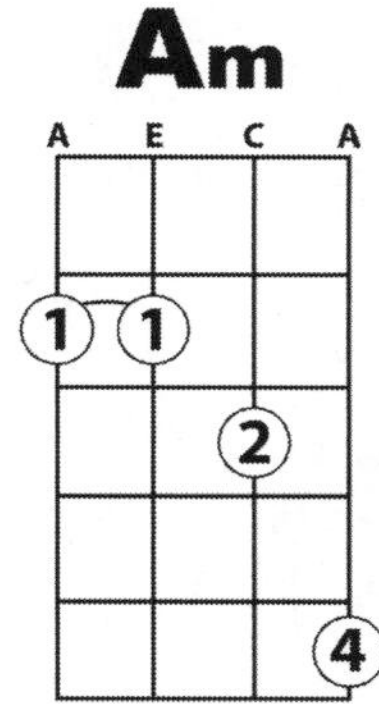

Additional Verses

It's 'round Cape Horn we've got to go,
Go down you blood red roses, go down.
Chasing whales through ice and snow,
Go down you blood red roses, go down.
Oh, you pinks and posies;
Go down, you blood red roses, go down.

Oh my old mother she wrote to me,
Go down you blood red roses, go down.
My darling son come home from the sea,
Go down you blood red roses, go down.
Oh, you pinks and posies;
Go down, you blood red roses, go down.

Oh it's one more pull and that will do,
Go down you blood red roses, go down.
For we're the bullies to kick her through,
Go down you blood red roses, go down.
Oh, you pinks and posies;
Go down, you blood red roses, go down.

Blood Red Roses (continued)

Basic Melody
Key of G

```
  G                                                               C
E ─────────────────────────────────────────────────────────────────────────────────────────────
A ─────────────────────────────────────────────────────────────────────────────────────────────
D 0───────────────────────────────────────────0───2──3──0──5──5─────3───0──────────────────────
G ──────0──────────2───4──────────5────────────────────────────────────────────────────────────
  Our boots and clothes are all in pawn, go down you blood
```

```
      Em        C                       G
E ─────────────────────────────────────────────────────────────────────────────────────────────
A ─────────────────────────────────────────────────────────────────────────────────────────────
D 2───3──0───5──5───────0───0─────────────────────────────────0──────2──────3──0───────────────
G ────────────────────────────────────0─────2───4───5──────────────────────────────────────────
  Red roses, go down. And it's mighty drafty 'round Cape Horn!
```

```
  C                           Em       G
E ─────────────────────────────────────────────────────────────────────────────────────────────
A ─────────────────────────────────────────────────────────────────────────────────────────────
D 5──5──────3────0───────2────3───0────5──5────────────────────────────────────────────────────
G ─────────────────────────────────────────────────────────────────────────────────────────────
  Go down you blood red roses, go down.
```

```
  G                               C                           Em        G
E ─────────────────────────────────────────────────────────────────────────────────────────────
A 5───3────0──────2────3───0───────────────────────────────────────────────────────────────────
D ────────────────────────────────5───5─────3────0───────2────3───0────5──5────────────────────
G ─────────────────────────────────────────────────────────────────────────────────────────────
  Oh, you pinks and posies; go down you blood red roses, go down.
```

Chord Forms

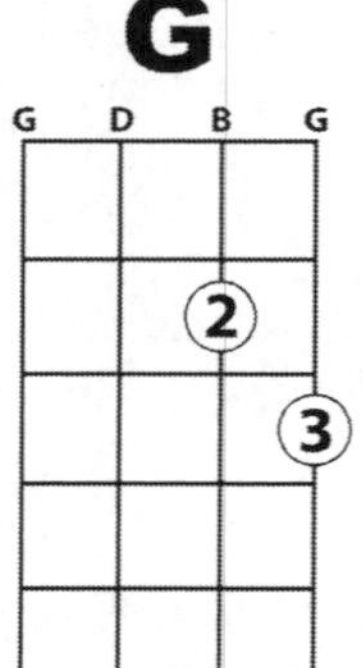

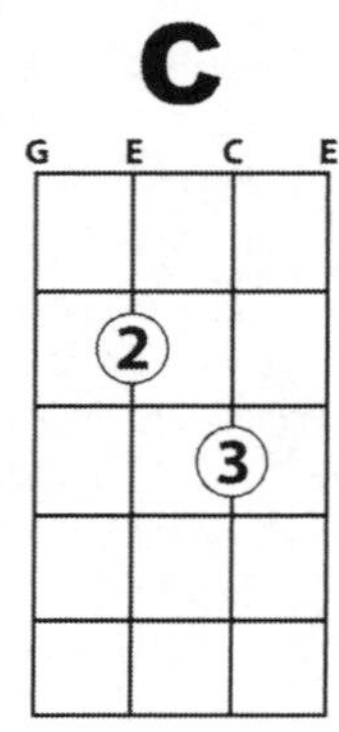

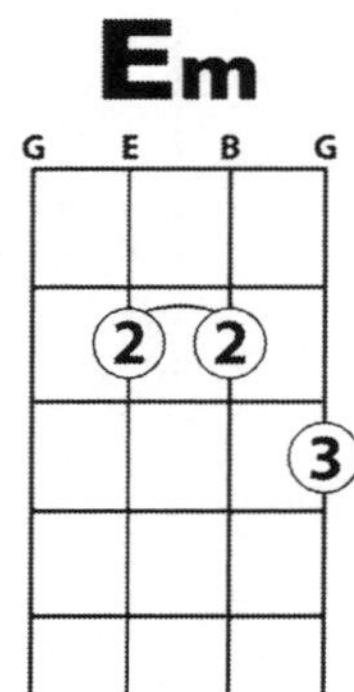

Blood Red Roses (continued)

Melody & Chords
Key of G

```
  G                                                   C
E ------------------------------------------------------------------------------------
A ------------------------------------------------------------------------------------
D 0----------------------------------0----2---3---0---5---5-----3----0----------------
G 0----0------2----4--------5--------0----0---0---0---5---5-----5----0----------------
  Our boots and clothes are all in pawn, go down you blood
```

```
    Em      C                         G
E ------------------------------------------------------------------------------------
A ------------------------------------------------------------------------------------
D 2----3---0----5---5-------0----0-------------------------0-------2------3---0-------
G 5----4---4----5---5-------0----0-----0----2---4----5-----0-------0------0---0-------
  Red roses, go down. And it's mighty drafty 'round Cape Horn!
```

```
  C                          Em       G
E ------------------------------------------------------------------------------------
A ------------------------------------------------------------------------------------
D 5--5------3----0------2----3---0----5---5-------------------------------------------
G 5--5------5----0------5----4---4----0---0-------------------------------------------
  Go down you blood red roses, go down.
```

```
  G                                  C                            Em       G
E ------------------------------------------------------------------------------------
A 5----3----0------2----3---0-----------------------------------------------------------
D 0----0----0------0----0---0-----5---5------3-----0------2----3----0------5---5------
G 0---------2-------------------2-----5---5------5-----0------5----4----4------5---5-----
  Oh, you pinks and posies; go down you blood red roses, go down.
```

Chord Forms

G

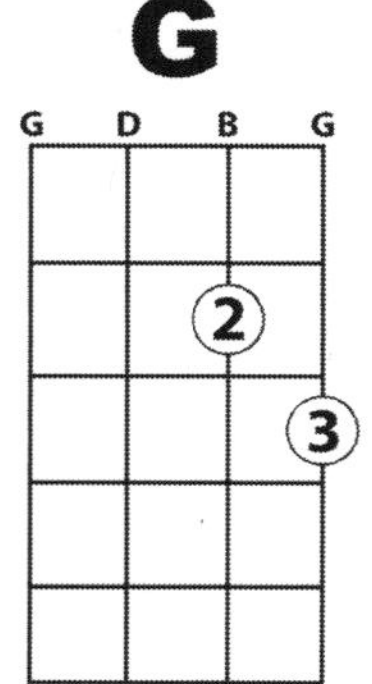

C

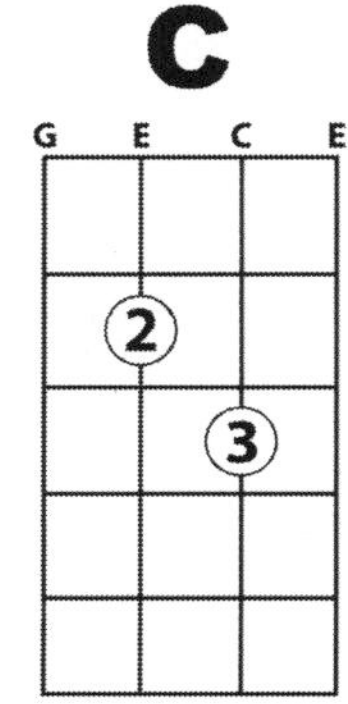

Em

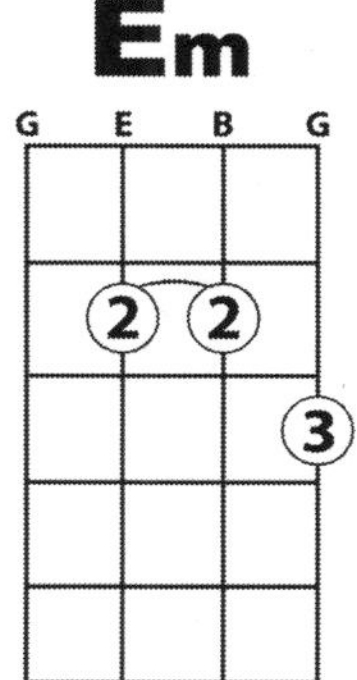

Blow, Boys, Blow

Basic Melody
Key of C (Low)

Words and Music
Traditional

The lyrics of this old sea shanty were well-suited for name substitution, such that the sailors could put in their own names, or those of their ship's current captain and mates. It is officially classified as a "long-drag (or topsail) halyard" style of shanty, and probably dates to the days of the West African slave trade. As with many such songs, various other verses have been added over the years.

```
   C                              F                        Dm       Am       F
E ───────────────────────────────────────────────────────────────────────────────────────────
A ───────────────────────────────────────────────────────────────────────────────────────────
D 5─2──2────2───────────────────0────────────────────────0────────2────────3─────────────────
G ────────────────────5──────────────────5─────2─5───────────────────────────────────────────
  A Yankee ship comes down the river, blow, boys, blow!

     C       G7                    C        F           C            G                C
E ───────────────────────────────────────────────────────────────────────────────────────────
A 0──────────────────────────────────────────────────────────────────────────────────────────
D ──5──2────3──────0──────0───────────────────3──────2────────5───0───0───5──────────────────
G ─────────────────────────────────5───0────5──────────────────────────────────────────5─────
  A Yankee ship with a Yankee skipper, blow, my bully boys, blow!
```

See Additional Verses on Next Page

Chord Forms

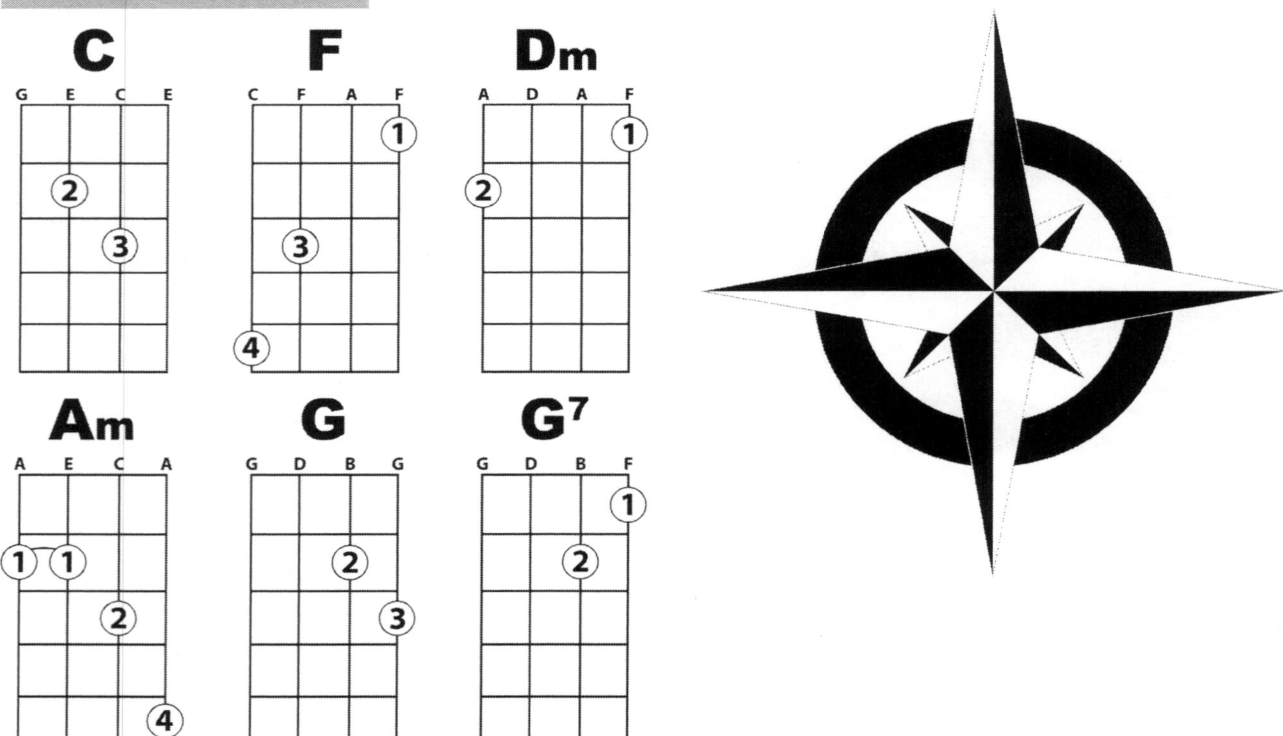

Blow, Boys, Blow (continued)

Additional Verses

How do you know she's a Yankee liner?
Blow, boys, blow...
The stars and stripes float out behind her!
Blow, my bully boys, blow.

And how d'you know she's a Yankee clipper?
Blow, boys, blow...
Her masts and yards they shine like silver!
Blow, my bully boys, blow.

Who d'you think is the captain of her?
Blow, boys, blow...
Why Billy Hays and there is no other.
Blow, my bully boys, blow.

And what d'you think they have for dinner?
Blow, boys, blow...
Why, monkey's tails and pickled liver!
Blow, my bully boys, blow.

Who do you think was first mate of her?
Blow, boys, blow...
Why, Shanghai Brown, the sailor robber!
Blow, my bully boys, blow.

What do you think she's got for cargo?
Blow, boys, blow...
Why, black sheep that have run the embargo
Blow, my bully boys, blow.

Yonder comes the Arrow packet,
Blow, boys, blow...
She fires the gun, can't you hear the racket?
Blow, my bully boys, blow.

Then blow, my bullies, all together!
Blow, boys, blow...
Blow, my boys, for better weather.
Blow, my bully boys, blow.

Blow, Boys, Blow (continued)

Two Versions
Key of C (High)

Basic Melody

```
  C                    F                    Dm     Am     F
E 3-0--0---0-------------------------------------------0------1-----------
A -------------------3------5-----3----0-3-----5-------------------------
D -----------------------------------------------------------------------
G -----------------------------------------------------------------------
  A Yankee ship comes down the river, blow, boys, blow!
```

```
    C      G7              C      F      C      G         C
E 5-3--0---1-------------------------------1-----0-----3--------3--------
A ----------------5-----5-3------3-----------------------5--5--------3---
D -----------------------------5-----------------------------------------
G -----------------------------------------------------------------------
  A Yankee ship with a Yankee skipper, blow, my bully boys, blow!
```

Melody & Chords

```
  C                    F                    Dm     Am     F
E 3-0--0---0-------------------------------------------0------1-----------
A 3-3--3---3-------3------5-----3----0-3-----5---------0------0-----------
D 2-2--2---2-------2------3-----3----3-3-----3---------2------3-----------
G --0--------------0------2----------2-------2---------------------------
  A Yankee ship comes down the river, blow, boys, blow!
```

```
    C      G7              C      F      C      G         C
E 5-3--0---1-------------------------------1-----0-----3--------3--------
A 3-3--3---2------5-----5-3------3----3----3-----3--5--5--2----------3---
D 3-2------0------0-----0-2--5---3---------2--------0--0--0----------2---
G ----------------0-----0-0-------------------------0----------------0---
  A Yankee ship with a Yankee skipper, blow, my bully boys, blow!
```

Chord Forms

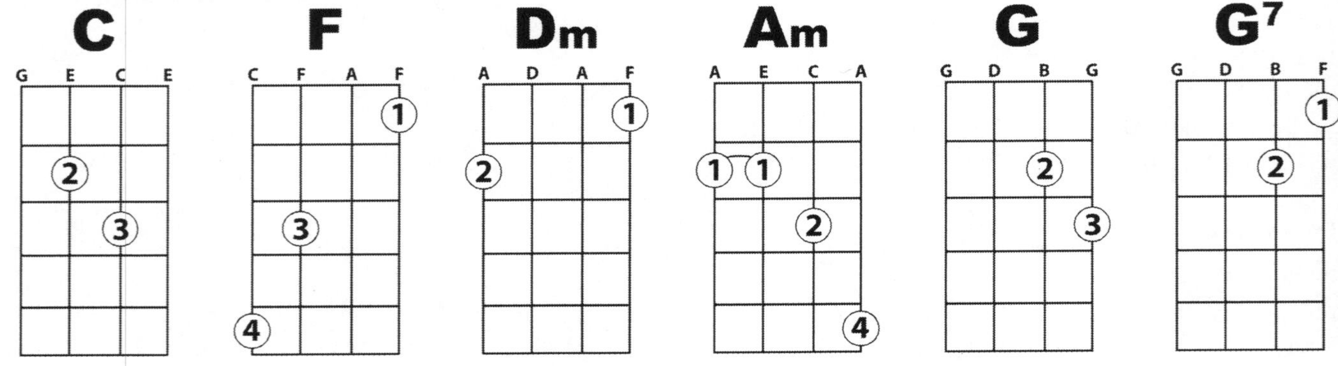

Blow, Boys, Blow (continued)

Two Versions
Key of G

Basic Melody

```
  G                    C               Am    Em    C
E ----------------------------------------------------------
A 5-2--2---2-----------0---------------0-----2-----3--------
D ---------------5---------5---2-5--------------------------
G ----------------------------------------------------------
  A Yankee ship comes down the river, blow, boys, blow!
```

```
    G      D7            G     C       G        D           G
E 0---------------------------------------------------------------
A --5--2---3----0----0-------------3----2-----5--0--0--5----------
D ---------------------5--0--5---------------------------5-------
G ----------------------------------------------------------------
  A Yankee ship with a Yankee skipper, blow, my bully boys, blow!
```

Melody & Chords

```
  G                    C               Am    Em    C
E ----------------------------------------------------------
A 5-2--2---2-----------0---------------0-----2-----3--------
D 0-0--0---0-----5-----2---5---2-5-----2-----2-----2--------
G 0-0------0-----0-----0---5---5-5-----2-----4-----0--------
  A Yankee ship comes down the river, blow, boys, blow!
```

```
    G      D7            G     C       G        D           G
E 0---------------------------------------------------------------
A 3-5--2---3----0----0-------------3----2-----5--0--0--5----------
D 2-0--0---0----0----0-5--0--5-----2----0-----0--0--0--0-----5----
G --0------2----2-------0--0--5-----0----0---------2-----2---0----
  A Yankee ship with a Yankee skipper, blow, my bully boys, blow!
```

Chord Forms

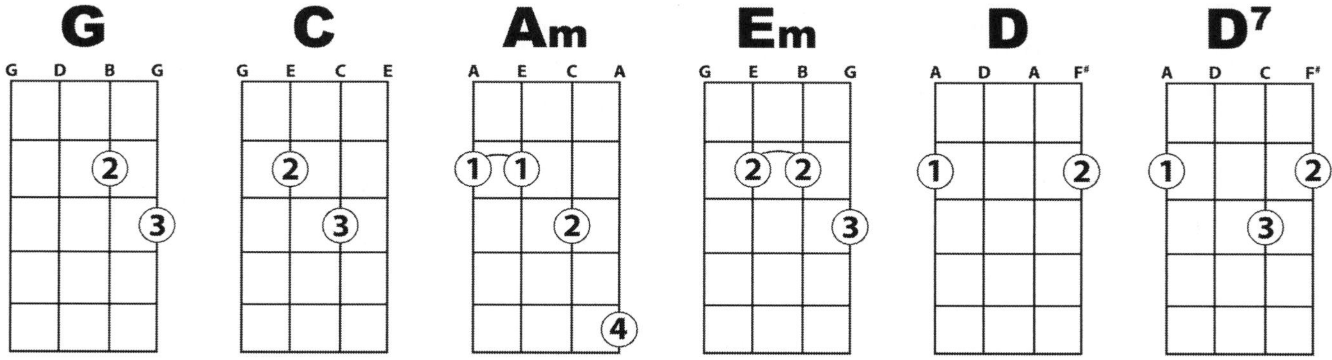

SEA SHANTY

Blow the Man Down

Basic Melody
Key of C (Low)

Words and Music
Traditional

This old sea shanty (seafaring/sailor folk song) is of English origin. The exact origins are unknown, but it is thought to have gotten its start in the 1860's. It was sung in a "call and response" style, with one singer calling out the first and third lines, and the rest of the crew responding back with the second and fourth. In a way, 1 & 3 are the "verse" and 2 & 4 are the "chorus". There are many verses to this song, some more bawdy than others; we present just a few of the tamer ones here.

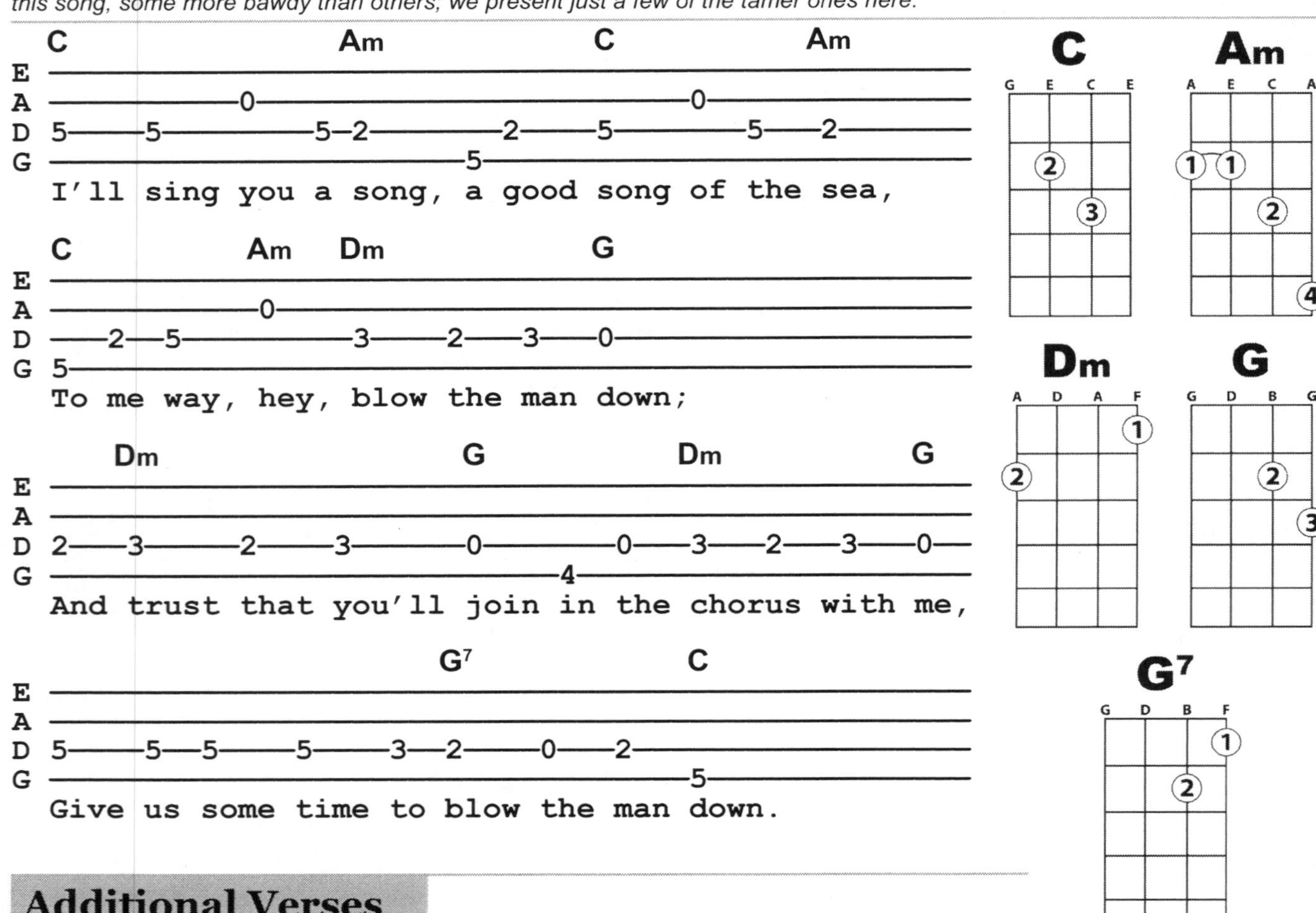

Additional Verses

A bonnie good mate and a captain too... (To me way, hey...)
A bonnie good ship and a bonnie good crew... (Give us some time...)

It's now we are sailing on th' ocean so wide...
Where the deep and blue waters dash by our black side...

It's now when we enter the channel so wide...
All hands are ordered to scrub the ship's side...

And now, my fine boys, we are round the rock...
And soon, oh! Soon, we will be in the dock...

Then all our hands will bundle ashore...
Perhaps some will never to sea go more...

Blow the Man Down
(continued)

Melody & Chords

Key of C (Low)

```
   C                 Am            C           Am
E ------------------------------------------------------------
A ------------0-------------------------------0---------------
D 5----5------2----5--2--------2----5----2--5----2------------
G 5----5-----------5--2-----5--2----5--------5----2-----------
  I'll sing you a song, a good song of the sea,
```

```
   C          Am    Dm          G
E ------------------------------------------------------------
A ------------0-----------------------------------------------
D ---2--5-----2-----3-----2---3---0---------------------------
G 5--5--5-----2-----2-----2---2---0---------------------------
  To me way, hey, blow the man down;
```

```
      Dm                 G            Dm          G
E ------------------------------------------------------------
A ------------------------------------------------------------
D 2--3-----2----3-------0-------0---3----2--3-----0--
G 0--2-----2----2-------0----4--0---2----2--2-----0--
  And trust that you'll join in the chorus with me,
```

```
                         G7          C
E ------------------------------------------------------------
A ------------------------------------------------------------
D 5-----5--5-----5-----3--2-----0---2-------------------------
G 0-----0--4-----4-----4--4-----4---4---5---------------------
  Give us some time to blow the man down.
```

Chord Forms

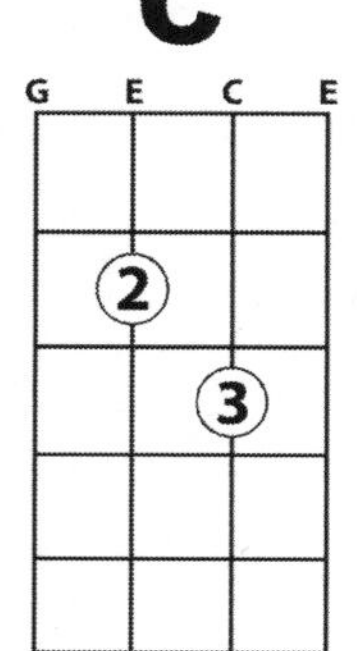

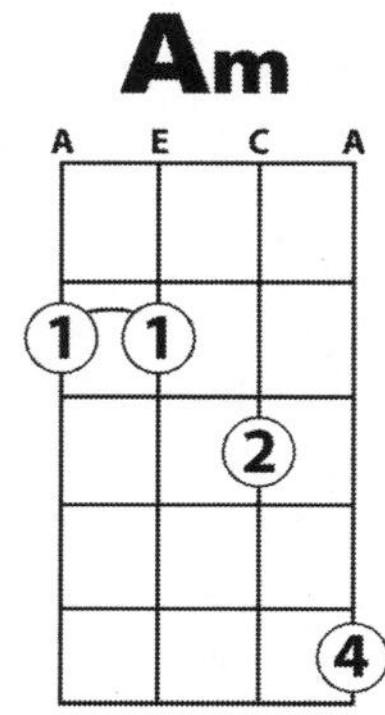

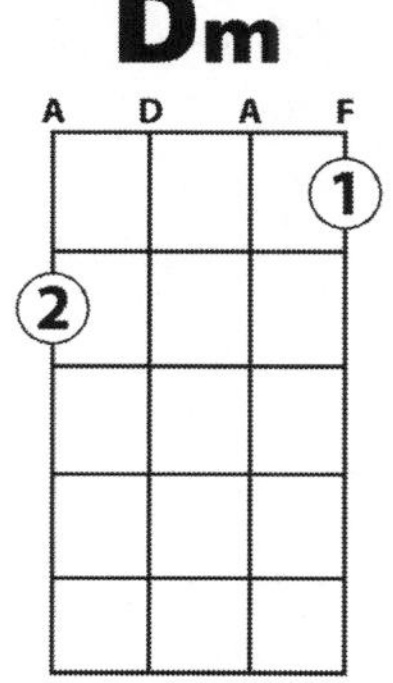

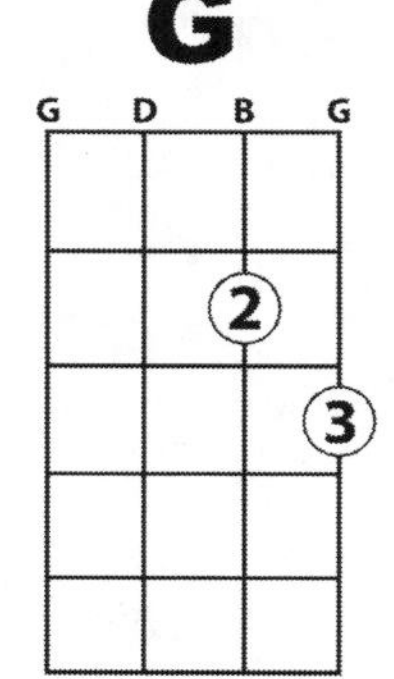

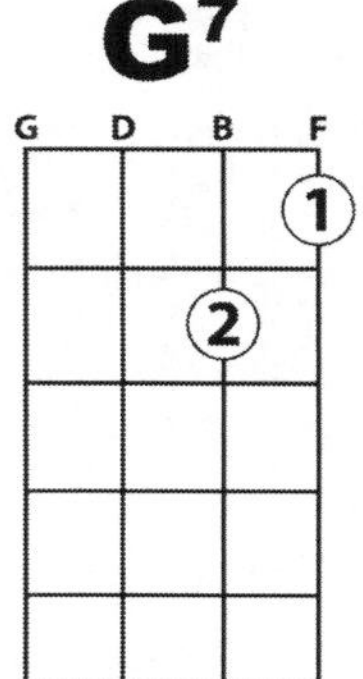

Blow the Man Down
(continued)

Basic Melody

Key of C (High)

```
   C                     Am               C               Am
E 3----3----5---3-0----------0----3----5---3----0-------------
A -----------------------3------------------------------------
D ------------------------------------------------------------
G ------------------------------------------------------------
  I'll sing you a song, a good song of the sea,
```

```
   C           Am    Dm               G
E ----0--3----5-----1-----0---1------------------------------
A 3--------------------------------5--------------------------
D ------------------------------------------------------------
G ------------------------------------------------------------
  To me way, hey, blow the man down;
```

```
      Dm                       G              Dm              G
E 0---1------0----1--------------------------1----0----1------------
A ----------------------------5-----2--5-----------------------5----
D ------------------------------------------------------------------
G ------------------------------------------------------------------
  And trust that you'll join in the chorus with me,
```

```
                            G7            C
E 3----3--3-----3-----1--0---------0-----------------------
A ---------------------------5----------3------------------
D ---------------------------------------------------------
G ---------------------------------------------------------
  Give us some time to blow the man down.
```

Chord Forms

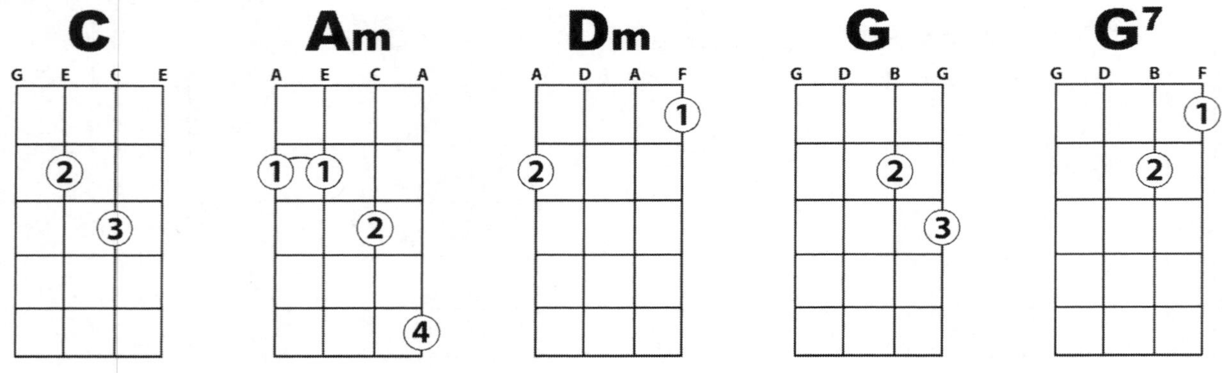

Blow the Man Down
(continued)

Melody & Chords

Key of C (High)

```
   C                      Am                   C              Am
E  3------3------5----3--0---------------0------3------5----3-----0------------
A  3------3------3----3--0-----------3--0------3------3----3-----0------------
D  2------2--------------2-----------2---------2-----------2-----2------------
G  -------0------------------------2---------------------------2------------
   I'll sing you a song, a good song of the sea,
```

```
   C              Am    Dm               G
E  -----0---3-----5-----1------0----1----------------------------------------
A  3---3---3------3-----0------0----0----5-----------------------------------
D  2----------2----2----0-----------0----0-----------------------------------
G  ---------------------2----------------0-----------------------------------
   To me way, hey, blow the man down;
```

```
       Dm                        G               Dm             G
E  0----1-------0-----1--------------------------1-----0-----1-------------
A  2----0-------0-----0--------5------2---5------0-----0-----0------5------
D  -----0----------------------0------0---0------0------------------0------
G  -----2----------------------0-----------------2------------------0------
   And trust that you'll join in the chorus with me,
```

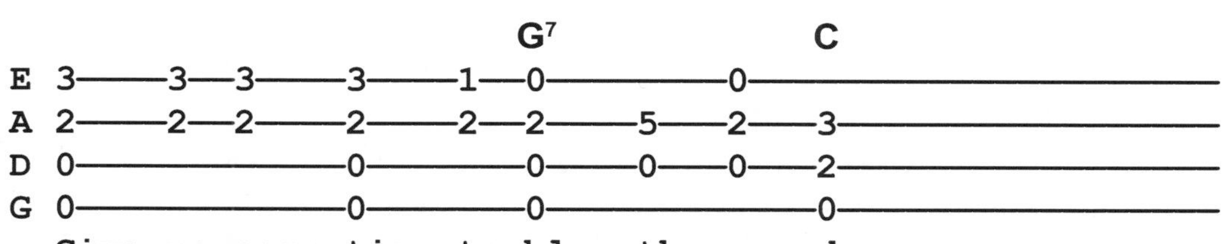

Chord Forms

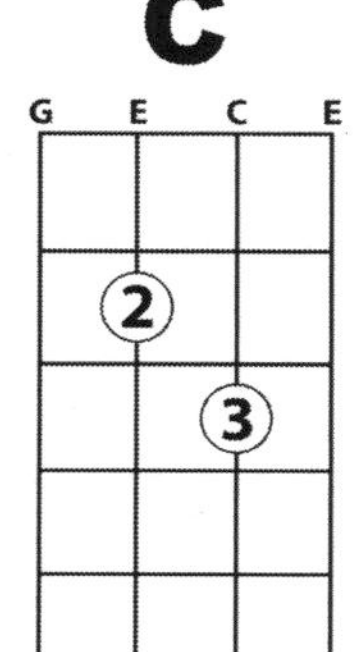

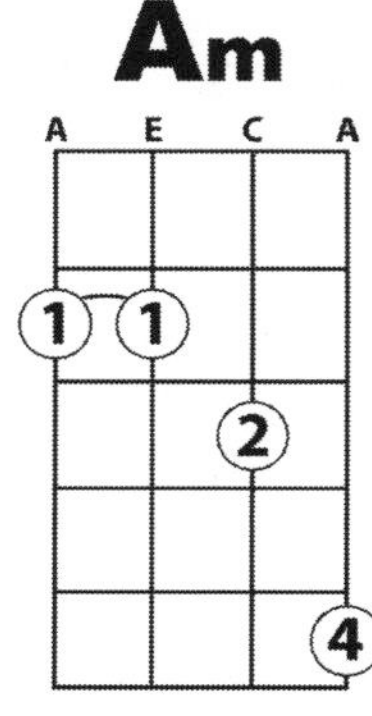

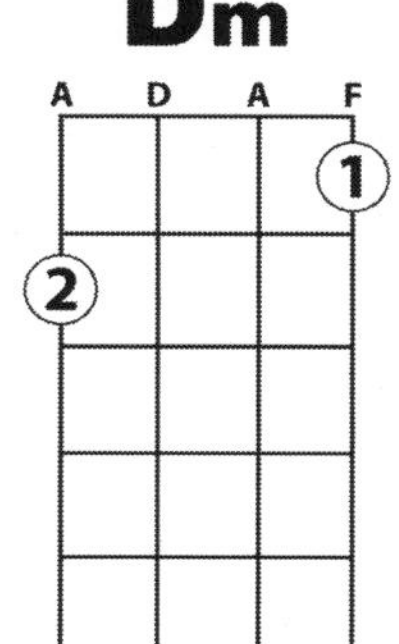

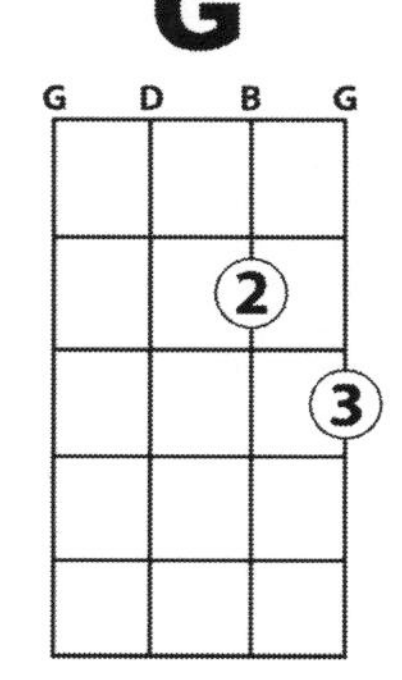

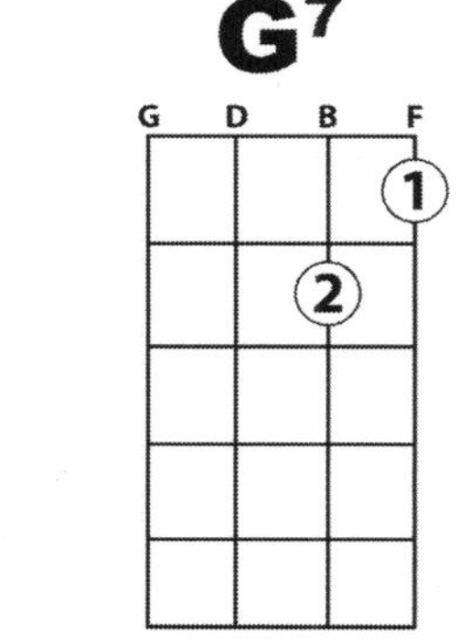

Blow the Man Down
(continued)

Basic Melody

Key of G

```
   G                   Em              G               Em
E ----------------0---------------------------0------------------------
A 5-----5-----------5--2----------2-----5--------5----2----------------
D -------------------------------5------------------------------------
G ---------------------------------------------------------------------
  I'll sing you a song, a good song of the sea,
```

```
   G          Em   Am            D
E ----------0-----------------------------------------------------
A ---2--5-------------3-----2----3---0----------------------------
D 5---------------------------------------------------------------
G ----------------------------------------------------------------
  To me way, hey, blow the man down;
```

```
      Am                  D            Am            D
E ----------------------------------------------------------------
A 2---3------2-----3--------0--------0----3----2----3----0--------
D ------------------------------4---------------------------------
G ----------------------------------------------------------------
  And trust that you'll join in the chorus with me,
```

```
                            D7              G
E ----------------------------------------------------------------
A 5-----5---5-----5-----3---2-----0---2---------------------------
D ----------------------------------------5-----------------------
G ----------------------------------------------------------------
  Give us some time to blow the man down.
```

Chord Forms

G
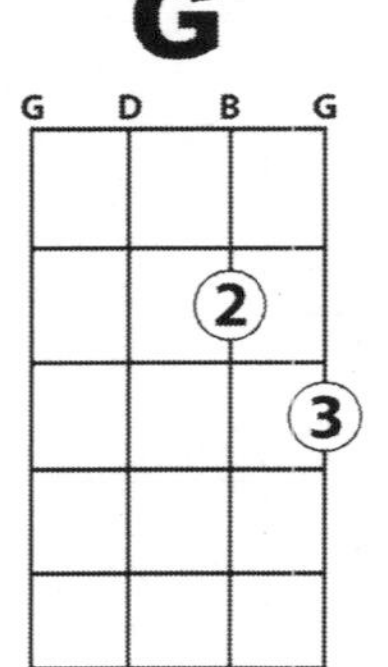

Em
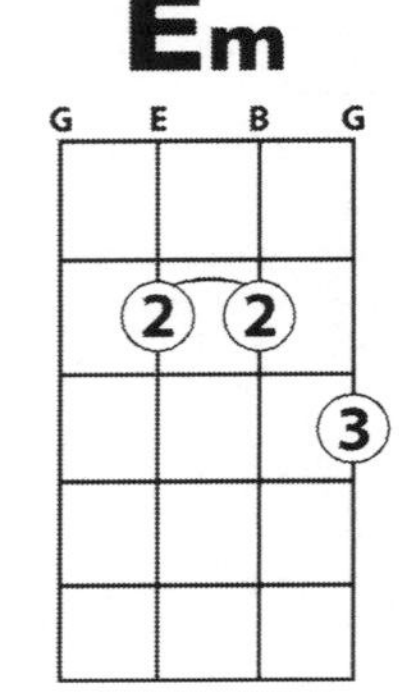

Am
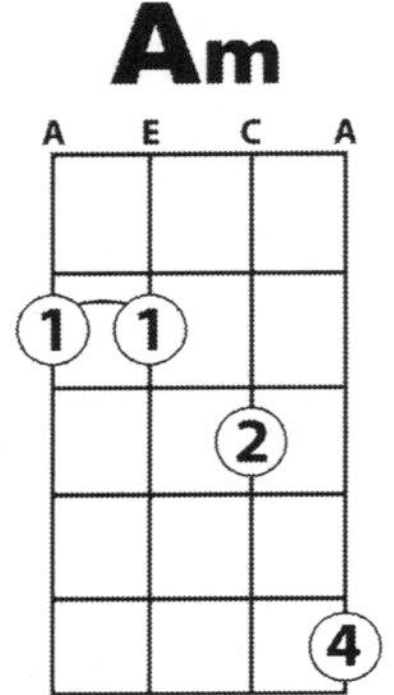

D
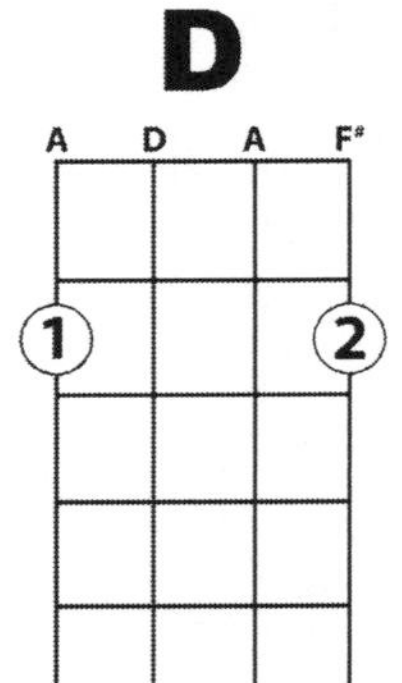

D^7
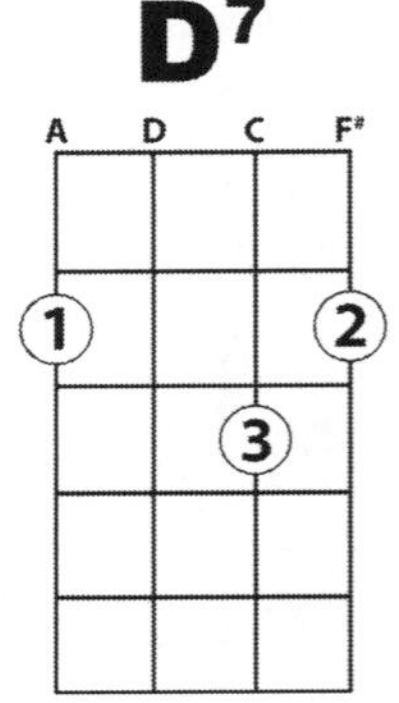

Blow the Man Down
(continued)

Melody & Chords

Key of G

```
   G                    Em                   G                    Em
E ─────────────────0──────────────────────────────────0───────────────────────
A 5──────5──────2──────5─2──────────2──────5──────2──5──────2─────────────────
D 0──────0─────────────0─2───────5─2──────0──────────0──────2─────────────────
G ───────0───────────────4────────4───────0─────────────────4─────────────────
  I'll sing you a song, a good song of the sea,
```

```
   G               Em     Am                 D
E ─────────────────0──────────────────────────────────────
A ───2──5──────2──────3──────2─────3──────0───────────────
D 5──2──0──────2──────2──────2─────2──────0───────────────
G 0─────0─────────────2───────────────────2───────────────
  To me way, hey, blow the man down;
```

```
      Am                           D                 Am              D
E ────────────────────────────────────────────────────────────────────────────
A 2────3────────2──────3───────────0──────────0─────3─────2─────3─────0───────
D 0────2────────2──────2───────────0──────4───0─────2─────2─────2─────0───────
G 2────2───────────────────────────2──────2─────────2─────────────────2───────
  And trust that you'll join in the chorus with me,
```

```
                             D7                 G
E ──────────────────────────────────────────────────────────────
A 5──────5──5──────5──────3──2──────0─────2─────────────────────
D 0──────0──0──────0──────0──0──────0─────0─────5───────────────
G 2────────────────2─────────2──────────────────0───────────────
  Give us some time to blow the man down.
```

Chord Forms

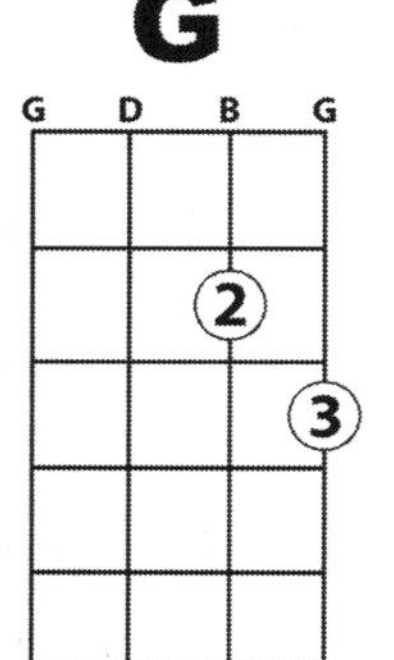

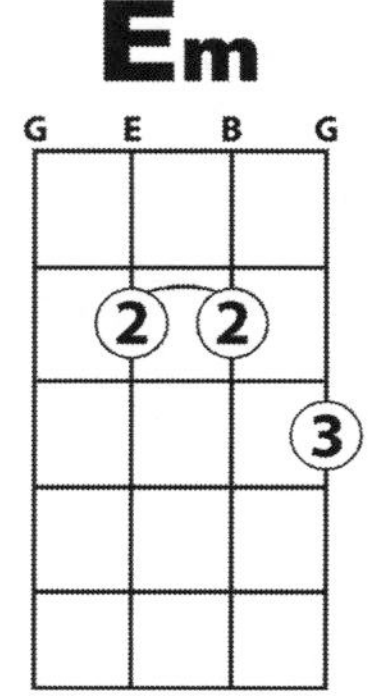

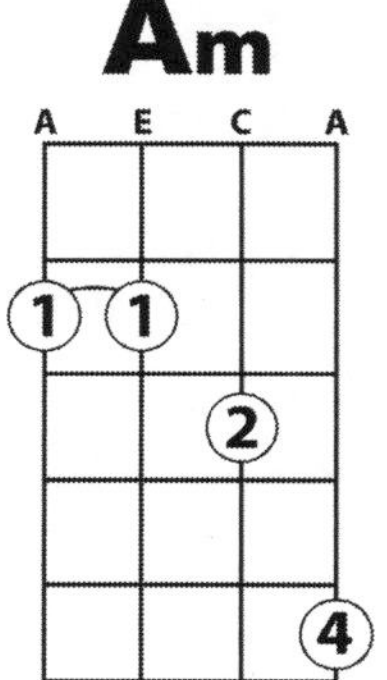

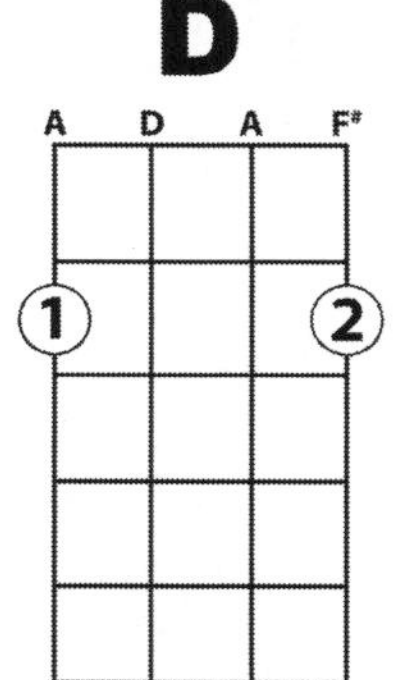

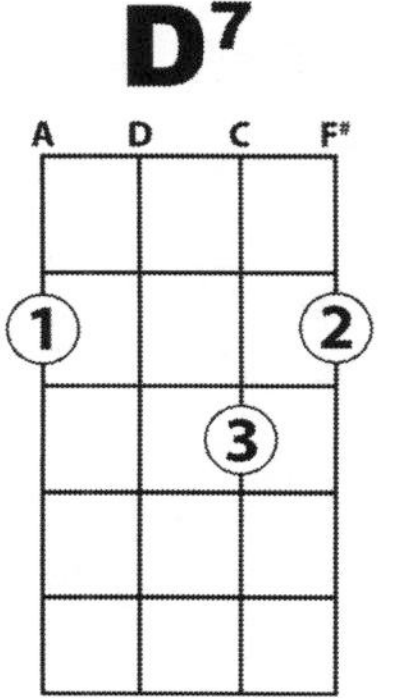

WHALING SONG

Blow Ye Winds

Basic Melody

Key of C (Low)

This old seafaring and sailing song has been around for a long time, and has been recorded by the likes of Pete Seeger, Burl Ives and many others. The subject of the song is the New England whaling trade in the 1800's. Unlike true sea shanties, this one was not sung to accompany work, but rather when the sailors were off-duty. This style of sea song is known as a "Fo'c'sle" (forecastle) song, and they were sung by sailors both on the ship and while ashore.

Words and Music

Traditional

```
  C
E ------------------------------------------------------------------
A ------------------------------------------------------------------
D -------------------------0----------------------------2-5---------
G -0----0-5--5----------------5-4-2----0---5----0---5---------------
  'Tis advertised in Bos-ton, New York and Buffalo,

       F                C            G
E ------------------------------------------------------------------
A ------------------------------------------------------------------
D 5----3--3----3-----0-2--0-----------------0-----0-----------------
G ---------------------------5------5-2-------------5--4------------
  Five hundred brave Amer-i-cans, a-whaling for to go.
```

Chorus

```
  G       C
E ------------------------------------------------------------------
A ------------------------------------------------------------------
D ---------------------------0---------------------------2-----5----
G 2--0-----5----4--5-----5--------5-4-2-0--5-----4--5---------------
  Singing blow ye winds in the morning, blow ye winds, high-ho!

     F               C                 G           C
E ------------------------------------------------------------------
A ------------------------------------------------------------------
D 5--3------3-3---0-----2--0---------------0-----5------------------
G ----------------------------5-----5-----------------5-------------
  Oh clear a-way your runnin' gear, and blow, boys, blow!
```

See Additional Verses on Next Page

Chord Forms

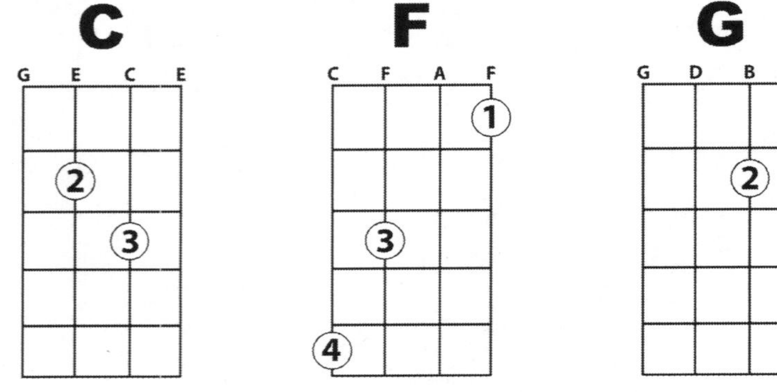

Blow Ye Winds (continued)

Additional Verses

They'll take you to New Bedford that famous whaling port,
And hand you to some land sharks to board and fit you out.

They tell you of the clipper ships a going in and out,
They say you'll take five hundred sperm before you're six months out.

And now we're out to sea my boys, the wind comes on to blow,
Half the watch is sick on deck, the other half below.

But as for our provisions, we don't get half enough,
A little piece of stinking beef and a blamed small bag of duff.

Next comes the running rigging which you're all supposed to know,
Lay aloft you son of a gun or overboard you'll go.

The skipper's on the quarter deck a squinting at the sails,
When up aloft the lookout spots a mighty school of whales.

Now clear away the boats my boys and after him we'll travel,
But if you get too near his fluke he'll kick you to the devil.

Now we've got him turned up we'll tow him alongside,
Over with our blubber hooks and we'll rob him of his hide.

Now comes the stowing down, my boy, 'twill take both night and day,
You'll all get two bits after six months to the day.

A 19th-century whaling station in Labrador.

Blow Ye Winds (continued)

Basic Melody

Key of C (High)

```
  C
E ---------------------------------------------------0-3------------
A --------3--3------5--3-2-0---------3--------3----------------------
D -5--5-----------------------5---------5-----------------------------
G -----------------------------------------------------------------------
  'Tis advertised in Bos-ton, New York and Buffalo,
```

```
      F                C           G
E 3----1--1----1--------0-------------------------------------------
A ---------------------5-----5-3------3-0--5-----5---3--2------------
D -----------------------------------------------------------------
G -----------------------------------------------------------------
  Five hundred brave Amer-i-cans, a-whaling for to go.
```

CHORUS

```
  G      C
E ----------------------------------------------------------0-----3----
A 0--------3-----2--3------3--5---3-2-0------3-----2--3-----------------
D ---5--------------------------------5-------------------------------
G ---------------------------------------------------------------------
  Singing blow ye winds in the morning, blow ye winds, high-ho!
```

```
    F                C                 G          C
E 3--1-----1-1-------0---------------------------3------------------
A ----------------5-------5----3-----3--5-----------3----------------
D -------------------------------------------------------------------
G -------------------------------------------------------------------
  Oh clear a-way your runnin' gear, and blow, boys, blow!
```

Chord Forms

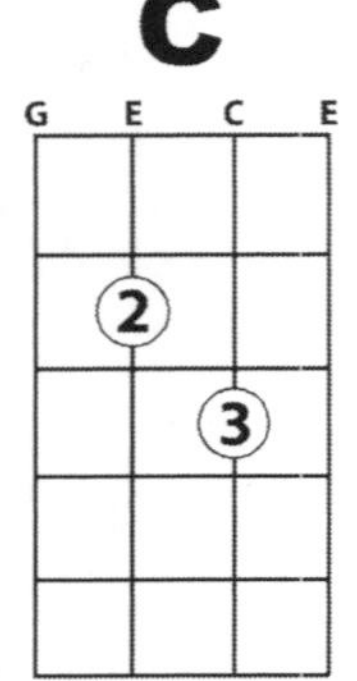

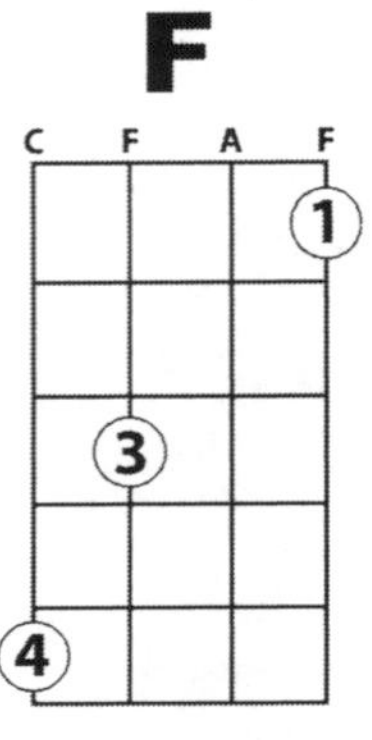

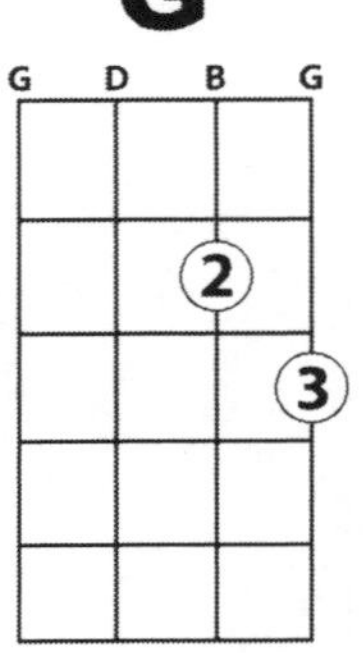

"Victims of the Whale Hunt", circa 1900.

Blow Ye Winds (continued)

Melody & Chords

Key of C (High)

```
    C
E ----------------------------------------------------------0-3----------
A ----------3--3-------5--3-2-0---------3-----------3--3-3--------------
D -5----5-2--2-------0--2-2-2-------5----2-------5----2----2------------
G -5----5-----0-----------0---------5----0-------5----0-----------------
  'Tis advertised in Bos-ton, New York and Buffalo,
```

```
        F                    C               G
E 3-----1--1------1----------0----------------------------------------------
A 3-----0--0------0-------5-3--5-3--------3-0--5-------5----3--2-----------
D 2-----3---------2-------3-2--2-2--------2-0--0-------0----0--0-----------
G --------------------------------0--------0---------0--------0-----------
  Five hundred brave Amer-i-cans, a-whaling for to go.
```

Chorus

```
  G       C
E --------------------------------------------------------------0------3----
A 0-------3-----2--3-------3--5----3-2-0-----3------2--3-------3------3----
D 0--5----2-----2--2-------2--2----2-2-2-5---2------2--2---------------2----
G ---0----0--------0---------------0-------5--0----------------------------
  Singing blow ye winds in the morning, blow ye winds, high-ho!
```

```
     F                    C                  G            C
E 3--1-------1-1----------0--------------------------3-----------------
A 3--0-------0-0----5-----3--5------3------3---5-----2-------3---------
D 2--3--------3-----3-----2--2------2------2---0-----0-------2---------
G ----------------------------------0----------0-------------0---------
  Oh clear a-way your runnin' gear, and blow, boys, blow!
```

Chord Forms

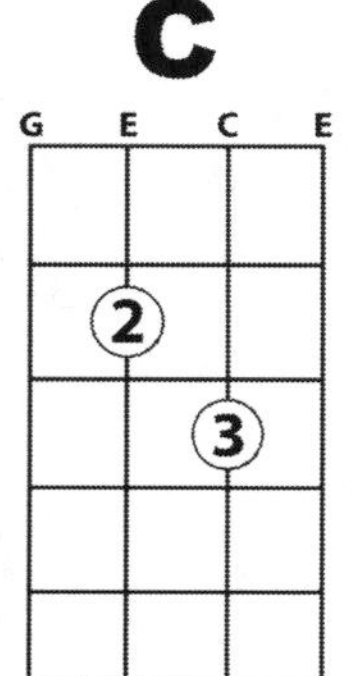

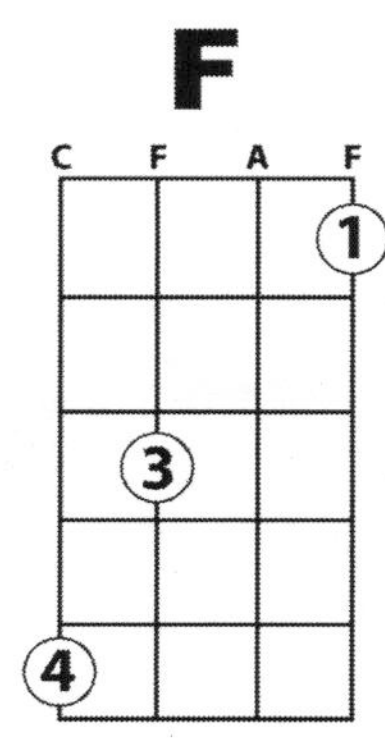

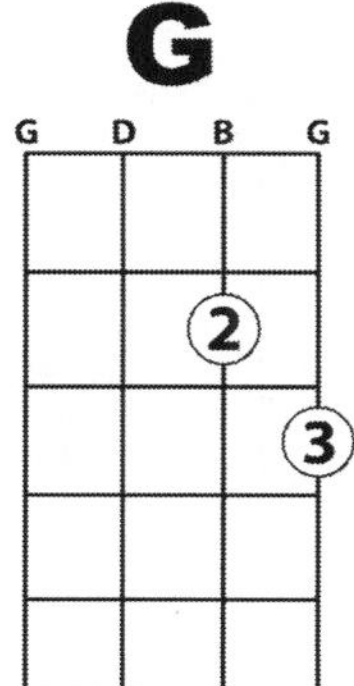

Blow Ye Winds (continued)

Basic Melody

Key of G

```
    G
E ------------------------------------------------------------------------
A ----------------------0------------------------------------2-5----------
D -0---0-5--5--------------5-4-2----0----5----0---5-----------------------
G ------------------------------------------------------------------------
  'Tis advertised in Bos-ton, New York and Buffalo,
```

```
        C                G              D
E ------------------------------------------------------------------------
A 5----3--3----3-----0-2-0----------------------0-----0-------------------
D ------------------------------5------5-2---------------5--4-------------
G ------------------------------------------------------------------------
  Five hundred brave Amer-i-cans, a-whaling for to go.
```

Chorus

```
  D      G
E ------------------------------------------------------------------------
A ------------------------------0--------------------------------2----5---
D 2--0----5----4--5------5-------5-4-2-0--5----4--5-----------------------
G ------------------------------------------------------------------------
  Singing blow ye winds in the morning, blow ye winds, high-ho!
```

```
      C               G                D           G
E ------------------------------------------------------------------------
A 5--3------3-3---0----2--0--------------0-----5--------------------------
D ---------------------------------5-----5----------------5---------------
G ------------------------------------------------------------------------
  Oh clear a-way your runnin' gear, and blow, boys, blow!
```

Chord Forms

G

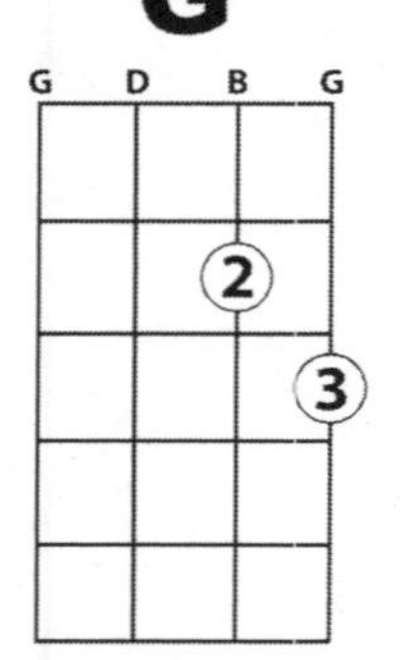

C

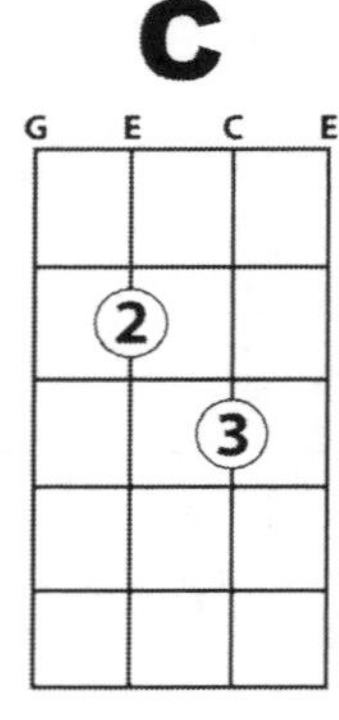

D

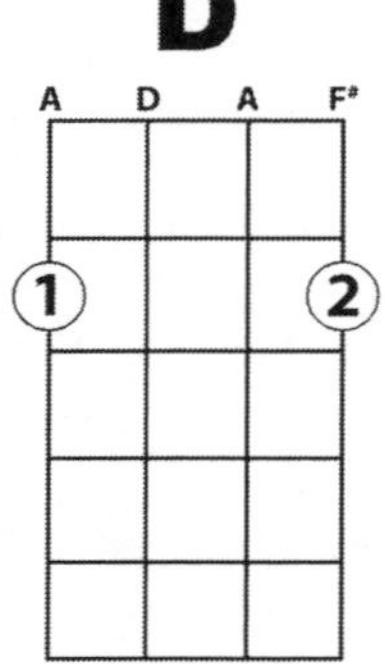

Blow Ye Winds (continued)

Melody & Chords

Key of G

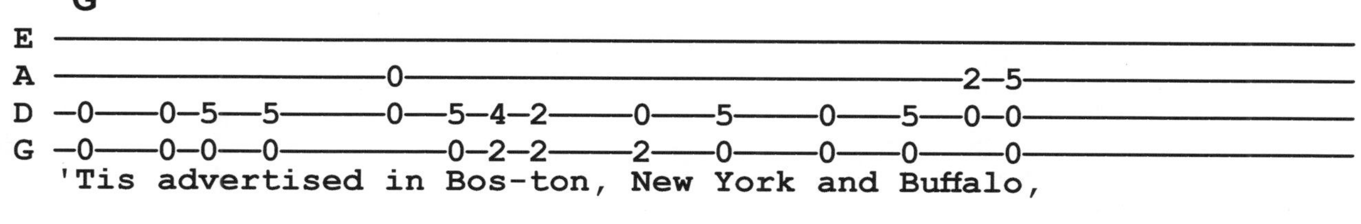


```
      C                G            D
E ——————————————————————————————————————————————
A 5——3—3——3——0–2—0——————————0——0———————————
D 0——2—2——2——2–0—0–5—————5–2—0——0——5—4———
G 0——0————0——0——0——0–2————2——2—2———
  Five hundred brave Amer-i-cans, a-whaling for to go.
```

Chorus

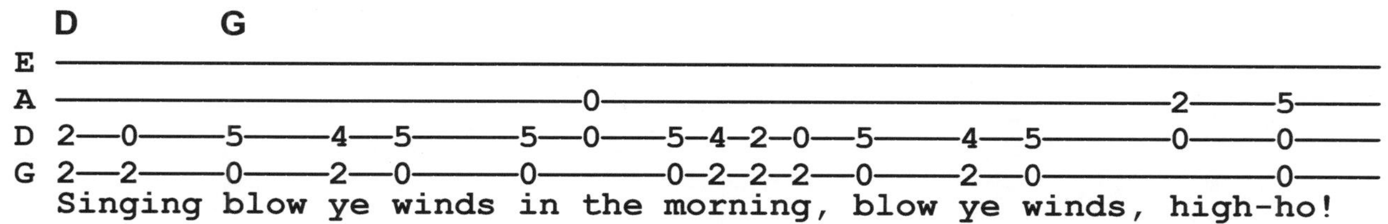


```
    C               G                 D          G
E ——————————————————————————————————————————————————
A 5—3————3–3—0——2—0——————————————0——5————————————
D 0—2————2–2——2——0—0——5———5—0——0——5———
G 0—0—————0————0————0———0—2——2——0———
  Oh clear a-way your runnin' gear, and blow, boys, blow!
```

Chord Forms

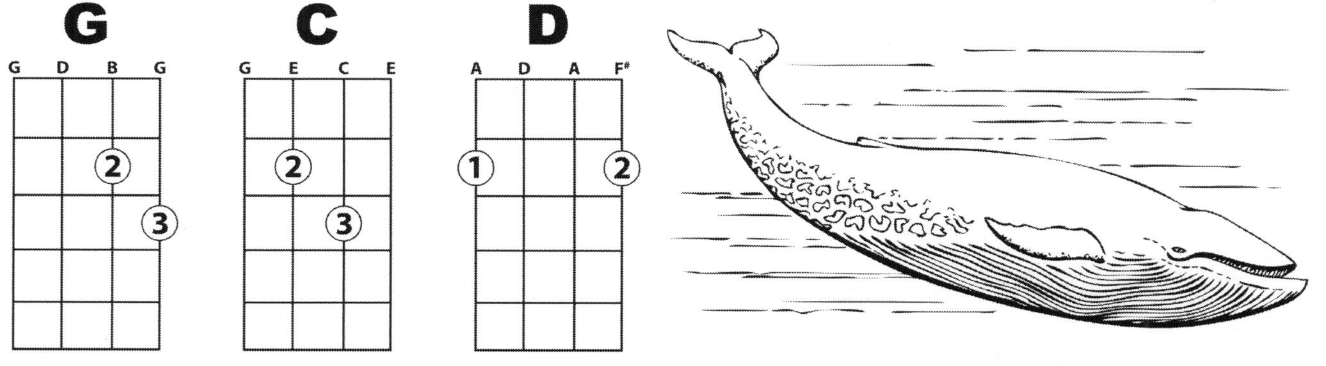

Bonnie Hieland Laddie

Basic Melody
Key of A Minor (Low)

A number of different lyrics have been set to this old folk tune. The most traditional lyrics are Robert Burns' poem "Highland Laddie", but the ones below are better known today. Even Beethoven took a turn arranging and setting words to the tune.

Words and Music
Traditional

```
  Am
E ----------------------------------------------------------------
A ----------------------------------------------------------------
D ---0---2-2--3--0--2-----0-------0--2------------0---------------
G 5-------------------------5---------------5--4---5--------------
  Was you ever in Quebec? Bonnie laddie, hieland laddie;
```

```
  Am                                      Em      Am
E ----------------------------------------------------------------
A ----------------------------------------------------------------
D ---0---2--2---3--0---2----2--0----------------------------------
G 5------------------------------5---4--0----2--2-----------------
  Loading timber on the deck, my bonnie hieland laddie.
```

Chorus

```
  F   C   G7        C   Em              Am
E ----------------------------------------------------------------
A 0---------------------------------------------------------------
D ---5----3-3---5--2---0-----0--2--------------0------------------
G ---------------------5-------------5--4---5---------------------
  Hey-ho, a-way we go, bonnie laddie, hieland laddie;
```

```
  F   C   G7        C      Em             Am
E ----------------------------------------------------------------
A 0---------------------------------------------------------------
D ---5----3-3---5--2----2--0--------------------------------------
G ---------------------------5---4--0----2--2---------------------
  Hey-ho, a-way we go, my bonnie hieland laddie.
```

See Additional Verses on Next Page

Chord Forms

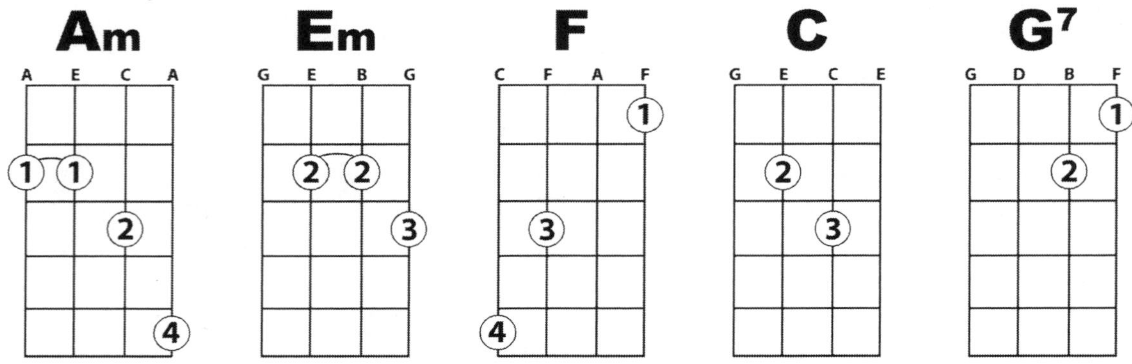

Bonnie Hieland Laddie
(continued)

Melody & Chords

Key of A Minor (Low)

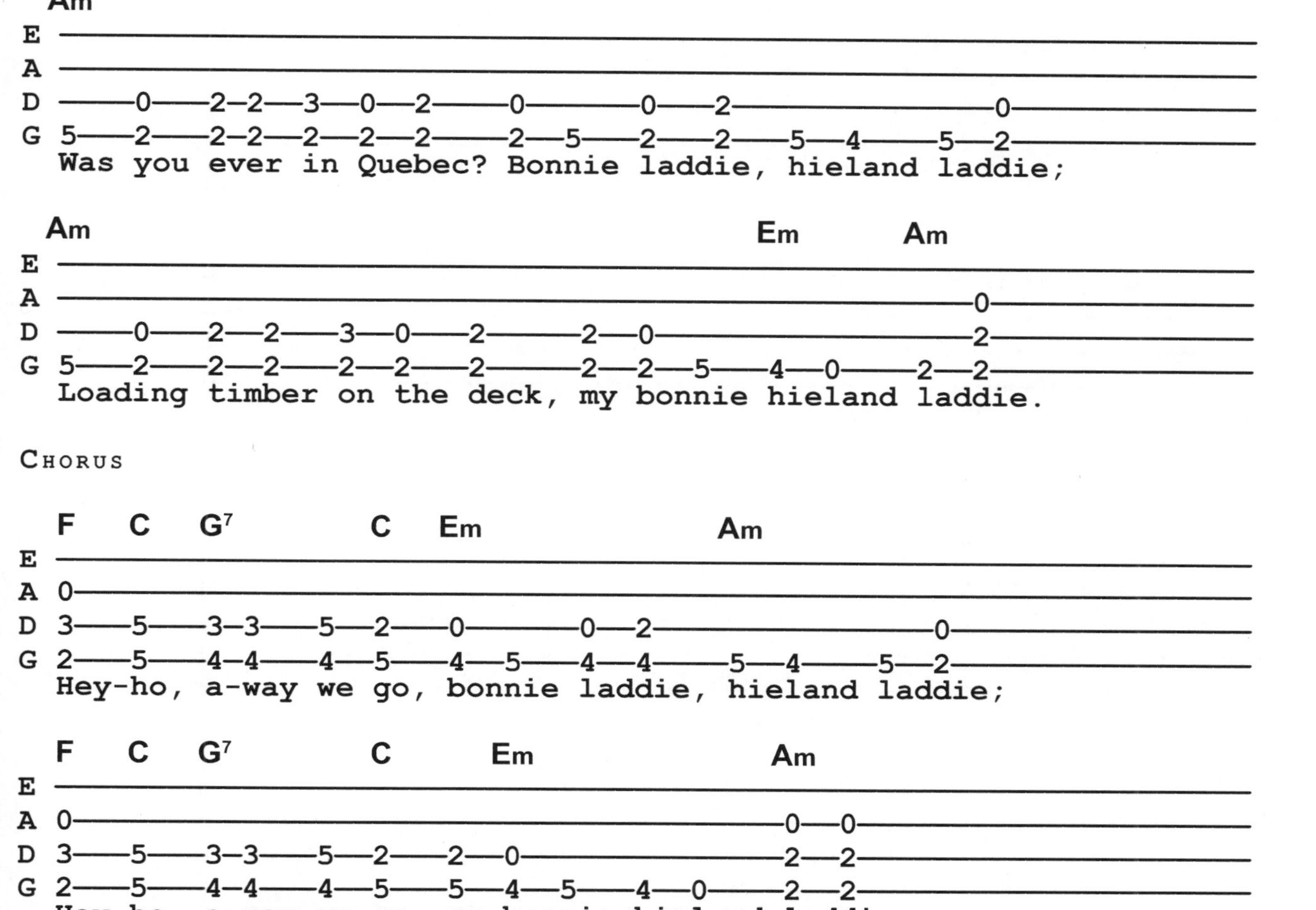

Additional Verses

Was you ever in Callao,
Bonnie laddie, hieland laddie;
Where the girls are never slow?
My bonnie hieland laddie.

Was you ever in Baltimore,
Bonnie laddie, hieland laddie;
Dancing on the sanded floor?
My bonnie hieland laddie.

Was you ever in Mobile Bay,
Bonnie laddie, hieland laddie;
Screwing cotton by the day?
My bonnie hieland laddie.

Was you on the Brummalow,
Bonnie laddie, hieland laddie;
Where Yankee boys are all the go?
My bonnie hieland laddie.

See Additional Verses on Next Page

Bonnie Hieland Laddie
(continued)

Basic Melody

Key of A Minor (High)

```
 Am
E ----------0--0--1-----0-----------------0-----------------------
A 3--5-----------------5------5--3--5---------3--2----3--5---------
D -----------------------------------------------------------------
G -----------------------------------------------------------------
  Was you ever in Quebec? Bonnie laddie, hieland laddie;
```

```
 Am                                      Em       Am
E ----------0--0--1------0-----0-----------------------------------
A 3--5------------------5-----------5--3--2---------0--0-----------
D ----------------------------------------------5------------------
G -----------------------------------------------------------------
  Loading timber on the deck, my bonnie hieland laddie.
```

CHORUS

```
  F   C   G7        C   Em               Am
E 5---3---1--1---3--0-----------------0----------------------------
A ----------------------5--3--5------------3--2----3--5------------
D -----------------------------------------------------------------
G -----------------------------------------------------------------
  Hey-ho, a-way we go, bonnie laddie, hieland laddie;
```

```
  F   C   G7        C     Em              Am
E 5---3---1--1---3--0---0------------------------------------------
A -----------------------5--3--2---------0--0----------------------
D ------------------------------5----------------------------------
G -----------------------------------------------------------------
  Hey-ho, a-way we go, my bonnie hieland laddie.
```

Chord Forms

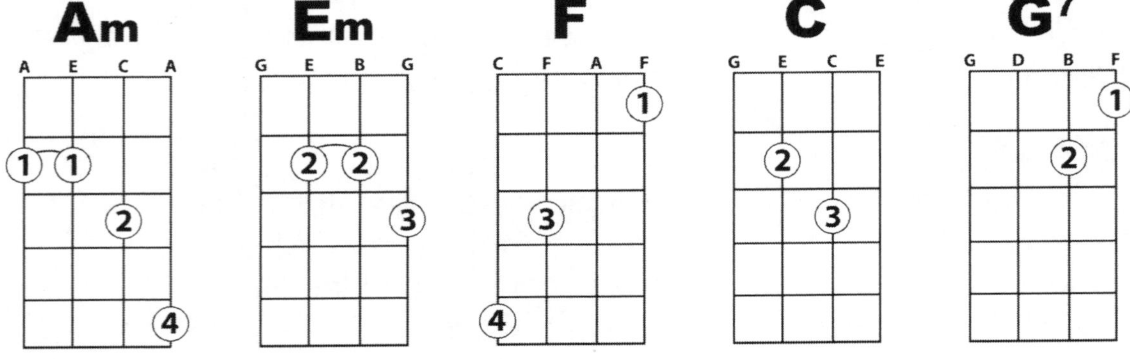

Bonnie Hieland Laddie
(continued)

Melody & Chords

Key of A Minor (High)

```
  Am
E ———————0—0—1————0———————————————————0——————————————————————
A 3——5——0—0——0——5——0————5——3———5———0———3——2————3——5———————————
D 2——2——2—————0——0——2————2——2———2————————2——2————2——0——————————
G 2—————————————————————2——————2————————2————————2————————————
  Was you ever in Quebec? Bonnie laddie, hieland laddie;
```

```
  Am                                        Em       Am
E ———————0——0———1——————0————0——————————————————————————————————
A 3——5——0——0————0——5————0————0——5——3———2————————0——0————————————
D 2——2——2————————0——0————2————2——2——2———2——5—————2——2————————————
G 2——————————————————————————2———————————4——4—————2——2————————————
  Loading timber on the deck, my bonnie hieland laddie.
```

CHORUS

```
  F   C   G7        C    Em              Am
E 5——3——1-1——3——0———————————————0——————————————————————————————
A 3——3——2-2——2——3———5——3———5——2————3——2————3——5————————————————
D 3——2——0———————2———2——2———2——2————2——2————2——2————————————————
G ————————————————————————————————2—————————2—————————————————
  Hey-ho, a-way we go, bonnie laddie, hieland laddie;
```

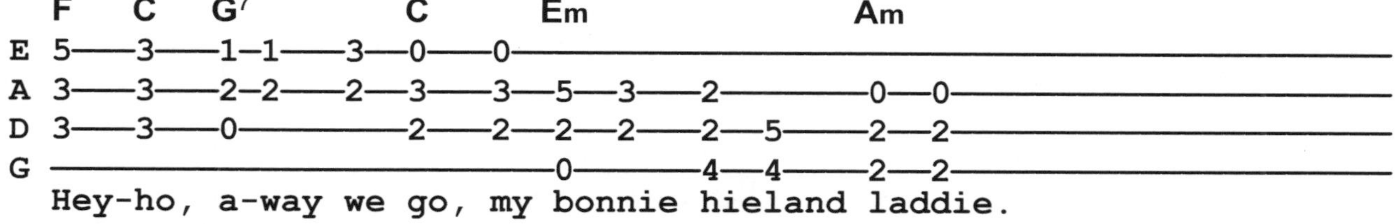

Chord Forms

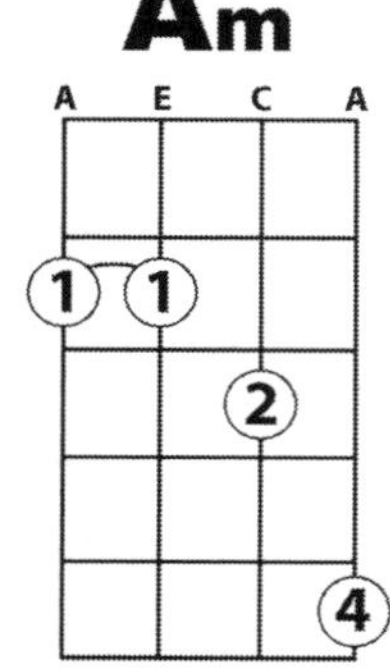

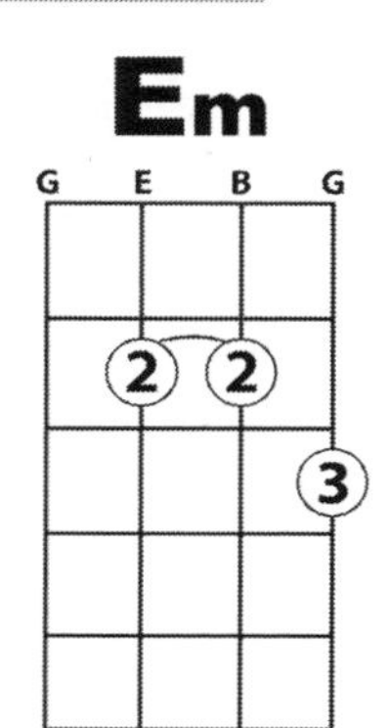

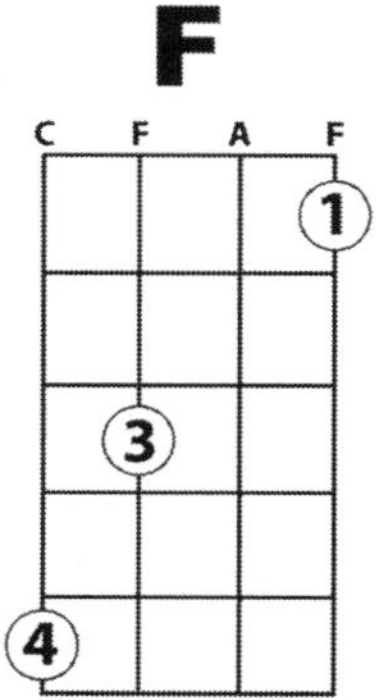

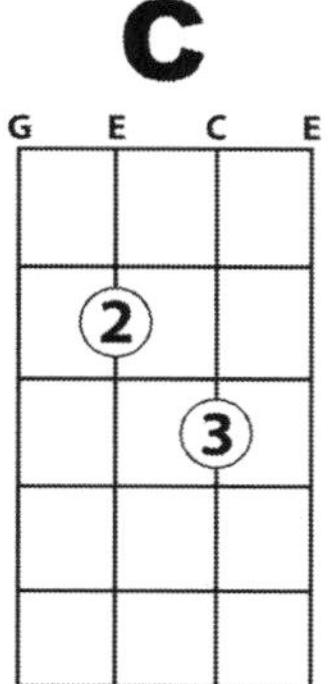

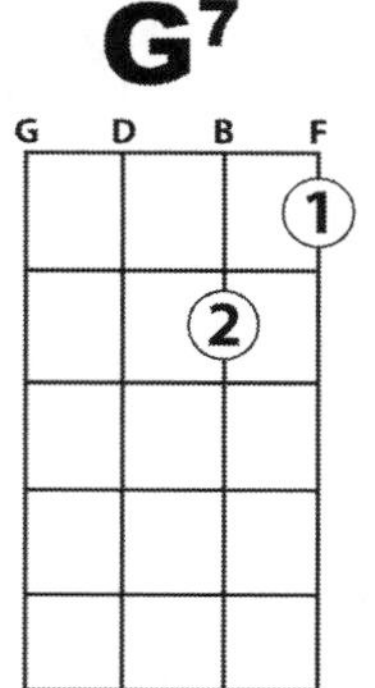

Bonnie Hieland Laddie
(continued)

Basic Melody

Key of E Minor

```
  Em
E -----------------------------------------------------------------------------
A -----0-----2--2---3---0---2-------0--------0---2-------------------0---------
D 5-----------------------------------5-----------5---4-----5------------------
G -----------------------------------------------------------------------------
  Was you ever in Quebec? Bonnie laddie, hieland laddie;

  Em                                          Bm       Em
E -----------------------------------------------------------------------------
A -----0-----2---2----3---0----2------2---0------------------------------------
D 5------------------------------------------5----4---0-----2---2--------------
G -----------------------------------------------------------------------------
  Loading timber on the deck, my bonnie hieland laddie.
```

Chorus

```
  C    G    D7        G    Bm           Em
E 0----------------------------------------------------------------------------
A -----5-----3--3----5---2----0---------0---2-------------------0--------------
D -------------------------------5-----------------5---4-----5-----------------
G -----------------------------------------------------------------------------
  Hey-ho, a-way we go, bonnie laddie, hieland laddie;

  C    G    D7        G         Bm             Em
E 0----------------------------------------------------------------------------
A -----5-----3--3----5---2----2---0--------------------------------------------
D -----------------------------------5----4---0-----2---2----------------------
G -----------------------------------------------------------------------------
  Hey-ho, a-way we go, my bonnie hieland laddie.
```

Chord Forms

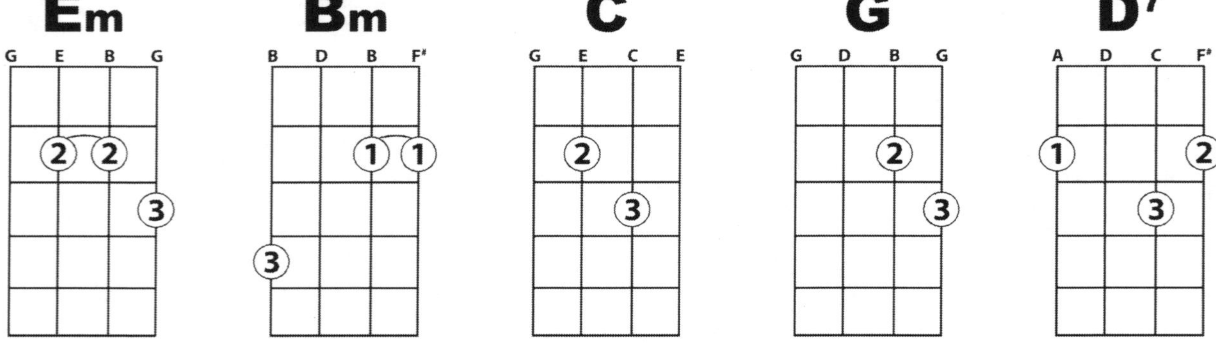

Bonnie Hieland Laddie
(continued)

Melody & Chords

Key of E Minor

```
  Em
E ----------------------------------------------------------------
A ---0---2-2--3--0--2-----0-------0--2-------------------0--------
D 5--2---2-2--2--2--2-----2--5----2--2----5--4-----5--2--------
G 4------4----4-----4-----4--4--------------4--4-----4--4--------
  Was you ever in Quebec? Bonnie laddie, hieland laddie;
```

```
  Em                                    Bm      Em
E ----------------------------------------------------------------
A ---0---2--2---3--0---2-----2--0---------------------------------
D 5--2---2--2---2--2---2-----2--2--5----4--0-----2--2-------------
G 4------4------4------4--------4--4----4--2-----4--4-------------
  Loading timber on the deck, my bonnie hieland laddie.
```

Chorus

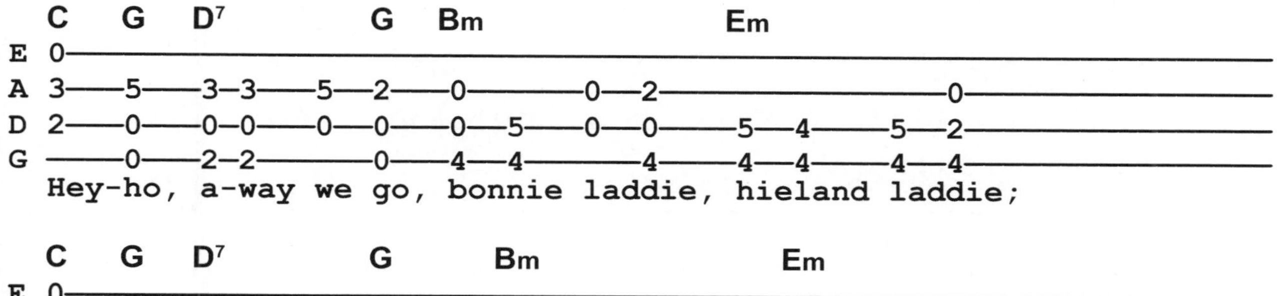

```
  C   G   D7      G   Bm              Em
E 0---------------------------------------------------------------
A 3---5---3-3---5--2---0--------0--2-----------------0------------
D 2---0---0-0---0--0---0--5-----0--0------5--4-----5--2-----------
G ----0---2-2------0---4--4--------4------4--4-----4--4-----------
  Hey-ho, a-way we go, bonnie laddie, hieland laddie;
```

```
  C   G   D7      G        Bm            Em
E 0---------------------------------------------------------------
A 3---5---3-3---5--2---2--0---------------------------------------
D 2---0---0-0---0--0---0--0--5----4--0-----2--2-------------------
G 0---0-----2------0------4--4----4--4-----4--4-------------------
  Hey-ho, a-way we go, my bonnie hieland laddie.
```

Chord Forms

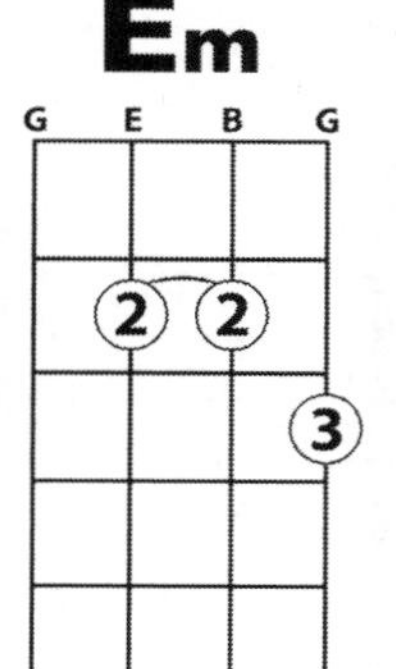

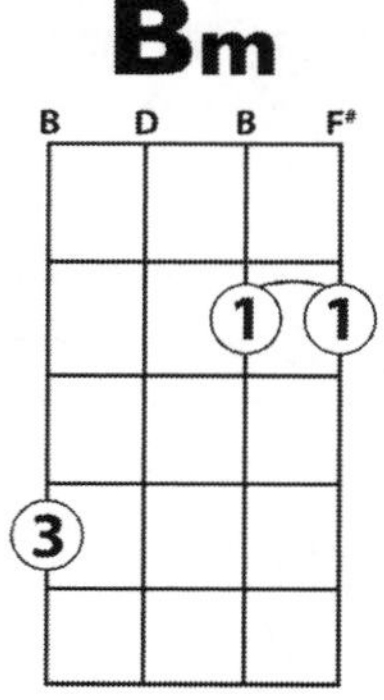

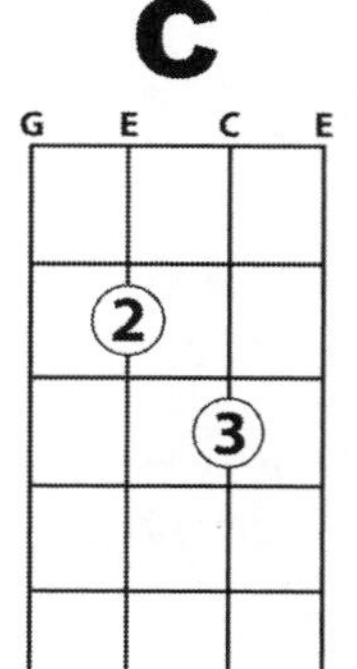

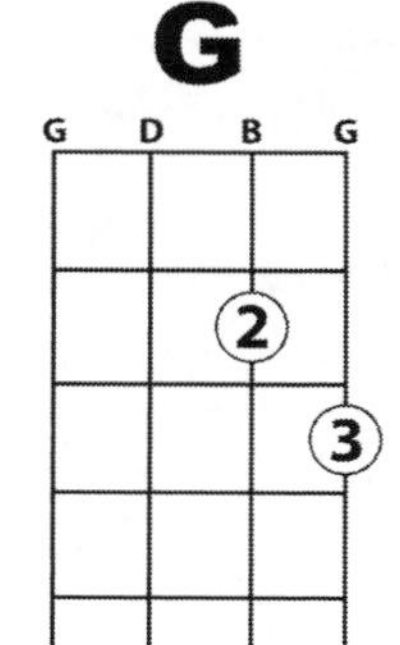

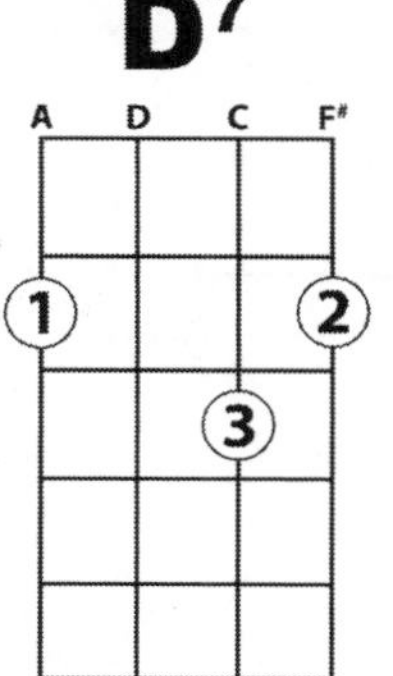

Bonnie Ship the Diamond

Basic Melody
Key of A Minor (Low)

This old sea shanty and whaling song was written about a ship named The Diamond, which was caught in the ice west of Greenland and sank in 1819 along with a number of other ships. The song is said to have originated in Scotland, and The Corries recorded what is probably the best-known version of it today.

Words and Music

Traditional

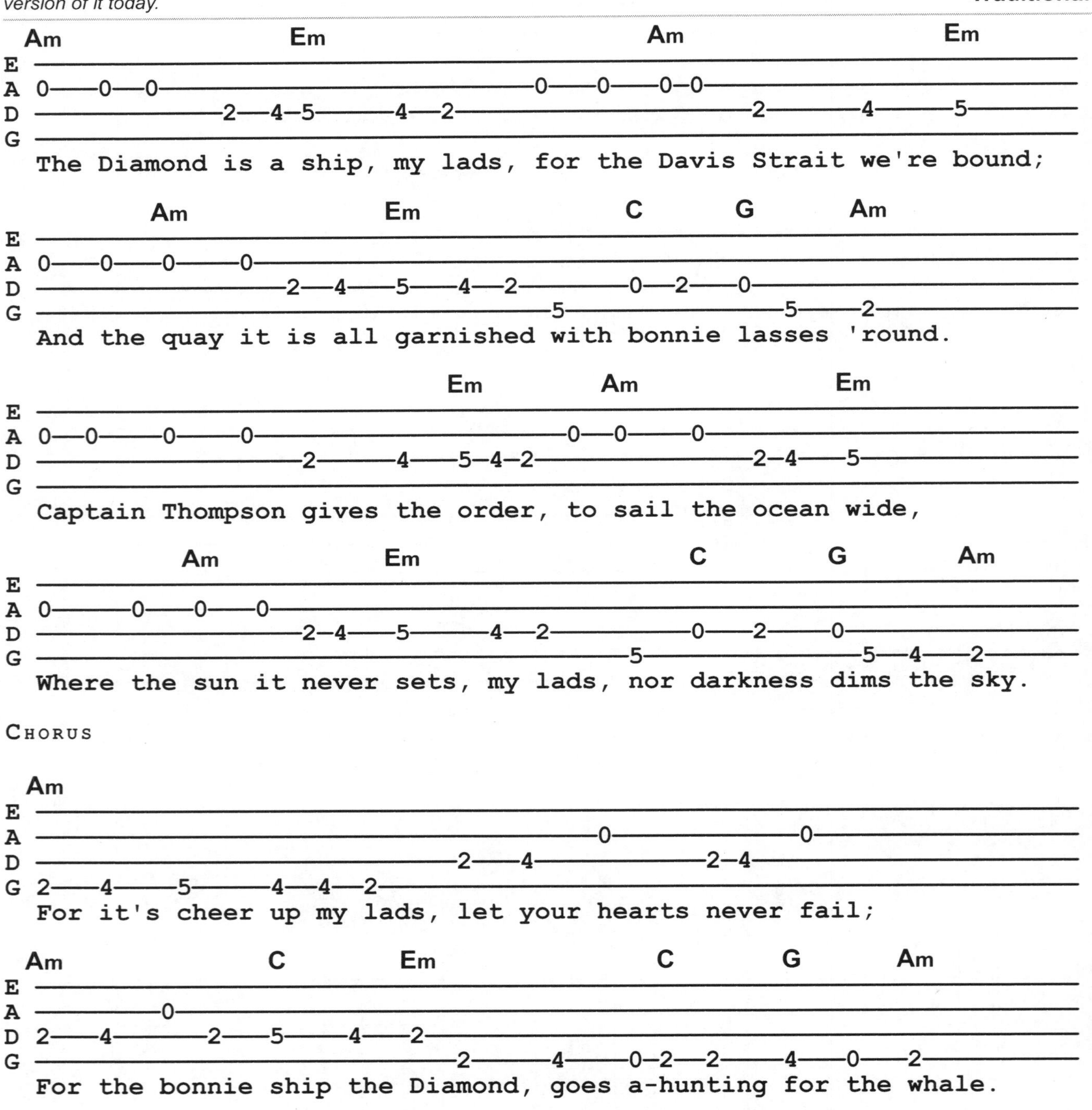

See Chord Forms and Additional Verses on Next Page

Bonnie Ship the Diamond
(continued)

Chord Forms and Additional Verses

Chord Forms

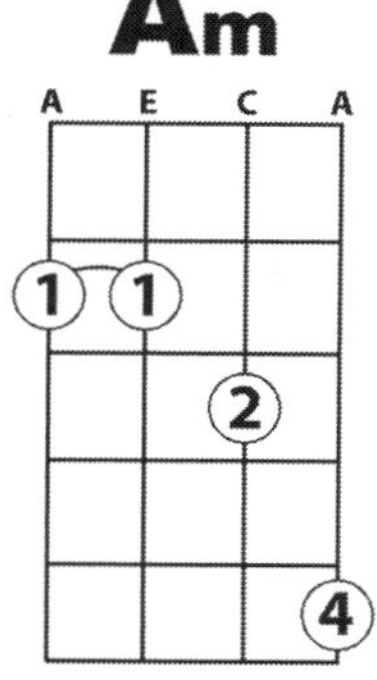

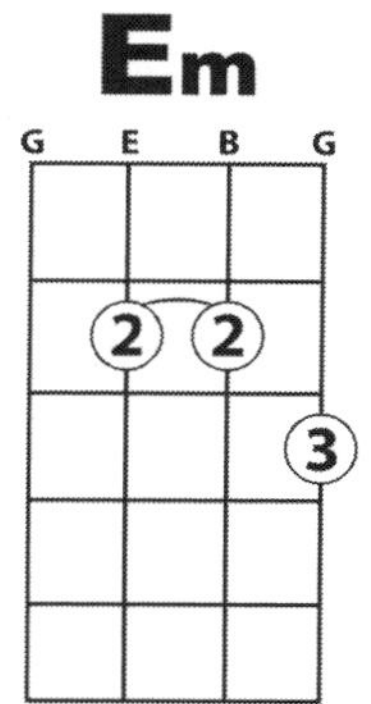

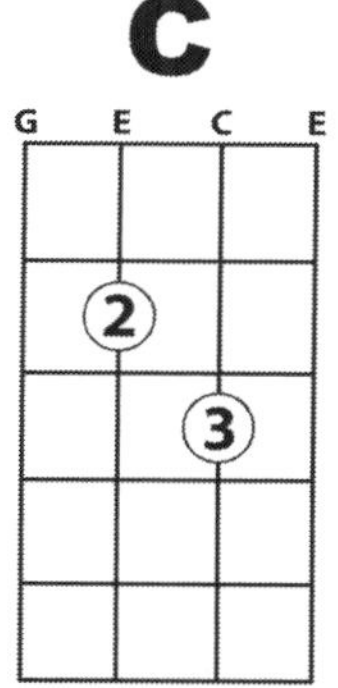

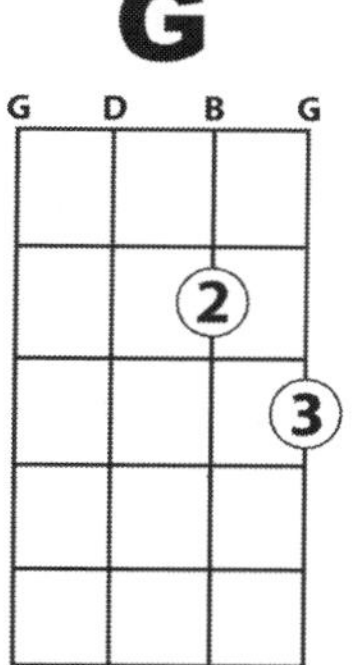

Additional Verses

Along the quay at Peterhead, the lasses stand around,
With their shawls all pulled around them, and the salt tears runnin' down.
Don't you weep, my bonnie wee lass, though you be left behind;
For the rose will grow on Greenland's ice, before we change our mind.

Here's a health to the Resolution, likewise the Eliza Swan;
Three cheers for the Battler of Montrose, and the Diamond, ship of fame.
We wear the trousers o' the white, the jackets o' the blue,
When we get back to Peterhead, we'll hae sweethearts enou'.

It will be bright both day and night, when the Greenland lads come hame,
Our ship full up with oil, my lads, and money to our name.
We'll make the cradles for to rock, and the blankets for to tear,
And every lass in Peterhead sing, "Hushabye, my dear."

Bonnie Ship the Diamond
(continued)

Basic Melody

Key of A Minor (High)

```
   Am                Em                      Am                  Em
E 5--5--5---0--2-3------2--0------5---5---5-5---0---------2------3-----
A ---------------------------------------------------------------------
D ---------------------------------------------------------------------
G ---------------------------------------------------------------------
  The Diamond is a ship, my lads, for the Davis Strait we're bound;

          Am            Em               C      G       Am
E 5--5--5----5--0--2---3---2--0---------0----------------------------
A ------------------------------3---5--------5--3---0----------------
D -------------------------------------------------------------------
G -------------------------------------------------------------------
  And the quay it is all garnished with bonnie lasses 'round.

                             Em     Am             Em
E 5--5----5----5---0-----2---3-2-0--5--5-----5---0-2---3-------------
A -------------------------------------------------------------------
D -------------------------------------------------------------------
G -------------------------------------------------------------------
  Captain Thompson gives the order, to sail the ocean wide,

            Am        Em                  C        G        Am
E 5------5---5---5--0-2---3------2--0-------------0--------------------
A -------------------------------------3---5----------5-3---2---0-----
D ---------------------------------------------------------------------
G ---------------------------------------------------------------------
  Where the sun it never sets, my lads, nor darkness dims the sky.
```

Chorus

```
   Am
E ---------------------------0---2----5------0-2---5------------------
A 0--2---3-----2--2--0-------------------------------------------------
D ---------------------------------------------------------------------
G ---------------------------------------------------------------------
  For it's cheer up my lads, let your hearts never fail;

   Am            C          Em              C       G        Am
E 0--2--5--0---3---2---0-----------------------------------------------
A ---------------------------0-----2-----0--0----2-------0------------
D ----------------------------------5-------------5--------------------
G ---------------------------------------------------------------------
  For the bonnie ship the Diamond, goes a-hunting for the whale.
```

Am (A E C A): 1 1 2 4

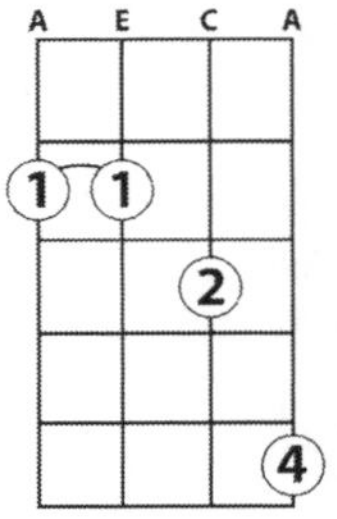

Em (G E B G): 2 2 3

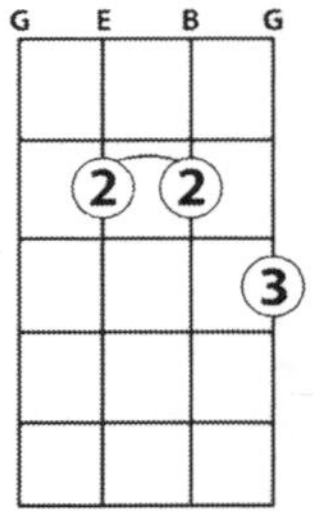

C (G E C E): 2 3

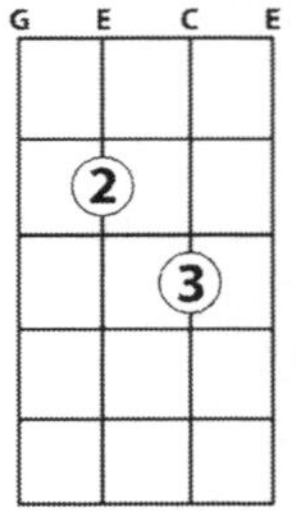

G (G D B G): 2 3

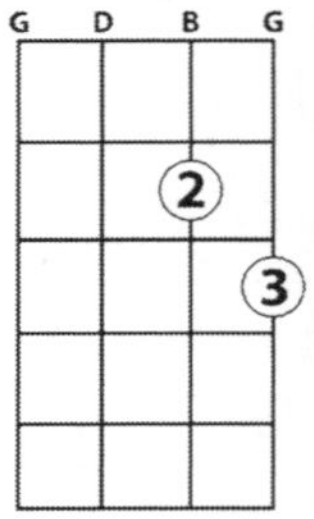

Bonnie Ship the Diamond
(continued)

Melody & Chords

Key of A Minor (High)

```
Am                Em                      Am                  Em
E 5--5--5---0--2-3----2--0----5---5---5-5---0------2------3---
A 3--3--3---2--0-2----2--2----0---0---3-3---2------0------2---
D 2--2-----------2-------2--------------2-----------------2---
G ------------------------------------------------------------
  The Diamond is a ship, my lads, for the Davis Strait we're bound;
```

```
       Am            Em               C       G      Am
E 5--5--5---5--0--2--3--2--0----------0-----------------------
A 5--5--3---3--2--3--2--2--2--3---5---3---5---3---0-----------
D ------2------------2--------2---0---2---0---2---2-----------
G ------------------------------0-----------0-----2-----------
  And the quay it is all garnished with bonnie lasses 'round.
```

```
                            Em       Am          Em
E 5--5----5----5--0-----2---3-2-0--5--5----5---0-2--3---------
A 3--3----3----3--2-----2---2-2-2--0--3----3---2-2--2---------
D 2-------2-----------------2---2-----2--------2----2---------
G ------------------------------------------------------------
  Captain Thompson gives the order, to sail the ocean wide,
```

```
         Am          Em                  C       G       Am
E 5------5--5---5--0-2--3-----2--0------------0---------------
A 5------5--3---3--2-3--2-----2--2----3---5---3----5-3--2--0--
D -----------2----------2-------------2---0---2----0-2--0--2--
G ----------------------------------------0--------0-------2--
  Where the sun it never sets, my lads, nor darkness dims the sky.
```

CHORUS

```
Am
E -------------------------0---2----5-------0-2---5-----------
A 0---2----3----2--2--0----0---0----3-------2-2---3-----------
D 2---2----2----2--2--2----2--------2-------------2-----------
G 2--------2----------2---------------------------------------
  For it's cheer up my lads, let your hearts never fail;
```

```
Am           C          Em             C        G        Am
E 0---2---5--0---3----2---0-----------------------------------
A 0---0---3--2---3----0---2--0------2-----0--0----2------0----
D 2-------2------2--------2--2------2---5-2--2----0---5--2----
G ---------------------------0------0---0-5-------0---0--2----
  For the bonnie ship the Diamond, goes a-hunting for the whale.
```

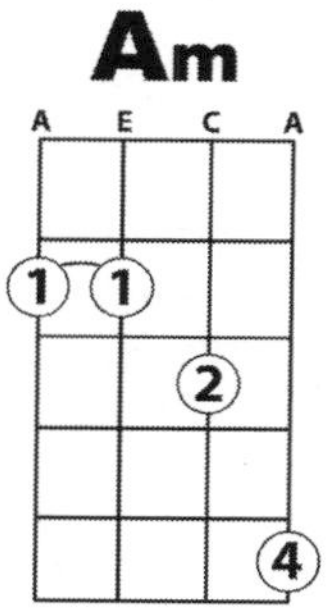

Am (A E C A): ① ① ② ④

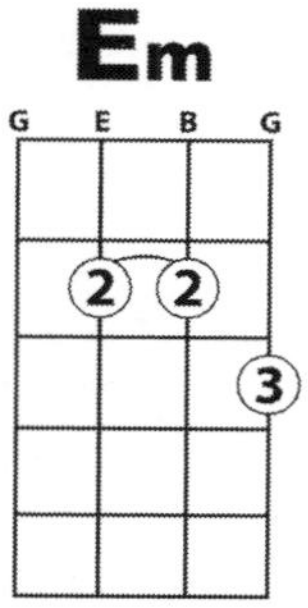

Em (G E B G): ② ② ③

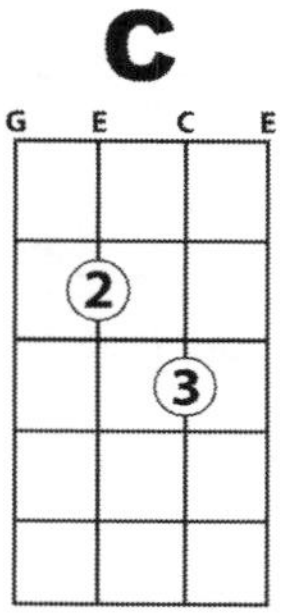

C (G E C E): ② ③

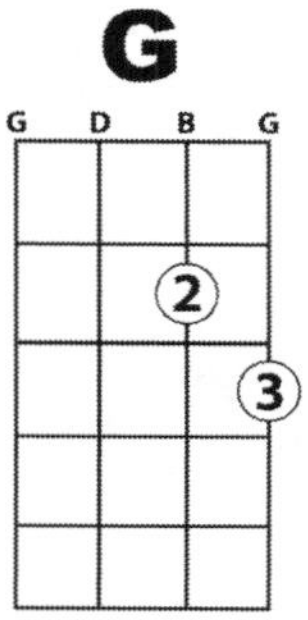

G (G D B G): ② ③

Bonnie Ship the Diamond
(continued)

Basic Melody

Key of E Minor

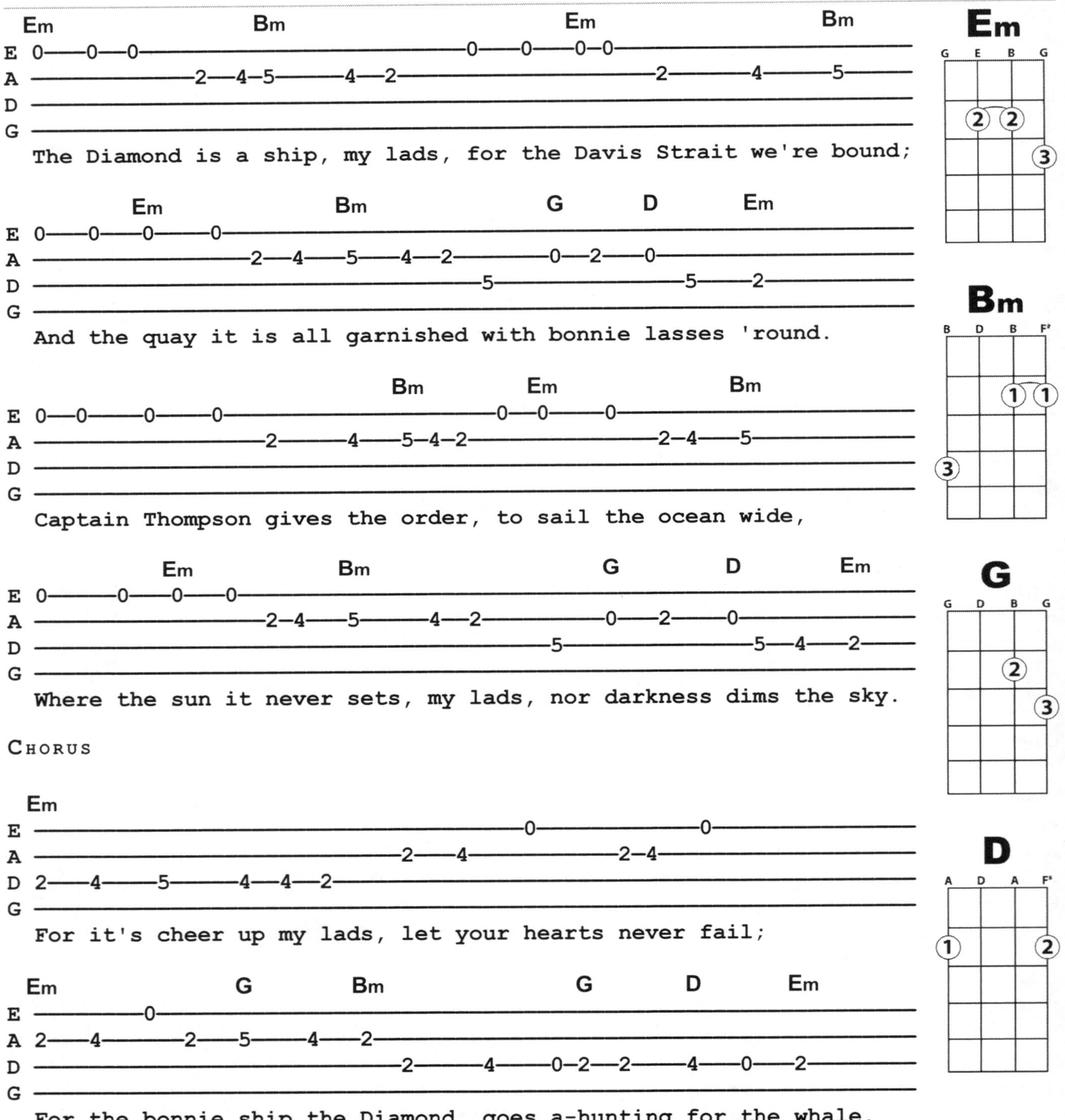

Bonnie Ship the Diamond

(continued)

Basic Melody

Key of E Minor

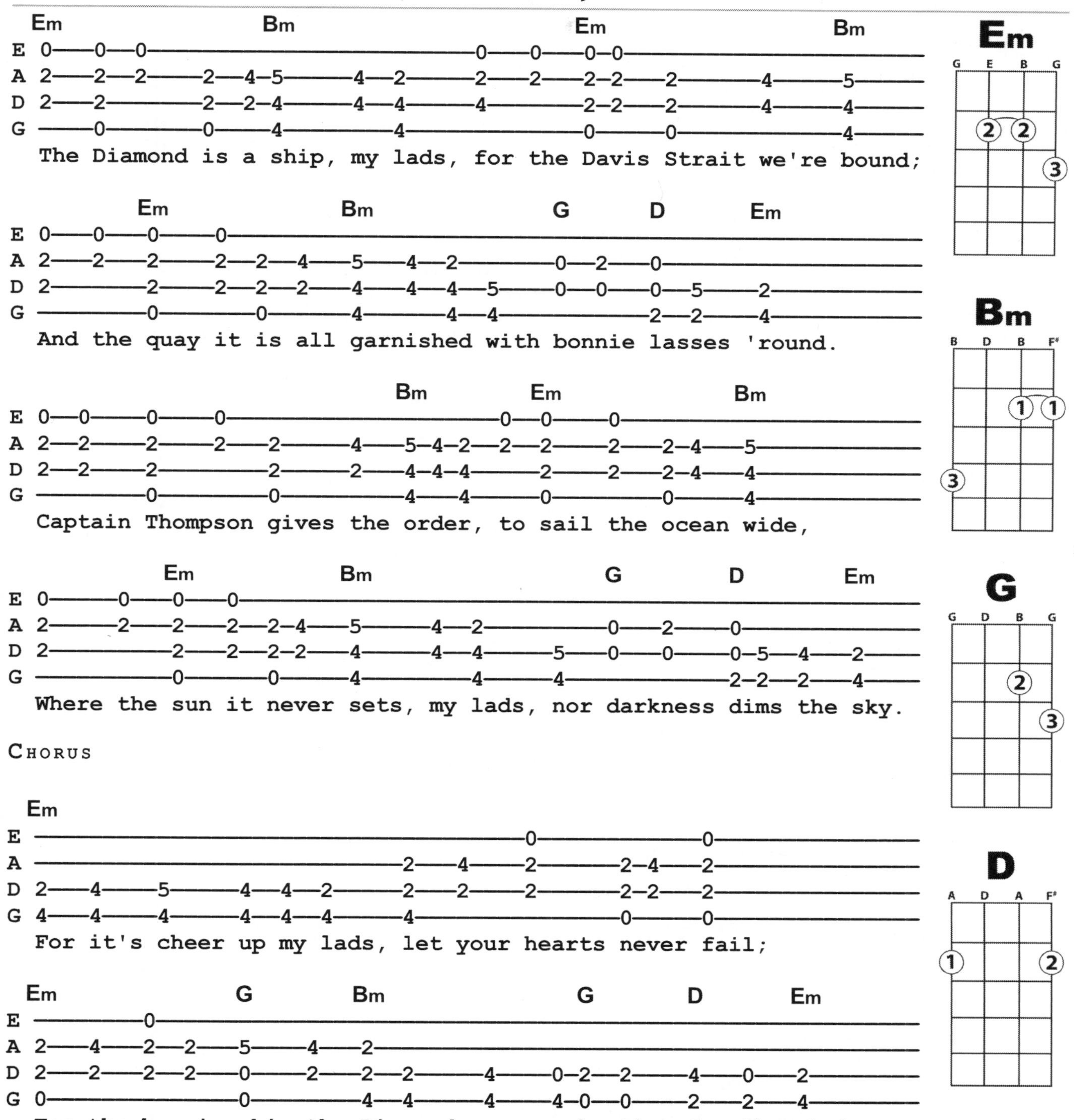

Botany Bay

Basic Melody

Key of C (Low)

This old Irish song was first collected in Australia, and tells the tale of a bricklayer named Pat who emigrates to Australia to find his fortune. Before he goes he makes sure to let his former boss knows what he thinks of the old job.

Words and Music
Traditional

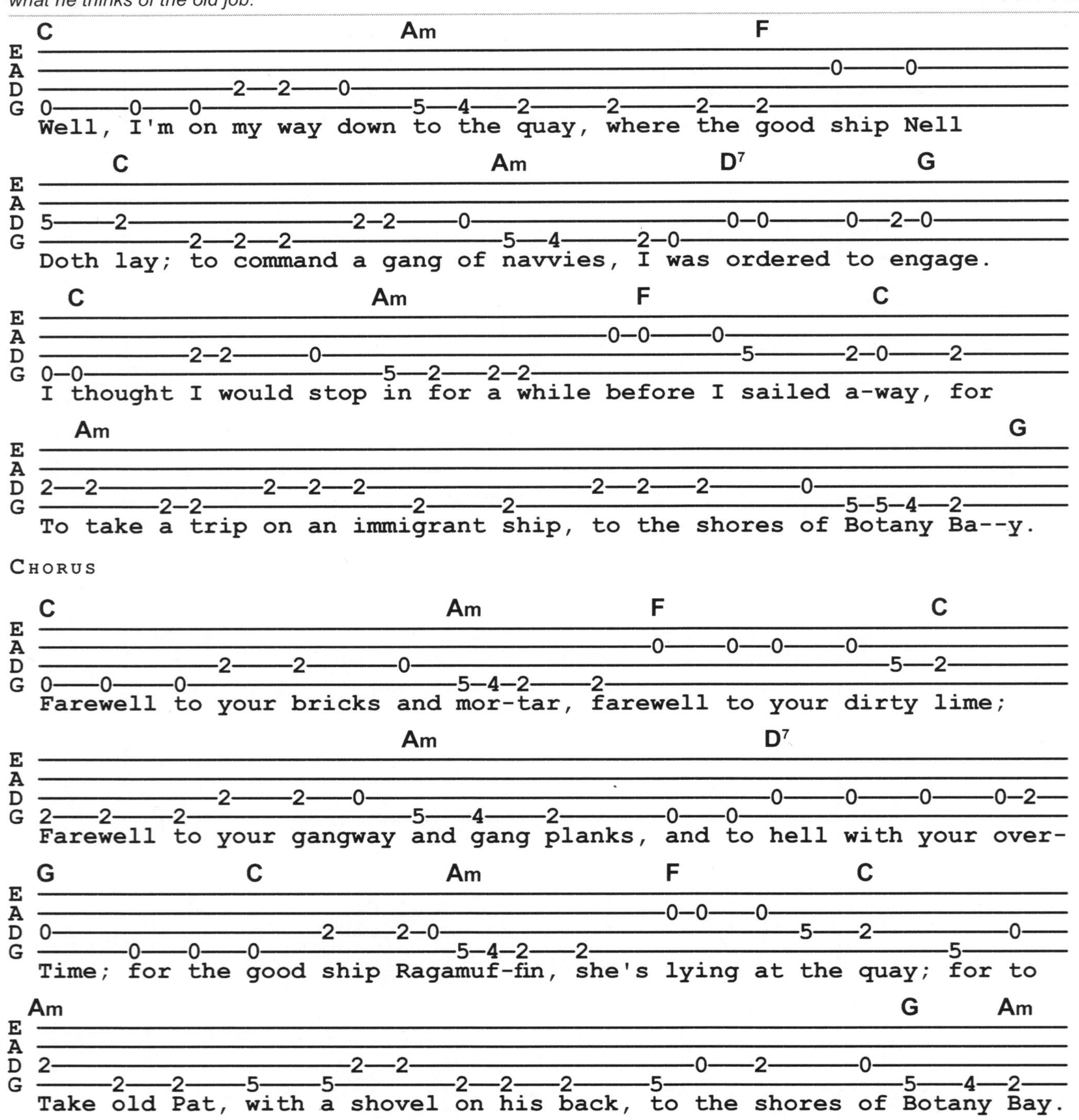

See Chord Forms and Additional Verses on Next Page

Botany Bay (continued)

Chord Forms and Additional Verses

Chord Forms (Key of C)

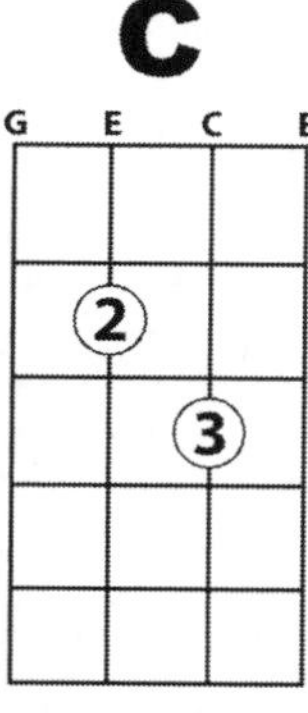

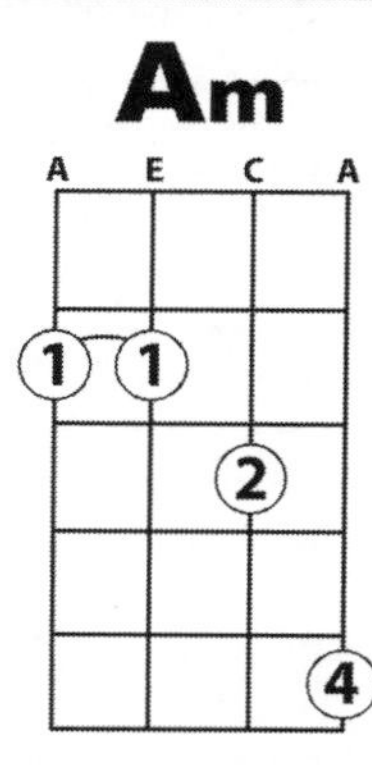

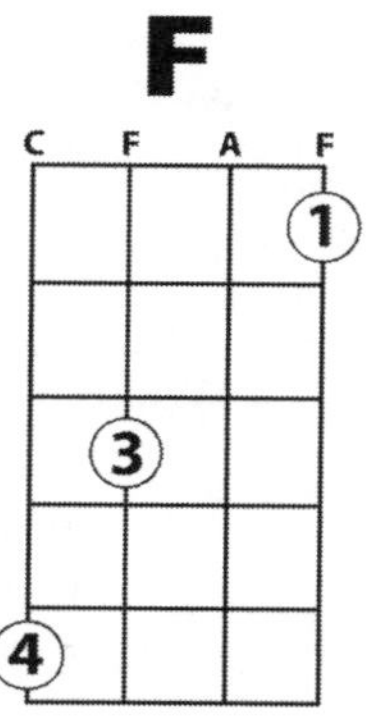

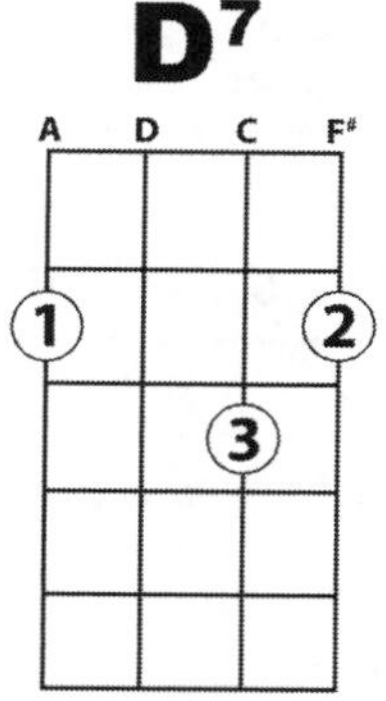

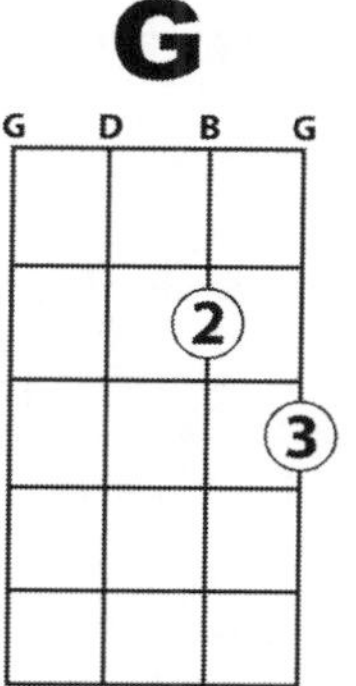

Additional Verses

The best years of our life we spend at working on the docks;
Building mighty wharves and quays, of earth and ballast rocks.
Though pensions keep our jobs secure, I shan't rue the day;
When I take a trip on an immigrant ship, to the shores of Botany Bay.

Well, the boss comes up this morning, and he says, "Why, Pat, hello;
If you do not mix the mortar quick, to be sure you'll have to go."
Well, of course he did insult me, I demanded all me pay;
And I told him straight I was going to emigrate, to the shores of Botany Bay.

When I reach Australia, I'll go and search for gold;
There's plenty there for digging up, or so I have been told.
Or maybe I'll go back to me trade, eight hundred bricks I'll lay;
For an eight hour shift and an eight bob pay, on the shores of Botany Bay.

Chord Forms (Key of G)

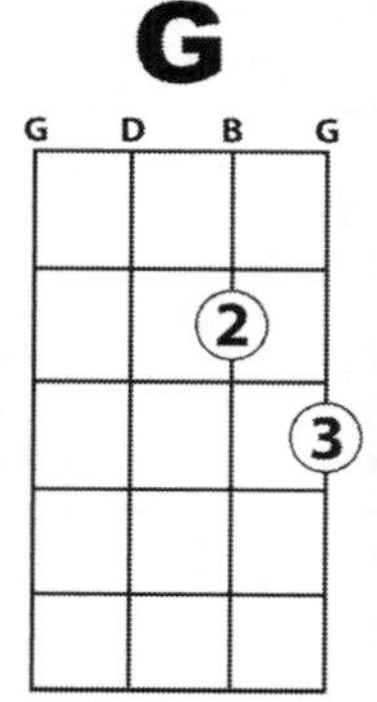

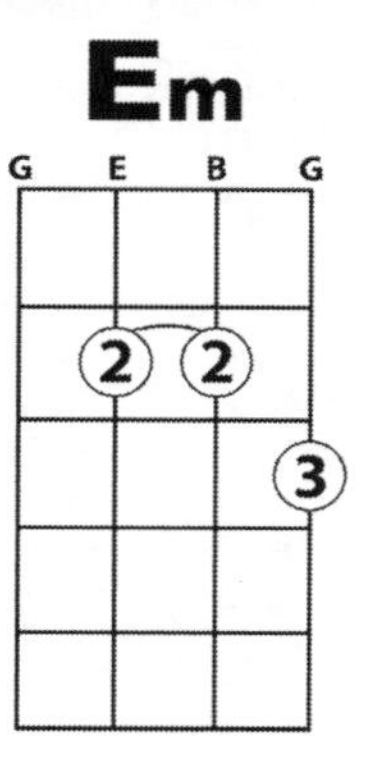

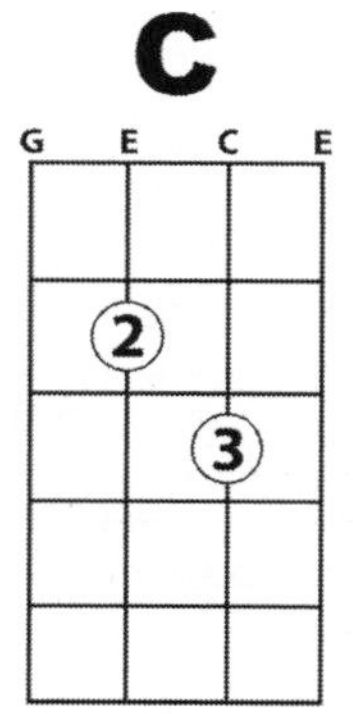

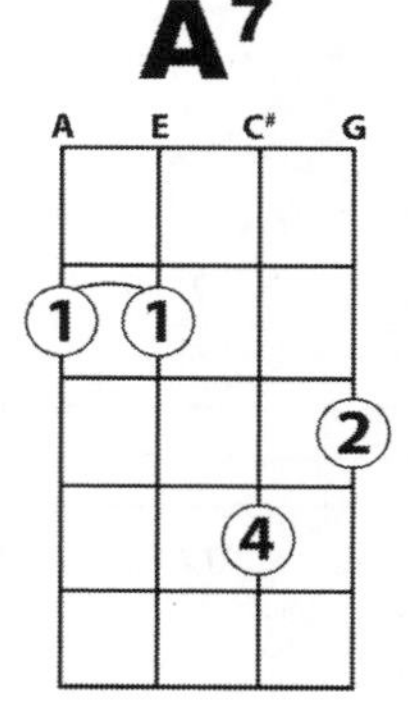

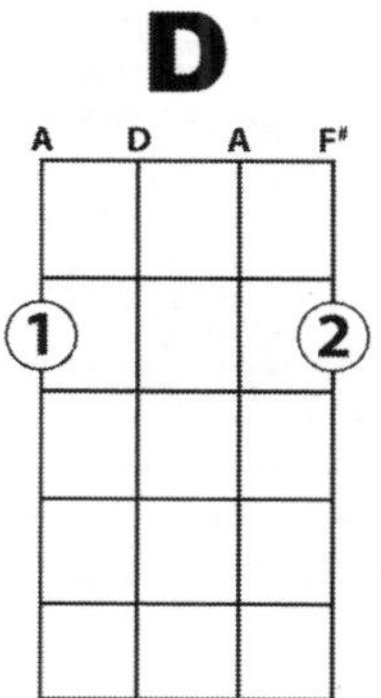

Botany Bay (continued)

Basic Melody

Key of C (High)

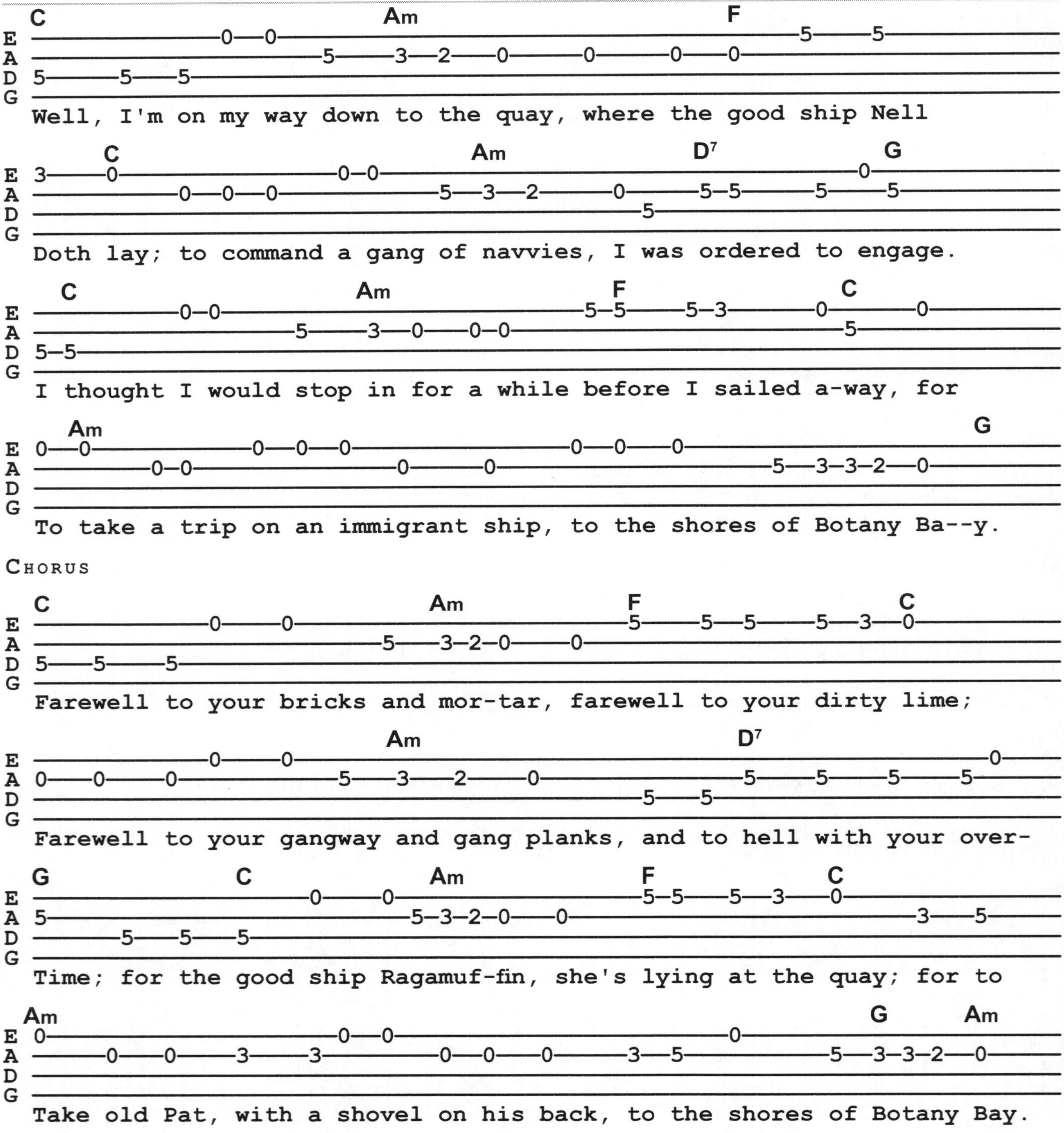

```
  C                            Am                               F
E ------------------0--0-----------------------------------------------5----5-----
A -------------------------5---3--2---0-----0-----0--0------------------------------
D 5----5---5-----------------------------------------------------------------------
G --------------------------------------------------------------------------------
  Well, I'm on my way down to the quay, where the good ship Nell
```

```
      C                           Am                 D7          G
E 3---0---------------------0-0------------------------------0-----------
A ----------0--0--0------------------5--3--2----0-----5-5----5--5---------
D -------------------------------------------------5---------------------
G ------------------------------------------------------------------------
  Doth lay; to command a gang of navvies, I was ordered to engage.
```

```
    C                       Am                    F                C
E -----------0-0--------------------------------5-5---5-3-----0---------0---
A ---------------------5----3--0---0-0----------------------------5-----------
D 5-5--------------------------------------------------------------------------
G -----------------------------------------------------------------------------
  I thought I would stop in for a while before I sailed a-way, for
```

```
    Am                                                                  G
E 0-0-----------0--0--0-----------------0--0--0------------------------------
A -------0-0-----------------0-----0----------------------5--3-3-2--0--------
D ---------------------------------------------------------------------------
G ---------------------------------------------------------------------------
  To take a trip on an immigrant ship, to the shores of Botany Ba--y.
```

CHORUS

```
  C                           Am                F                       C
E -----------------0-----0--------------------5-----5--5-----5--3--0---------
A --------------------------------5---3-2-0----0-------------------------------
D 5---5-----5-----------------------------------------------------------------
G -----------------------------------------------------------------------------
  Farewell to your bricks and mor-tar, farewell to your dirty lime;
```

```
                               Am                           D7
E -----------------0-----0--------------------------------------------------0--
A 0---0----0-----------------5---3---2----0------------------5----5----5----5-----
D -------------------------------------------------5---5--------------------------
G ---------------------------------------------------------------------------------
  Farewell to your gangway and gang planks, and to hell with your over-
```

```
  G                C           Am                F                C
E ---------------------0----0-----------------------5-5---5--3---0--------------
A 5-----------------------------5-3-2-0---0------------------------------3---5---
D -------5---5---5---------------------------------------------------------------
G --------------------------------------------------------------------------------
  Time; for the good ship Ragamuf-fin, she's lying at the quay; for to
```

```
  Am                                                                  G       Am
E 0-----------------------------0-0--------------------------0------------------
A -------0----0-----3-----3-----------0--0--0------3--5-----------5--3-3-2--0----
D --------------------------------------------------------------------------------
G --------------------------------------------------------------------------------
  Take old Pat, with a shovel on his back, to the shores of Botany Bay.
```

See Chord Forms on Previous Page

Botany Bay (continued)

Melody & Chords
Key of C (High)

```
  C                          Am                          F
E ------------0--0------------------------------------------------------------
A ------------3--3---5----3--2--0-----0-----0--0----5----5-------------------
D 5-----5--5--2--2---0----2--2--2-----2-----2--3----3----3-------------------
G 0-----0--0--------------2-----2-----2--------2---------3-------------------
  Well, I'm on my way down to the quay, where the good ship Nell

      C                         Am                D7               G
E 3---0--------------0-0--------------------------------------0------------
A 3---3----0--0--0---3-3----5---3---2------0-----5-5-----5--0-5------------
D -----2---2--2--2---2-2----0---2---2------2-5---0-0-----0----0------------
G ---------0--------------------2----------2-2---2-------2----0------------
  Doth lay; to command a gang of navvies, I was ordered to engage.

  C                         Am                  F                 C
E ----------0-0-----------------------------5-5----5-3-----0-------0------
A ----------3-3------5----3--0---0-0--------3-3----3-3-----3-5-----3------
D 5-5-------2-2------0----2--2---2-2--------3------3---------0-----2------
G 0-0---------------------2------2------------------------------------------
  I thought I would stop in for a while before I sailed a-way, for

    Am                                                                 G
E 0-0-------------0--0--0-----------------0--0--0-------------------------
A 3-0------0-0----0--0--0----0-----0------0--0--0------5--3-3-2--0--------
D ---2-----2-2----2-----2----2-----2------2-----2------2--2-2-2--2---5----
G ---------2-2---------------------2--------------------2--------2---0----
  To take a trip on an immigrant ship, to the shores of Botany Ba--y.
```

CHORUS

```
  C                            Am                F                     C
E -----------0----0------------------------------5-----5--5-----5--3--0----
A -----------3----3------5---3-2-0------0--------3-----3--3-----3--3--3----
D 5---5---5--2----2------0---2-2-2------2--------3--------------3--3--3----
G 0---0---0------------------2---2------2---------------------------3--2----
  Farewell to your bricks and mor-tar, farewell to your dirty lime;

                            Am                        D7
E -----------0----0-------------------------------------------------------0--
A 0---0---0--3----3----5----3----2-----0--------------5----5-----5----5-0----
D 2---2---2--2----2----0----2----2-----2------5---5---0----0-----0----0------
G ----0---------------------2----------2------0---0---2-----------------2----
  Farewell to your gangway and gang planks, and to hell with your over-

  G                C            Am                 F                C
E -----------------------0------0--------------------5-5----5--3----0-----------
A 5----------------------3------3-5-3-2-0-----0------3-3----3--3----3-----3----5--
D 0-----5----5----5------2------2-0-2-2-2-----2------3------3-------2-----2----0--
G 0-----0----0----0-----------------2---2-----2---------------------------0-------
  Time; for the good ship Ragamuf-fin, she's lying at the quay; for to

 Am                                                         G        Am
E 0---------------------0-0--------------------------0-------------------------
A 0----0----0----3-----3-0-0----0----0----0----3-5---0------5--3-3-2--0--------
D 2----2----2----2-----2-2------2----2----2----2-0---2------0--0-0-2--2--------
G -----------2------------------2---------2----2-----2------------------2-------
  Take old Pat, with a shovel on his back, to the shores of Botany Bay.
```

See Chord Forms Two Pages Previous

Botany Bay (continued)

Basic Melody

Key of G

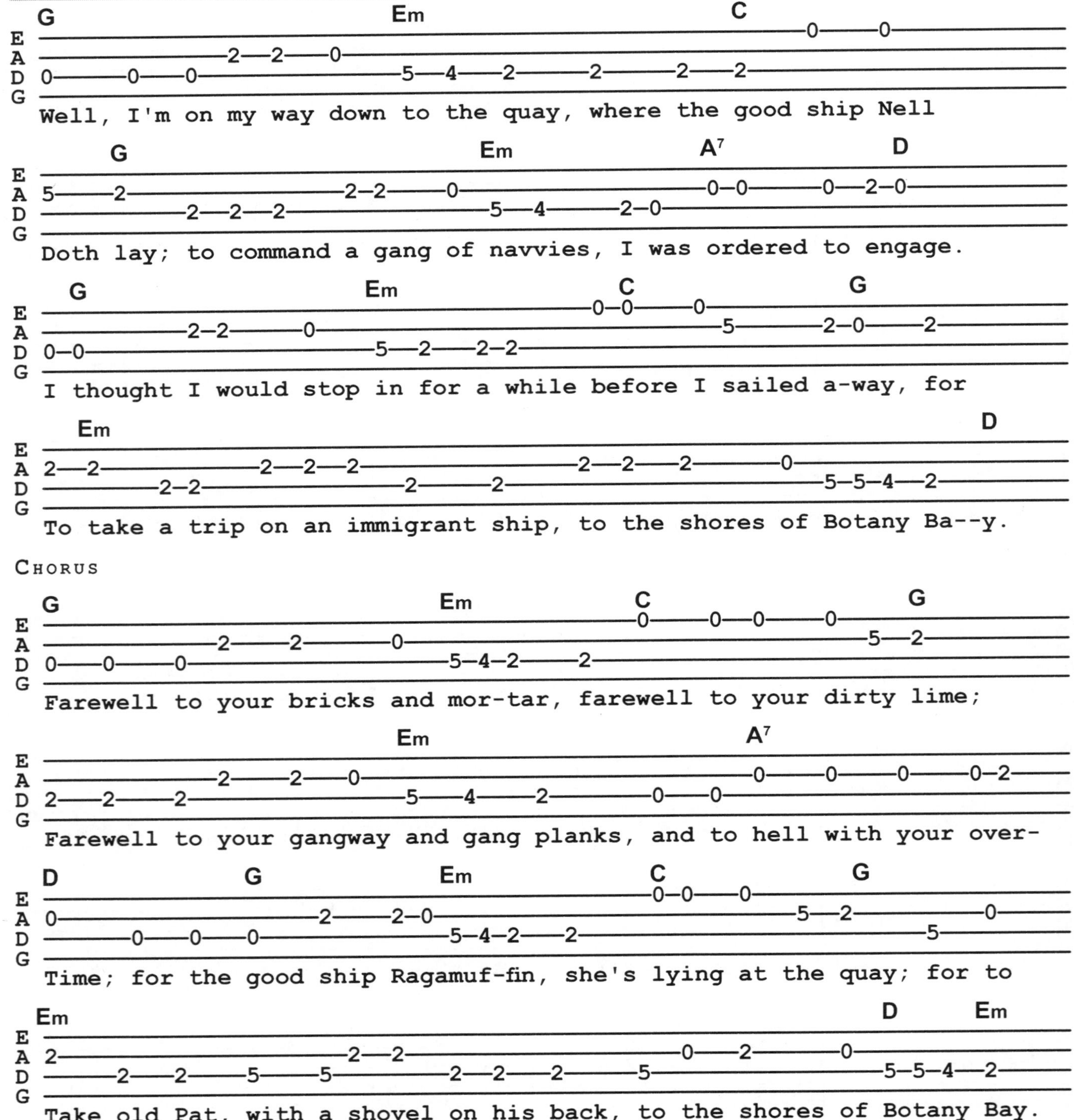

See Chord Forms Three Pages Previous

Botany Bay (continued)

Melody & Chords
Key of G

```
  G                         Em                            C
E ---------------------------------------------------------0------0----
A -------------2--2---0----------------------------------3------3----
D 0------0---0--0--0---0----5--4---2-----2-----2--2----------2----
G 0------0---0-----0--------4--4---4-----4-----4--5--------------
  Well, I'm on my way down to the quay, where the good ship Nell
```

```
      G                       Em          A7          D
E ----------------------------------------------------------------
A 5----2----------------2-2----0----------------0-0-----0--2--0---
D 2----0----2--2--2-----0-0----0--5--4-----2-0--2-2-----2--2--0---
G ------0----0--0--0-------0-------4--4-----4-4--2-----------2----
  Doth lay; to command a gang of navvies, I was ordered to engage.
```

```
    G                  Em                C              G
E ------------------------------------0-0----0-----------------------
A -----------2-2------0---------------2-3----3-5-------2-0-----2----
D 0-0--------0-0------0----5--2---2-2---2-2------2------2-0-----0----
G 2-0----------0-----------4--4---4-4----------------------0--------
  I thought I would stop in for a while before I sailed a-way, for
```

```
    Em                                                           D
E -------------------------------------------------------------------
A 2--2-----------2--2--2-----------------2--2--2------0-------------
D 0--2----2--2---2--2--2---2-----2-------2--2--2------2--5-5-4--2--0-
G ----4----4--4--------4---4-----4--------------4--------4-4-4--4--2-
  To take a trip on an immigrant ship, to the shores of Botany Ba--y.
```

Chorus

```
  G                        Em            C                    G
E -------------------------------------0------0--0------0------------
A -----------2----2-------0------------3------3--3------3--5--2-----
D 0--0----0--0----0-------0--5-4-2---2--2----------------2--2--0-----
G 0--0----0-------0----------4-4-4---4-----------------------0------
  Farewell to your bricks and mor-tar, farewell to your dirty lime;
```

```
                        Em                         A7
E -------------------------------------------------------------------
A -----------2----2---0---------------------------0-----0----0----0-2-
D 2--2----2--0----0---0----5----4----2------0---0--2-----2----2----2-2-
G 0--0----0-------0--------4----4----4------4---4--2--------------2---
  Farewell to your gangway and gang planks, and to hell with your over-
```

```
  D           G              Em            C              G
E ------------------------------------------0-0----0------------------
A 0--------------------2-----2-0------------3-3----3----5---2---------0-
D 0------0---0---0-----0-----0-0-5-4-2---2---2-------2----2---0-----5---0-
G 2------2---2---0-----------0---4-4-4---4---------------------0-----0---
  Time; for the good ship Ragamuf-fin, she's lying at the quay; for to
```

```
  Em                                                       D       Em
E ---------------------------------------------------------------------
A 2--------------------2-2-----------------0---2---------0------------
D 2----2---2----5------5-2--2---2---2----5--2---2--------2--5-5-4--2---
G 4----4---4----4------4-4------4---4---4----4-----4--------2-2-2--4---
  Take old Pat, with a shovel on his back, to the shores of Botany Bay.
```

See Chord Forms Four Pages Previous

Bully In the Alley

Basic Melody

Key of C (Low)

Words and Music

Traditional

Another popular and easy-to-sing traditional shanty, this one is often done a cappella but we give chord suggestions below in case you want to strum along. One explanation for the title and lyrics states that "bully" was another term for drunk/incapacitated, which was a common state for sailors while ashore. Interestingly, there was a "Shinbone Alley" in New York City, which ran near some other streets mentioned in other shanties.

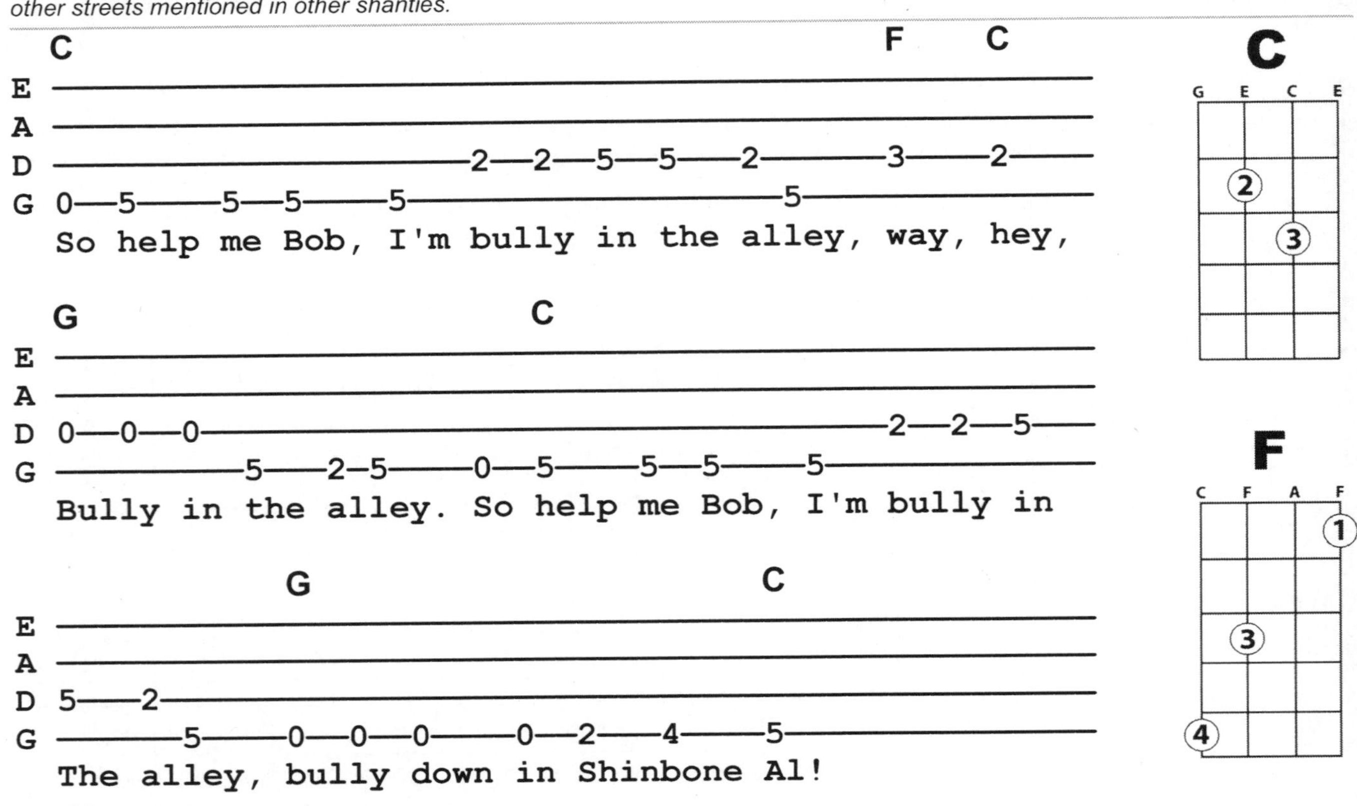

Additional Verses

Sally is a girl that I love dearly,
Way, hey, bully in the alley;
Sally is a girl that I spliced nearly,
Bully down in Shinbone Al.

For seven long years I courted Sally,
Way, hey, bully in the alley;
All she did was dilly-dally,
Bully down in Shinbone Al.

I left Sal and went a-sailing,
Way, hey, bully in the alley;
Signed on a ship, I went a-whaling,
Bully down in Shinbone Al.

I'll leave Sal and become a sailor,
Way, hey, bully in the alley;
I'll leave Sal and ship on a whaler,
Bully down in Shinbone Al.

Then I'll come back and marry Sally,
Way, hey, bully in the alley;
We'll have kids and count 'em by the tally,
Bully down in Shinbone Al.

I thought I heard the old man saying,
Way, hey, bully in the alley;
One more chorus then we're belaying,
Bully down in Shinbone Al.

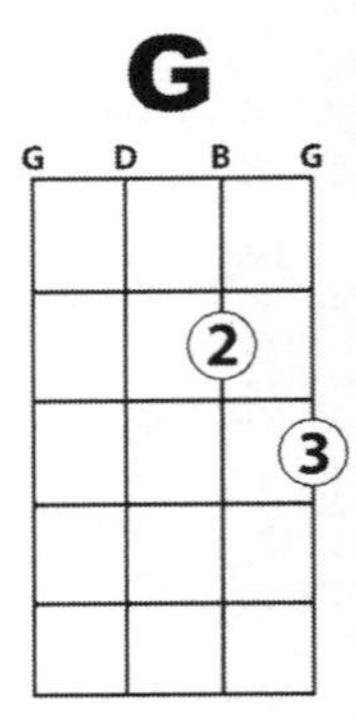

Bully In the Alley (continued)

Two Versions

Key of C (High)

Basic Melody

```
  C                                               F     C     G
E ─────────────────────────────0──0──3──3───0──────1──────0───────────────────────────
A ───3─────3──3─────3───────────────────────────3─────────────────5──5──5──3───0─3───
D 5───────────────────────────────────────────────────────────────────────────────────
G ────────────────────────────────────────────────────────────────────────────────────
  So help me Bob, I'm bully in the alley, way, hey, bully in the alley.

     C                                            G                            C
E ─────────────────────────────0──0──3──3───0─────────────────────────────────────────
A ───3─────3──3─────3───────────────────────────3────────────────────0────2─────3─────
D 5──────────────────────────────────────────────────5──5──5────5─────────────────────
G ────────────────────────────────────────────────────────────────────────────────────
  So help me Bob, I'm bully in the alley, bully down in Shinbone Al!
```

Melody & Chords

```
  C                                               F     C     G
E ─────────────────────────────0──0──3──3───0──────1──────0───────────────────────────
A ───3─────3──3─────3────3──3──3──3───3─3──────0──────3──────5──5──5──3───0─3───
D 5──2─────2──2─────2────2─────2──────2─2──────3──────2──────0──0──0──0───3─3───
G 0──0────────0─────────────────────────0────────────────────0─────0────────────
  So help me Bob, I'm bully in the alley, way, hey, bully in the alley.

     C                                            G                            C
E ─────────────────────────────0──0──3──3───0─────────────────────────────────────────
A ───3─────3──3─────3────3──3──3──3───3─3──────────────────────0────2─────3─────
D 5──2─────2──2─────2────2─────2──────2─2──5──5──5────5──3────3─────2─────
G 0──0────────0─────────────────────────0──0──0──0────0─────────────0─────
  So help me Bob, I'm bully in the alley, bully down in Shinbone Al!
```

Chord Forms

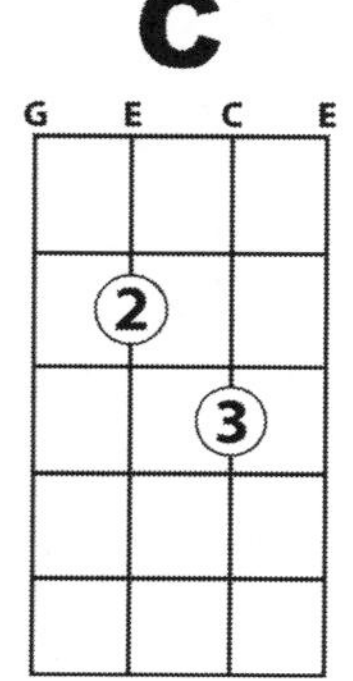

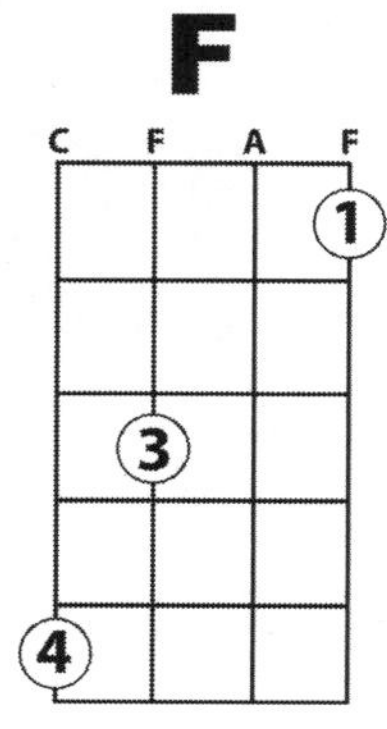

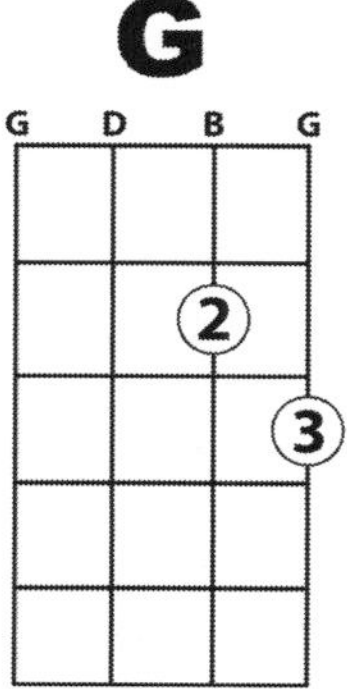

Bully In the Alley (continued)

Basic Melody

Key of G

```
   G                                                     C     G
E ---------------------------------------------------------------------
A -------------------------------2--2--5--5---2--------3-----2--------
D 0--5-----5--5-----5-------------------------5------------------------
G ---------------------------------------------------------------------
  So help me Bob, I'm bully in the alley, way, hey,

   D                        G
E ---------------------------------------------------------------------
A 0--0--0-------------------------------------------------2--2--5-----
D -----------5---2-5----0--5----5--5----5------------------------------
G ---------------------------------------------------------------------
  Bully in the alley. So help me Bob, I'm bully in

               D                         G
E ---------------------------------------------------------------------
A 5---2----------------------------------------------------------------
D ------5----0--0--0----0--2---4----5----------------------------------
G ---------------------------------------------------------------------
  The alley, bully down in Shinbone Al!
```

Chord Forms

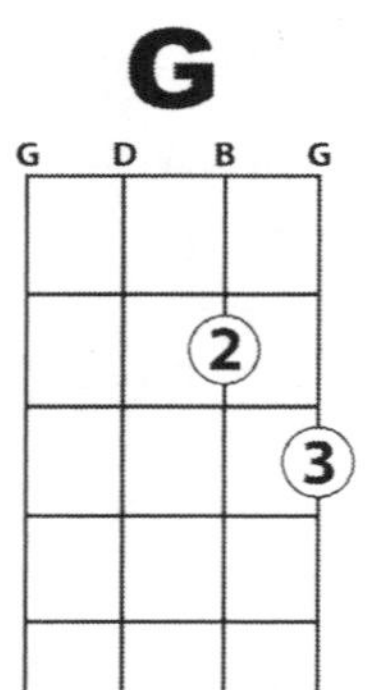

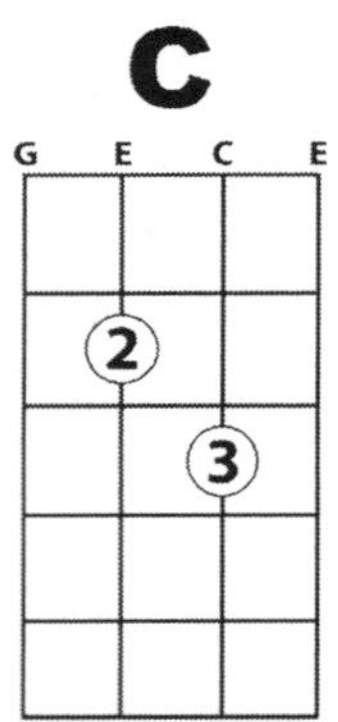

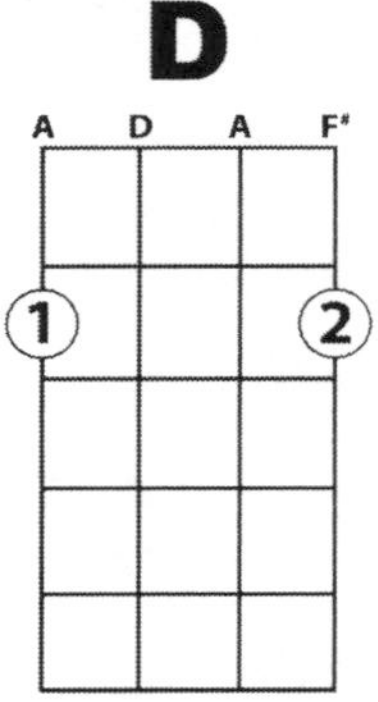

A historic view of Shinbone Alley in New York City, from Bond Street.

Bully In the Alley (continued)

Melody & Chords

Key of G

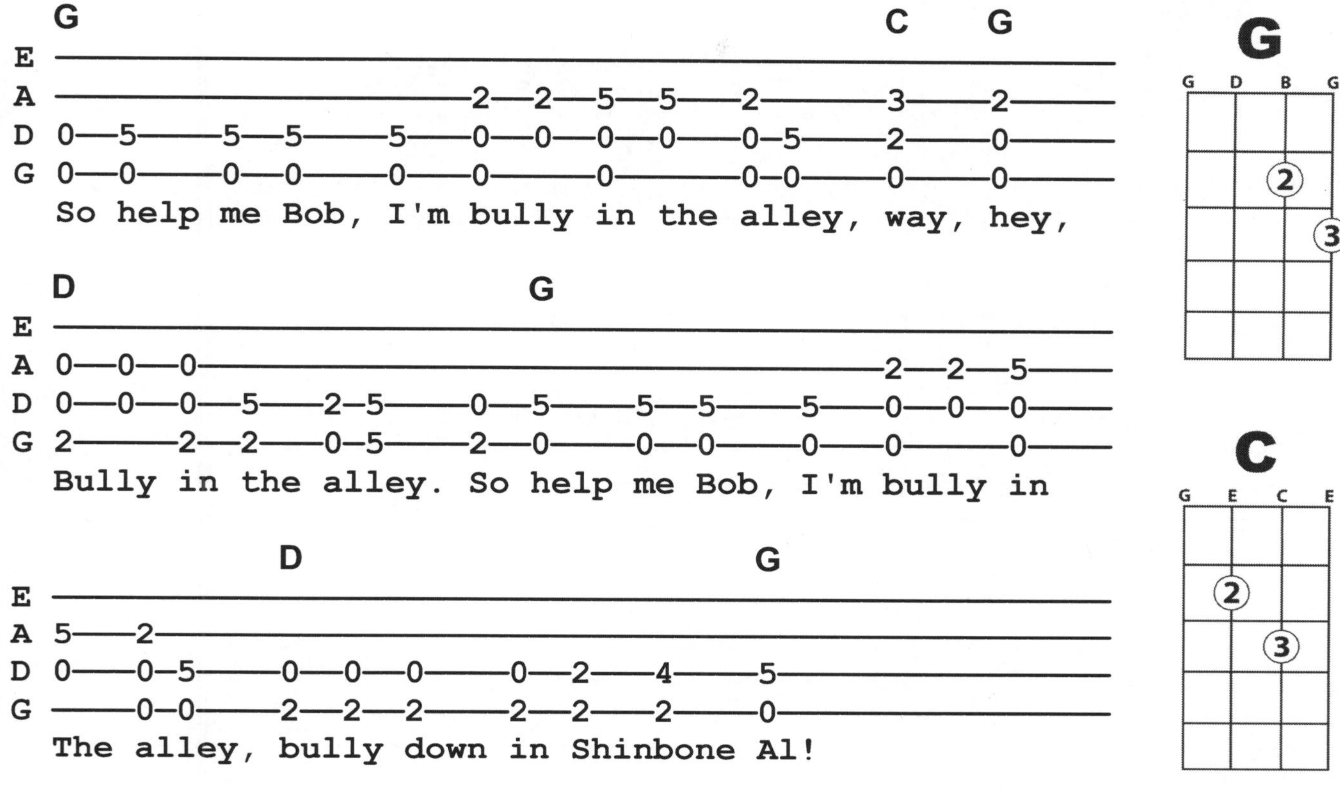

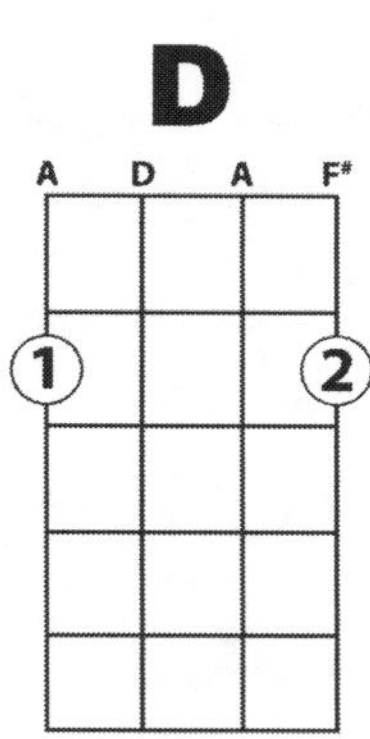

D G
E
A 5 2
D 0 0 5 0 0 0 0 2 4 5
G 0 0 2 2 2 2 2 2 0
The alley, bully down in Shinbone Al!

A modern view of Shinbone Alley from Google street view, with the Bond Street side walled off, and still paved with Belgian paver blocks.

The Coast of High Barbary

Basic Melody

Key of A Minor

Words and Music Traditional

This old sea song/shanty tells of a ship encountering pirates off of the coast of "High Barbary", which is what northwestern Africa was known as back then. The good guys are victorious over the pirates and leave them to drown. There have been many variations of the lyrics over the years.

```
   Am                                               E7        Am
E ---------------------------------------------------------------------
A ------------0----0---2---2-------0------3----2----------0-----------
D 2------2----------------------------------------5-------------------
G ---------------------------------------------------------------------
  There were two lofty ships from old England came,
```

```
                       G          F          E7
E -----0--------------------------------------0-----------------------
A 5--------------3------5-------2-----0-2-3---5-----------------------
D ---------------------------------------------------------------------
G ---------------------------------------------------------------------
  Blow high! Blow low! And s-o sailed we.
```

```
      Am                      G                    F                   Em
E -----0----0----0---------------------------------------0-------------------
A 5-------------------------3--5-5-----5----2----3-5-------------0-----------
D ----------------------------------------------------------------------5----
G ---------------------------------------------------------------------------
  One was the Prince of Luther and the other Prince of Wales,
```

```
    Am                                   G     E7     Am
E ---------------------------------------0-----------------------------
A --0---0------0------2-----3------5-----------2---2---0--------------
D 2--------------------------------------------------------------------
G ---------------------------------------------------------------------
  A-sailing down the coast of High Barbary.
```

Chord Forms

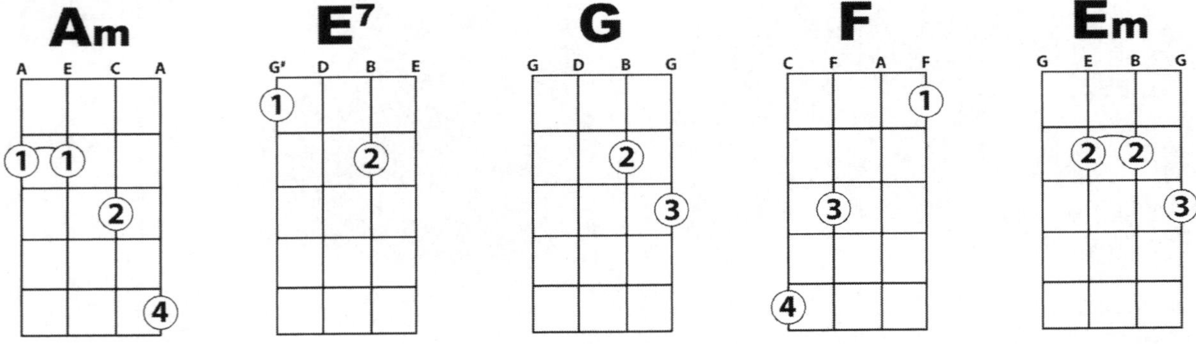

See Additional Verses on Next Page

The Coast of High Barbary

(continued)

Melody & Chords

Key of A Minor

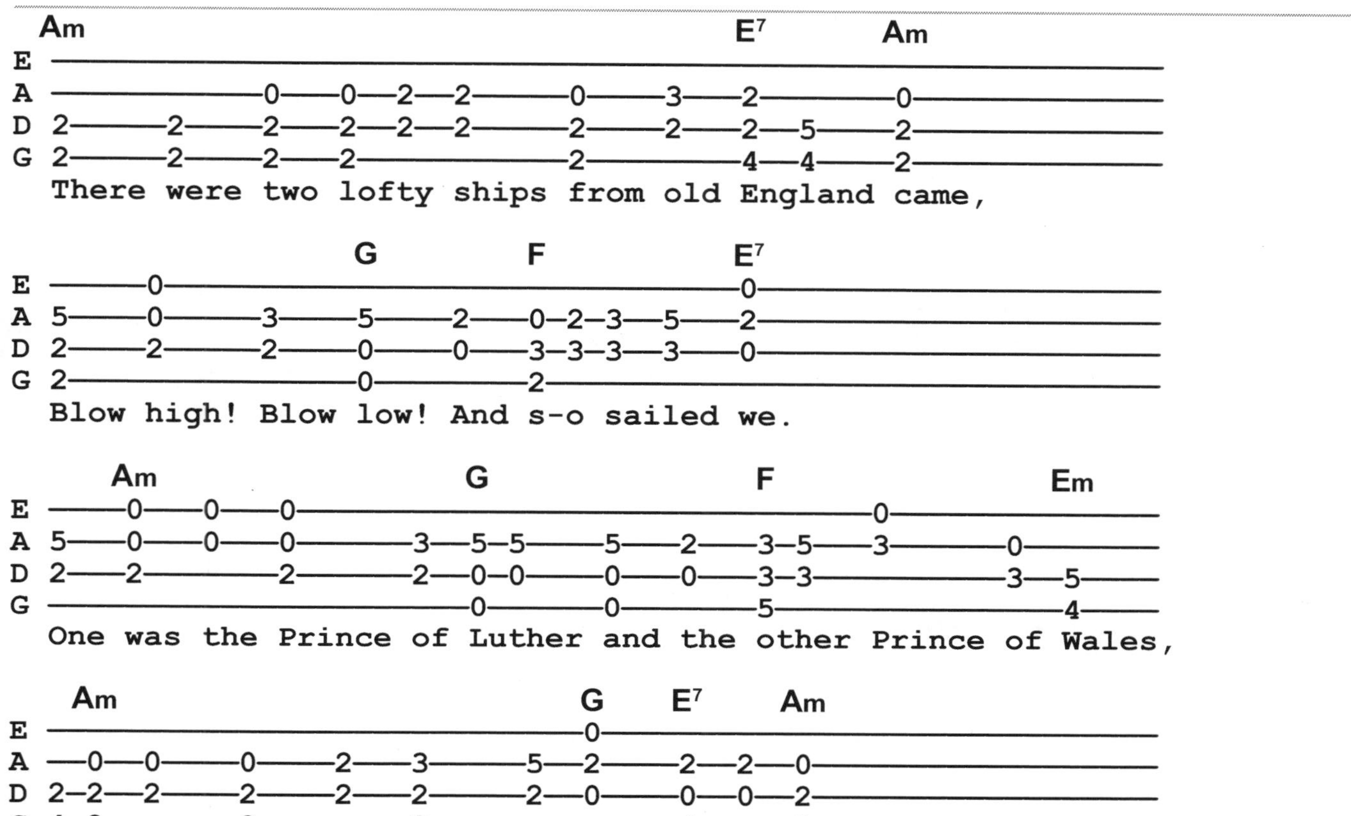

Additional Verses

"Aloft there, aloft " our jolly bosun cried,
Blow high, blow low, and so sail we;
"Look ahead, look astern,
Look the weather look a-lee,"
All a-cruisin' down the coast of High Barbary.

"There's naught upon the stern, sir,
There's naught upon our lee,
Blow high, blow low, and so sail we;
But there's a lofty ship to wind'ard,
An' she's sailin' fast and free",
All a-cruisin' down the coast of High Barbary.

"Oh hail her, oh hail her", our gallant captain cried,
Blow high, blow low, and so sail we;
"Are you a man-o-war, or a privateer," cried he,
All a-cruisin' down the coast of High Barbary.

"I am not a man-o-war, a privateer," said he,
Blow high, blow low, and so sail we;
"But I am a salt sea pirate a-looking for me fee,"
All a-cruisin' down the coast of High Barbary.

For Broadside, for broadside, a long time we lay,
Blow high, blow low, and so sail we;
Until the Prince of Luther
Shot the pirate's mast away,
All a-cruisin' down the coast of High Barbary.

"For quarter, for quarter", the pirates they did cry,
Blow high, blow low, and so sail we;
But the answer that we gave them,
We sunk them in the sea,
All a-cruisin' down the coast of High Barbary.

The Coast of High Barbary (continued)

Basic Melody

Key of E Minor (Low)

```
 Em                                         B7        Em
E ------------------------------------------------------------------
A ------------------------------------------------------------------
D -------------2---2--4--4-----2-----5---4--0----2------------------
G 4-----4-----------------------------------------------------------
  There were two lofty ships from old England came,

                    D          C           B7
E ------------------------------------------------------------------
A 0----2------------0------------------0---2------------------------
D -------------5-------------4---2-4-5------------------------------
G ------------------------------------------------------------------
  Blow high! Blow low! And s-o sailed we.

     Em                   D               C                 Bm
E ------------------------------------------------------------------
A 0---2---2---2-----------0-0----0-----------0---2------------------
D ---------------------5----------------4---5--------------2--0-----
G ------------------------------------------------------------------
  One was the Prince of Luther and the other Prince of Wales,

   Em                             D     B7     Em
E ------------------------------------------------------------------
A -------------------------------0---2------------------------------
D --2--2----2----4---5-------------------4---4--2-------------------
G 4-----------------------------------------------------------------
  A-sailing down the coast of High Barbary.
```

Chord Forms

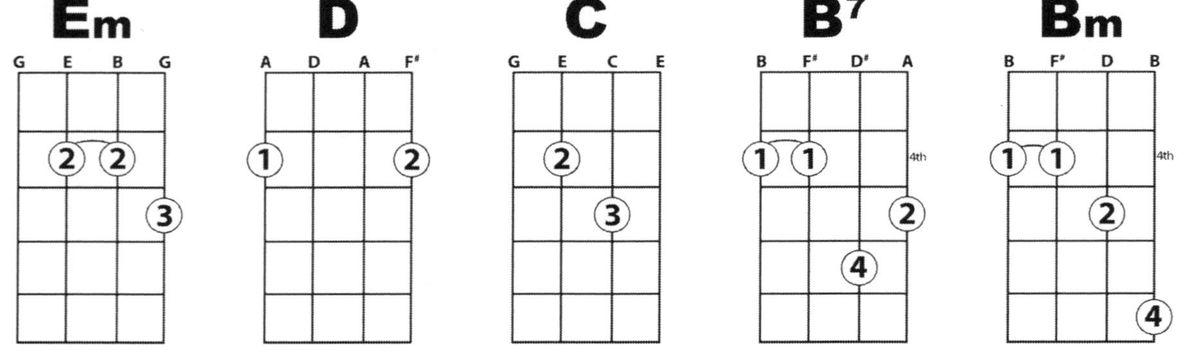

The Coast of High Barbary (continued)

Melody & Chords

Key of E Minor (Low)

```
  Em                                        B7      Em
E ---------------------------------------------------------------
A ---------------------------------------------------------------
D ----------2---2---4---4-----2----5----4---0----2---------------
G 4----4----4---4---2---2-----4----4----4---4----4---------------
  There were two lofty ships from old England came,
```

```
                    D        C          B7
E ---------------------------------------------------------------
A 0----2------------0-------------------0---2--------------------
D 2----2-----5------0-----4---2-4-5-----2---1--------------------
G 4----4-----4------2-----2---5-5-5---------4--------------------
  Blow high! Blow low! And s-o sailed we.
```

```
     Em                   D              C                Bm
E ---------------------------------------------------------------
A 0---2---2---2-----------0-0-----0----------0---2---------------
D 0---2---2---2-------5---0-0-----0----4---5-2---2-------2---0---
G ----4-------5-------4---2-------2----2---5-------------5---4---
  One was the Prince of Luther and the other Prince of Wales,
```

```
   Em                           D    B7    Em
E ---------------------------------------------------------------
A -----------------------------0---2-----------------------------
D --2--2----2----4----5--------2---0----4---4---2----------------
G 4-4--4----4----4----4------------2----4---4---4----------------
  A-sailing down the coast of High Barbary.
```

Chord Forms

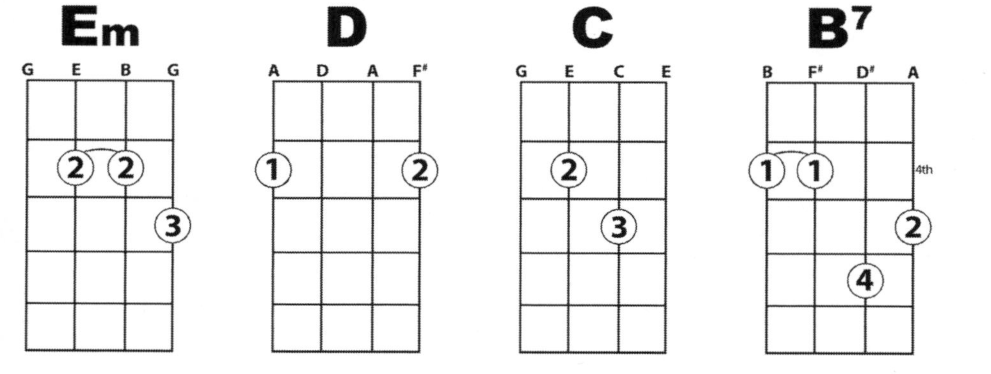

The Coast of High Barbary (continued)

Basic Melody

Key of E Minor (High)

```
  Em                                                  B7         Em
E ───────────────0───0───2───2──────0─────3───2──────────0──────────────────
A 2──────2────────────────────────────────────────5─────────────────────────
D ──────────────────────────────────────────────────────────────────────────
G ──────────────────────────────────────────────────────────────────────────
  There were two lofty ships from old England came,

                      D           C           B7
E 5────7──────3─────5─────2────0─2─3───5────7───────────────────────────────
A ──────────────────────────────────────────────────────────────────────────
D ──────────────────────────────────────────────────────────────────────────
G ──────────────────────────────────────────────────────────────────────────
  Blow high! Blow low! And s-o sailed we.

      Em                    D                 C                  Bm
E 5───7───7───7─────────3───5─5──────5────2────3─5────7─────────0────────────
A ────────────────────────────────────────────────────────────────5──────────
D ──────────────────────────────────────────────────────────────────────────
G ──────────────────────────────────────────────────────────────────────────
  One was the Prince of Luther and the other Prince of Wales,

     Em                              D     B7     Em
E ──0───0──────0──────2─────3──────5───7─────2───2───0───────────────────────
A 2─────────────────────────────────────────────────────────────────────────
D ──────────────────────────────────────────────────────────────────────────
G ──────────────────────────────────────────────────────────────────────────
  A-sailing down the coast of High Barbary.
```

Chord Forms

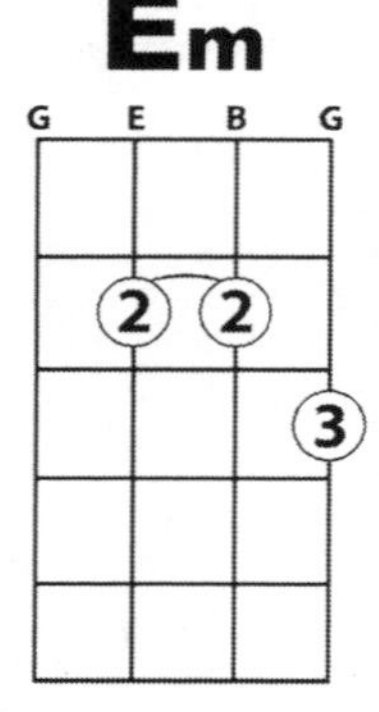

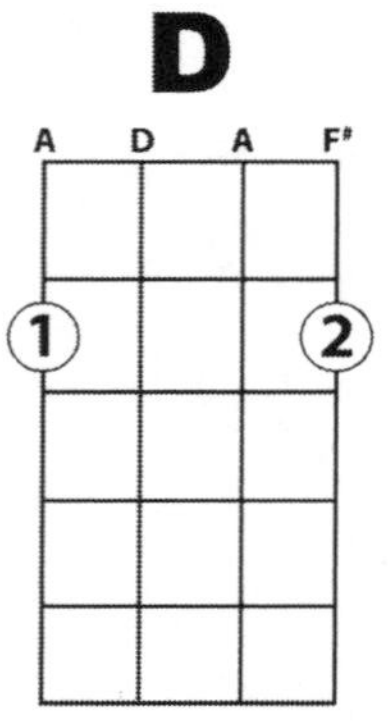

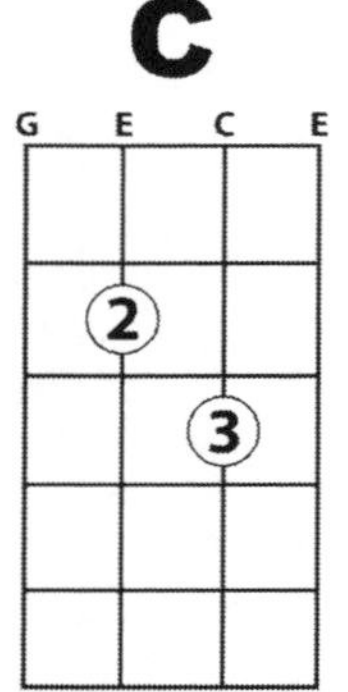

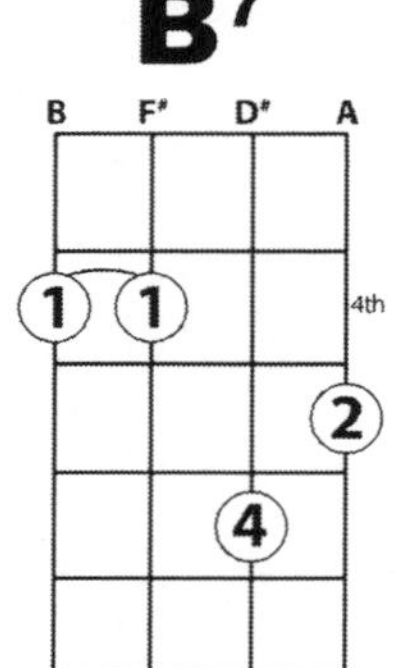

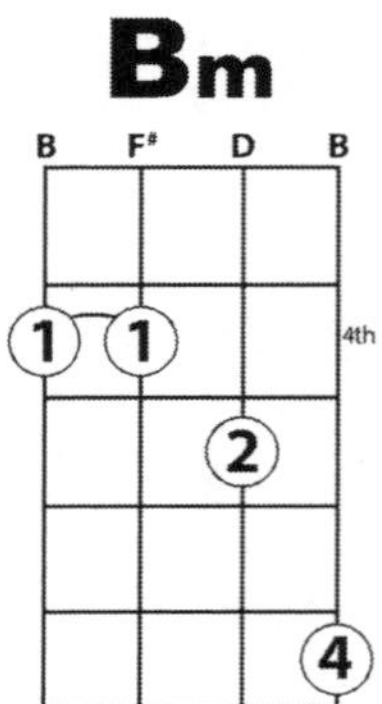

The Coast of High Barbary (continued)

Melody & Chords

Key of E Minor (High)

```
  Em                                                      B7          Em
E ───────────────0────0───2───2────────0──────3────2──────────0──────────
A 2────────2─────2────2───2───2────────2──────2────0────5─────2──────────
D 2────────2─────2────2───────2────────2───────────1────4─────2──────────
G 4──────────────────────────────────────────────────────────────────────
  There were two lofty ships from old England came,
```

```
                        D           C           B7
E 5─────7───────3───────5──────2────0──2──3───5────7─────────────────────
A 2─────7───────2───────0──────0────3──3──3───3────6─────────────────────
D 2─────5───────2───────0──────0────2──────────────7─────────────────────
G ───────────────────────────────────────────────────────────────────────
  Blow high! Blow low! And s-o sailed we.
```

```
      Em                         D                 C                   Bm
E 5───7───7───7─────────3───5──5───────5───2───3──5───7────────0──────────
A 7───7───7───7─────────2───0──0───────0───0───3──3───5────────3───5──────
D ────5───────5──────────────0─────────0───────2───────────────────4──────
G ─────────────────────────────────────────────────────────────────4──────
  One was the Prince of Luther and the other Prince of Wales,
```

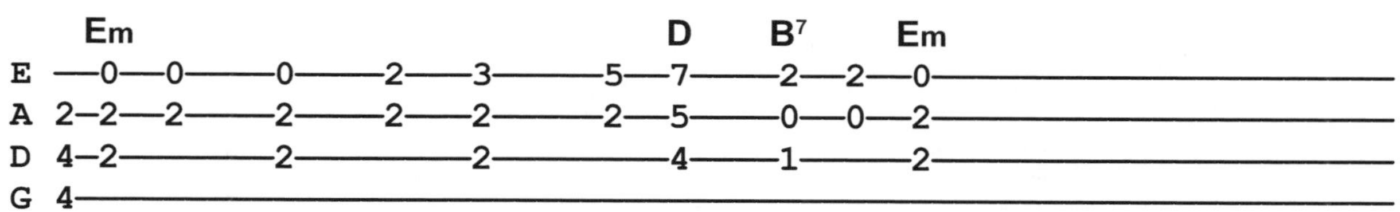

A-sailing down the coast of High Barbary.

Chord Forms

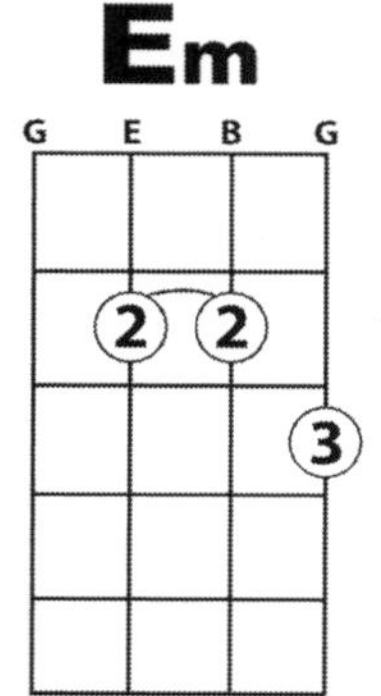

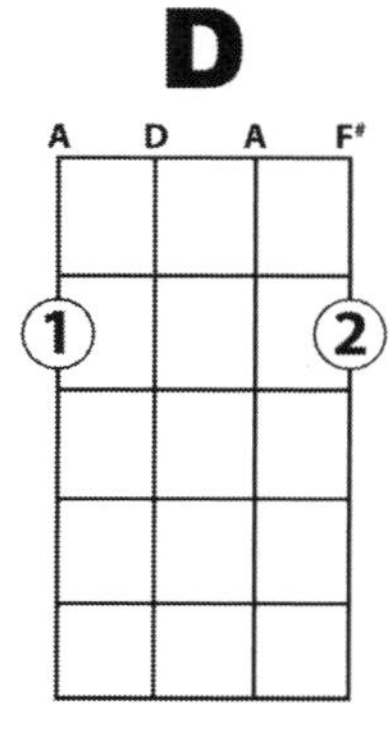

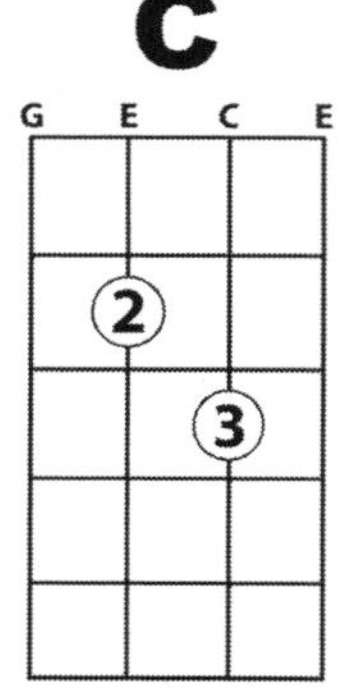

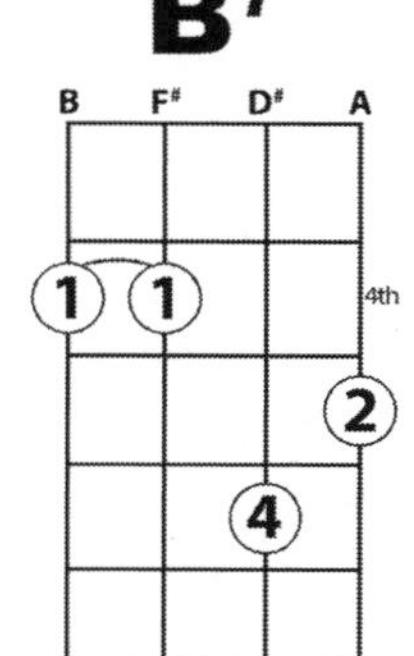

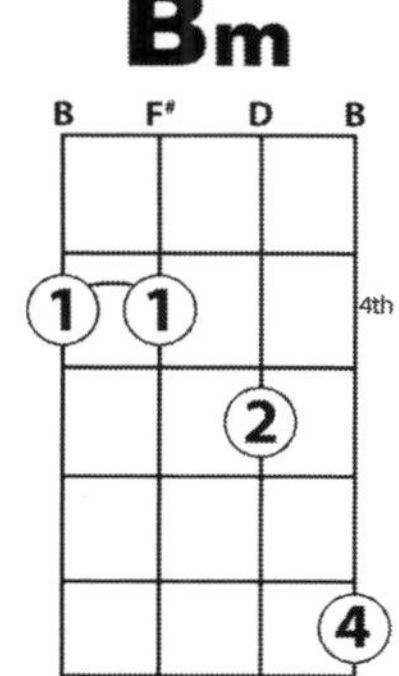

Cruising 'Round Yarmouth

Basic Melody
Key of C

This is another bawdy old sailor's song, in which nautical terms for the parts of a ship are used for the features of a rather friendly woman. This song has long been a part of the folk tradition, and was collected in the 1950's from one of the most prolific of the English folk singers, Harry Fox.

Words and Music
Traditional

```
  C                                        F                       C
E ---------------------------0-----0-----------------------------------------
A ----------------------------------------5----0----0-0----------------------
D 2--3--5---5----5------5-----------------------------------5-5---5-5--------
G ---------------------------------------------------------------------------
  While cruisin' round Yarmouth one day for a spree, I met a fair
```

```
                          G                C
E --------------0--------------------------0--------------0----0-------------
A ---3----5-----------5---3---5------3---5-------3-5-----------------3-------
D 5--------------------------------------------------------------------------
G ---------------------------------------------------------------------------
  Damsel, the wind blowing free;  "I'm a fast-going clipper, my
```

```
  F                C           F                                        C
E ---------------------------------------------------------------------------
A 5----3-----5-----3------5----3--0--0---0--3---0-----------0----------------
D -------------------------------------------------5------------5------2-----
G ---------------------------------------------------------------------------
  Kind sir," said she, "I'm ready for cargo, my hold is quite free."
```

CHORUS

```
  C                                  F
E ---------------------------0----0------------------------------------------
A -----------------------------------5----0----0----0------------------------
D 2--3-----5----5----5----5--------------------------------------------------
G ---------------------------------------------------------------------------
  Singin' fal der ral laddie and fal der ral day,
```

```
  C                      G         C
E --------------0----0-------------------------------------------------------
A -------------------------5---3---2---3-------------------------------------
D 5---5---5---5--------------------------------------------------------------
G ---------------------------------------------------------------------------
  Fal der ral laddie and fal der ral day.
```

Chord Forms

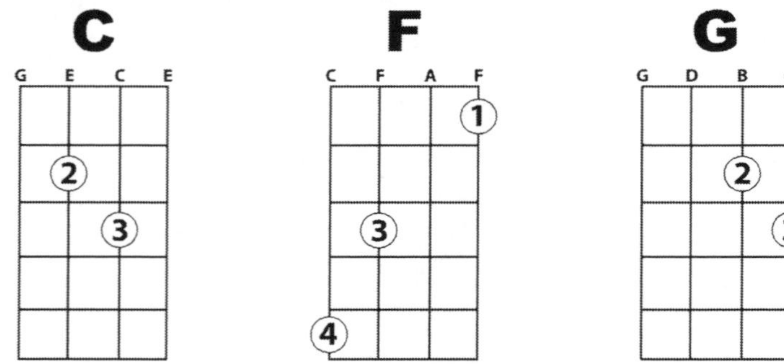

See Additional Verses on Next Page

Cruising 'Round Yarmouth (continued)

Melody & Chords

Key of C

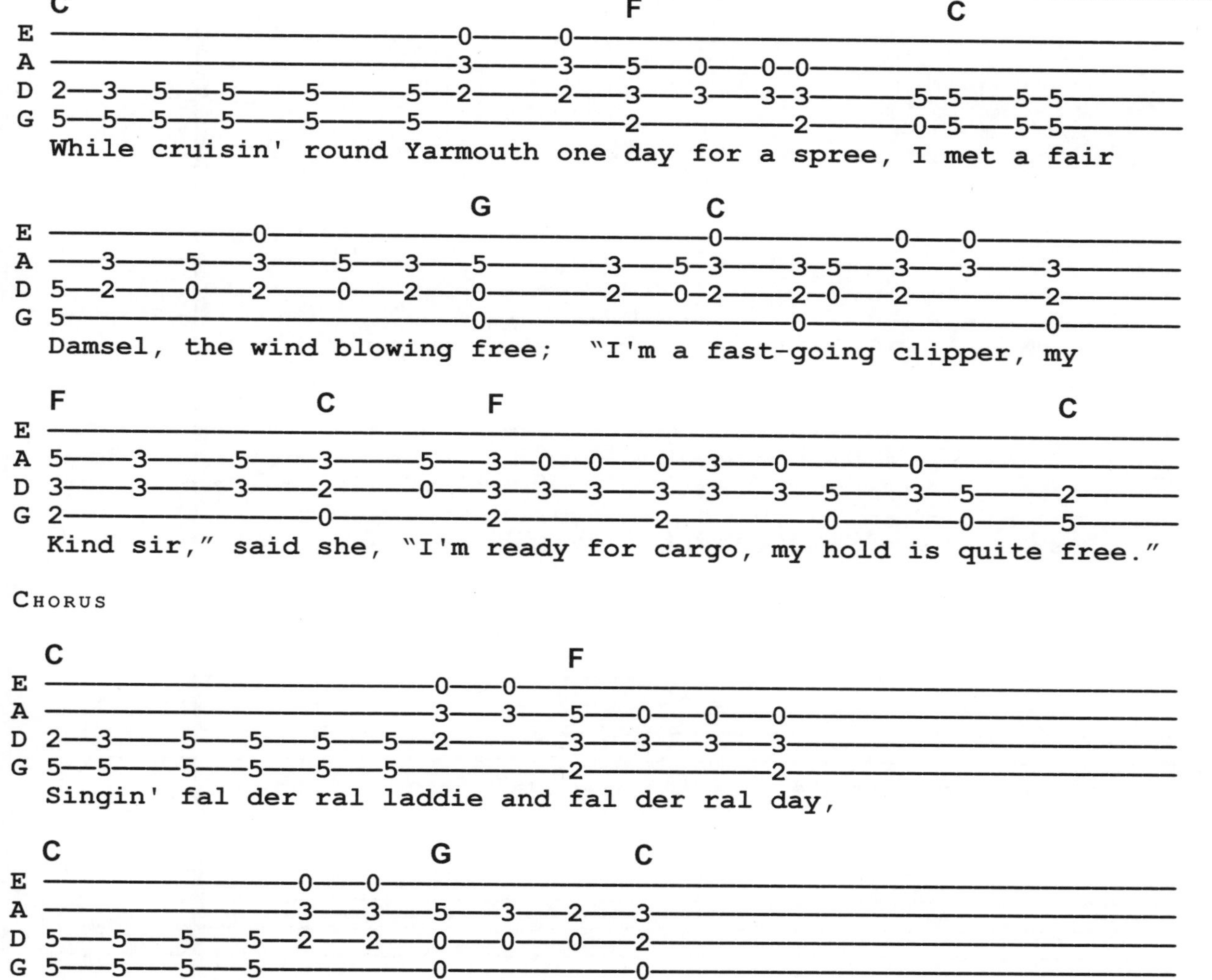

Additional Verses

The country she came from, I could not tell which,
But by her appearance I thought she was Dutch;
Her flag wore its colors, her masthead was low,
She was round at the quarters and bluff in the bow.

She took me upstairs and her topsail she lowered,
In a neat little harbor she soon had me moored;
She laid in her foresails, her staysails and all,
With her lily white hand on my reef-tackle fall.

I said, "Pretty fair maid, it's time to give o'er,
For 'twixt wind and water, you've run me ashore;
Me shot-locker's empty, me powder's all spent,
I can't fire a shot, for it's choked to the vent..."

Here's luck to the girl with the black curly locks,
Here's luck to the girl who ran Jack on the rocks;
Here's luck to the doctor who eased all his pain,
He's squared his main yard, he's cruising' again...

Cruising 'Round Yarmouth
(continued)

Basic Melody

Key of G (Low)

```
   G                                                 C                    G
E -----------------------------------------------------------------------------------
A ------------------------------------------2-------2----0---------------------------
D ---------0-----0------0--------0---------------------------2----2--2--------0--0----0--0----
G 4--5-------------------------------------------------------------------------------
  While cruisin' round Yarmouth one day for a spree, I met a fair
```

```
                              D                G
E -----------------------------------------------------------------------------------
A ---------0----2----0--------0----------------0-2---------0----2----2-----------------
D 0--5---------------------5---------------5-----------5---------------------5-------
G -----------------------------------------------------------------------------------
  Damsel, the wind blowing free;  "I'm a fast-going clipper, my
```

```
  C                 G          C                                                   G
E -----------------------------------------------------------------------------------
A 0-----------0-----------0----------------------------------------------------------
D -------5-----------5-----------5--2--2---2--5---2---0----2--0----------------------
G -----------------------------------------------------------------------------4-----
  Kind sir," said she, "I'm ready for cargo, my hold is quite free."
```

Chorus

```
  G                                      C
E -----------------------------------------------------------------------------------
A --------------------------------2----2----0----------------------------------------
D ---------0----0----0----0-----------------------2----2----2------------------------
G 4--5-------------------------------------------------------------------------------
  Singin' fal der ral laddie and fal der ral day,
```

```
  G                           D            G
E -----------------------------------------------------------------------------------
A -------------------2----2----0-----------------------------------------------------
D 0----0----0----0----------------5----4----5----------------------------------------
G -----------------------------------------------------------------------------------
  Fal der ral laddie and fal der ral day.
```

Chord Forms

G

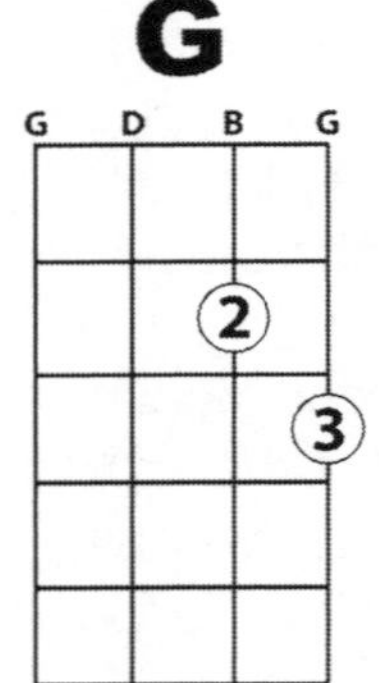

C

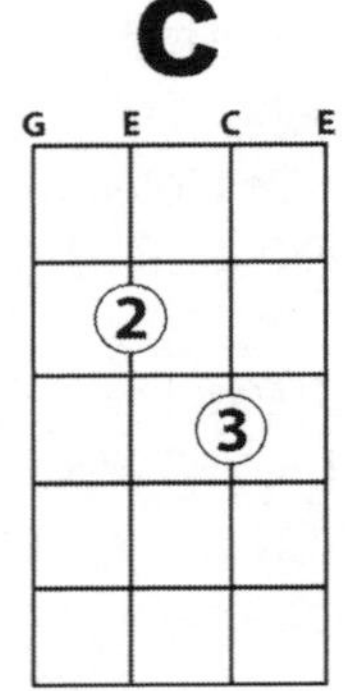

D

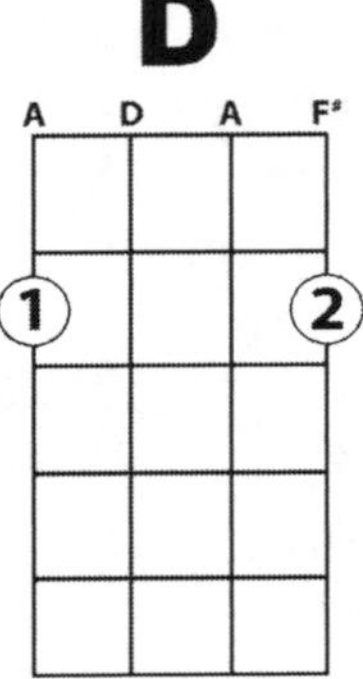

Cruising 'Round Yarmouth
(continued)

Melody & Chords

Key of G (Low)

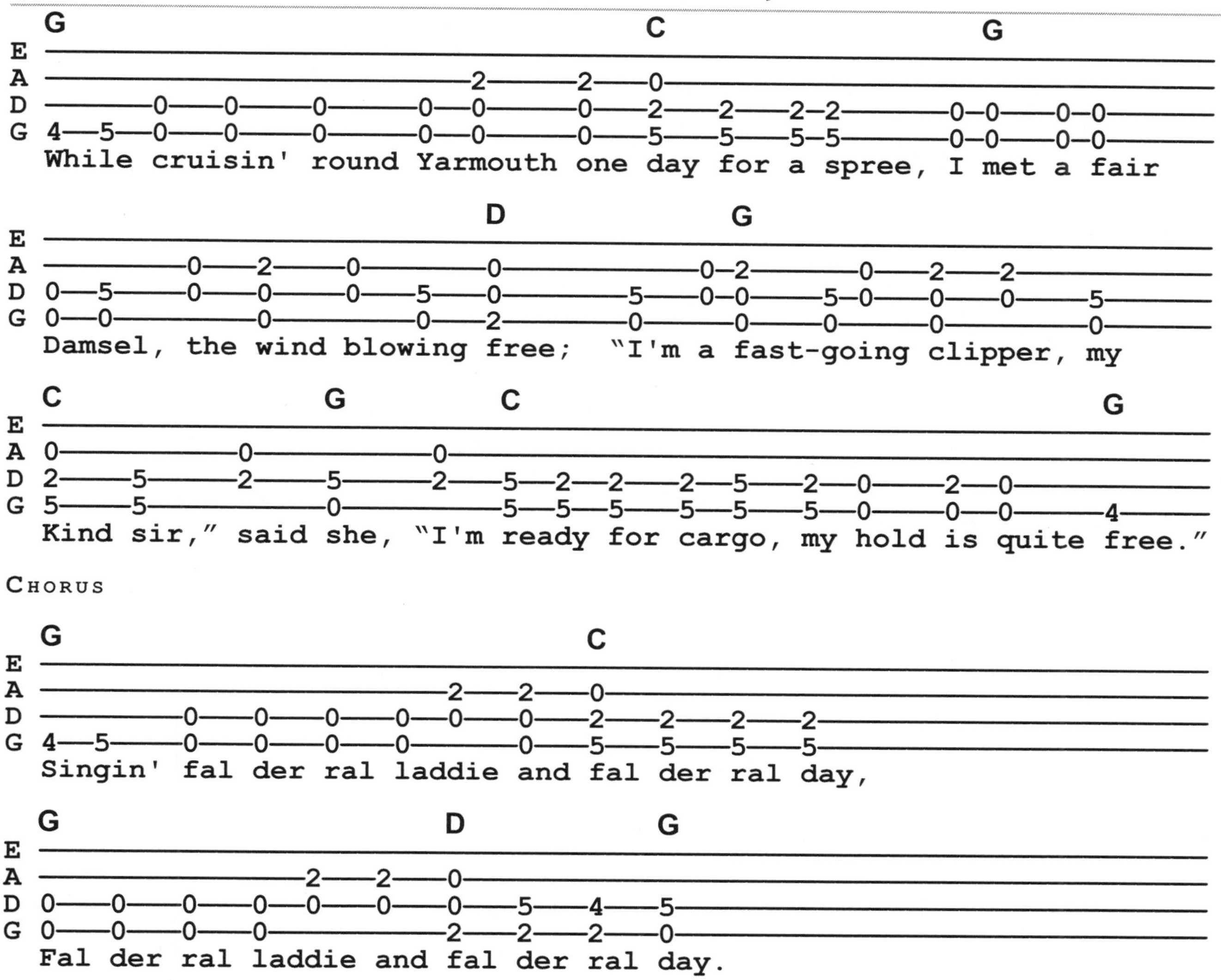

```
    G                                                      C                             G
E ---------------------------------------------------------------------------------------------------
A ------------------------------------------2---------2----0-----------------------------------------
D ----------0-----0------0--------0--0---------0-----2----2----2-2---------0-0-----0-0---------------
G 4--5-----0-----0------0--------0--0---------0-----5----5----5-5---------0-0-----0-0----------------
  While cruisin' round Yarmouth one day for a spree, I met a fair
```

```
                                           D                    G
E ---------------------------------------------------------------------------------------------------
A -------------0----2-------0--------------0------------------0-2----------0-----2----2--------------
D 0--5---------0----0-------0----5---------0-----------5------0-0-------5--0-----0-----0------5------
G 0--0--------------0--------------0-------2-----------0--------0-------0--------0------------0------
  Damsel, the wind blowing free;  "I'm a fast-going clipper, my
```

```
  C                        G              C                                                G
E ---------------------------------------------------------------------------------------------------
A 0----------------0-----------------0---------------------------------------------------------------
D 2-------5--------2------5----------2-----5---2---2-----2----5------2----0------2----0--------------
G 5-------5---------------0----------------5---5---5-----5----5------5----0------0----0---------4----
  Kind sir," said she, "I'm ready for cargo, my hold is quite free."
```

Chorus

```
    G                                                C
E ---------------------------------------------------------------------------------------------------
A ---------------------------------------2-----2-----0-----------------------------------------------
D ----------0-----0-----0-----0-----0----------0-----2-----2-----2-----2-----------------------------
G 4--5------0-----0-----0-----0----------------0-----5-----5-----5-----5-----------------------------
  Singin' fal der ral laddie and fal der ral day,
```

```
    G                                     D                 G
E ---------------------------------------------------------------------------------------------------
A --------------------------2-----2-----0------------------------------------------------------------
D 0-----0-----0-----0-----0-----0-----0-----5-----4-----5--------------------------------------------
G 0-----0-----0-----0-------------------2-----2-----2-----0------------------------------------------
  Fal der ral laddie and fal der ral day.
```

Chord Forms

G

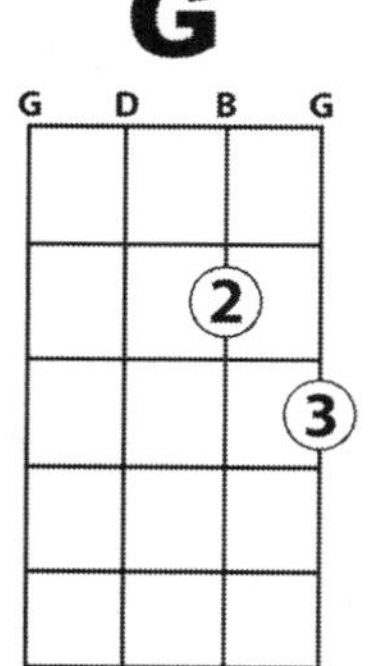

C

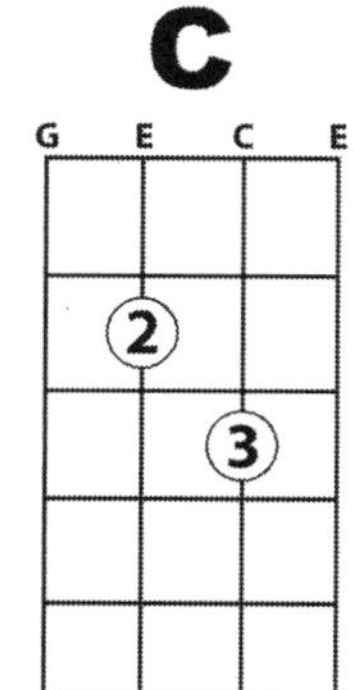

D

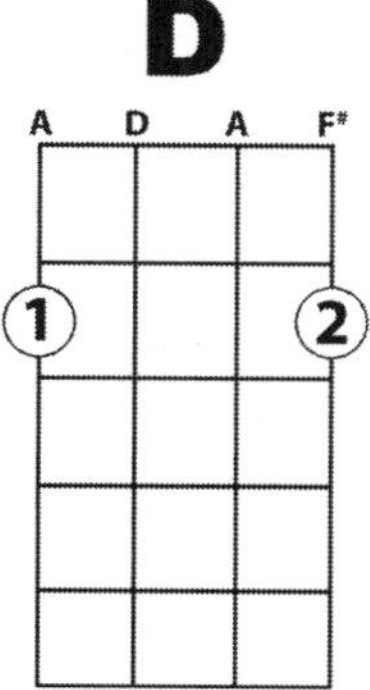

Cruising 'Round Yarmouth
(continued)

Basic Melody

Key of G (High)

```
  G                                          C                   G
E ─────────────────────────────7─────7──5───0───0─0───────────────────────────
A 2──3──5───5────5─────5───────────────────────────────5─5───5─5──────────────
D ────────────────────────────────────────────────────────────────────────────
G ────────────────────────────────────────────────────────────────────────────
  While cruisin' round Yarmouth one day for a spree, I met a fair
```

```
                            D            G
E ──3────5───7────5───3───5─────────3───5─7─────3─5───7────7─────3────────────
A 5───────────────────────────────────────────────────────────────────────────
D ────────────────────────────────────────────────────────────────────────────
G ────────────────────────────────────────────────────────────────────────────
  Damsel, the wind blowing free;  "I'm a fast-going clipper, my
```

```
  C                  G           C                                          G
E 5────3─────5────3─────5───3──0──0───0──3───0──────────0─────────────────────
A ─────────────────────────────────────────────────5──────────5──────2────────
D ────────────────────────────────────────────────────────────────────────────
G ────────────────────────────────────────────────────────────────────────────
  Kind sir," said she, "I'm ready for cargo, my hold is quite free."
```

CHORUS

```
  G                                   C
E ──────────────────────────7───7───5───0───0───0─────────────────────────────
A 2──3────5───5───5───5───────────────────────────────────────────────────────
D ────────────────────────────────────────────────────────────────────────────
G ────────────────────────────────────────────────────────────────────────────
  Singin' fal der ral laddie and fal der ral day,
```

```
  G                         D         G
E ────────────────7───7───5───3───2───3───────────────────────────────────────
A 5───5───5───5───────────────────────────────────────────────────────────────
D ────────────────────────────────────────────────────────────────────────────
G ────────────────────────────────────────────────────────────────────────────
  Fal der ral laddie and fal der ral day.
```

Chord Forms

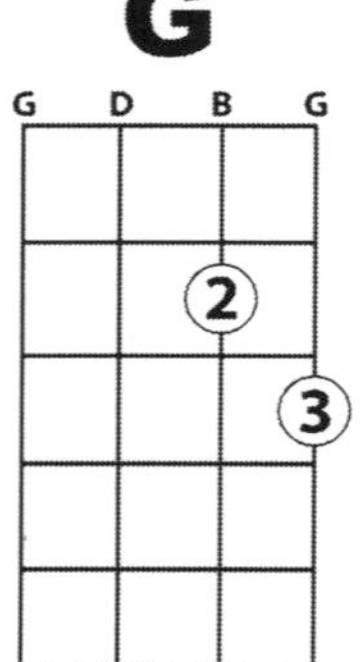

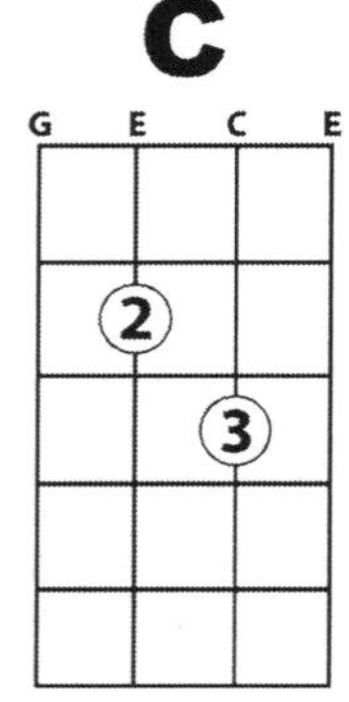

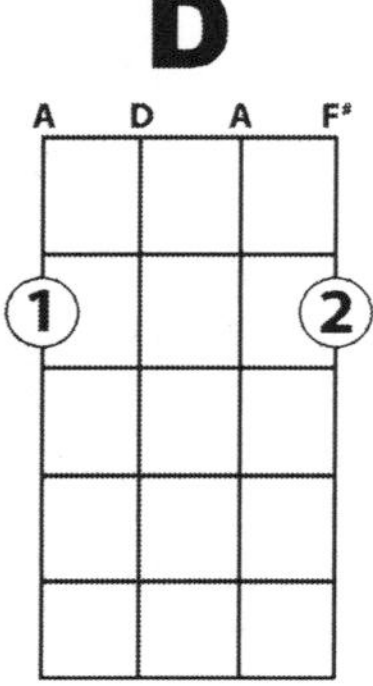

Cruising 'Round Yarmouth

(continued)

Melody & Chords

Key of G (High)

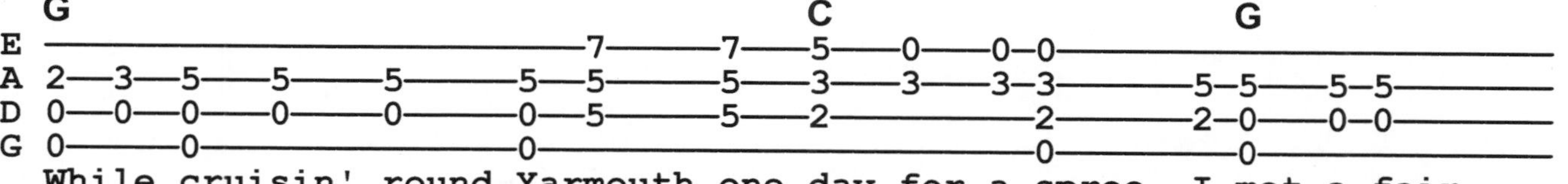

While cruisin' round Yarmouth one day for a spree, I met a fair

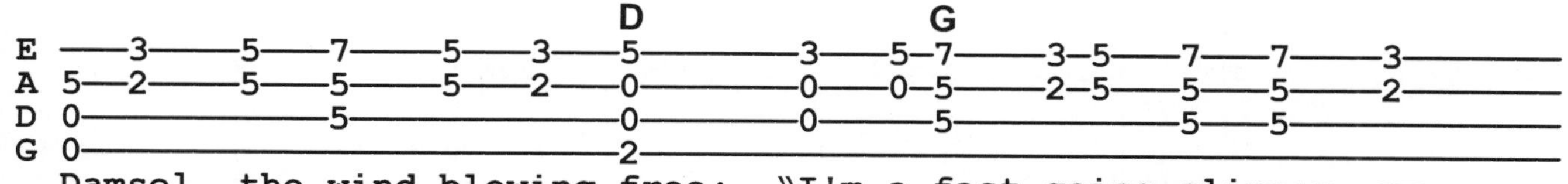

Damsel, the wind blowing free; "I'm a fast-going clipper, my

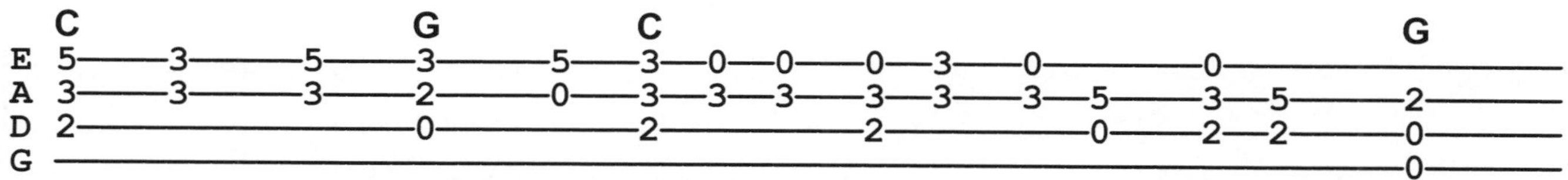

Kind sir," said she, "I'm ready for cargo, my hold is quite free."

Chorus

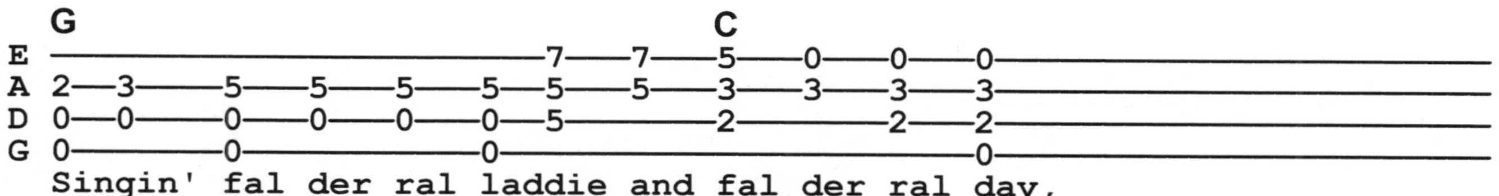

Singin' fal der ral laddie and fal der ral day,

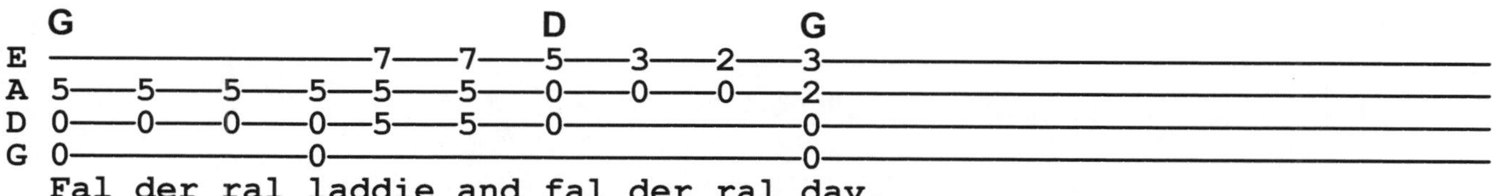

Fal der ral laddie and fal der ral day.

Chord Forms

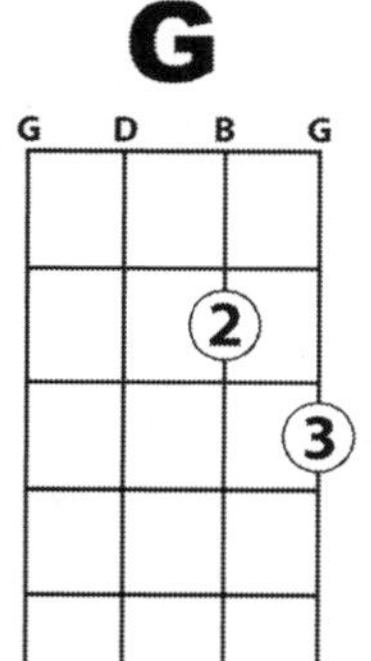

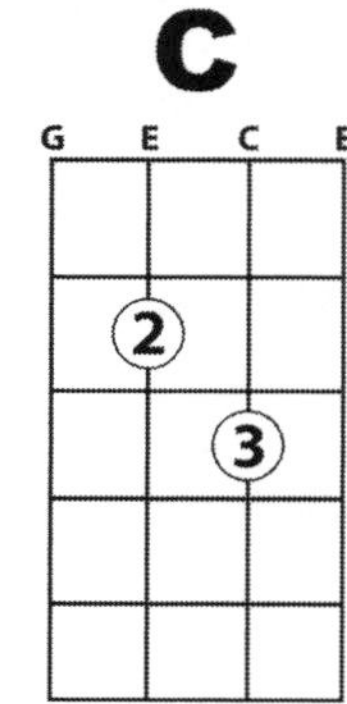

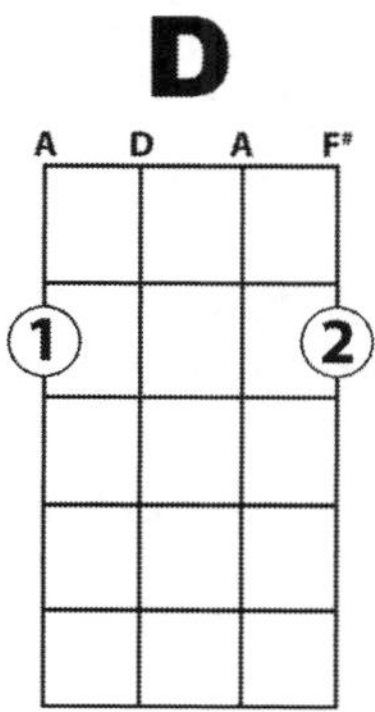

The Dead Horse

Basic Melody

Key of C

Also known as the Poor Old Man, this sailor's song goes bar a long ways and is tied to a peculiar ceremony that would take place on ship. See the historical snippet on the next page for more background on this traditional shanty.

Words and Music

Traditional

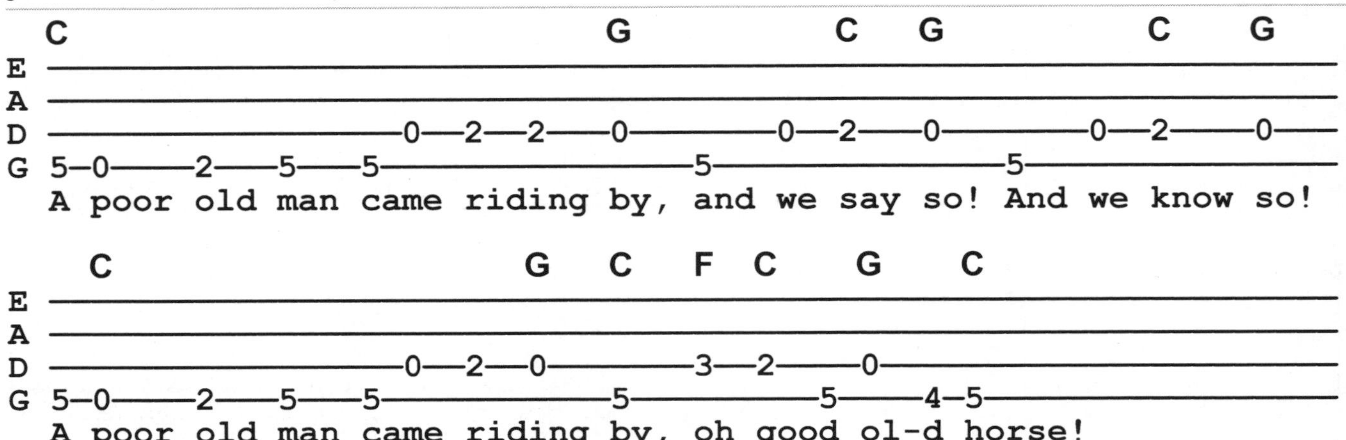

Chord Forms

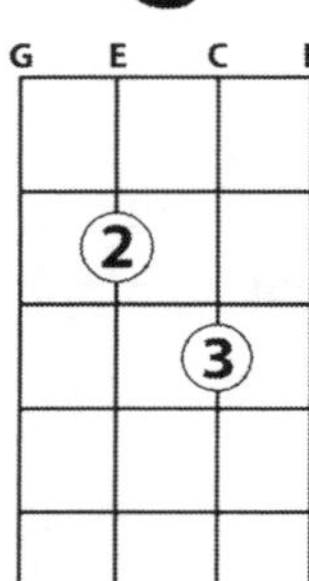

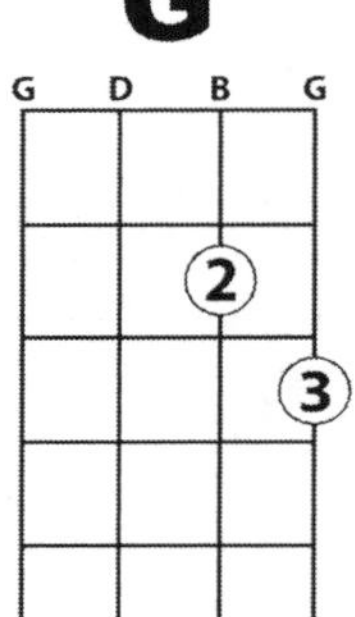

F

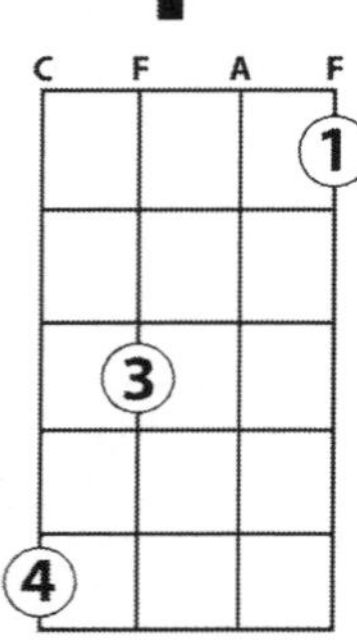

Additional Verses

Oh, poor old man your horse will die,
And we say so, and we know so!
Oh, poor old man your horse will die,
Oh, poor old man.

For thirty days I've ridden him,
And we say so, and we know so!
And when he dies we'll tan his skin,
Oh, poor old man.

We'll hoist him up to the main yardarm,
And we say so, and we know so!
We'll hoist him up to the main yardarm,
Oh, poor old man.

We'll drop him down to the depths of the sea,
And we say so, and we know so!
We'll drop him down to the bottom of the sea,
Oh, poor old man.

We'll sink him down with a long, low roll,
And we say so, and we know so!
Where the sharks'll have his body,
And the devil have his soul,
Oh, poor old man.

The Dead Horse (continued)

Two Versions
Key of C (High)

Basic Melody

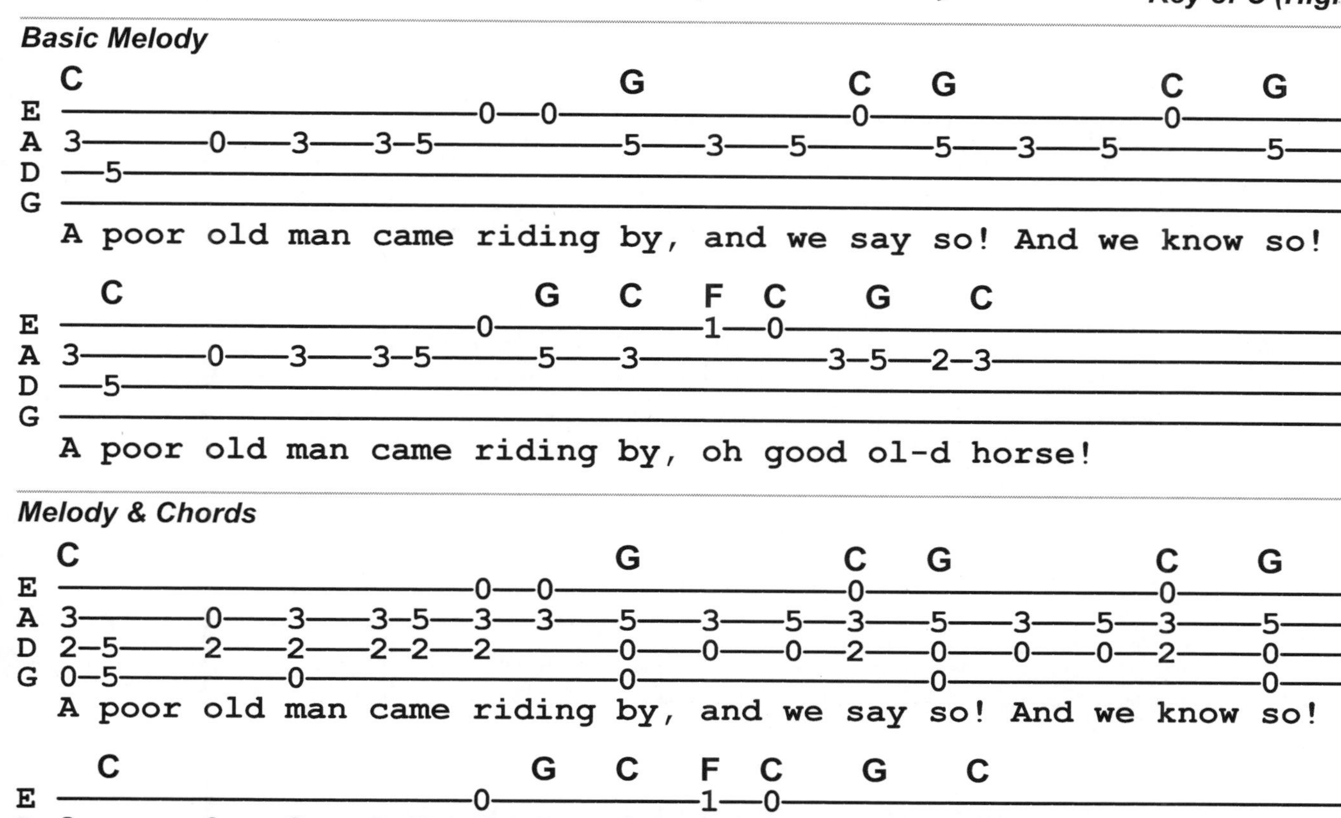

Chord Forms

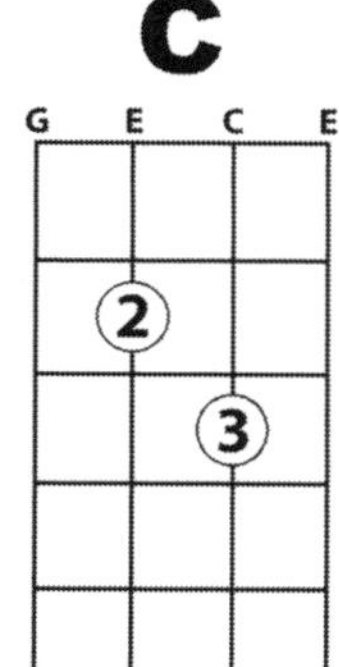

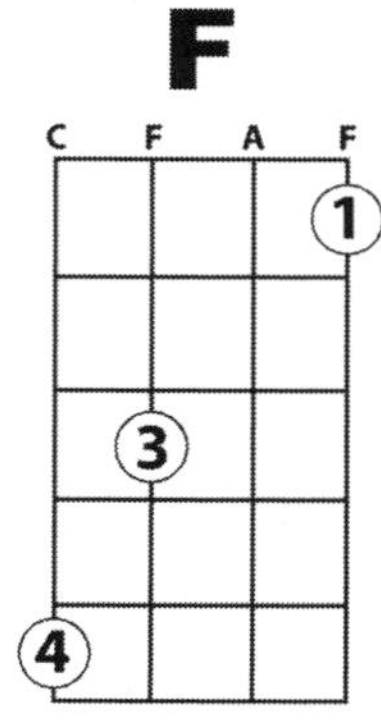

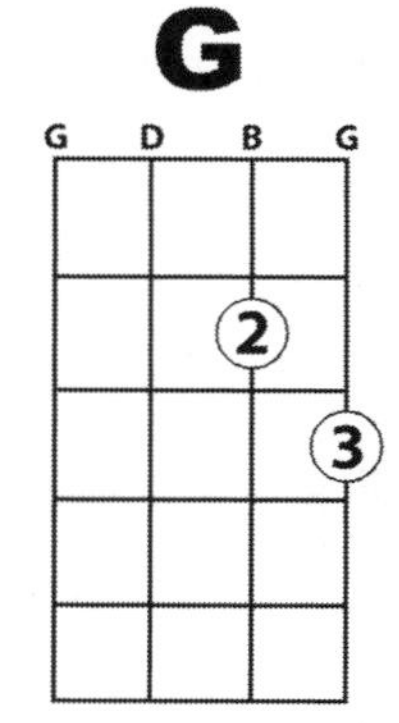

Historical Notes

According to Wikipedia and other sources, it was the custom in the old days of sailing for the men to be paid a month's wages in advance, for them to provision themselves for the journey.

But of course as many shanties and sea songs attest, they more often quickly spent the money on drink and other diversion, and were penniless by the time the ship set sail.

The pay advance was known as the "dead horse" and they spent their first month at sea working it off. After the thirty days were up, they would hoist a fake stuffed horse up the yardarm and then drop it into the sea, all while singing this very shanty... or so the story goes.

SEA SHANTY

The Dead Horse (continued)

Two Versions
Key of G (Low)

Basic Melody

```
   G                                        D               G     D                 G       D
E ------------------------------------------------------------------------------------------------
A ------------------------0---2---2---0------------0---2---0-------------0---2-------0-----
D 5-0------2-----5-----5---------------------5--------------------------5---------------------
G ------------------------------------------------------------------------------------------------
  A poor old man came riding by, and we say so! And we know so!
```

```
    G                                   D     G     C   G        D      G
E ------------------------------------------------------------------------------------------------
A ------------------------0---2---0----------------3---2------0-----------------------------------
D 5-0------2-----5-----5-----------------5------------------5------4-5---------------------------
G ------------------------------------------------------------------------------------------------
  A poor old man came riding by, oh good ol-d horse!
```

Melody & Chords

```
   G                                        D               G     D                 G       D
E ------------------------------------------------------------------------------------------------
A ------------------------0---2---2---0------------0---2---0-------------0---2-------0-----
D 5-0------2-----5-----5-0---0---0---0-----5----0---0------0-----5-----0---0-------0-----
G 0-0------0-----0-----0-----0--------2-----0----------0----2-----0-----------0-----2-----
  A poor old man came riding by, and we say so! And we know so!
```

```
    G                                   D     G     C   G        D      G
E ------------------------------------------------------------------------------------------------
A ------------------------0---2---0----------------3---2------0-----------------------------------
D 5-0------2-----5-----5-0---0---0-----5-----2---0---5-0---4-5---------------------------
G 0-0------0-----0-----0-----0---------0-----0---0---0-2---2-0---------------------------
  A poor old man came riding by, oh good ol-d horse!
```

Chord Forms

G

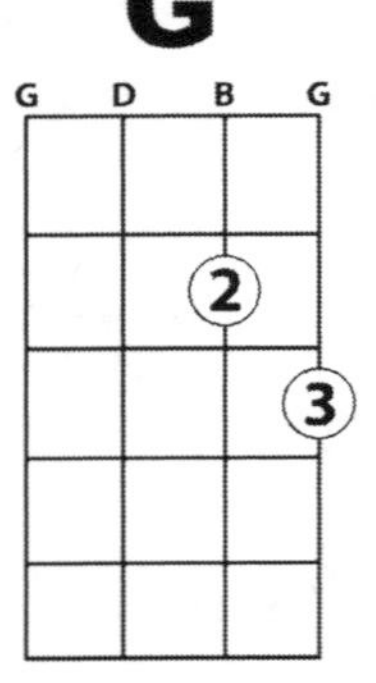

D

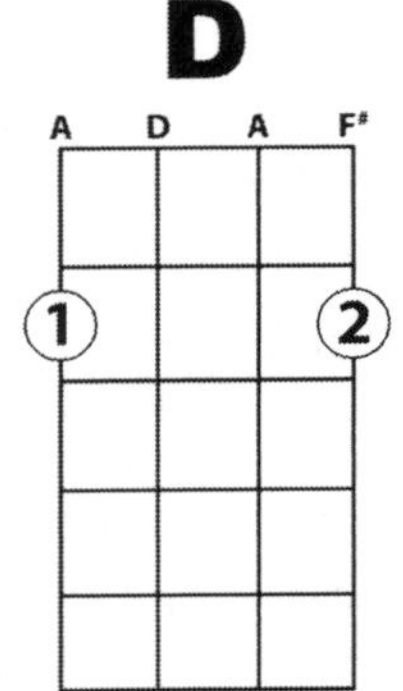

C

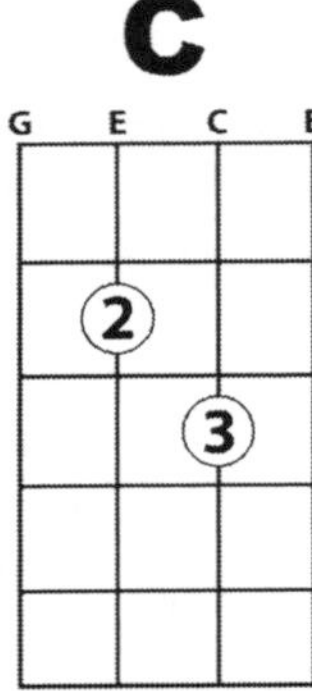

The Dead Horse (continued)

Two Versions
Key of G (High)

Basic Melody

```
   G                                   D              G    D               G     D
E 3———————0————3————3-5——7———7————5————3————5——7————5————3————5——7————5———
A ——5—————————————————————————————————————————————————————————————————————
D ————————————————————————————————————————————————————————————————————————
G ————————————————————————————————————————————————————————————————————————
  A poor old man came riding by, and we say so! And we know so!
```

```
     G                              D    G    C  G    D    G
E 3———————0————3————3-5——7———5————3————8——7——3-5——2-3———————————————
A ——5—————————————————————————————————————————————————————————————————
D ————————————————————————————————————————————————————————————————————
G ————————————————————————————————————————————————————————————————————
  A poor old man came riding by, oh good ol-d horse!
```

Melody & Chords

```
   G                                   D              G    D               G     D
E 3———————0————3————3-5——7———7————5————3————5——7————5————3————5——7————5———
A 2-5—————2————2————2-5——5———5————5————5————5——5————5————5————5——5————5———
D 0-0——————————0————0————5————————7———————————5————7——————————————5————7———
G ——0—————————————————————————————————————————————————————————————————————
  A poor old man came riding by, and we say so! And we know so!
```

```
     G                              D    G    C  G    D    G
E 3———————0————3————3-5——7———5————3————8——7——3-5——2-3———————————————
A 2-5—————2————2————2-5——5———5————2————7——5——5-5——0-2———————————————
D 0-0——————————0————0————5———7————0————5——5————7———0————————————————
G ——0—————————————————————————————————————————————————————————————————
  A poor old man came riding by, oh good ol-d horse!
```

Chord Forms

G

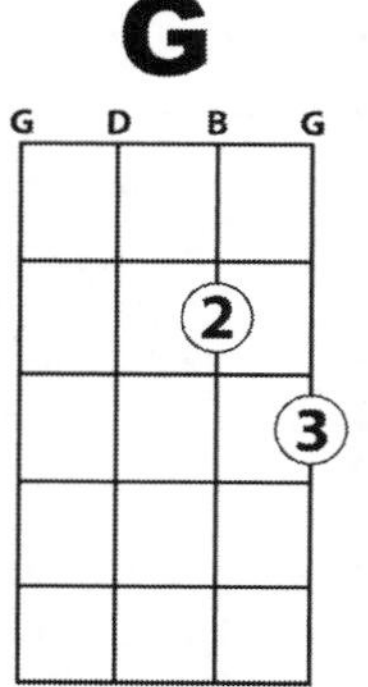

D

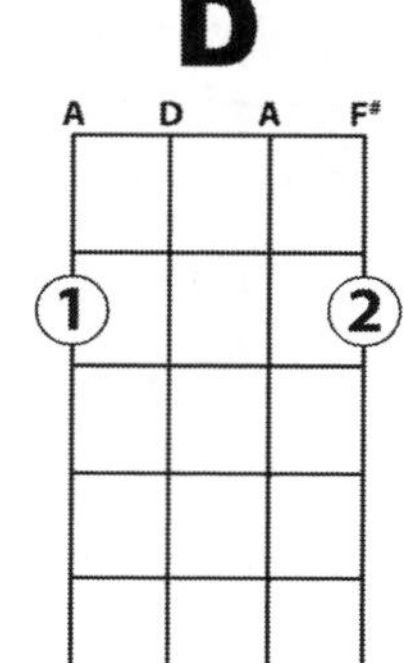

C

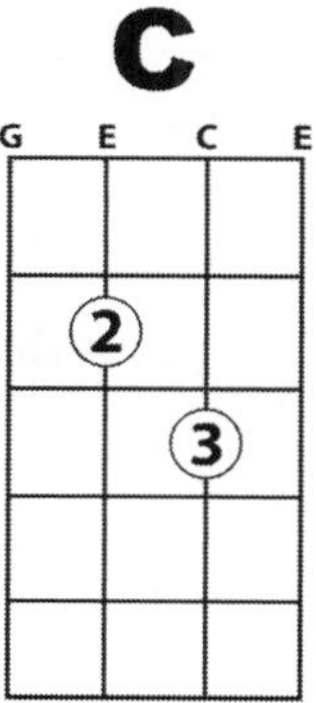

Don't Forget Your Old Shipmate

Basic Melody

Key of C (Low)

This is another traditional British naval song, which while not technically a true sea shanty has still become a part of the repertoires of many shanty singers. A version of this old song appeared in the 1978 movie Master and Commander, which helped increase its popularity.

Words and Music

Traditional

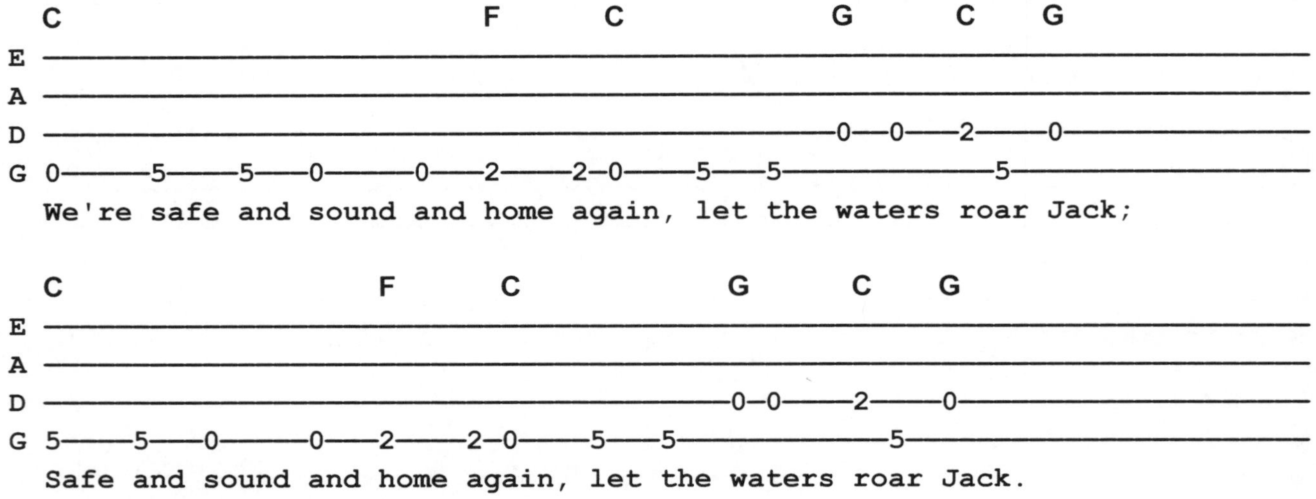

```
  C                          F      C              G       C    G
E -----------------------------------------------------------------------
A -----------------------------------------------------------------------
D ----------------------------------------------------0---0---2----0------
G 0-----5----5---0------0---2----2-0----5---5-------------------5---------
  We're safe and sound and home again, let the waters roar Jack;
```

```
  C                    F      C              G      C    G
E -----------------------------------------------------------------------
A -----------------------------------------------------------------------
D -------------------------------------------0-0-----2-----0--------------
G 5----5---0------0---2----2-0----5---5-------------5---------------------
  Safe and sound and home again, let the waters roar Jack.
```

CHORUS

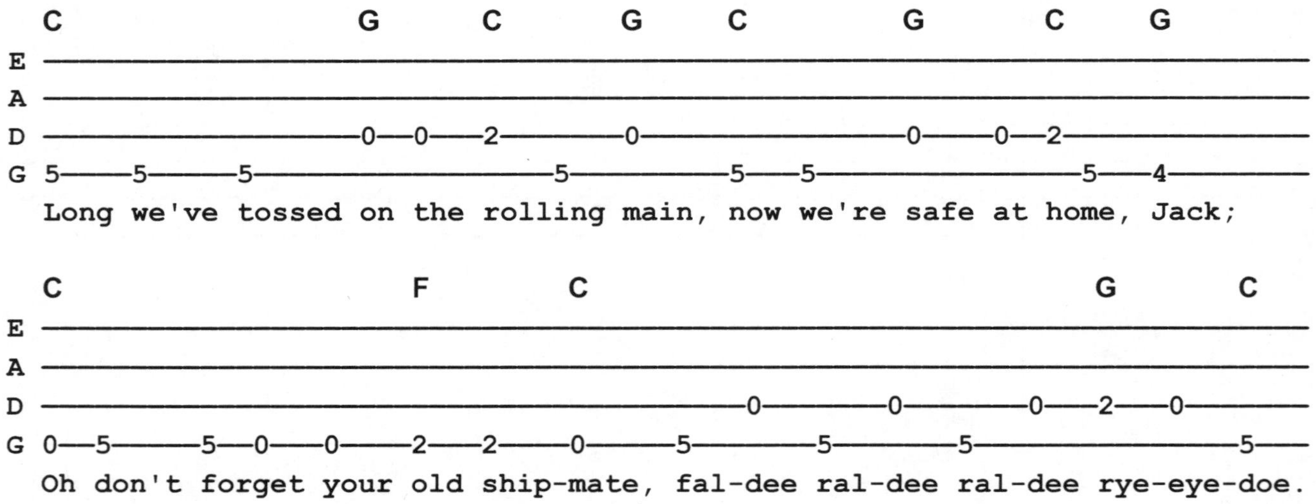

```
  C                   G       C       G       C         G       C     G
E -----------------------------------------------------------------------
A -----------------------------------------------------------------------
D ------------------------0---0---2-------0-----------------0-----0---2---
G 5----5-----5-------------------------5----------5---5-----------------5---4---
  Long we've tossed on the rolling main, now we're safe at home, Jack;
```

```
  C                     F         C                              G      C
E -----------------------------------------------------------------------
A -----------------------------------------------------------------------
D -----------------------------------------0-------0-------0---2---0-----
G 0--5------5--0---0-----2---2----0-----5-------5-------5---------------5--
  Oh don't forget your old ship-mate, fal-dee ral-dee ral-dee rye-eye-doe.
```

See Chord Forms and Additional Verses on Next Page

Don't Forget Your Old Shipmate (continued)

Chord Forms

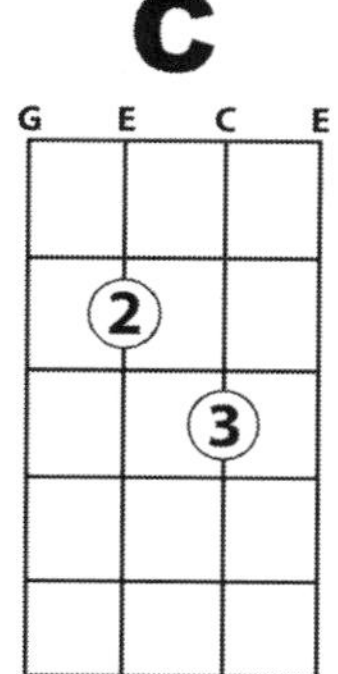

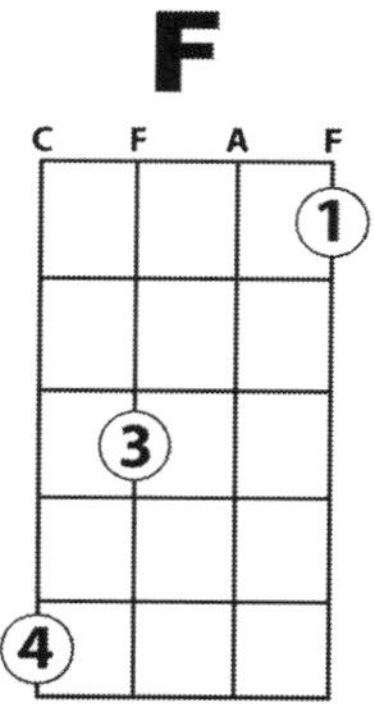

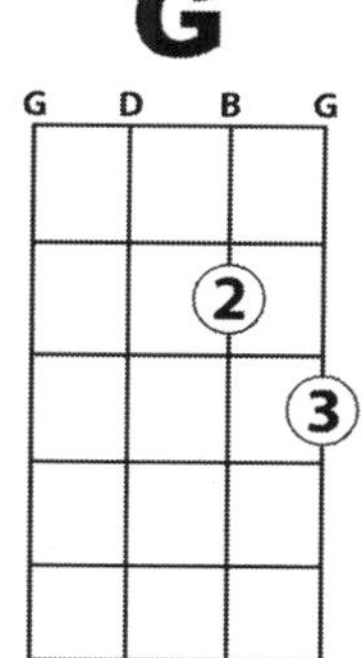

Additional Verses

Since we've sailed from Plymouth Sound,
Four years gone, or night, Jack;
Was there ever chummies, now,
Such as you and I, Jack?

We have worked the self-same gun,
Quarterdeck division;
Sponger I and loader you,
Through the whole commission.

Often times have we laid out,
Toil nor danger fearing;
Tugging out the flapping sail,
To the weather bearing.

When the middle watch was on,
And the time went slow, boy;
Who could choose a rousing stave,
Who like Jack or Joe, boy?

There she swings, an empty hulk,
Not a soul below now;
Number seven starboard mess,
Misses Jack and Joe now.

But the best of friends must part,
Fair or foul the weather;
Hand yer flipper for a shake,
Now a drink together.

Don't Forget Your Old Shipmate (continued)

Basic Melody

Key of C (High)

```
  C                                    F         C                   G         C      G
E ---------------------------------------------------------------------------0------------------
A ---------3-------3-------------------0-------0---------3-----3----5----5--------3---5---------
D 5-----------------------5--------5--------------------5---------------------------------------
G ----------------------------------------------------------------------------------------------
```

We're safe and sound and home again, let the waters roar Jack;

```
  C                         F         C                   G         C      G
E ---------------------------------------------------------------0-----------------------
A 3-----3-------------------0-------0---------3-----3----5---5--------3---5--------------
D -------------5--------5--------------5-------------------------------------------------
G ---------------------------------------------------------------------------------------
```

Safe and sound and home again, let the waters roar Jack.

CHORUS

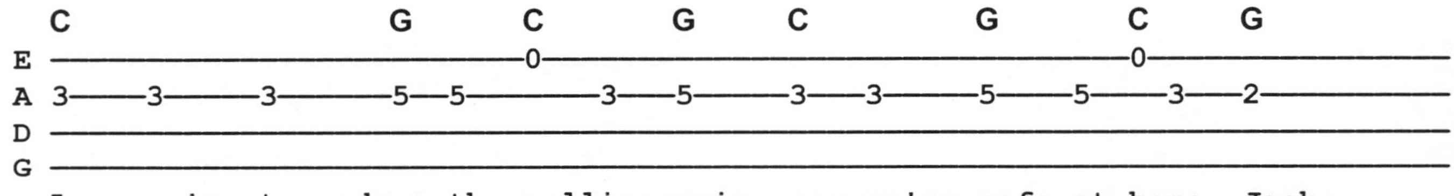

Long we've tossed on the rolling main, now we're safe at home, Jack;

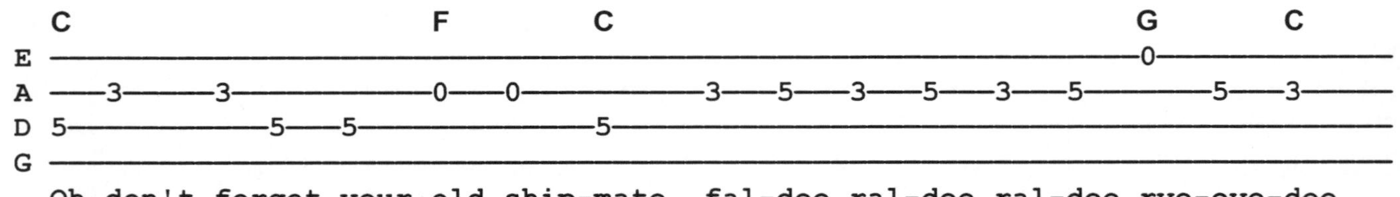

Oh don't forget your old ship-mate, fal-dee ral-dee ral-dee rye-eye-doe.

Chord Forms

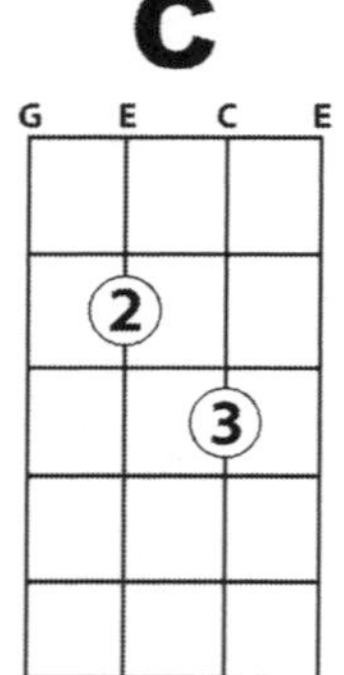

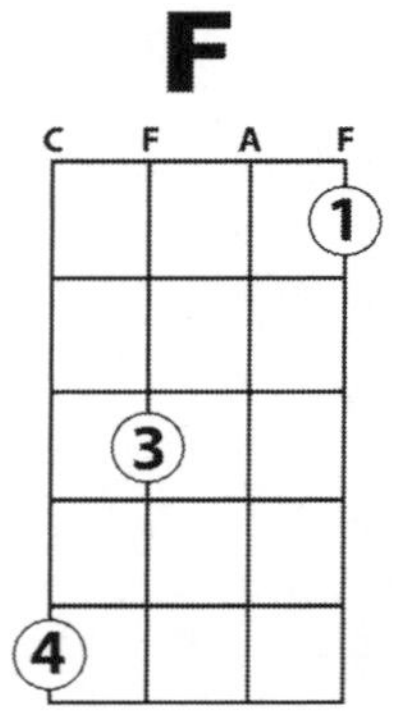

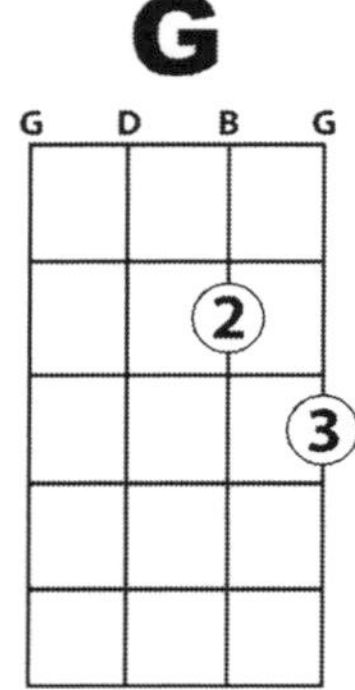

Don't Forget Your Old Shipmate (continued)

Melody & Chords

Key of C (High)

```
  C                                   F         C                 G         C      G
E ------------------------------------------------------------------------0----------------
A ---------3------3-------------------0------0---------3-----3----5----5---3--3---5--------
D 5--------2------2-----5--------5----3------3-5-------2-----2----0----0---2--2---0--------
G 5--------0------------5--------5----5--------5-------0----------0---------------0--------
  We're safe and sound and home again, let the waters roar Jack;
```

```
  C                         F        C                 G        C      G
E ----------------------------------------------------------------0------------------------
A 3------3------------------0--------0--------3-----3----5-5------3--3---5-----------------
D 2------2----5--------5----3--------3-5------2-----2----0-0------2--2---0-----------------
G 0-----------5--------5----5----------5------0----------0---------------0-----------------
  Safe and sound and home again, let the waters roar Jack.
```

CHORUS

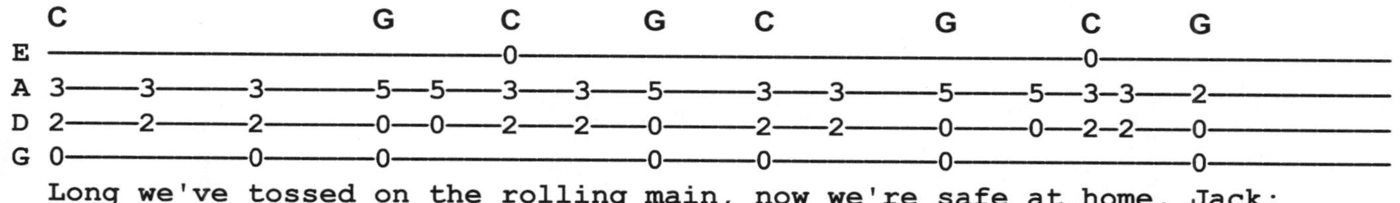

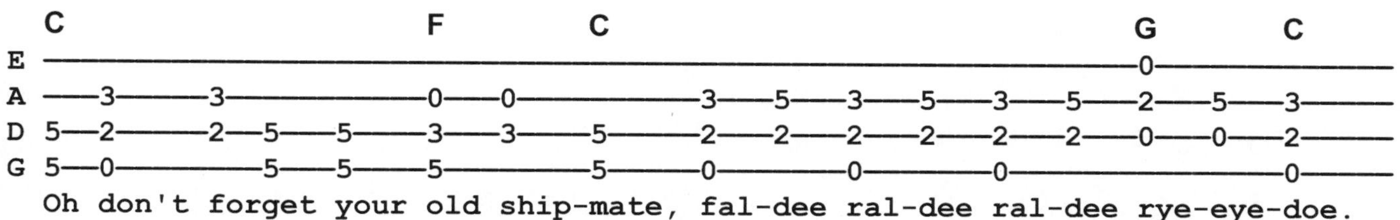

Chord Forms

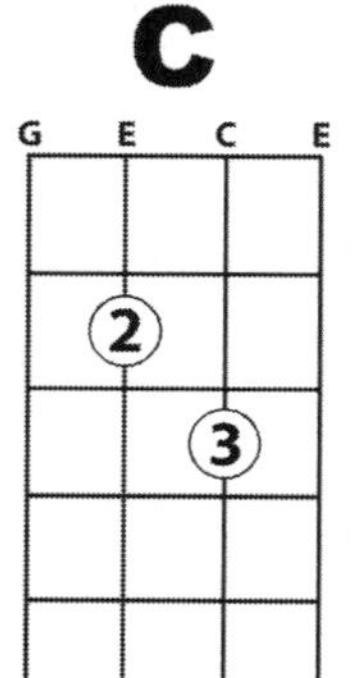

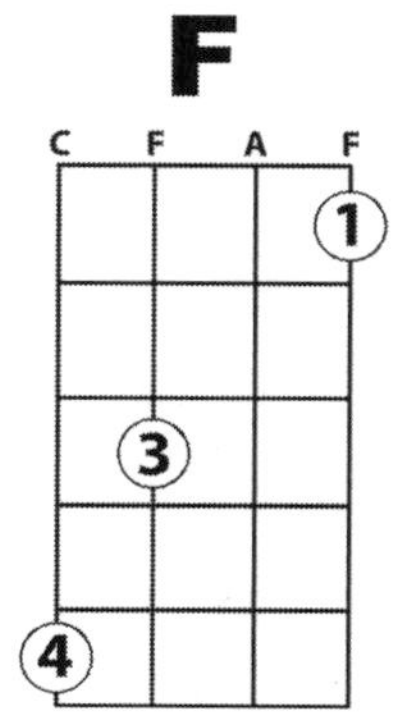

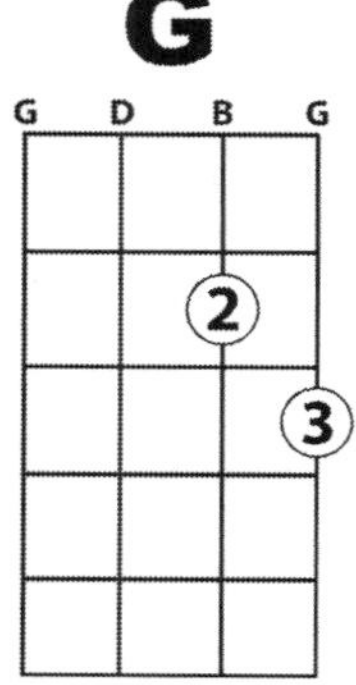

Don't Forget Your Old Shipmate (continued)

Basic Melody

Key of G (Low)

```
  G                         C       G               D       G      D
E -----------------------------------------------------------------------
A --------------------------------------------------0---0----2-----0-----
D 0-------5-----5----0-------0----2-----2-0-----5----5------------5------
G -----------------------------------------------------------------------
  We're safe and sound and home again, let the waters roar Jack;
```

```
  G                    C       G               D      G      D
E ------------------------------------------------------------------
A ---------------------------------------------0-0-----2-----0------
D 5------5----0-------0----2------2-0-----5----5------------5-------
G ------------------------------------------------------------------
  Safe and sound and home again, let the waters roar Jack.
```

Chorus

```
  G                   D       G        D      G          D        G      D
E ---------------------------------------------------------------------------
A ---------------------0---0----2--------0--------------0------0---2---------
D 5------5-------5-------------------5-----------5----5-------------5----4---
G ---------------------------------------------------------------------------
  Long we've tossed on the rolling main, now we're safe at home, Jack;
```

```
  G                      C          G                              D       G
E ----------------------------------------------------------------------------
A ---------------------------------------------0--------0-------0----2----0---
D 0--5--------5---0----0------2----2------0------5--------5--------5---------5---
G ----------------------------------------------------------------------------
  Oh don't forget your old ship-mate, fal-dee ral-dee ral-dee rye-eye-doe.
```

Chord Forms

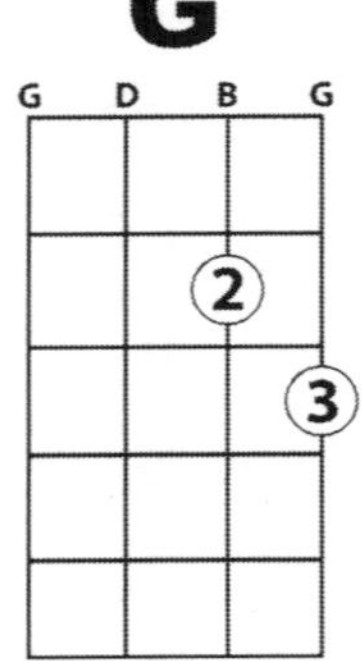

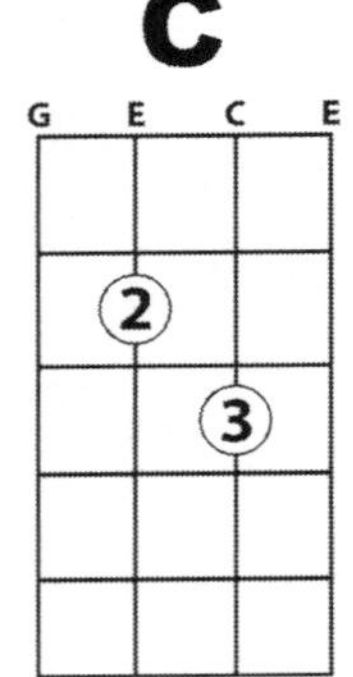

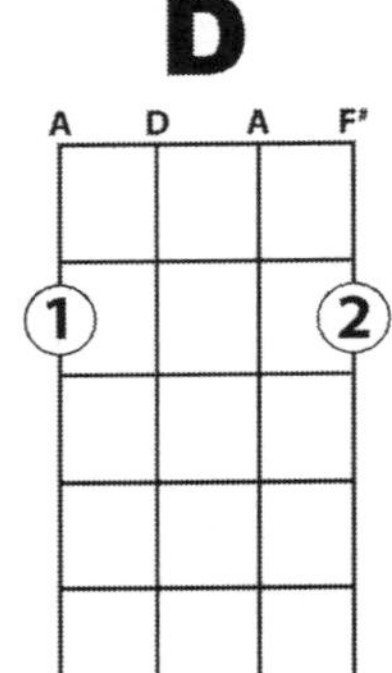

Don't Forget Your Old Shipmate (continued)

Basic Melody

Key of G (Low)

```
  G                          C        G                D        G      D
E ---------------------------------------------------------------------------------------------
A ----------------------------------------------------------------0--0----2-----0--------------
D 0-------5------5----0-------0----2------2-0------5----5----0--0----0-5---0-------------------
G 0-------0------0----0-------0----5------5-0------0----0----2-------0-0---2-------------------
  We're safe and sound and home again, let the waters roar Jack;
```

```
  G                    C        G                D        G      D
E ---------------------------------------------------------------------------------------
A -------------------------------------------------------0-0-----2-----0-----------------
D 5------5----0-------0----2------2-0------5----5-----0-0-----0-5---0-------------------
G 0------0----0-------0----5------5-0------0----0-----2-------0-0---2-------------------
  Safe and sound and home again, let the waters roar Jack.
```

Chorus

```
  G                       D        G         D        G            D          G       D
E ----------------------------------------------------------------------------------------------
A -------------------------0---0----2---------0-----------------------0-------0---2-------------
D 5------5-------5---------0---0----0----5----0--------5----5---------0-------0---0-5----4------
G 0------0-------0---------2--------0----0----2--------0----0---------2-----------0-0----2------
  Long we've tossed on the rolling main, now we're safe at home, Jack;
```

```
  G                         C          G                                           D          G
E ----------------------------------------------------------------------------------------------------
A ---------------------------------------------------------0---------0---------0----2----0------------
D 0--5-------5--0---0------2---2-----0-------5----0----5----0----5----0----0----0----5---------------
G 0--0-------0--0---0------5---5-----0-------0---------0---------0---------2---------0---------------
  Oh don't forget your old ship-mate, fal-dee ral-dee ral-dee rye-eye-doe.
```

Chord Forms

G

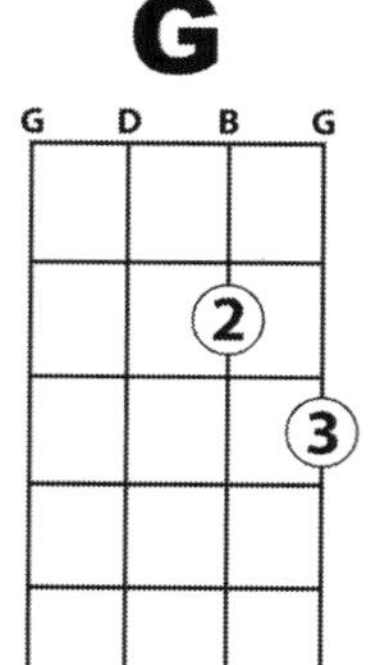

C

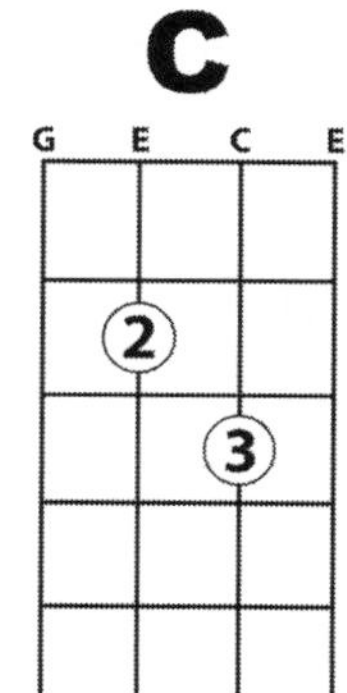

D

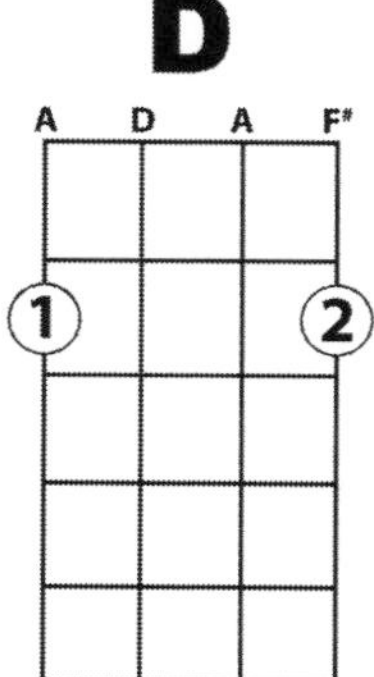

Don't Forget Your Old Shipmate (continued)

Basic Melody

Key of G (High)

```
  G                                 C       G                 D       G   D
E ---------3-----3-----------------0------0--------3----3----5---5---7--3--5----------
A 5------------------5------5-------------5---------------------------------------------
D ---------------------------------------------------------------------------------------
G ---------------------------------------------------------------------------------------
  We're safe and sound and home again, let the waters roar Jack;
```

```
  G                         C      G              D      G    D
E 3-----3------------------0------0--------3----3----5-5-----7-3---5--------------
A ------------5------5------------5----------------------------------------------
D ------------------------------------------------------------------------------
G ------------------------------------------------------------------------------
  Safe and sound and home again, let the waters roar Jack.
```

CHORUS

```
  G                     D      G       D        G           D        G     D
E 3-----3-------3------5--5---7----3---5-------3----3-------5-------5--7-3----2-------
A --------------------------------------------------------------------------------------
D --------------------------------------------------------------------------------------
G --------------------------------------------------------------------------------------
  Long we've tossed on the rolling main, now we're safe at home, Jack;
```

```
  G                         C        G                                      D       G
E ----3-------3-------------0----0-----------3----5----3----5----3----5----7----5----3-----
A 5---------------5---5--------------5------------------------------------------------------
D ------------------------------------------------------------------------------------------
G ------------------------------------------------------------------------------------------
  Oh don't forget your old ship-mate, fal-dee ral-dee ral-dee rye-eye-doe.
```

Chord Forms

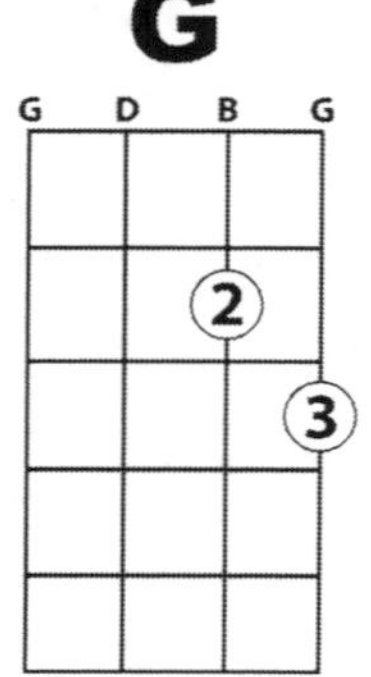

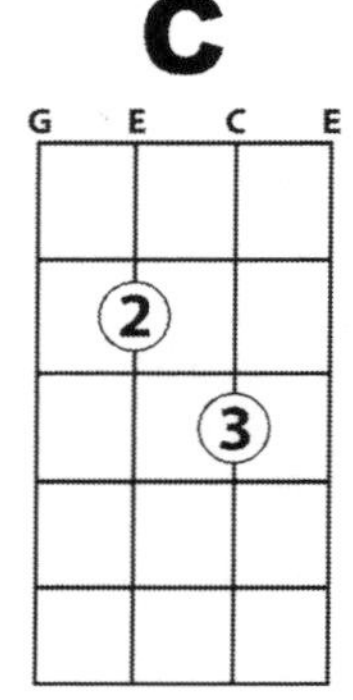

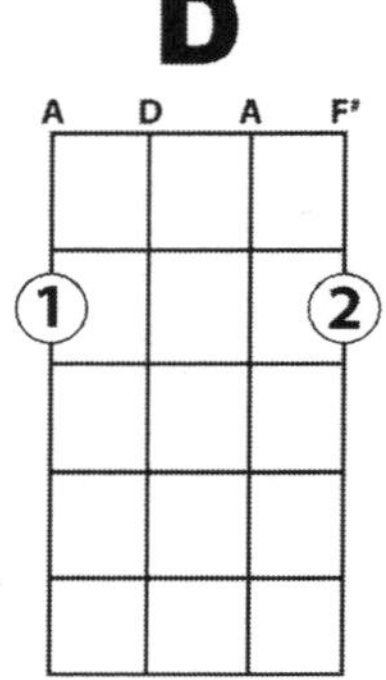

Don't Forget Your Old Shipmate (continued)

Melody & Chords

Key of G (Low)

```
  G                                    C        G              D       G    D
E ---------3-----3---------------------0--------0--------3-----3---5---5----7-3--5---------
A 5--------2-----2----5--------5-------3--------3-5------2-----2---0---0----5-2--0---------
D 0--------0----------0--------0-------2----------0------0---------0--------5----0---------
G 0-------------------0---------------------------0----------------------------------------
```

We're safe and sound and home again, let the waters roar Jack;

```
  G                        C        G           D      G    D
E 3-----3------------------0--------0-------3---3---5-5----7-3--5--------
A 2-----2----5-------5-----3--------3-5-----2---2---0-0----5-2--0--------
D 0----------0-------0-----2----------0-----0-------0------5----0--------
G ----------0-------------------------0-----------------------------------
```

Safe and sound and home again, let the waters roar Jack.

Chorus

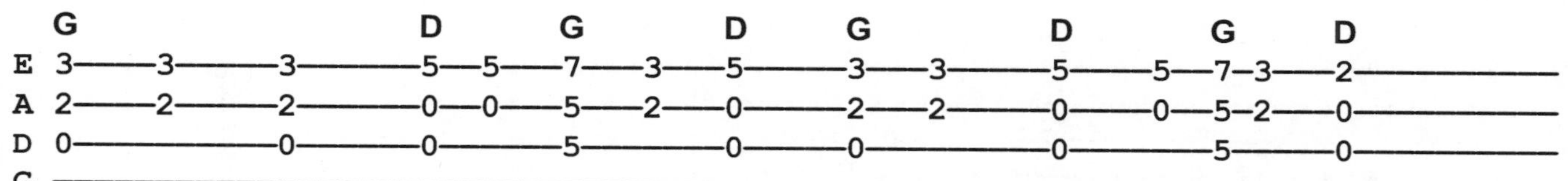

Long we've tossed on the rolling main, now we're safe at home, Jack;

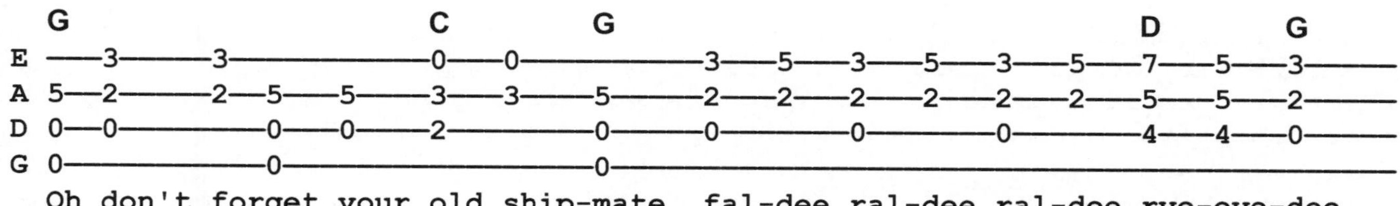

Oh don't forget your old ship-mate, fal-dee ral-dee ral-dee rye-eye-doe.

Chord Forms

G

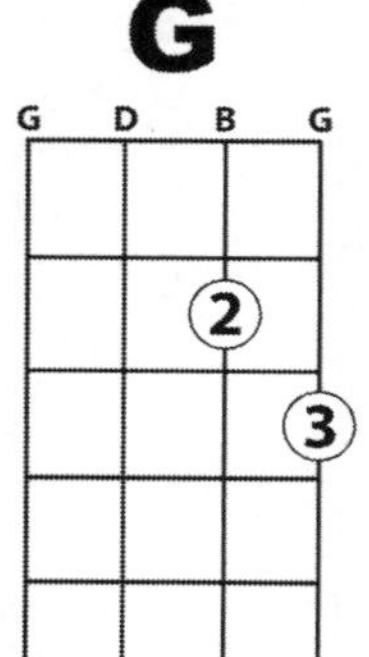

C

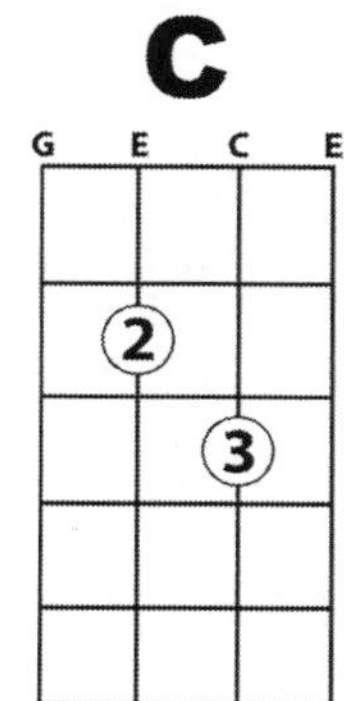

D

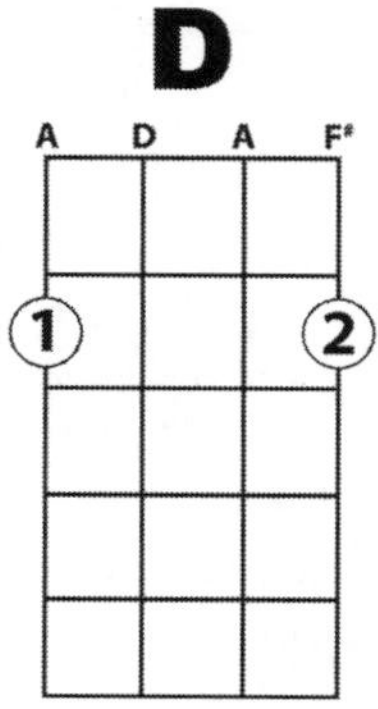

Donkey Riding

Basic Melody

Key of A Minor (Low)

This old work song appeared in the mid 1800's, and is based on the older Scottish song "Bonnie Hieland Laddie." The "donkey" in the song is thought to be an old "steam donkey" steam-powered winch engine used for logging and other hard work, rather than the farm animal. This is a great song for belting out while downing a few pints of beer with friends.

Words and Music

Traditional

```
  Am                 F       C                                 G
E ----------------------------------------------------------------------
A ----------------------------------------------------------------------
D ------------2-2--3--0--2-----2----0---------0-------2--0----0--------
G 2---5--------------------------------------------5--------------5----
  Was you ever in Quebec, launching timber on the deck,

  Am                          F          C      G             Am
E ----------------------------------------------------------------------
A ----------------------------------------------------------------------
D ---------2------2---3---0-----2------2-------0-----------------------
G 2------5-----------------------------------5--------4--2--2----------
  Where ya break yer bleedin' neck, riding on a donkey.
```

CHORUS

```
  F   C      F        C   Am               G
E ----------------------------------------------------------------------
A 0---------------------------------------------------------------------
D ----5----3-3---5--2---2--0---0---------2--0---0-----------------------
G ---------------------------------5--------------5---------------------
  Way hey a-way we go, donkey riding donkey riding,

  F   C      F        C   G             Am
E ----------------------------------------------------------------------
A 0---------------------------------------------------------------------
D ----5----3-3---5--2---2-------0---------------------------------------
G -----------------------5-------4--2--2--------------------------------
  Way hey a-way we go, riding on a donkey.
```

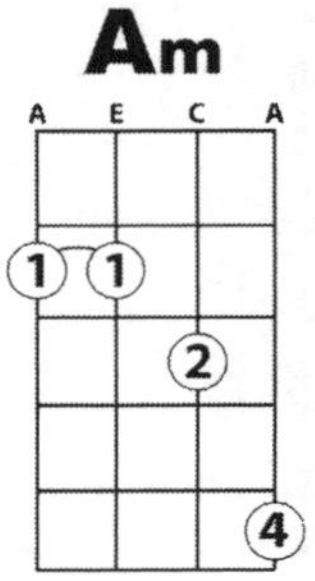

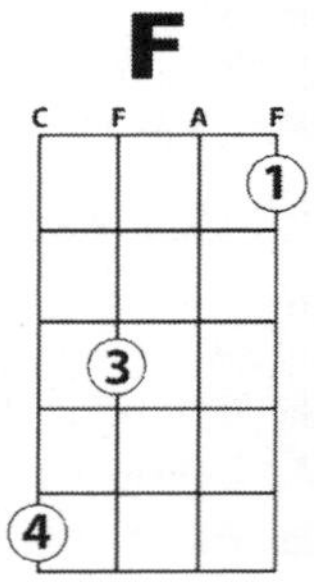

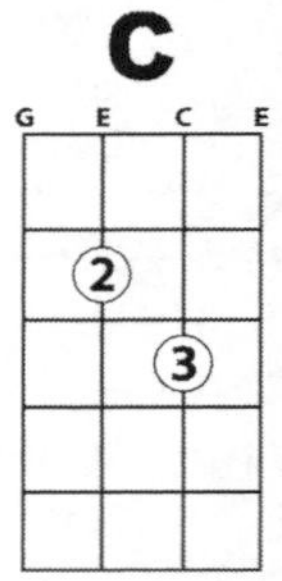

Am
A E C A
1 1
2
4

F
C F A F
1
3
4

C
G E C E
2
3

G
G D B G
2
3

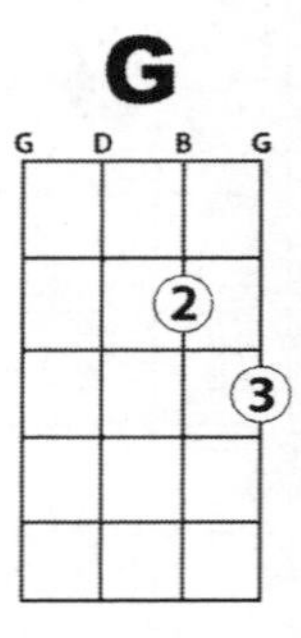

Additional Verses

Was you ever 'round Cape Horn, where the weather's never warm,
Wish to God you'd never been born, riding on a donkey.

Was you ever in Miramichi, where they tie you to a tree,
Have a girl sit on your knee, riding on a donkey.

Was you ever in Fortune Bay, hear the girls all shout hurray,
Here comes Jack with last month's pay, riding on a donkey.

Was you ever in Fredericton, see the king he does come down,
See the king in his golden crown, riding on a donkey.

Donkey Riding (continued)

Basic Melody
Key of A Minor (Low)

```
  Am                F     C                        G
E ──────────────────────────────────────────────────────────────
A ──────────────────────────────────────────────────────────────
D ──────────2─2──3──0──2─────2───0──────0───────2──0───0────────
G 2───5─────2─2──2──2──5─────5───0──────0──5────0──0───0──5─────
  Was you ever in Quebec, launching timber on the deck,

  Am                     F          C      G           Am
E ──────────────────────────────────────────────────────────────
A ──────────────────────────────────────────────────────0───────
D ─────────────2──────2──3───0──────2──────2──────0─────2───────
G 2──────5──2─────────2──2───2──────5──────0──5───0──4─2─2──────
  Where ya break yer bleedin' neck, riding on a donkey.
```

Chorus

```
  F   C     F      C   Am            G
E ──────────────────────────────────────────────────────────────
A 0─────────────────────────────────────────────────────────────
D 3───5───3─3───5──2───2──0───0──────2───0───0──────────────────
G 2───5───5─5───5──5───2──2───2─5────0───0───0─5────────────────
  Way hey a-way we go, donkey riding donkey riding,

  F   C     F      C   G           Am
E ──────────────────────────────────────────────────────────────
A 0───────────────────────────────────0─────────────────────────
D 3───5───3─3───5──2───2──────0───────2─────────────────────────
G 2───5───5─5───5──5───0─5────0──4─2──2─────────────────────────
  Way hey a-way we go, riding on a donkey.
```

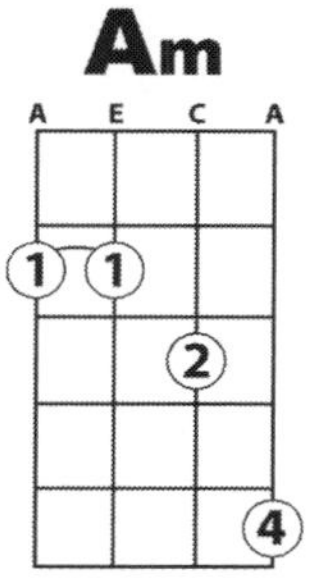

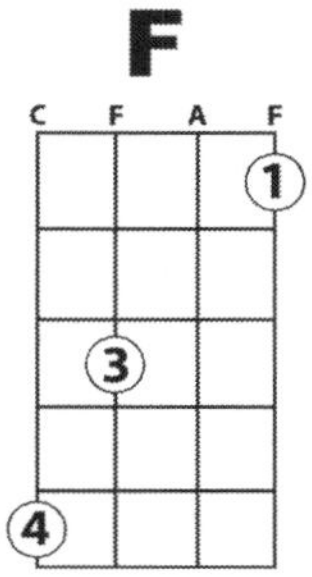

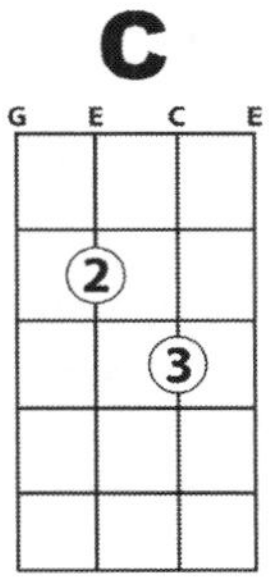

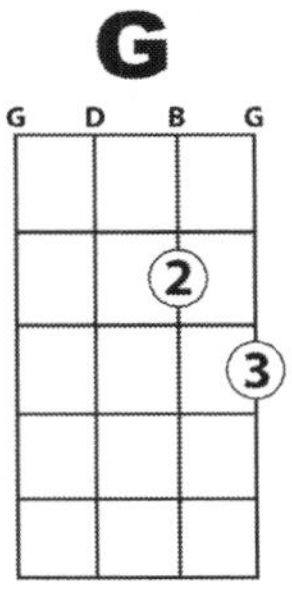

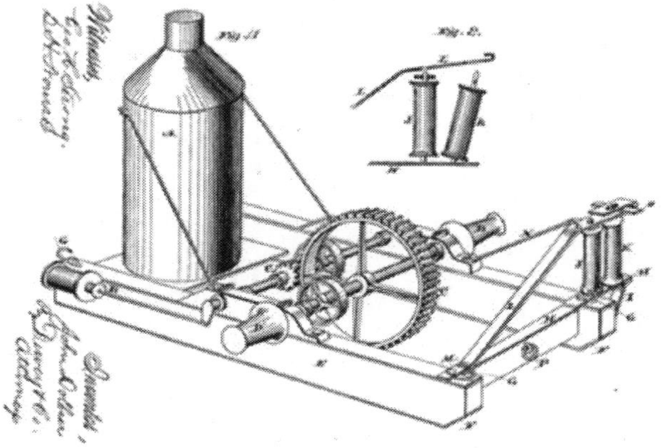

Am
A E C A

F
C F A F

C
G E C E

G
G D B G

Diagram from an 1882 steam donkey patent.

Donkey Riding (continued)

Basic Melody
Key of A Minor (High)

```
  Am                   F     C                               G
E ──────────0─0──1───────0─────0────────────────────────────────0──────────────────
A 0───3──────────────5───────────────────5──────5──3─────────5───5──3──
D ─────────────────────────────────────────────────────────────────────────────────
G ─────────────────────────────────────────────────────────────────────────────────
  Was you ever in Quebec, launching timber on the deck,
```

```
  Am                          F         C       G             Am
E ─────────────0──────0───1──────────0──────0──────────────────────────
A 0──────3──────────────────────5──────────────────3─────5──2─0──0─────
D ─────────────────────────────────────────────────────────────────────
G ─────────────────────────────────────────────────────────────────────
  Where ya break yer bleedin' neck, riding on a donkey.
```

CHORUS

```
  F    C      F        C   Am                G
E 5───3───1─1───3──0───0─────────────────────0─────────────────────
A ───────────────────────────5────5─3────────────5────5─3──────────
D ─────────────────────────────────────────────────────────────────
G ─────────────────────────────────────────────────────────────────
  Way hey a-way we go, donkey riding donkey riding,
```

```
  F    C      F        C   G              Am
E 5───3───1─1───3──0───0───────────────────────────────────────────
A ─────────────────────────3────5──2─0──0──────────────────────────
D ─────────────────────────────────────────────────────────────────
G ─────────────────────────────────────────────────────────────────
  Way hey a-way we go, riding on a donkey.
```

Chord Forms

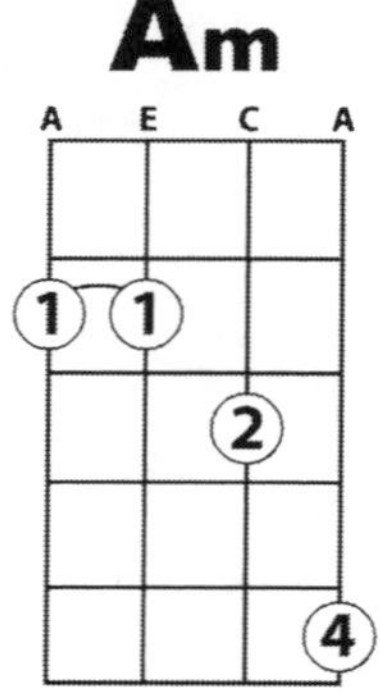

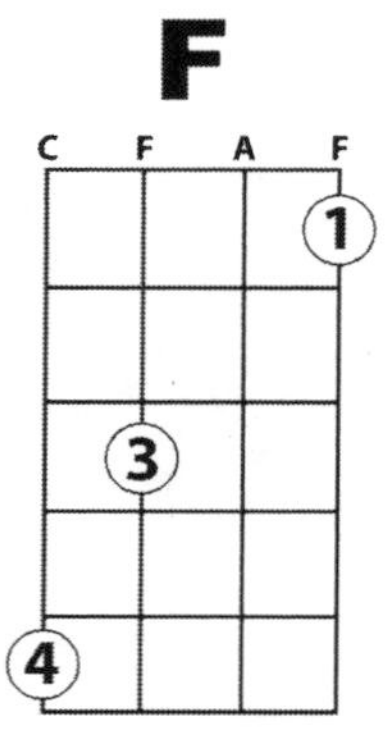

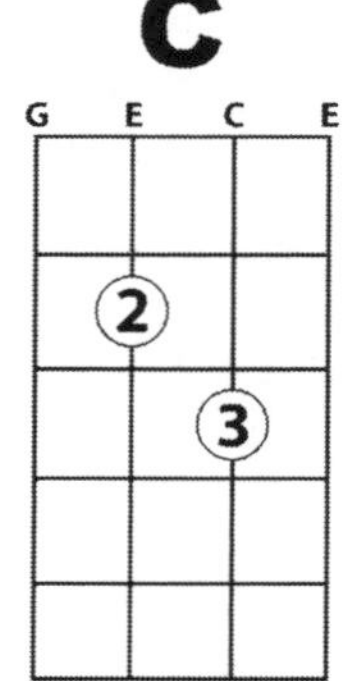

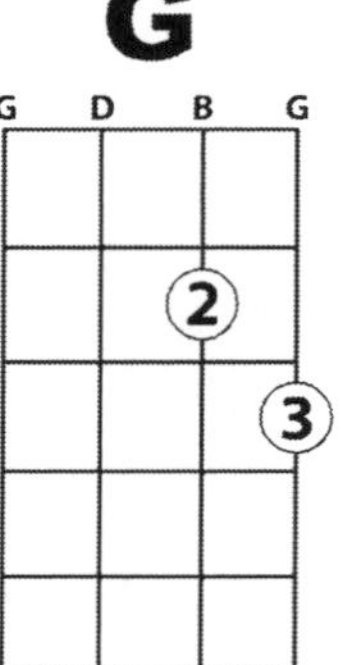

Donkey Riding (continued)

Melody & Chords
Key of A Minor (High)

```
  Am                F     C                               G
E ──────────0─0──1──────0──────0──────────────────────────0───────────────
A 0────3────0─0──0──5───3──────3────5────────5───3────────2───5────5───3──
D 2────2────2────3──3───2──────2────0────────2───2────────0───0────0───0──
G 2─────────────────────0─────────────────────────────────────────0───────
  Was you ever in Quebec, launching timber on the deck,

  Am                          F          C       G             Am
E ────────────0─────────0────1───────────0───────0────────────────────────
A 0──────3────0─────────0────0────5──────3───────2─3──────5──2─0──0───────
D 2──────2────2─────────2────3────3──────2───────0─0──────0──0─2──2───────
G 2───────────────────────────────────────────────────────0────2──2───────
  Where ya break yer bleedin' neck, riding on a donkey.
```

Chorus

```
  F    C     F       C    Am                   G
E 5────3─────1─1─────3────0────0───────────────0──────────────────────
A 3────3─────3─0─────0────3────0───5────5──3───2────5────5──3─────────
D 3────2───────3──────────2────2───0────2──2───0────0────0──0─────────
G ───────────────────────────────────────2─────────────0──────────────
  Way hey a-way we go, donkey riding donkey riding,

  F    C     F       C    G             Am
E 5────3─────1─1─────3────0───────────────────────────────────────────
A 3────3─────0─0─────3────3────2─3──────5──2─0──0─────────────────────
D 3────2───────3──────────2────0─0──────0──0─2──2─────────────────────
G ──────────────────────────────────────0─────2──2────────────────────
  Way hey a-way we go, riding on a donkey.
```

Chord Forms

Am

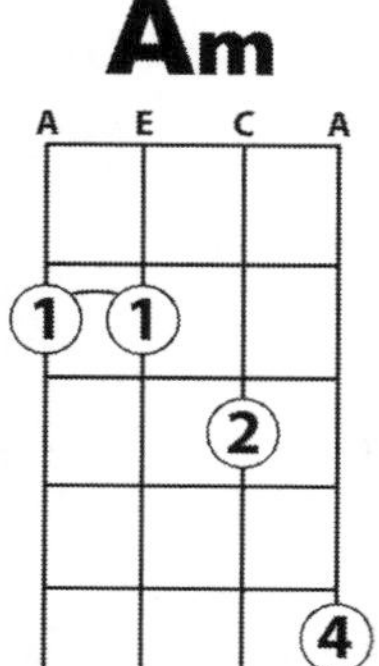

F

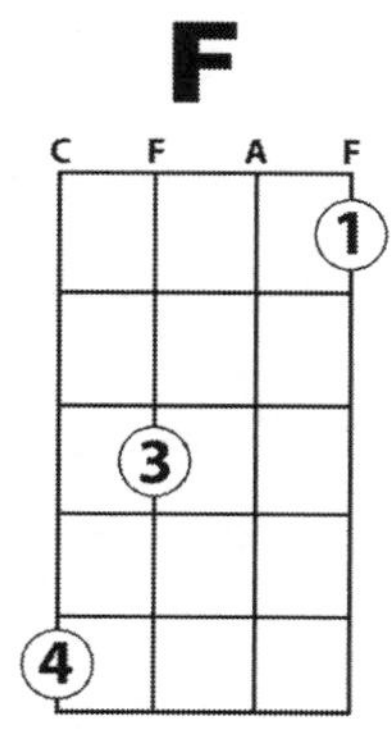

C

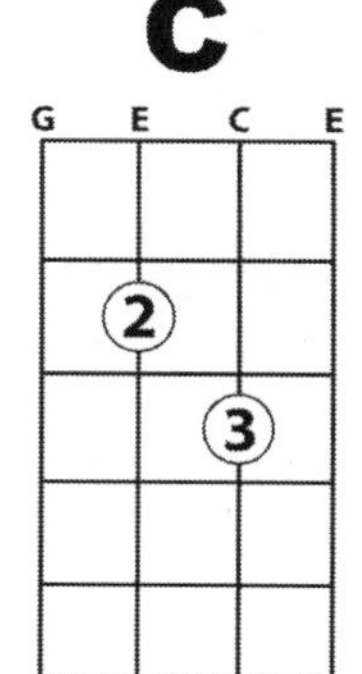

G

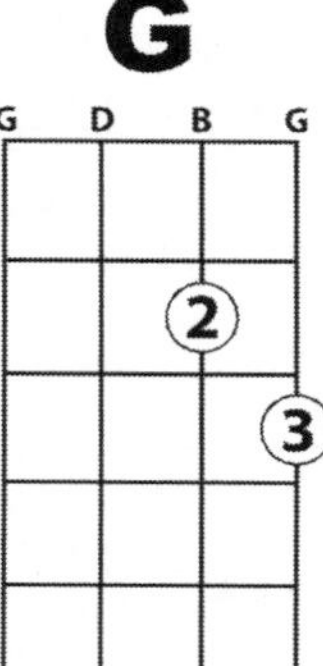

Donkey Riding (continued)

Basic Melody
Key of E Minor

```
  Em                 C      G                                D
E ───────────────────────────────────────────────────────────────────
A ──────────2─2──3──0──2──────2─────0──────────0─────────2──0───0─────
D 2───5─────────────────────────────────────────────5─────────────────5──
G ───────────────────────────────────────────────────────────────────
  Was you ever in Quebec, launching timber on the deck,
```

```
  Em                      C           G      D            Em
E ───────────────────────────────────────────────────────────────────
A ────────────2────────2────3────0────2──────2──────0────────────────
D 2─────5────────────────────────────────────────5──────4──2──2──────
G ───────────────────────────────────────────────────────────────────
  Where ya break yer bleedin' neck, riding on a donkey.
```

CHORUS

```
  C    G      C        G   Em              D
E 0──────────────────────────────────────────────────────────────────
A ────5────3──3────5──2────2──0────0──────────2──0───0───────────────
D ──────────────────────────────────────5────────────────5───────────
G ───────────────────────────────────────────────────────────────────
  Way hey a-way we go, donkey riding donkey riding,
```

```
  C    G      C        G   D            Em
E 0──────────────────────────────────────────────────────────────────
A ────5────3──3────5──2────2───────0─────────────────────────────────
D ────────────────────────────5─────────4──2──2──────────────────────
G ───────────────────────────────────────────────────────────────────
  Way hey a-way we go, riding on a donkey.
```

Chord Forms

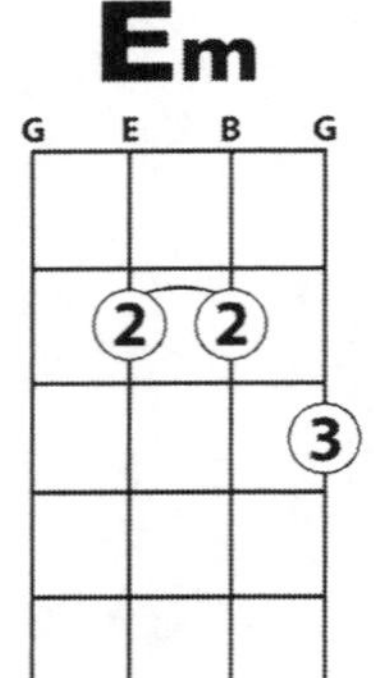

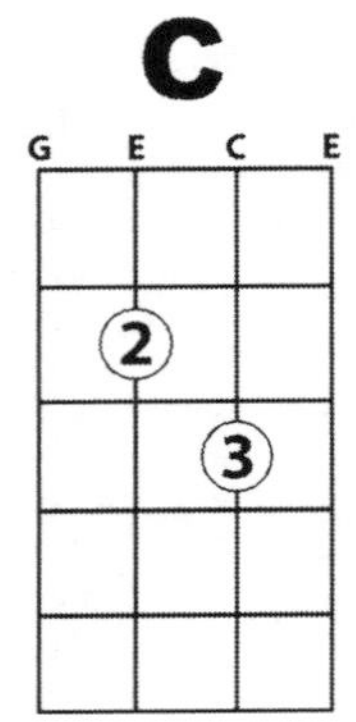

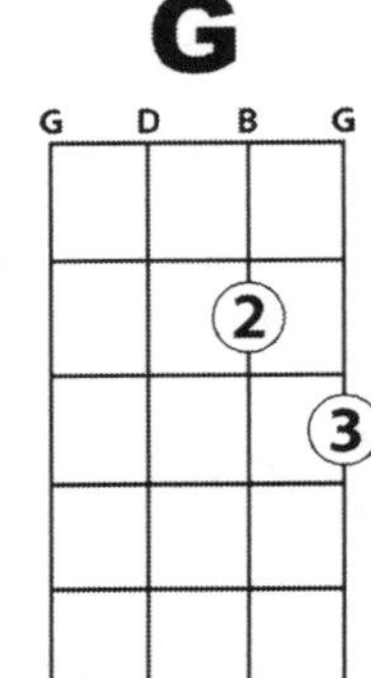

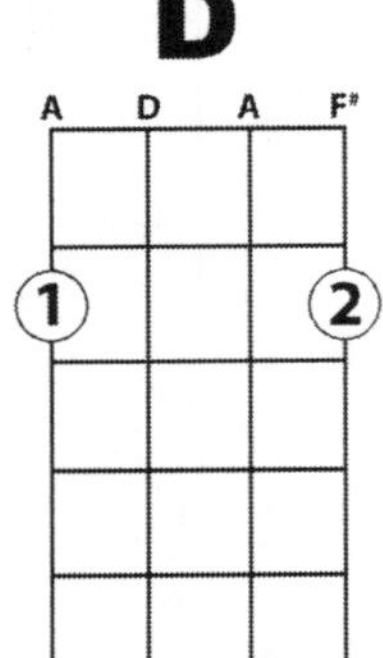

Donkey Riding (continued)

Basic Melody
Key of E Minor

```
  Em               C      G                                D
E ---------------------------------------------------------------------
A ---------2-2--3--0--2------2----0-------0--------2--0----0-----------
D 2---5----2-2--2--2--0------0----0-------0--5-----0--0----0--5--------
G 4---4----4-------0--------0----0----------------0--2---------2--0----
  Was you ever in Quebec, launching timber on the deck,
```

```
  Em                         C          G      D             Em
E ---------------------------------------------------------------------
A ---------2--------2----3----0-----2------2--------0------------------
D 2-----5--2--------2----2----2-----0------0--5-----0--4-2--2----------
G 4-----4--4-------------0----------0------2--0-----2--2-4--4----------
  Where ya break yer bleedin' neck, riding on a donkey.
```

Chorus

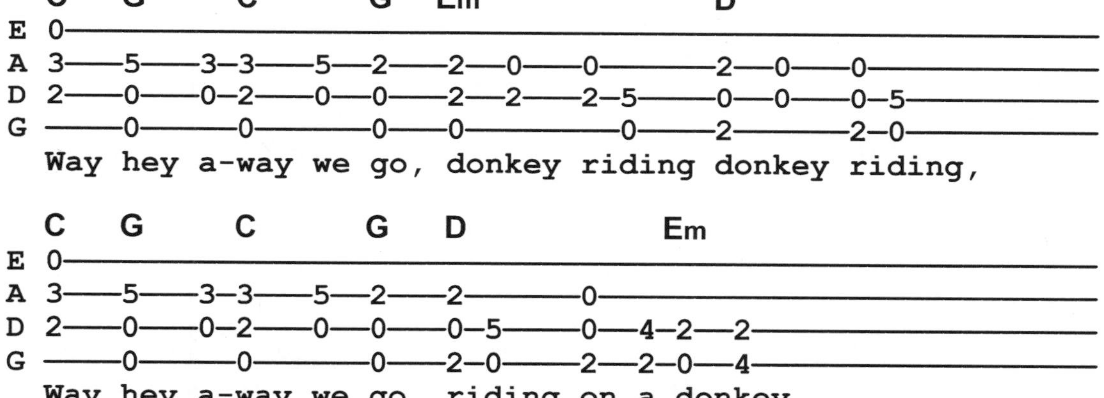

Chord Forms

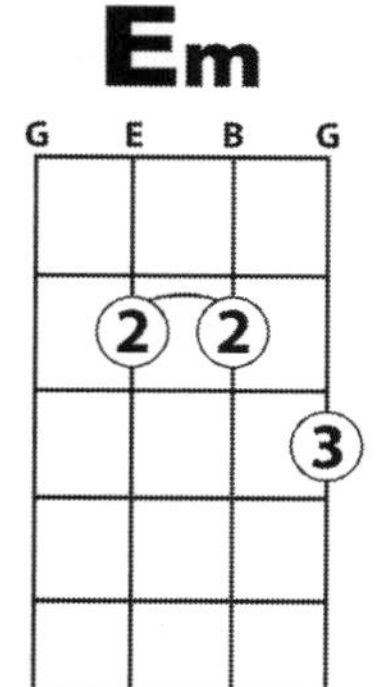

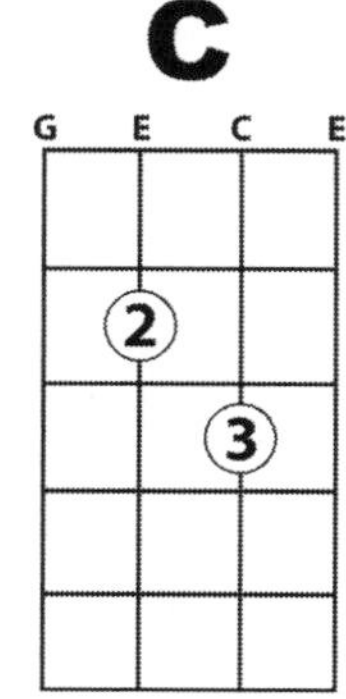

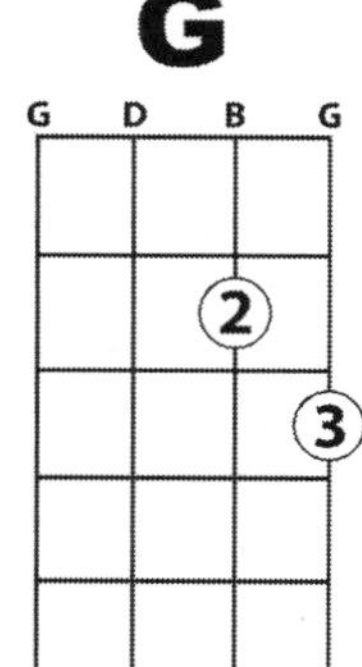

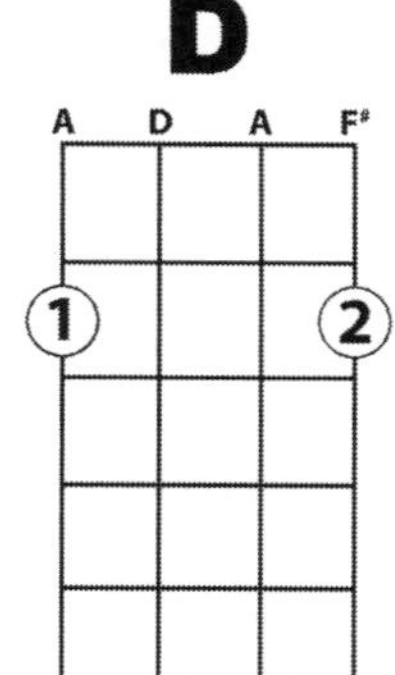

Farewell to Nova Scotia

Basic Melody
Key of C / A Minor

Words and Music
Traditional

This old seafaring song is thought to be descended from an older Scottish ballad entitled "The Soldier's Adieu." This is a popular song in the Canadian Maritime provinces and also New England, where you have a good chance of hearing it sung at pub singing sessions.

```
  C                                         Am
E ------------------------------------------------------------------
A 3---3---5---3--------------------3--2--0-----2-----3----3---5-----
D ---------------2--3---5---5--2--5---------------------------------
G ------------------------------------------------------------------
  The sun was sett-ing in th-e west, th-e birds were singing on

                 C      G                                    Am
E 0--------------0--0--------------------------------------0--------
A ---0---0----3-5-------5------5-2--------------2-5----3--5-----3---
D ---------------------------------5------5-------------------------
G ------------------------------------------------------------------
  Ev'ry tree. A-ll nature seemed i-n-clined fo-r rest, bu-t still

        F       Am
E ------------------------------------------------------------------
A 3---2--0--2-0--------0---0----------------------------------------
D --------------5-2-------------------------------------------------
G ------------------------------------------------------------------
  The-re wa-s n-o rest for me.
```

CHORUS

```
 Am   C                                                  Am
E ------------------------------------------------------------------
A 0--2-3---2--3-5--3--------------------------3---2----0----2-------
D ------------------2----3---5---5--2--5----------------------------
G ------------------------------------------------------------------
  Fa-rewell to Nova Scotia, the sea-bound coast, let your mountains

                                  C          G
E -----------0--------------------0--0--0-----------------------------
A 3----5---------0----0---3---5--------------5-5---5--2-----------2---
D ---------------6-----------------------------------------5--5--5----
G --------------------------------------------------------------------
  Dark and drear-y be, for when I am far a-way on the briny ocean

                 Am           F            Am
E ----------------0-------------------------------------------------
A 5-----3----5----5---3----2-0--2--0---------------0---0------------
D ------------------------------------5-2---------------------------
G ------------------------------------------------------------------
  Tossed will you e-ver heave a si-gh and a wish for me?
```

See Chord Forms and Additional Verses on Next Page

Farewell to Nova Scotia
(continued)

Chord Forms and Additional Verses

Chord Forms

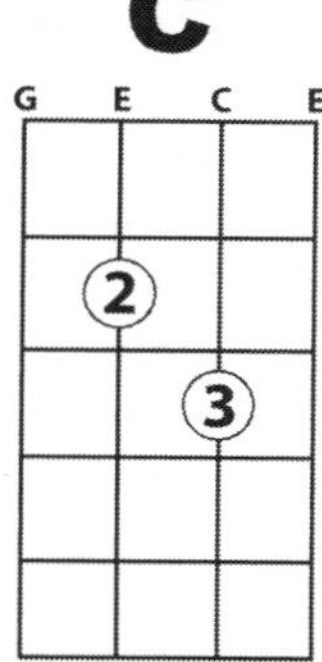

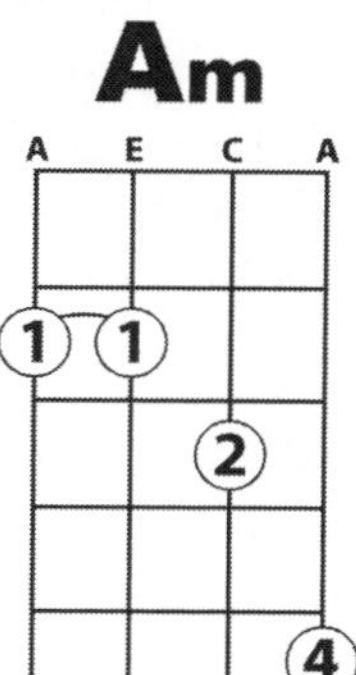

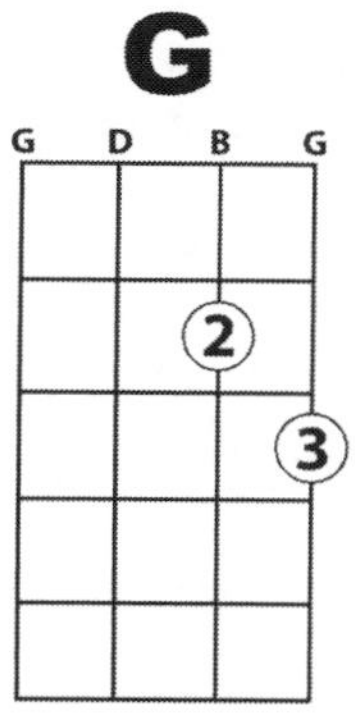

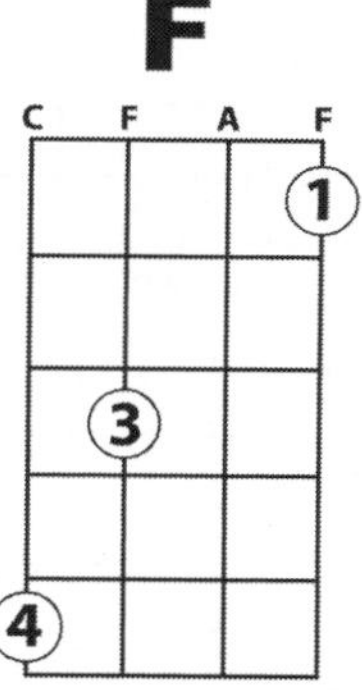

Additional Verses

I grieve to leave my native land,
I grieve to leave my comrades all;
And my parents, whom I held so dear,
And my bonny, bonny lassie that I do adore.

The drums do beat and the wars do alarm,
My captain calls, I must obey;
So farewell, farewell to Nova Scotia's Charm,
For it's early in the morning, I'll be far, far away.

I have three brothers and they are at rest,
Their arms are folded on their breasts;
But a poor and simple sailor, just like me,
Must be tossed and driven on the dark blue sea.

A 1764 print depicting the town and harbor of Halifax, Nova Scotia.

Farewell to Nova Scotia
(continued)

Basic Melody

Key of G / E Minor (Low)

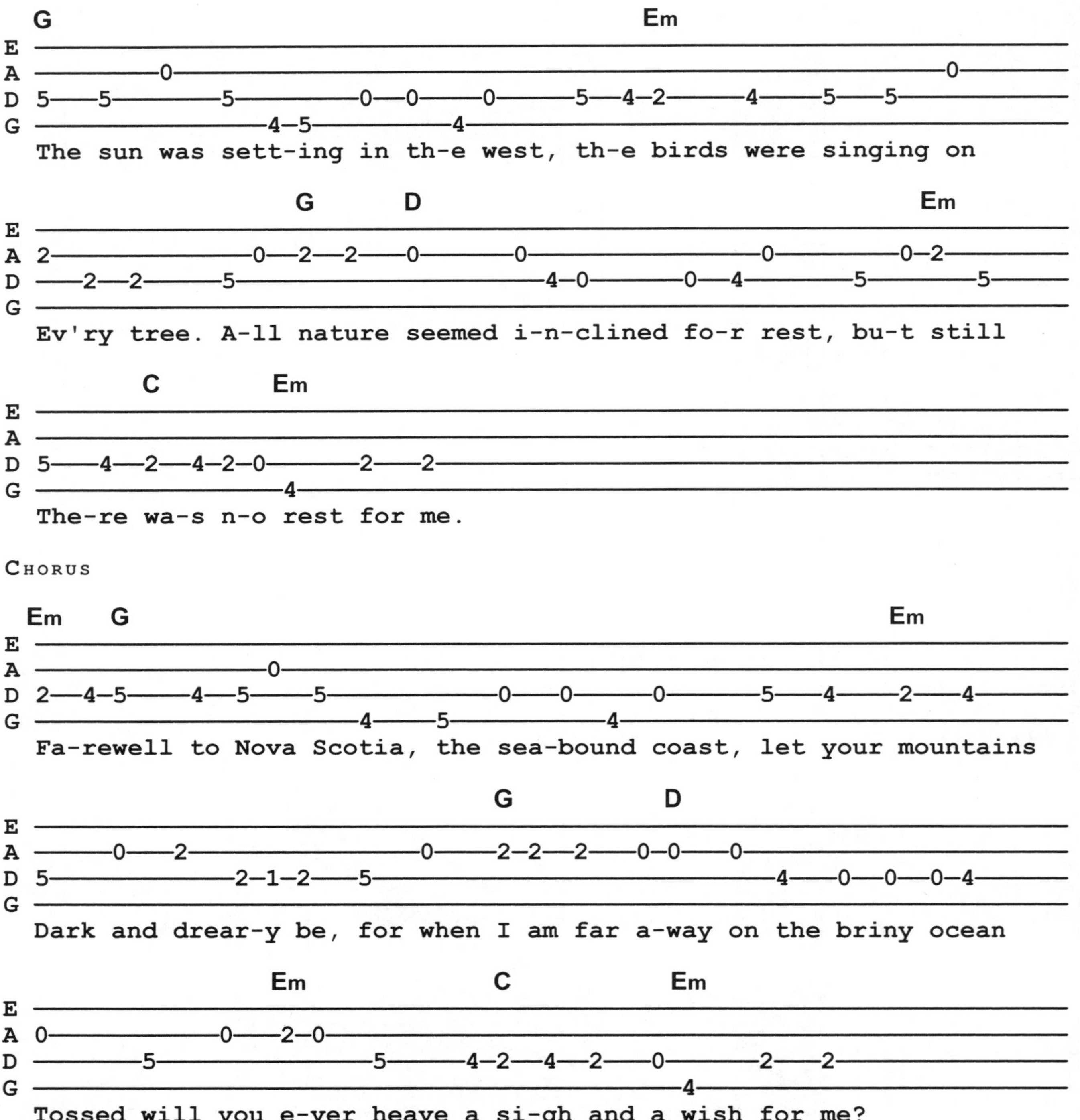

See Chord Forms on Next Page

Farewell to Nova Scotia
(continued)

Melody & Chords

Key of G / E Minor (Low)

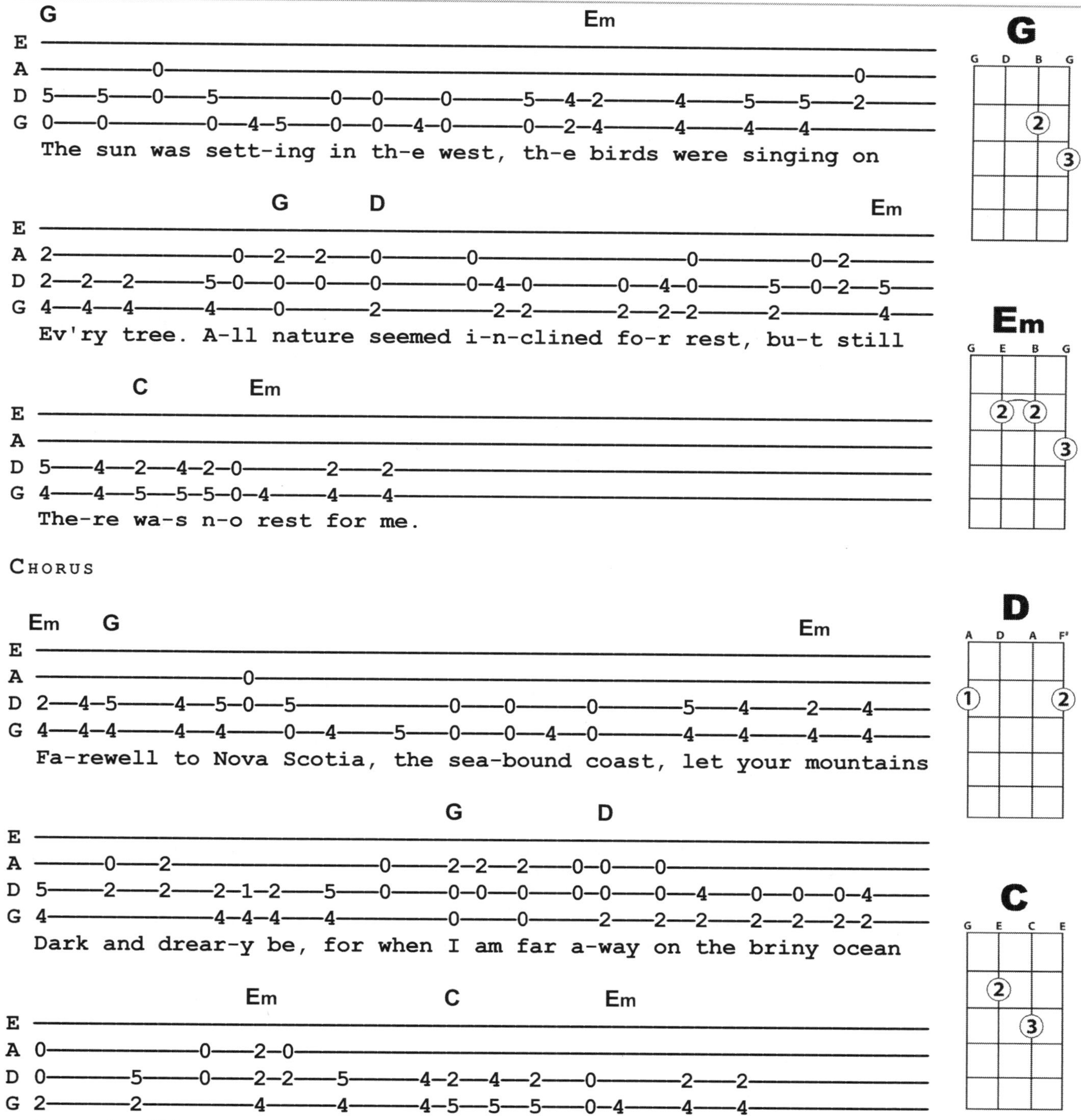

NOVA SCOTIAN SEA BALLAD

Farewell to Nova Scotia
(continued)

Basic Melody

Key of G / E Minor (High)

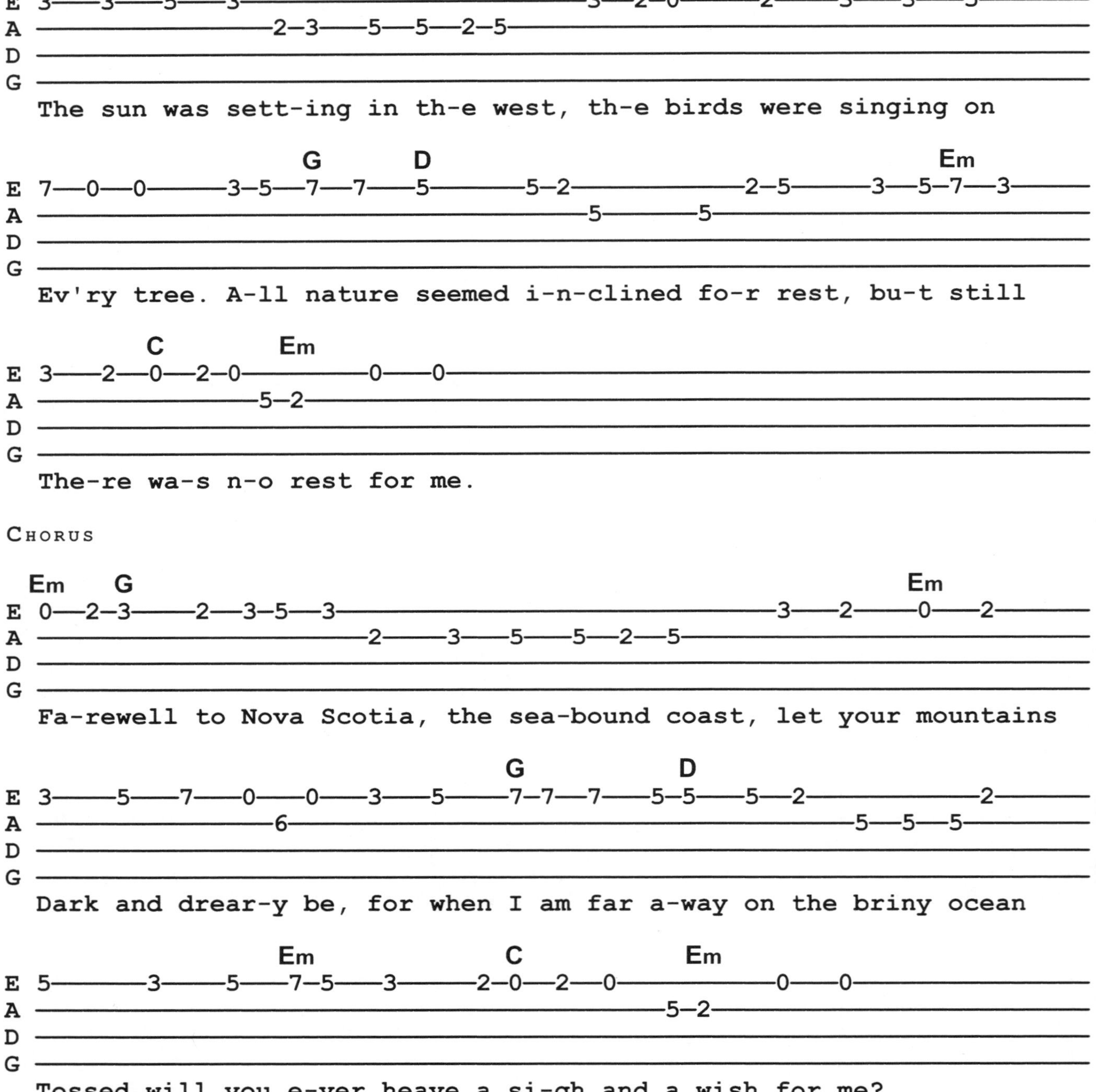

See Chord Forms on Next Page

Farewell to Nova Scotia
(continued)

Melody & Chords

Key of G / E Minor (High)

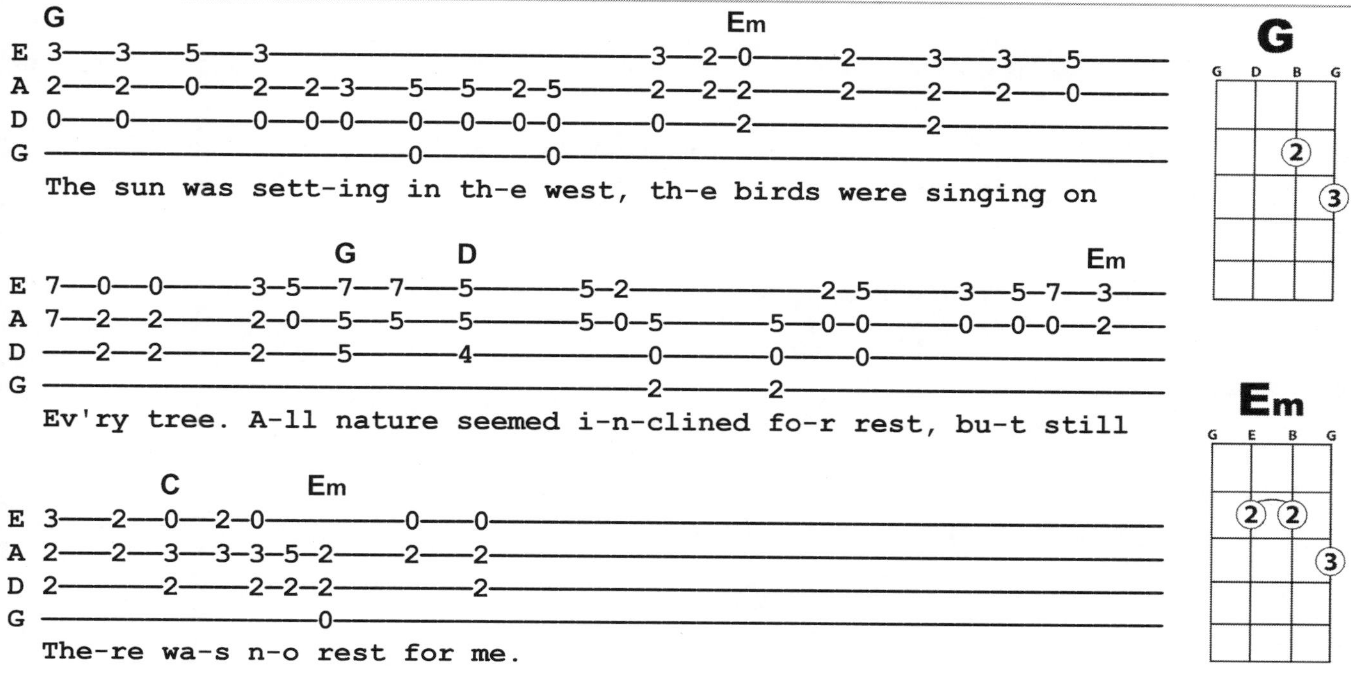

CHORUS

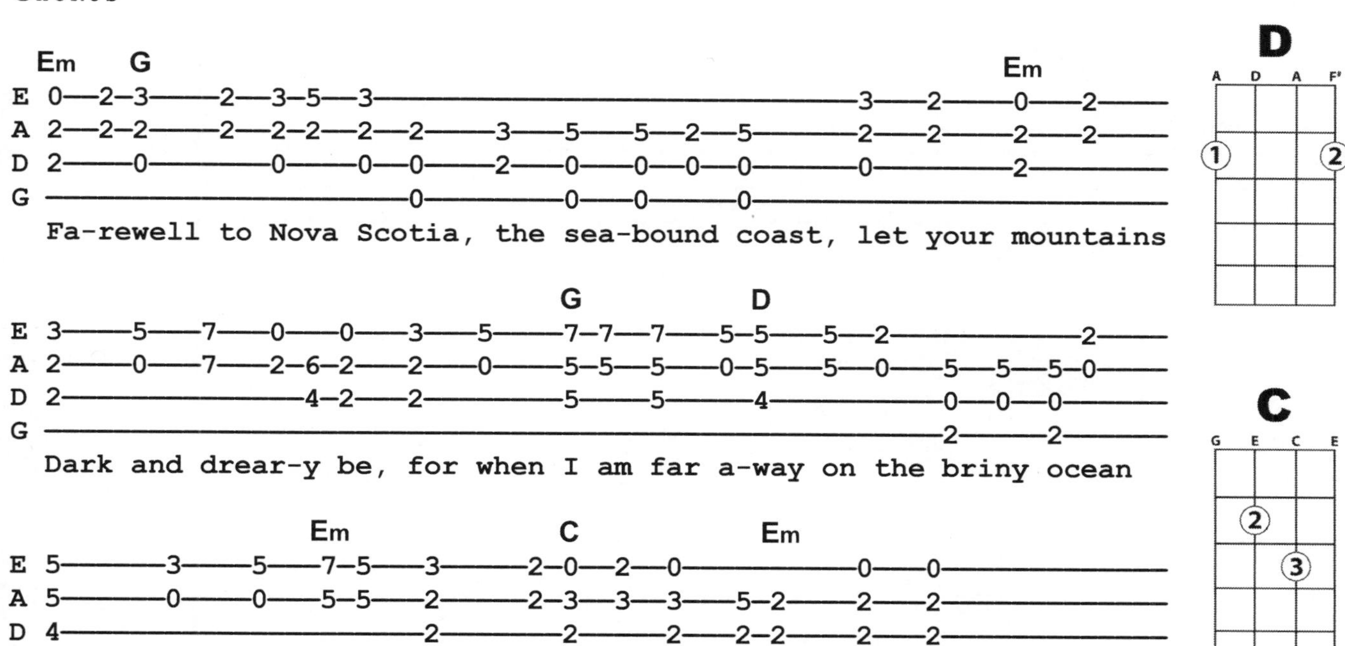

Farewell to Tarwathie

Basic Melody
Key of C (Low)

This traditional whaling song comes down from Scotland in the mid 1800's, and is attributed to a man named George Scroggie of Aberdeenshire. Signing onto whaling ships was a major source of income from men in the British Isles during that time, especially when times were tougher.

Words and Music by
George Scroggie

```
   C                                       F                     C
E ---------------------------------------------------------------------------------
A ---------------------------------------------------------------------------------
D -----2-----------------------------------------------------0-------2-------------
G 5-------------5-----5----2--0--------0--2-------5-------------------------------
  Fareweel tae Tarwathie, a-dieu, Mormond Hill,

                                                       F               C
E ---------------------------------------------------------------------------------
A ---------------------------------------------------------------------------------
D -------------2----------------------------------------------------0--------------
G 5----5---------------5-------5---2---0---------0--2----5-------------5----------
  And the dear land o' Crimond, I bid you fareweel.

                                       F      C             G             Am
E ---------------------------------------------------------------------------------
A -------------------------------------0-------------------------------------------
D --0-----------2-----5--------------------5------2-----0---------0---2-----------
G 5------5----------------------------------------------------5-------------------
  I am bound now for Greenland and ready to sail,

       C                                    F          G     C
E ---------------------------------------------------------------------------------
A ---------------------------------------------------------------------------------
D ----2-------------------------------------------------0-------------------------
G 5------------5---5----2--0-------0--2----5----------------5---------------------
  In hopes to find riches a-hunting the whale.
```

Chord Forms

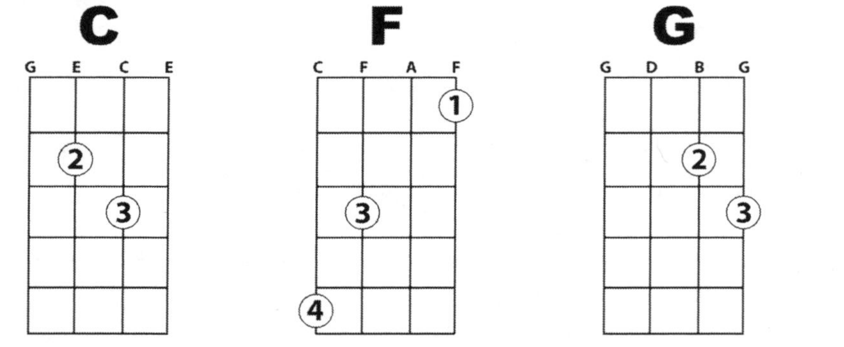

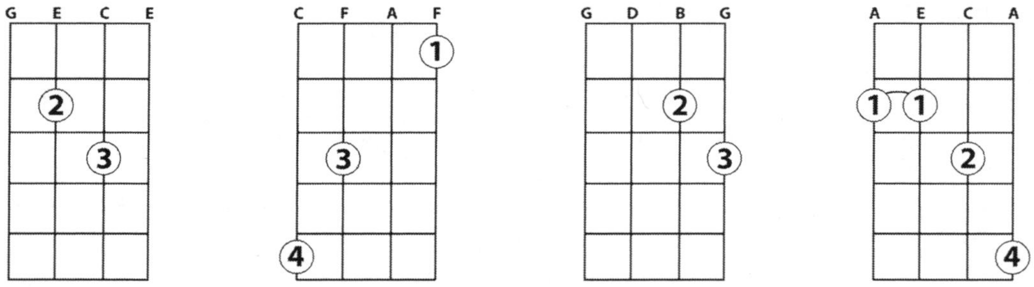

See Additional Verses on Next Page

Farewell to Tarwathie
(continued)

Additional Verses

Our ship is well-rigged and ready to sail,
Our crew they are anxious to follow the whale;
Where the icebergs do float and the stormy winds blow,
And the land and the ocean are covered wi' snow.

The cold coast o' Greenland is barren and bare,
No seed-time nor harvest is ever known there;
And the birds here sing sweetly on mountain and dale,
But there aren't any birds there, to sing to the whale.

There is no habitation for a man to live there,
And the king of that country is the wild Greenland bear;
And there'll be no temptation to tarry long there,
With our ship bumper full we will homeward repair.

Arctic Ocean whaling in the mid-1800's.

Farewell to Tarwathie
(continued)

Basic Melody

Key of C (High)

```
  C                                          F                       C
E ------0------------------------------------------------------------0--------------
A 3-------------3----3---0-------------------0-------3---5-------------------------
D -------------------------------5-------5-----------------------------------------
G ---------------------------------------------------------------------------------
  Fareweel tae Tarwathie, a-dieu, Mormond Hill,
```

```
                                                    F               C
E ------------0--------------------------------------------------------------------
A 3----3-------------------3------3---0------------0-----3------5-----3------------
D ---------------------------------------5-------5---------------------------------
G ---------------------------------------------------------------------------------
  And the dear land o' Crimond, I bid you fareweel.
```

```
                          F      C           G            Am
E ----------------0----3----5------3------0-------------------0--------------------
A 3-5---3----------------------------------------5---3---5-------------------------
D ---------------------------------------------------------------------------------
G ---------------------------------------------------------------------------------
  I am bound now for Greenland and ready to sail,
```

```
      C                                     F          G    C
E ----0----------------------------------------------------------------------------
A 3-------------3---3------0----------------0---3-------5----3---------------------
D ----------------------------5-------5--------------------------------------------
G ---------------------------------------------------------------------------------
  In hopes to find riches a-hunting the whale.
```

Chord Forms

C

G E C E

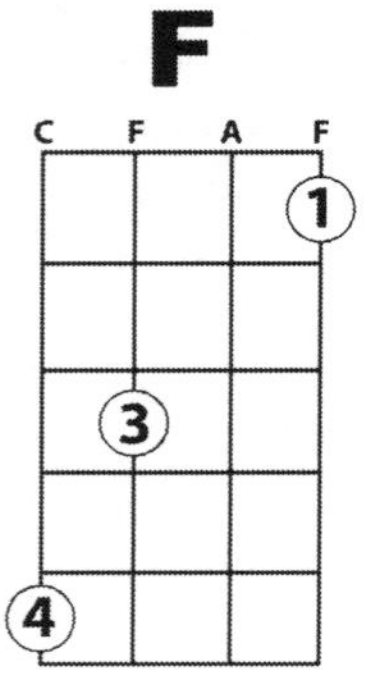

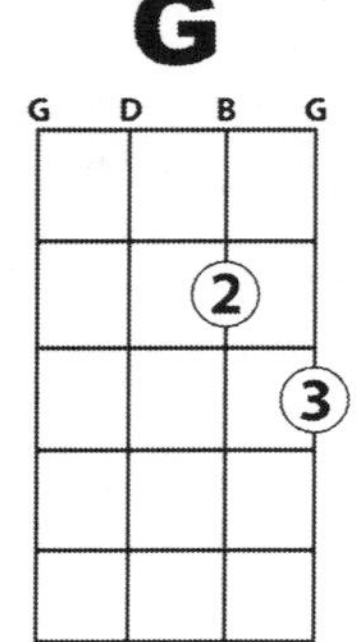

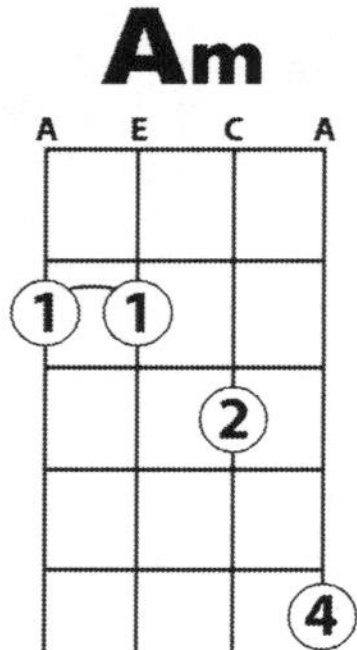

Farewell to Tarwathie

(continued)

Melody & Chords

Key of C (High)

```
   C                                F                 C
E ---0-------------------------------------------------0------
A 3--3----3----3--0---------------0------3--5----------3------
D 2--2----2----2--2-5---------5-3--------3--3----------2------
G 0-----------------0---------0-2----------------------0------
  Fareweel tae Tarwathie, a-dieu, Mormond Hill,
```

```
                                          F            C
E ---------0--------------------------------------------------
A 3--3--3-----3-----3--0------------------0----3----5---3-----
D 2--2--2-----2-----2--2--5---------5-3--------3----3---2-----
G 0-----------0-----------0---------0-2-----------------0-----
  And the dear land o' Crimond, I bid you fareweel.
```

```
                          F     C          G         Am
E ----------------0----3--5-----3----0--------------0------
A 3-5--3----------3----3--3-----3----3---5--3--5----0------
D 2-3--2----------2-------3-----2----2---0--0--0----2------
G 0----0---------------------------------0-----------------
  I am bound now for Greenland and ready to sail,
```

```
     C                                F        G    C
E ---0-----------------------------------------------------
A 3--3--------3--3--0-----------0--3-----5----3------------
D 2--2--------2--2--2-5------5-3--3------0----2------------
G 2-----------0--0----0------0-2---------0----0------------
  In hopes to find riches a-hunting the whale.
```

Chord Forms

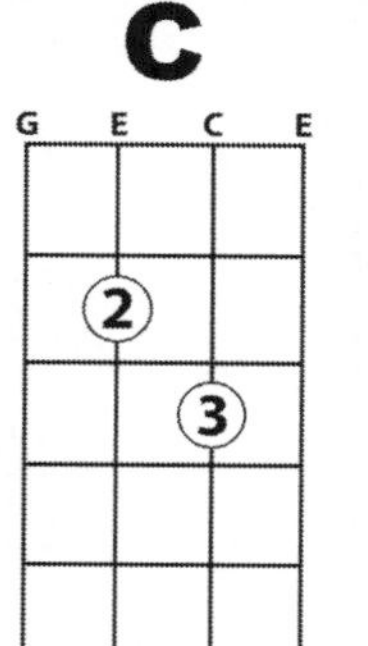

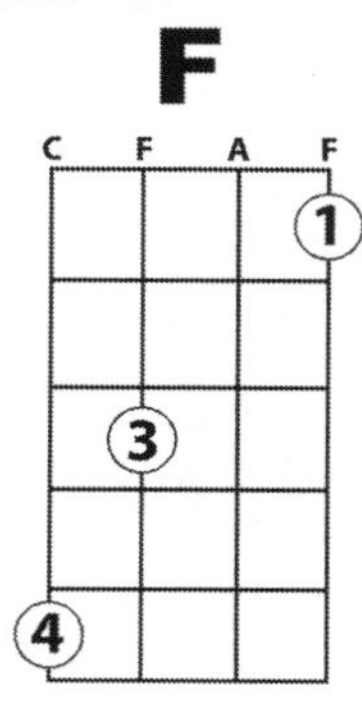

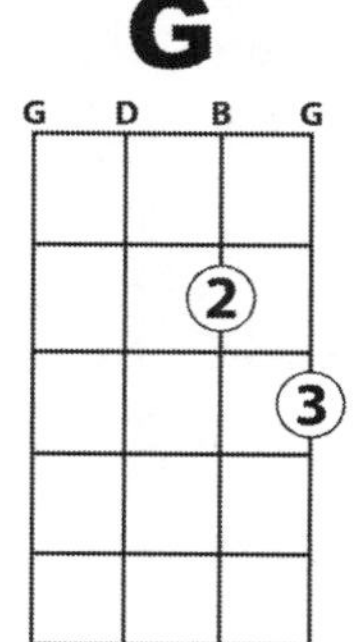

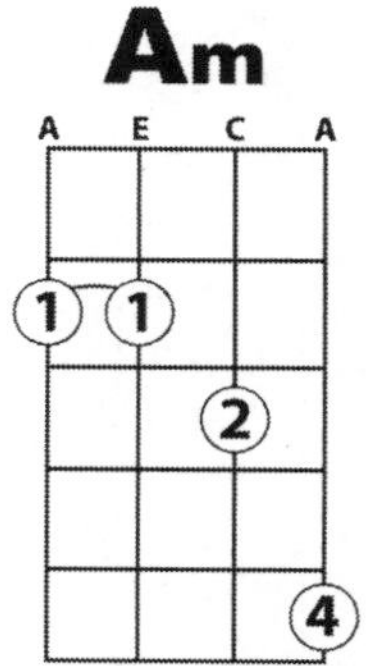

Farewell to Tarwathie
(continued)

Basic Melody

Key of G

```
  G                                    C                   G
E -------------------------------------------------------------------------
A -----2-----------------------------------------------0------2------------
D 5-----------5----5---2--0-------0--2-------5-------------------------------
G -------------------------------------------------------------------------
  Fareweel tae Tarwathie, a-dieu, Mormond Hill,
```

```
                                               C                 G
E -------------------------------------------------------------------------
A -----------2----------------------------------------------0--------------
D 5----5-------------5------5---2---0--------0--2----5-------------5--------
G -------------------------------------------------------------------------
  And the dear land o' Crimond, I bid you fareweel.
```

```
                                C      G           D           Em
E ------------------------------0------------------------------------------
A --0---------2----5-------------------5------2-----0--------0---2----------
D 5------5---------------------------------------------5-------------------
G -------------------------------------------------------------------------
  I am bound now for Greenland and ready to sail,
```

```
      G                                 C          D     G
E -------------------------------------------------------------------------
A ----2-----------------------------------------------0--------------------
D 5------------5---5------2--0------0--2---5------------5------------------
G -------------------------------------------------------------------------
  In hopes to find riches a-hunting the whale.
```

Chord Forms

G

G D B G

2 3

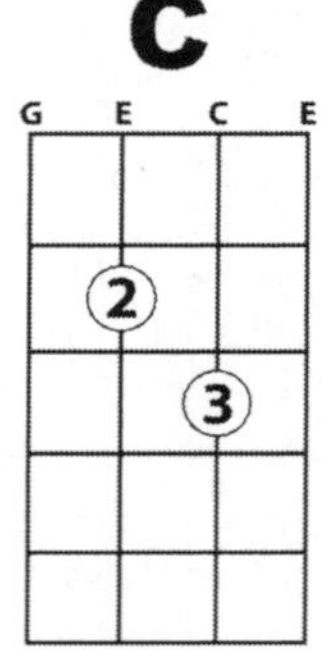

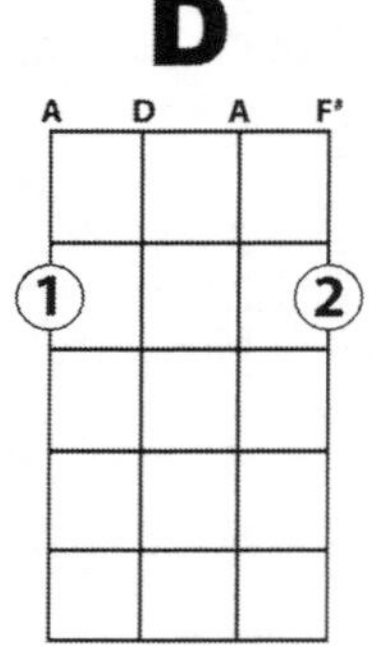

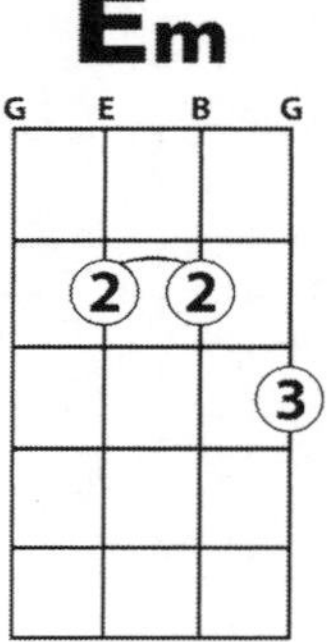

Farewell to Tarwathie
(continued)

Melody & Chords

Key of G

```
   G                                  C                  G
E ------------------------------------------------------------------------
A ---2-----------------------------------------------0-----2--------------
D 5--0-----5----5--2-0--------0-2-------5--2-------0--------------
G 0--0-----0----0--0-0--------0-5-------5----------0--------------
  Fareweel tae Tarwathie, a-dieu, Mormond Hill,

                                          C             G
E ------------------------------------------------------------------------
A ---------2---------------------------------------0----------------------
D 5--5-----0-----5-----5--2--0--------0-2----5----2----5----------
G 0--0-----0-----0-----0--0--0--------0-5----5---------0----------
  And the dear land o' Crimond, I bid you fareweel.

                          C     G          D          Em
E ------------------------0-----------------------------------------------
A --0-----------2----5----3-----5------2----0-------0--2------------------
D 5-0--5--------0----0----2-----0------0----0---5---0--2------------------
G 0----0------------------------0-----------2---0------4------------------
  I am bound now for Greenland and ready to sail,

     G                              C          D   G
E ------------------------------------------------------------------------
A ---2-------------------------------------------0------------------------
D 5--0------5--5---2-0-----0-2--5--------0----5---------------------------
G 4--0------0--0---0-0-----0-5--5--------2----0---------------------------
  In hopes to find riches a-hunting the whale.
```

Chord Forms

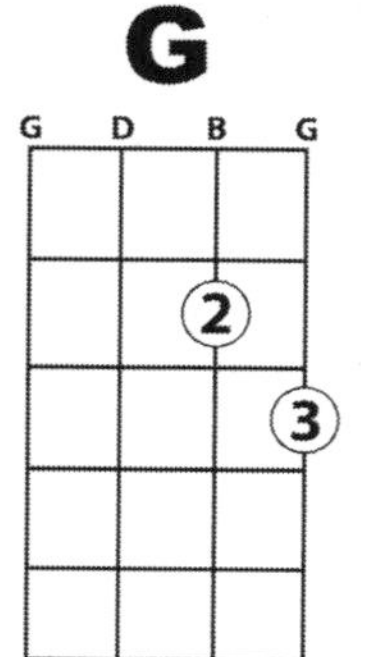

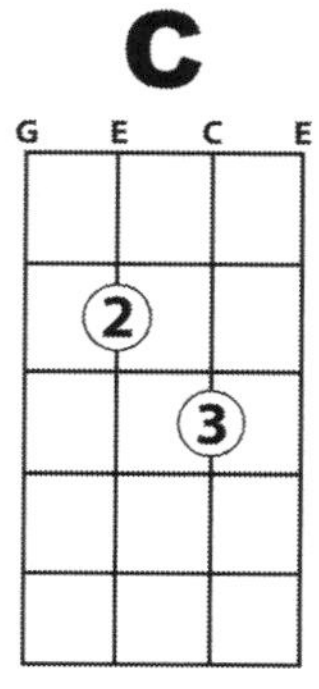

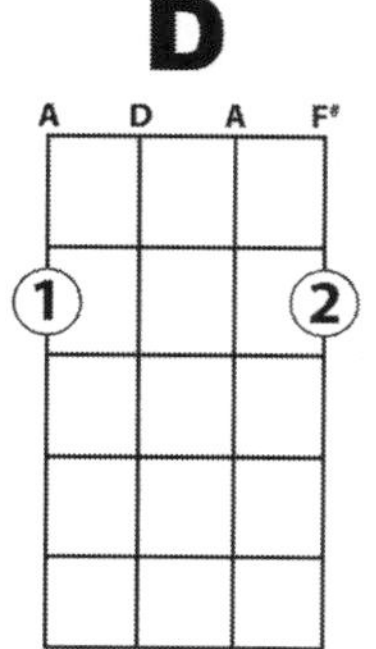

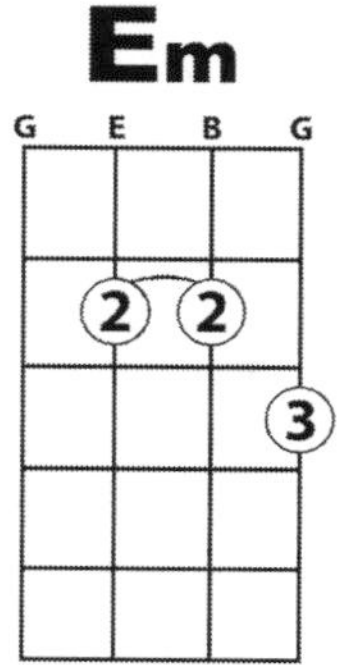

Go To Sea No More

Basic Melody

Key of A Minor (Low)

This old sea song tells the darker side of life as a sailor. Luke Kelly and The Dubliners recorded a great version of this song back in the 1970's - you can find it on YouTube if you are looking to learn how it is supposed to go. Like many of the old sea songs it is more bawdy in nature than many that we include in our songbooks.

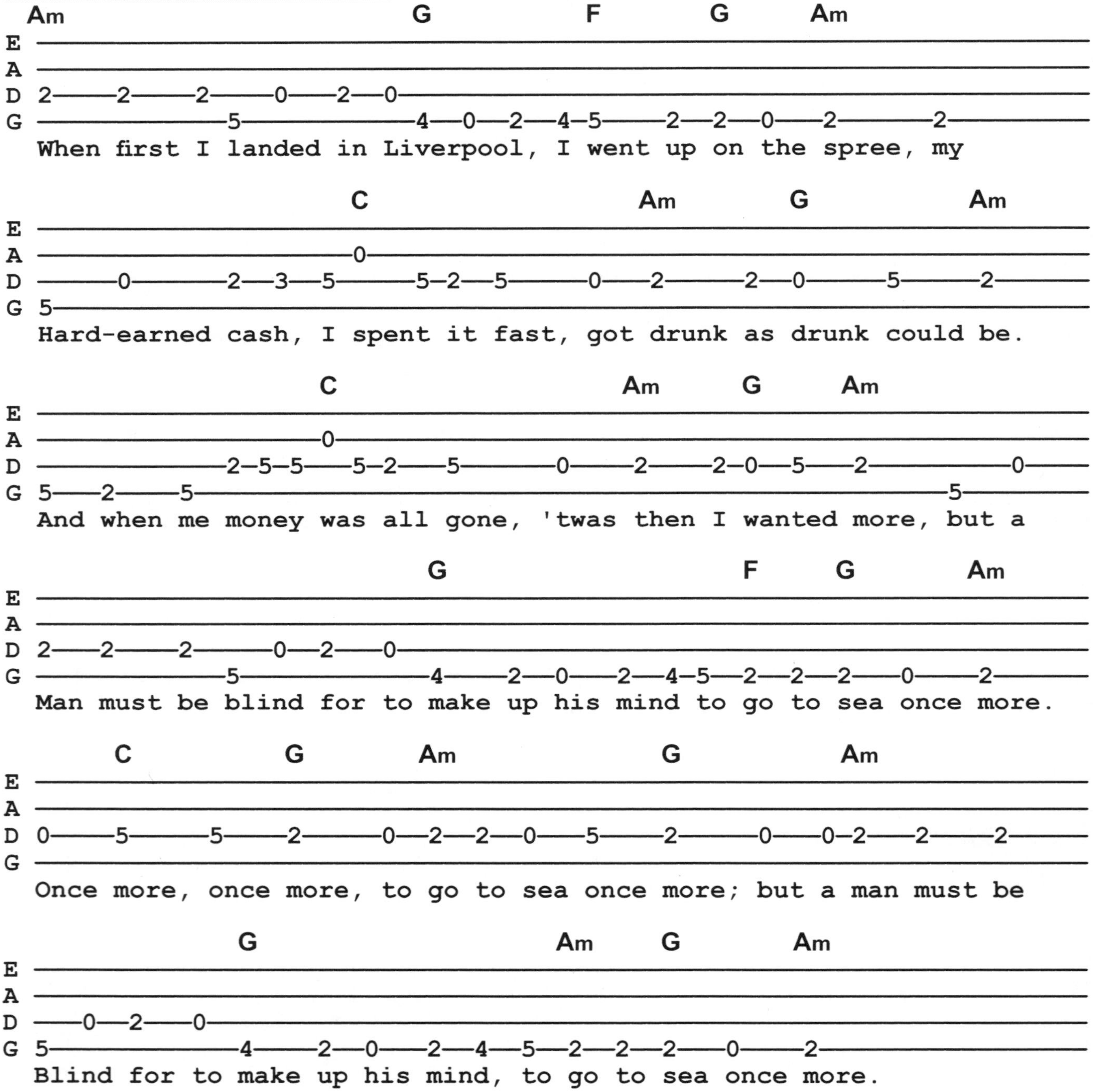

Words and Music

Traditional

```
Am                                 G          F       G      Am
E ---------------------------------------------------------------------
A ---------------------------------------------------------------------
D 2----2----2----0---2--0----------------------------------------------
G ---------------5-----------4--0--2--4-5----2--2--0---2-------2-------
  When first I landed in Liverpool, I went up on the spree, my

                    C                  Am        G           Am
E ---------------------------------------------------------------------
A --------------------0------------------------------------------------
D -----0------2--3--5-----5-2--5-----0--2-----2--0-----5-----2---------
G 5--------------------------------------------------------------------
  Hard-earned cash, I spent it fast, got drunk as drunk could be.

                  C                   Am       G      Am
E ---------------------------------------------------------------------
A ------------------0--------------------------------------------------
D -------------2-5-5--5-2---5------0----2----2-0--5---2---------0------
G 5--2----5--------------------------------------------------5---------
  And when me money was all gone, 'twas then I wanted more, but a

                              G                  F      G       Am
E ---------------------------------------------------------------------
A ---------------------------------------------------------------------
D 2---2----2-----0--2---0----------------------------------------------
G ---------------5------------4----2--0---2--4-5--2--2--2---0----2-----
  Man must be blind for to make up his mind to go to sea once more.

     C          G        Am              G          Am
E ---------------------------------------------------------------------
A ---------------------------------------------------------------------
D 0----5-----5----2-----0--2--2--0---5----2-----0---0-2---2----2-------
G ---------------------------------------------------------------------
  Once more, once more, to go to sea once more; but a man must be

                G                  Am      G        Am
E ---------------------------------------------------------------------
A ---------------------------------------------------------------------
D ---0--2---0----------------------------------------------------------
G 5--------------4----2--0---2--4--5--2--2--2---0----2-----------------
  Blind for to make up his mind, to go to sea once more.
```

See Chord Forms and Additional Verses on Next Page

Go To Sea No More
(continued)

Chord Forms and Additional Verses

Chord Forms

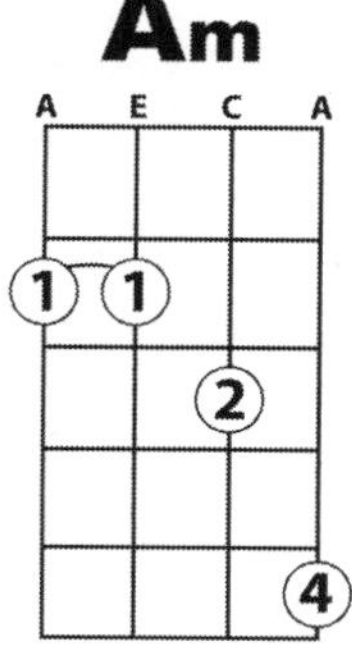

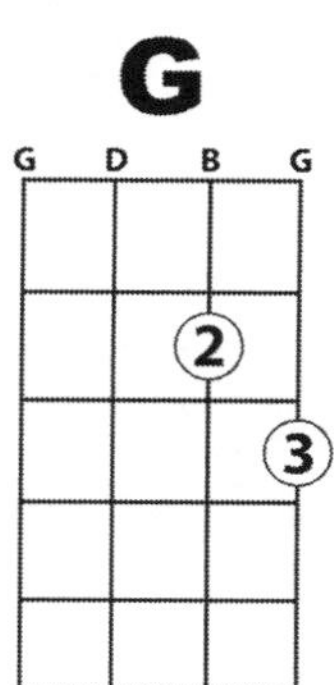

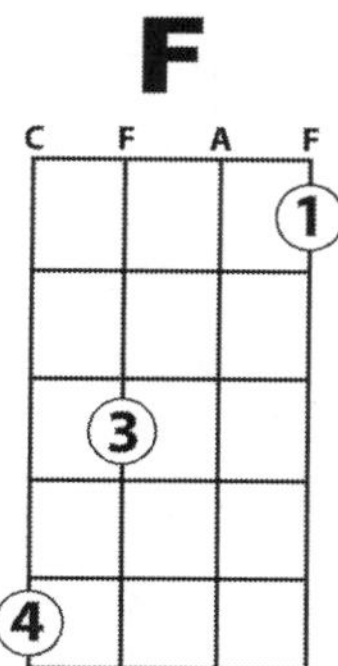

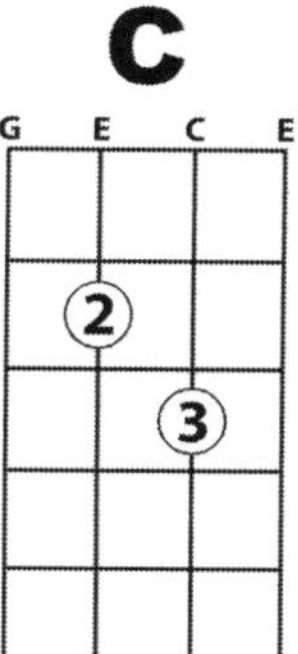

Additional Verses

I spent the night with Angeline, too drunk to roll in bed;
Me watch was new and me money too, in the morning with them she fled.
And as I walked the streets about, the whores they all did roar,
There goes Jack Strapp, the poor sailor lad, he must go to sea once more!
Once more, boys, once more, go to sea once more;
There goes Jack Strapp, the poor sailor lad, he must go to sea once more.

And as I walked the streets about, I met with the Rapper Brown;
I asked him for to take me on, and he looked at me with a frown.
He said last time you was paid off, with me you could no score;
But I'll give you a chance and I'll make your advance, and I'll send you to sea once more.
Once more, boys, once more, go to sea once more;
But I'll give you a chance and I'll make your advance, and I'll send you to sea once more.

He shipped me on board of a whaling ship, bound for the arctic seas;
Where cold winds blow through the frost and snow, and Jamaica rum would freeze.
But worse to bear, I'd no hard weather gear, for I'd spent all money on shore;
'Twas then that I wished that I was dead, and could go to sea no more.
No more, boys, no more, go to sea no more;
'Twas then that I wished that I was dead and could go to sea no more

So come all you bold seafaring men, who listen to me song;
When you come off them long trips, I'll have you not go wrong.
Take my advice, drink no strong drink, don't go sleeping with them whores;
Get married instead and spend all night in bed, and go to sea no more.
No more, boys, no more, go to sea no more;
Get married instead and spend all night in bed, and go to sea no more!

Go To Sea No More
(continued)

Basic Melody

Key of A Minor (High)

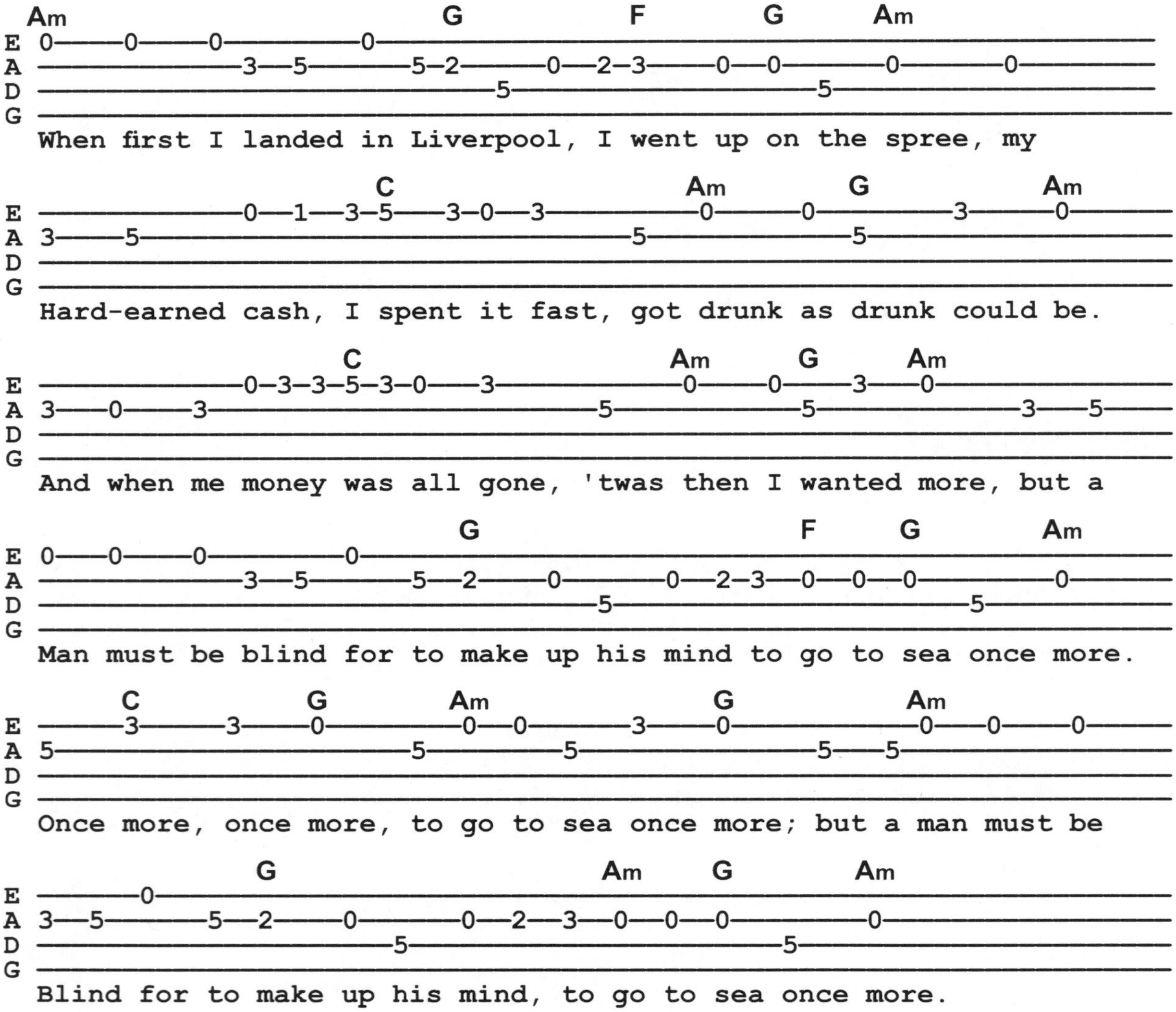

```
  Am                                        G                 F           G         Am
E 0-------0-------0--------------0------------------------------------------------------------------
A -----------------------3---5----------5---2-------0---2---3-------0---0---------0----------0------
D ---------------------------------------------5-----------------------------5----------------------
G --------------------------------------------------------------------------------------------------
  When first I landed in Liverpool, I went up on the spree, my
```

```
                              C                            Am        G            Am
E -----------------------0---1---3---5---3---0---3-----------------0-------0-----------3-------0-----
A 3-------5------------------------------------------------5------------------5-----------------------
D ----------------------------------------------------------------------------------------------------
G ----------------------------------------------------------------------------------------------------
  Hard-earned cash, I spent it fast, got drunk as drunk could be.
```

```
                            C                              Am       G       Am
E ----------------------0---3---3---5---3---0------3-----------------0------0------3------0-------------------
A 3------0-------3-----------------------------------------5------------------5---------------3-------5-------
D ------------------------------------------------------------------------------------------------------------
G ------------------------------------------------------------------------------------------------------------
  And when me money was all gone, 'twas then I wanted more, but a
```

```
                                          G                      F       G            Am
E 0------0-------0-----------0--------------------------------------------------------------------
A -----------------------3---5------5---2------0----------0---2---3---0---0---0--------------0-----
D -----------------------------------------------5--------------------------------5----------------
G -------------------------------------------------------------------------------------------------
  Man must be blind for to make up his mind to go to sea once more.
```

```
        C           G         Am                   G           Am
E ------3------3----0-----------0---0--------3-----0-----------0------0-------0-----
A 5-------------------------5--------------5--------------5----5--------------------
D ----------------------------------------------------------------------------------
G ----------------------------------------------------------------------------------
  Once more, once more, to go to sea once more; but a man must be
```

```
                    G                         Am      G          Am
E ----------0------------------------------------------------------------------
A 3---5---------5---2------0-----------0---2---3---0---0---0-----------0-------
D ------------------------------5------------------------------5---------------
G -----------------------------------------------------------------------------
  Blind for to make up his mind, to go to sea once more.
```

Chord Forms

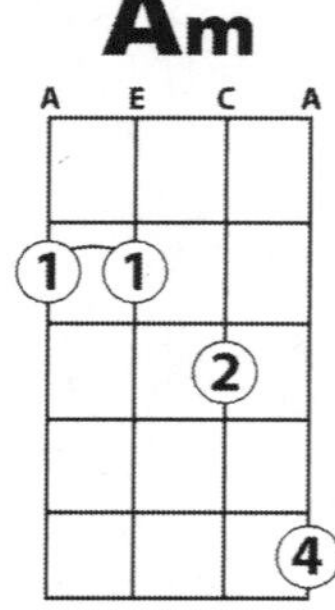

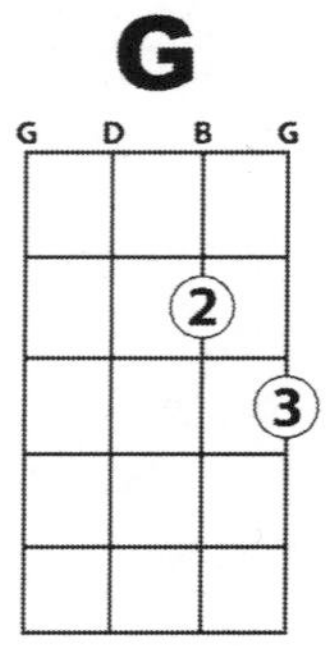

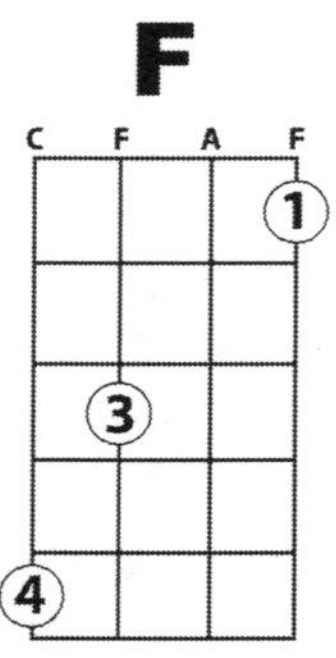

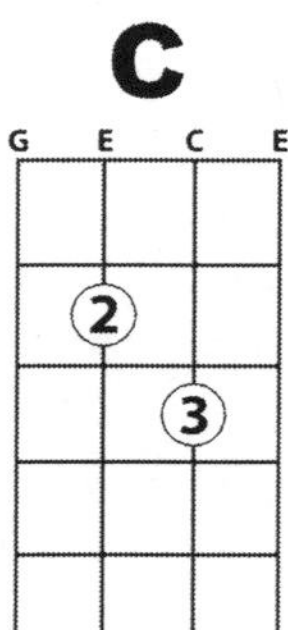

Go To Sea No More
(continued)

Melody & Chords

Key of A Minor (High)

```
   Am                                      G               F           G          Am
E 0------0------0------------0---------------------------------------------------------------
A 0------0------0--3---5-----2---5--2----------0---2--3------0---0---------0---------0-------
D 2------2-------------2--3--2---0--0--5-------0---0--3------3---0---5-----2---------2-------
G ---------------------2-------------------0--0----------2-----------------0---2-------------
  When first I landed in Liverpool, I went up on the spree, my

                             C                                      Am         G             Am
E -----------------------0---1---3-5----3--0---3--------------------0----------0----------3--------0-----
A 3------5---------------0---0---3-3----3--3---3--------------5-----0----------0---5------2--------0-----
D 2------3---------------2-------------------------2----------3-----2--------------0------0--------2-----
G 2--------------------------------------------------------------------------------0-------------------
  Hard-earned cash, I spent it fast, got drunk as drunk could be.

                            C                                    Am        G       Am
E -----------------------0--3--3--5--3--0----3-------------------0------0------3---0----------------------
A 3----0--------3-----0--3--3--3--3--3------3-----------5--------0------0--5---2---0---------3-----5------
D 2----2--------2-----2-------3--------------2----------3--------2---------0---0---2---------2-----3------
G 2------------------------------------------------------------------------0---------------2--------------
  And when me money was all gone, 'twas then I wanted more, but a

                                          G                                   F        G             Am
E 0----0-------0-------------0----------------------------------------------------------------------------
A 0----0-------0-----3----5--0----5---2---------0-----------0--2--3---0---0---0------------0--------------
D 2------------------2----2--2----2---0---------0----5------0--0--0---3---3---0------5-----2--------------
G ------------------------------------0--------------0----------------2-------0------0-----2--------------
  Man must be blind for to make up his mind to go to sea once more.

         C            G           Am                      G                 Am
E -------3------3-----0-----------0----0--------3---------0----------------0-------0-------0-----
A 5------3------3-----2------5----0----0----5---0---------2--------5-----5-0-------0-------0-----
D 0------2------------2------0--------------0-------------2--------0-----0-2-------2-------------
G ---------------------------0------------------------------------0-----------------------------
  Once more, once more, to go to sea once more; but a man must be

                  G                            Am       G              Am
E ---------0----------------------------------------------------------------------
A 3--5--3------5--2------0----------0--2--3---0---0--0-------------0--------------
D 2--3---------0--0------0-----5----0--0--0---2---2--0-------5-----2--------------
G 2---------------0------------0--------------2--------0-----0-----2--------------
  Blind for to make up his mind, to go to sea once more.
```

Chord Forms

Am

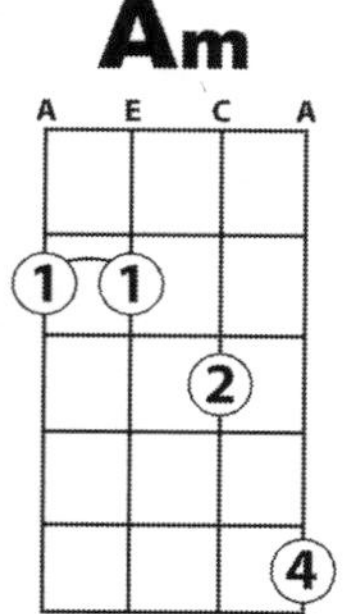

G

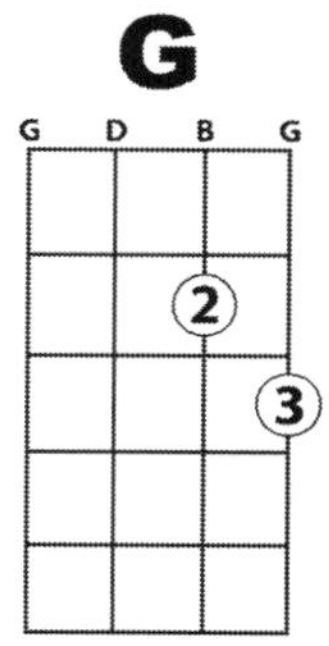

F

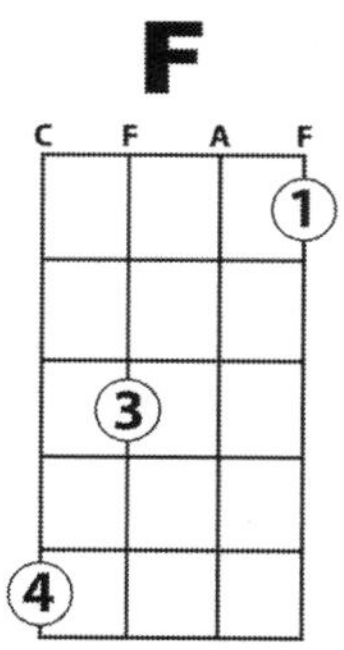

C

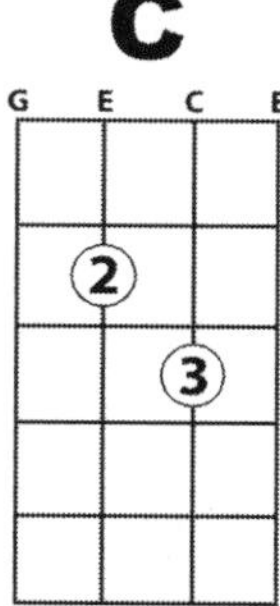

Go To Sea No More
(continued)

Basic Melody

Key of E Minor

```
  Em                                     D               C           D          Em
E ---------------------------------------------------------------------------------------------------
A 2------2------2------0-----2---0-------------------------------------------------------------------
D -----------------------5------------------4---0---2---4-5-------2---2---0-----2----------2---------
G ---------------------------------------------------------------------------------------------------
  When first I landed in Liverpool, I went up on the spree, my
```

```
                              G                            Em            D                Em
E ----------------------------0--------------------------------------------------------------------
A ---------0---------2---3---5-------5-2---5--------0-----2--------2---0---------5---------2--------
D 5------------------------------------------------------------------------------------------------
G -------------------------------------------------------------------------------------------------
  Hard-earned cash, I spent it fast, got drunk as drunk could be.
```

```
                           G                          Em          D          Em
E -------------------------0-------------------------------------------------------------------
A ---------------------2-5-5----5-2-----5-----------0------2-------2-0---5-----2------------0---
D 5-----2------5---------------------------------------------------------------------5--------
G ---------------------------------------------------------------------------------------------
  And when me money was all gone, 'twas then I wanted more, but a
```

```
                                           D                        C        D          Em
E ----------------------------------------------------------------------------------------------
A 2----2------2-------0----2-----0-------------------------------------------------------------
D -----------------------5------------------4------2---0-----2---4-5---2---2---2-----0-----2------
G ----------------------------------------------------------------------------------------------
  Man must be blind for to make up his mind to go to sea once more.
```

```
         G               D             Em                      D                Em
E ---------------------------------------------------------------------------------------------
A 0------5------5------2--------0---2---2---0-----5------2--------0-----0-2----2------2--------
D ---------------------------------------------------------------------------------------------
G ---------------------------------------------------------------------------------------------
  Once more, once more, to go to sea once more; but a man must be
```

```
                      D                            Em       D            Em
E ---------------------------------------------------------------------------------------------
A ----0---2----0-------------------------------------------------------------------------------
D 5------------------4------2---0-----2---4---5---2---2---2-----0------2-----------------------
G ---------------------------------------------------------------------------------------------
  Blind for to make up his mind, to go to sea once more.
```

Chord Forms

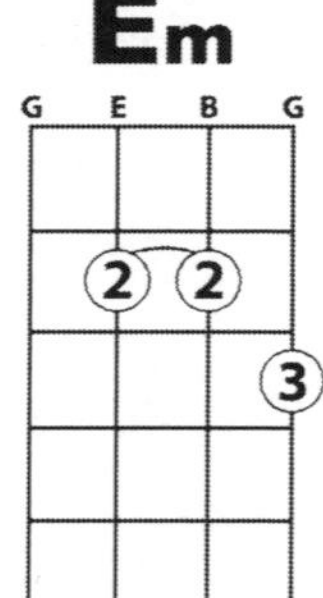

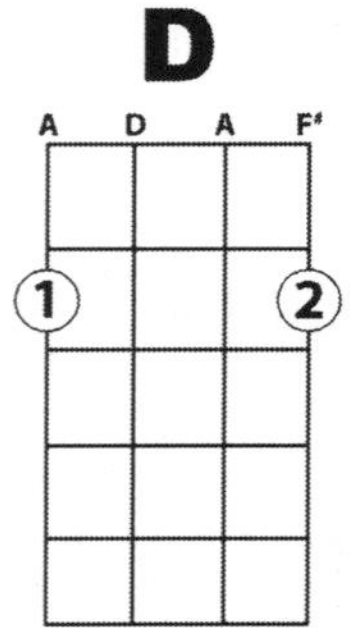

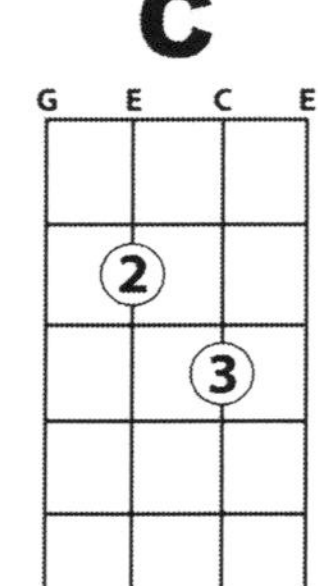

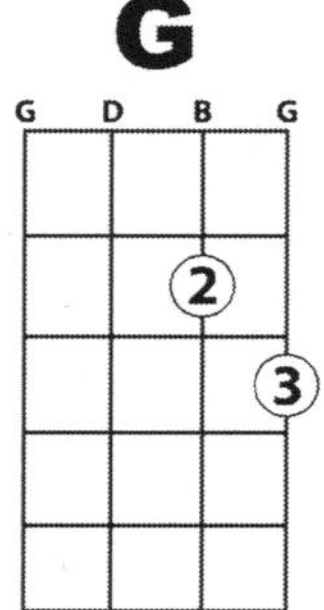

Go To Sea No More
(continued)

Melody & Chords

Key of E Minor

```
 Em                                   D          C         D       Em
E ------------------------------------------------------------------------------------
A 2----2----2----0----2---0-----------------------------------------------------------
D 2----2----2-5--2----2---2-4---0---2---4-5------2---2---0----2---------2-------------
G 0----0--------0---------0-----2---2---2---2-5--------5---2---2----2---------2-------
  When first I landed in Liverpool, I went up on the spree, my

                          G                       Em        D             Em
E ------------------------0-----------------------------------------------------------
A --------0--------2---3--5-2----5-2---5------0----2------2---0------5-------2--------
D 5-------2--------2---2--2-0----0-0---0------0----2------2---0------0-------2--------
G 0----------------0-------------------0-----------0----------2--------------0--------
  Hard-earned cash, I spent it fast, got drunk as drunk could be.

                       G                       Em        D      Em
E ---------------------0--------------------------------------------------------------
A ---------------2-5-5-2-5-2----5--------0------2------2-0--5----2------------0-------
D 5---2-----5----2-0-0-0-0-0----0--------0------2------2-0--0----2--------5---2-------
G 0---0-----0----0---------0----0---------------0----------2-------0------0-----------
  And when me money was all gone, 'twas then I wanted more, but a

                                D                           C      D          Em
E ------------------------------------------------------------------------------------
A 2---2----2------0---2----0----------------------------------------------------------
D 2---2----2--5---2---2----0---4-------2---0----2---4-5--2---2---2-----0------2-------
G 0---0-----------0---------0---------2-------2---2----2---2-0--5---5---2-----2-----0-------
  Man must be blind for to make up his mind to go to sea once more.

       G                D         Em                  D              Em
E ------------------------------------------------------------------------------------
A 0------5-------5------2------0---2---2---0----5--------2------0----0-2----2-----2---
D 2------0-------0------0------0---2---2---2----0--------0------0----0-2----2-----2---
G 4------0--------------2----------0---------------------2------2--------0------------
  Once more, once more, to go to sea once more; but a man must be

                   D                    Em      D        Em
E ------------------------------------------------------------------------------------
A ----0---2----0----------------------------------------------------------------------
D 5---2---2----2---4-------2---0----2---4---5---2---2---2----0------2-----------------
G 0-------0--------2-------2---2----2---2---4---4---4---2----2------4-----------------
  Blind for to make up his mind, to go to sea once more.
```

Chord Forms

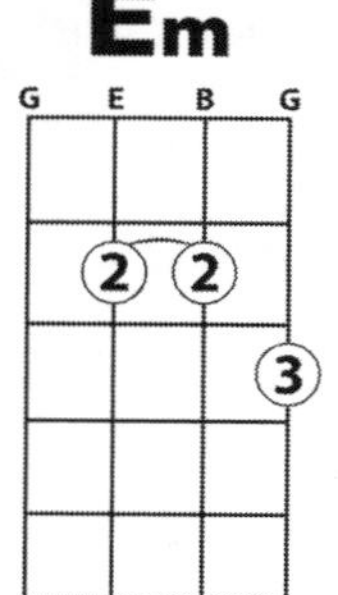

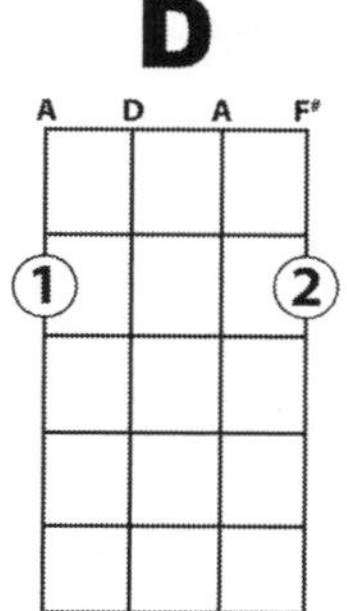

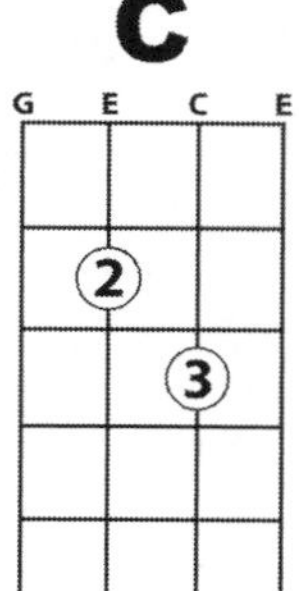

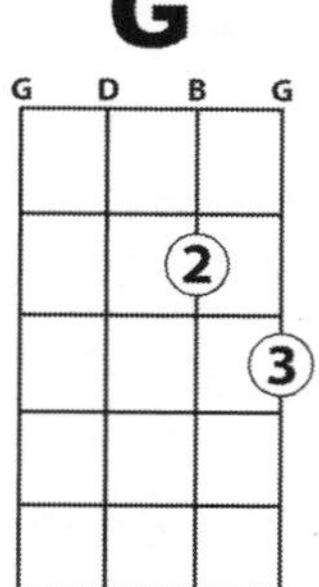

Greenland Whale Fisheries (version 1)

Two Versions

Key of C (Low)

This is one of the oldest of the whaling songs, with early versions dating back to the 1720's. It has had many versions of the lyrics and melody over the years; the ones presented below are some of the more traditional.

Words and Music

Traditional

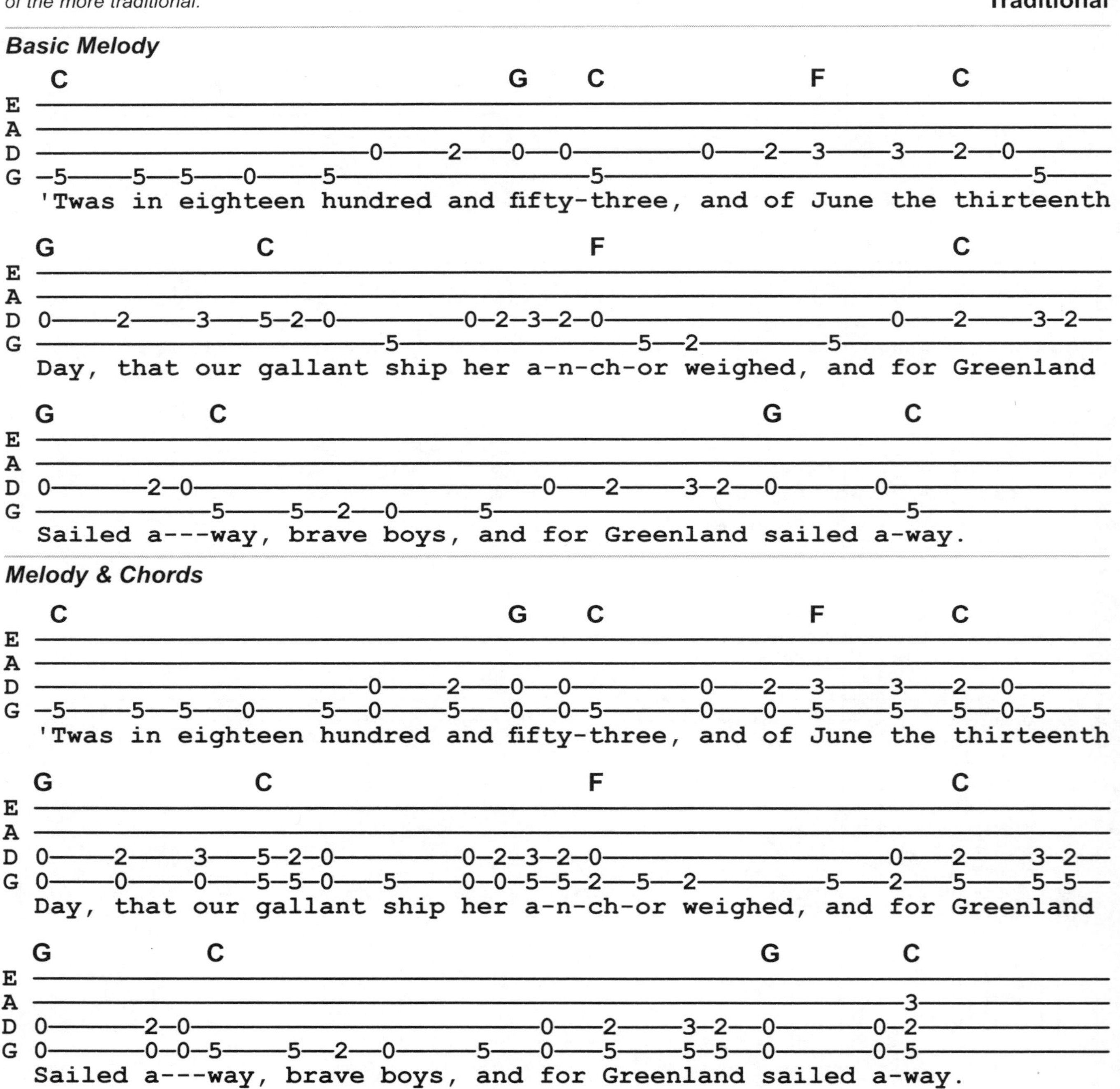

See Chord Forms and Additional Verses on Next Page

Greenland Whale Fisheries (version 1 - continued)

Chord Forms and Additional Verses

Chord Forms (Key of C)

C G F

Chord Forms (Key of G)

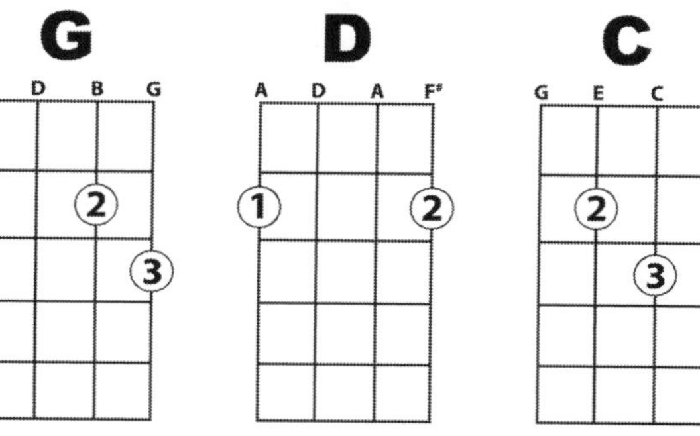

Additional Verses

The lookout in the crow's nest stood, with a spy-glass in his hand;
"There's a whale, there's a whale, there's a whale-fish he cried;
And she blows at every span, brave boys, she blows at every span."

The captain stood on the quarter-deck, and a brave old man was he;
"Haul away, haul away, let your davit tackles fall,
And put your boats to sea, brave boys, put your boats to sea!"

Well our boats got down, and the men all in, and the whale 'twas soon in view;
Resolved, resolved, were the whalermen so bold,
To strike when the whale-fish blew, brave boys, to strike when the whale-fish blew.

Well the whale was struck and the line played out, but she gave a flourish with her tail;
And our boat capsized and four men were drowned,
And we never caught that whale, brave boys, and we never caught that whale.

"Oh to lose that whale," the captain sighed, "It grieves my heart right sore;
But to lose four of my brave, jolly men,
It grieves me ten times more, brave boys, it grieves me ten times more."

Oh Greenland is a dreadful place, a land that's never green, oh...
There's ice and snow and the whale-fishes blow,
And the daylight's seldom seen brave boys, the daylight's seldom seen.

Greenland Whale Fisheries (version 1 - continued)

Two Versions

Key of C (High)

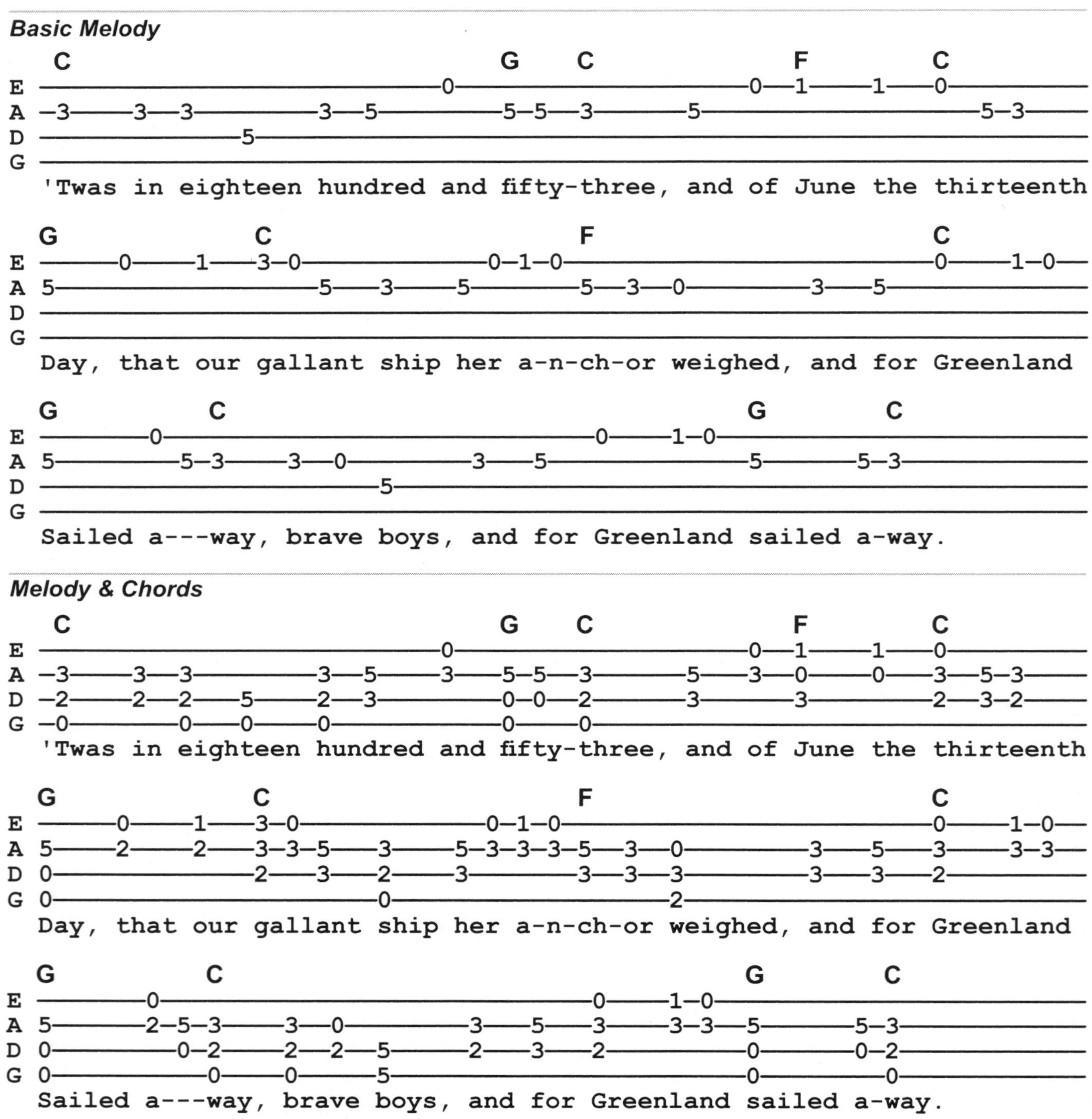

See Chord Forms and Additional Verses on Previous Page

Greenland Whale Fisheries (version 1 - continued)

Two Versions

Key of G

Basic Melody

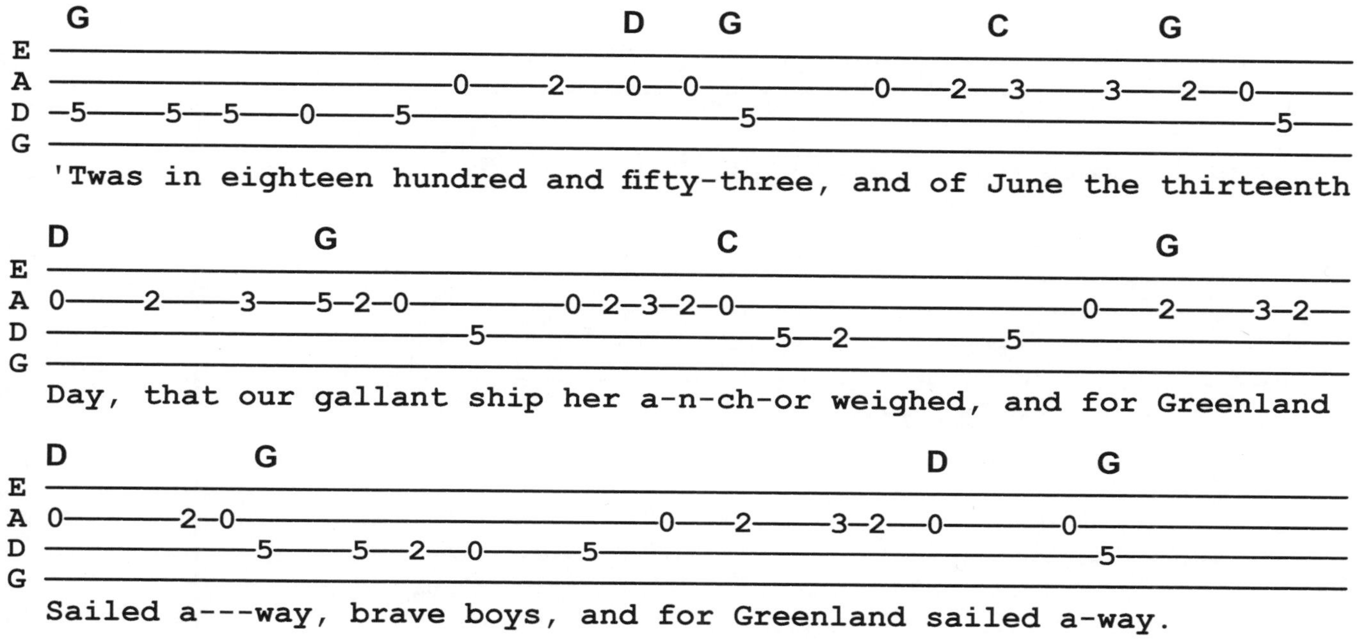

```
   G                                        D    G              C        G
E ---------------------------------------------------------------------------
A ---------------------------0-----2----0--0-----------0---2--3-----3---2--0----
D -5-----5--5----0-----5----------------------5-------------------------------5--
G ---------------------------------------------------------------------------
  'Twas in eighteen hundred and fifty-three, and of June the thirteenth
```

```
  D              G                     C                        G
E ---------------------------------------------------------------------------
A 0----2-----3----5-2-0----------0-2-3-2-0------------------0----2-----3-2--
D ----------------------------5------------------5---2---------5--------------
G ---------------------------------------------------------------------------
  Day, that our gallant ship her a-n-ch-or weighed, and for Greenland
```

```
  D          G                                         D         G
E ---------------------------------------------------------------------------
A 0--------2-0-------------------------0----2------3-2---0-------0-----------
D -------------5-----5--2---0-----5-----------------------------5------------
G ---------------------------------------------------------------------------
  Sailed a---way, brave boys, and for Greenland sailed a-way.
```

Melody & Chords

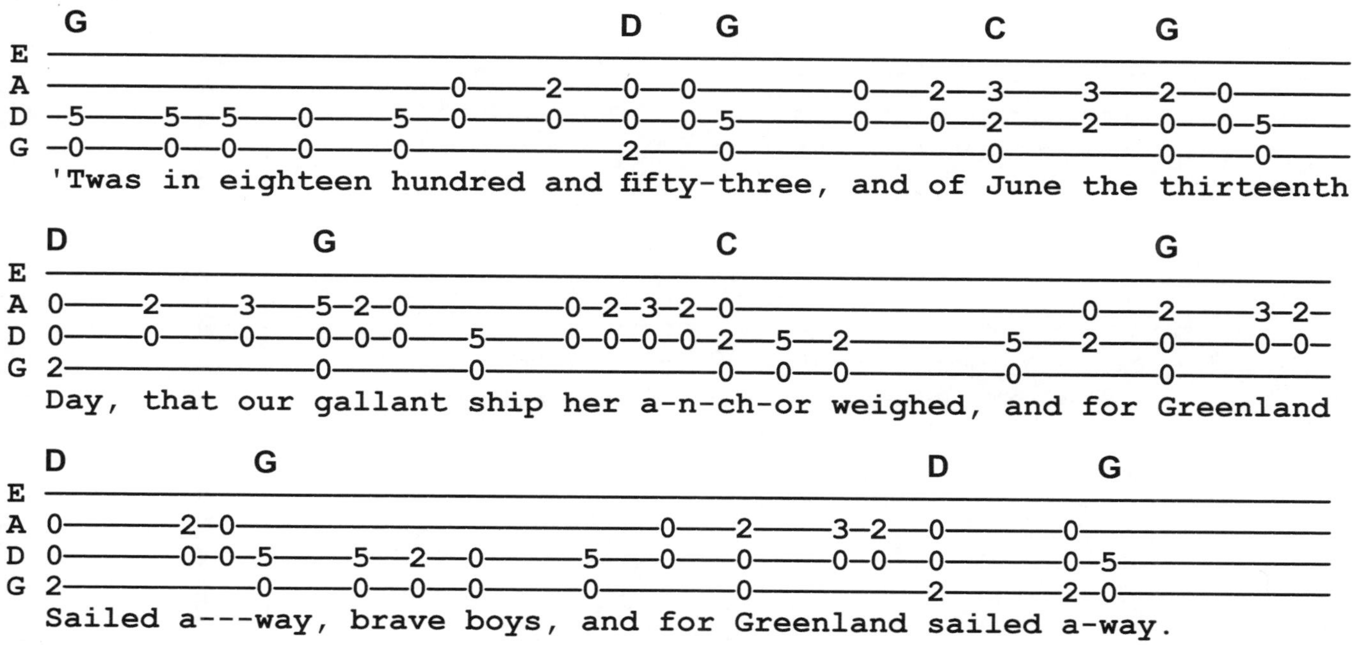

```
   G                                        D    G              C        G
E ---------------------------------------------------------------------------
A ---------------------------0-----2----0--0-----------0---2--3-----3---2--0----
D -5-----5--5----0-----5--0-----0----0--0-5------0---0--2-----2---0--0-5--
G -0-----0--0----0-----0-----------------2---0-------------0----------0----0--
  'Twas in eighteen hundred and fifty-three, and of June the thirteenth
```

```
  D              G                     C                        G
E ---------------------------------------------------------------------------
A 0----2-----3----5-2-0----------0-2-3-2-0------------------0----2-----3-2-
D 0----0-----0----0-0-0----5-----0-0-0-0-2---5---2----------5----2----0-----0-0-
G 2----------------0-------0------------0---0---0---------0---------0--------
  Day, that our gallant ship her a-n-ch-or weighed, and for Greenland
```

```
  D          G                                         D         G
E ---------------------------------------------------------------------------
A 0--------2-0-------------------------0----2------3-2---0-------0-----------
D 0--------0-0-5-----5--2---0-----5----0----0------0-0---0-------0-5---------
G 2------------0-----0--0---0-----0---------0------------2-------2-0---------
  Sailed a---way, brave boys, and for Greenland sailed a-way.
```

See Chord Forms and Additional Verses on Two Pages Previous

Greenland Whale Fisheries (version 2)

Basic Melody

Key of C / A Minor

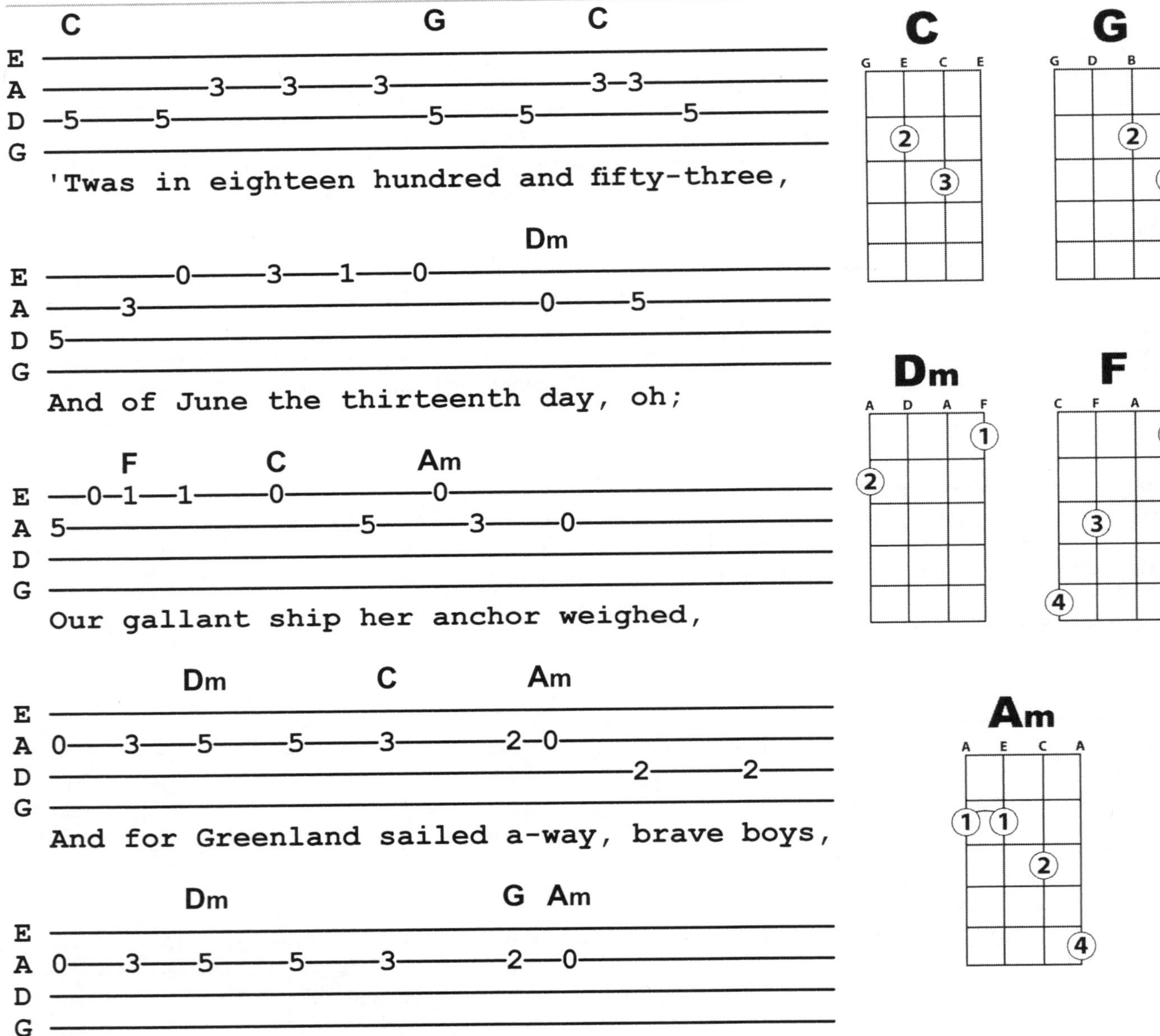

Greenland Whale Fisheries (version 2 - continued)

Melody & Chords

Key of C / A Minor

```
    C                           G          C
E ----------------------------------------------------------
A ------------3----3-----3----------------3--3--------------
D -5-------5--2----2-----2--5-------5-----2--2--5-----------
G -0-------0--0----------0--0-------0-----0-----0-----------
  'Twas in eighteen hundred and fifty-three,
```

```
                                      Dm
E -----------0-----3----1----0------------------------------
A -------3---3-----3----3----3--------0-----5---------------
D 5------2---2-----2------------------0-----3---------------
G 0-----------------------------------2-----2---------------
  And of June the thirteenth day, oh;
```

```
      F       C         Am
E --0-1--1----0---------0-----------------------------------
A 5-0-0--0----3------5--0-3------0--------------------------
D 3---3-------2------3----2-2----2--------------------------
G 2------------------------------2--------------------------
  Our gallant ship her anchor weighed,
```

```
           Dm          C          Am
E ----------------------------------------------------------
A 0----3----5------5-----3-------2-0------------------------
D 2----2----3------3-----2-------2-2-----2-------2----------
G 2---------2------------0---------2-----2-------2----------
  And for Greenland sailed a-way, brave boys,
```

```
           Dm                  G  Am
E ----------------------------------------------------------
A 0----3----5------5-----3-------2--0-----------------------
D 2----2----3------3-----3-------0--2-----------------------
G ----------2------------2-------0--2-----------------------
  And for Greenland sailed a--way.
```

Chord diagrams:

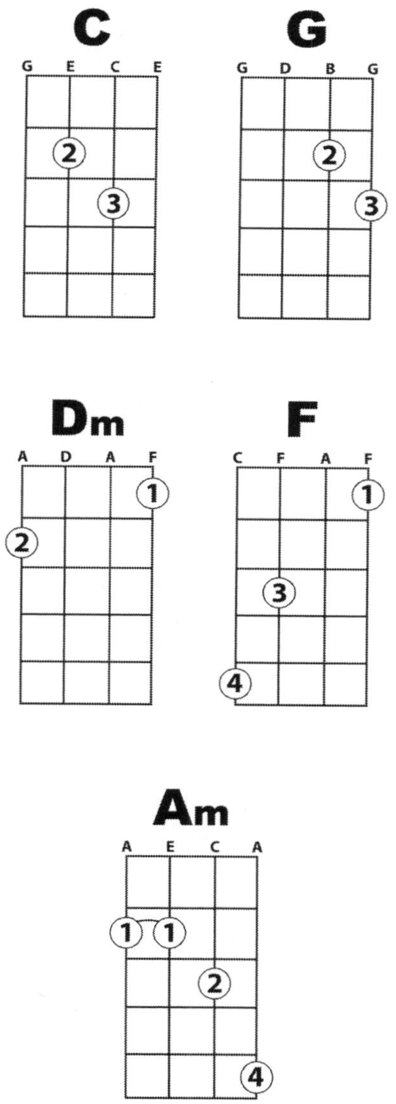

- **C** (G E C E): ② ③
- **G** (G D B G): ② ③
- **Dm** (A D A F): ① ②
- **F** (C F A F): ① ③ ④
- **Am** (A E C A): ① ① ② ④

Greenland Whale Fisheries (version 2 - continued)

Basic Melody

Key of G / E Minor

```
   G                          D           G
E ─────────────────────────────────────────────────────────
A ─────────────────────────────────────────────────────────
D ─0──────0───5────5─────5───0───────0─────5─5───0─────────
G ─────────────────────────────────────────────────────────
  'Twas in eighteen hundred and fifty-three,
```

```
                                             Am
E ─────────────────────────────────────────────────────────
A ────────2─────5────3────2──────────────0─────────────────
D 0────5────────────────────────2──────────────────────────
G ─────────────────────────────────────────────────────────
  And of June the thirteenth day, oh;
```

```
       C          G          Em
E ─────────────────────────────────────────────────────────
A 0─2─3───3───────2───────0────2───────────────────────────
D ────────────────────────────────5──────2─────────────────
G ─────────────────────────────────────────────────────────
  Our gallant ship her anchor weighed,
```

```
           Am           G          Em
E ─────────────────────────────────────────────────────────
A ───────────0──────0──────────────────────────────────────
D 2────5─────────────────────5──────4─2────────────────────
G ────────────────────────────────────────────4───────4────
  And for Greenland sailed a-way, brave boys,
```

```
           Am                     D  Em
E ─────────────────────────────────────────────────────────
A ───────────0──────0──────────────────────────────────────
D 2────5─────────────────────5──────4───2──────────────────
G ─────────────────────────────────────────────────────────
  And for Greenland sailed a--way.
```

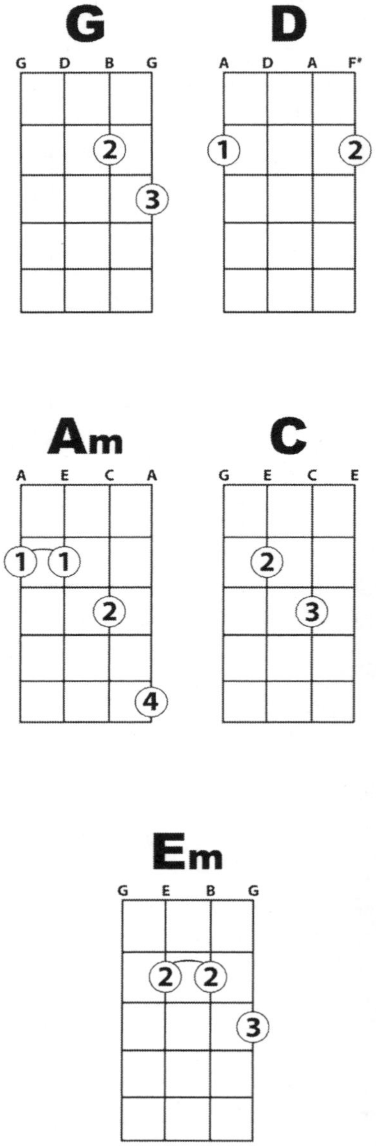

Chord diagrams: G (G D B G), D (A D A F#), Am (A E C A), C (G E C E), Em (G E B G)

Greenland Whale Fisheries (version 2 - continued)

Melody & Chords

Key of G / E Minor

```
    G                         D         G
E ——————————————————————————————————————————————————————
A ——————————————————————————————————————————————————————
D —0————0——5———5————5——0————0————5–5——0—————————————————
G —0————0——0———0————0——2————2————0–0——0—————————————————
  'Twas in eighteen hundred and fifty-three,

                                 Am
E ——————————————————————————————————————————————————————
A ———————2———5———3———2—————————————0————————————————————
D 0———5——0———————0———0———0—————2———2————————————————————
G 0———0——0———————————————————————2———2——————————————————
  And of June the thirteenth day, oh;

     C        G        Em
E ——————————————————————————————————————————————————————
A 0–2–3——3————2————0———2————————————————————————————————
D 2–2–2——2————0————0———2–5————2—————————————————————————
G 2————0——————0————————0–4————4—————————————————————————
  Our gallant ship her anchor weighed,

          Am          G         Em
E ——————————————————————————————————————————————————————
A ——————————0————0——————————————————————————————————————
D 2————5————2————2————5————4–2——————————————————————————
G 4————4————2—————————0————0–4————4————4————————————————
  And for Greenland sailed a-way, brave boys,

          Am                  D  Em
E ——————————————————————————————————————————————————————
A ——————————0————0——————————————————————————————————————
D 2————5————2————2————5————4——2—————————————————————————
G 4————4————2—————————5————2——4—————————————————————————
  And for Greenland sailed a--way.
```

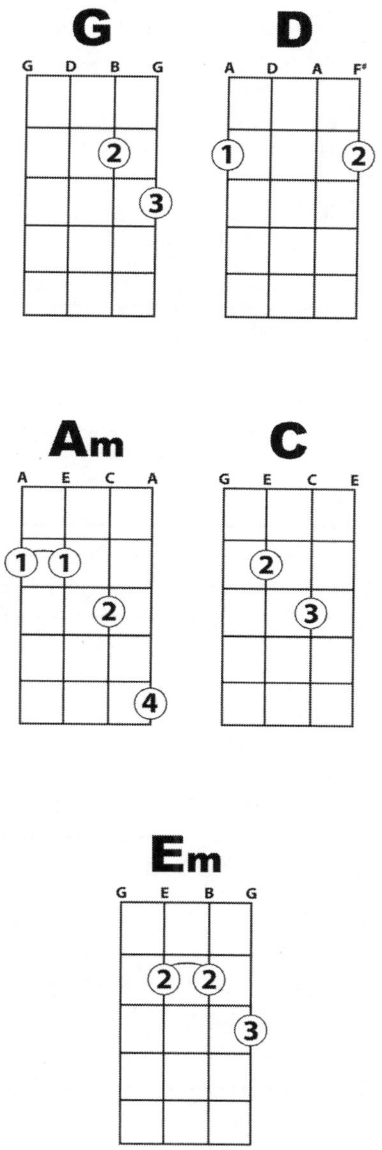

G (G D B G): A string fret 2 (finger 2), E string fret 3 (finger 3)

D (A D A F#): G string fret 2 (finger 1), E string fret 2 (finger 2)

Am (A E C A): G & D strings fret 2 (finger 1, barre), A string fret 3 (finger 2), E string fret 5 (finger 4)

C (G E C E): D string fret 2 (finger 2), A string fret 3 (finger 3)

Em (G E B G): D & A strings fret 2 (finger 2, barre), E string fret 3 (finger 3)

Haul Away Joe

Basic Melody

Key of A Minor (Low)

Words and Music

Traditional

This is one of the quintessential sea shanties, best belted out at top volume with friends. It is a favorite in singing sessions in New England and elsewhere. Usually this is sung a cappella, but we give the chords below so you can strum along if you want.

```
  Am                Em               Dm               Em
E ---------------------------------------------------------------------------
A 0-----0--0-----------------------------------------------------------------
D --------------2-5----5---5-2---0---0--------0----2-----5----5--5-----------
G ---------------------------------------5-----------------------------------
  When I was a little boy, so my father told me (t' me!)

  Am             Em             Dm          E    Am
E ---------------------------------------------------------------------------
A 0----0-------------------------------------------0-----0--0--0-------------
D ------------2-5----2------0-----0-2------------------------------2---------
G -----------------------------------------2---------------------------------
  Way haul a-way, we'll haul a-way Joe. That if I did not

  Em                      Dm                        Em
E ---------------------------------------------------------------------------
A ---------------------------------------------------------------------------
D 5-----5----5---------2--0-----0----------0-----2--5----5--5----------------
G -----------------------------------5---------------------------------------
  Kiss the girls, my lips would all grow moldy (t' me!)

  Am             Em             Dm          E    Am
E ---------------------------------------------------------------------------
A 0----0---------------------------------------------------------------------
D ------------2-5----2------0-----0-2----------------------------------------
G -----------------------------------------2---------------------------------
  Way haul a-way, we'll haul a-way Joe.
```

CHORUS

```
  Am                 Em            Dm                    Em
E ---------------------------------------------------------------------------
A -----0----0----------------------------------------------------------------
D 2---------------2--5-----2------0-------0-------0----2--5------------------
G -------------------------------------------5-------------------------------
  Oh, way haul a-way, we're bound for better weather.

  Am             Em             Dm            E    Am
E ---------------------------------------------------------------------------
A 0----0---------------------------------------------------------------------
D ------------2-5----2------0-----0---2--------------------------------------
G -------------------------------------------2-------------------------------
  Way haul a--way, we'll haul a--way Joe.
```

Am (A E C A): 1 1 2 4

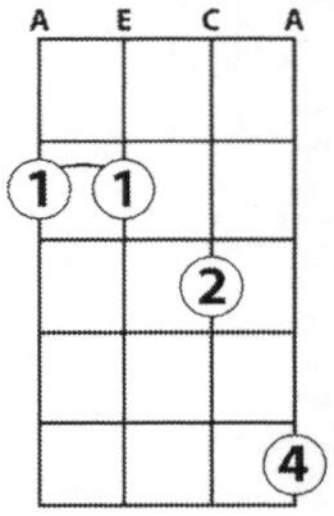

Em (G E B G): 2 2 3

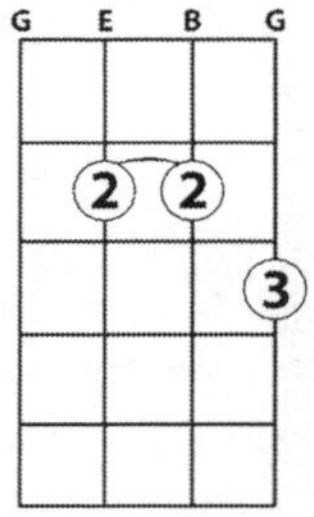

Dm (A D A F): 1 2

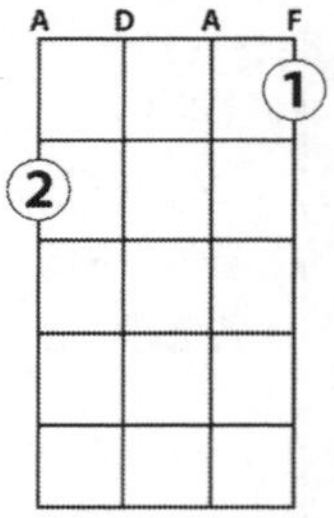

E (B E B G#): 1 1 2 3

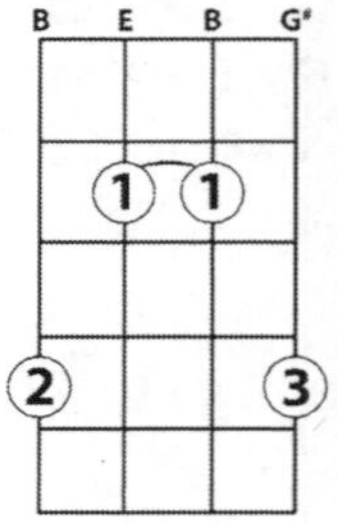

See Additional Verses on Next Page

Haul Away Joe (continued)

Melody & Chords
Key of A Minor (Low)

```
  Am                 Em               Dm                Em
E ---------------------------------------------------------------------------
A 0------0--0-----------------------------------------------------------------
D 2------2--2-----2--5-----5---5--2---0---0-------0----2-----5----5---5-----
G 2---------2-----2--4-----4---4--4---2---2---5---2----4-----4----0---0-----
  When I was a little boy, so my father told me (t' me!)
```

```
  Am          Em            Dm        E    Am
E ---------------------------------------------------------------------------
A 0----0--------------------------------------------0-----0---0--0------------
D 2----2-------2--5------2-------0------0--2--------2-----2---2--2-----2------
G 2----2-------2--4------4-------2------2--4----2---2-----2------2-----2------
  Way haul a-way, we'll haul a-way Joe. That if I did not
```

```
  Em                      Dm                        Em
E ---------------------------------------------------------------------------
A ---------------------------------------------------------------------------
D 5------5---5-------2---0-------0------------0-----2---5-----5---5---------
G 4------4---4-------4---2-------2-------5----2-----4---4-----0---0---------
  Kiss the girls, my lips would all grow moldy (t' me!)
```

```
  Am          Em            Dm        E    Am
E ---------------------------------------------------------------------------
A 0----0-------------------------------------0--------------------------------
D 2----2------2--5------2-------0------0--2--2--------------------------------
G 2----2------2--4------4-------2------2--4--2--------------------------------
  Way haul a-way, we'll haul a-way Joe.
```

CHORUS

```
  Am                  Em             Dm                    Em
E ---------------------------------------------------------------------------
A -----0----0-----------------------------------------------------------------
D 2----2----2------2--5-----2-------0------0--------0-----2---5--------------
G 2----2----2------2--4-----4-------2------2----5---2-----4---4--------------
  Oh, way haul a-way, we're bound for better weather.
```

```
  Am          Em            Dm        E    Am
E ---------------------------------------------------------------------------
A 0----0--------------------------------------0-------------------------------
D 2----2------2--5------2-------0------0--2---2-------------------------------
G 2----2------2--4------4-------2------2--4---2-------------------------------
  Way haul a-way, we'll haul a--way Joe.
```

Am
A E C A

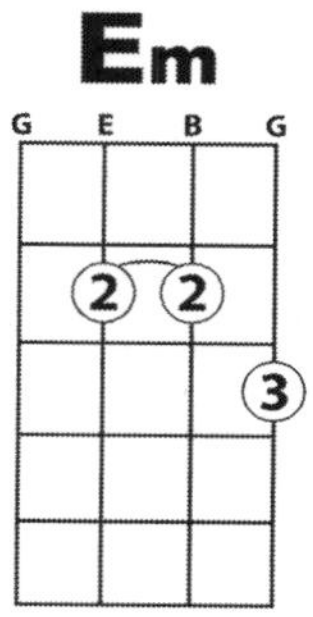

Em
G E B G

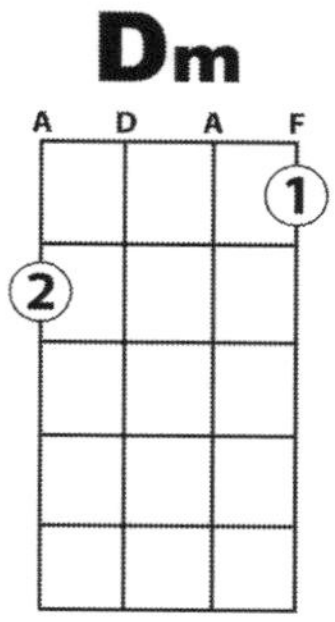

Dm
A D A F

E

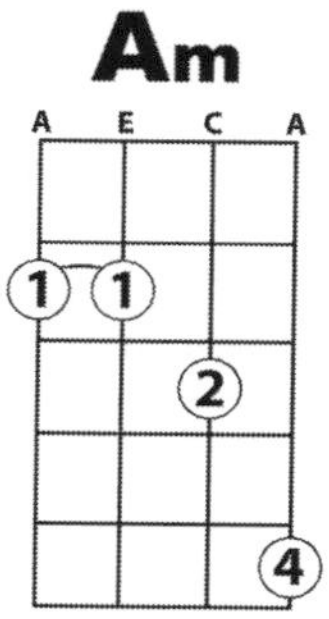

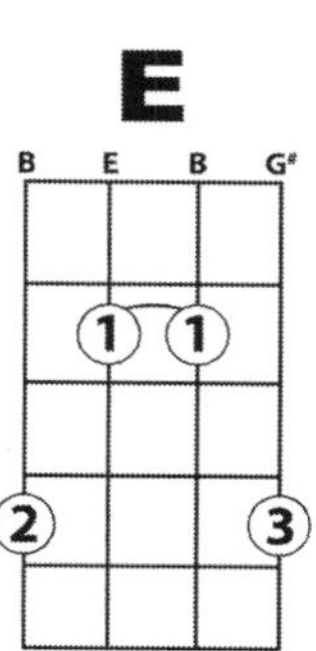

Additional Verses

King Louis was the king of France,
Before the revolution;
And then he got his head chopped off,
It spoiled his constitution.

Saint Patrick was a gentleman,
He came from decent people;
He built a church in Dublin town,
And on it put a steeple.

Once I was in Ireland,
A-digging turf and taties;
But now I'm on a Yankee ship,
A haulin' on the braces.

Once I had a Yankee girl,
But she was fat and lazy;
And then I got an Irish girl,
She damn near drove me crazy.

Haul Away Joe (continued)

Basic Melody
Key of A Minor (High)

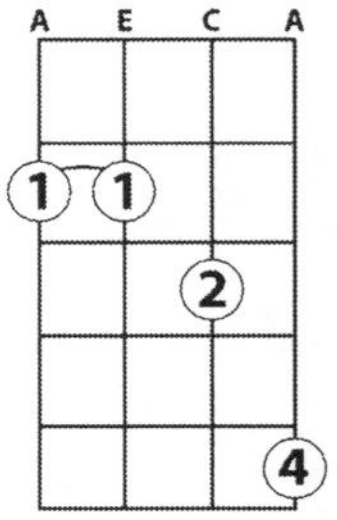

```
  Am                  Em                 Dm                  Em
E 5------5-5-----0-3-----3---3-0---------------------------0------3-----3---3---------
A ---------------------------------------5---5---3---5--------------------------------
D ------------------------------------------------------------------------------------
G ------------------------------------------------------------------------------------
  When I was a little boy, so my father told me (t' me!)

  Am             Em             Dm           E     Am
E 5---5------0-3-----0-----------------------0------------5------5---5-5----0----
A -------------------------------5------5----------0-----------------------------
D -------------------------------------------------------------------------------
G -------------------------------------------------------------------------------
  Way haul a-way, we'll haul a-way Joe. That if I did not

  Em                          Dm                         Em
E 3-----3-----3--------0-----------------------------------0---3-----3---3-------
A ----------------------------5------5--------3---5------------------------------
D -------------------------------------------------------------------------------
G -------------------------------------------------------------------------------
  Kiss the girls, my lips would all grow moldy (t' me!)

  Am             Em             Dm           E     Am
E 5---5------0-3-----0-----------------------0-----------------------------------
A -------------------------------5------5----------0-----------------------------
D -------------------------------------------------------------------------------
G -------------------------------------------------------------------------------
  Way haul a-way, we'll haul a-way Joe.
```

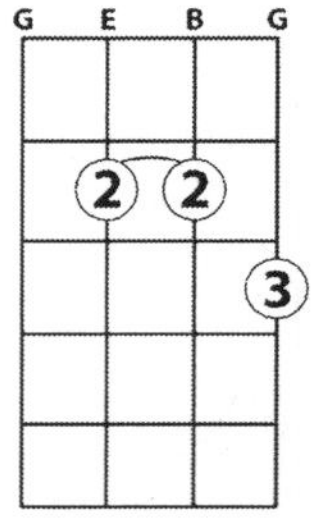

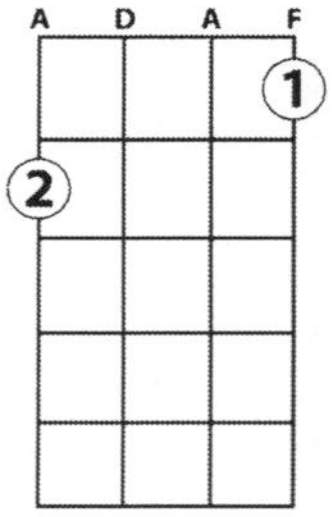

Chorus

```
  Am                     Em              Dm                            Em
E 0----5-----5-----0---3------0--------------------------------------0---3-------
A -----------------------------------5-------5----3---5--------------------------
D -------------------------------------------------------------------------------
G -------------------------------------------------------------------------------
  Oh, way haul a-way, we're bound for better weather.

  Am             Em             Dm           E     Am
E 5---5------0-3-----0-----------------------0-----------------------------------
A -------------------------------5------5----------0-----------------------------
D -------------------------------------------------------------------------------
G -------------------------------------------------------------------------------
  Way haul a-way, we'll haul a--way Joe.
```

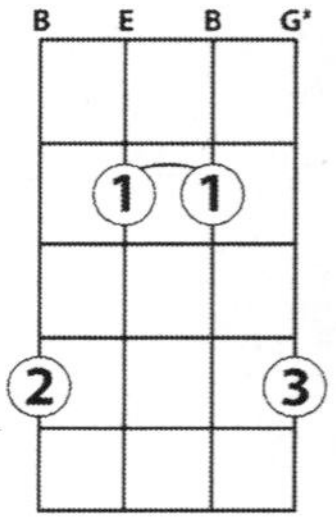

Sometimes an alternate line is sung for the first line of the chorus:
"Oh, way haul away, the good ship now is rolling."
You can also choose to add the "t' me" to the first line of the chorus.

Am
A E C A

Em
G E B G

Dm
A D A F

E
B E B G#

Haul Away Joe (continued)

Melody & Chords
Key of A Minor (High)

```
Am                    Em                  Dm                   Em
E 5------5-5----0-3----3---3-0--------------------------------0------3-----3---3------
A 3------3-3----3-2----2---2-3---5---5---3---5----2------2-----2---2------
D 2---------2--------2-----------2-----3---3---3---3  --2------2-------------------
G -------------------------------------2-----------------------------------------------
  When I was a little boy, so my father told me (t' me!)
```

```
Am                 Em                 Dm          E    Am
E 5----5------0-3------0--------------------------0-------------5------5---5---5-----0----
A 3----3------3-2------2--------5------5-2-----0-------------3------3---3---3-----3----
D 2----2----------2--------------------3------3-2-----2-------------2------2-------2---------
G ------------------------------------2-----------------2------------------------------------
  Way haul a-way, we'll haul a-way Joe. That if I did not
```

```
Em                              Dm                              Em
E 3------3----3----------0------------------------------------0---3----3---3-----
A 2------2----2----------2---5--------5--------3------5-------2---2----2---2-----
D 2-----------2-------------------3--------3--------3------3-------2---2-----------
G ----------------------------------2-----------------------------------------------
  Kiss the girls, my lips would all grow moldy (t' me!)
```

```
Am                 Em                 Dm          E    Am
E 5----5------0-3------0--------------------------0-------------------------------------
A 3----3------3-2------2--------5------5-2-----0--------------------------------------
D 2----2----------2--------------------3------3-2-----2---------------------------------
G ------------------------------------2-----------------2-------------------------------
  Way haul a-way, we'll haul a-way Joe.
```

CHORUS

```
Am                          Em              Dm                         Em
E 0----5----5----0----3--------0----------------------------------------0---3--------
A 2----3----3----3----2--------2--------5--------5----3----5----2---2--------
D 2----2----2-----------2------------------3--------3----3----3----2---2--------
G ------------------------------------------2--------------------2-----------------
  Oh, way haul a-way, we're bound for better weather.
```

```
Am                 Em                 Dm          E    Am
E 5----5------0-3------0--------------------------0-------------------------------------
A 3----3------3-2------3--------5------5----2-----0-----------------------------------
D 2----2----------2--------------------3------3----2-----2------------------------------
G ------------------------------------2-------------------2-----------------------------
  Way haul a--way, we'll haul a--way Joe.
```

Am (A E C A): 1 1 2 4

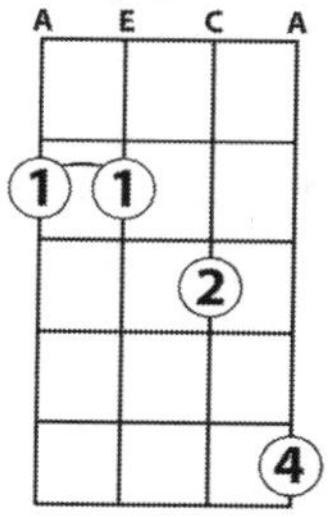

Em (G E B G): 2 2 3

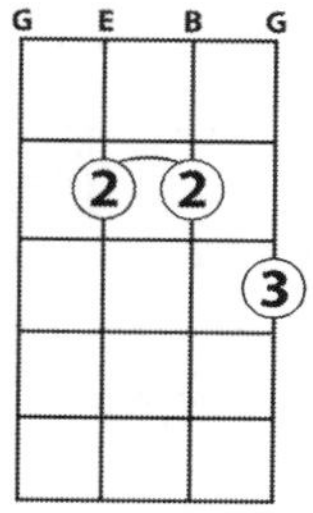

Dm (A D A F): 1 2

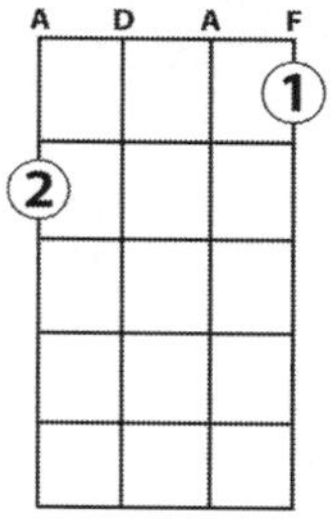

E (B E B G#): 1 1 2 3

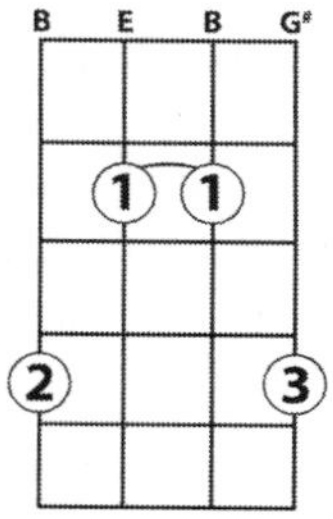

Haul Away Joe (continued)

Basic Melody
Key of E Minor

```
  Em                   Bm                 Am                  Bm
E 0-------0--0------------------------------------------------------------------------
A ---------------------2--5----5---5--2---0----0---------0-----2-------5-----5---5-----
D -------------------------------------------------5----------------------------------
G -------------------------------------------------------------------------------------
  When I was a little boy, so my father told me (t' me!)
```

```
  Em              Bm              Am          B    Em
E 0-----0-------------------------------------------------0--------0---0--0-----------
A -------------------2--5------2---------0-------0--2------------------------------2---
D -----------------------------------------------------2--------------------------------
G -------------------------------------------------------------------------------------
  Way haul a-way, we'll haul a-way Joe. That if I did not
```

```
  Bm                            Am                              Bm
E --------------------------------------------------------------------------------------
A 5-----5-----5--------2---0-------0----------------0-------2---5------5---5-----------
D -----------------------------------------------5---------------------------------------
G --------------------------------------------------------------------------------------
  Kiss the girls, my lips would all grow moldy (t' me!)
```

```
  Em              Bm              Am          B    Em
E 0-----0------------------------------------------------------------------------------
A -------------------2--5------2---------0-------0--2-----------------------------------
D -----------------------------------------------------2--------------------------------
G --------------------------------------------------------------------------------------
  Way haul a-way, we'll haul a-way Joe.
```

CHORUS

```
  Em                        Bm              Am                            Bm
E ------0-----0--------------------------------------------------------------------------
A 2-----------------------2---5-------2--------0---------0---------0----2----5----------
D -----------------------------------------------------------5---------------------------
G ---------------------------------------------------------------------------------------
  Oh, way haul a-way, we're bound for better weather.
```

```
  Em              Bm              Am           B    Em
E 0-----0--------------------------------------------------------------------------------
A -------------------2--5------2---------0-------0---2-----------------------------------
D ------------------------------------------------------2---------------------------------
G ----------------------------------------------------------------------------------------
  Way haul a-way, we'll haul a--way Joe.
```

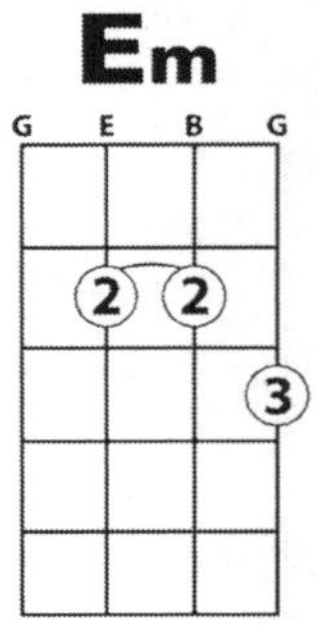

Em
G E B G

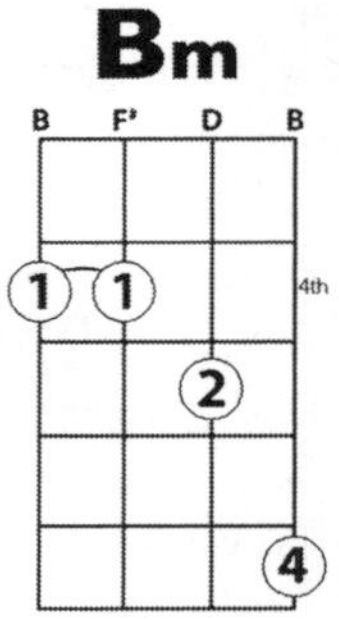

Bm
B F# D B
4th

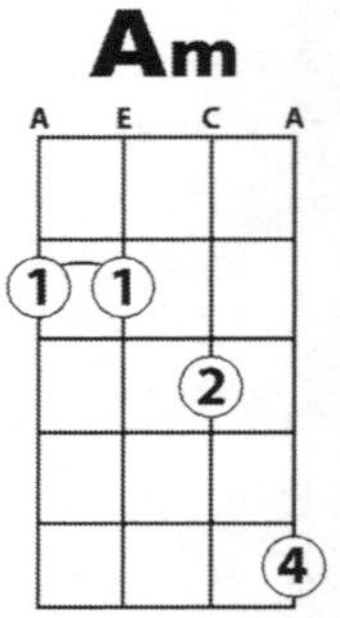

Am
A E C A

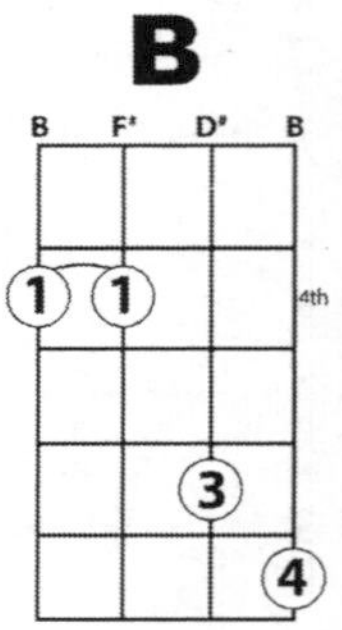

B
B F# D# B
4th

Haul Away Joe (continued)

Melody & Chords

Key of E Minor

```
Em                     Bm                    Am                 Bm
E 0------0-0---------------------------------------------------------------
A 2------2-2-----2-5-----5-----5-2---0---0----------0----2------5----5---5--
D 2--------2-----2-4-----4-----4-4---2---2----5-----2----2------4----4---4--
G ---------------4-------------4-----2--------2-----------------4-----------
  When I was a little boy, so my father told me (t' me!)
```

```
Em               Bm               Am          B    Em
E 0---0-------------------------------------------------0------0---0-0------
A 2---2-------2-5------2--------0-------0-2-------------2------2---2-2----2-
D 2---2-------2-4------4--------2-------2-1-----2-------2------2-----2----2-
G -------------4----------------2---------4-----4---------------------------
  Way haul a-way, we'll haul a-way Joe. That if I did not
```

```
Bm                          Am                           Bm
E --------------------------------------------------------------------------
A 5------5----5---------2--0-------0------------0-----2--5-----5--5--------
D 4------4----4---------4--2-------2-------5----2-----4--4-----4--4--------
G 4-----------4------------2---------------2----------4--------------------
  Kiss the girls, my lips would all grow moldy (t' me!)
```

```
Em               Bm               Am          B    Em
E 0---0---------------------------------------------------------------------
A 2---2-------2-5------2--------0-------0-2---------------------------------
D 2---2-------2-4------4--------2-------2-1-----2---------------------------
G -------------4----------------2---------4-----4---------------------------
  Way haul a-way, we'll haul a-way Joe.
```

CHORUS

```
Em                    Bm            Am                            Bm
E -----0----0---------------------------------------------------------------
A 2----2----2----2--5------2--------0--------0---------0----2---5----------
D 2----2----2----2--4------4--------2--------2----5----2----4---4----------
G -------------------4--------------2----------------2--------4------------
  Oh, way haul a-way, we're bound for better weather.
```

```
Em               Bm               Am          B    Em
E 0---0---------------------------------------------------------------------
A 2---2-------2-5------2--------0-------0-2---------------------------------
D 2---2-------2-4------4--------2-------2-1-----2---------------------------
G -------------4----------------2---------4-----0---------------------------
  Way haul a-way, we'll haul a--way Joe.
```

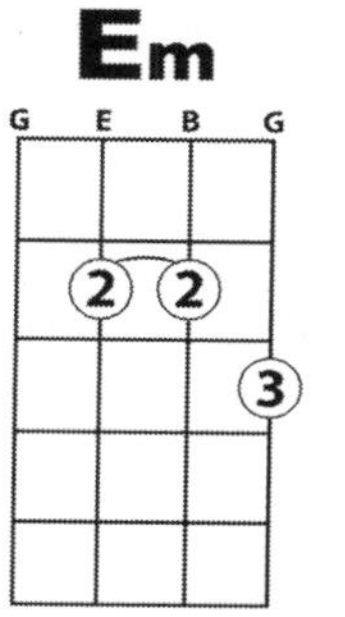

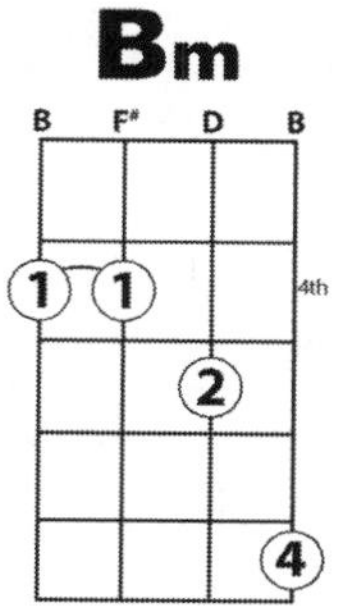

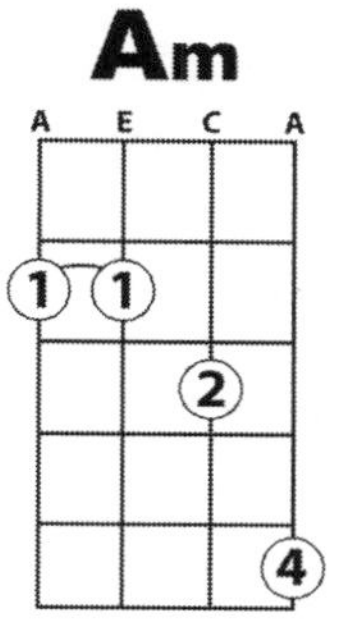

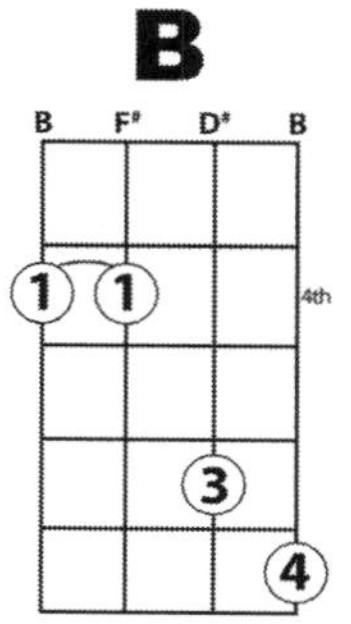

Em

G E B G

Bm

B F# D B

4th

Am

A E C A

B

B F# D# B

4th

IRISH SEA SONG

The Holy Ground

Basic Melody

Key of C

This is one of those Irish songs that is perfect for shouting out while drinking some Guinness. In fact the "FINE GIRL YOU ARE" lines in the chorus are literally meant to be shouted out rather than sung. The version of this song by the Clancy Brothers and Tommy Makem is highly recommended.

Words and Music

Traditional

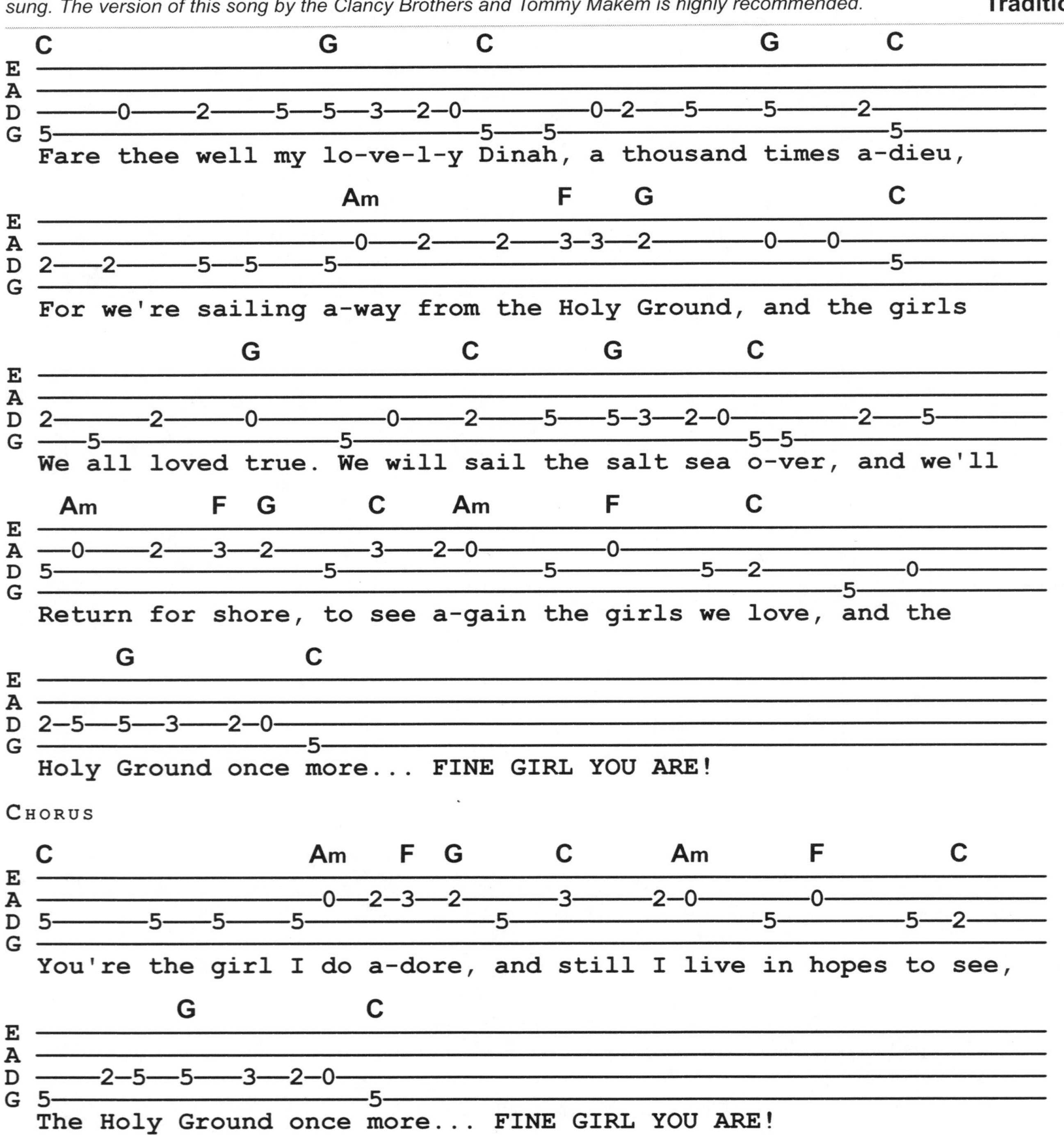

See Chord Forms and Additional Verses on Next Page

The Holy Ground (continued)

Chord Forms and Additional Verses

Chord Forms

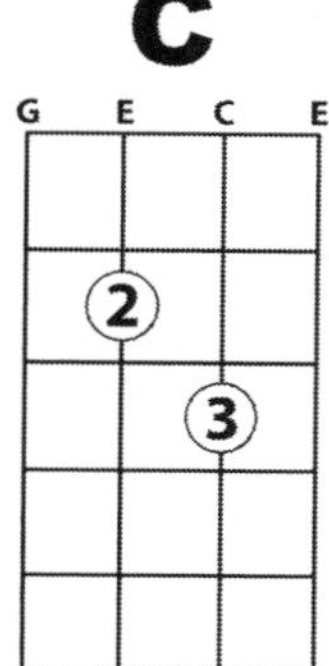

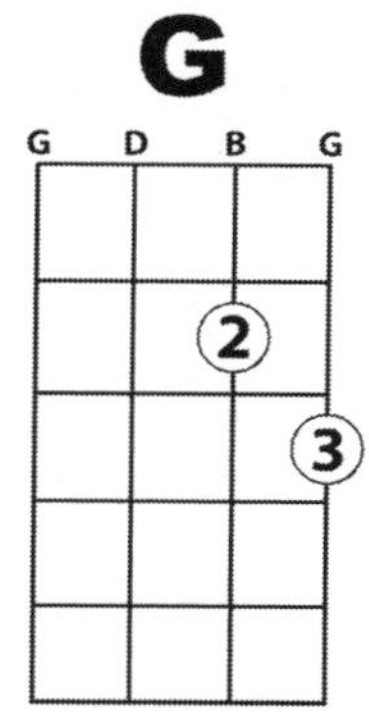

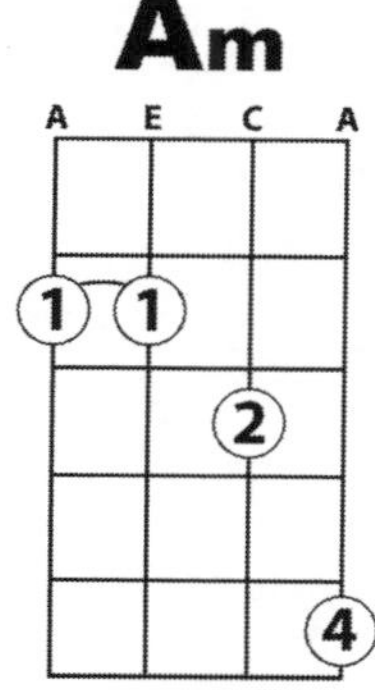

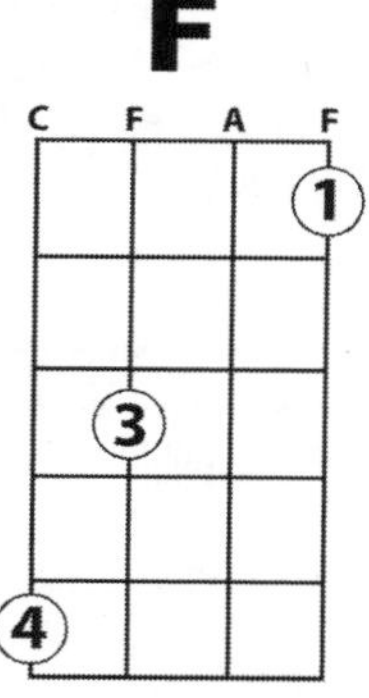

Additional Verses

And now the storm is raging,
And we are far from shore;
And the good old ship is tossing about,
And the rigging is all torn.
And the secrets of my life, my love,
You're the girl I do adore!
And still I live in hopes to see
The Holy Ground once more...
FINE GIRL YOU ARE!

And now the storm is over,
And we are safe and well.
We will go into a public house,
And we'll sit and drink black ale!
We will drink strong ale and porter,
And we'll make the rafters roar,
And when our money is all spent
We'll go to sea once more...
FINE GIRL YOU ARE!

The Holy Ground (continued)

Melody & Chords
Key of C

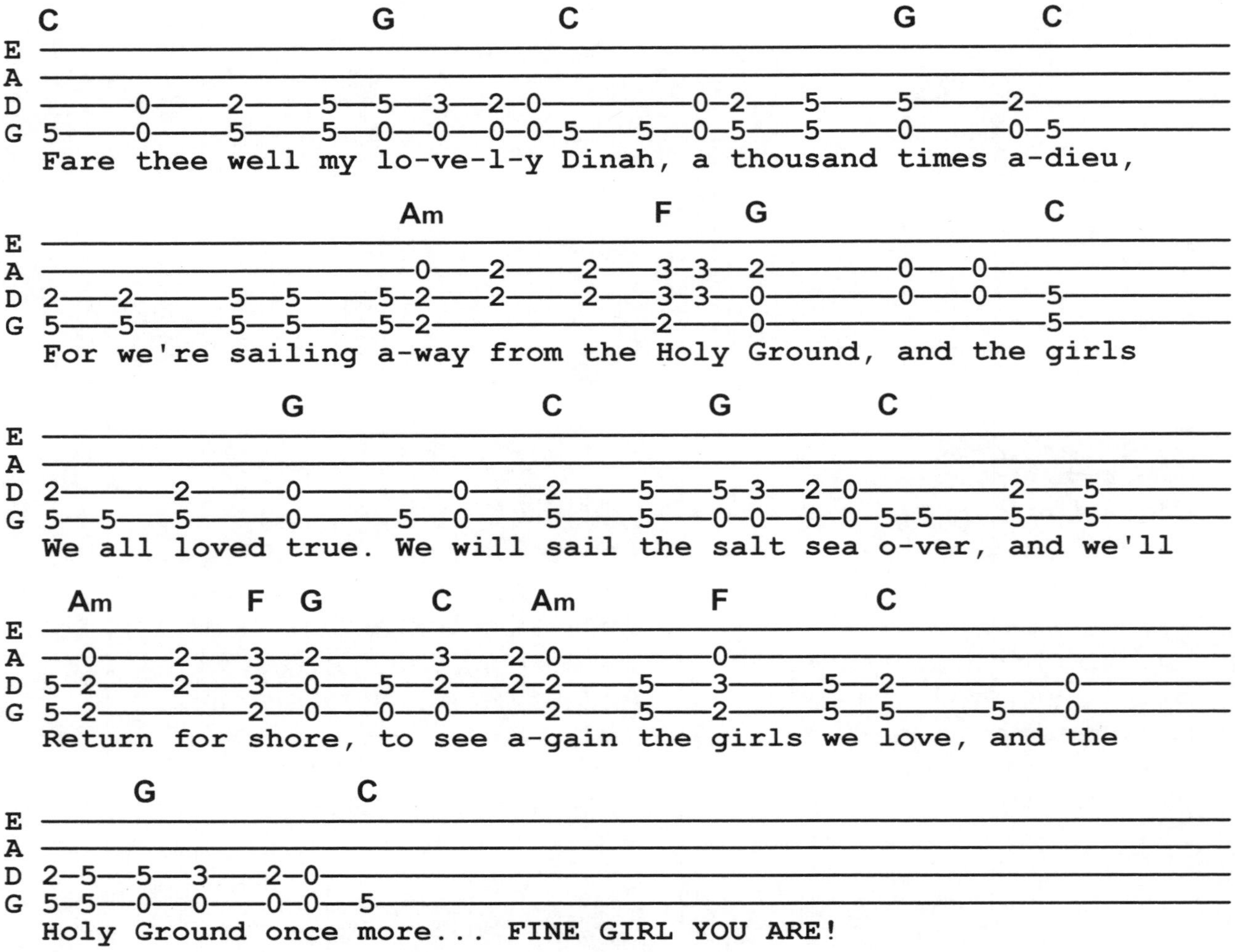

```
  C                  G         C                  G       C
E ------------------------------------------------------------------
A ------------------------------------------------------------------
D -----0----2----5--5--3--2-0---------0-2---5-----5-----2-----------
G 5----0----5----5--0--0--0-0-5---5--0-5---5-----0-----0-5---------
  Fare thee well my lo-ve-l-y Dinah, a thousand times a-dieu,
```

```
                    Am           F    G               C
E ------------------------------------------------------------------
A -------------------0---2---2---3-3--2-------0---0-----------------
D 2--2---5--5---5-2---2---2---3-3--0-------0---0---5----------------
G 5--5---5--5---5-2-----------2----0---------------5----------------
  For we're sailing a-way from the Holy Ground, and the girls
```

```
             G             C        G        C
E ------------------------------------------------------------------
A ------------------------------------------------------------------
D 2-----2----0-------0----2----5---5-3--2-0--------2---5------------
G 5--5--5----0----5--0----5----5---0-0--0-0-5-5----5---5------------
  We all loved true. We will sail the salt sea o-ver, and we'll
```

```
   Am       F  G      C     Am       F        C
E ------------------------------------------------------------------
A --0----2---3--2------3---2-0-------0------------------------------
D 5-2----2---3--0---5--2---2-2---5---3-----5--2-------0-------------
G 5-2--------2--0---0--0-----2---5---2-----5--5----5--0-------------
  Return for shore, to see a-gain the girls we love, and the
```

```
       G          C
E ------------------------------------------------------------------
A ------------------------------------------------------------------
D 2-5--5--3---2-0---------------------------------------------------
G 5-5--0--0---0-0--5------------------------------------------------
  Holy Ground once more... FINE GIRL YOU ARE!
```

CHORUS

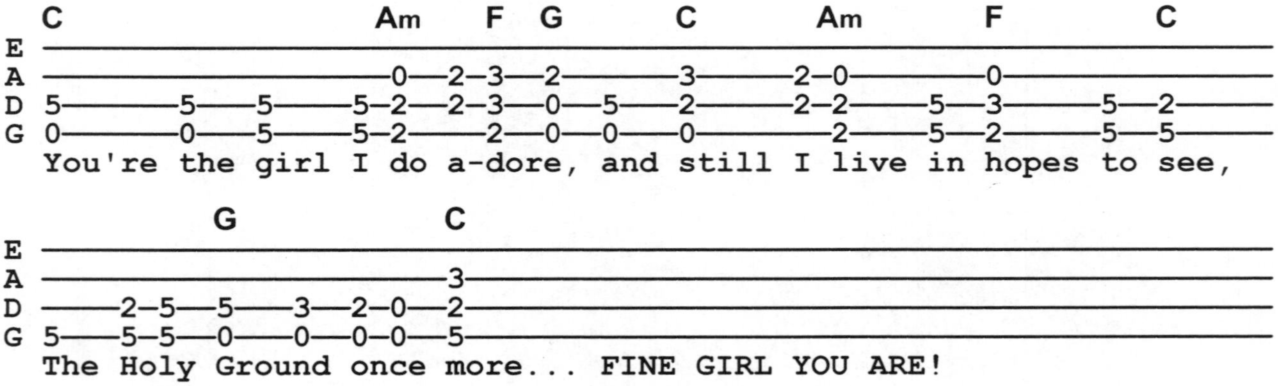

```
  C                 Am   F  G      C       Am       F        C
E ------------------------------------------------------------------
A -------------------0--2-3--2------3-----2-0-------0---------------
D 5-----5---5----5-2--2-3--0--5---2-----2-2----5--3------5--2-------
G 0-----0---5----5-2----2--0--0---0-------2----5--2------5--5-------
  You're the girl I do a-dore, and still I live in hopes to see,
```

```
          G           C
E ------------------------------------------------------------------
A ---------------------3--------------------------------------------
D ----2-5--5---3--2-0--2--------------------------------------------
G 5---5-5--0---0--0-0--5--------------------------------------------
  The Holy Ground once more... FINE GIRL YOU ARE!
```

See Chord Forms on Previous Page

The Holy Ground (continued)

Basic Melody
Key of G (Low)

```
  G                              D              G                                        D          G
E ---------------------------------------------------------------------------------------------------------
A ---------------------------------------------------------------------------------------------------------
D --------------------------0--0--------------------------------------0-------0-----------------------------
G 0-----2-----4----------------------5--4-2-0----0--2-4----------------------------------4--0--------------
  Fare thee well my lo-ve-l-y Dinah, a thousand times a-dieu,

                                Em                  C      D                      G
E ---------------------------------------------------------------------------------------------------------
A ---------------------------------------------------------------------------------------------------------
D ------------------0---0------0-2----4------4----5--5---4-----------2----2-----0-------------------------
G 4---4----------------------------------------------------------------------------------------------------
  For we're sailing a-way from the Holy Ground, and the girls

                        D                   G           D           G
E ---------------------------------------------------------------------------------------------------------
A ---------------------------------------------------------------------------------------------------------
D ------------------------------------------------0----0-------------------------------------0-------------
G 4--0---4-------2--------0--2--------4-------------------5--4-2-0-0------4--------------------------------
  We all loved true. We will sail the salt sea o-ver, and we'll

    Em              C  D          G        Em            C              G
E ---------------------------------------------------------------------------------------------------------
A ---------------------------------------------------------------------------------------------------------
D 0-2-----4----5---4----0---5-----4-2-------0------2---------0---------------------------------------------
G --------------------------------------------------------------4---------0-----2--------------------------
  Return for shore, to see a-gain the girls we love, and the

           D                  G
E ---------------------------------------------------------------------------------------------------------
A ---------------------------------------------------------------------------------------------------------
D ---0--0--------------------------------------------------------------------------------------------------
G 4--------5----4-2---0------------------------------------------------------------------------------------
  Holy Ground once more... FINE GIRL YOU ARE!
```

CHORUS

```
  G                        Em     C   D          G          Em           C             G
E ---------------------------------------------------------------------------------------------------------
A ---------------------------------------------------------------------------------------------------------
D 0---------0----0-------0-2---4-5---4---0----5---------4-2-------0---2---------0--------------------------
G ---------------------------------------------------------------------------------------4-----------------
  You're the girl I do a-dore, and still I live in hopes to see,

                D                G
E ---------------------------------------------------------------------------------------------------------
A ---------------------------------------------------------------------------------------------------------
D ------------0---0----------------------------------------------------------------------------------------
G 0---4-------------------5---4-2---0----------------------------------------------------------------------
  The Holy Ground once more... FINE GIRL YOU ARE!
```

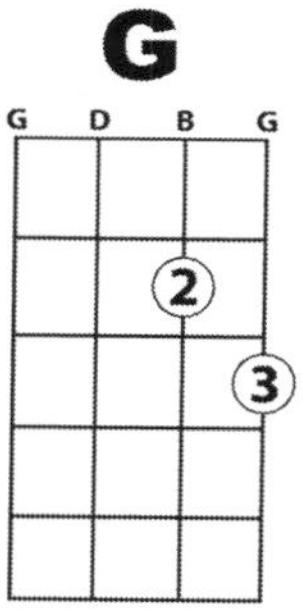

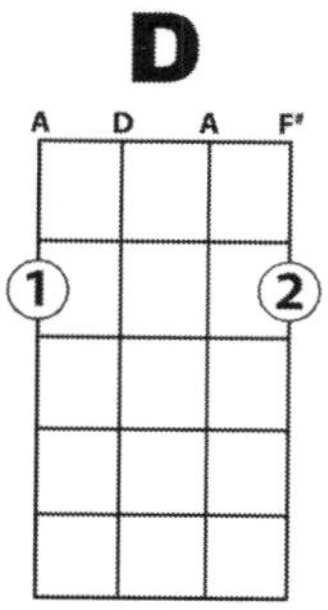

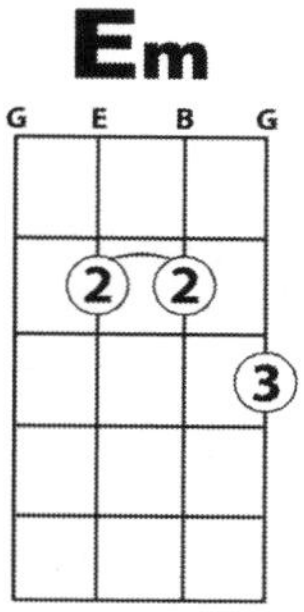

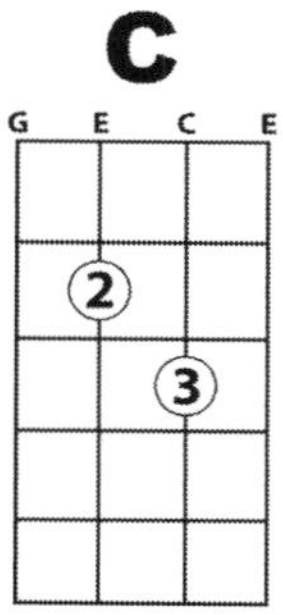

The Holy Ground (continued)

Basic Melody
Key of G (High)

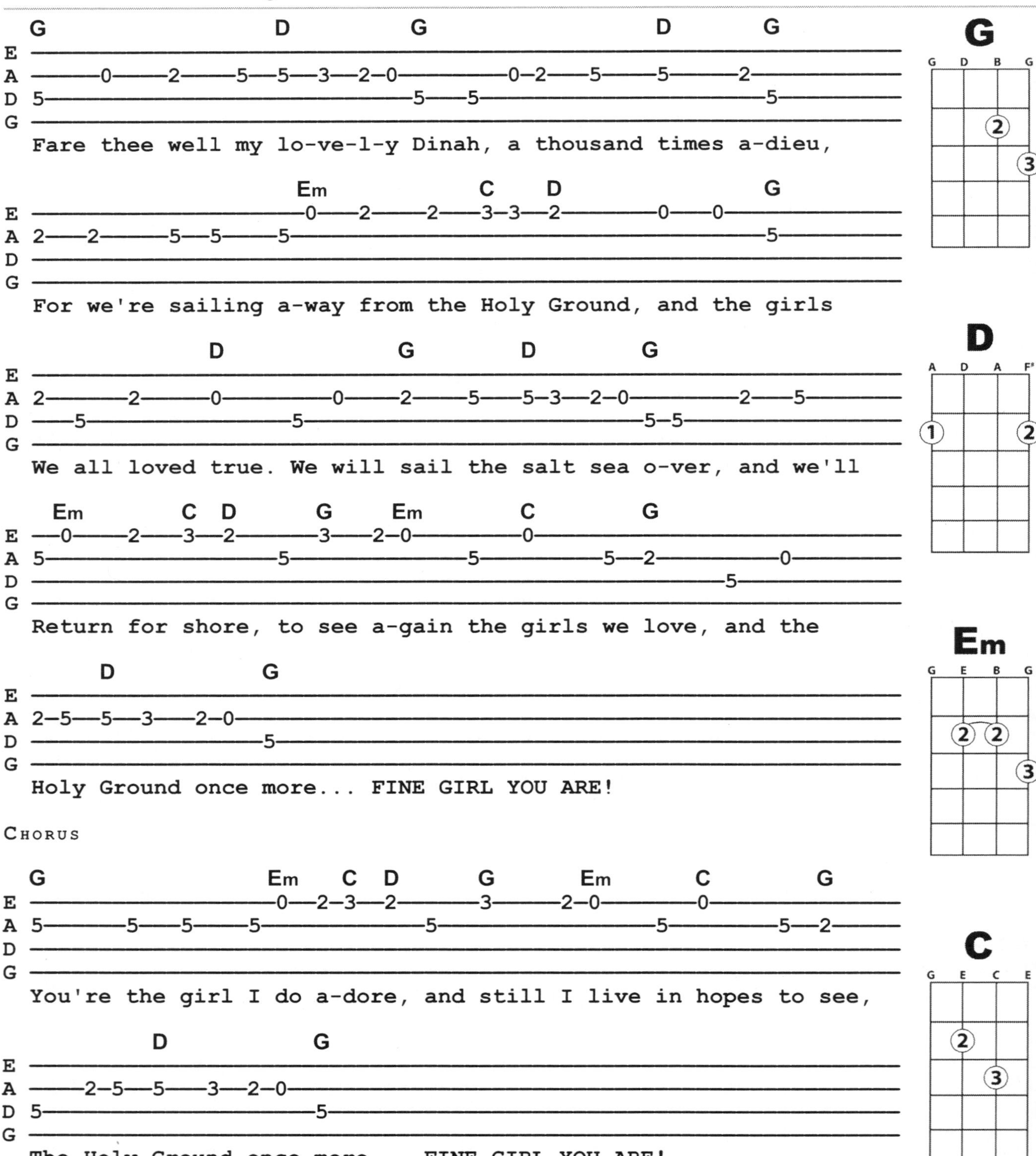

The Holy Ground (continued)

Melody & Chords
Key of G (High)

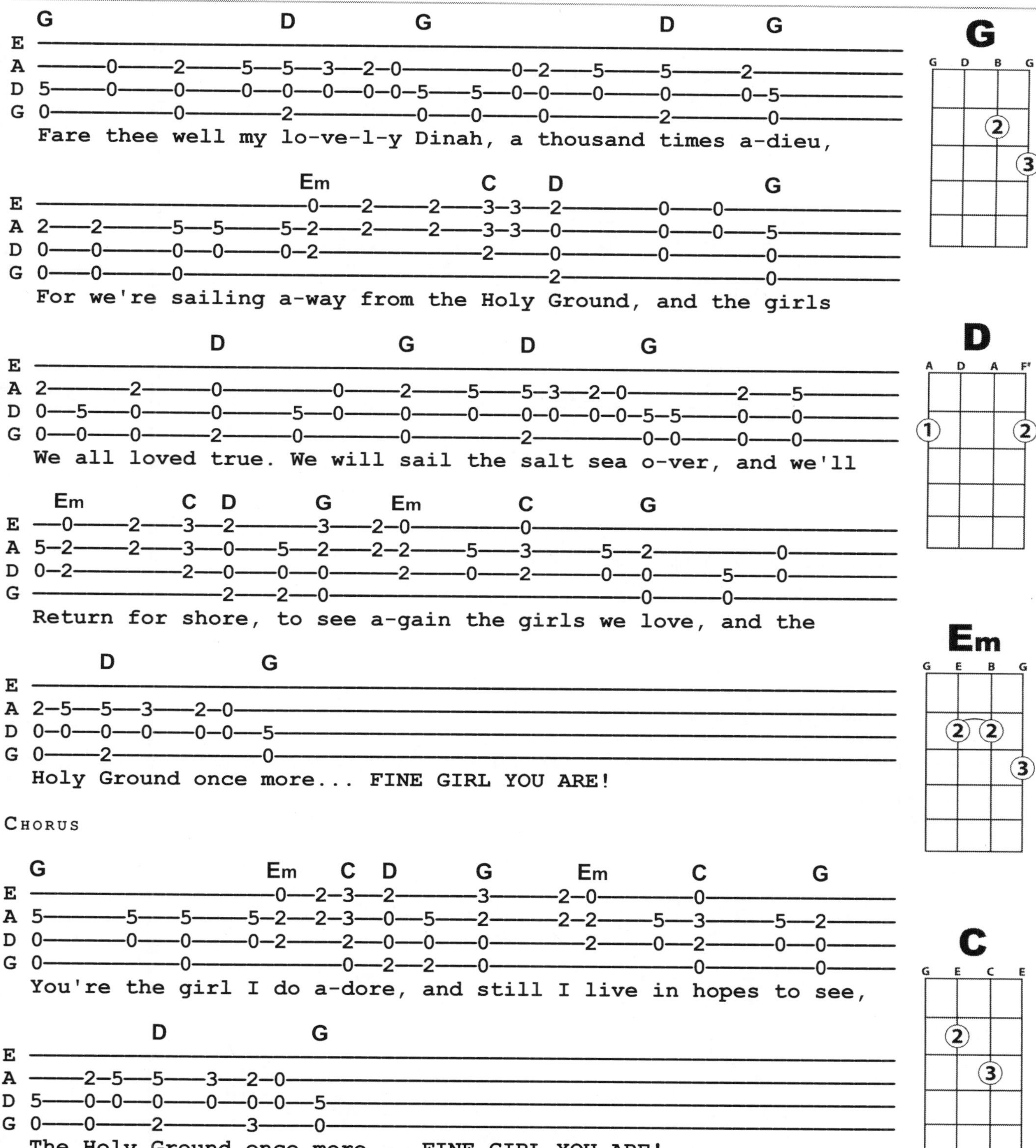

Homeward Bound

Basic Melody

Key of C (Low)

This was one of the most popular of the shanties that sailors would sing when heading homewards. According to tradition, it was most often sung at the windlass or the capstan on the ship. Like many shanties it tells the tale of the sailors going ashore with pockets full of pay, and quickly spending it all and having to go to sea again. The words of the final chorus were often changed to "Outward Bound" instead of homeward bound, to reflect this.

Words and Music

Traditional

```
  C                                        G7       C         F
E ----------------------------------------------------------------------------------
A ------------------------------------------------------------0--------3----0-------
D 5--3----2------2---2----2-----------0-----------------5---------3-----------------
G -------------------------------5---------5-5--------------------------------------
  To the West Indies docks I bid a-dieu, to lovely Sal and

       C               G7                           C
E ----------------------------------------------------------------------------------
A 0-----------------------------------0---------------------------------------------
D -----5------5------2----3-----------3------------3----2-------2-5-----------------
G ----------------------------------------------------------------------------------
  Charming Sue; our ship's unmoored, our sails unfurled,

        Am                          F       G
E ----------------------------------------------------------------------------------
A -------3--------------------------------------------------------------------------
D 5-------------------5--2----------3-3-0-------------------------------------------
G -----------------------------5------------4---------------------------------------
  We're bound to plow this watery world.
```

CHORUS

```
  G  C          G          C          F          G         C
E ----------------------------------------------------------------------------------
A -----------------------------------------3---0------------------------------------
D -----------------------------0-------2-5----------3-------5---5-------------------
G 0--5---5-------4-------------------5--------------------------------5-------------
  Hurrah we're homeward bound, hurrah we're homeward bound!
```

Chord Forms

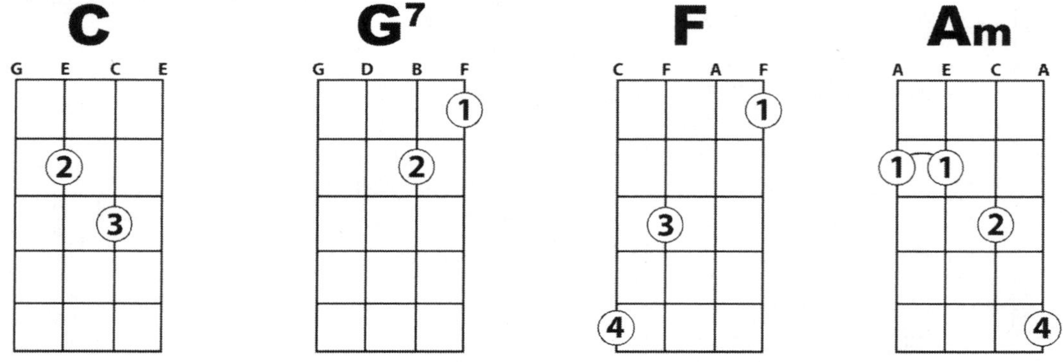

See Additional Verses on Next Page

Homeward Bound (continued)

Melody & Chords
Key of C (Low)

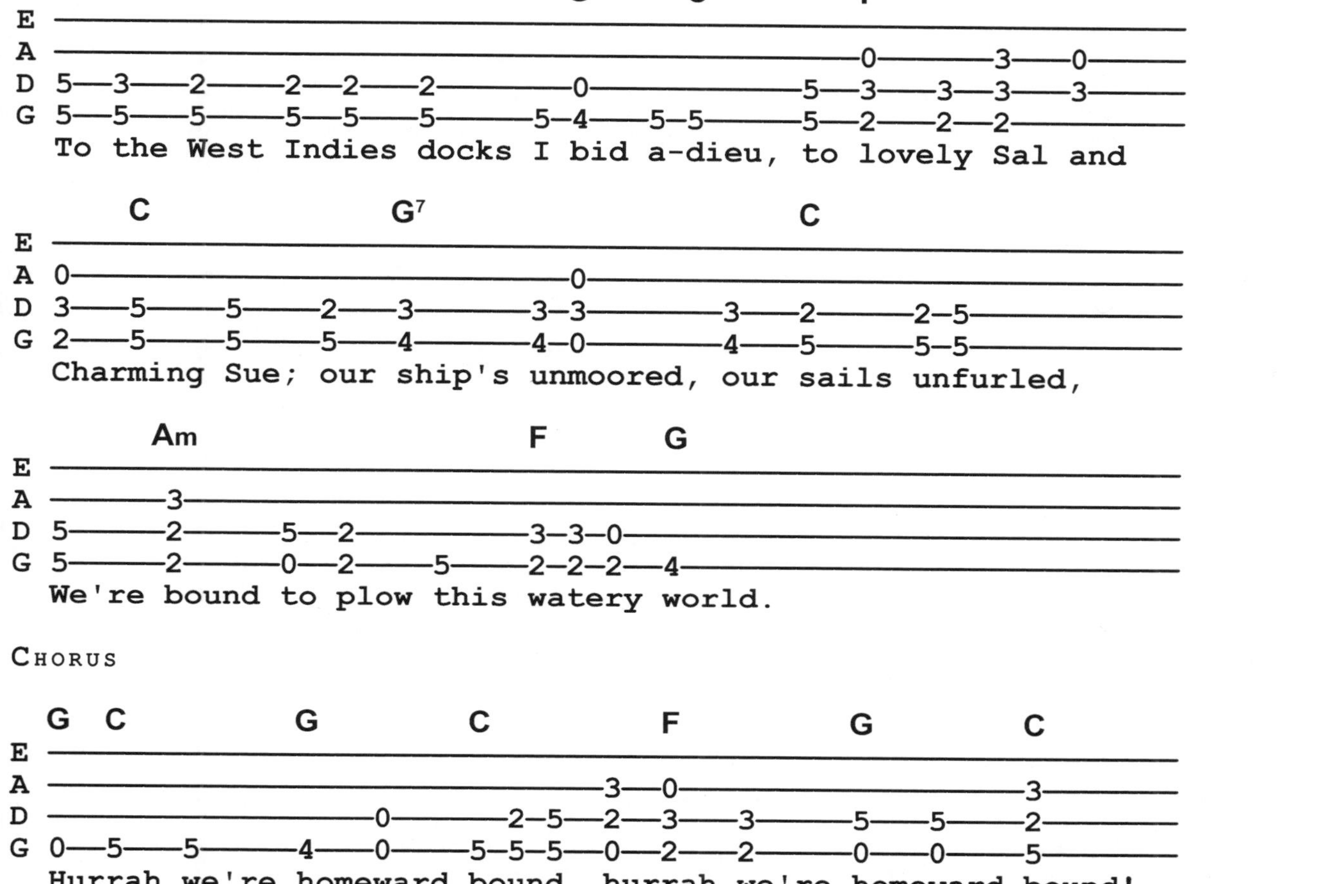

Additional Verses

The wind blew a gale from the sou'sou'east,
Our ship did make nine knots at least,
Our purser well our wants supplied:
While we have grub we will never say die.

When we arrive at Malabar,
Or any port that's twice as far,
Our thundering great guns we'll let fly:
While we have shot we'll never say die.

When we arrive at the West Indies docks,
The girls of the town come down in flocks,
And if you listen you will hear them say,
"Here comes our Jack with three months' pay."

When we arrive at the Dog and Bell,
Where the best of liquors they do sell,
In comes the landlord with a smile,
"Come drink my boys, it's worth your while."

Now my money's all gone and spent,
There's none to be borrowed and none to be lent;
In comes the landlord with a frown,
It's "Rise up, Jack, let John sit down!"

Homeward Bound (continued)

Basic Melody
Key of C (High)

```
  C                                    G7     C         F
E 3--1---0----0--0---0-------------------------------3--5---1--8---5-----
A ------------------------------------3-5---3-3--------------------------
D -----------------------------------------------------------------------
G -----------------------------------------------------------------------
  To the West Indies docks I bid a-dieu, to lovely Sal and
```

```
      C              G7                        C
E 5---3----3----0---1------1-5-------1---0-----0-3------
A ------------------------------------------------------
D ------------------------------------------------------
G ------------------------------------------------------
  Charming Sue; our ship's unmoored, our sails unfurled,
```

```
       Am                       F      G
E 3----8-----3--0--------------1-1----------------------
A --------------------3-----------5--2------------------
D ------------------------------------------------------
G ------------------------------------------------------
  We're bound to plow this watery world.
```

Chorus

```
  G  C          G         C        F        G       C
E --------------------------0-3--8-5---1------3---3-------
A ---3---3------2---5-----3-----------------------------3-
D 5-------------------------------------------------------
G --------------------------------------------------------
  Hurrah we're homeward bound, hurrah we're homeward bound!
```

Chord Forms

C

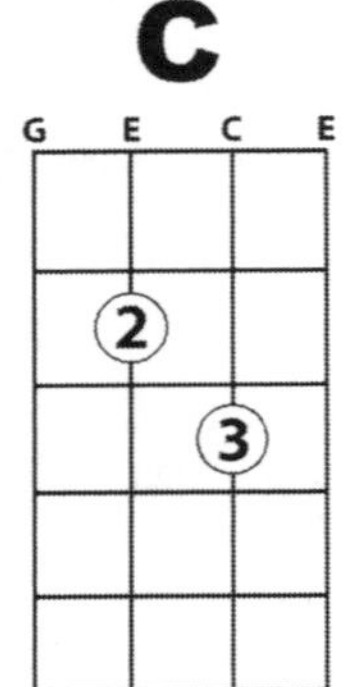

G7

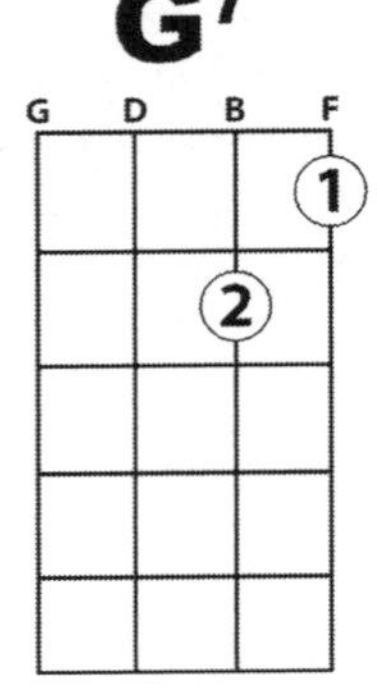

F

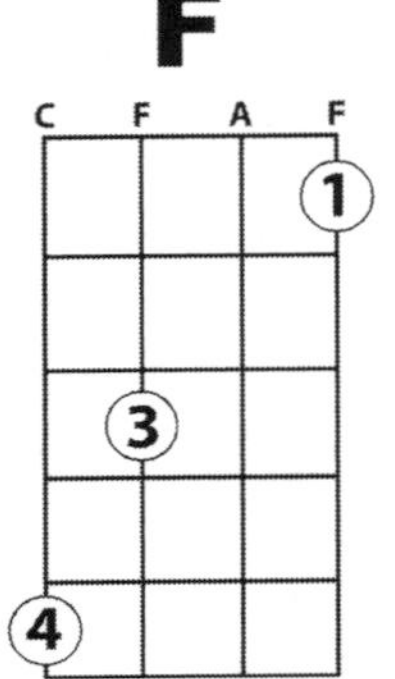

Am

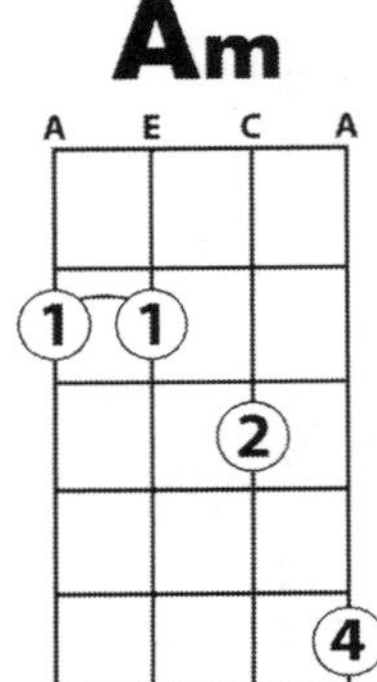

Homeward Bound (continued)

Melody & Chords
Key of C (High)

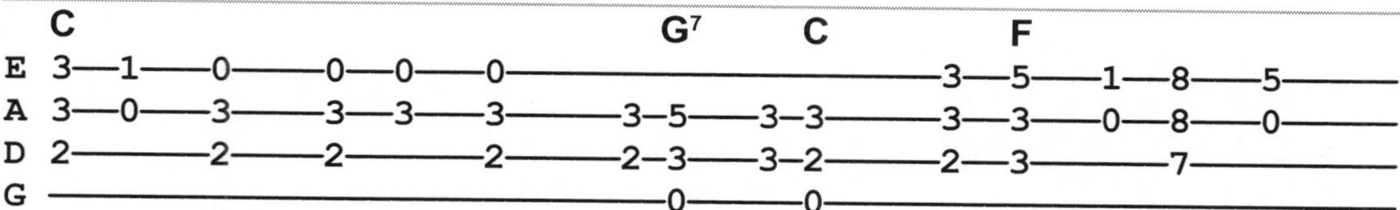

To the West Indies docks I bid a-dieu, to lovely Sal and

```
     C               G7                   C
E 5——3———3———0——1————1–5———————1——0————0–3——————
A 3——3———3———3——2————2–0———————2——3————3–3——————
D 3——————2———2——0———————————————0——2——————2——————
G ——————————————————————————————————————————————
```

Charming Sue; our ship's unmoored, our sails unfurled,

```
      Am                      F     G
E 3————8—————3——0—————————————1–1——————————————
A 3————8—————3——0————3————————0–0–5——2——————————
D 2—————————————2————2————3———————3——0——————————
G ———————————————————————————————————0——————————
```

We're bound to plow this watery world.

Chorus

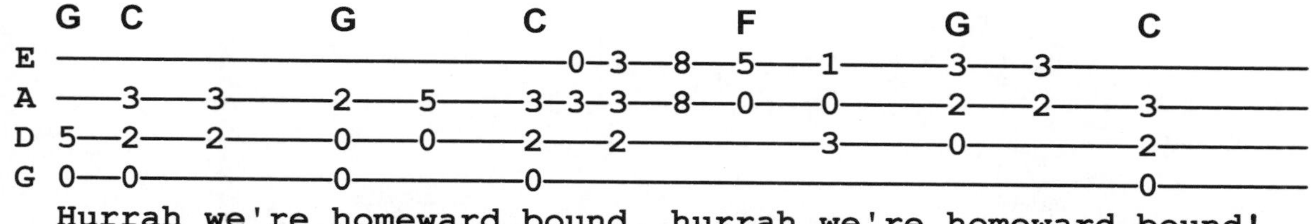

Hurrah we're homeward bound, hurrah we're homeward bound!

Chord Forms

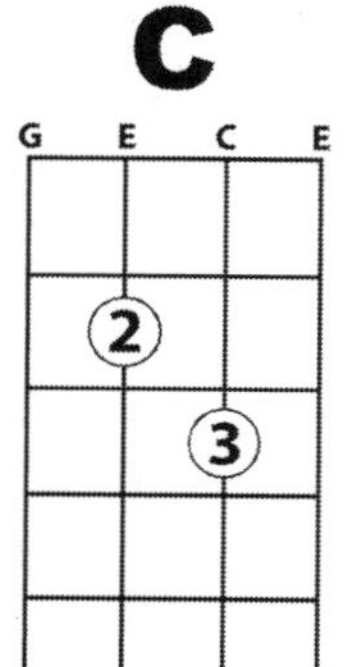

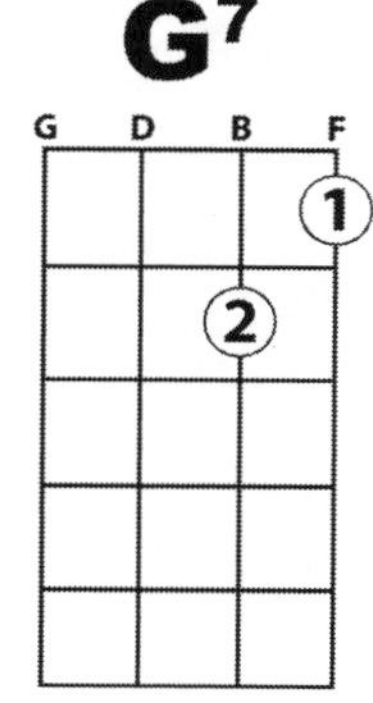

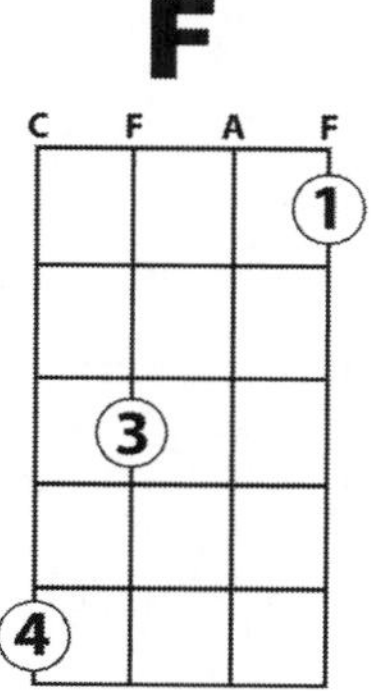

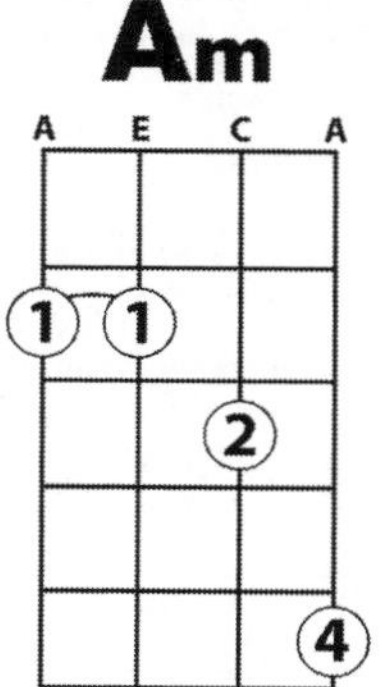

Homeward Bound (continued)

Basic Melody
Key of G

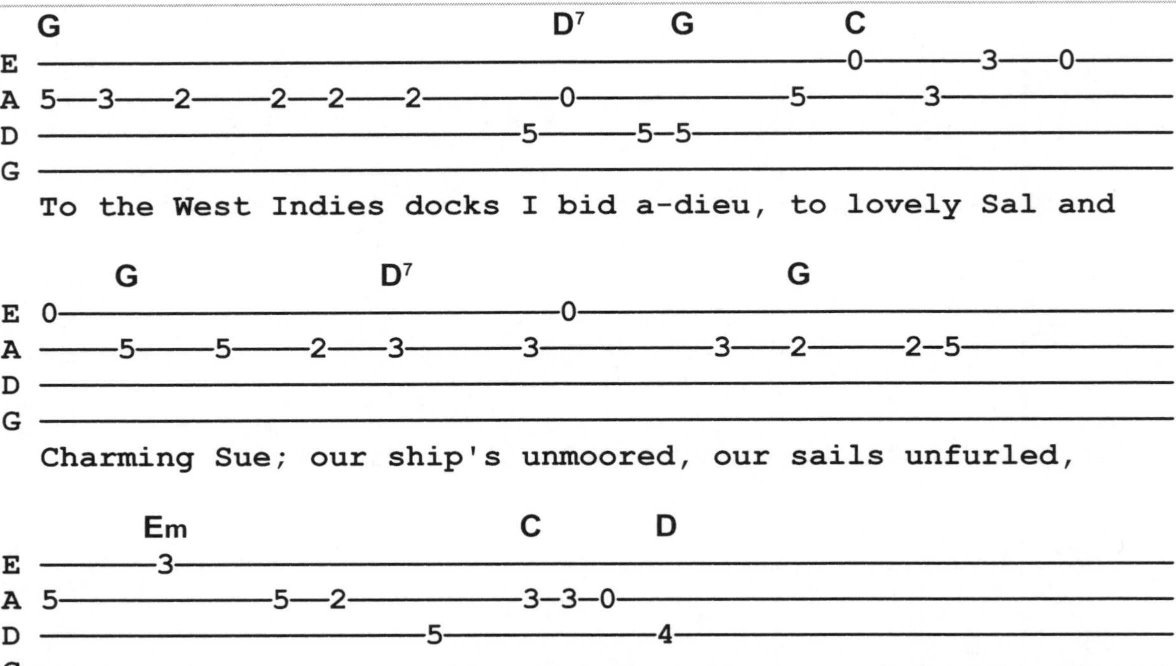

Chorus

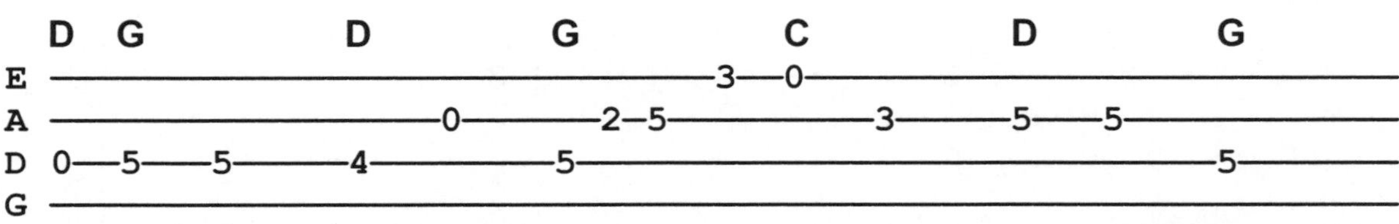

Chord Forms

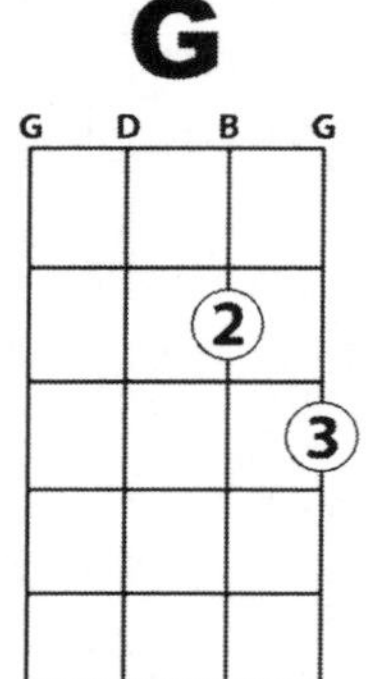

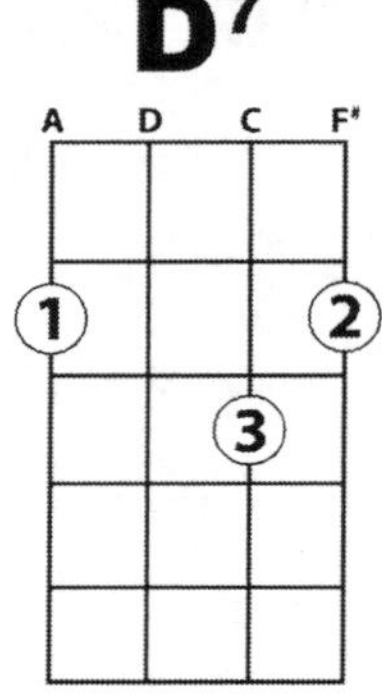

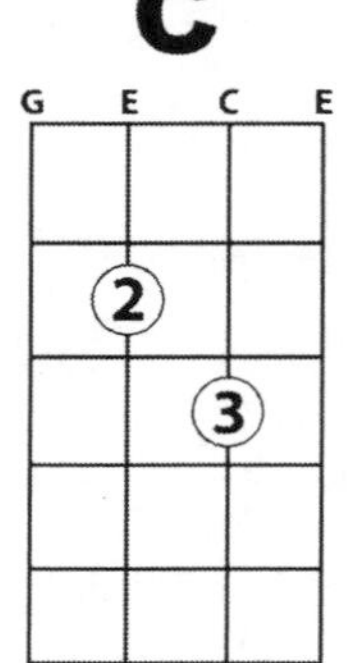

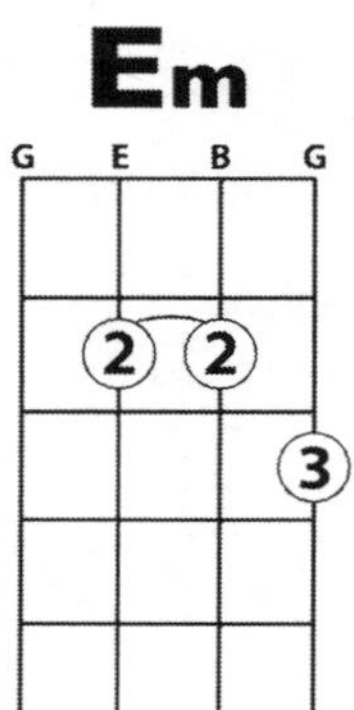

Homeward Bound (continued)

Melody & Chords
Key of G

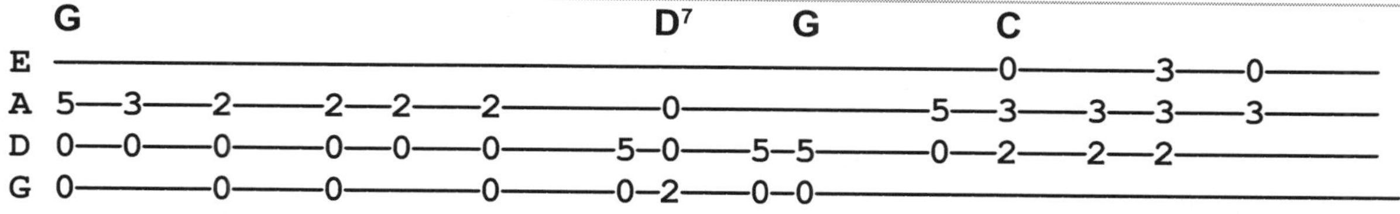

To the West Indies docks I bid a-dieu, to lovely Sal and

```
    G              D7                     G
E 0———————————————————————————0——————————————————————
A 3——5———5————2——3——————3—0————————3——2—————2—5——————
D 2——0———0————0——0——————0—0————————0——0—————0—0——————
G ———————0———————2—————————————————2——0—————0————————
```

Charming Sue; our ship's unmoored, our sails unfurled,

```
       Em                    C      D
E ———————3——————————————————————————————————————————
A 5——————2—————5——2————————3—3—0————————————————————
D 0——————2—————0——2————5———2—2—2——4—————————————————
G 0———————————————0————0———0————0——2————————————————
```

We're bound to plow this watery world.

CHORUS

```
  D  G        D        G        C        D       G
E ——————————————————————————3——0————————————————————
A ————————————————0—————2—5—2——3———3————5———5———————
D 0——5———5————4———0—————5—0—0——0—2———2————0———0————5———
G 2——0———0————2———2—————0———————————————————2————————0———
```

Hurrah we're homeward bound, hurrah we're homeward bound!

Chord Forms

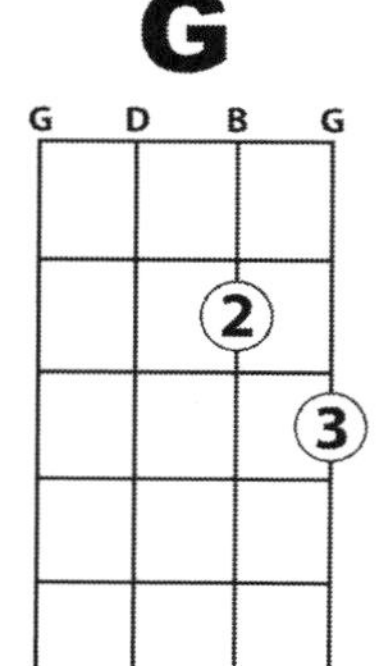

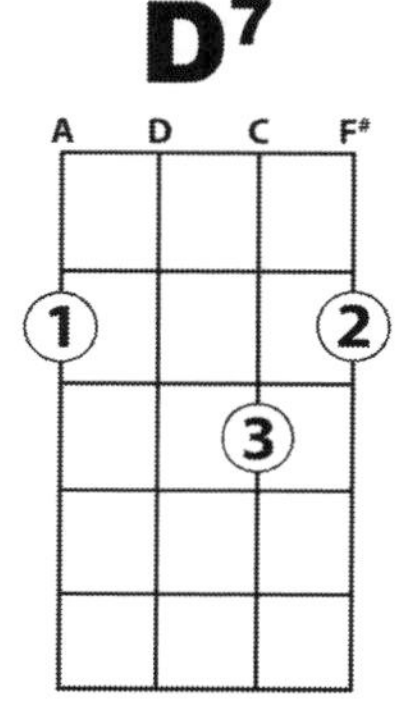

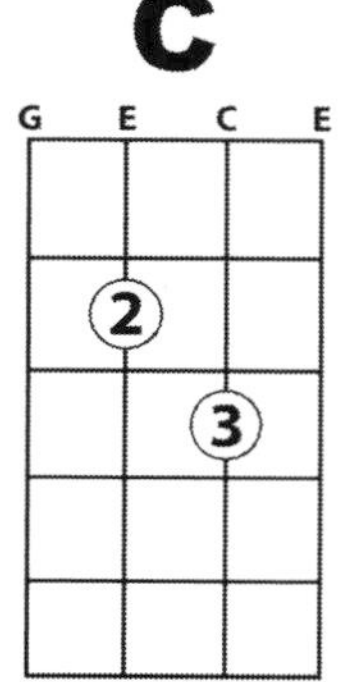

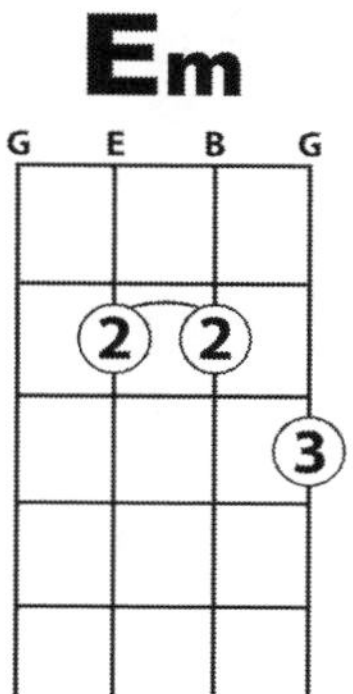

The Irish Rover

Basic Melody

Key of C

This lively song tells the story of the mythical ship the Irish Rover and its crew, and its sad demise. It is a good example of the Irish tendency towards exaggeration when spinning a tale. This song has been recorded at one time or another by most of the well-known Irish bands, including the Clancy Brothers and Tommy Makem, and also (not surprisingly) by the band that took their name from the song: The Irish Rovers.

Words and Music

Traditional

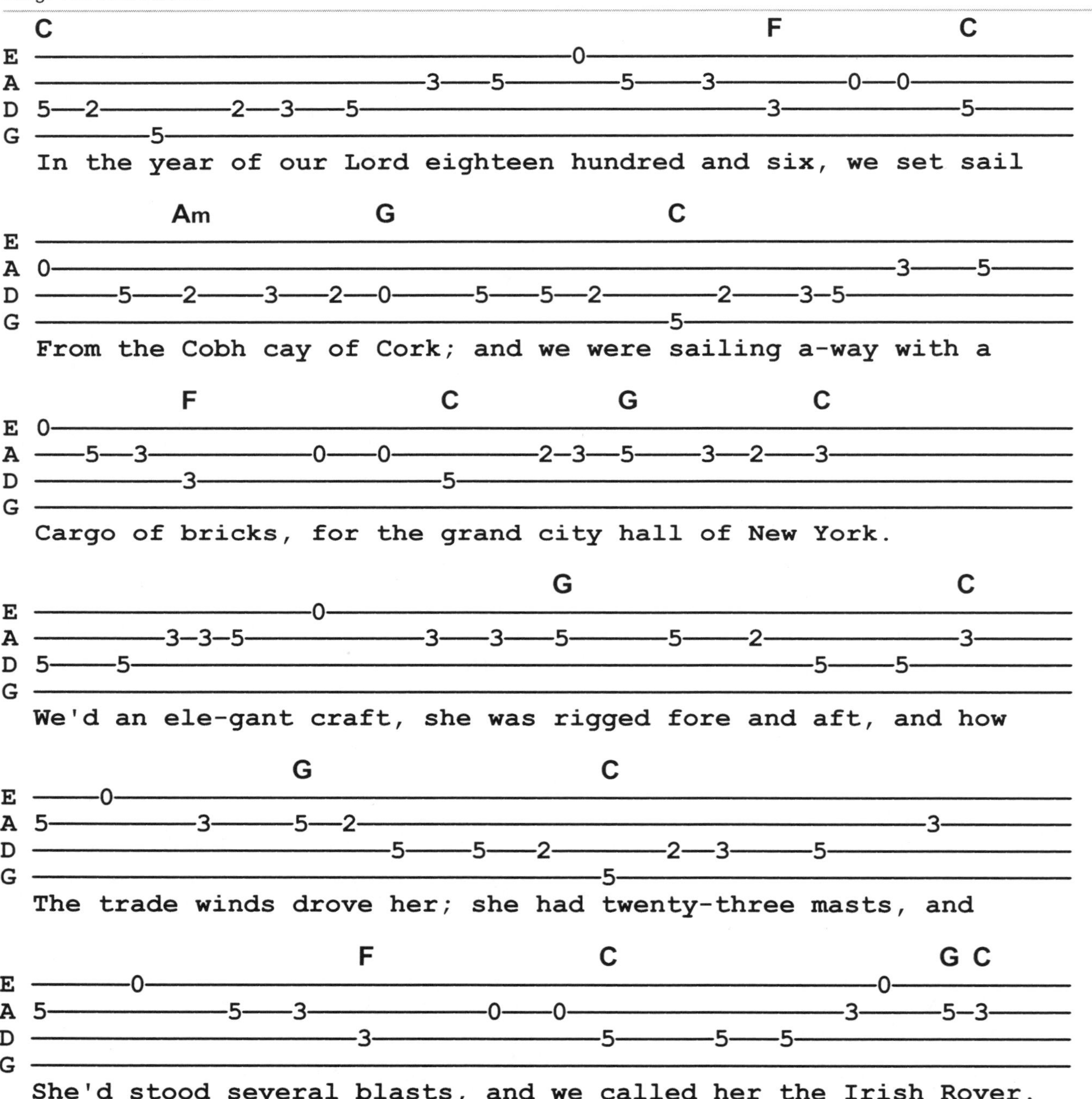

See Chord Forms and Additional Verses on Next Page

The Irish Rover (continued)

Chord Forms and Additional Verses

Chord Forms

C

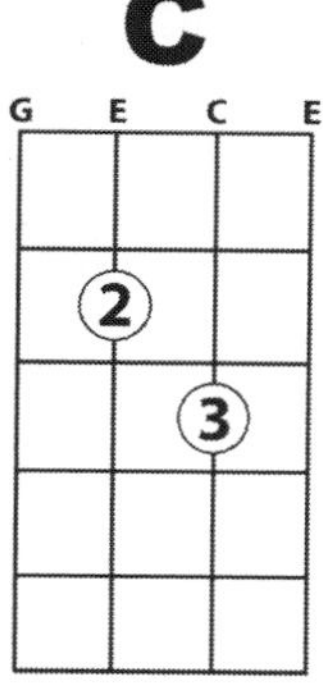

F

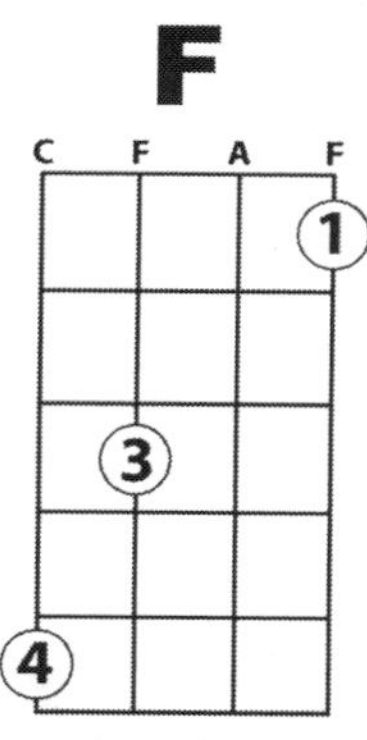

Am

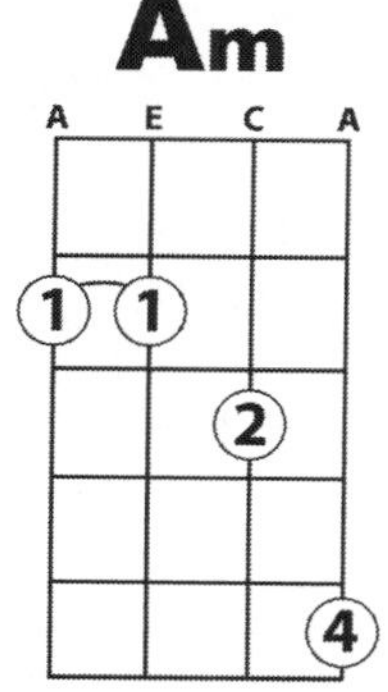

G

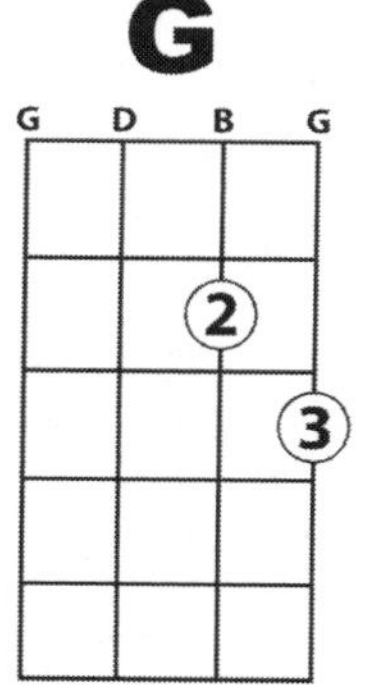

Additional Verses

We had one million bags of the best Sligo rags,
We had two million barrels of stone.
And we had three million bales of old nanny goats' tails
We had four million barrels of bone.
We had five million hogs, and six million dogs,
And seven million barrels of porter.
We had eight million sides of old blind horses' hides,
In the hold of the Irish Rover!

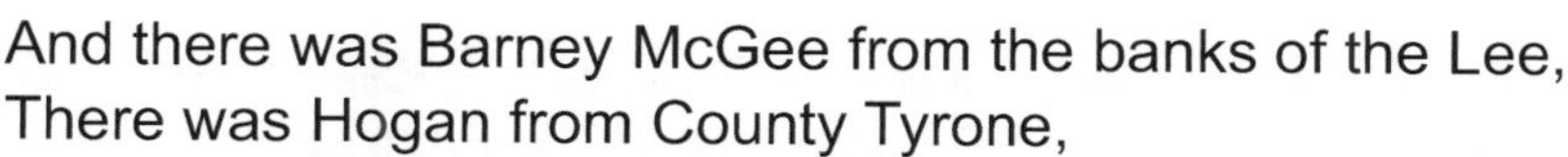

And there was Barney McGee from the banks of the Lee,
There was Hogan from County Tyrone,
And there was Johnny McGirk, who was scared stiff of work,
And a chap from Westmeath named Malone.
There was Slugger O'Toole who was drunk as a rule,
And fightin' Charlie Boyle from Dover,
And yer man Mick McGann, from the banks of the Ban,
Was the skipper of the Irish Rover.

We had sailed seven years when the measles broke out,
And the ship lost her way in a fog (GREAT FOG!)
And the whole of the crew was reduced unto two,
Just meself and the captain's old dog.
And then the ship struck a rock, oh Lord what a shock,
I nearly tumbled over... turned nine times around,
And the poor old dog was drowned...
I'm the last of the Irish Rover!

The Irish Rover (continued)

Melody & Chords
Key of C

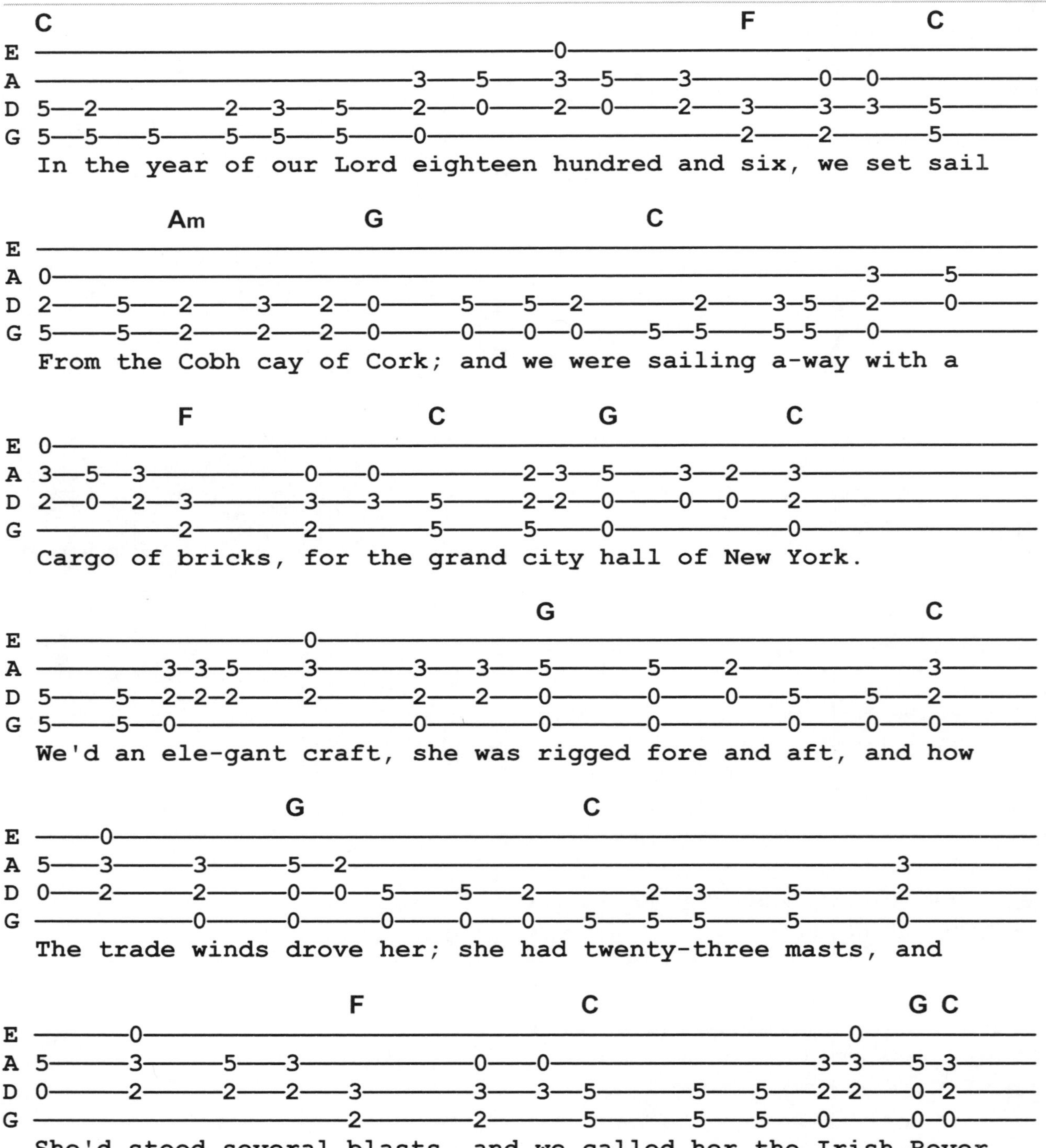

See Chord Forms on Previous Page

The Irish Rover (continued)

Basic Melody
Key of G (Low)

```
  G                                                          C              G
E ------------------------------------------------------------------------------
A -----------------------------------0-----2--0---------------------------------
D 0------------------------0-----5------------------5----------2--2---0--------
G ---4---0-----4--5------------------------------------------5------------------
  In the year of our Lord eighteen hundred and six, we set sail
```

```
           Em             D                    G
E ------------------------------------------------------------------------------
A ------------------------------------------------------------------------0-----
D 2----0--------------------------0----0------------------------0---5-----------
G ---------4----5---4--2-------------------4-----0---4-----5--------------------
  From the Cobh cay of Cork; and we were sailing a-way with a
```

```
            C                     G            D           G
E ------------------------------------------------------------------------------
A 2--0-----------------------------------------0--------------------------------
D --------5-------------2---2----0------4--5-------------5---4----5-------------
G ----------------5-------------------------------------------------------------
  Cargo of bricks, for the grand city hall of New York.
```

```
                                             D                            G
E ------------------------------------------------------------------------------
A -------------------0------2---------------0--------0--------------------------
D 0-----0--5--5------------------5----5-----------------------------------------
G -----------------------------------------------------------4----0-----0----5--
  We'd an ele-gant craft, she was rigged fore and aft, and how
```

```
                    D                     G
E ------------------------------------------------------------------------------
A 0---2-------------0-----------------------------------------------------------
D -------------5---------4---0------0-------------------------0-------5---------
G ----------------------------------------4----0----4---5-----------------------
  The trade winds drove her; she had twenty-three masts, and
```

```
                         C                   G                         D G
E ------------------------------------------------------------------------------
A 0------2-------0-----------------------------------------------2----0---------
D -----------------------5------------2---2---0-------0----0----5---------5-----
G ----------------------------5-------------------------------------------------
  She'd stood several blasts, and we called her the Irish Rover.
```

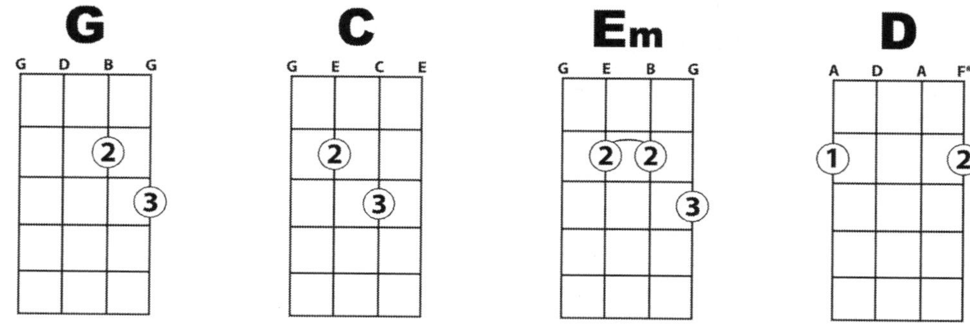

The Irish Rover (continued)

Basic Melody
Key of G (High)

```
  G                                              C           G
E ---------------------------3---5----7--5----3-------------0--0--------------
A 5--2-------------2--3--5--------------------------3--------------5----------
D --------5-------------------------------------------------------------------
G ----------------------------------------------------------------------------
  In the year of our Lord eighteen hundred and six, we set sail
```

```
          Em          D                G
E 0---------------------------------------------------------3-----5-----
A -----5---2----3---2--0-----5---5--2-----------2-----3-5---------------
D ----------------------------------------5-----------------------------
G ----------------------------------------------------------------------
  From the Cobh cay of Cork; and we were sailing a-way with a
```

```
          C                 G          D         G
E 7--5--3-----------0---0-----------2-3--5----3--2---3-------------------
A ----------3-------------------5----------------------------------------
D -----------------------------------------------------------------------
G -----------------------------------------------------------------------
  Cargo of bricks, for the grand city hall of New York.
```

```
                                     D                             G
E ---------3-3-5-----7-------3----3---5--------5-----2----------------3--------
A 5----5-----------------------------------------------------5----5------------
D -----------------------------------------------------------------------------
G -----------------------------------------------------------------------------
  We'd an ele-gant craft, she was rigged fore and aft, and how
```

```
                   D                 G
E 5---7------3-----5--2----------------------------------------3--------
A -----------------------5----5---2-----------2---3------5--------------
D -----------------------------------5----------------------------------
G ----------------------------------------------------------------------
  The trade winds drove her; she had twenty-three masts, and
```

```
                          C                   G                     D G
E 5------7------5----3-----------------0---0-------------------3--7---5-3-----
A ------------------------3-------------------5--------5---5------------------
D ----------------------------------------------------------------------------
G ----------------------------------------------------------------------------
  She'd stood several blasts, and we called her the Irish Rover.
```

Chord Forms

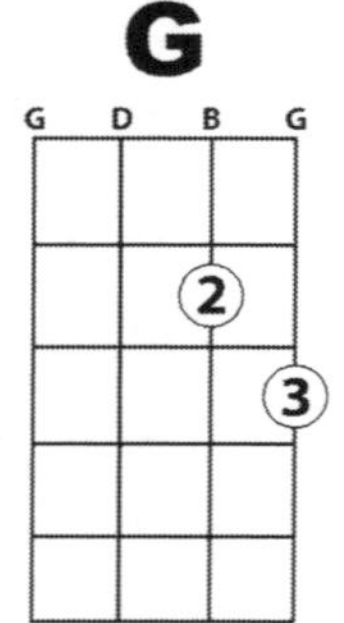

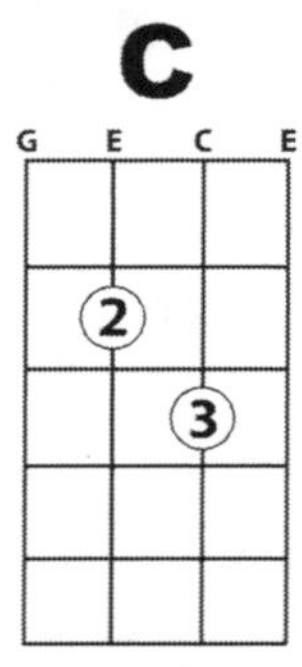

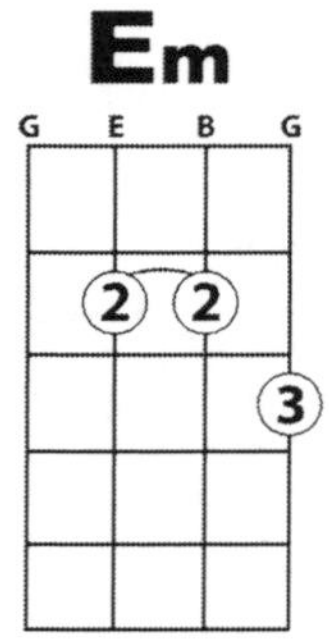

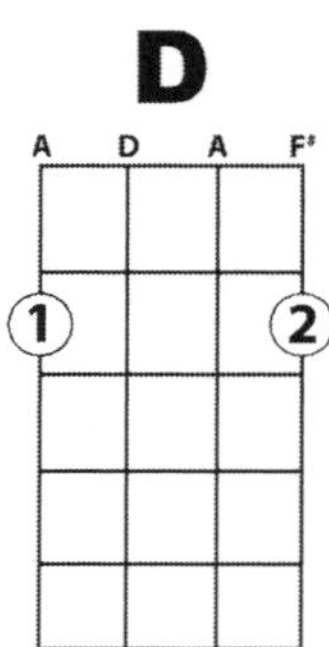

The Irish Rover (continued)

Melody & Chords
Key of G (High)

```
   G                                                C          G
E ──────────────────────────3──5───7──5───3─────────────0──0──────────
A 5──2──────────2──3───5────2──5───5──5───2──3──────3──3──5──────────
D 0──0───5──────0──0───0────0──────5─────────2──────2─────0──────────
G 0──────0──────0──────0─────────────────────0────────────0──────────
  In the year of our Lord eighteen hundred and six, we set sail
```

```
          Em           D                  G
E 0──────────────────────────────────────────────────────3─────5──────
A 2───5──2───3──2──0─────5───5──2──────────2───3─5──2─────5──────
D ────0──2───2──2──0─────0───0──0───5──0───────0─0──0────────────
G ───────0─────────2────────────────0──────────0─────────────────
  From the Cobh cay of Cork; and we were sailing a-way with a
```

```
          C                  G          D          G
E 7──5──3────────────0──0───────────2─3─5─────3──2──3──────────────
A 5──5──2──3─────────3──3───5───────0─2─0─────0──0──2──────────────
D 5────────2─────────2──────0───────────0─────0──0──0──────────────
G ─────────0────────────────0─────────────────────────────────────
  Cargo of bricks, for the grand city hall of New York.
```

```
                                       D                        G
E ──────────3─3─5────7──────3───3───5──────5───2──────────────────3────
A 5────5──2─2─5────5──────2───2───0──────0───0───5────5────2────
D 0────0──0────────5──────0───────0──────0───0───0────0────0────
G 0──────────────────────────────────────────────2────2─────────
  We'd an ele-gant craft, she was rigged fore and aft, and how
```

```
                   D                      G
E 5──7───────3───5──2─────────────────────────────────────3──────
A 5──5───────2───0──0──5────5───2───────2──3─────5────────2──────
D ───5───────────0─────0────0───0───5───0──0─────0────────0──────
G ─────────────────────2────2───────0────────────0───────────────
  The trade winds drove her; she had twenty-three masts, and
```

```
                       C                G                   D G
E 5────7────5──3───────────────0──0─────────────────3─7────5─3────
A 5────5────5──2───3───────────3──3───5────5───5───2─5────0─2────
D ─────5───────────2───────────2──────0────0───0───0─5────0─0────
G ─────────────────0──────────────────0────0─────────────────────
  She'd stood several blasts, and we called her the Irish Rover.
```

Chord Forms

G
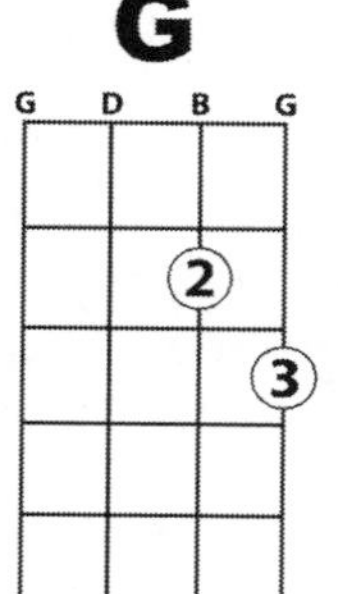

C
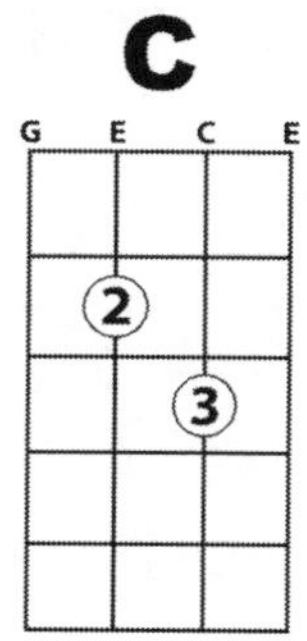

Em
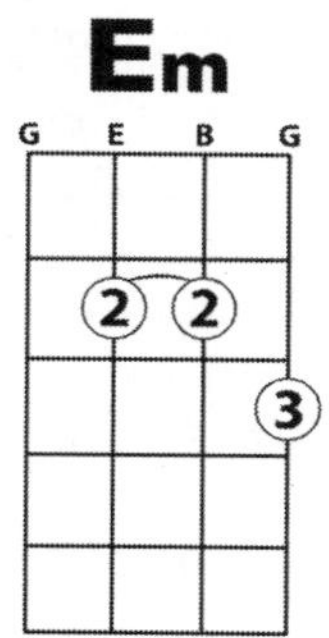

D
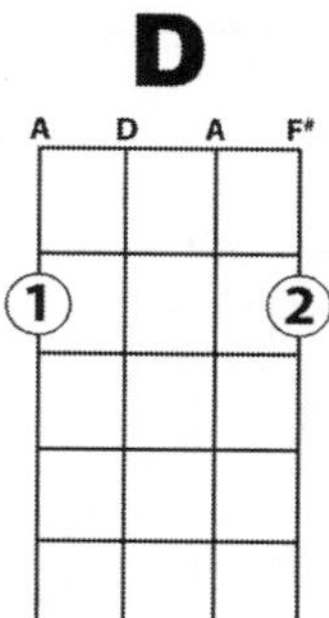

The John B. Sails

Basic Melody
Key of C (Low)

This old folk song of the sea comes down from the Caribbean, specifically around the port of Nassau in the Bahamas. It has been recorded many times over the years, with the best-known version undoubtedly being that recorded by the Beach Boys in 1966. The song tells the tale of a young sailor and his grandfather whose time ashore isn't going so great, and who aren't all that happy with their ship and its crew.

Words and Music

Traditional

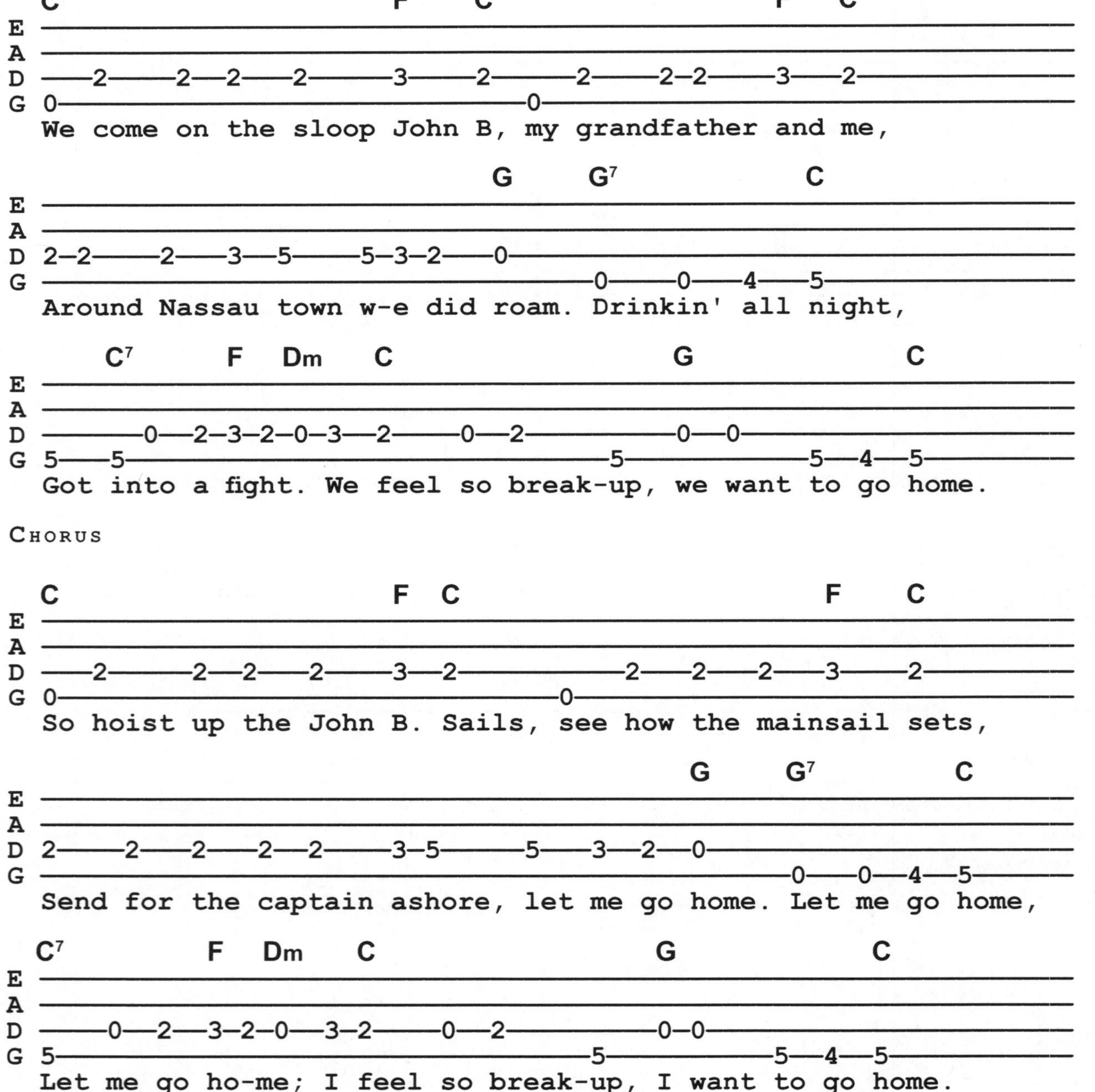

See Chord Forms and Additional Verses on Next Page

The John B. Sails (continued)

Chord Forms and Additional Verses

Chord Forms

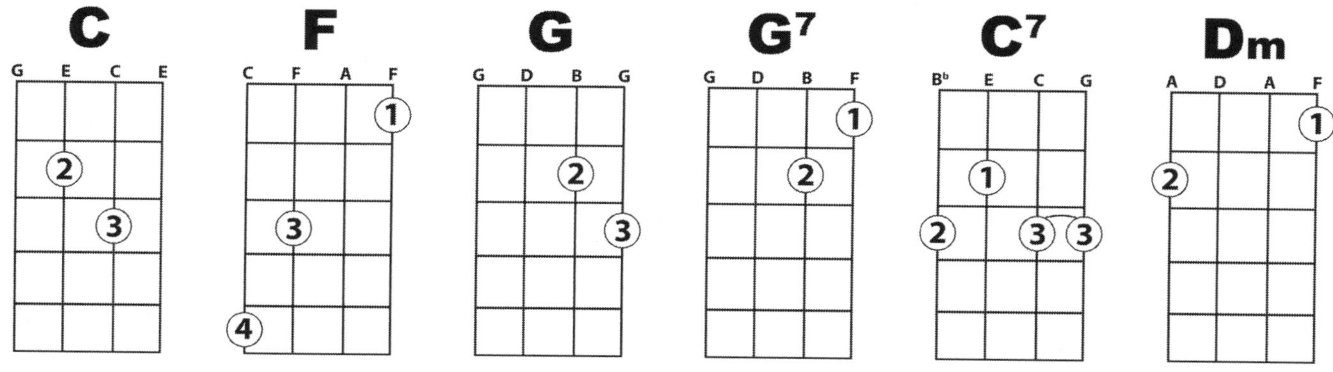

Additional Verses

The first mate he got drunk,
Broke in the captain's trunk,
Constable come aboard, take him away.
Mr. John Stone, leave me alone,
I feel so break-up, I want to go home.

The poor cook got the fits,
Throw away all of my grits,
Captain's pig done eat up all o' my corn.
Lemme go home, I want to go home,
I feel so break-up, I want to go home.

Steamboat go by steam,
Sailboat go by sail,
My girl's hat 'ain't got no tail.
Lemme go home, I want to go home,
I feel so break-up, I want to go home.

Send all the things from ashore,
Let all the breezes blow,
I'm so sorry that I can longer stay,
Good-by to you, tra-la-la-lu,
This is the worst trip since I was born.

The John B. Sails (continued)

Basic Melody
Key of C (High)

```
  C                        F    C                      F    C
E ——0————0—0———0—————1————0—————0—————0-0————1———0————————————
A ————————————————————————————————————————————————————————————
D 5————————————————————————————5——————————————————————————————
G ————————————————————————————————————————————————————————————
  We come on the sloop John B, my grandfather and me,
```

```
                                  G      G7            C
E 0—0————0———1——3————3—1—0————————————————————————————————————
A —————————————————————————————5———————————————2———3——————————
D ————————————————————————————————————5————5——————————————————
G ————————————————————————————————————————————————————————————
  Around Nassau town w-e did roam. Drinkin' all night,
```

```
        C7        F   Dm     C                        G            C
E ——————————————0—1—0———1——0——————0—————————————————————————————————
A 3———3—5——————————————5——————————5————————3———5——5————3——2——3——————
D ——————————————————————————————————————————————————————————————————
G ——————————————————————————————————————————————————————————————————
  Got into a fight. We feel so break-up, we want to go home.
```

CHORUS

```
  C                        F   C                            F     C
E ——0——————0——0———0———————1——0————————————0————0———0———1—————0———————
A ——————————————————————————————————————————————————————————————————
D 5——————————————————————————————5——————————————————————————————————
G ——————————————————————————————————————————————————————————————————
  So hoist up the John B. Sails, see how the mainsail sets,
```

```
                                                G      G7         C
E 0————0———0————0——0—————1—3——————3———1——0——————————————————————————
A ——————————————————————————————————————————————5———————————2———3———
D ————————————————————————————————————————————————————5————5————————
G ——————————————————————————————————————————————————————————————————
  Send for the captain ashore, let me go home. Let me go home,
```

```
  C7            F   Dm     C                        G            C
E ——————————0———1—0——————1—0——————————0———————————————————————————————
A 3———5——————————————5————————————5————————3———5—5————3——2——3—————————
D ————————————————————————————————————————————————————————————————————
G ————————————————————————————————————————————————————————————————————
  Let me go ho-me; I feel so break-up, I want to go home.
```

Chord Forms

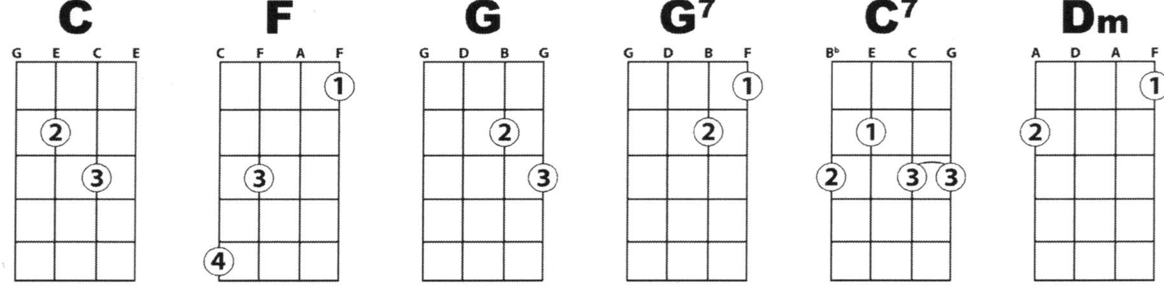

The John B. Sails (continued)

Melody & Chords
Key of C (High)

```
  C                              F    C                        F    C
E --0----0--0---0------1----0-------0----0-0----1----0---------
A --3----3--3---3------0----3-------3----3-3----0----3---------
D 5-2-----------2------3----2--5----2----2------3----2---------
G 0----------------------------0-------------------------------
  We come on the sloop John B, my grandfather and me,
```

```
                                  G     G7              C
E 0-0---0--1--3---3-1-0---------------------------------------
A 3-3---3--3--3---3-0-0---5-------------------2---3-----------
D -2---2------2---2-------0-----5-----5---0---2---------------
G ------------------------0-----0-----0-------0---------------
  Around Nassau town w-e did roam. Drinkin' all night,
```

```
     C7      F  Dm   C                        G                C
E -----------0-1-0----1--0--------0-------------------------------
A 3--3-5---3-0-0-5--0--3------5---3------3---5---5----3--2--3-----
D 2--2-2---2-3------3--0--2---0---2------2---0---0----0--0--2-----
G 0----------------2---------------------0---0---0----------0-----
  Got into a fight. We feel so break-up, we want to go home.
```

CHORUS

```
  C                           F  C                          F     C
E --0-----0--0---0------1---0---------------0----0----0---1-----0---
A --3-----3--3---3------0---3---------------3----3----3---0-----3---
D 5-2------------2------3---2---------5-----2---------2---3-----2---
G 0-----------------------------------0-----------------------------
  So hoist up the John B. Sails, see how the mainsail sets,
```

```
                                                 G      G7          C
E 0----0----0----0----0----1-3------3----1--0---------------------------
A 3----3----3----3----3----0-3------3----0--0---5-------------2---3-----
D 2----2---------2-----------2------2-----------0-----5---5---3---2-----
G -----------------------------------------------0-----0---0-------0-----
  Send for the captain ashore, let me go home. Let me go home,
```

```
  C7          F  Dm   C                        G                C
E ---------0--1-0----1-0-------0--------------------------------------
A 3---5--3--0-0-5--0-3------5--3-------3----5-5------3---2---3--------
D 2---2-----3------3--0-2---2--2-------2----0-0------0---0---2--------
G 0----------------2------------------------0-0--------------0--------
  Let me go ho-me; I feel so break-up, I want to go home.
```

Chord Forms

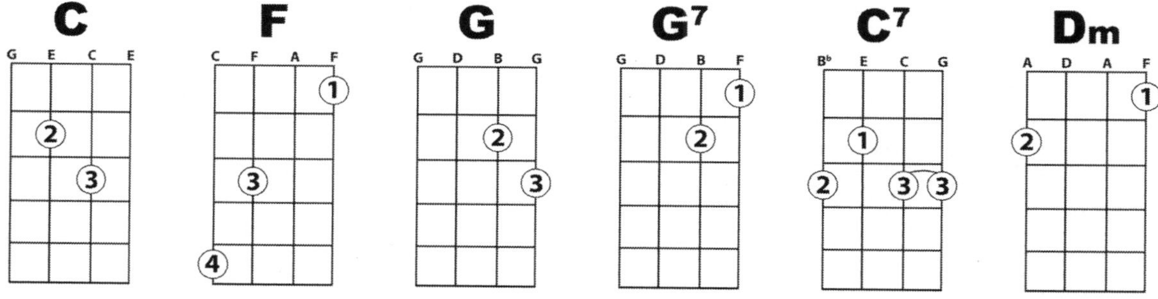

The John B. Sails (continued)

Basic Melody
Key of G

```
  G                    C    G                     C    G
E ---------------------------------------------------------------
A ---2----2--2---2-----3----2-----2-----2-2-----3----2-----------
D 0-------------------------------0------------------------------
G ---------------------------------------------------------------
  We come on the sloop John B, my grandfather and me,

                                   D     D7         G
E ---------------------------------------------------------------
A 2-2----2---3--5-----5-3-2----0---------------------------------
D ----------------------------------0-----0----4----5------------
G ---------------------------------------------------------------
  Around Nassau town w-e did roam. Drinkin' all night,

     G7      C   Am    G                D            G
E ---------------------------------------------------------------
A -------0--2-3-2-0-3--2-----0--2-----------0--0-----------------
D 5---5-------------------------------5-------------5--4--5------
G ---------------------------------------------------------------
  Got into a fight. We feel so break-up, we want to go home.
```

Chorus

```
  G                    C  G                         C    G
E ---------------------------------------------------------------
A ---2------2--2---2---3--2---------2---2---2---3-----2----------
D 0-----------------------------0--------------------------------
G ---------------------------------------------------------------
  So hoist up the John B. Sails, see how the mainsail sets,

                                             D     D7         G
E ---------------------------------------------------------------
A 2----2---2---2--2----3-5-----5---3--2--0-----------------------
D ---------------------------------------------0---0--4--5-------
G ---------------------------------------------------------------
  Send for the captain ashore, let me go home. Let me go home,

  G7           C    Am    G                D            G
E ---------------------------------------------------------------
A -----0--2--3-2-0--3-2-----0--2-----------0-0-------------------
D 5-------------------------------------5---------5--4--5--------
G ---------------------------------------------------------------
  Let me go ho-me; I feel so break-up, I want to go home.
```

Chord Forms

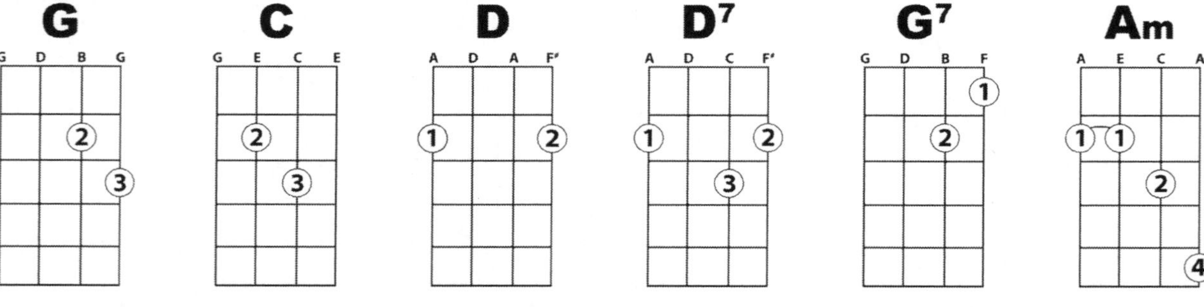

The John B. Sails (continued)

Melody & Chords

Key of G

```
 G                          C    G                          C   G
E -------------------------------------------------------------------------
A ---2-----2--2----2-------3-----2--------2------2--2------3----2----------
D 0--0-----0--0----0-------2-----0---0----0------0--0------2----0----------
G 0--0-------------0-------0-----0---0----0----------------0----0----------
  We come on the sloop John B, my grandfather and me,
```

```
                                     D      D7              G
E -------------------------------------------------------------------------
A 2-2-----2----3--5-----5-3-2-----0----------------------------------------
D 0-0-----0----0--0-----0-0-0-----0--------0-------0----4----5-------------
G --0-----0-------0-----0---------2--------2-------2----2----0-------------
  Around Nassau town w-e did roam. Drinkin' all night,
```

```
     G7        C   Am   G                          D                 G
E -------------------------------------------------------------------------
A ---------0--2-3-2-0-3--2------0--2----------------0--0-------------------
D 5---5-3---3-2-0-2-2----0------0--0-------5--------0--0------5---4---5----
G 0---0----------0--2-2--0---------0-------0-------2--2-------2---2---0----
  Got into a fight. We feel so break-up, we want to go home.
```

CHORUS

```
 G                          C   G                            C      G
E -------------------------------------------------------------------------
A ---2-------2--2---2-------3---2--------------2----2----2----3------2-----
D 0--0-------0--0---0-------2---0--------0-----0----0----0----2------0-----
G 0--0--------------0-------0---0--------0-----0---------0----0------0-----
  So hoist up the John B. Sails, see how the mainsail sets,
```

```
                                                  D      D7             G
E -------------------------------------------------------------------------
A 2----2----2----2--2-----3-5------5----3--2---0---------------------------
D 0----0----0----0--0-----0-0------0----0--0---0--------0----0---4---5-----
G 0----0---------0--------0--------0-----------2--------2----2---2---0-----
  Send for the captain ashore, let me go home. Let me go home,
```

```
 G7          C    Am    G                        D                G
E -------------------------------------------------------------------------
A -----0--2---3-2-0---3-2------0--2---------------0-0-----------------------
D 5----0--0---2-2-2---2-0------0--0--------5------0-0-------5---4---5------
G 0-----------0---2---2-0---------0--------0-----2-2-------2---2---0------
  Let me go ho-me; I feel so break-up, I want to go home.
```

Chord Forms

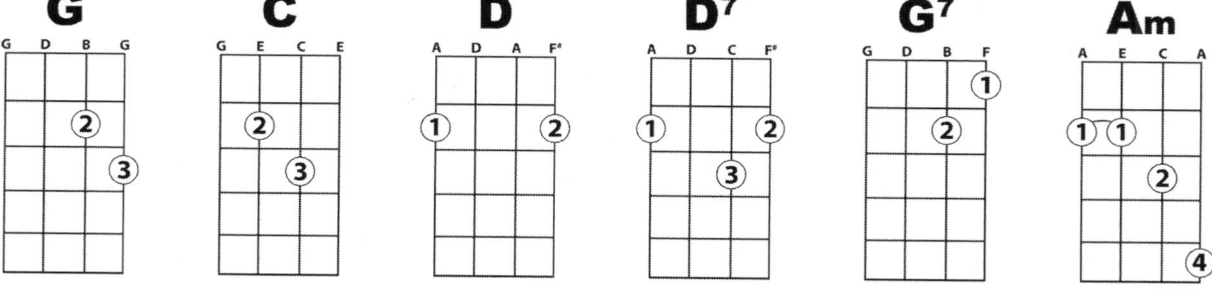

SEA SHANTY

Leave Her, Johnny, Leave Her

Basic Melody

Key of C (Low)

Words and Music

Traditional

This shanty was usually sung at the very end of a voyage, when the sailors were completing the final tasks before going ashore. It is a beautiful song - despite being excited to go ashore, it tells of a sort of melancholy longing for the sea now that the voyage is over. In some versions, the lyrics are critical of the ship's officers, since the sailors could now speak freely at the end of their work.

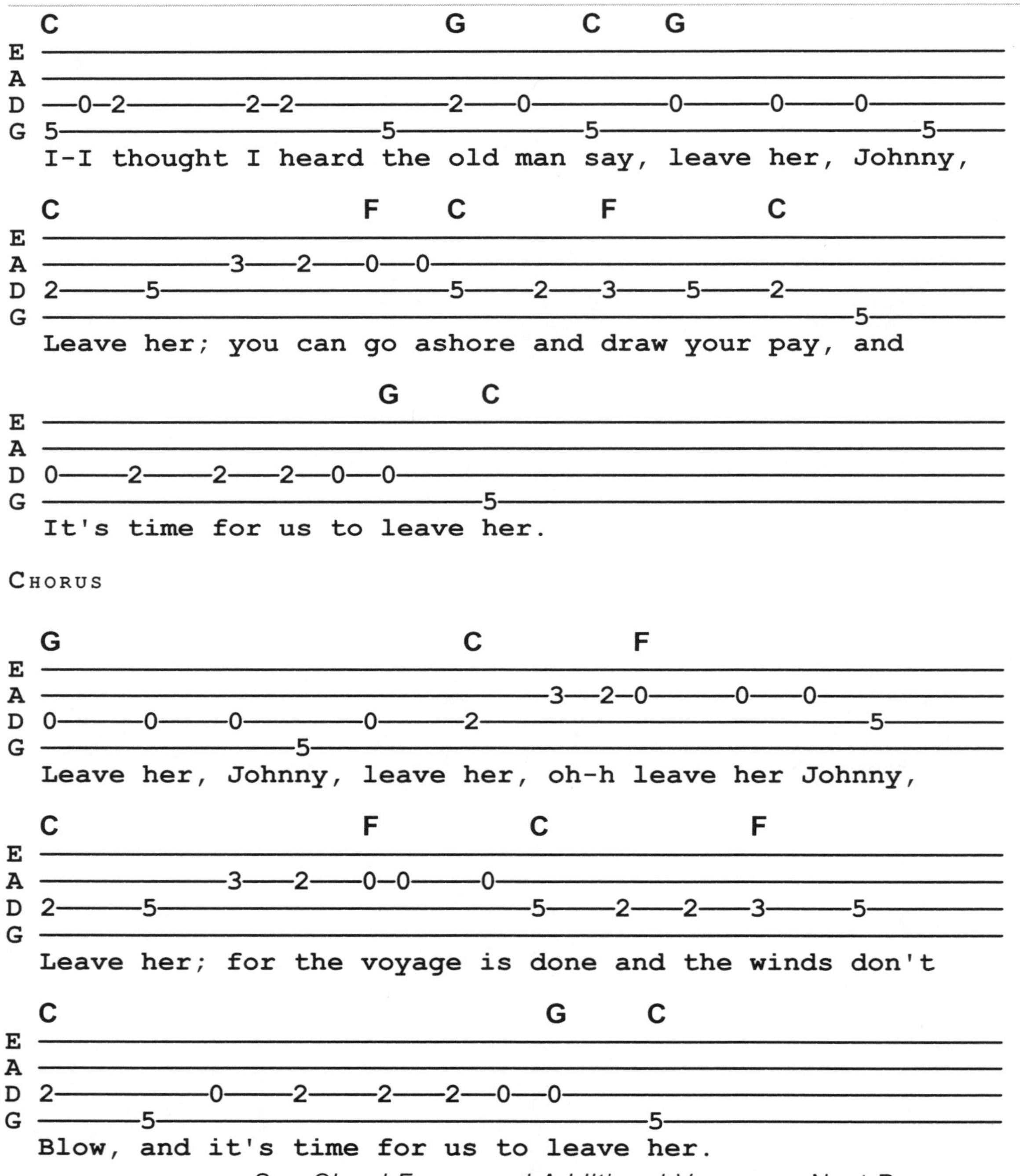

See Chord Forms and Additional Verses on Next Page

Leave Her, Johnny, Leave Her (continued)

Chord Forms and Additional Verses

Chord Forms

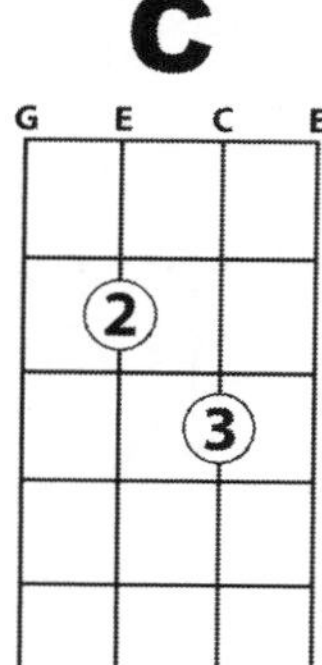

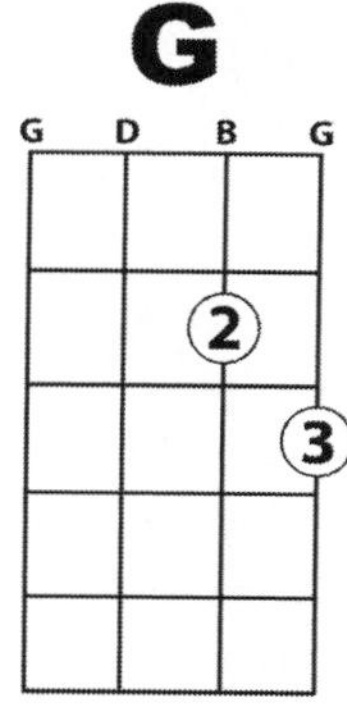

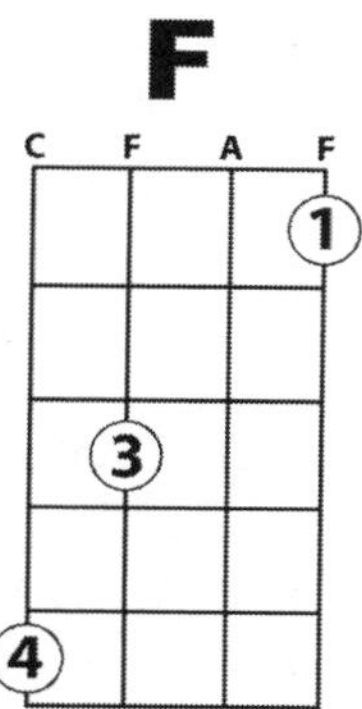

Additional Verses

You may make her fast and pack your gear,
Leave her, Johnny, leave her;
And leave her moored to the West Street Pier,
And it's time for us to leave her.

The winds were foul and the work was hard,
Leave her, Johnny, leave her;
From Liverpool docks to the Brooklyn yard,
And it's time for us to leave her.

She would not steer nor ware nor stay,
Leave her, Johnny, leave her;
She shipped green water night and day,
And it's time for us to leave her.

Beware these packet ships I say,
Leave her, Johnny, leave her;
They steal your stores and clothes away,
And it's time for us to leave her.

She shipped it green and made us curse,
Leave her, Johnny, leave her;
The mate's a devil and the old man's worse,
And it's time for us to leave her.

The winds were foul, the ship was slow,
Leave her, Johnny, leave her;
The grub was bad, the wages low,
And it's time for us to leave her.

The winds were foul, the trip was long,
Leave her, Johnny, leave her;
But before we go we'll sing this song,
And it's time for us to leave her.

Well I hate to sail on this rotten tub,
Leave her, Johnny, leave her;
No rum allowed, and rotten grub,
And it's time for us to leave her.

Two nights ashore then we sail again,
Leave her, Johnny, leave her;
And we won't be home 'til God knows when,
And it's time for us to leave her.

The verses above are a combination of those traditionally attributed to this song, as well as those of another shanty with the same melody, entitled "Across the Western Ocean."

Leave Her, Johnny, Leave Her (continued)

Melody & Chords

Key of C (Low)

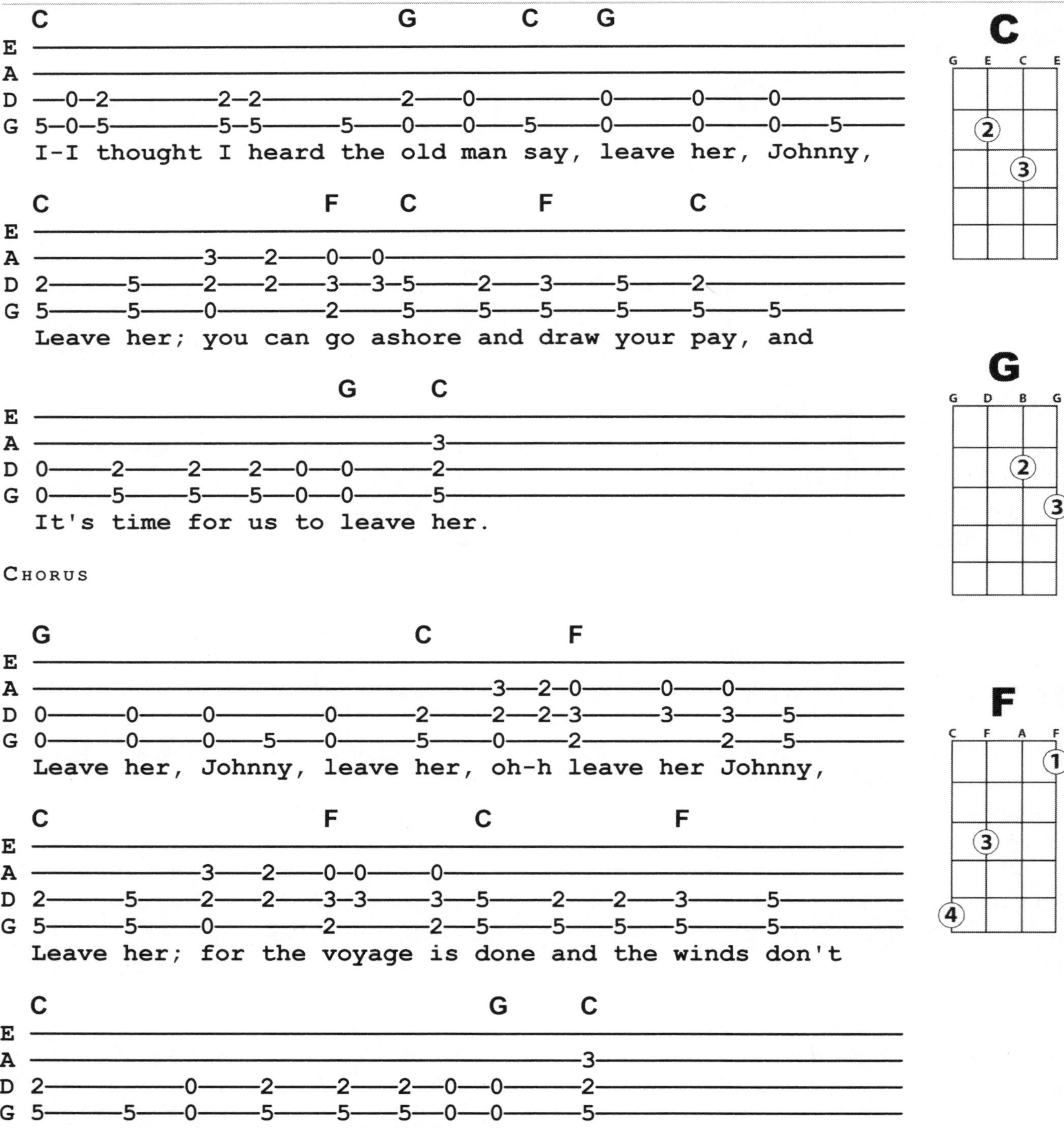

About Sea Shanties

Shanties were the songs sung by sailors as they went about their work on the ships. They are a particular class of work songs, related to field hollers and chain gang songs of the American south, and many of them are believed by musicologists to have had roots in African singing traditions.

According to the Encyclopedia Britannica, the majority of the sea shanties from before the 19th century (pre-1800) were of British origin, and many of those from the 1800's are of American origin - though often built on older tunes and incorporating older lyrical structures.

One of the main purposes of any work song, including sea shanties, is to keep the workers in rhythm so their efforts are all applied in a synchronized way - such as when hoisting a huge, heavy main sail up the mast of a ship. Of course the singing had other less obvious purposes as well - such as artistic expression and spiritual release for a group of men whose lives were often brutal and short.

There where three primary types of sea shanties sung aboard-ship:

- **Short-haul or Short-drag Shanties -** these were short, simple songs or phrases sung for shorter jobs when only a few short bursts of action were needed.
- **Halyard Shanties** - longer songs and tunes for jobs such as hoisting a sail, where a repeated action (pull the rope, relax a moment, pull again) was needed. One example of this style is *Blow the Man Down*, included in this collection.
- **Windlass or Capstan Shanties -** longer slower songs with a steady plodding beat for when synchronized footsteps were needed - such as when hoisting an anchor, which involved men turning a circular winch as shown in the illustration to the right. *Shenandoah*, which is included in this book, is an example of a capstan shanty.

Another class of sea song sung by sailors were the forecastles or fore-bitters, which were not work songs but rather sung for enjoyment. There were two distinct varieties - those sung when outward bound on a new voyage, and those song when homeward bound.

Examples of the latter in this songbook include *Rolling Down to Old Maui, Leave Her Johnny Leave Her, Rolling Home and Homeward Bound.*

Leave Her, Johnny, Leave Her (continued)

Basic Melody

Key of C (High)

```
   C                                 G        C    G
E ———0————————0–0————————————————0———————————————————————————————————
A 3–5————————————————————3————————————5————3————5——————5—————5————3———
D ————————————————————————————————————————————————————————————————————
G ————————————————————————————————————————————————————————————————————
  I-I thought I heard the old man say, leave her, Johnny,

  C                        F    C          F          C
E 0—————3—————8————7————5——5–3—————0————1—————3——————0————————————————
A ————————————————————————————————————————————————————————————3———————
D ————————————————————————————————————————————————————————————————————
G ————————————————————————————————————————————————————————————————————
  Leave her; you can go ashore and draw your pay, and

                              G      C
E —————0—————0————0———————————————————————————————————————————————————
A 5—————————————————————5————5——————3—————————————————————————————————
D ————————————————————————————————————————————————————————————————————
G ————————————————————————————————————————————————————————————————————
  It's time for us to leave her.
```

CHORUS

```
  G                                  C          F
E ——————————————————————————————————0—————8————7–5—————5————5————3————
A 5—————5—————5————3————5—————————————————————————————————————————————
D ————————————————————————————————————————————————————————————————————
G ————————————————————————————————————————————————————————————————————
  Leave her, Johnny, leave her, oh-h leave her Johnny,

  C                        F          C                 F
E 0—————3—————8————7————5–5——————5————3—————0————0————1——————3————————
A ————————————————————————————————————————————————————————————————————
D ————————————————————————————————————————————————————————————————————
G ————————————————————————————————————————————————————————————————————
  Leave her; for the voyage is done and the winds don't

  C                                       G      C
E 0————————————————0——————0————0——————————————————————————————————————
A ——————3————5————————————————————————5———5——————3————————————————————
D ————————————————————————————————————————————————————————————————————
G ————————————————————————————————————————————————————————————————————
  Blow, and it's time for us to leave her.
```

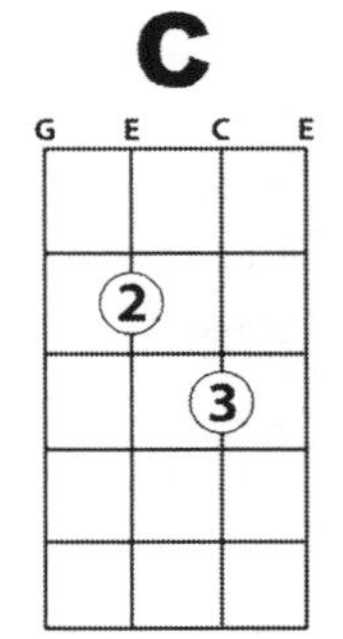

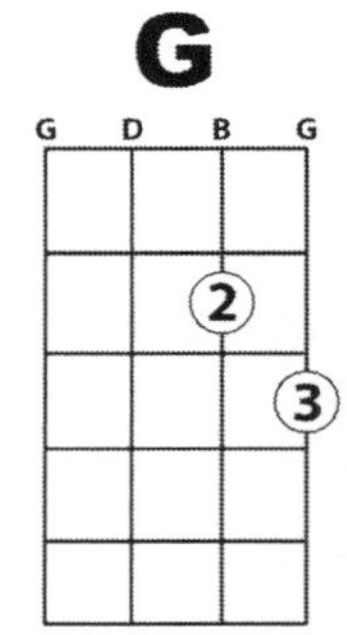

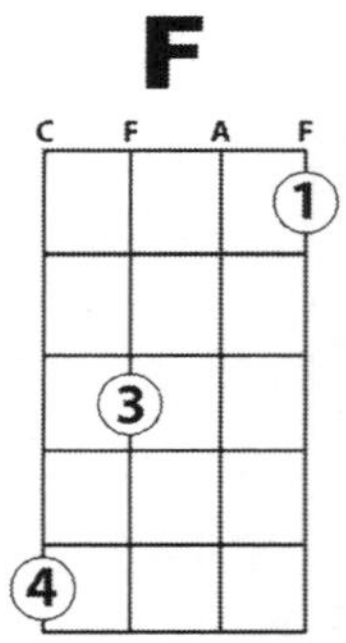

C (G E C E): 2 on E string, 3 on C string

G (G D B G): 2 on B string, 3 on G string

F (C F A F): 1 on F string, 3 on F string, 4 on C string

Leave Her, Johnny, Leave Her (continued)

Melody & Chords

Key of C (High)

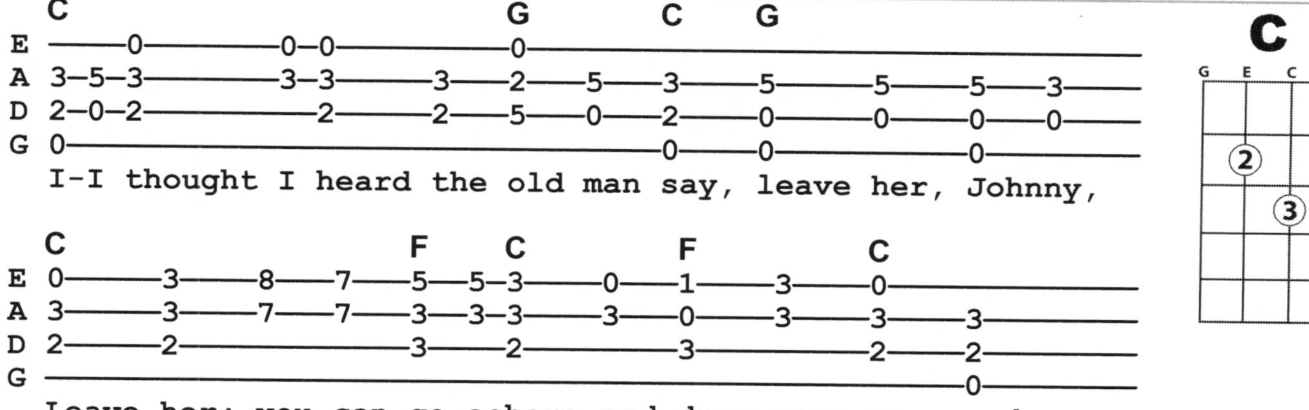


```
                              G       C
E ———0————0———0——————————————————————————
A 5——3————3———3——5——5—————3——————————————
D 0——2————————2——0——0—————2——————————————
G ——————————————————0—————0——————————————
  It's time for us to leave her.
```

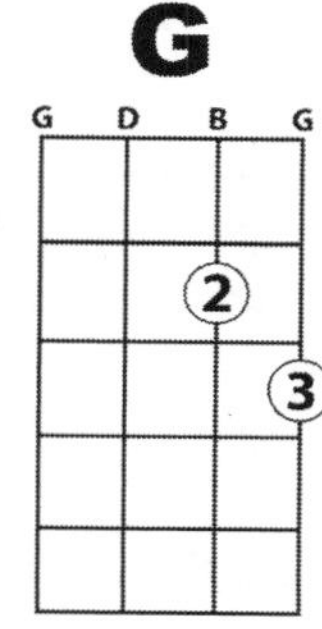

Chorus

```
  G                             C        F
E ——————————————————————————————0————8——7–5————5————5————3————
A 5————5————5————3————5—————————3————7——7–3————3————3————3————
D 0————0————0————0————0—————————2————————3——————————3—————————
G 0—————————0—————————0———————————————————————————————————————
  Leave her, Johnny, leave her, oh-h leave her Johnny,
```

```
  C                      F        C             F
E 0————3————8————7————5–5————5——3————0————0————1————3————
A 3————3————7————7————3–3————3——3————3————3————0————3————
D 2————2——————————————3——————3——2————2—————————3—————————
G ———————————————————————————————————————————————————————
  Leave her; for the voyage is done and the winds don't
```

```
  C                                  G       C
E 0————————————————0————0————0———————————————————————
A 3————3————5——————3————3————3——5——5————————3————————
D 2————2————0——————2—————————2——0——0————————2————————
G —————0———————————————————————————0————————0————————
  Blow, and it's time for us to leave her.
```

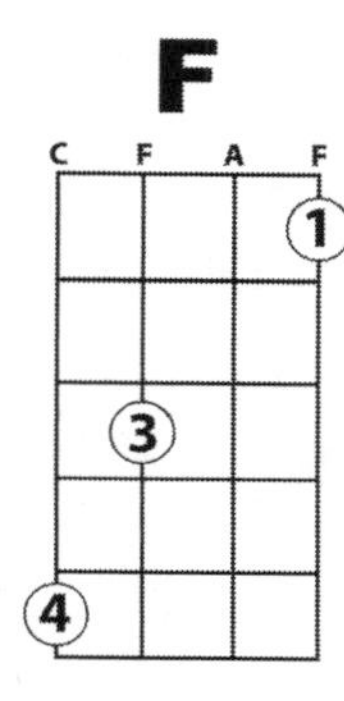

Leave Her, Johnny, Leave Her (continued)

Basic Melody

Key of G

```
  G                                   D          G       D
E ---------------------------------------------------------------------------------------
A ---0--2-------------2--2---------------2-----0------------0--------0-------0-----------
D 5-------------------------------5-----------------5------------------------------5-----
G ---------------------------------------------------------------------------------------
  I-I thought I heard the old man say, leave her, Johnny,
```

```
  G                          C       G            C              G
E ----------------3-----2-----0---0-----------------------------------------------
A 2-------5------------------------------5-------2------3------5-----2------------
D -------------------------------------------------------------------------5------
G --------------------------------------------------------------------------------
  Leave her; you can go ashore and draw your pay, and
```

```
                              D        G
E ---------------------------------------------------------
A 0-------2-------2-----2----0----0------------------------
D -------------------------------------5-------------------
G ---------------------------------------------------------
  It's time for us to leave her.
```

Chorus

```
  D                                      G             C
E ---------------------------------------------------3----2--0---------0------0----------
A 0---------0-------0-------------0-------2-------------------------------------------5---
D -----------------------------5----------------------------------------------------------
G ----------------------------------------------------------------------------------------
  Leave her, Johnny, leave her, oh-h leave her Johnny,
```

```
  G                          C             G                     C
E ----------------3-----2-----0--0-------0---------------------------------------------
A 2-------5------------------------------------5-------2------2------3--------5--------
D -------------------------------------------------------------------------------------
G -------------------------------------------------------------------------------------
  Leave her; for the voyage is done and the winds don't
```

```
  G                                             D        G
E -----------------------------------------------------------------------
A 2-------------0-------2-------2-----2----0----0------------------------
D --------5--------------------------------------------5-----------------
G -----------------------------------------------------------------------
  Blow, and it's time for us to leave her.
```

G
G D B G 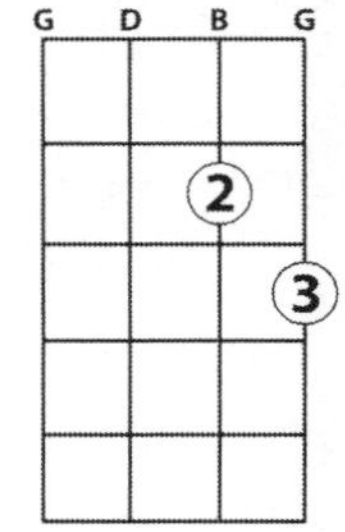
2
3

D
A D A F#
1
2

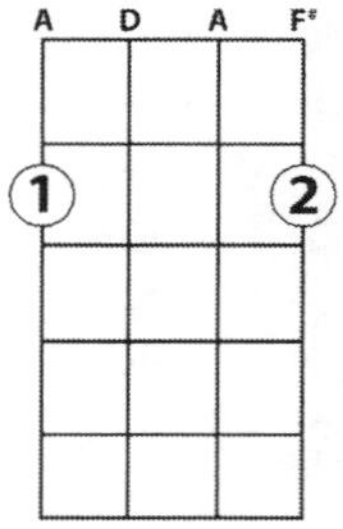

C
G E C E 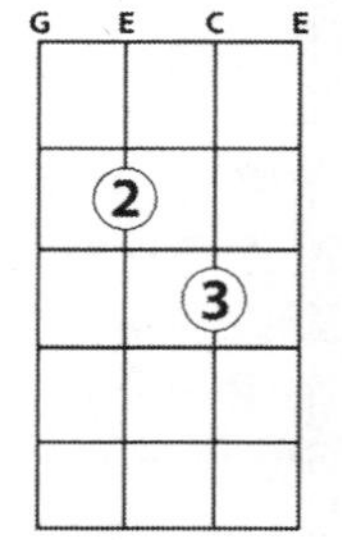
2
3

Leave Her, Johnny, Leave Her (continued)

Melody & Chords

Key of G

```
   G                                D        G      D
E -------------------------------------------------------------------
A --0-2--------2-2----------2----0--------0-------0-------0---------
D 5-0-0--------0-0----5-----0----0----5---0-------0-------0----5----
G 0---0----------0----0-----2---------0---2---------------2----0----
  I-I thought I heard the old man say, leave her, Johnny,
```

```
  G                         C    G          C          G
E -------------3---2---0--0-----------------------------------------
A 2------5-----2---2---3--3-5-------2----3-------5-------2----------
D 0------0-----0-------2-----0------0----2-------0-------0-----5----
G 0------0-------------------0-----------0---------------0-----0----
  Leave her; you can go ashore and draw your pay, and
```

```
                         D      G
E -------------------------------------------------------------------
A 0-----2-----2----2---0---0---------------------------------------
D 0-----0-----0----0---0---0-------5-------------------------------
G ------0----------0-------2-------0-------------------------------
  It's time for us to leave her.
```

G

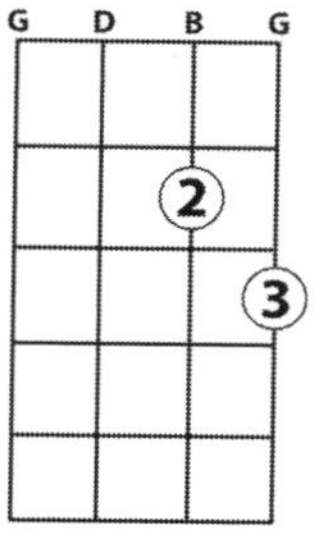

D

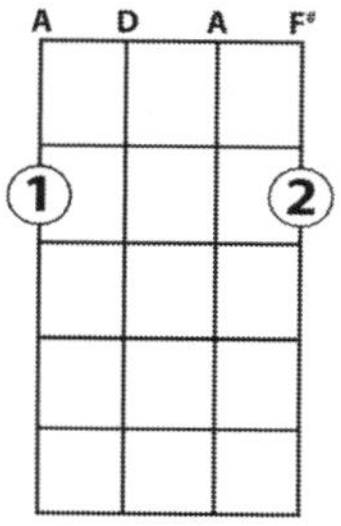

C

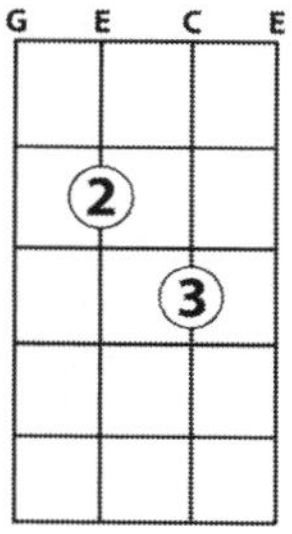

Chorus

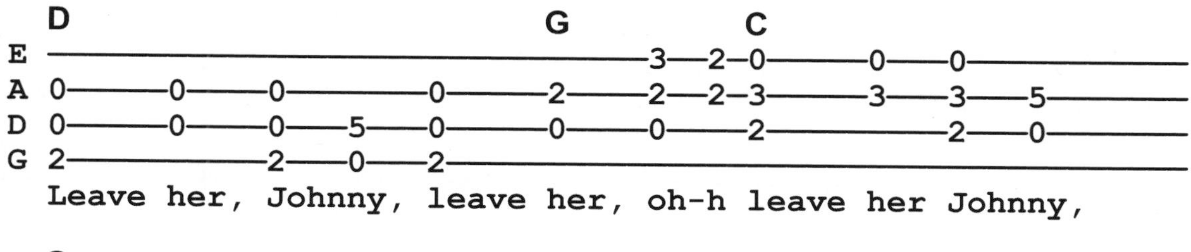

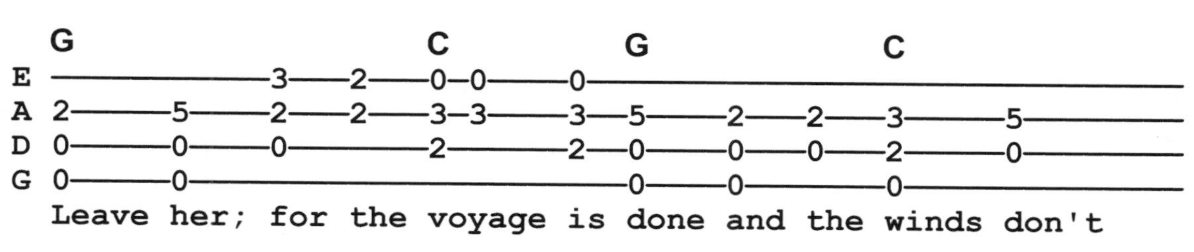

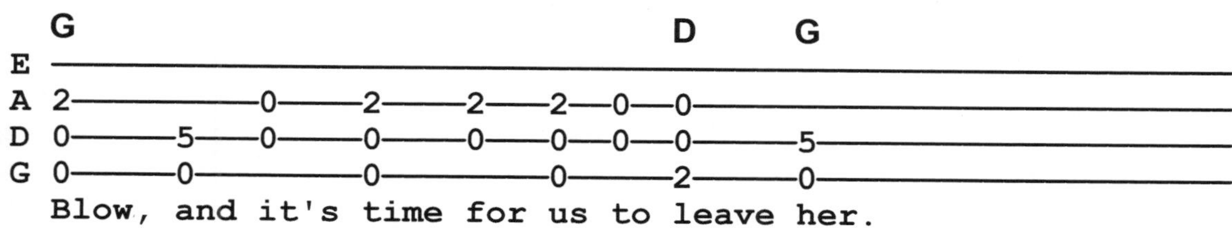

The Leaving of Liverpool

Basic Melody

Key of C

This old sea song tells the story of a sailor saying farewell to his own true love, whom he is leaving behind in Liverpool, England. It is thought that this song was written sometime around 1870, when Captain Burgess was an actual sea captain on the American clipper ship the Davy Crockett. The author of the song is not known, but it has been recorded by most folk and Irish performers over the years, including the Dubliners and the Clancy Brothers with Tommy Makem.

Words and Music

Traditional

```
   C                                    F        C                                          G
E ---------------------------------------------------------------------------------------------------------
A ------------------------------------3----0----------------------------------------0------------------------
D ---0--2------5---3--2--0--------------------5-----------0---2--5--------5--2-----0----------0-------------
G 5---------------------------------5-------------------5------------------------------5---------5---------------
  Farewell to you m-y own true love, I am going far a---way; I am

   C                                F        C                                      G          C
E ---------------------------------------------------------------------------------------------------------
A --------------------------------3------0-------------------------------------------------------------------
D 2--------5-----3--2--0----------------------5----------0--2-------5--------5------2--0--------------------
G ------------------------------5--------------------5----------------------------------------------5------5---
  Bound for Cal-i---forn-aye-ay, but I know that I'll return some day.
```

CHORUS

```
   C  G                                F          C
E ---------------------------------------------------------------------------------------------------------
A 3---5------2---------------5---3----0-----------------------------------------------------------------------
D ----------------------5---------------------------5-----------0-------2--5--5------------------------------
G -----------------------------------------------------------5-----------------------------------------------
  So fare thee well, my own true love, and when I return

                               G                   C
E ---------------------------------------------------------------------------------------------------------
A ---0--------------------------------------------------------------------------------------------------------
D 5-----5-----2--------------0----5------5-----3-----2---2-------5---3--2---0--------------------------------
G ---------------------5--------------------------------------------------------------------------------------
  Uni-ted we will be; it's not the leaving of Liverpool

         F          C                                  G          C
E ---------------------------------------------------------------------------------------------------------
A --------3----0----------------------------------------------------------------------------------------------
D ----------------------5------------0---2---5------5------2--0-----------------------------------------------
G 5----------------------------5-------------------------------------------5---5-----------------------------
  That grieves me, but my darling when I think of thee.
```

Chord Forms

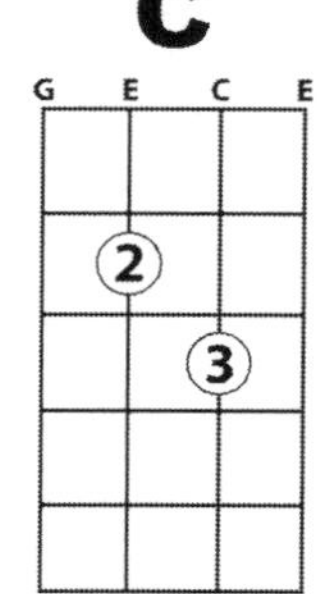

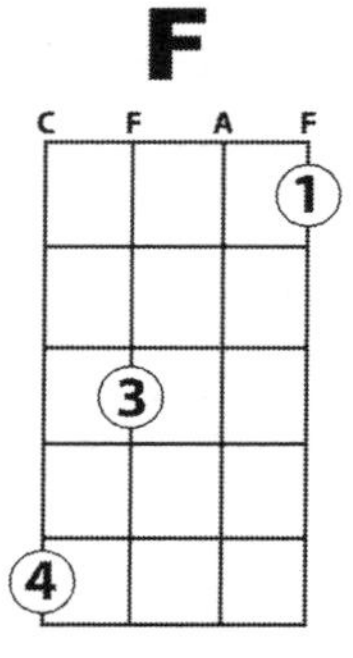

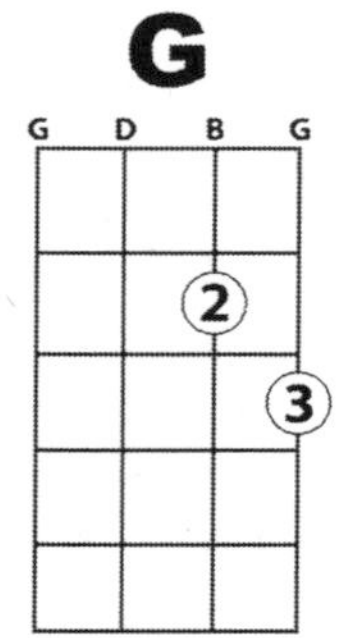

See Additional Verses on Next Page

The Leaving of Liverpool

(continued)

Melody & Chords

Key of C

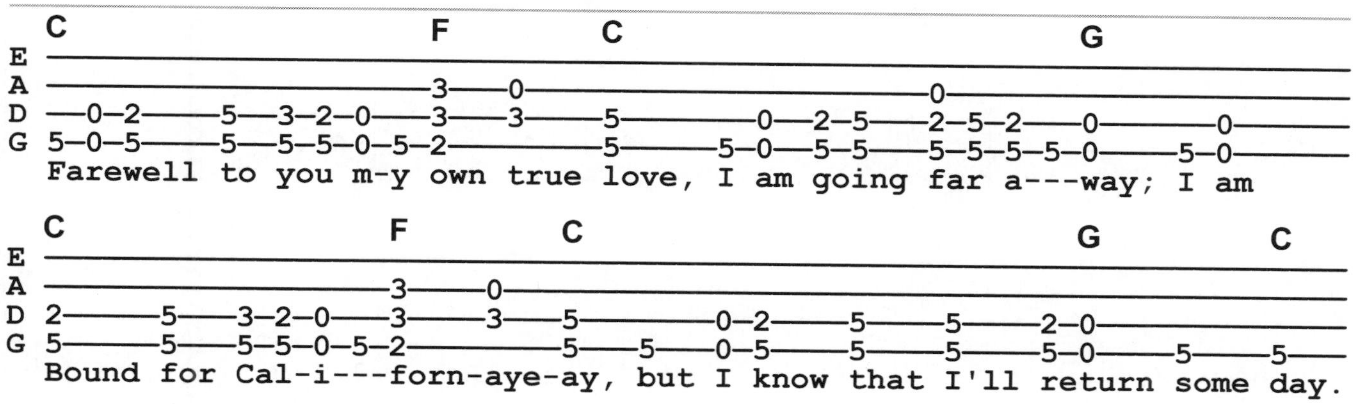

```
  C                             F      C                            G
E ------------------------------------------------------------------------------
A ------------------------------3-----0---------------------------0--------------
D --0-2-----5--3-2-0-----3------3------5--------0--2-5----2-5-2----0---------0----
G 5-0-5-----5--5-5-0-5-2----------------5------5-0--5-5----5-5-5-5-0------5-0----
  Farewell to you m-y own true love, I am going far a---way; I am
```

```
  C                        F      C                                  G       C
E ------------------------------------------------------------------------------
A -------------------------3------0------------------------------------------------
D 2--------5----3-2-0------3------3----5-------0-2------5------5-----2-0-----------
G 5--------5----5-5-0-5-2--------------5----5--0-5------5------5-----5-0-----5----5--
  Bound for Cal-i---forn-aye-ay, but I know that I'll return some day.
```

Chorus

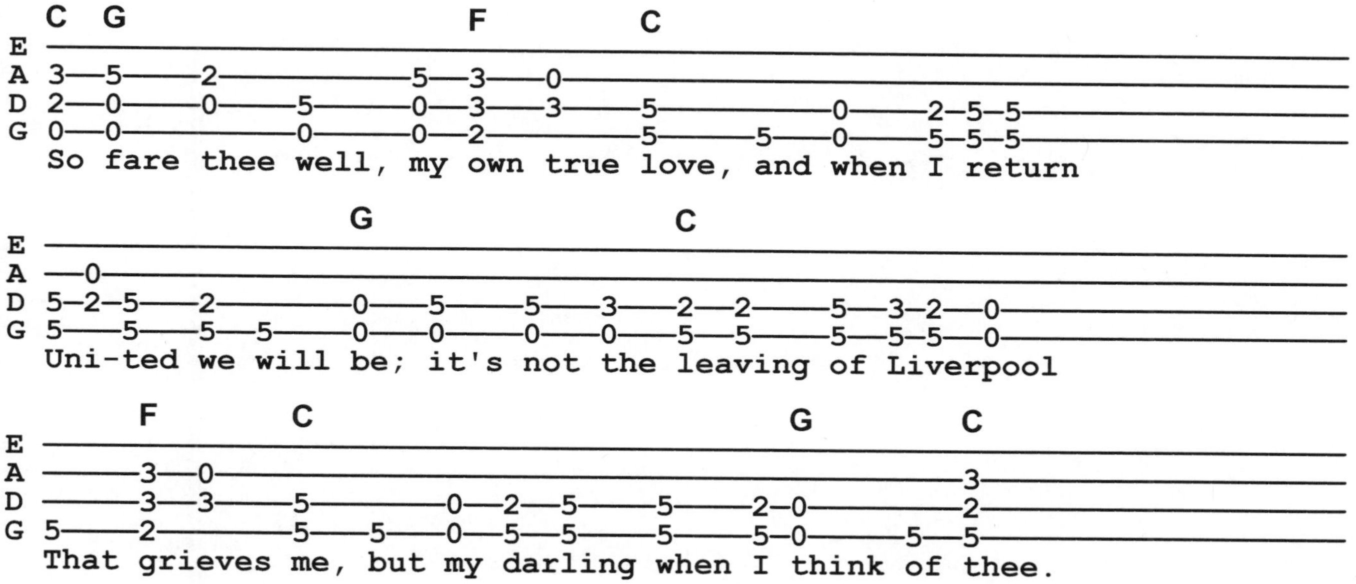

```
  C  G                      F       C
E ------------------------------------------------------------------------------
A 3--5----2-------------5--3---0-------------------------------------------------
D 2--0----0-----5-------0--3---3------5----------0------2-5-5--------------------
G 0--0----------0-------0--2----------5------5---0------5-5-5--------------------
  So fare thee well, my own true love, and when I return
```

```
                    G                 C
E ------------------------------------------------------------------------------
A --0---------------------------------------------------------------------------
D 5-2-5---2-------0----5-----5----3----2--2------5--3-2--0----------------------
G 5---5---5--5----0----0-----0----0----5--5------5--5-5--0----------------------
  Uni-ted we will be; it's not the leaving of Liverpool
```

```
       F        C                                    G        C
E ------------------------------------------------------------------------------
A -----3--0----------------------------------------------------3-----------------
D -----3--3------5--------0--2--5------5------2-0--------------2-----------------
G 5----2---------5----5---0--5--5------5------5-0--------5-----5-----------------
  That grieves me, but my darling when I think of thee.
```

Additional Verses

Oh I'm bound to California,
By way of the stormy Cape Horn;
And I'll write to you a letter, my love,
When I am homeward bound.

I have signed on a Yankee sailing ship,
'Davy Crockett' is her name;
And Burgess is the Captain of her,
And they say she's a floating shame.

I have sailed with Burgess once before,
And I think I know him right well;
If a man's a sailor he will get along,
But if not then he's surely in hell.

Now the sun is on the harbor, love,
And I wish I could remain;
For I know it will be a long, long time,
Before I see you again.

The Leaving of Liverpool
(continued)

Basic Melody

Key of G (Low)

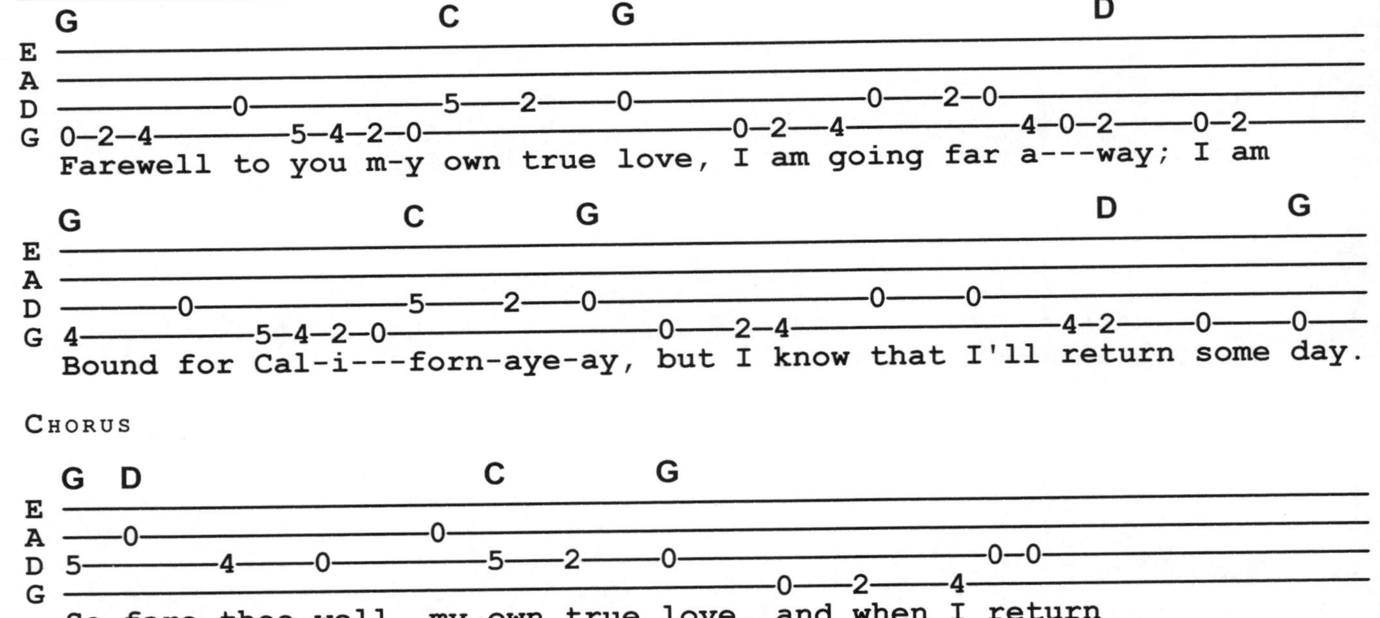

CHORUS

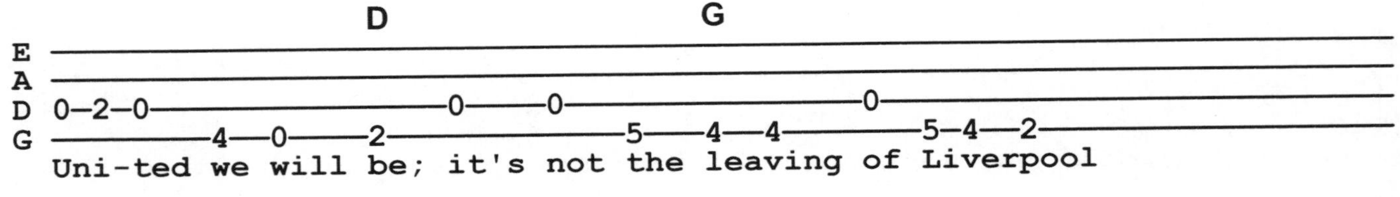

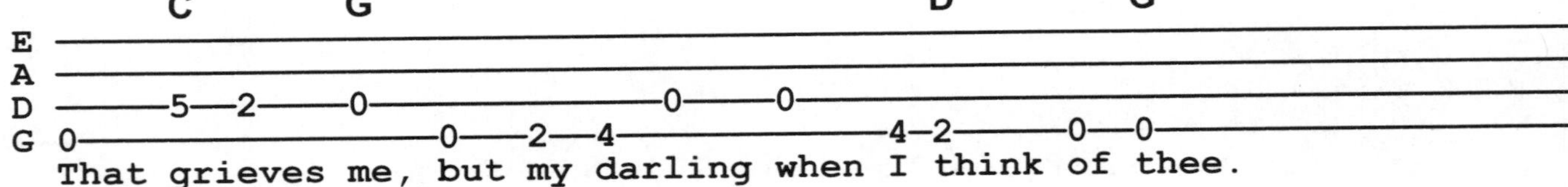


```
       C      G                      D       G
E ------------------------------------------------------
A ------------------------------------------------------
D -----5--2----0-------------0---0---------------------
G 0-----------------0--2--4-----------4-2----0--0------
  That grieves me, but my darling when I think of thee.
```

Chord Forms

G

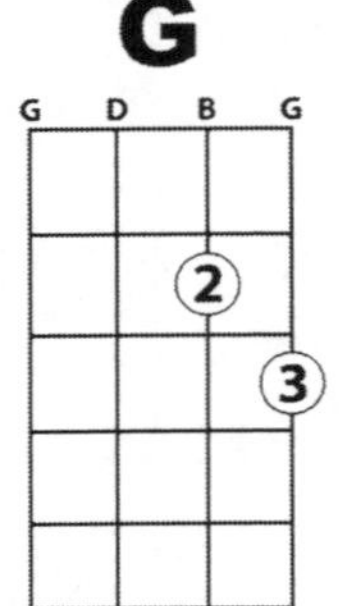

C

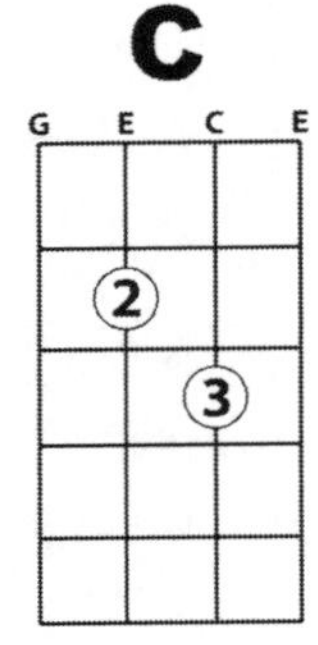

D

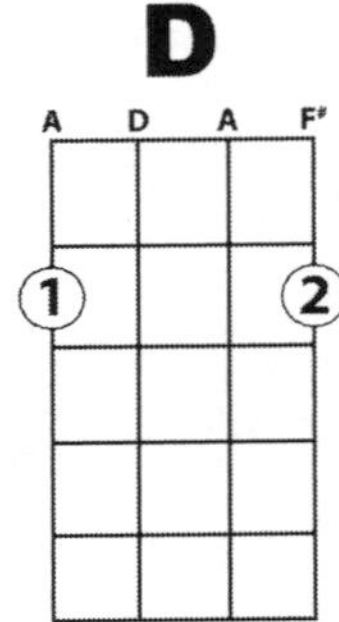

The port city of Liverpool, England has had a long and rich history amongst seafarers and sailors. The song "The Leaving of Liverpool" reflects the fact that it was a common port of departure for many sailors from the British Isles.

The illustration above depicts Liverpool harbor in the 1800's, and the photo below shows a corner of it around 1910.

The Leaving of Liverpool

(continued)

Basic Melody

Key of G (High)

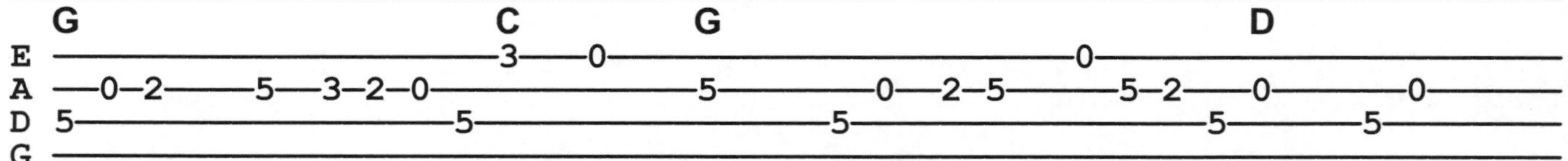

Farewell to you m-y own true love, I am going far a---way; I am

```
G                 C     G                               D        G
E ----------------3-----0-------------------------------------------
A 2----5---3-2-0------------5------0-2----5----5----2-0-------------
D --------------5-------------5----------------------------5----5---
G ------------------------------------------------------------------
```

Bound for Cal-i---forn-aye-ay, but I know that I'll return some day.

CHORUS

```
G D                 C     G
E 3--5---2--------5--3---0---------------------------------------
A -------------5---------------5-----------0----2-5-5------------
D ------------------------------------5--------------------------
G ---------------------------------------------------------------
```

So fare thee well, my own true love, and when I return

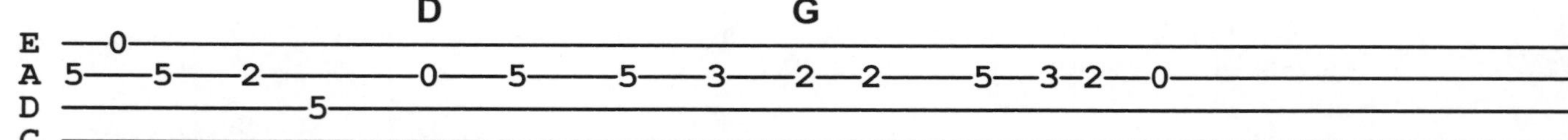

Uni-ted we will be; it's not the leaving of Liverpool

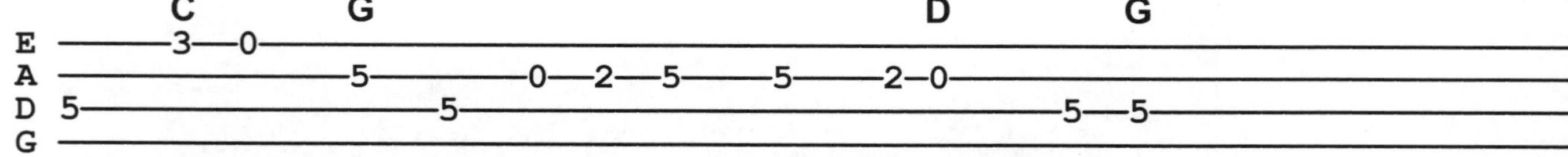

That grieves me, but my darling when I think of thee.

Chord Forms

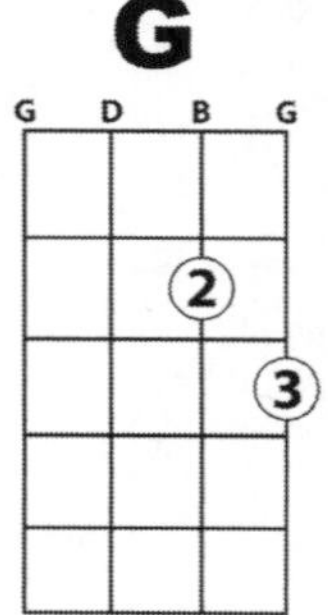

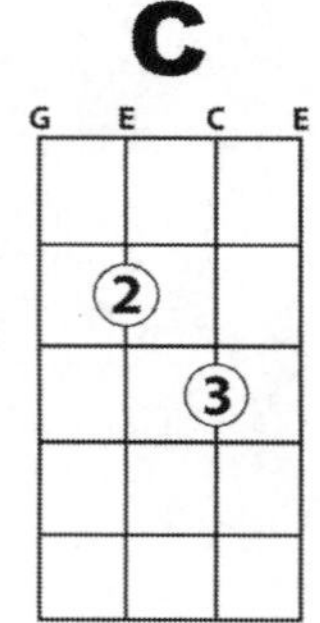

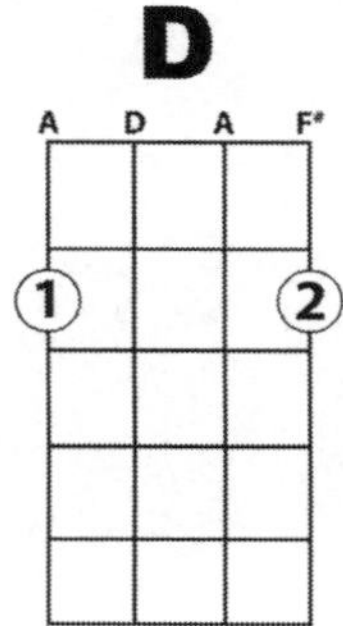

The Leaving of Liverpool
(continued)

Melody & Chords

Key of G (High)

```
  G                          C      G                              D
E ---------------------------3--0-----------------------------0-------------------------
A --0-2----5--3-2-0----3--3----5-----------0--2-5---2-5-2---0---------0--
D 5-0-0----0--0-0-0-5-2----2----0--------5-0--0-0----0----0-5-0------5-0-
G 0---0----0----------0------------0--------0----0-------------0-0-2------0-2-
  Farewell to you m-y own true love, I am going far a---way; I am
```

```
  G                         C      G                                   D        G
E --------------------------3----0---------------------------------------------------
A 2--------5----3-2-0----3------3---5-----------0-2-------5-------5-------2-0-------------
D 0--------0----0-0-0-5-2-------2---0------5----0-0-------0-------0-------0-0------5-----5--
G 0-------------0-------0-----------0------0--------0-------------0----------2-----0-----0--
  Bound for Cal-i---forn-aye-ay, but I know that I'll return some day.
```

Chorus

```
  G  D                          C       G
E 3--5------2-------------5--3----0------------------------------------------
A 2--0------0------5------0--3----3-----5-------------0-------2-5-5-----------
D 0--0-------------0------0--2----------0-------5-----0-------0-0-0-----------
G ------------------2-------------------0-------0-------------0---0-----------
  So fare thee well, my own true love, and when I return
```

```
                          D                       G
E --0----------------------------------------------------------------------------
A 5-2-5-----2-------------0----5------5-----3-----2---2-------5---3-2---0--------
D 0----0----0----5--------0----0------0-----0-----0---0-------0---0-0---0--------
G -------------0---0------2----2--------------------0-----------0-----------------
  Uni-ted we will be; it's not the leaving of Liverpool
```

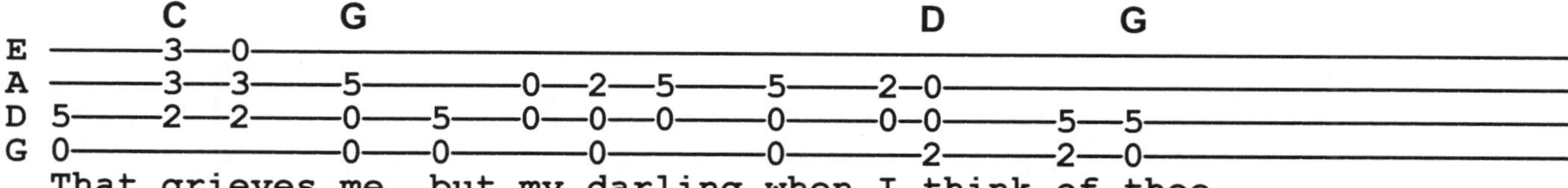

```
         C    G                                            D          G
E --------3--0---------------------------------------------------------------------
A --------3--3-------5-------------0--2--5--------5-------2-0----------------------
D 5-------2--2-------0------5------0--0--0--------0-------0-0--------5---5---------
G 0------------------0------0------------0--------0-----------2------2-0---------
  That grieves me, but my darling when I think of thee.
```

Chord Forms

G

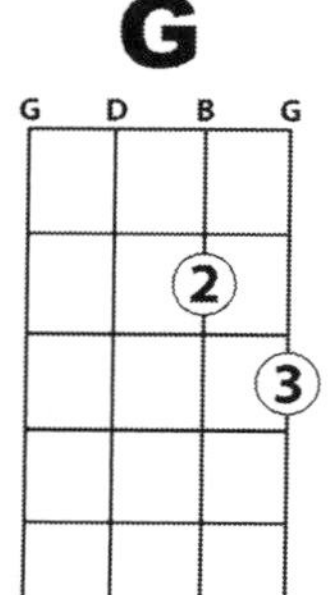

C

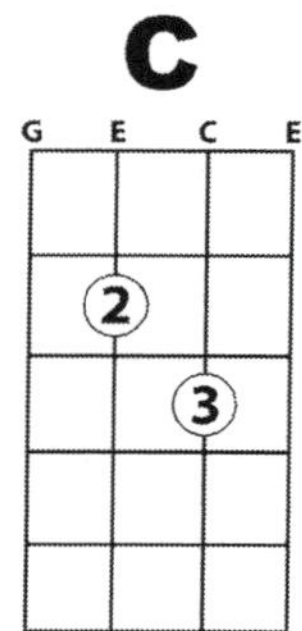

D

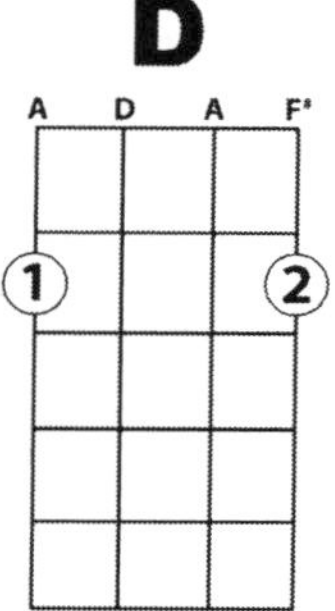

Lowlands Away

Two Versions

Key of C

Words and Music

Traditional

This slow and mournful old shanty tells the tale of a drowned sailor (or in some versions, the drowned girl of a sailor). There has been some confusion over the years as to whether this was a true shanty (a sailor work song) or a ballad, but today it is considered by many singers to be a true shanty, and as such we include it here. The Lowlands referred to Holland. We present two versions of the lyrics, from both the man's and woman's points of view.

Basic Melody

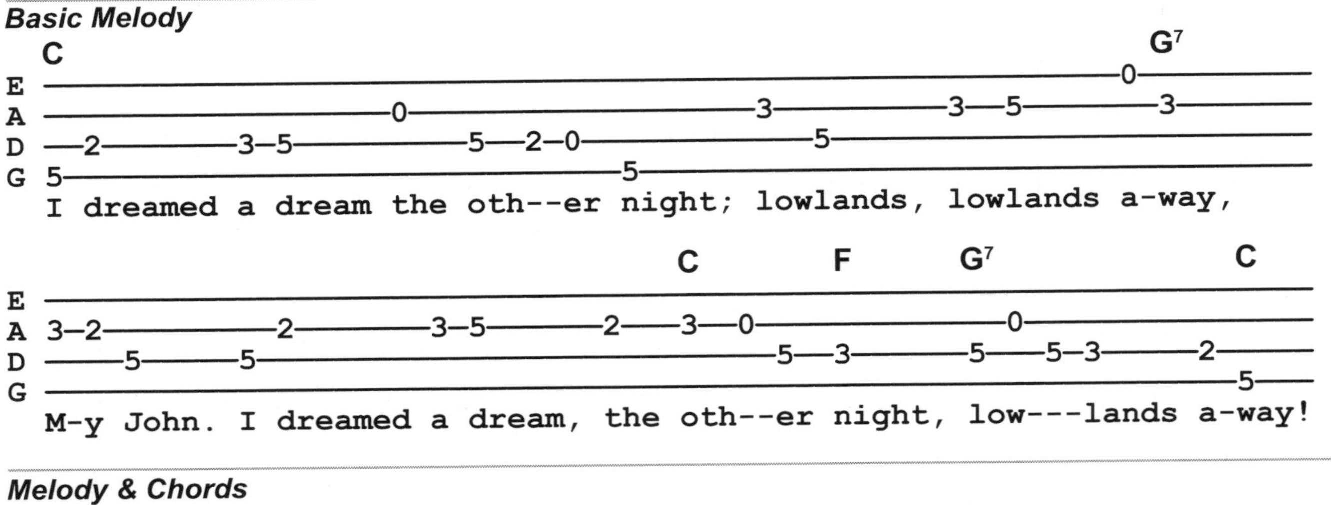

Melody & Chords

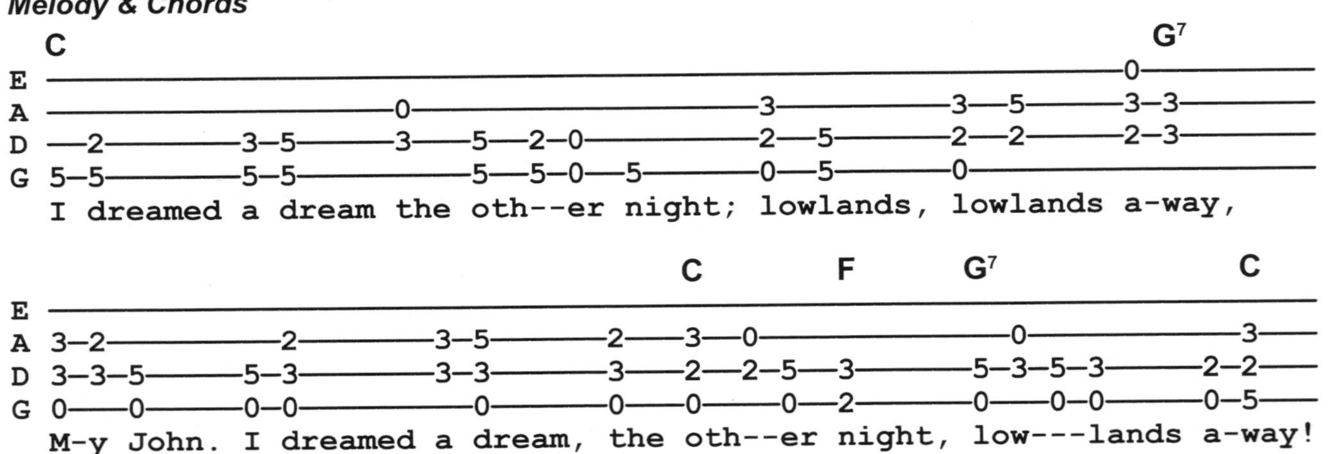

Chord Forms

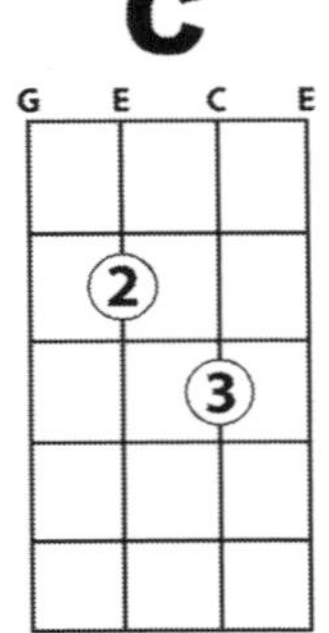

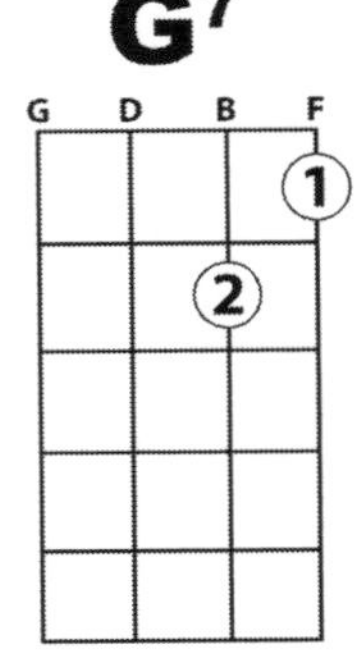

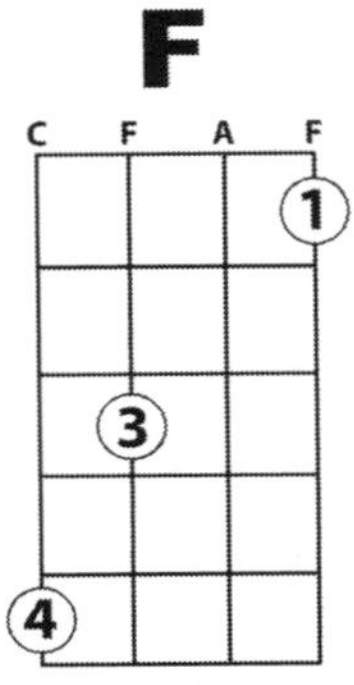

Lowlands Away (continued)

Additional Verses

Female Point of View Lyrics

I dreamt I saw my own true love,
Lowlands, lowlands, away my John;
He stood so still, he did not move... lowlands, away.

I knew my love was drowned and dead,
Lowlands, lowlands, away my John;
He stood so still, no word he said... lowlands, away.

All dank his hair, all dim his eye,
Lowlands, lowlands, away my John;
I knew that he had said goodbye... lowlands, away

All green and wet with weeds so cold,
Lowlands, lowlands, away my John;
Around his form green weeds had hold... lowlands, away

'I'm drowned in the Lowland Seas,' he said,
Lowlands, lowlands, away my John;
'Oh, you an' I will ne'er be wed...' my lowlands, away

'I shall never kiss you more,' he said,
Lowlands, lowlands, away my John;
'Never kiss you more --- for I am dead...' lowlands, away.

'I will cut my breasts until they bleed.'
Lowlands, lowlands, away my John;
His form had gone, in the green weed... lowlands, away.

'I will cut away my bonnie hair,
Lowlands, lowlands, away my John;
No other man will think me fair...' lowlands, away.

I bound the weeper round my head,
Lowlands, lowlands, away my John;
For now I knew my love was dead... lowlands, away.

My love is drowned in the windy lowlands,
Lowlands, lowlands, away my John;
My love is drowned in the windy lowlands... lowlands, away.

Three Versions

Lowlands Away (continued)

Key of G

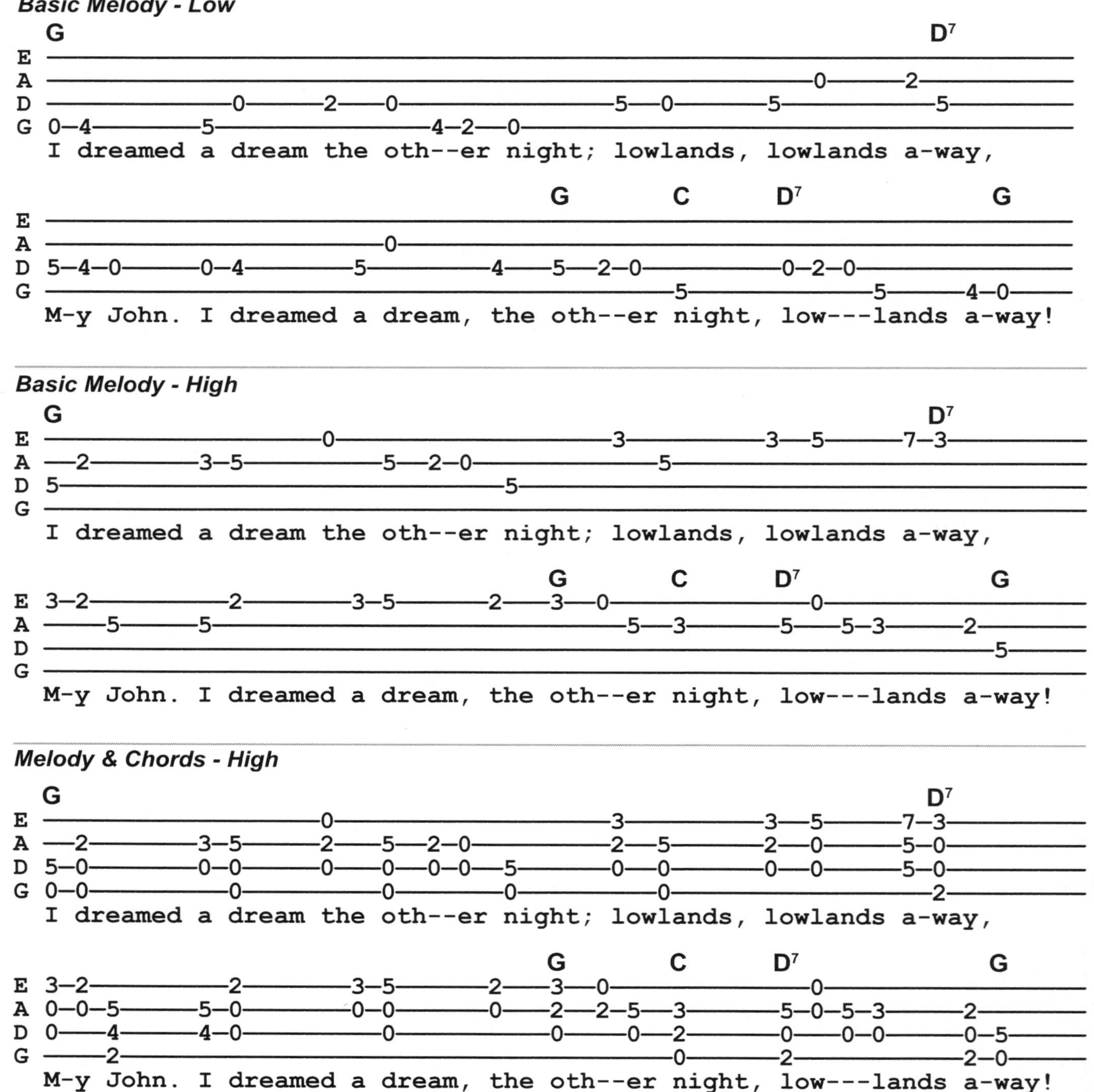

See Chords and Alternate Verses on Next Page

Lowlands Away (continued)

Chord Forms

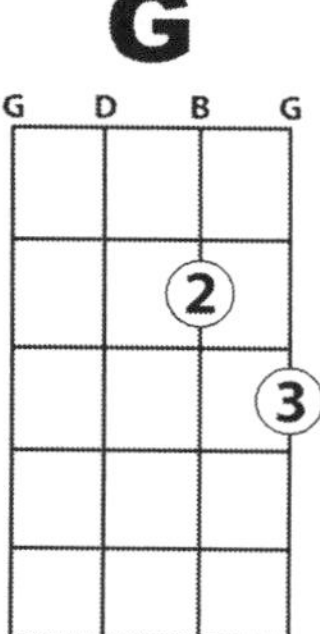

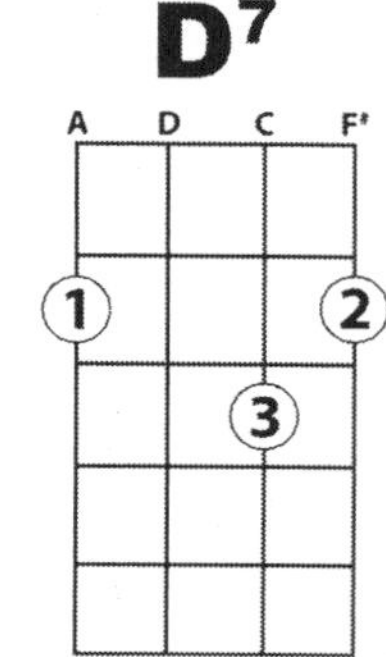

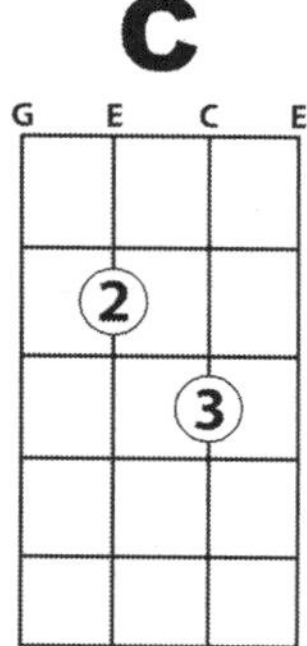

Additional Verses

Male Point of View Lyrics

I dreamed a dream, the other night...
Lowlands, lowlands away, my John.
My love she came, dressed all in white...
Lowlands away.

I dreamt my love came in my sleep...
Lowlands, lowlands away, my John.
Her cheeks were wet, her eyes did weep...
Lowlands away.

She came to me at my bedside...
Lowlands, lowlands away, my John.
All dressed in white, like some fair bride...
Lowlands away.

And bravely in her bosom fair...
Lowlands, lowlands away, my John.
A red, red rose, my love did wear...
Lowlands away.

She made no sound, no word she said...
Lowlands, lowlands away, my John.
And then I knew my love was dead...
Lowlands away.

Then I awoke to hear the cry...
Lowlands, lowlands away, my John.
All watch on deck, all watch ahoy...
Lowlands away.

Lowlands, Low

Basic Melody

Key of A Minor

Words and Music
Traditional

This song, also known as The Island Lass, is one of a number of songs that have been known as "Lowlands Low" over the years. This version seems to have been an authentic halyard shanty in classic call-and-response style.

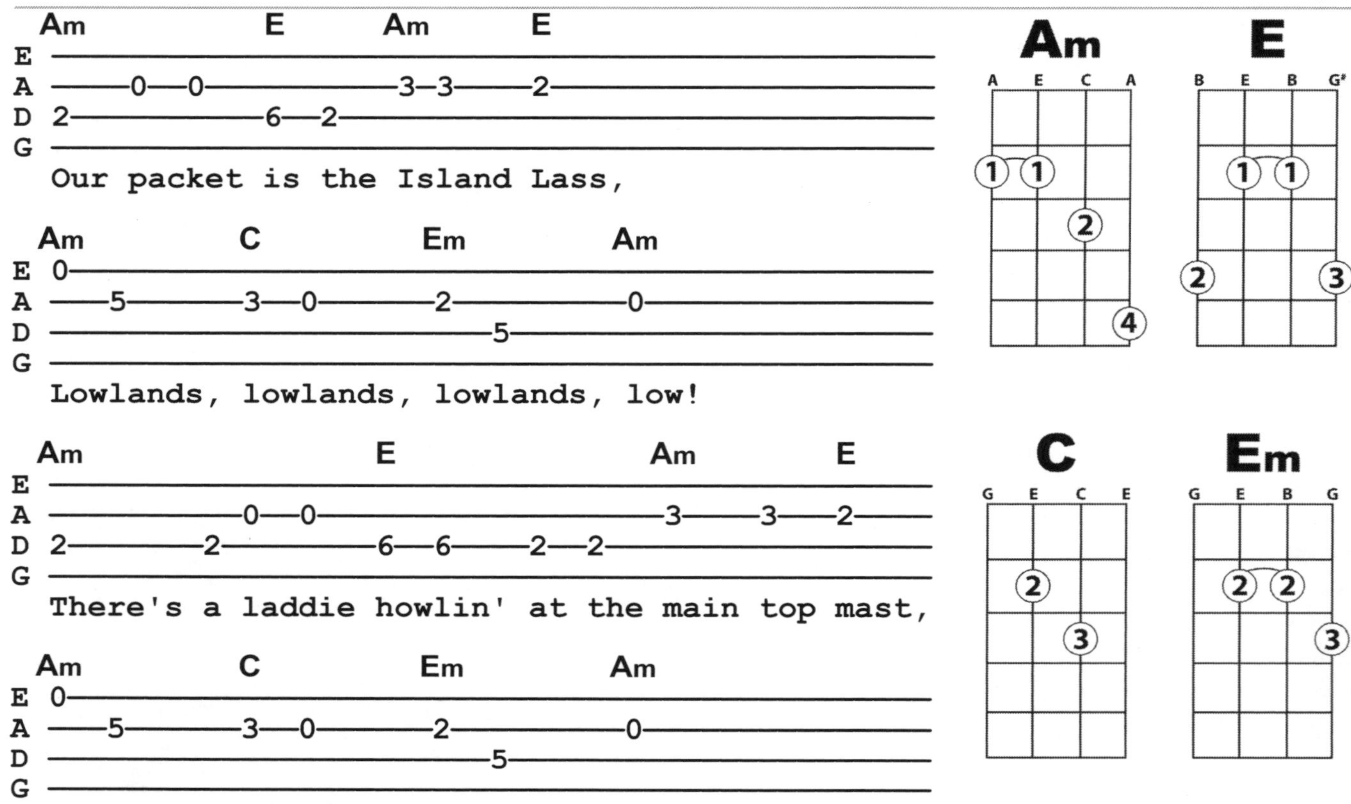

Additional Verses

The old man hails from Barbados,
Lowlands, lowlands, lowlands, low!
He's got the name of "Hammer Toes",
Lowlands, lowlands, lowlands, low!

He gives us bread as hard as brass,
Lowlands, lowlands, lowlands, low!
Our junk's as salt as a bailer's arse,
Lowlands, lowlands, lowlands, low!.

The monkey's rigged in a soldier's clothes,
Lowlands, lowlands, lowlands, low!
Where he got 'em from, God only knows,
Lowlands, lowlands, lowlands, low!

We'll haul 'em high and let 'em dry,
Lowlands, lowlands, lowlands, low!
We'll trice them up into the sky,
Lowlands, lowlands, lowlands, low!

It's up aloft that yard must go,
Lowlands, lowlands, lowlands, low!
Up aloft from down below,
Lowlands, lowlands, lowlands, low!

Lowlands, me boys, and up she goes,
Lowlands, lowlands, lowlands, low!
Get changed, me boys, to your shore-going clothes,
Lowlands, lowlands, lowlands, low!

Lowlands, Low (continued)

Melody & Chords

Key of A Minor

```
  Am            E     Am      E
E ------------------------------------------------
A ----0--0-----------3-3----2---------------------
D 2---2--2---6--2----2-2----2---------------------
G 2---2------4--4----2------4---------------------
  Our packet is the Island Lass,
```

```
  Am          C         Em          Am
E 0-----------------------------------------------
A 0--5--------3--0------2-----------0-------------
D 2--2--------2--2------2--5--------2-------------
G ------------0---------4--4--------2-------------
  Lowlands, lowlands, lowlands, low!
```

```
  Am                  E                Am        E
E -----------------------------------------------------
A ----------0--0-------------------------3-----3---2---
D 2--------2-2--2----6--6-----2--2-------2-----2---2---
G 2--------2-2-------4--4-----4--4-------2---------4---
  There's a laddie howlin' at the main top mast,
```

```
  Am          C         Em          Am
E 0-----------------------------------------------
A 0--5--------3--0------2-----------0-------------
D 2--2--------2--2------2--5--------2-------------
G ------------0---------4--4--------2-------------
  Lowlands, lowlands, lowlands, low!
```

Chord Forms

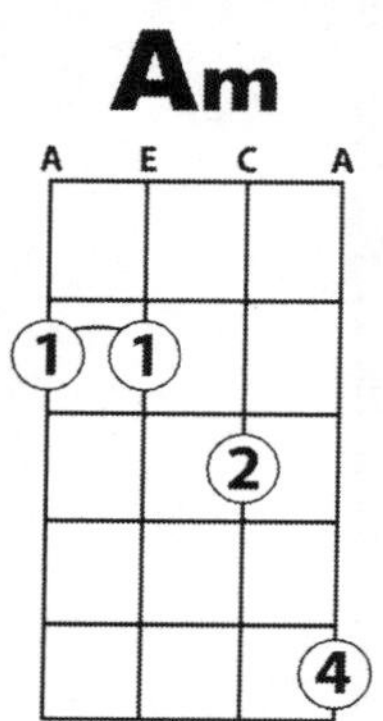

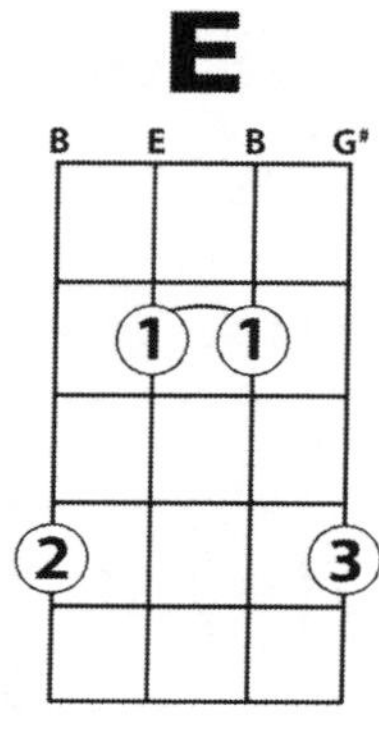

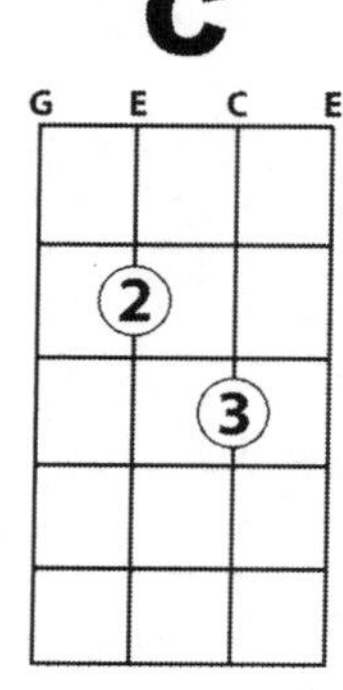

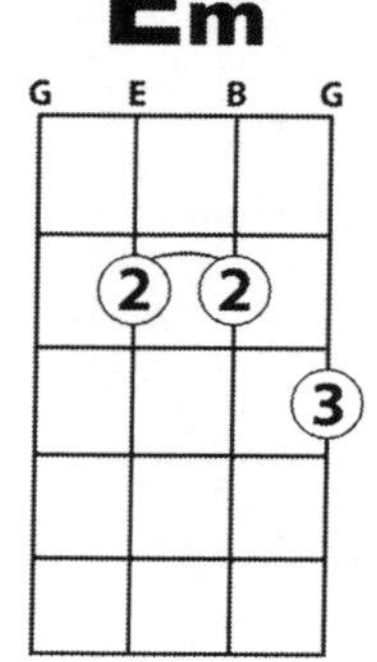

Lowlands, Low (continued)

Basic Melody

Key of E Minor (Low)

```
  Em          B      Em     B
E ──────────────────────────────────────────────────
A ──────────────────────────────────────────────────
D ────2──2───1──────5─5─────4───────────────────────
G 4─────────────4───────────────────────────────────
  Our packet is the Island Lass,
```

```
  Em         G         Bm         Em
E ──────────────────────────────────────────────────
A 2──0──────────────────────────────────────────────
D ──────────5──2────────4──0──────2─────────────────
G ──────────────────────────────────────────────────
  Lowlands, lowlands, lowlands, low!
```

```
  Em                 B                 Em        B
E ──────────────────────────────────────────────────
A ──────────────────────────────────────────────────
D ──────────2──2───1──1────────────────5────5───4───
G 4──────4─────────────────────4──4─────────────────
  There's a laddie howlin' at the main top mast,
```

```
  Em         G         Bm         Em
E ──────────────────────────────────────────────────
A 2──0──────────────────────────────────────────────
D ──────────5──2────────4──0──────2─────────────────
G ──────────────────────────────────────────────────
  Lowlands, lowlands, lowlands, low!
```

Chord Forms

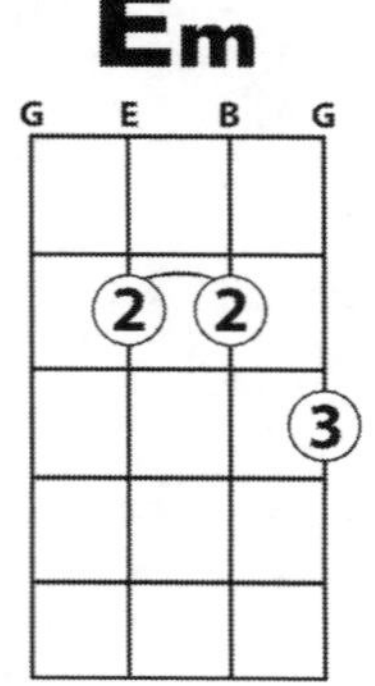

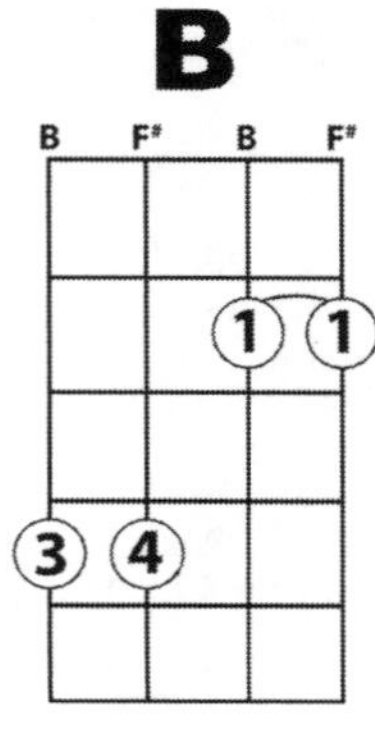

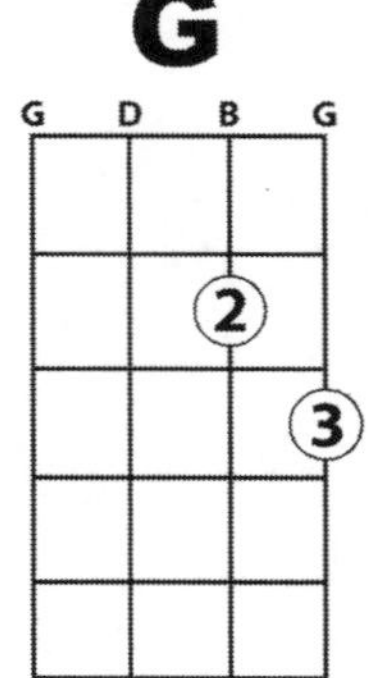

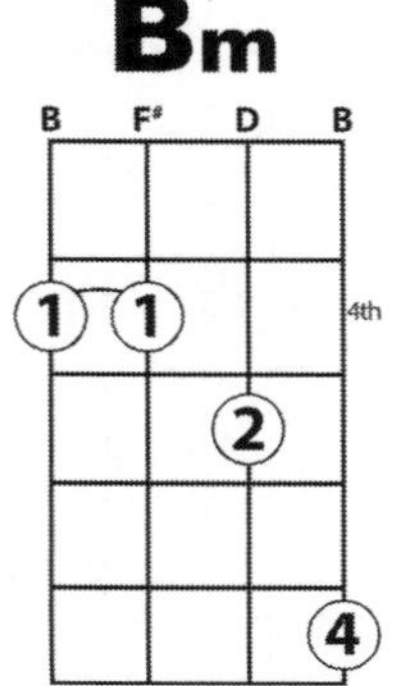

Lowlands, Low (continued)

Melody & Chords

Key of E Minor (Low)

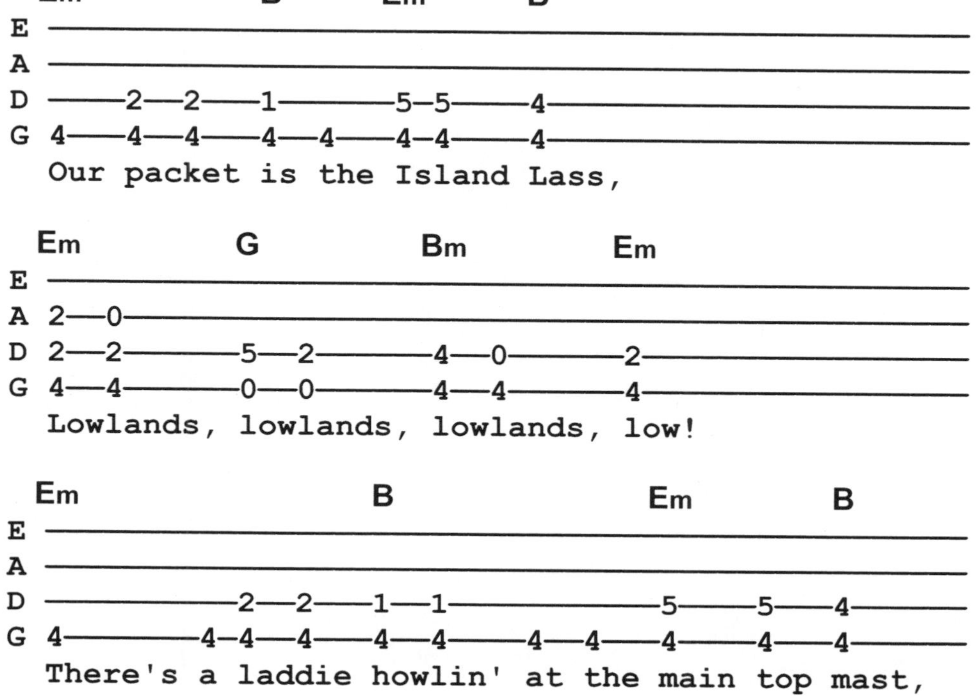


```
Em         G          Bm         Em
E ——————————————————————————————————————
A 2—0———————————————————————————————————
D 2—2————5—2————4—0————2————————————————
G 4—4————0—0————4—4————4————————————————
Lowlands, lowlands, lowlands, low!
```

Chord Forms

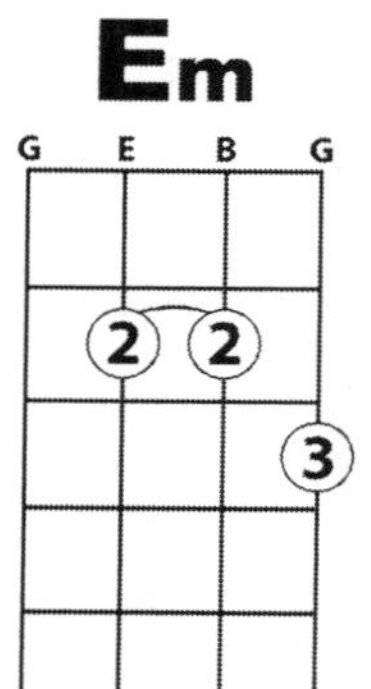

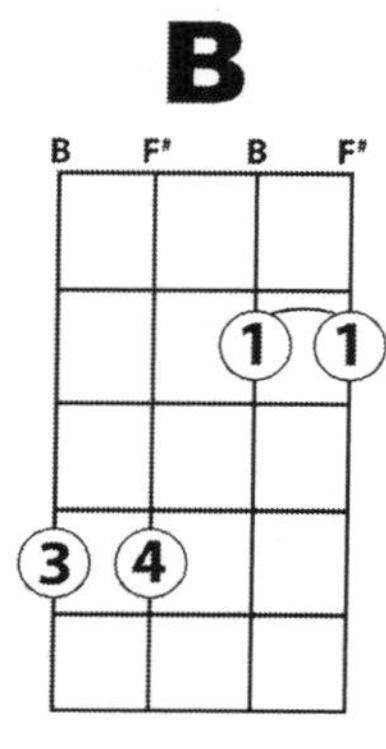

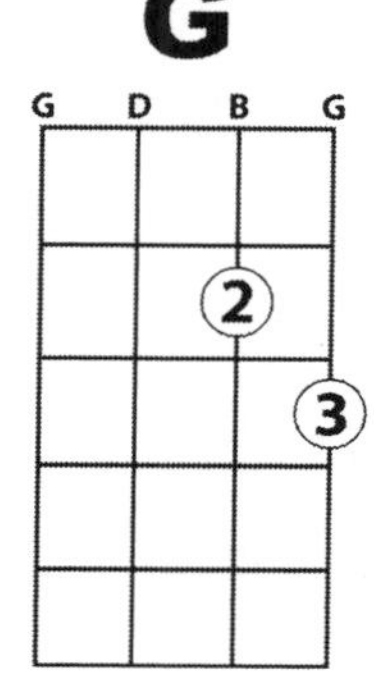

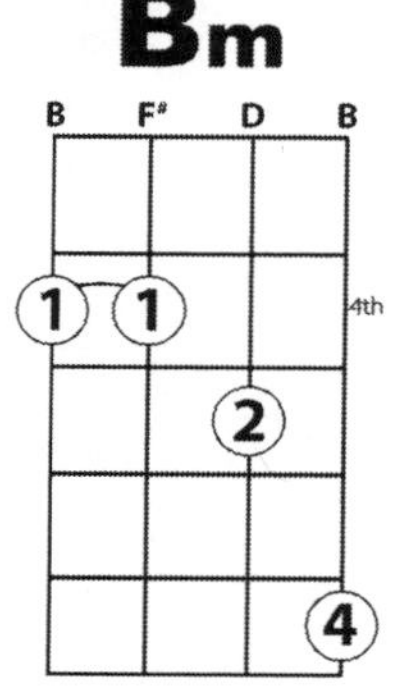

Lowlands, Low (continued)

Basic Melody

Key of E Minor (High)

```
   Em          B      Em     B
E ----0--0-----------3--3----2------------
A 2-----------6--2------------------------
D ----------------------------------------
G ----------------------------------------
  Our packet is the Island Lass,
```

```
   Em         G          Bm        Em
E 7--5--------3--0-------2---------0------
A -----------------------------5----------
D ----------------------------------------
G ----------------------------------------
  Lowlands, lowlands, lowlands, low!
```

```
   Em                 B                Em        B
E ----------0--0--------------------3-----3----2---
A 2-------2----------6--6----2--2------------------
D --------------------------------------------------
G --------------------------------------------------
  There's a laddie howlin' at the main top mast,
```

```
   Em         G          Bm        Em
E 7--5--------3--0-------2---------0------
A -----------------------------5----------
D ----------------------------------------
G ----------------------------------------
  Lowlands, lowlands, lowlands, low!
```

Chord Forms

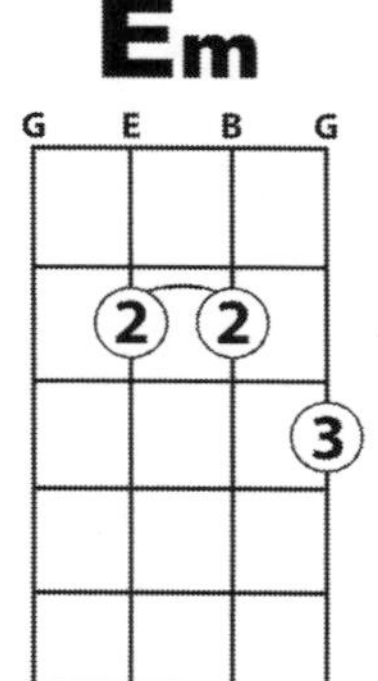

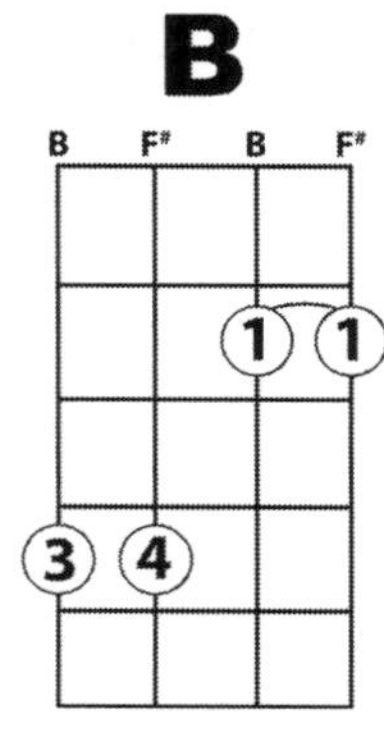

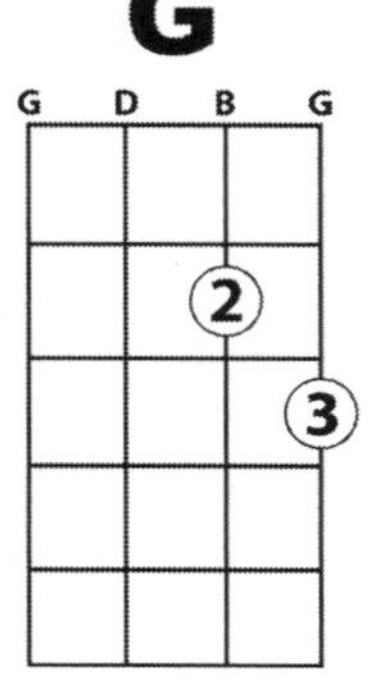

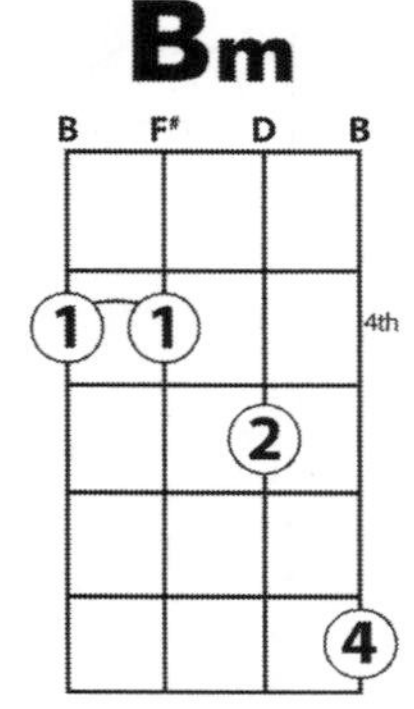

Lowlands, Low (continued)

Melody & Chords

Key of E Minor (High)

```
  Em           B     Em    B
E ------0--0-----------3-3---2------------------
A 2-----2--2---6--2----2-2---2------------------
D 2-----2------4--4----2-----4------------------
G 0------------4--------------------------------
  Our packet is the Island Lass,

  Em         G          Bm        Em
E 7--5-------3--0-------2---------0-------------
A 7--7-------2--2-------2--5------2-------------
D 5--5-------0----------4--4------2-------------
G ----------------------------------------------
  Lowlands, lowlands, lowlands, low!

  Em                   B                 Em      B
E ----------0--0-------------------------3----3---2-----
A 2------2-2--2----6--6----2--2----2----2---2-----
D 2------2-2-------4--4----4--4----2----2---4-----
G 0----------------4-------4--------------------------
  There's a laddie howlin' at the main top mast,

  Em         G          Bm        Em
E 7--5-------3--0-------2---------0-------------
A 7--7-------2--2-------2--5------2-------------
D 5--5-------0----------4--4------2-------------
G ----------------------------------------------
  Lowlands, lowlands, lowlands, low!
```

Chord Forms

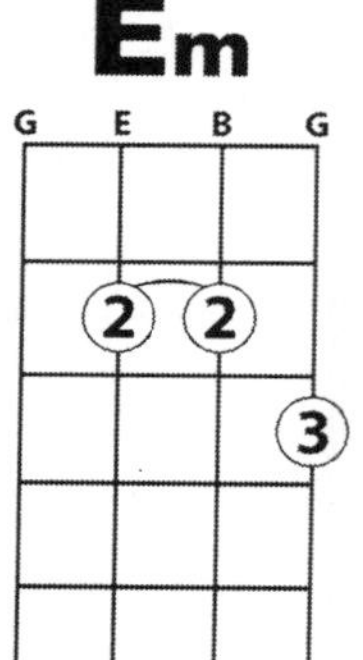

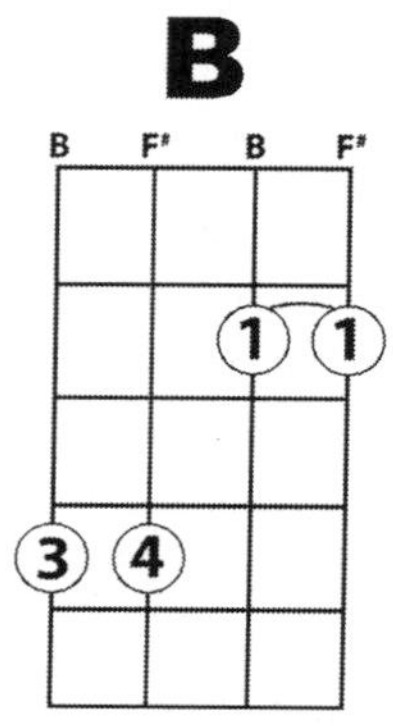

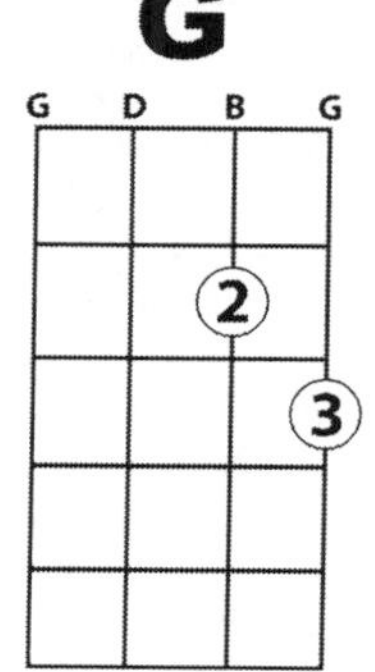

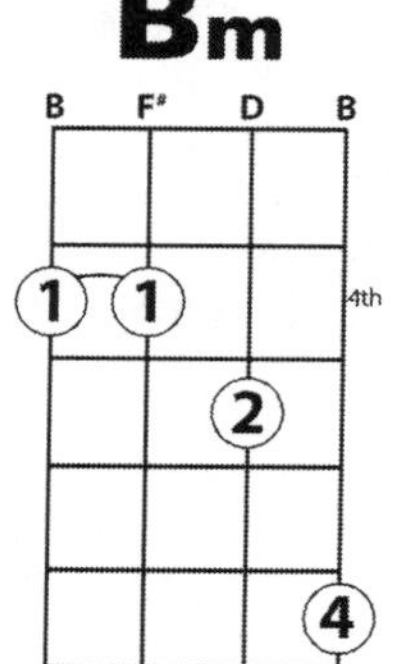

The Mermaid

Basic Melody

Key of C (Low)

This old seafaring ballad is thought to date to the mid 1700's, probably of English origin. It is still sung around the fire at children's summer camps and is also in the set lists of many Irish bands and singers. It is frequently heard at Irish singing sessions in the coastal regions of New England.

Words and Music Traditional

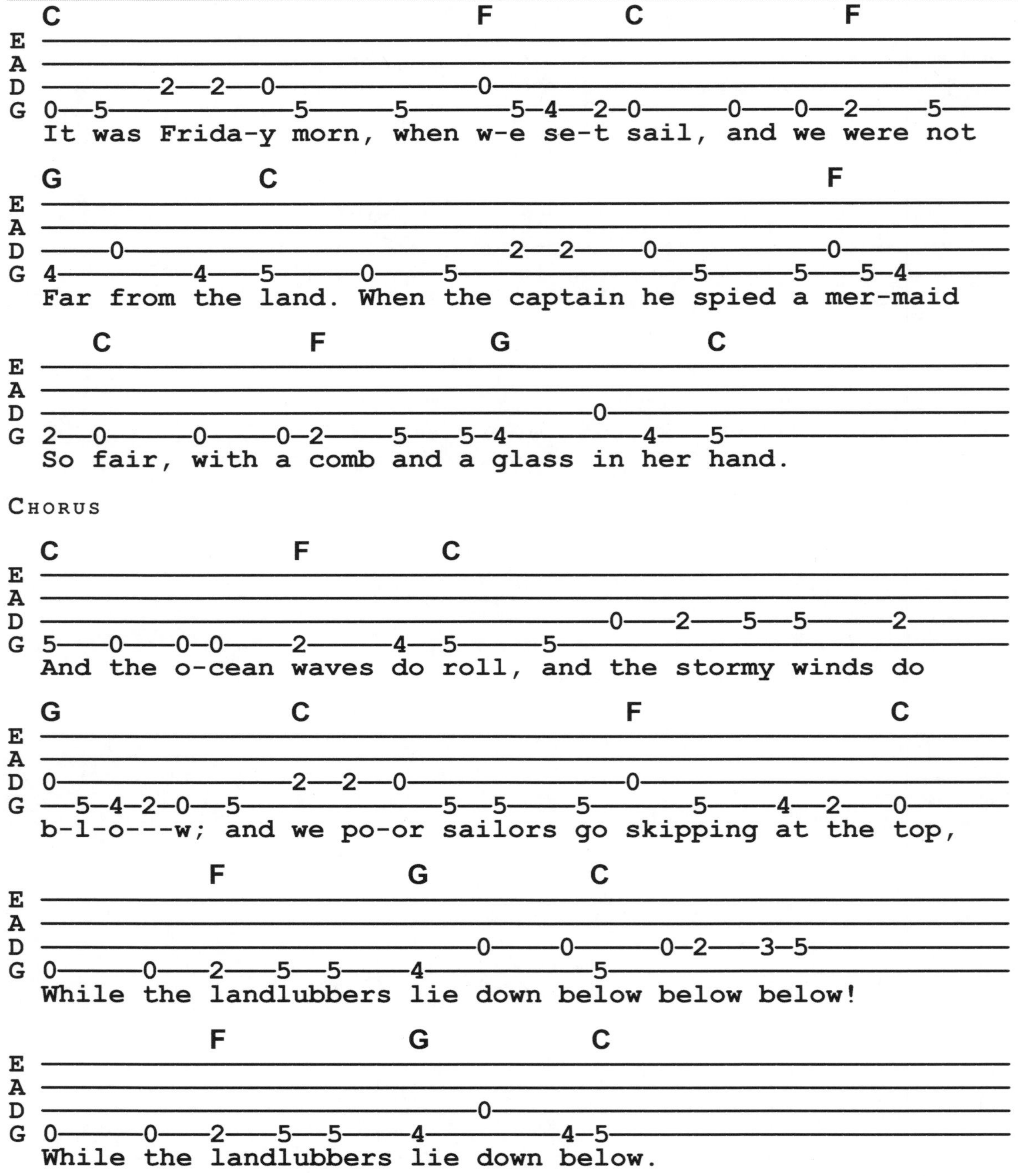

See Chord Forms and Additional Verses on Next Page

The Mermaid (continued)

Chord Forms

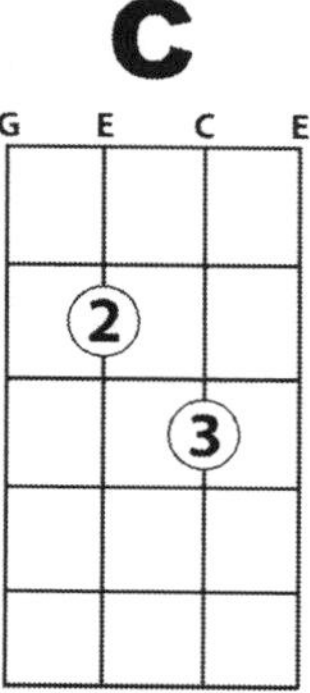

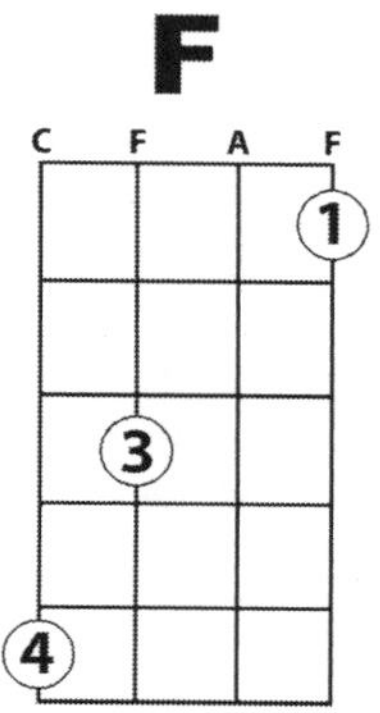

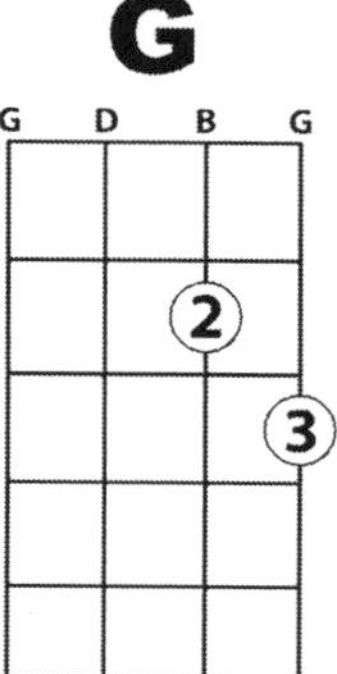

Additional Verses

Then up spoke the captain of our gallant ship,
And a fine old gentleman was he.
He said, “This fishy mermaid has warned me of our fate,
We shall sink to the bottom of the sea.”

Then up spoke the first mate of our gallant ship,
And a well-spoken gentleman was he.
He said, “I have me a wife in Portsmouth by the sea,
And tonight she a widow she'll be.”

Then up spoke the cook of our gallant ship,
And a crazy old butcher was he.
He said, “I care much more for my pots and my pans,
Than I do for the bottom of the sea.”

Then up spoke the cabin boy of our gallant ship,
And a fine young lad was he.
He said, “I have me a girlfriend in Salem by the sea,
And tonight she'll be weeping for me.”

Then it was three times ‘round, spun our gallant ship,
And three times ‘round spun she.
Yes it was three times ‘round, spun our gallant ship:
And she sank to the bottom of the sea!

The Mermaid (continued)

Basic Melody

Key of C (High)

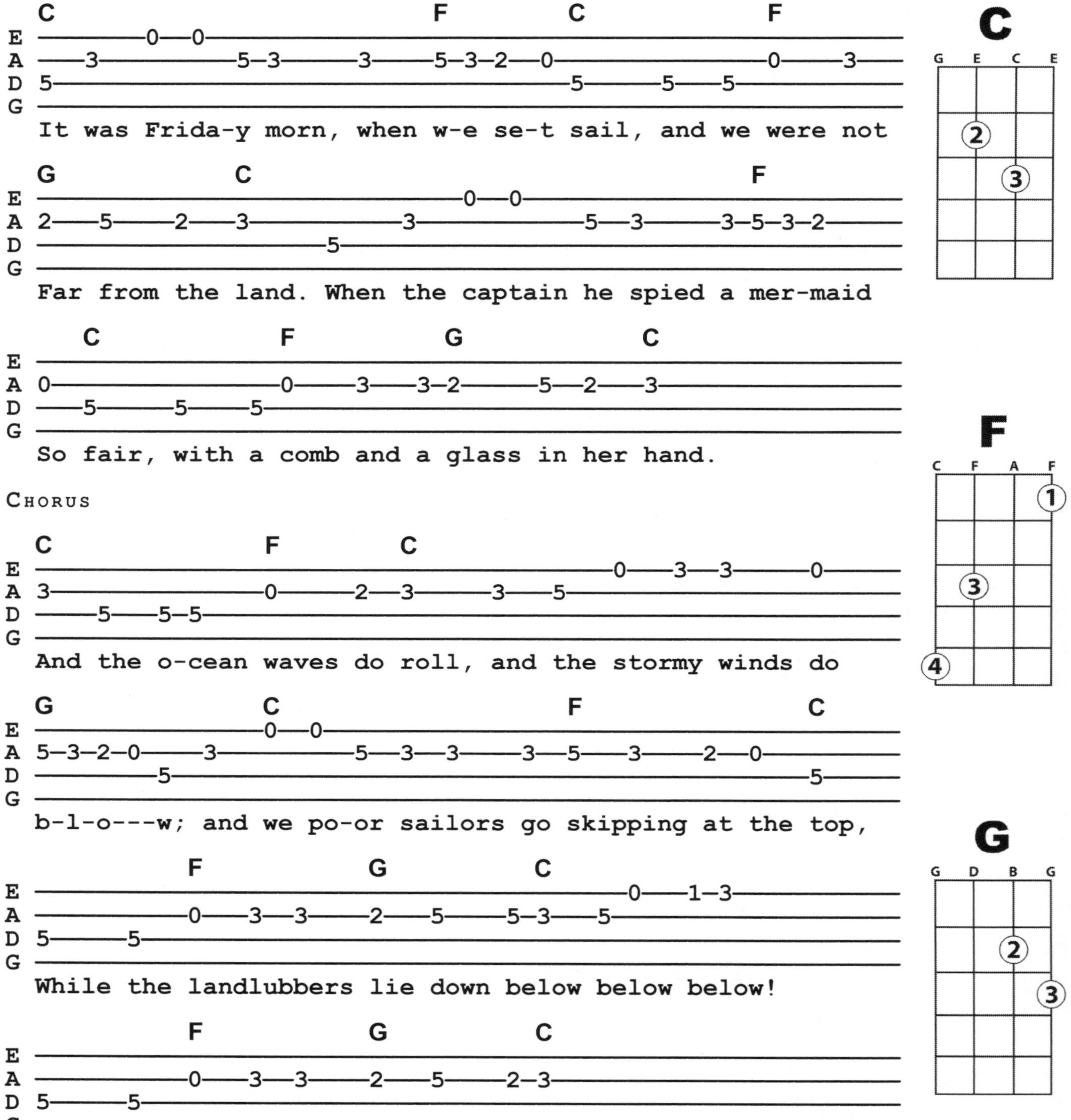

The Mermaid (continued)

Melody & Chords

Key of C (High)

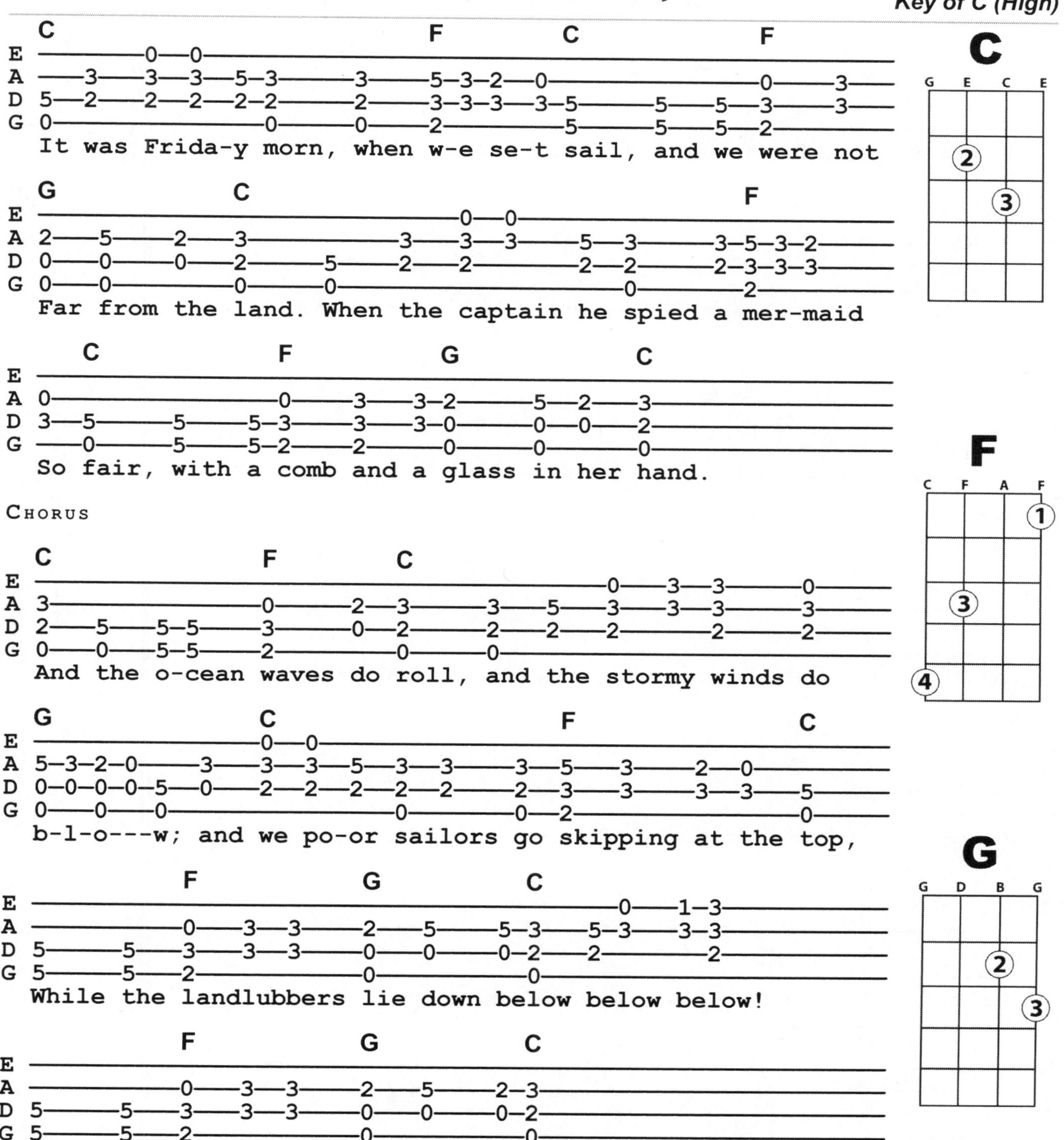

The Mermaid (continued)

Basic Melody

Key of G

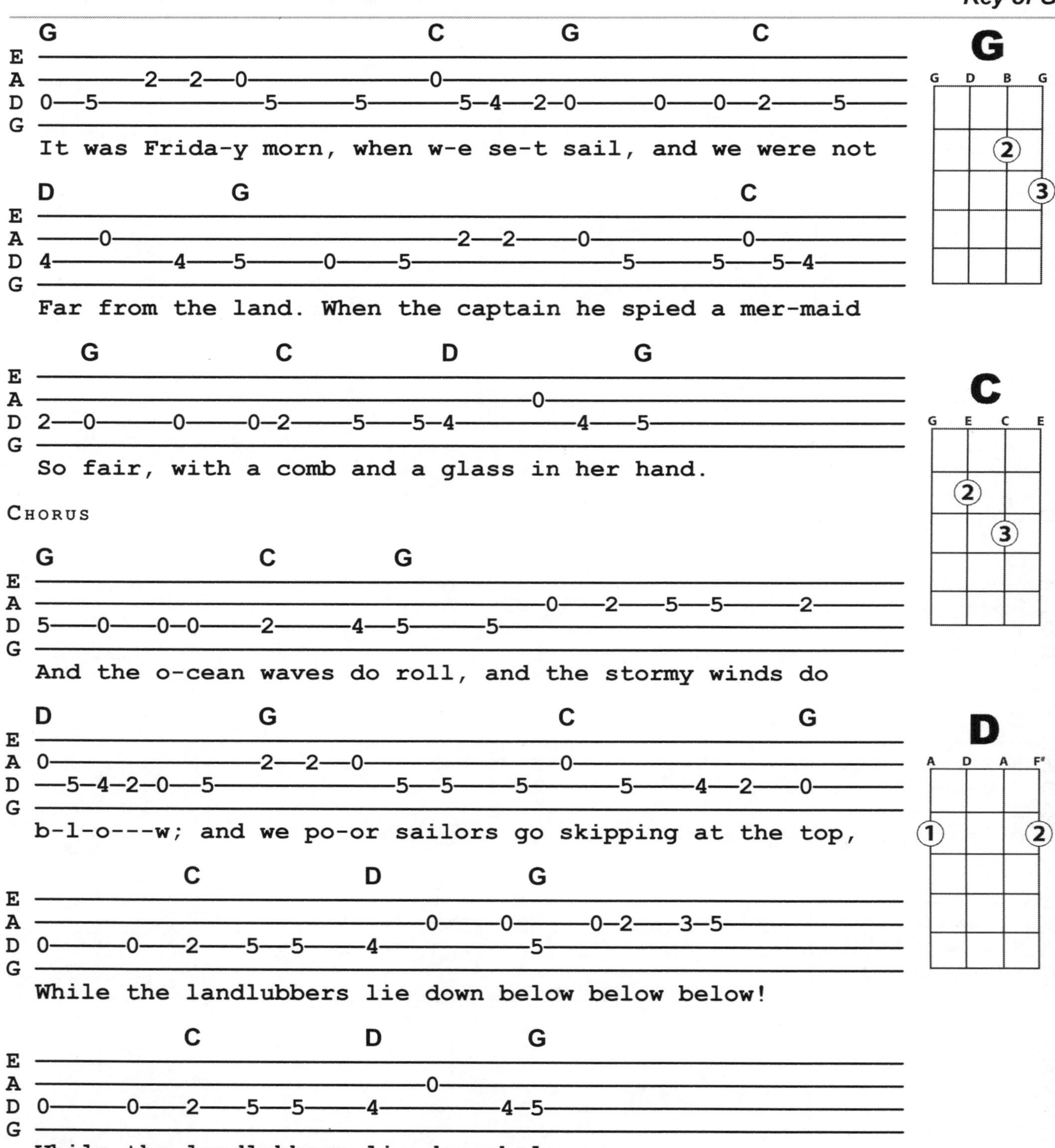

The Mermaid (continued)

Melody & Chords

Key of G

```
  G                                               C             G              C
E ───────────────────────────────────────────────────────────────────────────────────
A ─────────2──2──0─────────────────────────0─────────────────────────────────────────
D 0──5─────0──0──0──5─────────5────────2-5-4──2-0─────────0─────0──2─────5──
G 0──0─────0──────────0───────0────────0-0-2──0-0─────────0─────0──5─────5──
  It was Frida-y morn, when w-e se-t sail, and we were not
```

```
  D                 G                                                  C
E ───────────────────────────────────────────────────────────────────────────────────
A ────0────────────────────────────────2──2─────0──────────────0─────────────────────
D 4───0─────4───5──────0──────5────0──0──────0──5───────5-2-5-4───
G 2───2─────2───0──────0──────0────0─────────────0──────0-0-0-2───
  Far from the land. When the captain he spied a mer-maid
```

```
     G                  C              D                 G
E ───────────────────────────────────────────────────────────────────────────────────
A ─────────────────────────────────────────────0─────────────────────────────────────
D 2──0────────0──────0-2──────5────5-4─────0───4───5────────────────
G 0──0────────0──────0-5──────5────5-2─────2───2───0────────────────
  So fair, with a comb and a glass in her hand.
```

Chorus

```
  G                    C            G
E ───────────────────────────────────────────────────────────────────────────────────
A ──────────────────────────────────────────────0────2────5──5───────2──────────────
D 5───0────0-0──────2──────4──5──────5──0────0────0──0───────0──────────────
G 0───0────0-0──────5──────2──0──────0───────0───────0──────────────────────
  And the o-cean waves do roll, and the stormy winds do
```

```
  D                    G                         C                    G
E ───────────────────────────────────────────────────────────────────────────────────
A 0────────────────2──2──0─────────────────────0──────────────────────────────────────
D 0-5-4-2-0──5─────0──0──0──5──5────5──2─────5──────4──2────0──────
G 2-2-2-2-2──0─────0──0─────0──0────0──0─────0──────2──0────0──────
  b-l-o---w; and we po-or sailors go skipping at the top,
```

```
                C              D            G
E ───────────────────────────────────────────────────────────────────────────────────
A ───────────────────────────────────0─────0───────0-2─────3-5──────────────────────
D 0──────0───2───5──5──────4───0─────0-5───0-0─────0-0─────────────
G 0──────0───5───5──5──────2───2─────0─────────────0───────────────
  While the landlubbers lie down below below below!
```

```
                C              D            G
E ───────────────────────────────────────────────────────────────────────────────────
A ───────────────────────────────────0───────────────────────────────────────────────
D 0──────0───2───5──5──────4───0─────4-5──────────────────────────
G 0──────0───5───5──5──────2───2─────2-0──────────────────────────
  While the landlubbers lie down below.
```

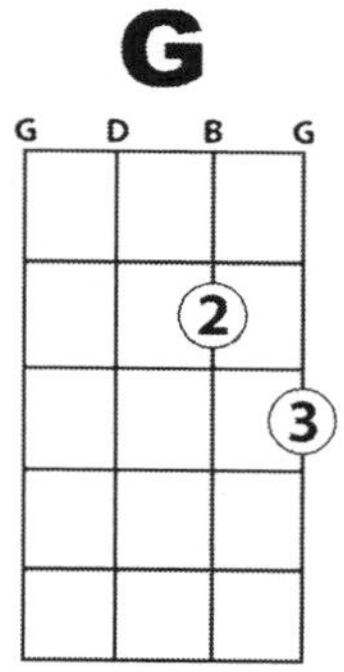

G

G D B G

②
③

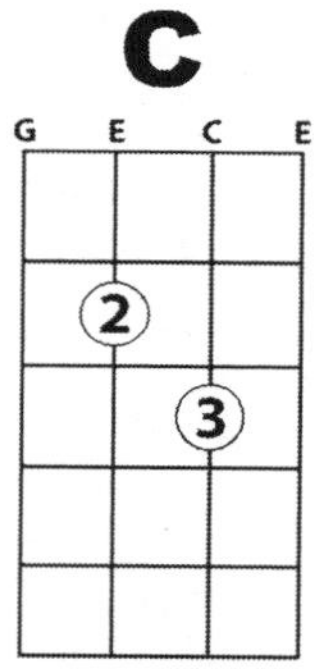

C

G E C E

②
③

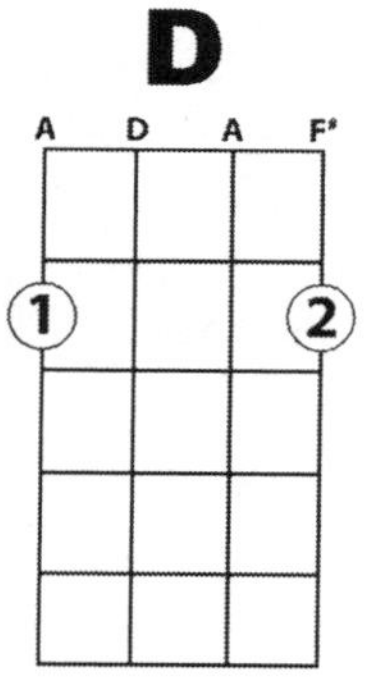

D

A D A F#

① ②

Mingulay Boat Song

Basic Melody

Key of C (Low)

The origins of this old song are lost in time, but it first came to wider notice when published in a book of songs of the British Isles in the 1930's by Hugh Roberton. The source of the tune is thought to be an older Scottish air. This song has been performed and re-worked by many folk artists over the years.

Words by Hugh Roberton

Music Traditional

CHORUS AND FIRST VERSE

```
  C
E ------------------------------------------------
A ------------------------------------------------
D ---------------------------5---2---2-0----------
G 5---0---2-4---5---5--------------------5--------
  And hee-l ya ho, boys, let her g-o boys,

  C          G                     F
E ------------------------------------------------
A ------------------------------------------------
D 2---0---------0-----0-----0-2-0-----------------
G ---------5-----------------------5---2-4-5------
  Br-ing her head 'round int-o the weather.

           C
E ------------------------------------------------
A ------------------------------------------------
D -------------------------5---2---2-0------------
G 0---2-4---5---5------------------------5--------
  Hee-l ya ho, boys, let her g-o, boys,

  C        G                     F     C
E ------------------------------------------------
A ------------------------------------------------
D 2---0-------0---0-----0---2---0-----------------
G ---------5-----------------------5-5----5-------
  Sa-iling homeward to Mi-ng-u-la---y!
```

C

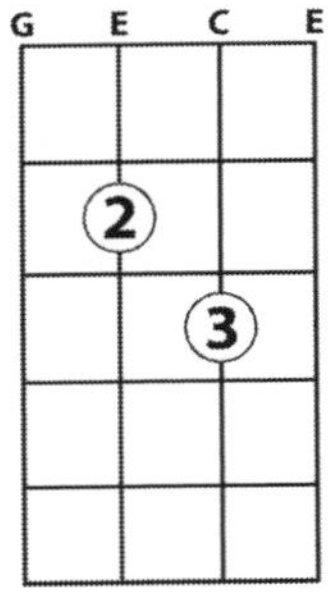

G E C E

G

G D B G

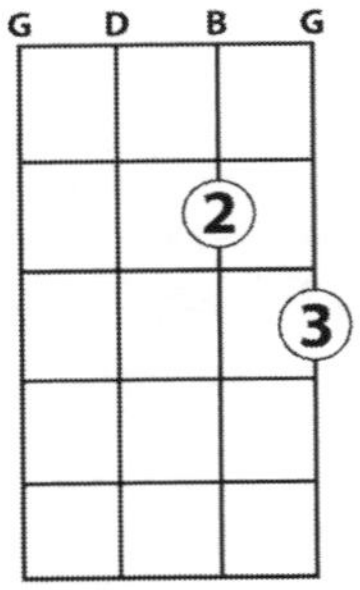

Additional Verses

What care we tho' white the Minch is,
What care we for the wind and weather?
Bring her round, boys, every inch is
Closer homeward to Mingulay.

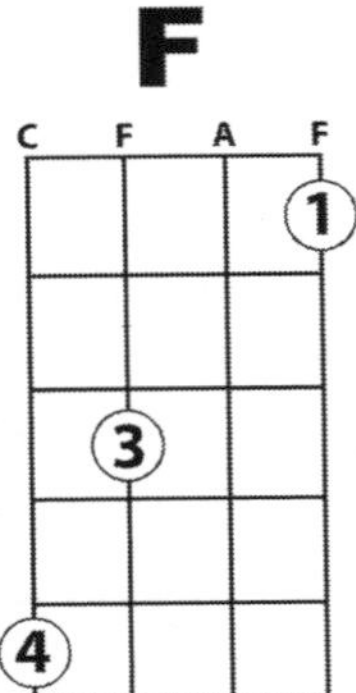

Wives are waiting on the beach head,
Looking seaward from the heather;
Bring her round boys, and we'll anchor,
E're the sun sets on Mingulay.

Minguláy Boat Song

(continued)

Basic Melody

Key of C (High)

CHORUS AND FIRST VERSE

```
  C
E -------------------------------3---0---0-----------
A 3-------0-2--3---3---------------------------5-3---
D ----5----------------------------------------------
G ---------------------------------------------------
  And hee-l ya ho, boys, let her g-o boys,

  C           G                          F
E 0-----------------------------0--------------------
A ---5---3----5------5----------5---5-3----0-2-3-----
D ---------------------------------------------------
G ---------------------------------------------------
  Br-ing her head 'round int-o the weather.

            C
E ------------------------3---0---0------------------
A -----0-2--3---3---------------------5--3-----------
D 5--------------------------------------------------
G ---------------------------------------------------
  Hee-l ya ho, boys, let her g-o, boys,

  C         G                          F     C
E 0-----------------------0--------------------------
A ---5-3----5----5----5-------5--3-3----3------------
D ---------------------------------------------------
G ---------------------------------------------------
  Sa-iling homeward to Mi-ng-u-la---y!
```

Chord Forms

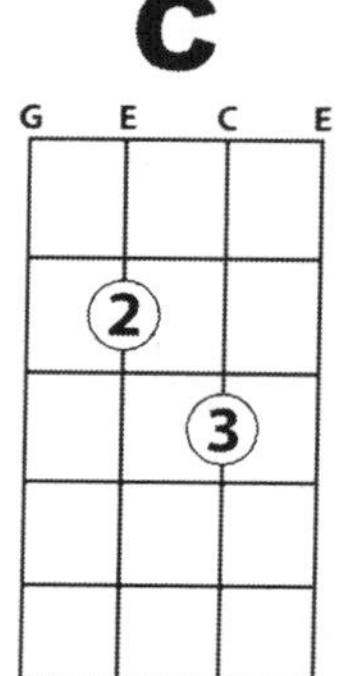

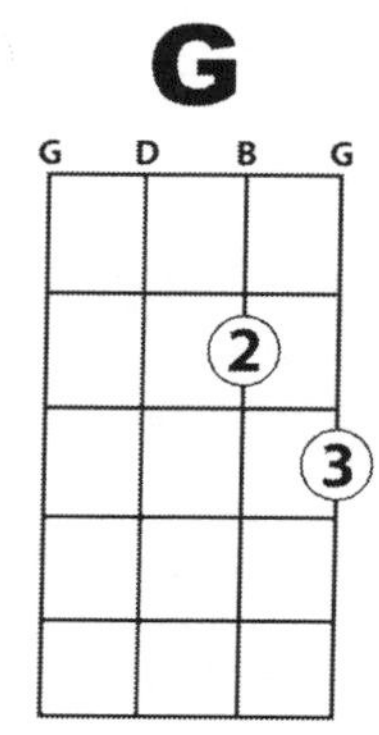

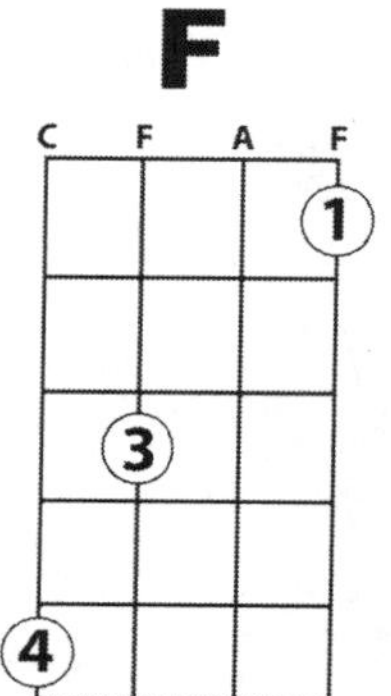

Mingulay Boat Song
(continued)

Melody & Chords

Key of C (High)

CHORUS AND FIRST VERSE

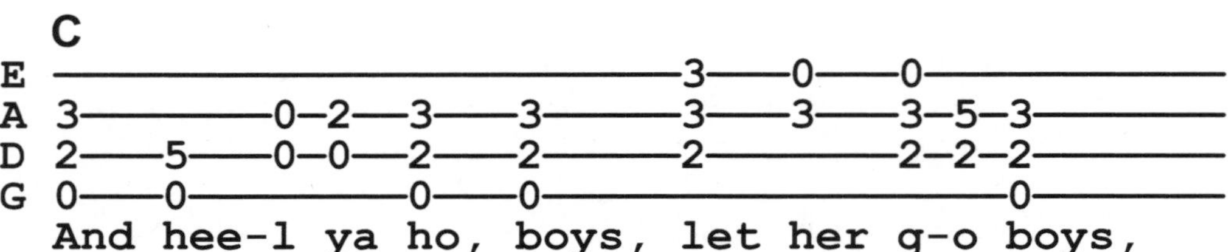


```
C           G                      F
E 0-------------------------0----------------
A 3--5---3---5-----5-----5-2-5-3---0-2-3-----
D 2--2---2---0-----0-----0---0-0---3-3-3-----
G ------------0-----0---------------2---2-----
Br-ing her head 'round int-o the weather.
```

```
          C
E --------------------3---0---0-----------
A ----0-2--3---3------3---3---3-5--3------
D 5---0-0--2---2------2-------2-2--2------
G 0--------0---0-------------------0------
Hee-l ya ho, boys, let her g-o, boys,
```

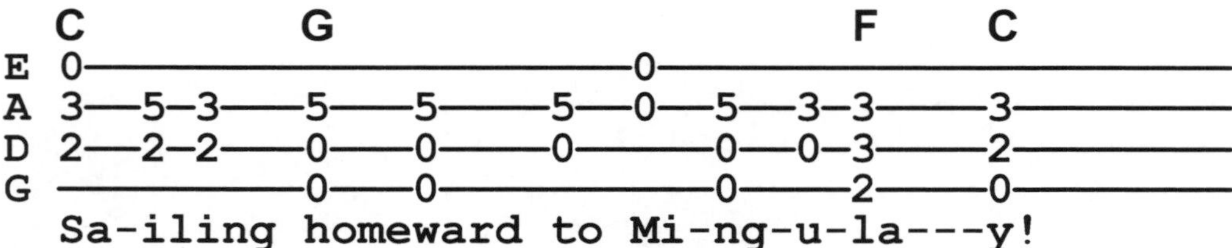

Chord Forms

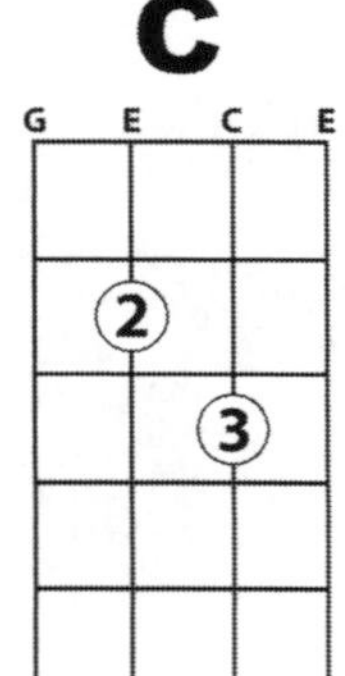

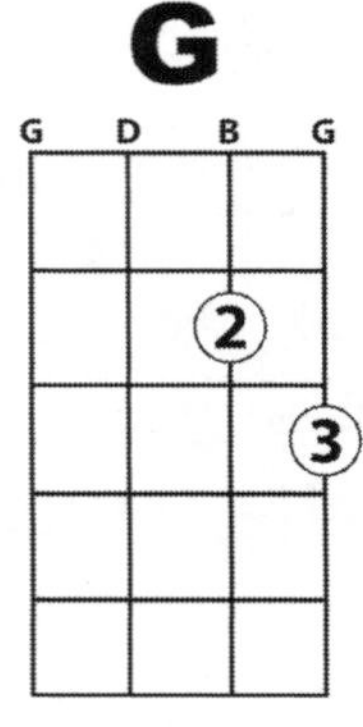

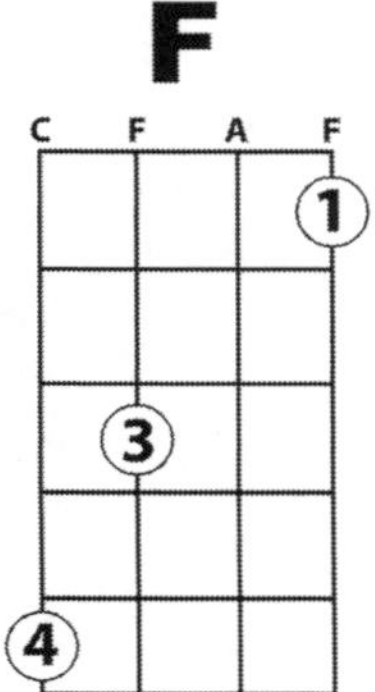

The Ghost Island of Mingulay

Mingulay is an actual island located in the Outer Hebrides chain off the north-western coast of Scotland. While its history of settlement is believed to date back to the Iron Age, settlement on the island was abandoned in 1912 and today only a few wind-worn ruins remain of the village shown above.

Roberton's decision to use the island's name in his sea song was likely purely romantic and artistic in nature, as it is unlikely he had ever been there himself - the island had already been uninhabited for a quarter of a century by the time he wrote the words to this song, and no residents of the island ever sang the song.

After being abandoned by its year-round residents, the island was used for sheet grazing and was seasonally populated by shepherds. It is now owned by the National Trust for Scotland and is regularly visited by naturalists and by rock-climbing enthusiasts wanting to test their skills on the extraordinarily high sea cliffs.

According to Wikipedia, there is a local tradition that French gold was hidden in a sea cave on the island, intended to help support the 1745 Jacobite rebellion in Scotland, though no trace has ever been found.

Mingulay Boat Song
(continued)

Basic Melody

Key of G

CHORUS AND FIRST VERSE

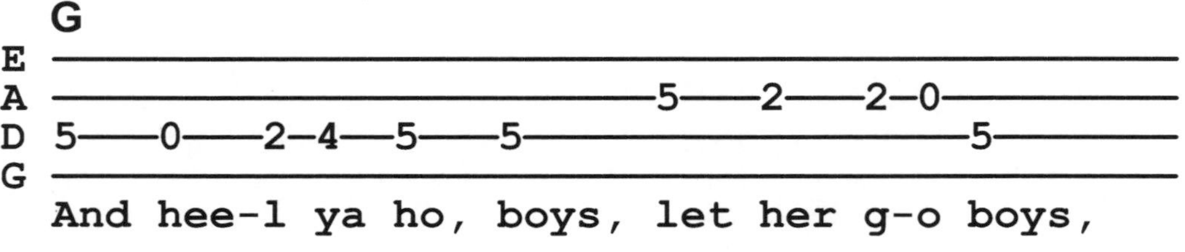

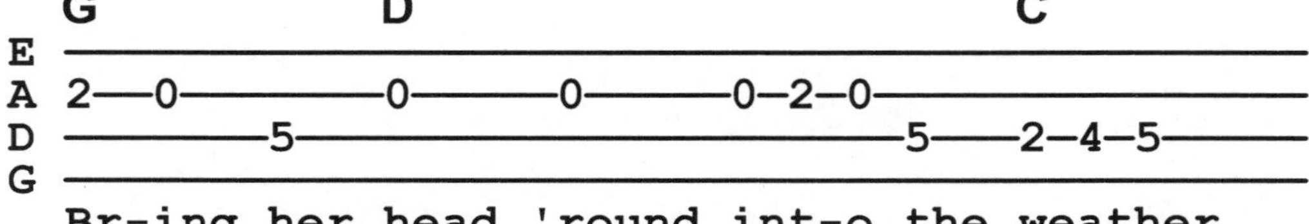

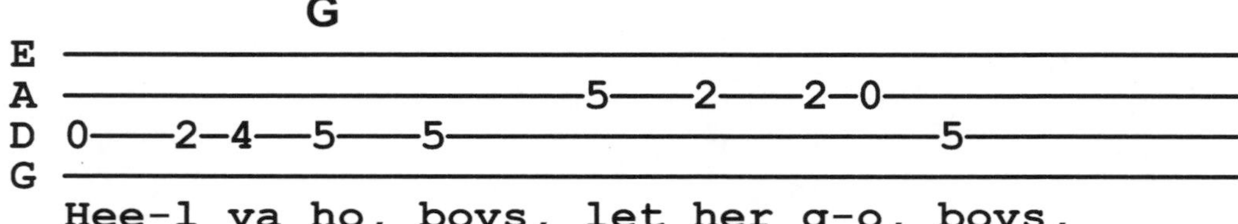

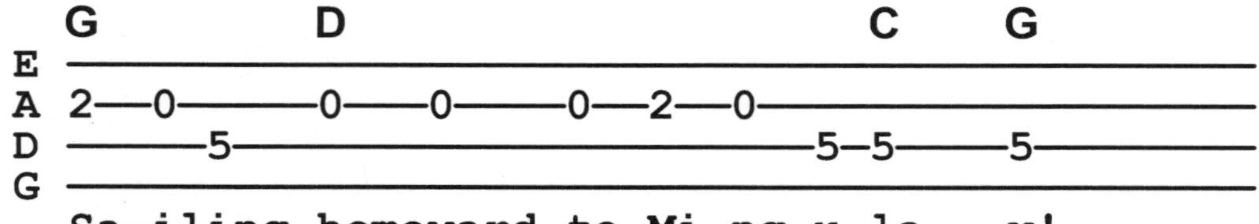

Chord Forms

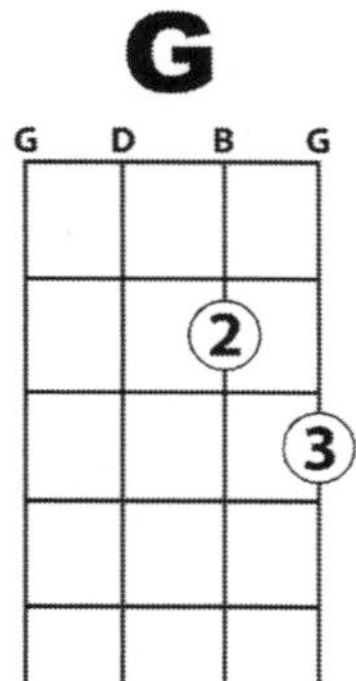

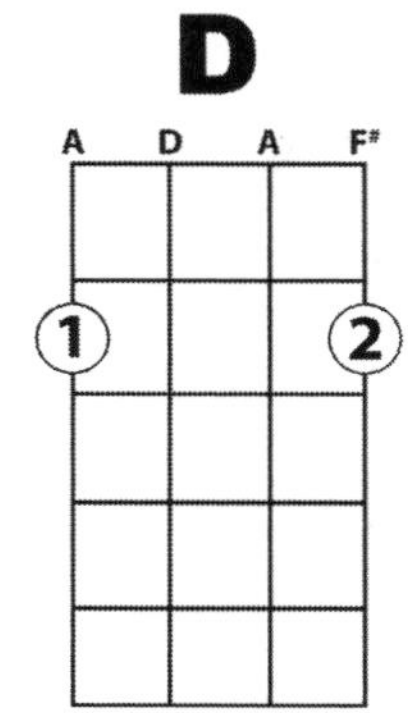

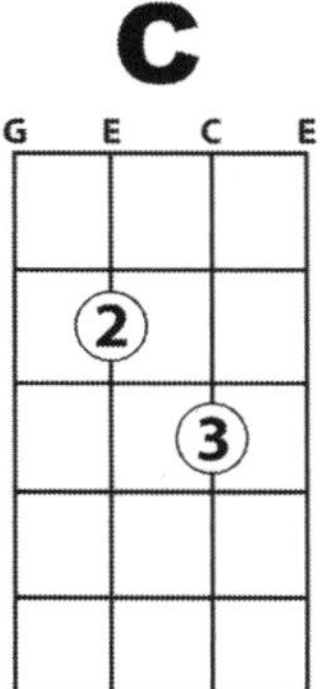

Mingulay Boat Song
(continued)

Melody & Chords

Key of G

CHORUS AND FIRST VERSE

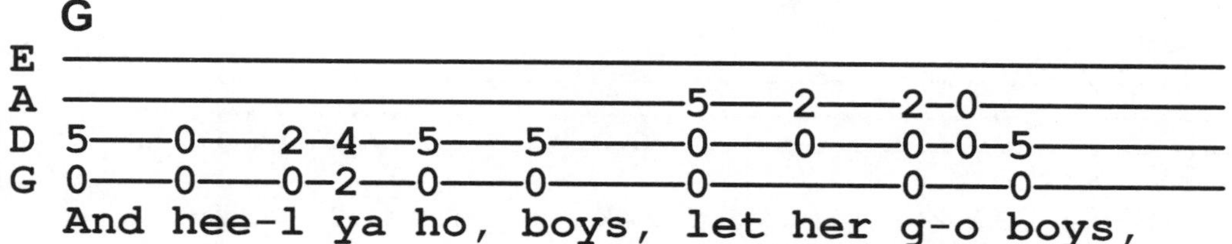

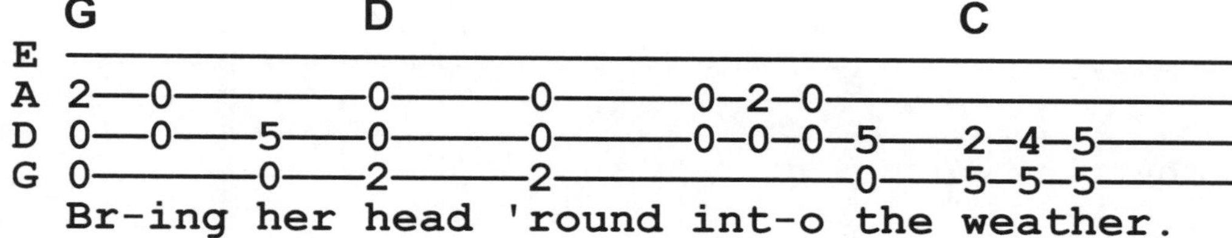

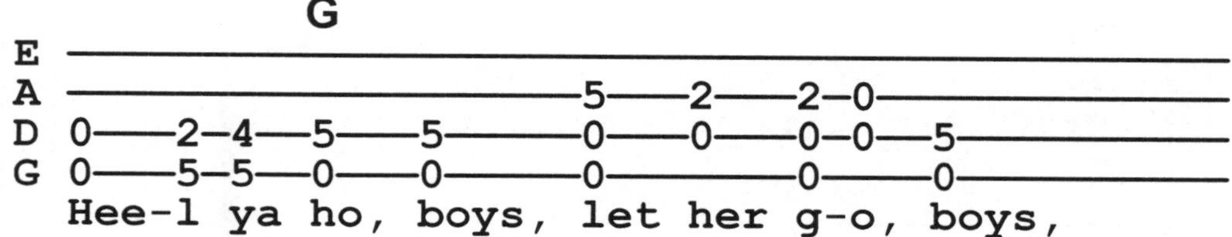


```
  G          D                   C    G
E ————————————————————————————————————————
A 2—0————0——0————0—2—0———————————————————
D 0—0–5——0——0————0—0—0——5–5————5————————
G 0————0——2——2————————2————0–5————0——————
  Sa-iling homeward to Mi-ng-u-la---y!
```

Chord Forms

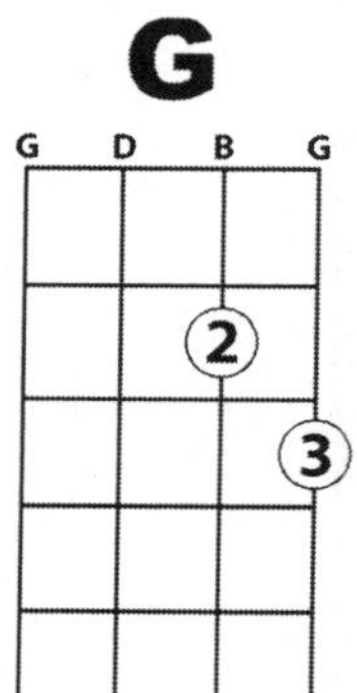

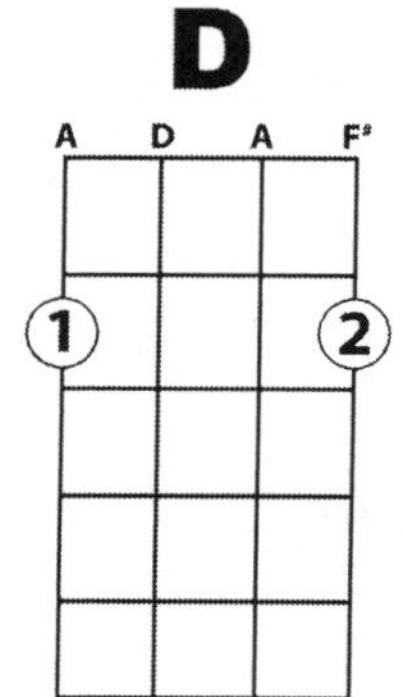

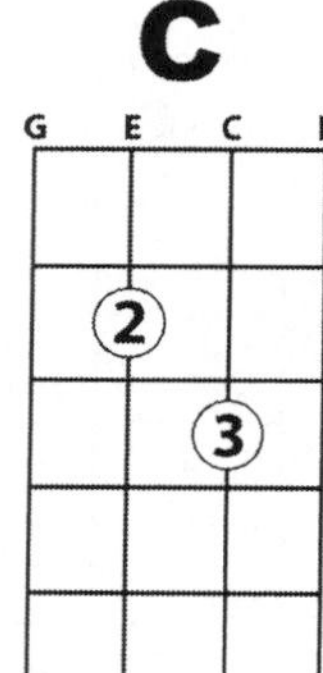

The Morning Glory (page 1)

Basic Melody

Key of C

Words and Music

Traditional

This is another "love" song that does not entirely follow the traditional form. In it a sailor tells the story of the results of his courtship of the four daughters of the landlord of a local pub. When he returns from sea, the results of his amorous adventures await him. Liam Clancy's rendition of this one as part of Makem & Clancy is highly recommended.

```
  C                       G     C                 F          C
E -------------------------------------------------------------------------------
A -------------------------------------------------------------------------------
D 5--5--------------------0----0--2------2--2---2-----3--------3--5--------5--5--
G ---------5----5---5------------------------------------------------------------
  At the end of the day I like a little drink to raise my voice
```

```
  F   C               F                       C                      D
E -------------------------------------------------------------------------------
A -------------------------------0---0-------------------------------------------
D 3----2--------2----2--3--3-----------------5--3--2-----5--5------5----2----0--0-
G -------------------------------------------------------------------------------
  And sing; and another or two of a pint of brew and I'm ready
```

```
          G                 C            G                  C        F
E -------------------------------------------------------------------------------
A -------------------------------------------------------------------------------
D 0----2----0-------5--5-------------------0----0-------0-------2----2------3----
G -----------5--------------------5-----5----------------------------------------
  For anything. At the cross Keys Inn there were sisters four,
```

```
      C                  F     C           F
E -------------------------------------------------------------------------------
A -------------------------------------------------0---0-------------------------
D 3----5----5--------5------3------2-------2----3----------------5------3--------
G -------------------------------------------------------------------------------
  The landlord's daughters fair; and every night when they'd
```

```
  C                          D                 G
E -------------------------------------------------------------------------------
A -------------------------------------------------------------------------------
D 2-----5----5----5-------2----0----0----2---4----5-----------5--5---------------
G -------------------------------------------------------------------------------
  Turn out the light I'd tip toe up the stairs, singin':
```

Chord Forms

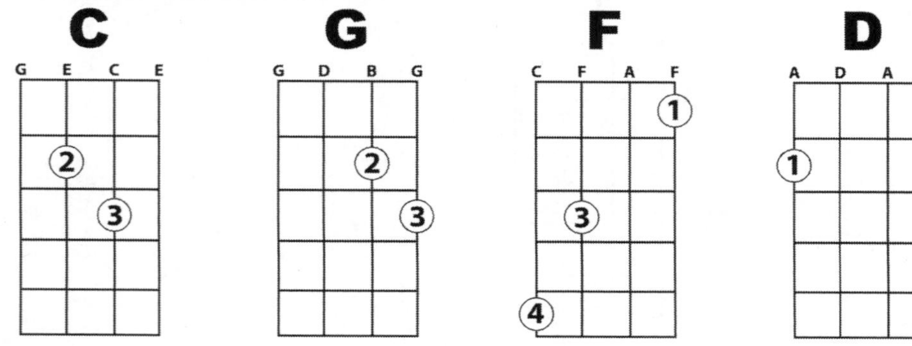

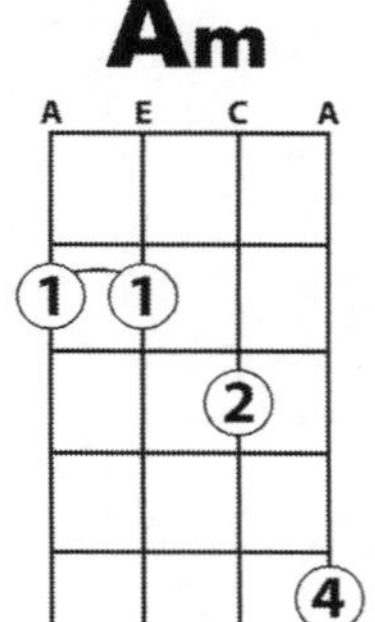

The Morning Glory (page 2)

Basic Melody

Key of C

CHORUS

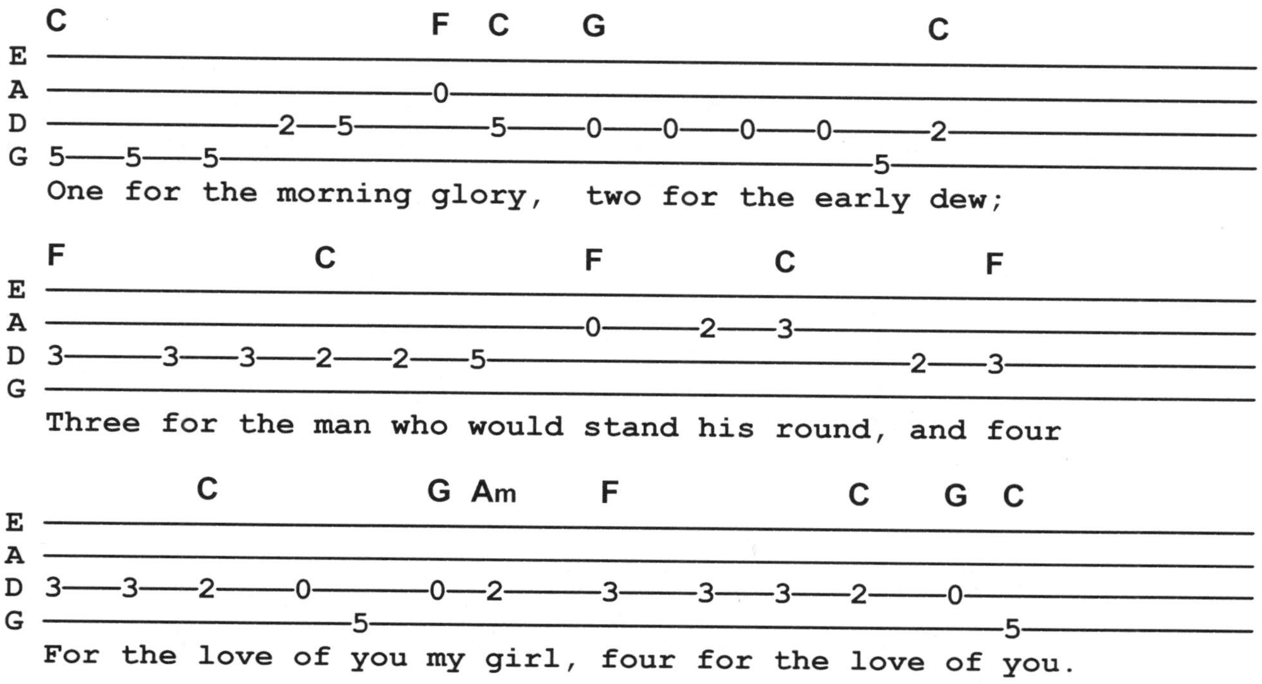

```
  C                        F   C    G                      C
E ------------------------------------------------------------------------
A --------------------------0---------------------------------------------
D ----------------2---5---------5----0----0----0----0-------2------------
G 5---5---5-------------------------------------------5------------------
  One for the morning glory,  two for the early dew;

  F                 C                F           C          F
E ------------------------------------------------------------------------
A -----------------------------------0-----2----3-------------------------
D 3-----3----3----2----2----5---------------------------2----3------------
G ------------------------------------------------------------------------
  Three for the man who would stand his round, and four

           C             G  Am     F              C      G   C
E ------------------------------------------------------------------------
A ------------------------------------------------------------------------
D 3---3---2-----0--------0--2------3-----3----3----2-----0----------------
G ----------------------5----------------------------------------5--------
  For the love of you my girl, four for the love of you.
```

Additional Verses

Well I got the call from foreign shores, to go and fight the foe;
Though I thought no more of the sisters four, still I was sad to go.
We sailed away on a ship, the Morning Glory was her name;
And we'd all fall down when the rum went 'round,
Then we'd get up and start again... singin':

Well we sailed once more to our native shore, farewell to the rolling sea;
The Cross Keys Inn it was beckonin', and my heart was full of glee.
But there on the shore were the sisters four, with a bundle on each knee;
There were three little girls and a bouncin' boy,
And they all looked just like me... singing':

The Morning Glory

(continued - page 1)

Melody & Chords

Key of C

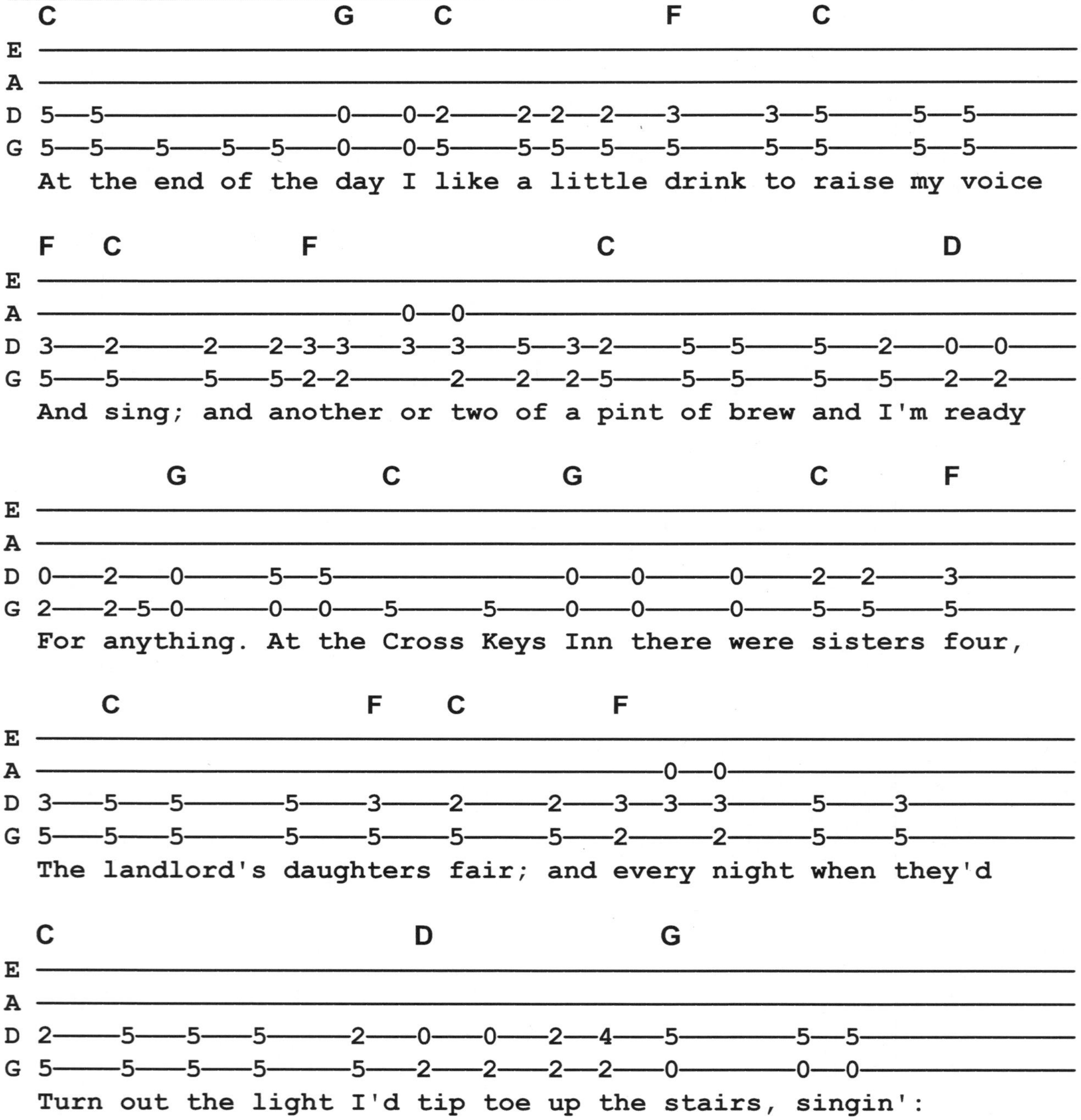

```
  C                  G     C              F         C
E ─────────────────────────────────────────────────────────────────
A ─────────────────────────────────────────────────────────────────
D 5──5──────────────0───0─2────2─2──2───3──────3──5──────5──5──────
G 5──5──5───5──5──0───0─5────5─5──5───5──────5──5──────5──5──────
  At the end of the day I like a little drink to raise my voice

  F   C         F                 C                    D
E ─────────────────────────────────────────────────────────────────
A ───────────────────────────0──0──────────────────────────────────
D 3───2─────2───2─3─3───3──3───5──3─2──────5──5─────5───2───0──0───
G 5───5─────5───5─2─2──────2───2──2─5──────5──5─────5───5───2──2───
  And sing; and another or two of a pint of brew and I'm ready

          G            C          G              C       F
E ─────────────────────────────────────────────────────────────────
A ─────────────────────────────────────────────────────────────────
D 0───2───0─────5──5─────────────────0───0─────0─────2───2─────3───
G 2───2─5─0─────0──0───5──────5──────0───0─────0─────5───5─────5───
  For anything. At the Cross Keys Inn there were sisters four,

      C                F    C         F
E ─────────────────────────────────────────────────────────────────
A ─────────────────────────────────────────0──0────────────────────
D 3───5───5──────5────3────2─────2───3──3──3──────5────3───────────
G 5───5───5──────5────5────5─────5───2─────2──────5────5───────────
  The landlord's daughters fair; and every night when they'd

  C                     D              G
E ─────────────────────────────────────────────────────────────────
A ─────────────────────────────────────────────────────────────────
D 2─────5───5───5──────2───0───0───2──4───5─────────5──5───────────
G 5─────5───5───5──────5───2───2───2──2───0─────────0──0───────────
  Turn out the light I'd tip toe up the stairs, singin':
```

The Morning Glory

(continued - page 2)

Melody & Chords

Key of C

CHORUS

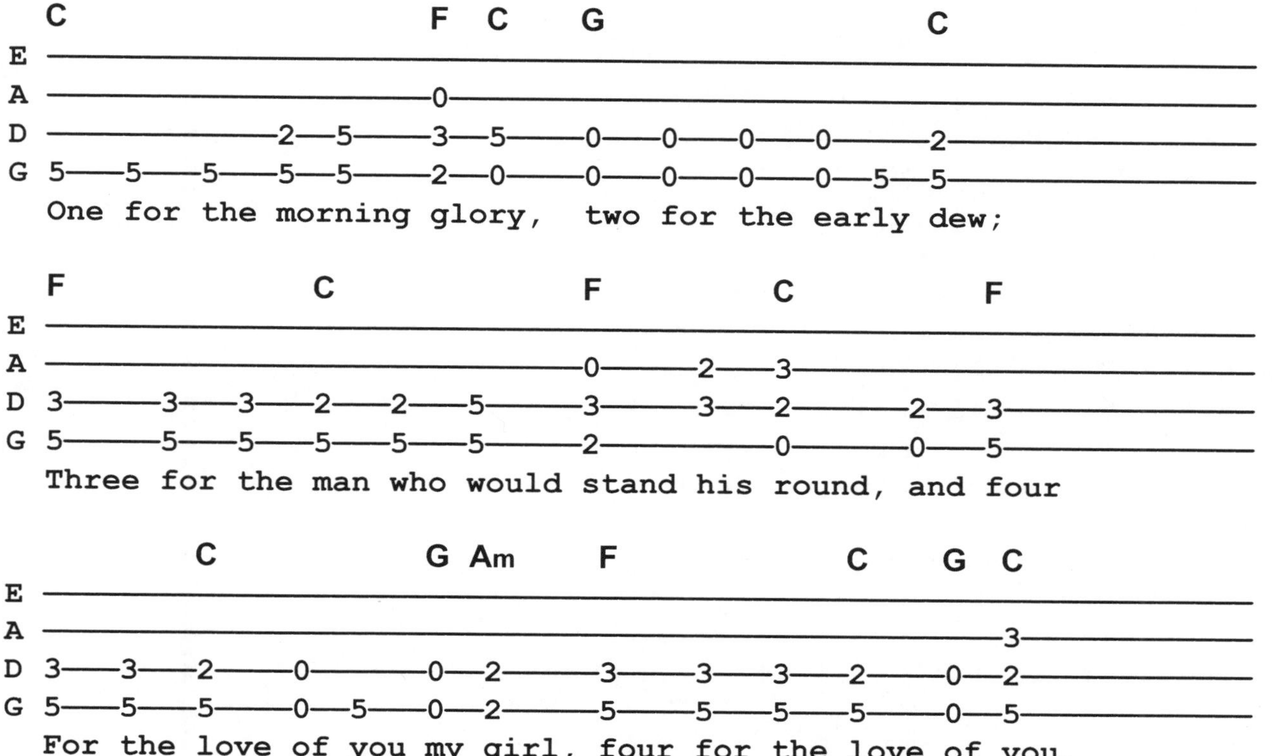

Chord Forms

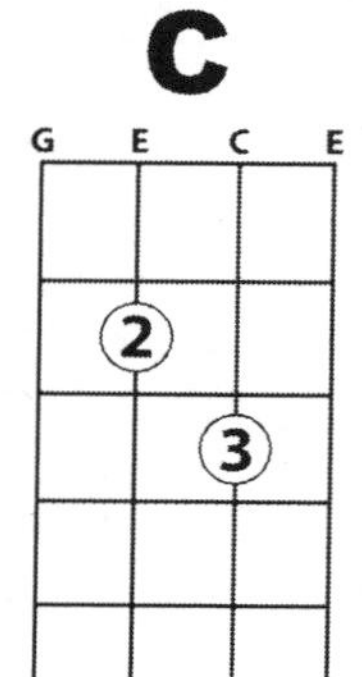

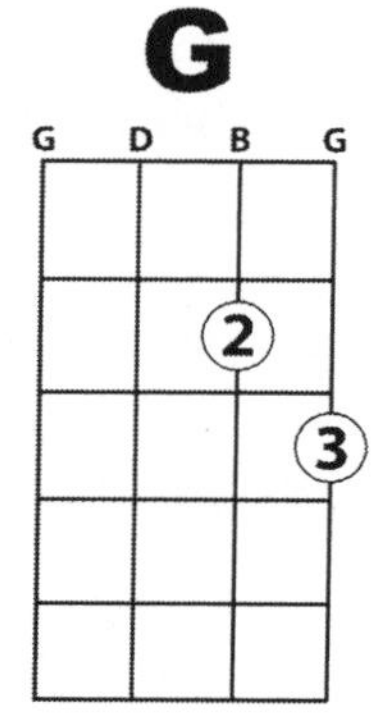

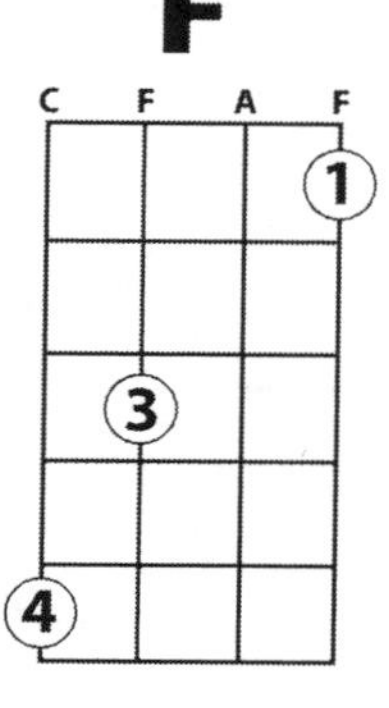

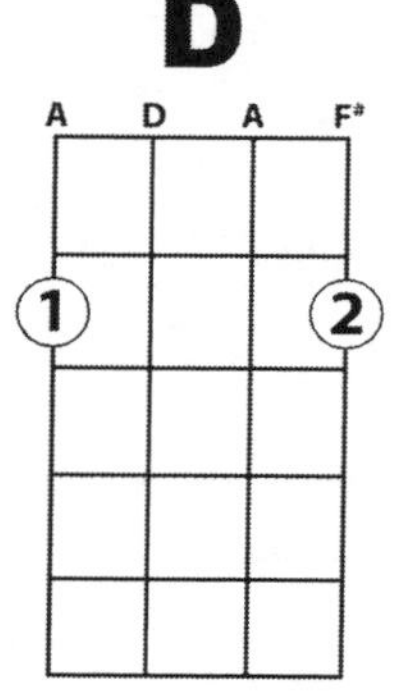

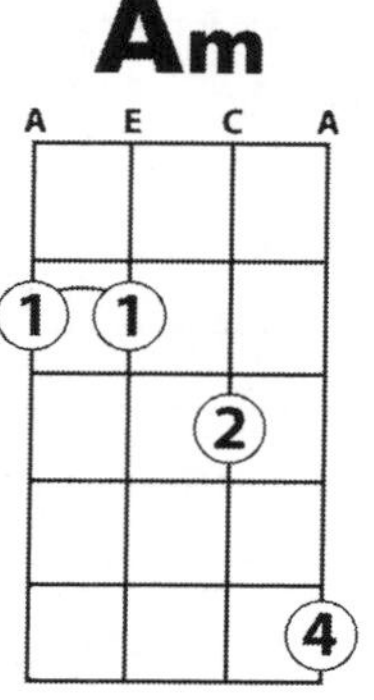

The Morning Glory
(continued - page 1)

Basic Melody

Key of G (Low)

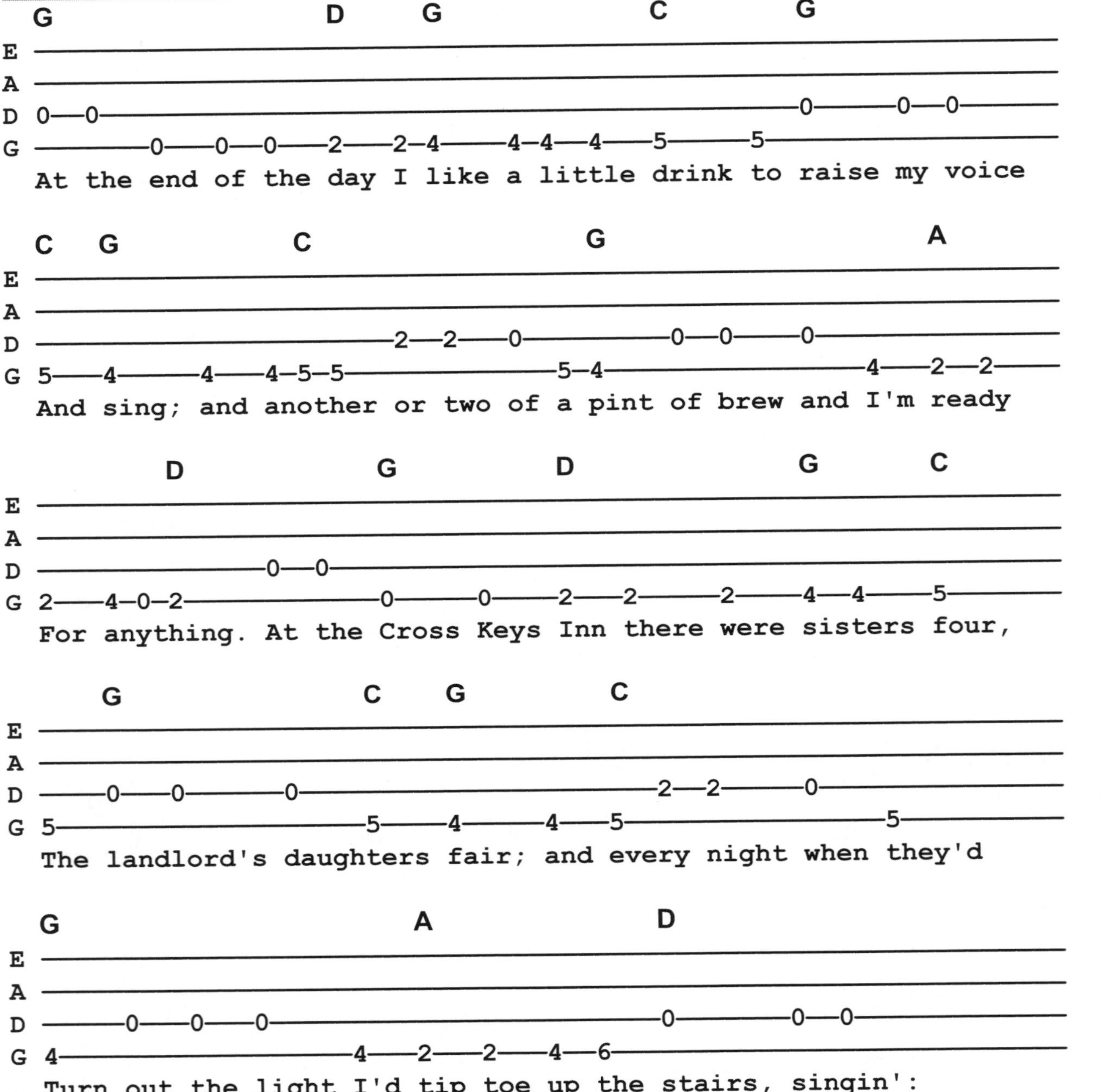

The Morning Glory

(continued - page 2)

Basic Melody

Key of G (Low)

CHORUS

```
  G                        C  G  D                     G
E ------------------------------------------------------------
A ------------------------------------------------------------
D -------------------0----2--0--------------------------------
G 0---0---0---4----------------2---2---2---2--0--4-------------
  One for the morning glory,  two for the early dew;
```

```
  C             G             C         G          C
E ------------------------------------------------------------
A ------------------------------------------------------------
D ---------------------------0-----2-----4---5----------------
G 5-----5---5---4---4-----------------------------4----5-------
  Three for the man who would stand his round, and four
```

```
        G           D  Em    C            G     D  G
E ------------------------------------------------------------
A ------------------------------------------------------------
D ------------------------------------------------------------
G 5---5---4----2--0---2--4-----5----5---5---4----2--0---------
  For the love of you my girl, four for the love of you.
```

Chord Forms

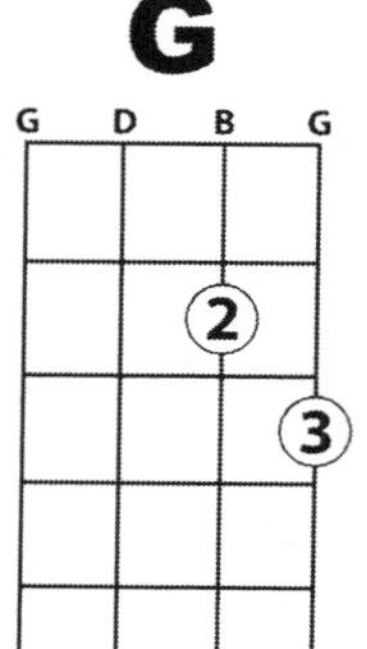

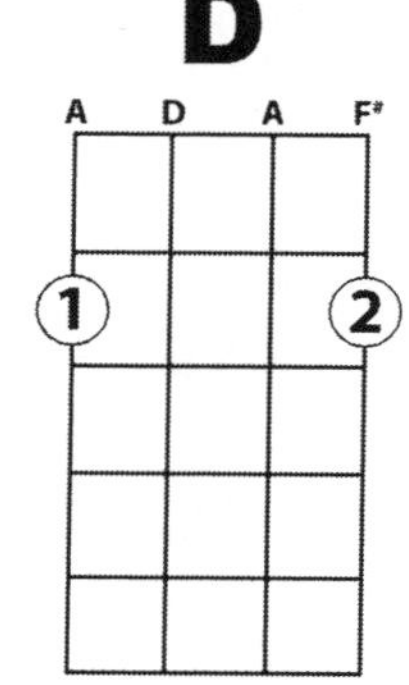

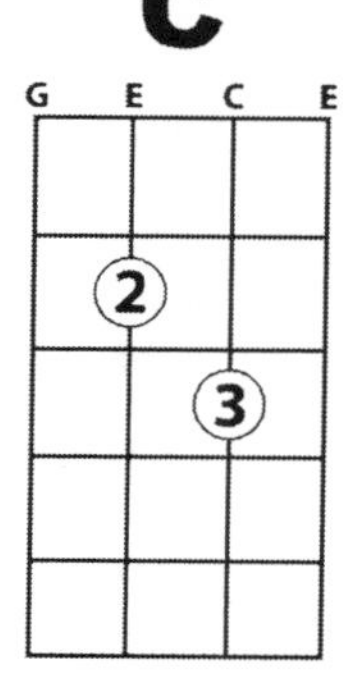

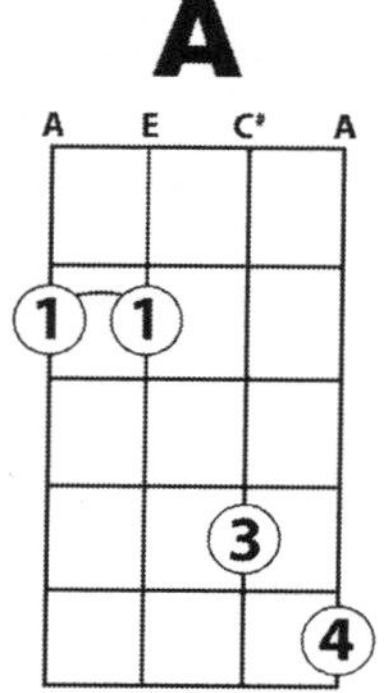

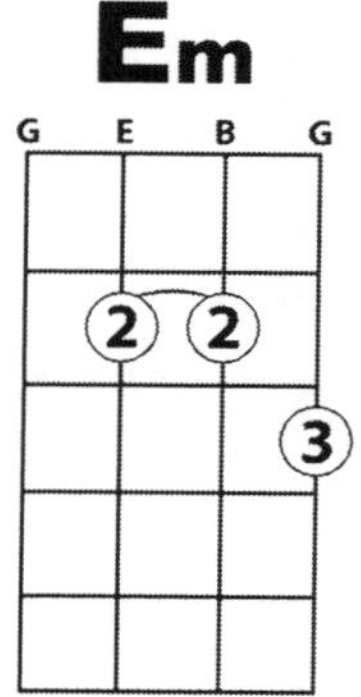

The Morning Glory

(continued - page 1)

Basic Melody

Key of G (High)

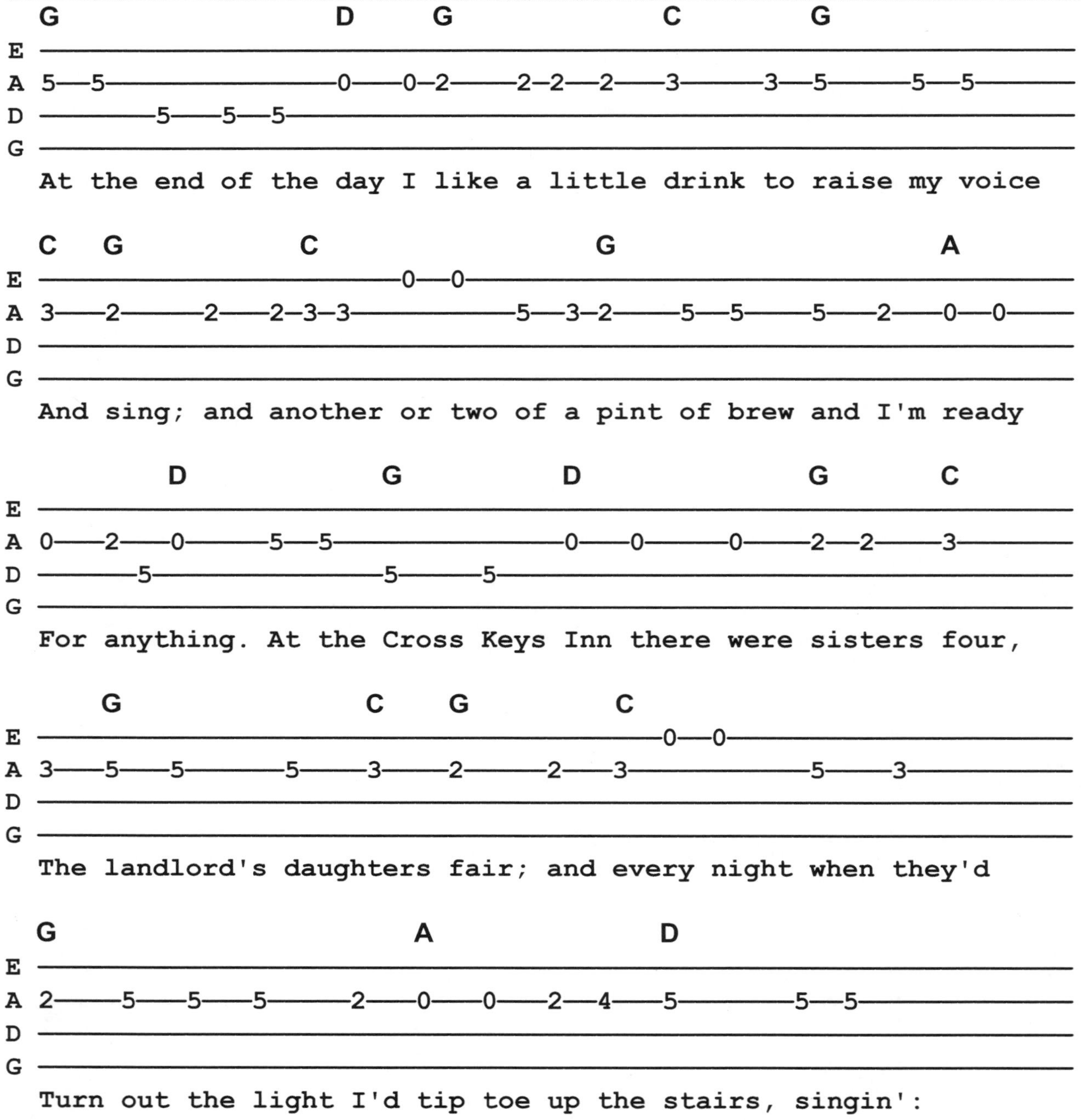

```
  G                  D    G             C        G
E ----------------------------------------------------------------
A 5--5---------------0---0-2----2-2--2---3-----3--5------5--5------
D ------5---5--5---------------------------------------------------
G ----------------------------------------------------------------
  At the end of the day I like a little drink to raise my voice

  C   G          C                  G                    A
E ------------------------0--0------------------------------------
A 3---2------2---2-3-3-------------5--3-2----5--5----5---2---0--0--
D ----------------------------------------------------------------
G ----------------------------------------------------------------
  And sing; and another or two of a pint of brew and I'm ready

          D             G          D               G       C
E ----------------------------------------------------------------
A 0---2---0-----5--5-----------------0---0------0------2--2----3---
D --------5-------------------5-----5-----------------------------
G ----------------------------------------------------------------
  For anything. At the Cross Keys Inn there were sisters four,

      G                C    G         C
E --------------------------------------0--0-----------------------
A 3---5---5------5----3----2-----2---3------------5----3-----------
D ----------------------------------------------------------------
G ----------------------------------------------------------------
  The landlord's daughters fair; and every night when they'd

  G                       A              D
E ----------------------------------------------------------------
A 2-----5---5---5-----2---0---0---2--4---5-------5--5--------------
D ----------------------------------------------------------------
G ----------------------------------------------------------------
  Turn out the light I'd tip toe up the stairs, singin':
```

The Morning Glory

(continued - page 2)

Basic Melody

Key of G (High)

CHORUS

```
  G                        C  G    D                    G
E ------------------------0---------------------------------------
A ----------------2--5---------5----0----0----0----0------2-------
D 5--5--5----------------------------------------------5----------
G ----------------------------------------------------------------
  One for the morning glory,  two for the early dew;

  C                 G                C        G          C
E ---------------------------------0------2---3--------------------
A 3-----3---3---2---2---5--------------------------2---3-----------
D -----------------------------------------------------------------
G -----------------------------------------------------------------
  Three for the man who would stand his round, and four

            G                D  Em   C                G    D  G
E -----------------------------------------------------------------
A 3---3---2-----0----------0--2------3-----3----3----2-----0-------
D ----------------------5----------------------------------5-------
G -----------------------------------------------------------------
  For the love of you my girl, four for the love of you.
```

Chord Forms

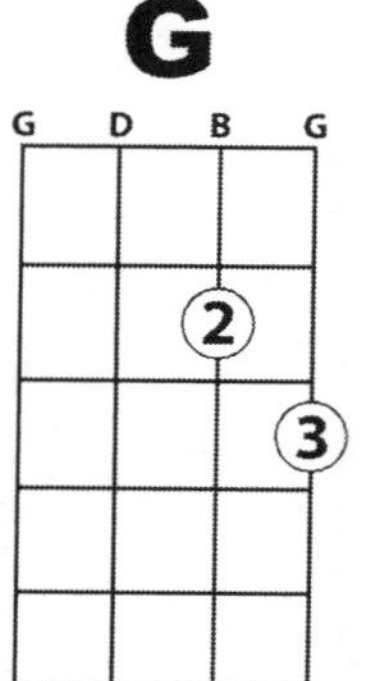

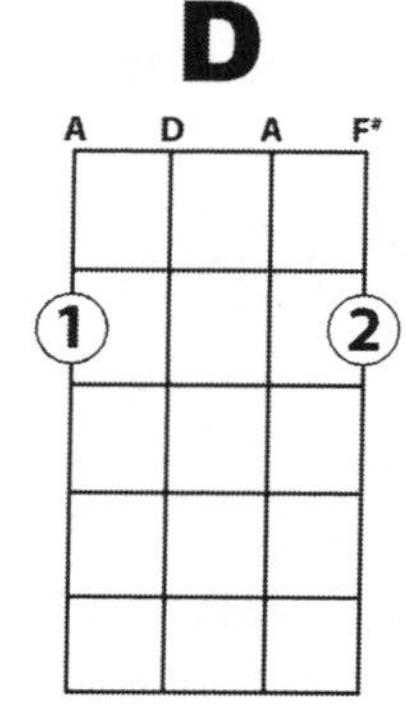

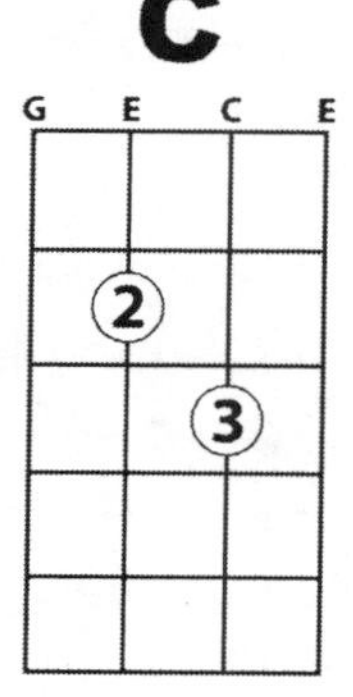

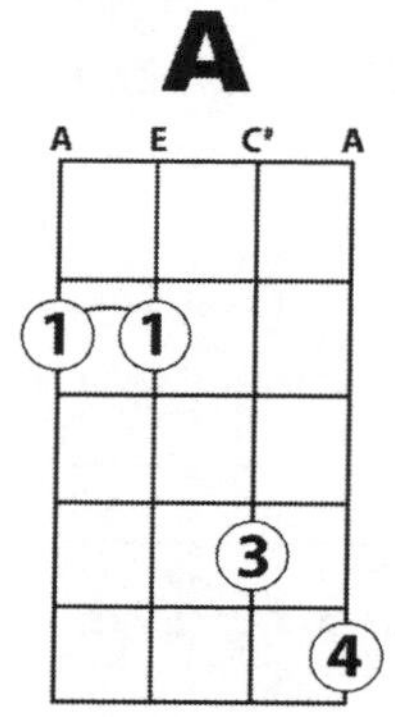

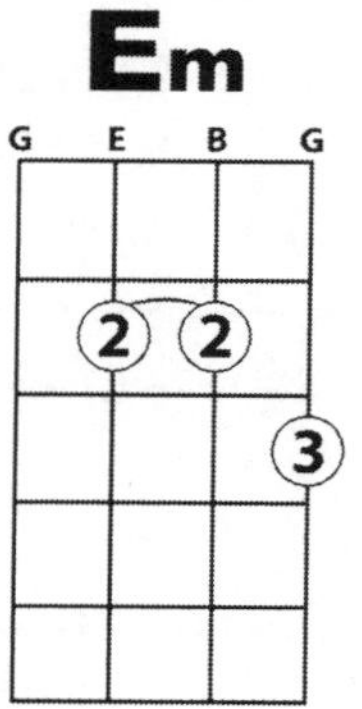

The Morning Glory

(continued - page 1)

Melody & Chords

Key of G (High)

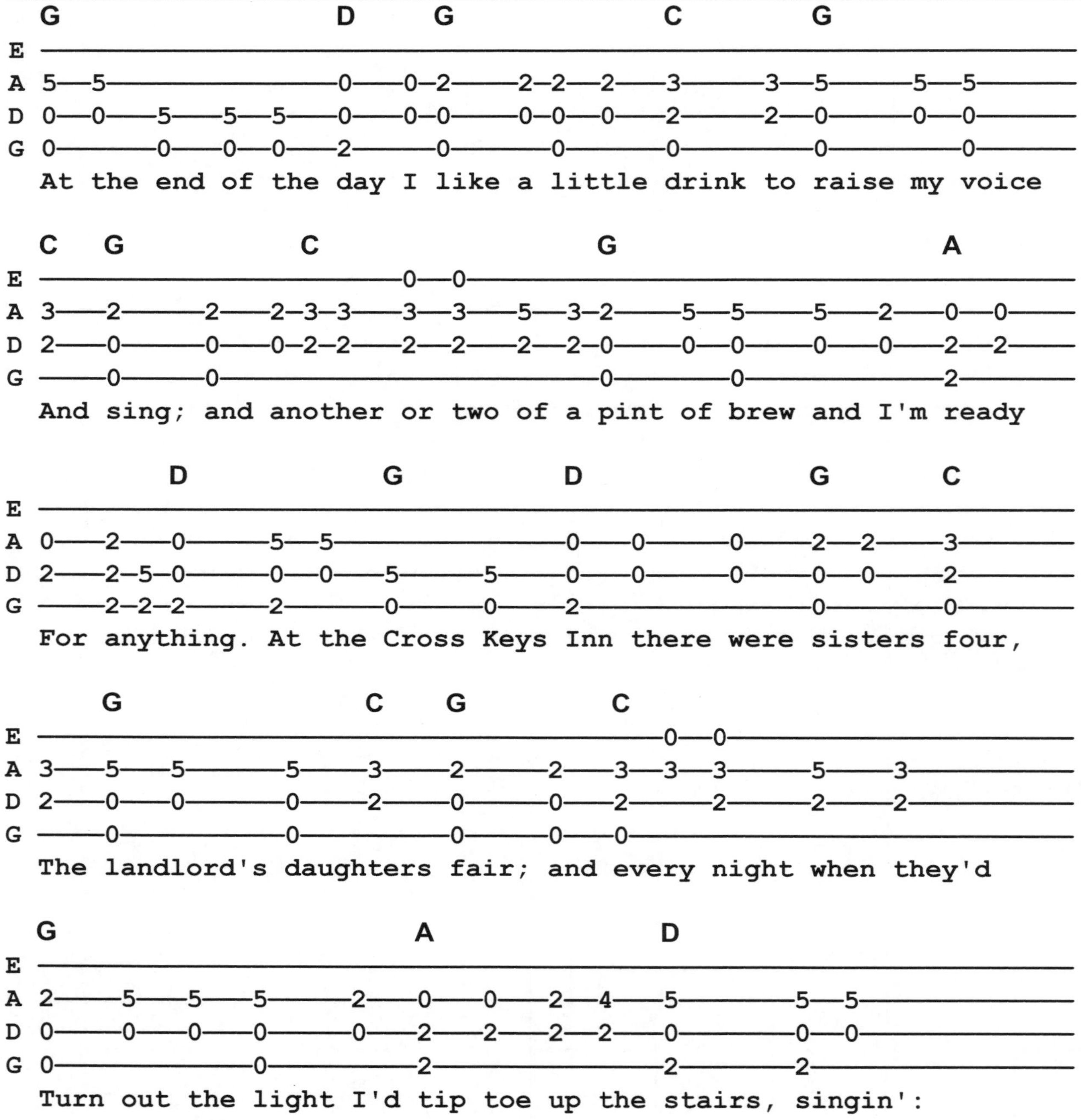

```
  G                 D     G             C        G
E -----------------------------------------------------------------
A 5--5--------------0---0-2---2-2--2----3-----3--5------5--5-------
D 0--0---5---5--5---0---0-0---0-0--0----2-----2--0------0--0-------
G 0------0---0--0---2-----0------0------0--------0---------0-------
  At the end of the day I like a little drink to raise my voice
```

```
  C   G           C                 G                   A
E -----------------------0--0-------------------------------------
A 3---2-----2---2-3-3----3--3---5--3-2----5--5----5---2---0--0----
D 2---0-----0---0-2-2----2--2---2--2-0----0--0----0---0---2--2----
G -----0-----0--------------------------0-----0-----------2-------
  And sing; and another or two of a pint of brew and I'm ready
```

```
          D            G          D              G       C
E -----------------------------------------------------------------
A 0---2---0-----5--5---------------0---0-----0---2--2----3---------
D 2---2-5-0-----0--0---5-----5-----0---0-----0---0--0----2---------
G -----2-2-2----2------0-----0-----2---------------0-----0---------
  For anything. At the Cross Keys Inn there were sisters four,
```

```
      G              C    G         C
E ----------------------------------------0--0---------------------
A 3---5---5------5---3----2-----2---3--3--3------5----3------------
D 2---0---0------0---2----0-----0---2-----2------2----2------------
G -----0---------0--------0-----0---0------------------------------
  The landlord's daughters fair; and every night when they'd
```

```
  G                      A              D
E -----------------------------------------------------------------
A 2----5---5---5-----2---0---0---2--4---5-------5--5---------------
D 0----0---0---0-----0---2---2---2--2---0-------0--0---------------
G 0------------0---------2--------------2-------2------------------
  Turn out the light I'd tip toe up the stairs, singin':
```

The Morning Glory

(continued - page 2)

Melody & Chords

Key of G (High)

CHORUS

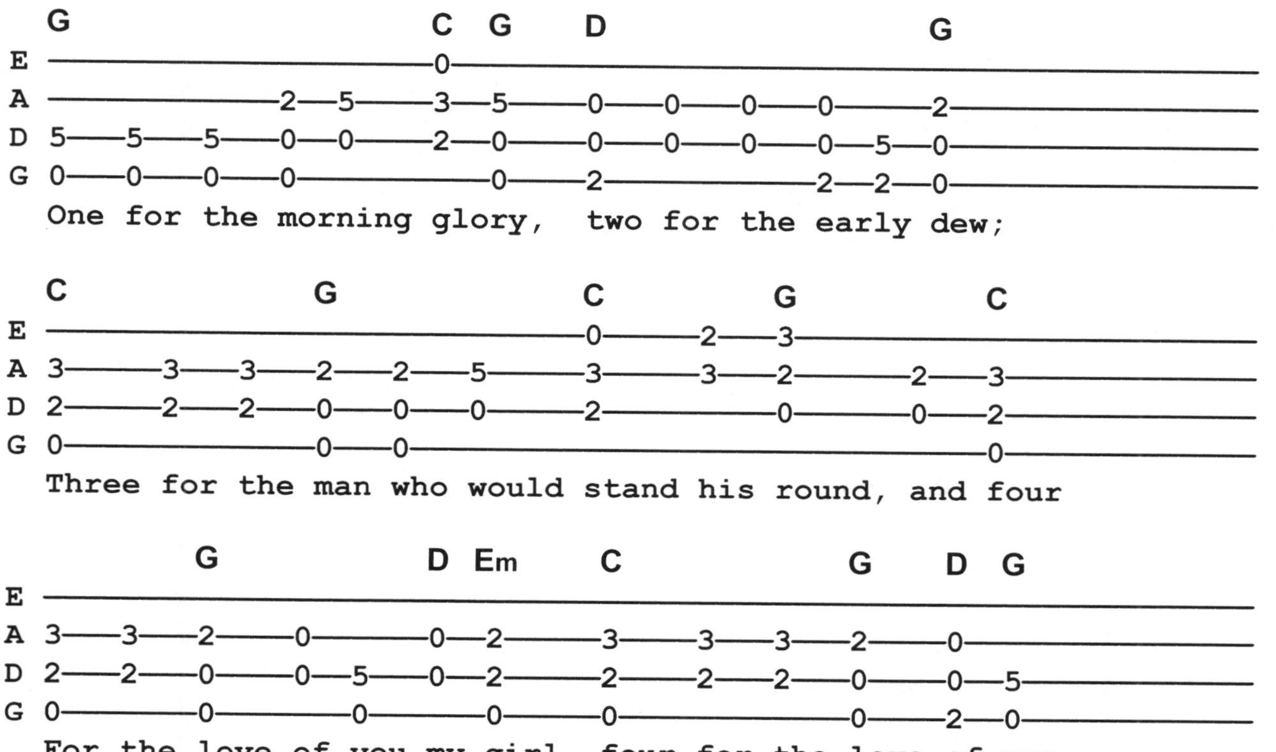

Chord Forms

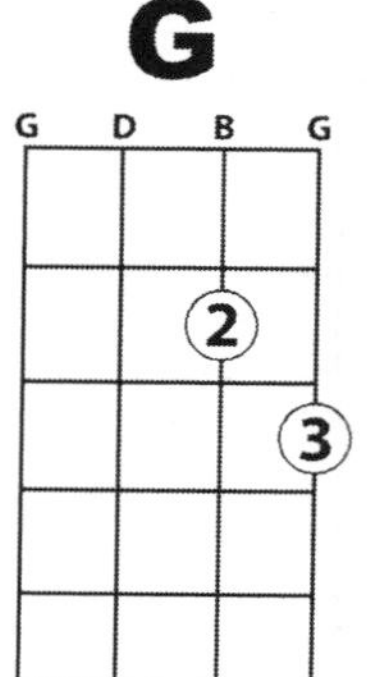

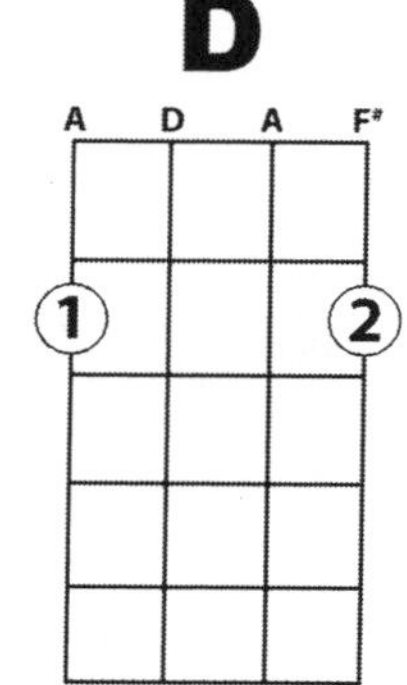

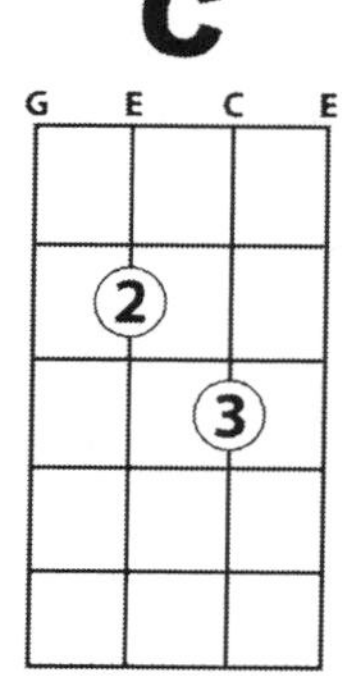

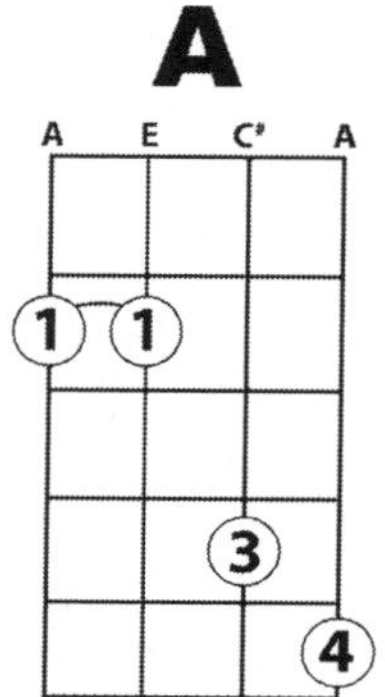

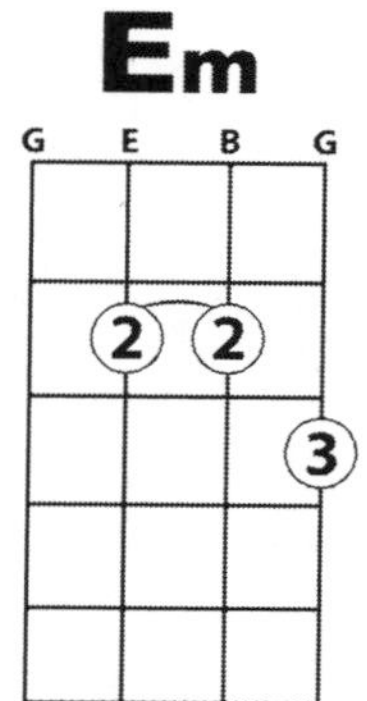

Paddy Doyle's Boots

Basic Melody

Key of C (Low)

Words and Music

Traditional

According to folk history, this was a sea shanty specifically for "bunting" the main sail of the old sailing ships. The rhythm and words were timed to the men's' movements, and the "yah" on each line was where the sailors would have to perform a particularly heavy heave of the bundled sail. Each of the lines below is technically a separate verse.

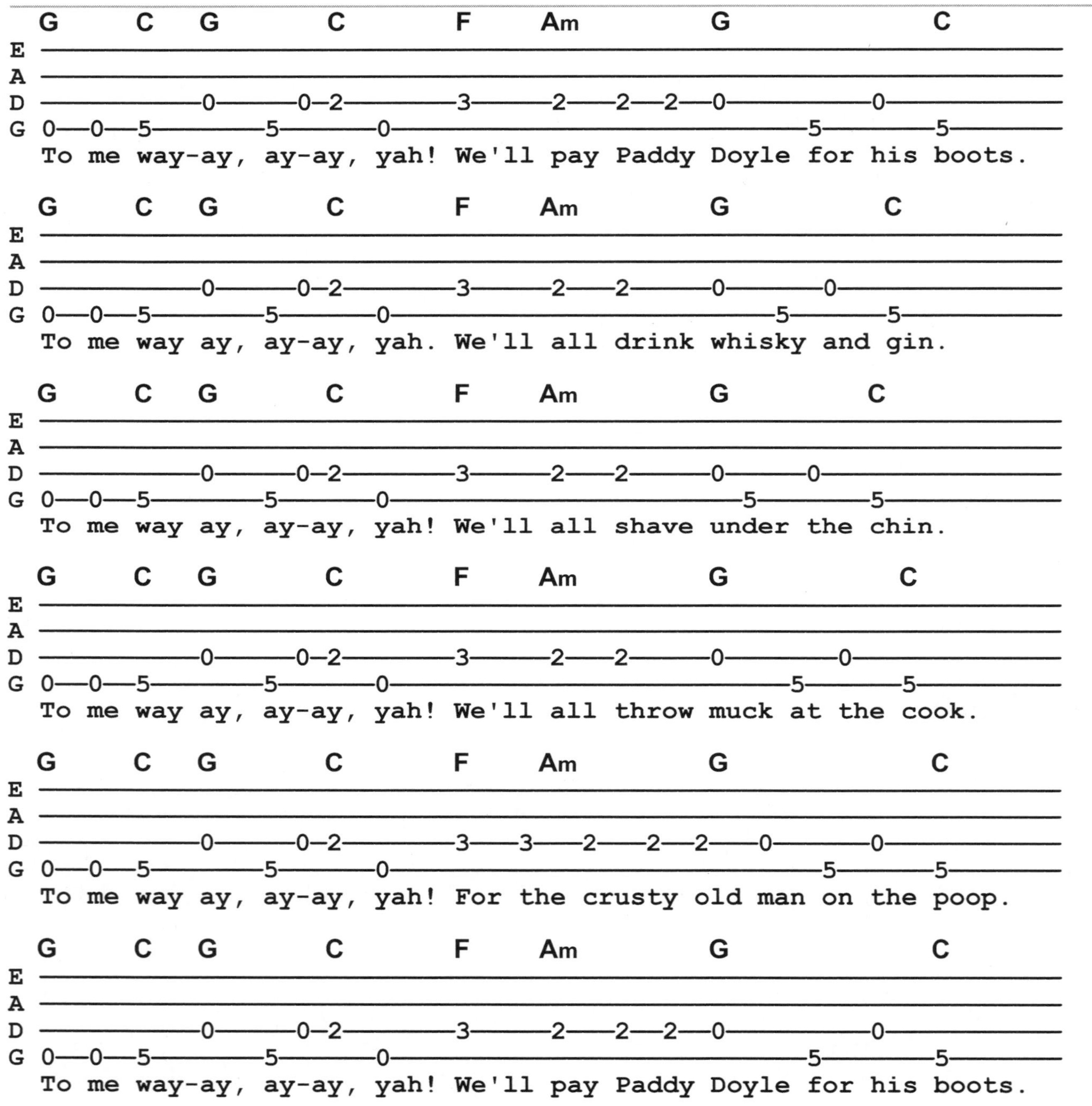

See Chord Forms on Next Page

Paddy Doyle's Boots (continued)

Melody & Chords
Key of C (Low)

```
  G    C  G      C       F    Am       G          C
E ---------------------------------------------------------
A -------------------------------------------------3-------
D ---------0-----0-2-------3----2--2--2--0-------0--2-------
G 0--0--5--0--5-0-5--0-----2----2--2--2--0----5--0--5-------
  To me way-ay, ay-ay, yah! We'll pay Paddy Doyle for his boots.
```

```
  G    C  G      C       F    Am       G       C
E ---------------------------------------------------------
A --------------------------------------------3-------------
D ---------0-----0-2-------3----2--2-----0----0--2-----------
G 0--0--5--0--5-0-5--0-----2----2--2-----0--5--0--5----------
  To me way ay, ay-ay, yah. We'll all drink whisky and gin.
```

```
  G    C  G      C       F    Am       G      C
E ---------------------------------------------------------
A ------------------------------------------3---------------
D ---------0-----0-2-------3----2--2-----0----0--2-----------
G 0--0--5--0--5-0-5--0-----2----2--2-----0-5--0--5-----------
  To me way ay, ay-ay, yah! We'll all shave under the chin.
```

```
  G    C  G      C       F    Am       G        C
E ---------------------------------------------------------
A ---------------------------------------------3------------
D ---------0-----0-2-------3----2--2-----0-------0--2--------
G 0--0--5--0--5-0-5--0-----2----2--2-----0----5--0--5--------
  To me way ay, ay-ay, yah! We'll all throw muck at the cook.
```

```
  G    C  G      C       F       Am       G        C
E ---------------------------------------------------------
A ---------------------------------------------------------
D ---------0-----0-2-------3--3--2--2--2--0------0-----------
G 0--0--5--0--5-0-5--0-----2--2--2--2--2-------5-----5-------
  To me way ay, ay-ay, yah! For the crusty old man on the poop.
```

```
  G    C  G      C       F    Am       G          C
E ---------------------------------------------------------
A -------------------------------------------------3-------
D ---------0-----0-2-------3----2--2--2--0-------0--2-------
G 0--0--5--0--5-0-5--0-----2----2--2--2--0----5--0--5-------
  To me way-ay, ay-ay, yah! We'll pay Paddy Doyle for his boots.
```

Chord Forms

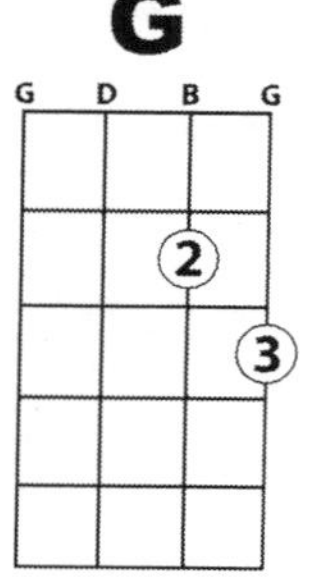

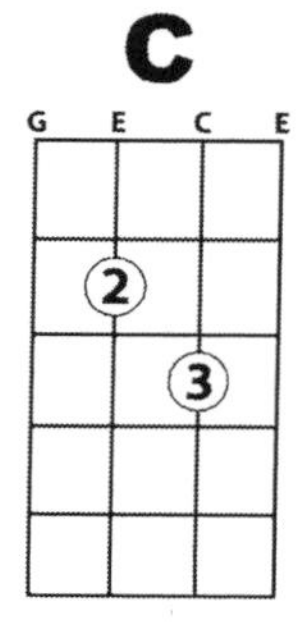

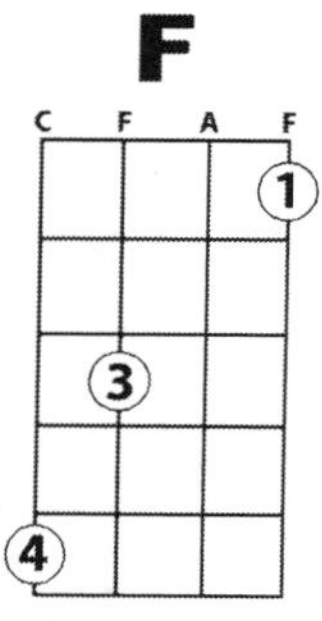

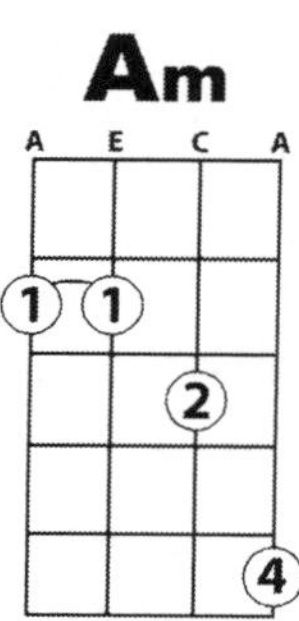

Paddy Doyle's Boots (continued)

Basic Melody
Key of C (High)

```
   G     C  G         C      F    Am          G           C
E ───────────────────0──────1─────0───0──0──────────────────────
A ──────3───5───3─5──────────────────────────5─────3───5───3────
D 5──5──────────────────5────────────────────────────────────────
G ───────────────────────────────────────────────────────────────
  To me way-ay, ay-ay, yah! We'll pay Paddy Doyle for his boots.
```

```
   G     C  G         C      F    Am          G          C
E ───────────────────0──────1─────0───0─────────────────────────
A ──────3───5───3─5──────────────────────────5───3───5───3──────
D 5──5──────────────────5────────────────────────────────────────
G ───────────────────────────────────────────────────────────────
  To me way ay, ay-ay, yah. We'll all drink whisky and gin.
```

```
   G     C  G         C      F    Am          G        C
E ───────────────────0──────1─────0───0─────────────────────────
A ──────3───5───3─5──────────────────────────5─3───5───3────────
D 5──5──────────────────5────────────────────────────────────────
G ───────────────────────────────────────────────────────────────
  To me way ay, ay-ay, yah! We'll all shave under the chin.
```

```
   G     C  G         C      F    Am          G           C
E ───────────────────0──────1─────0───0─────────────────────────
A ──────3───5───3─5──────────────────────────5─────3───5───3────
D 5──5──────────────────5────────────────────────────────────────
G ───────────────────────────────────────────────────────────────
  To me way ay, ay-ay, yah! We'll all throw muck at the cook.
```

```
   G     C  G         C      F        Am           G          C
E ───────────────────0──────1───1───0────0──0───────────────────
A ──────3───5───3─5───────────────────────────────5───3───5───3─
D 5──5──────────────────5────────────────────────────────────────
G ───────────────────────────────────────────────────────────────
  To me way ay, ay-ay, yah! For the crusty old man on the poop.
```

```
   G     C  G         C      F    Am          G           C
E ───────────────────0──────1─────0───0──0──────────────────────
A ──────3───5───3─5──────────────────────────5─────3───5───3────
D 5──5──────────────────5────────────────────────────────────────
G ───────────────────────────────────────────────────────────────
  To me way-ay, ay-ay, yah! We'll pay Paddy Doyle for his boots.
```

Chord Forms

G

G D B G

C

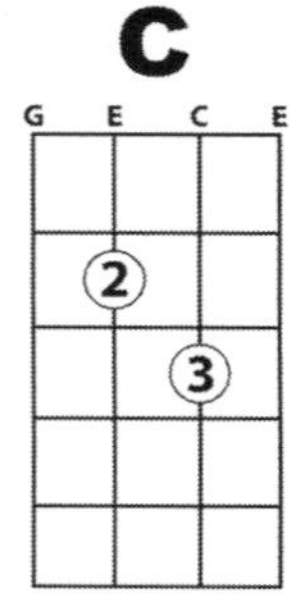

F

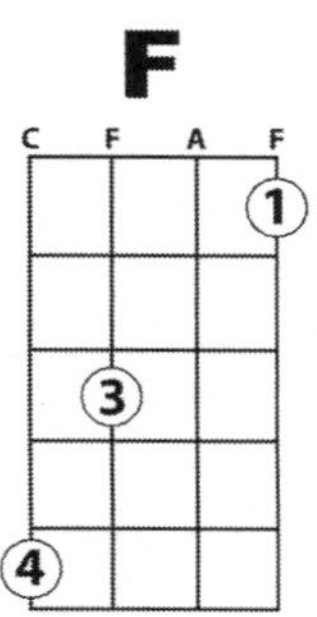

Am

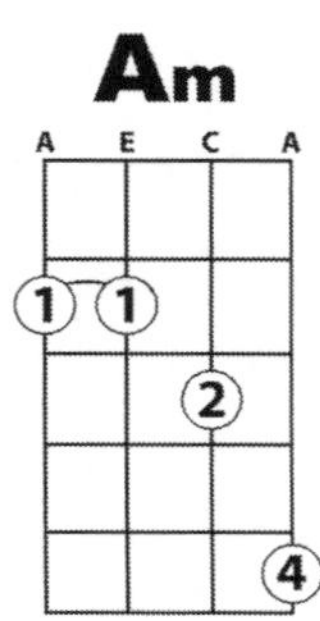

Paddy Doyle's Boots (continued)

Melody & Chords
Key of C (High)

```
   G     C   G       C       F    Am          G           C
E ──────────────────0───────1────0───0──0────────────────────────
A ──────3───5───3─5─3───────0────0───0──0──5─────3───5───3───────
D 5──5──2───0───0─0─2──5────3────2───2─────0─────0───0───2───────
G 0──0──0───0──────────5───────────────────0─────────────0───────
  To me way-ay, ay-ay, yah! We'll pay Paddy Doyle for his boots.
```

```
   G     C   G       C       F    Am          G        C
E ──────────────────0───────1────0───0───────────────────────────
A ──────3───5───3─5─3───────0────0───0────5───3───5───3──────────
D 5──5──2───0───0─0─2──5────3────2───2────0───0───0───2──────────
G 0──0──0───0──────────5──────────────────0───────────0──────────
  To me way ay, ay-ay, yah. We'll all drink whisky and gin.
```

```
   G     C   G       C       F    Am          G       C
E ──────────────────0───────1────0───0───────────────────────────
A ──────3───5───3─5─3───────0────0───0────5─3───5───3────────────
D 5──5──2───0───0─0─2──5────3────2────────0─0───0───2────────────
G 0──0──0───0──────────5──────────────────0─────────0────────────
  To me way ay, ay-ay, yah! We'll all shave under the chin.
```

```
   G     C   G       C       F    Am          G          C
E ──────────────────0───────1────0───0───────────────────────────
A ──────3───5───3─5─3───────0────0───0────5─────3───5───3────────
D 5──5──2───0───0─0─2──5────3────2────────0─────0───0───2────────
G 0──0──0───0──────────5──────────────────0─────────────0────────
  To me way ay, ay-ay, yah! We'll all throw muck at the cook.
```

```
   G     C   G       C       F      Am            G         C
E ──────────────────0───────1──1───0───0──0──────────────────────
A ──────3───5───3─5─3───────0──0───0───0──0───5───3───5───3─────
D 5──5──2───0───0─0─2──5────3──────2───2──────0───0───0───2─────
G 0──0──0───0──────────5──────────────────────0───────────0─────
  To me way ay, ay-ay, yah! For the crusty old man on the poop.
```

```
   G     C   G       C       F    Am          G           C
E ──────────────────0───────1────0───0──0────────────────────────
A ──────3───5───3─5─3───────0────0───0──0──5─────3───5───3───────
D 5──5──2───0───0─0─2──5────3────2───2─────0─────0───0───2───────
G 0──0──0───0──────────5───────────────────0─────────────0───────
  To me way-ay, ay-ay, yah! We'll pay Paddy Doyle for his boots.
```

Chord Forms

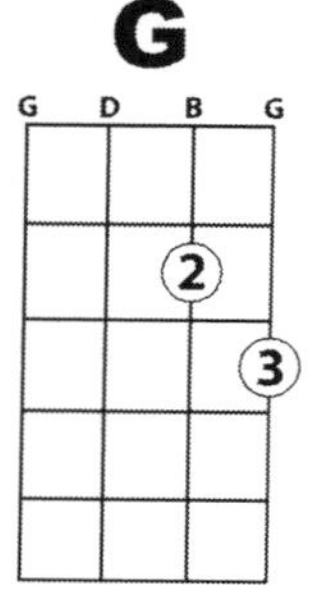

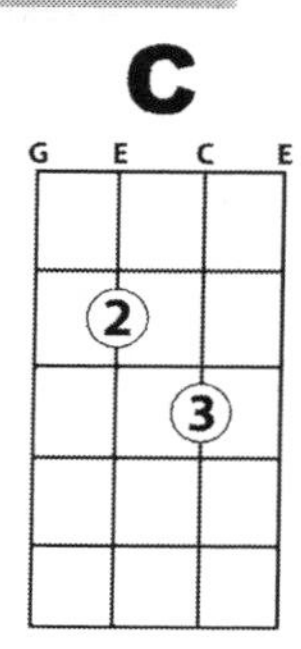

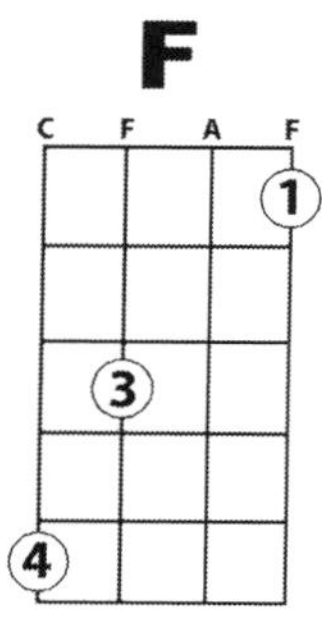

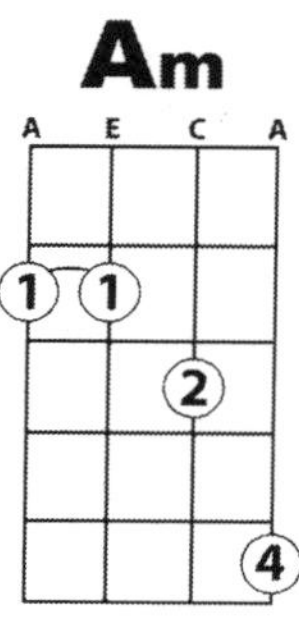

Paddy Doyle's Boots (continued)

Basic Melody
Key of G

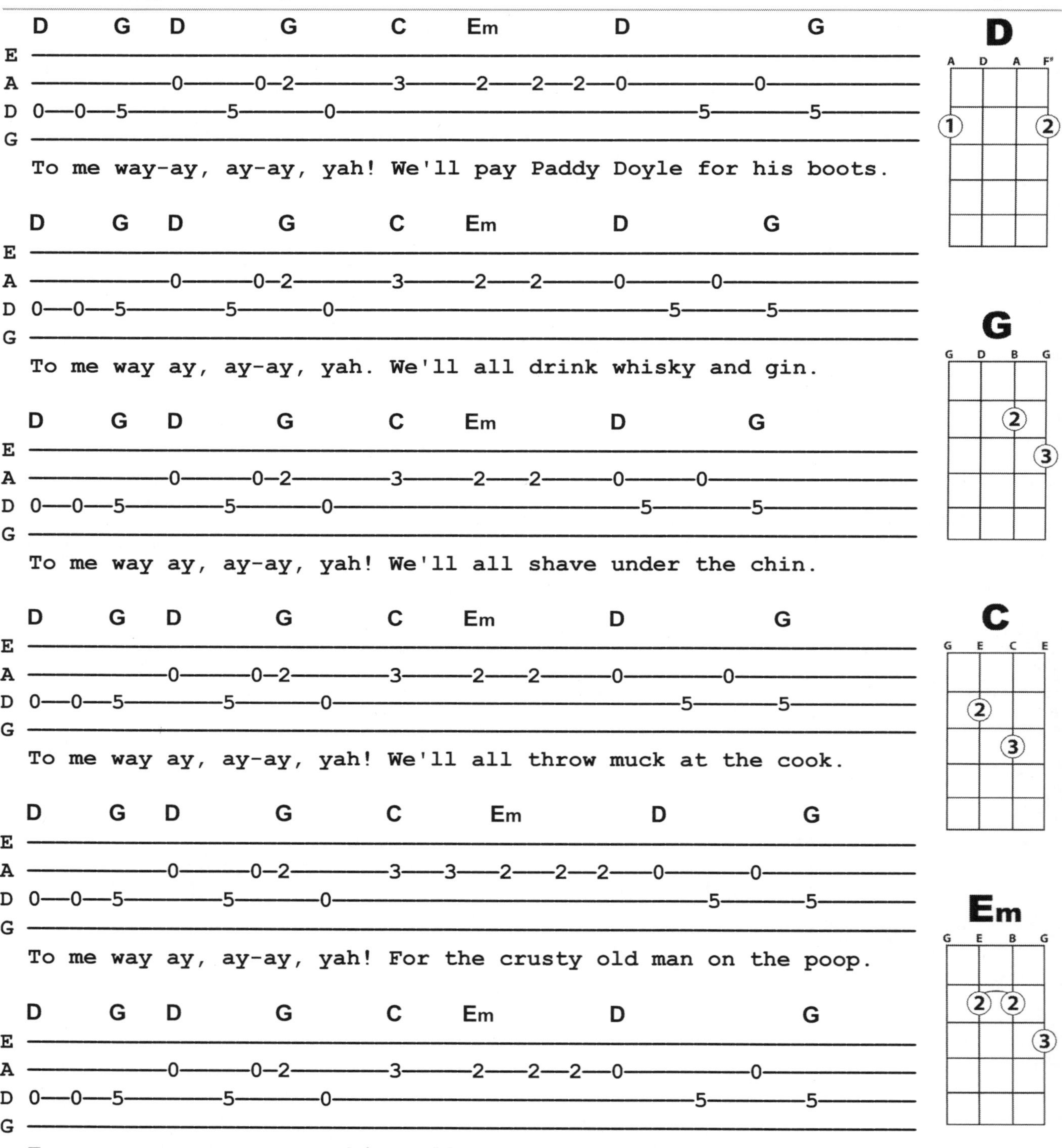

Paddy Doyle's Boots (continued)

Melody & Chords

Key of G

```
  D    G   D       G       C     Em         D            G
E ----------------------------------------------------------------
A ----------0-----0-2-------3-----2---2---2---0---------0---------
D 0--0--5---0---5-0--0--0---2-----2---2---2---0----5----0---5-----
G 2--2--0---2---2----0--0---0-----0---0-------2----2--------0-----
  To me way-ay, ay-ay, yah! We'll pay Paddy Doyle for his boots.
```

```
  D    G   D       G       C     Em         D         G
E ----------------------------------------------------------------
A ----------0-----0-2-------3-----2---2-------0-------0-----------
D 0--0--5---0---5-0--0--0---2-----2---2-------0---5---0---5-------
G 2--2--0---2---2----0--0---0-----0-----------2---2-------0-------
  To me way ay, ay-ay, yah. We'll all drink whisky and gin.
```

```
  D    G   D       G       C     Em         D         G
E ----------------------------------------------------------------
A ----------0-----0-2-------3-----2---2-------0-------0-----------
D 0--0--5---0---5-0--0--0---2-----2---2-------0-5-----0---5-------
G 2--2--0---2---2----0--0---0-----0-----------2-2---------0-------
  To me way ay, ay-ay, yah! We'll all shave under the chin.
```

```
  D    G   D       G       C     Em         D            G
E ----------------------------------------------------------------
A ----------0-----0-2-------3-----2---2-------0--------0----------
D 0--0--5---0---5-0--0--0---2-----2---2-------0----5---0---5------
G 2--2--0---2---2----0--0---0-----0-----------2----2-------0------
  To me way ay, ay-ay, yah! We'll all throw muck at the cook.
```

```
  D    G   D       G       C        Em          D            G
E ----------------------------------------------------------------
A ----------0-----0-2-------3---3---2---2---2---0-------0---------
D 0--0--5---0---5-0--0--0---2---2---2---2---2---0---5---0---5-----
G 2--2--0---2---2----0--0---0-------0-----------2---2-------0-----
  To me way ay, ay-ay, yah! For the crusty old man on the poop.
```

```
  D    G   D       G       C     Em         D            G
E ----------------------------------------------------------------
A ----------0-----0-2-------3-----2---2---2---0---------0---------
D 0--0--5---0---5-0--0--0---2-----2---2---2---0----5----0---5-----
G 2--2--0---2---2----0--0---0-----0-----------2----2--------0-----
  To me way-ay, ay-ay, yah! We'll pay Paddy Doyle for his boots.
```

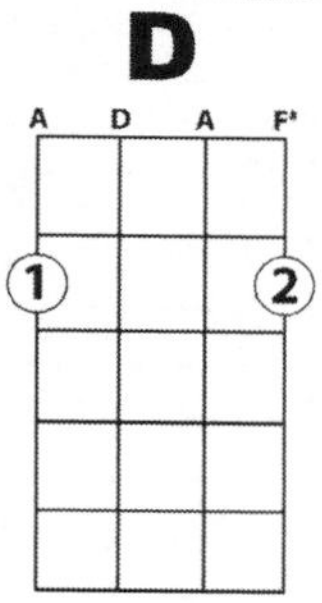

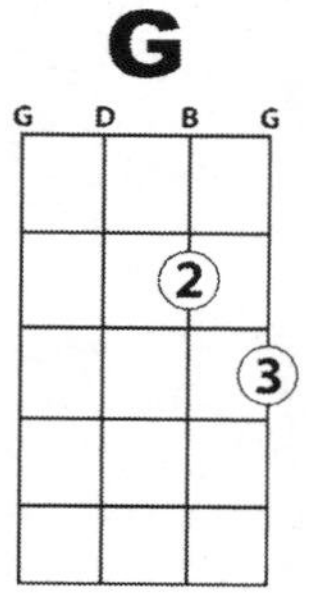

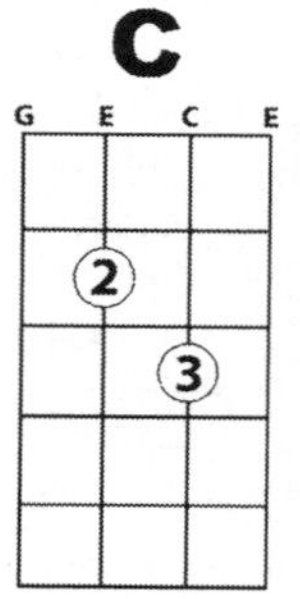

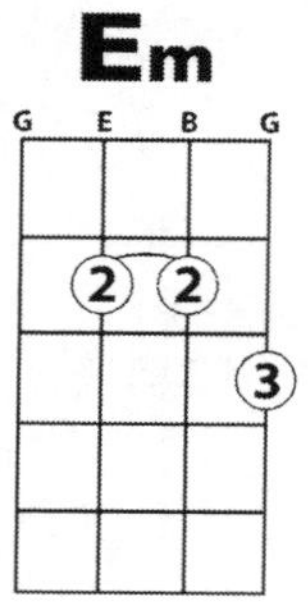

D (A D A F#) · G (G D B G) · C (G E C E) · Em (G E B G)

Paddy West (page 1)

Basic Melody
Key of C (Low)

This song hails from the late 1800's, when there may have been an actual Paddy West in Liverpool, the keeper of a boarding house and an ad-hoc trainer of would-be sailors. The verses outline Paddy's course of training, which was rather unconventional to say the least. This song was popular among sailors both at sea and ashore, and is still sung today.

Words and Music

Traditional

```
  C                                    Dm        F          G
E ---------------------------------------------------------------------------------
A ---------------------------------------------------------------------------------
D ---2--2---2--0---------------------0---2-------------------------------0---------
G 5------------------5-----2-------------------5-------2--0-----2--5--5------------
  As I was a-walking down London Road, I came to Paddy West's

  C                                        F          C
E ---------------------------------------------------------------------------------
A -----------------------------------------0---0--0--------------------------------
D ---------2--5------5--5--2------3--5-----------------5------2----0---------------
G 5-------------------------------------------------------------------5------------
  House; he gave me a feed of A-meri-can hash, and he called

                 Am           C                                     F
E ---------------------------------------------------------------------------------
A -----------------------------------------------------------------0---0-----------
D 2--0--0--------------------2---5-----5--------5--2-----3-------5-----------------
G ----------5-----2------------------------------------------------------------------
  It Liverpool scouse. He said there's a ship that's a-wanting

  C                                        Am          C
E ---------------------------------------------------------------------------------
A ---------------------------------------------------------------------------------
D 5-------2--------2--2------0-----------------------2------2--2--0----------------
G ------------5------------------------5--2------5-----------------5---------------
  Hands, and on 'er you'll quickly sign; the mate is a tyrant,

      Dm        F            G                        C
E ---------------------------------------------------------------------------------
A ---------------------------------------------------------------------------------
D -----0--2------------------------------------0-----------------------------------
G 2-------------5------2--0---2-----5-----------------5----------------------------
  The bosun's worse, but she will suit you fine.
```

Chord Forms

C

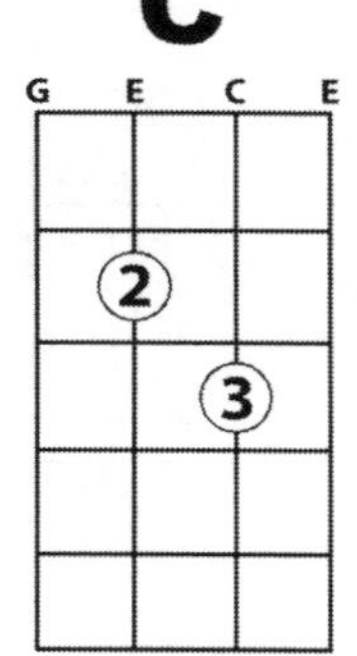

Dm

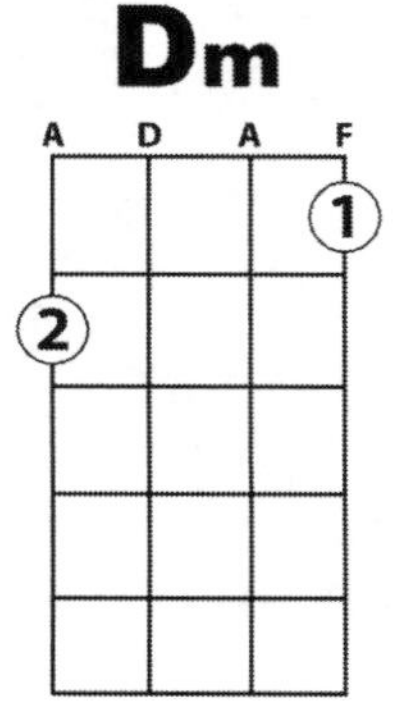

F

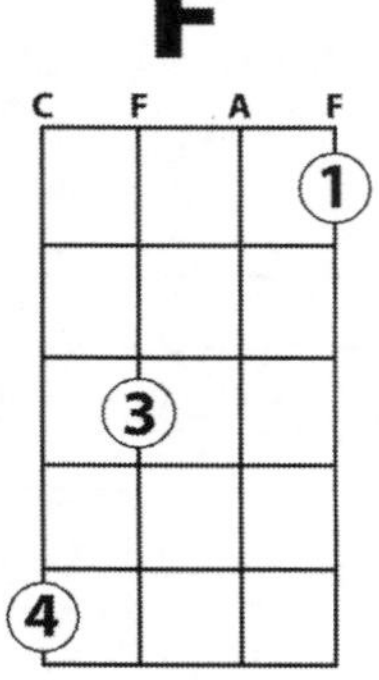

G

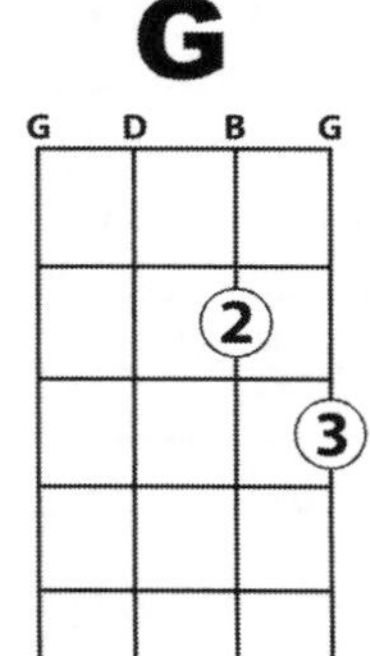

Am

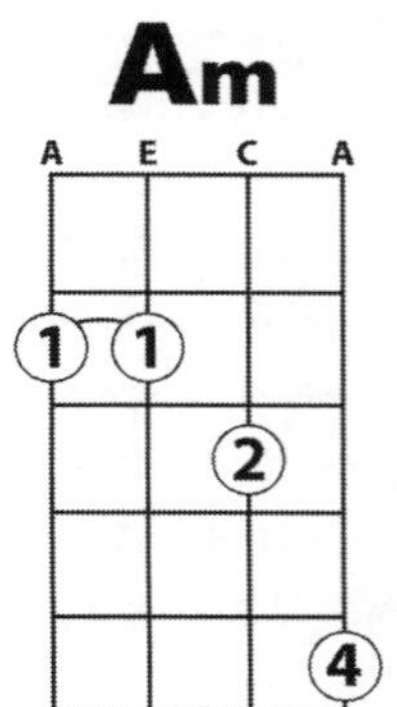

Paddy West (page 2)

Basic Melody
Key of C (Low)

CHORUS

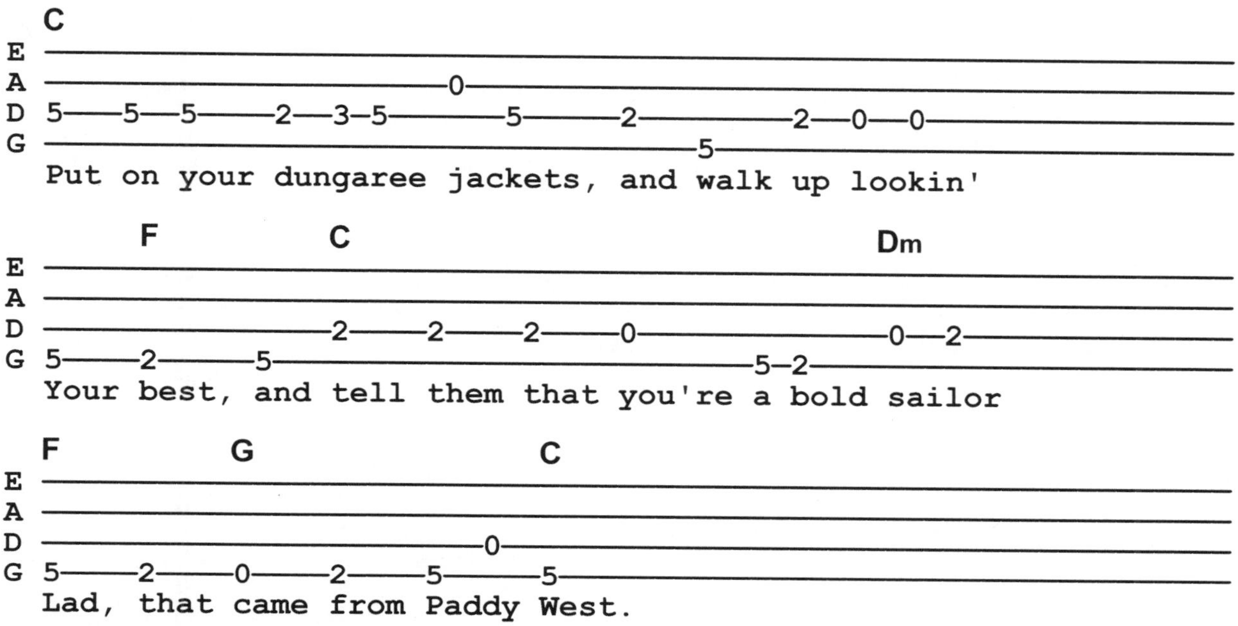

```
  C
E ------------------------------------------------------------------
A ---------------------------------0--------------------------------
D 5---5---5-----2---3--5-------------5-----2-----------2---0---0----
G -------------------------------------------5-----------------------
  Put on your dungaree jackets, and walk up lookin'
```

```
        F         C                                    Dm
E ------------------------------------------------------------------
A ------------------------------------------------------------------
D -------------------2-----2-----2-----0--------------0---2---------
G 5-----2------5---------------------------------5--2---------------
  Your best, and tell them that you're a bold sailor
```

```
  F         G               C
E ------------------------------------------------------------------
A ------------------------------------------------------------------
D ---------------------------------0--------------------------------
G 5-----2-----0-----2-----5-----5-----------------------------------
  Lad, that came from Paddy West.
```

Additional Verses

Well, when I'd had a feed, my boys, the wind began to blow;
He sent me up in the attic, the main-royal for to stow.
But when I got up in the attic, no main-royal could I find,
So I turned around to the window and I furled the window blind.

Now Paddy he piped all hands on deck, their stations for to man;
His wife stood in the doorway with a bucket in her hand.
And Paddy cries out, "Now let 'er rip!" and she flung the water our way,
Sayin', "Clew up your fore t'gan'sl, boys, she's takin' in the spray!"

Now seein' we're off to the south'ard, boys, to Frisco we was bound;
Old Paddy he called for a length of rope, and he laid it on the ground.
And we all stepped over and back again, And he says to me, "That's fine;
Now when they ask if you've been to sea, You can say you've crossed the Line."

"Now there's only one thing for you to do, before you sail away:
Just step around the table, where the bullock's horn does lay.
And if they ask you, 'Were you ever at sea?', you can say, 'Ten times 'round the Horn.'
You can tell him that you've been a sailor since the day that you were born."

Paddy West (continued - page 1)

Basic Melody
Key of C (High)

```
  C                               Dm     F       G
E ——0—0——0————————————————————————0—————————————————————————————————
A 3——————————5—3————0————5—————————————3——————0——————0—3—3—5————————
D ———————————————————————————————————————————5——————————————————————
G ——————————————————————————————————————————————————————————————————
  As I was a-walking down London Road, I came to Paddy West's
```

```
  C                                    F     C
E ——————0—3————3—3—0————1—3—5—5—5————3——————0———————————————————————
A 3——————————————————————————————————————————————————5—3————————————
D ——————————————————————————————————————————————————————————————————
G ——————————————————————————————————————————————————————————————————
  House; he gave me a feed of A-meri-can hash, and he called
```

```
              Am         C                                  F
E 0————————————————————0—3————3————————3—0————1————3—5—5————————————
A ———5—5—3————0—————————————————————————————————————————————————————
D ——————————————————————————————————————————————————————————————————
G ——————————————————————————————————————————————————————————————————
  It Liverpool scouse. He said there's a ship that's a-wanting
```

```
  C                                    Am         C
E 3———————0———————0—0—————————————————————————————0————0—0——————————
A ——————————————3——————————————5————3—0————3————————————————5—3——————
D ——————————————————————————————————————————————————————————————————
G ——————————————————————————————————————————————————————————————————
  Hands, and on 'er you'll quickly sign; the mate is a tyrant,
```

```
     Dm       F           G                   C
E ————————0—————————————————————————————————————————————————————————
A 0———5————————3——————0——————————0————3————5————3———————————————————
D ——————————————————————————5———————————————————————————————————————
G ——————————————————————————————————————————————————————————————————
  The bosun's worse, but she will suit you fine.
```

Chord Forms

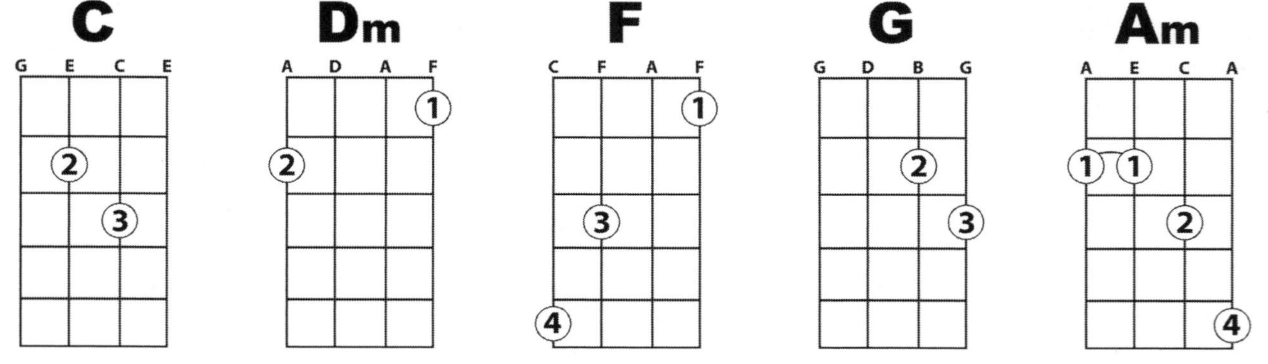

Paddy West (continued - page 2)

Basic Melody
Key of C (High)

CHORUS

```
  C
E 3---3--3----0--1-3---5--3-----0--------0------------------
A -----------------------------------3--------5--5----------
D ----------------------------------------------------------
G ----------------------------------------------------------
  Put on your dungaree jackets, and walk up lookin'
```

```
      F        C                       Dm
E ---------------0----0----0------------------0-------------
A 3----0-----3---------------------5------3-0----5----------
D ----------------------------------------------------------
G ----------------------------------------------------------
  Your best, and tell them that you're a bold sailor
```

```
  F        G          C
E ----------------------------------------------------------
A 3----0----------0----3--5--3------------------------------
D ------------5---------------------------------------------
G ----------------------------------------------------------
  Lad, that came from Paddy West.
```

Paddy West (continued - page 1)

Melody & Chords
Key of C (High)

```
  C                        Dm     F       G
E ----0-0---0-----------------0---------------------------------
A 3---3-3---3-5--3----0----5--0---3-----0------0--3--3--5-------
D 2---2-------2--2----2----3------3-----3-5----0--0--0--0-------
G 0-----------0------------2------2-------0-------0-------------
  As I was a-walking down London Road, I came to Paddy West's
```

```
  C                              F        C
E -------0---3----3--3-0---1--3--5--5-5---3-----0---------------
A 3------3---3----3--3-3---3--3--3--3-3---3-----3---5--3--------
D 2------2---2---------2---------3--------2---------2--2--------
G 0----------------------------------------------------0--------
  House; he gave me a feed of A-meri-can hash, and he called
```

```
               Am         C                            F
E 0--------------------0--3----3-------3-0----1------3-5--5-----
A 3--5-5--3----0-------0--3----3-------3-3----3------3-3--3-----
D 2--2-2--2----2-------2--2--------------2-------------3--------
G ---0---------5------------------------------------------------
  It Liverpool scouse. He said there's a ship that's a-wanting
```

```
  C                                Am        C
E 3------0-------0--0------------------------0----0--0----------
A 3------3---3---3--3------5----3--0-----3---3----3--3-5-3------
D 2----------2---2--2------2----2--2-----2---2---------2-2------
G -----------0-------------0-------5-------------------0--------
  Hands, and on 'er you'll quickly sign; the mate is a tyrant,
```

```
      Dm      F          G                 C
E ------0-------------------------------------------------------
A 0---5-0-----3------0-------0----3----5---3--------------------
D 2---3-------3------3---5---0----0----0---2--------------------
G ----2-------2----------0--------0--------0--------------------
  The bosun's worse, but she will suit you fine.
```

Chord Forms

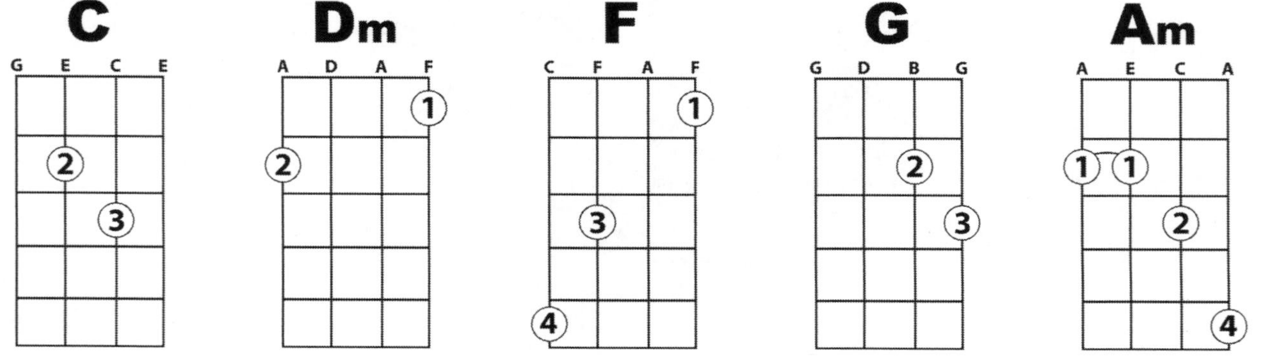

Paddy West (continued - page 2)

Melody & Chords
Key of C (High)

CHORUS

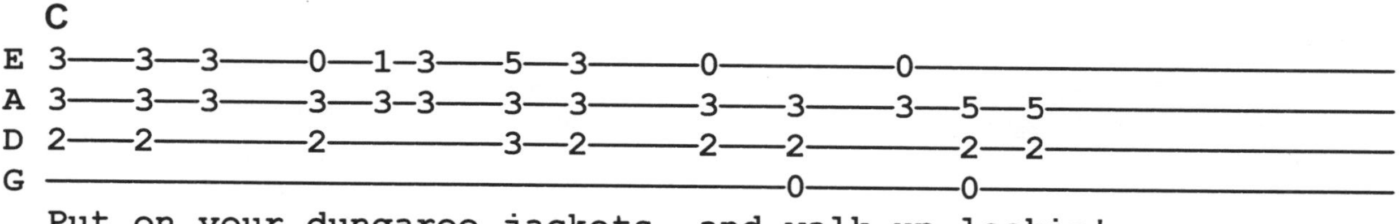

```
  C
E 3--3--3---0--1--3---5--3----0--------0------------
A 3--3--3---3--3--3---3--3----3---3----3--5--5------
D 2--2------2---------3--2----2---2-------2--2------
G ----------------------------------0-----0---------
  Put on your dungaree jackets, and walk up lookin'
```

```
      F       C                             Dm
E ------------0----0----0---------------------0-----
A 3---0----3--3----3----3----5-----3-0---5--0-----
D 2---3----3--2--------------2-----2-2---3--------
G 0---2----------------------0-----------2--------
  Your best, and tell them that you're a bold sailor
```

```
  F       G               C
E --------------------------------------------------
A 3----0--------0----3--5--3------------------------
D 3----3----5---0----0--0--2------------------------
G 2---------0--------0-----0------------------------
  Lad, that came from Paddy West.
```

Paddy West (continued - page 1)

Basic Melody
Key of G

```
   G                          Am     C       D
E ---------------------------------------------------------------
A ---2-2---2-0-------------0--2--------------------------0-------
D 5----------------5----2------------5-----2-0----2--5--5--------
G ---------------------------------------------------------------
  As I was a-walking down London Road, I came to Paddy West's

   G                                   C        G
E -------------------------------------0--0-0--------------------
A -------2--5----5--5-2----3--5----------------5----2---0--------
D 5-----------------------------------------------------------5--
G ---------------------------------------------------------------
  House; he gave me a feed of A-meri-can hash, and he called

              Em          G                                C
E ---------------------------------------------------------0--0--
A 2--0-0---------------2--5----5-------5-2----3-------5----------
D ---------5----2------------------------------------------------
G ---------------------------------------------------------------
  It Liverpool scouse. He said there's a ship that's a-wanting

   G                                Em         G
E ---------------------------------------------------------------
A 5------2-------2--2-----0--------------------2----2--2-0-------
D ------------5----------------------5--2----5---------------5---
G ---------------------------------------------------------------
  Hands, and on 'er you'll quickly sign; the mate is a tyrant,

      Am      C           D                  G
E ---------------------------------------------------------------
A ----0-2---------------------------------0----------------------
D 2-----------5------2----0----2----5---------5------------------
G ---------------------------------------------------------------
  The bosun's worse, but she will suit you fine.
```

Chord Forms

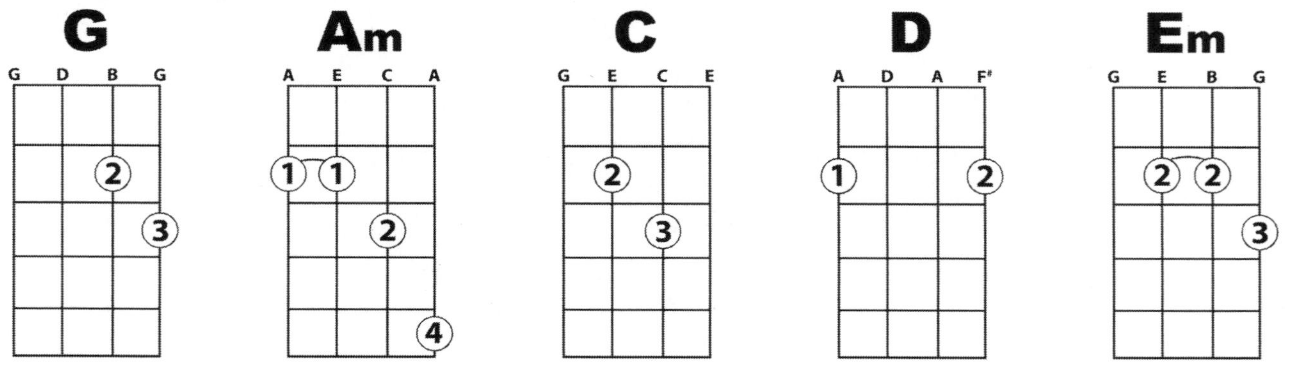

Paddy West (continued - page 2)

Basic Melody
Key of G

CHORUS

```
  G
E ----------------------------------0-----------------------------------------
A 5---5---5----2---3--5--------5------2-------------2---0---0---------------
D ------------------------------------------5----------------------------------
G ----------------------------------------------------------------------------
  Put on your dungaree jackets, and walk up lookin'

       C            G                                Am
E ----------------------------------------------------------------------------
A ---------------------2-----2-----2-----0---------------0---2--------------
D 5-----2------5---------------------------------5-2-------------------------
G ----------------------------------------------------------------------------
  Your best, and tell them that you're a bold sailor

  C          D               G
E ----------------------------------------------------------------------------
A -------------------------------0--------------------------------------------
D 5----2-----0-----2-----5------5--------------------------------------------
G ----------------------------------------------------------------------------
  Lad, that came from Paddy West.
```

Paddy West (continued - page 1)

Melody & Chords
Key of G

```
  G                        Am    C        D
E ---------------------------------------------------------------
A ---2--2---2-0------------0--2-------------------------0--------
D 5--0--0---0-0--5----2----2--2--5------2-0----2--5--5--0--------
G 0--0--------0--0----0----5-----5------5-2----2--2--2--2--------
  As I was a-walking down London Road, I came to Paddy West's
```

```
  G                             C        G
E ------------------------------0--0-0---------------------------
A -------2--5----5--5-2----3--5-3--3-3---5-----2---0-------------
D 5------0--0----0--0-0----0--0-2----2---0-----0---0--5----------
G 0---------0---------0------------------0------------0----------
  House; he gave me a feed of A-meri-can hash, and he called
```

```
              Em          G                            C
E -----------------------------------------------------0--0------
A 2--0-0---------------2--5----5-------5-2----3------5-3--3------
D 0--0-0--5----2-------2--0----0-------0-0----0------0-2---------
G ---0----0----4-------0--0--------------0-----------------------
  It Liverpool scouse. He said there's a ship that's a-wanting
```

```
  G                                Em        G
E ---------------------------------------------------------------
A 5------2-------2--2------0-----------------2----2--2-0---------
D 0------0---5---0--0------0----5--2-----5---0----0--0-0-5-------
G 0----------0-------------0----0--4-----4---0---------0-0-------
  Hands, and on 'er you'll quickly sign; the mate is a tyrant,
```

```
      Am      C          D                 G
E ---------------------------------------------------------------
A ----0-2------------------------------0-------------------------
D 2---2-2-----5------2---0---2----5----0---5---------------------
G 0---5-------5------5---2---2----2----2---0---------------------
  The bosun's worse, but she will suit you fine.
```

Chord Forms

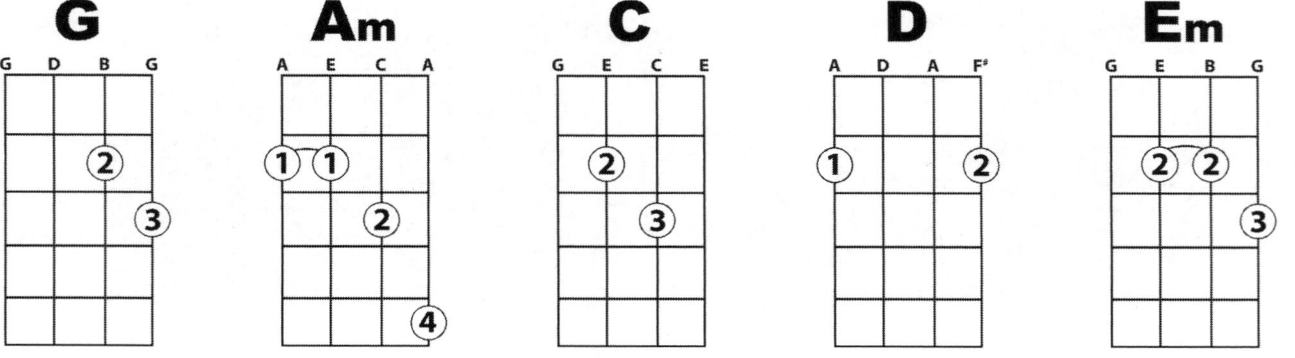

Paddy West (continued - page 2)

Melody & Chords
Key of G

CHORUS

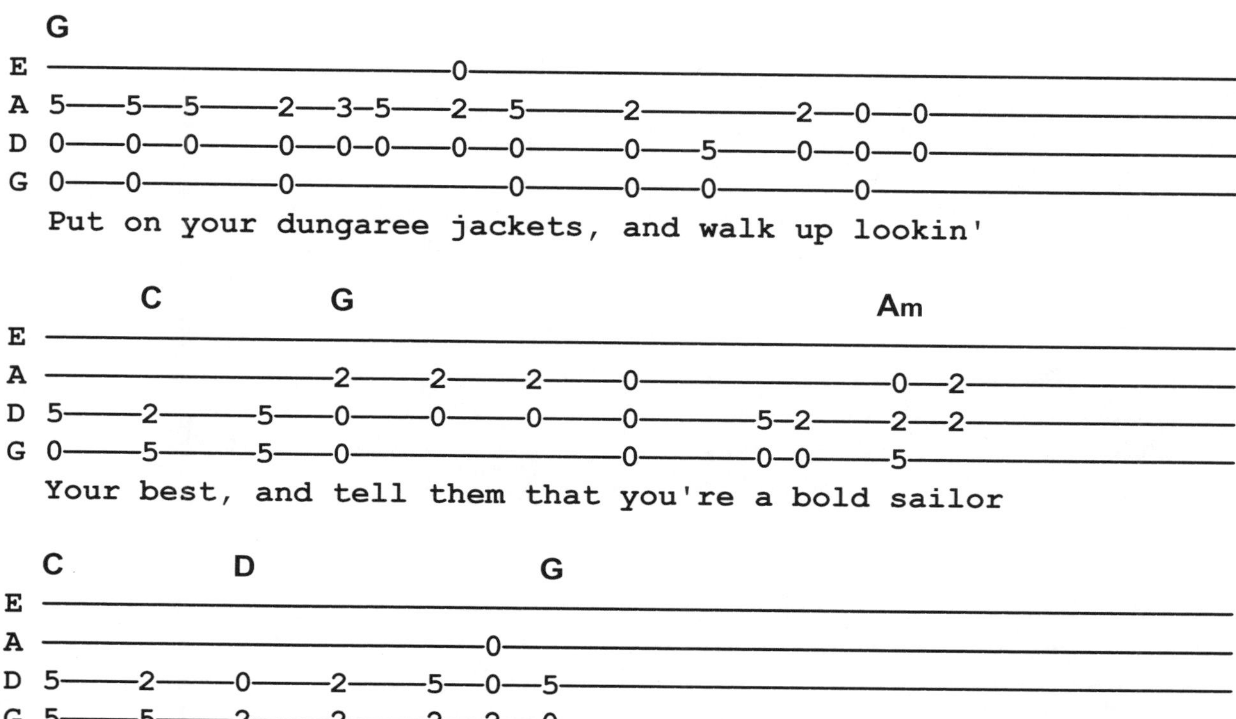

Quare Bungle Rye

Basic Melody
Key of C (Low)

This song hails from the late 1800's, when there may have been an actual Paddy West in Liverpool, the keeper of a boarding house and an ad-hoc trainer of would-be sailors. The verses outline Paddy's course of training, which was rather unconventional, to say the least. This song was popular among sailors both at sea and ashore, and is still sung today.

Words and Music

Traditional

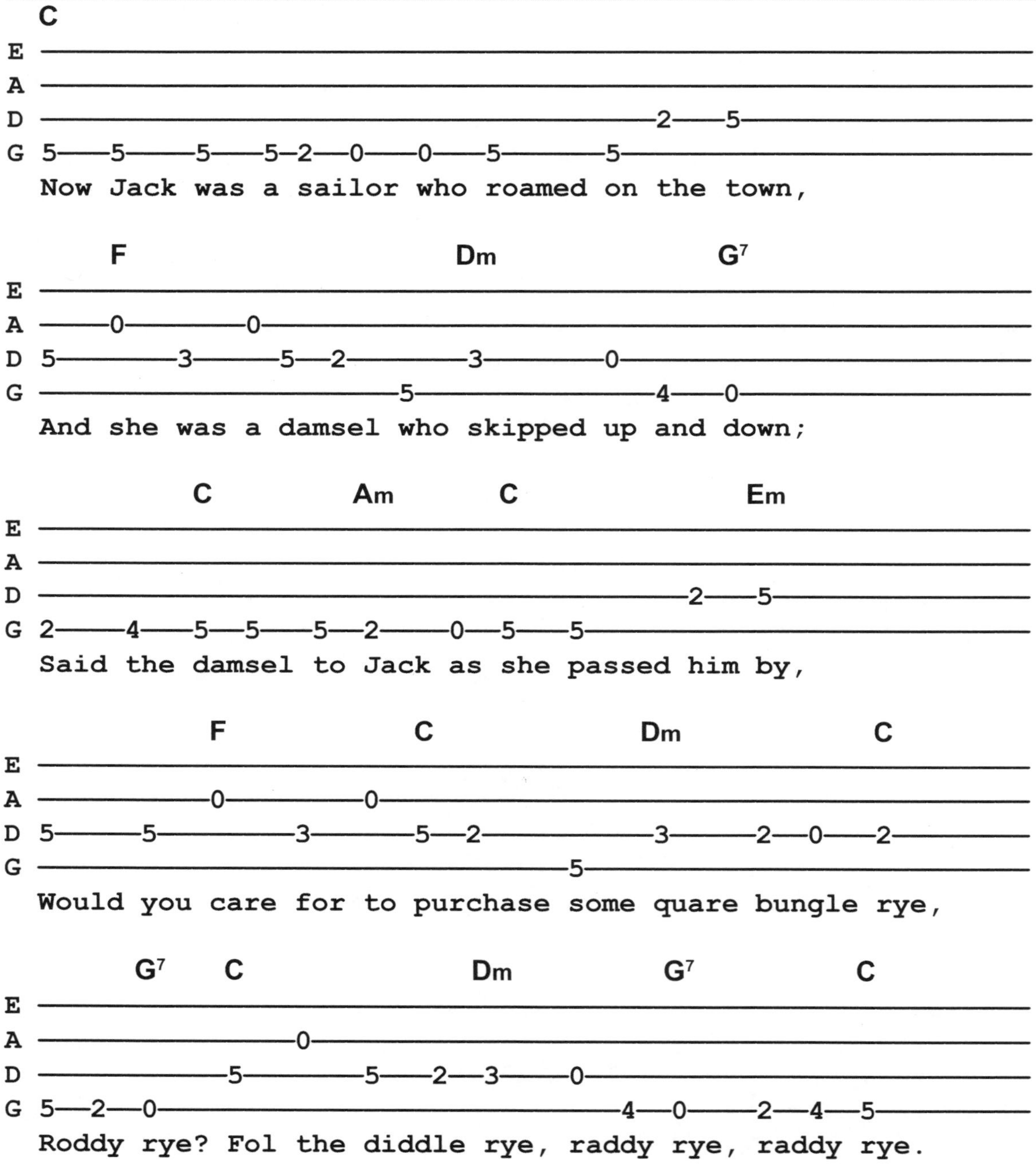

```
  C
E ---------------------------------------------------------
A ---------------------------------------------------------
D ---------------------------------------2---5-------------
G 5---5----5---5--2---0---0---5------5---------------------
  Now Jack was a sailor who roamed on the town,
```

```
     F                  Dm            G7
E ---------------------------------------------------------
A ---0-------0-----------------------------------------------
D 5------3------5--2------3------0---------------------------
G -----------------------5------------4---0------------------
  And she was a damsel who skipped up and down;
```

```
         C        Am      C             Em
E ---------------------------------------------------------
A ---------------------------------------------------------
D ----------------------------------------2---5------------
G 2----4---5--5---5--2----0---5---5------------------------
  Said the damsel to Jack as she passed him by,
```

```
          F          C           Dm         C
E ---------------------------------------------------------
A ----------0--------0---------------------------------------
D 5----5-------3-------5--2---------3-----2---0---2----------
G ------------------------------5----------------------------
  Would you care for to purchase some quare bungle rye,
```

```
      G7  C         Dm        G7       C
E ---------------------------------------------------------
A -------------0---------------------------------------------
D ----------5-------5---2--3----0----------------------------
G 5--2--0-------------------------4---0---2--4--5------------
  Roddy rye? Fol the diddle rye, raddy rye, raddy rye.
```

See Chord Forms and Additional Verses on Next Page

Quare Bungle Rye (continued)

Chord Forms and Additional Verses

Chord Forms

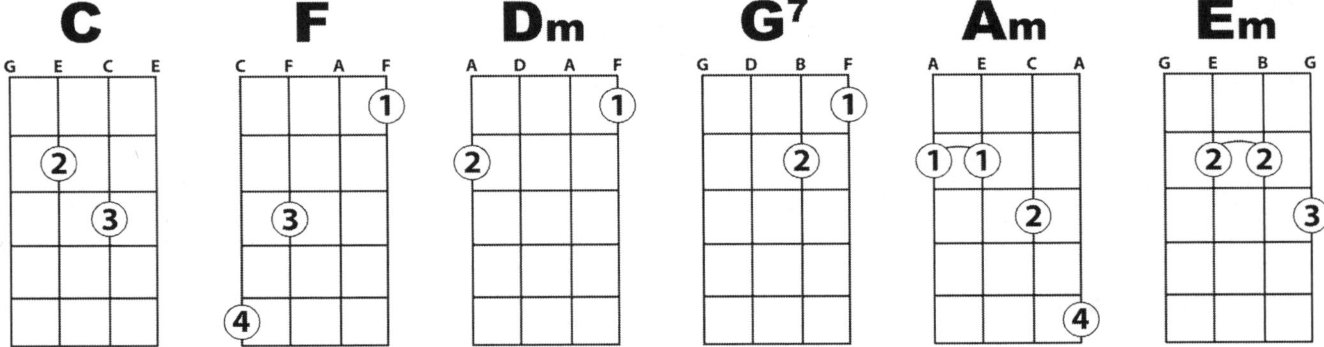

Additional Verses

Thought Jack to himself, "Now what can this be?
"But the finest old whiskey from old Germany;
Smuggled up in a basket and sold on the sly,
And the name that it goes by is quare bungle rye raddy rye."
Fol the diddle rye raddy rye raddy rye.

Jack hands her a shilling and he thought nothing strange.
Says she, "Here hold the basket 'til I run for your change."
Jack peeks in the basket and a babe he did spy.
"Why b'damn me," says Jack, "This is quare bungle rye raddy rye."
Fol the diddle rye raddy rye raddy rye.

Now to get the child christened was Jack's first intent,
So to get the child christened to the parson he went.
Says the parson to Jack, 'What's the name he'll go by?'
"Ah b'damn me," says Jack, "Call 'im quare bungle rye raddy rye."
Fol the diddle rye raddy rye raddy rye.

Says the parson to Jack, "That's a mighty quare name."
"Ah b'damn me," says Jack, 'It's a quare way he came;
Smuggled up in a basket and sold on the sly,
And the name that he'll go by is Quare Bungle Rye raddy rye."
Fol the diddle rye raddy rye raddy rye

Now all you young sailors who roam on the town,
Be wary of damsels that skip up and down.
Take a peek in their baskets as they pass you by,
Or else they may pawn on you quare bungle rye raddy rye.
Fol the diddle rye raddy rye raddy rye.

Quare Bungle Rye (continued)

Basic Melody
Key of C (High)

```
  C
E ---------------------------------------------------------------0---3--------------
A 3---3-----3---3-0-----------------3-----------3------------------------------------
D -------------------------5---5------------------------------------------------------
G ------------------------------------------------------------------------------------
  Now Jack was a sailor who roamed on the town,

        F                       Dm                     G7
E 3---5---1---5-3---0-----------1--------------------------------------------
A ------------------------3----------------5---2------------------------------
D ---------------------------------------------------5------------------------
G ----------------------------------------------------------------------------
  And she was a damsel who skipped up and down;

           C            Am        C                 Em
E ----------------------------------------------0---3-------------------------
A 0-----2---3---3---3---0---------3---3-----------------------------------------
D ---------------------------5--------------------------------------------------
G ------------------------------------------------------------------------------
  Said the damsel to Jack as she passed him by,

              F          C              Dm            C
E 3-----3---5-----1---5---3---0---------------1-------0-------0-------
A ----------------------------------3---------------------5-----------
D --------------------------------------------------------------------
G --------------------------------------------------------------------
  Would you care for to purchase some quare bungle rye,

        G7    C                 Dm              G7             C
E -------------3---5---3---0---1--------------------------------------
A 3--0------------------------------5---2------------0---2---3--------
D -------5-----------------------------------------5-----------------
G --------------------------------------------------------------------
  Roddy rye? Fol the diddle rye, raddy rye, raddy rye.
```

Chord Forms

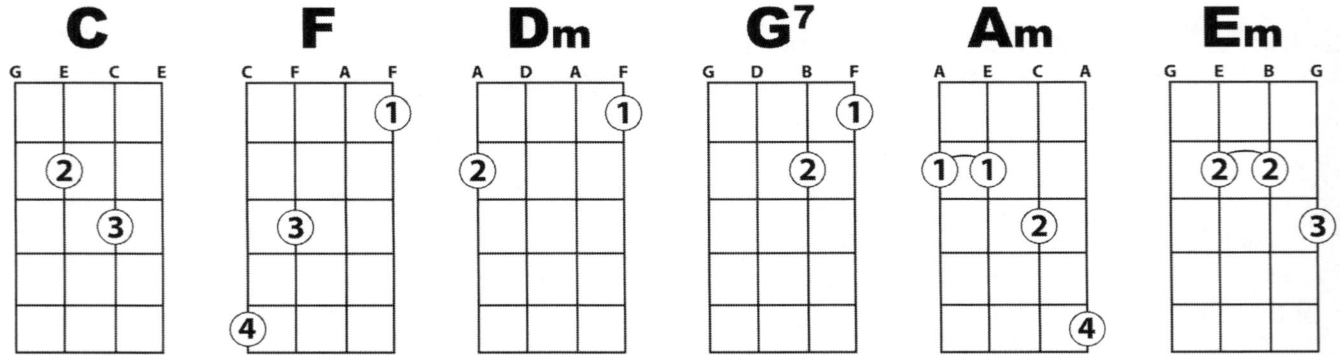

Quare Bungle Rye (continued)

Melody & Chords
Key of C (High)

```
  C
E -------------------------------------0---3------
A 3---3----3---3-0-----------3-----3--3---3------
D 2---2----2---2-2--5---5----2-----2------2------
G 0---0-----------5--5---5---0-------------------
  Now Jack was a sailor who roamed on the town,
```

```
     F                        Dm             G7
E 3--5--1--5-3--0-------------1--------------------
A 3--3--0--0-0--0----3--------0------5--2----------
D 2-------------3-3--3---3----0------0--0---5------
G ------------------------------------2------0------
  And she was a damsel who skipped up and down;
```

```
          C          Am       C              Em
E ---------------------------------------0---3-----
A 0----2--3--3---3--0--------3----3------3---2-----
D 0----0--2--2---2--2----5---2----2----------2-----
G 0--------0----------5--5---0----0----------------
  Said the damsel to Jack as she passed him by,
```

```
            F          C             Dm         C
E 3-----3---5----1---5-3--0-----------1----0-----0----
A 2-----2---3----0---0-3--3-------3---0----0--5--3----
D 2---------3------------2--------2---0-------0--2----
G ---------------------------------0-------------------
  Would you care for to purchase some quare bungle rye,
```

```
       G7    C              Dm          G7         C
E -----------3---5---3---0--1------------------------
A 3--0-------3---3---3---3--0----5--2-------0--2--3--
D 2--2--5----2-------2------0----0--0--5----3--3--2--
G 0-----0------------------------------0----4--4--0--
  Roddy rye? Fol the diddle rye, raddy rye, raddy rye.
```

Chord Forms

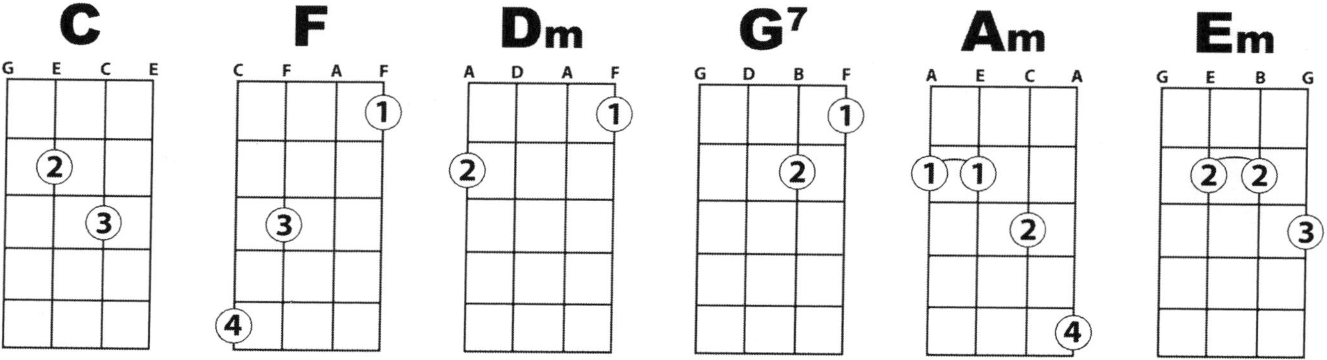

Quare Bungle Rye (continued)

Basic Melody
Key of G

```
  G
E ------------------------------------------------------
A ---------------------------------------2---5----------
D 5--5----5---5-2--0---0---5-----5----------------------
G ------------------------------------------------------
  Now Jack was a sailor who roamed on the town,
```

```
      C                    Am             D7
E ----0-------0-----------------------------------------
A 5-------3-------5--2-------3-------0------------------
D ---------------------5----------------4---0-----------
G ------------------------------------------------------
  And she was a damsel who skipped up and down;
```

```
          G        Em       G              Bm
E ------------------------------------------------------
A --------------------------------------2----5----------
D 2---4---5--5---5--2---0--5---5------------------------
G ------------------------------------------------------
  Said the damsel to Jack as she passed him by,
```

```
           C           G             Am          G
E ---------0-------0------------------------------------
A 5---5-------3-------5--2----------3------2--0---2-----
D --------------------------------5---------------------
G ------------------------------------------------------
  Would you care for to purchase some quare bungle rye,
```

```
      D7   G              Am        D7         G
E -------------0----------------------------------------
A ----------5------5--2--3---0--------------------------
D 5--2--0--------------------------4--0---2--4--5-------
G ------------------------------------------------------
  Roddy rye? Fol the diddle rye, raddy rye, raddy rye.
```

Chord Forms

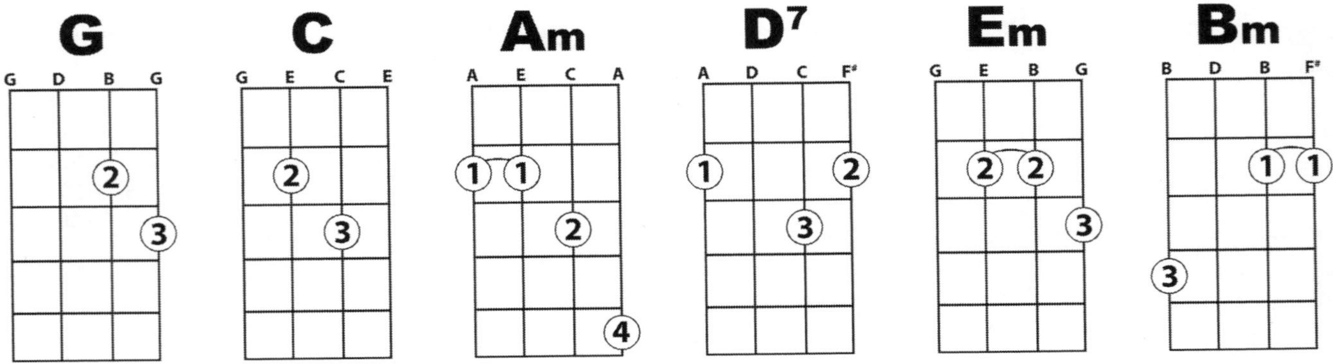

Quare Bungle Rye (continued)

Melody & Chords
Key of G

```
  G
E ----------------------------------------------------------------------
A ---------------------------------------------------2---5--------------
D 5---5----5---5-2--0----0----5--------5---0----0-----------------------
G 0---0----0---0-0--0----0----0--------0--------0-----------------------
  Now Jack was a sailor who roamed on the town,
```

```
       C                          Am                D7
E -----0---------0------------------------------------------------------
A 5----3----3----3-5--2-----------3--------0----------------------------
D 0----2----2---------2--2---5----2--------2---4---0--------------------
G ----------0----------------0----2------------2---2--------------------
  And she was a damsel who skipped up and down;
```

```
            G          Em        G                Bm
E ----------------------------------------------------------------------
A ---------------------------------------------2---5--------------------
D 2-----4---5--5----5--2----0---5----5---------0---4--------------------
G 2-----2---0--0----0--4----4---0----0-------------4--------------------
  Said the damsel to Jack as she passed him by,
```

```
               C            G                Am              G
E -------------0----------0---------------------------------------------
A 5------5-----3-----3----3---5--2-----------3-------2---0----2---------
D 4------4-----2-----2--------0--0-----5-----2-------2---2----0---------
G -----------------------------0-------0-----2----------------0---------
  Would you care for to purchase some quare bungle rye,
```

```
         D7     G                 Am           D7           G
E -------------------0--------------------------------------------------
A --------------5----2---5---2---3------0-------------------------------
D 5--2--0-------0--------0---0---2------2---4---0------2---4---5--------
G 0--0--2-------0--------0-------2----------2---2------2---2---0--------
  Roddy rye? Fol the diddle rye, raddy rye, raddy rye.
```

Chord Forms

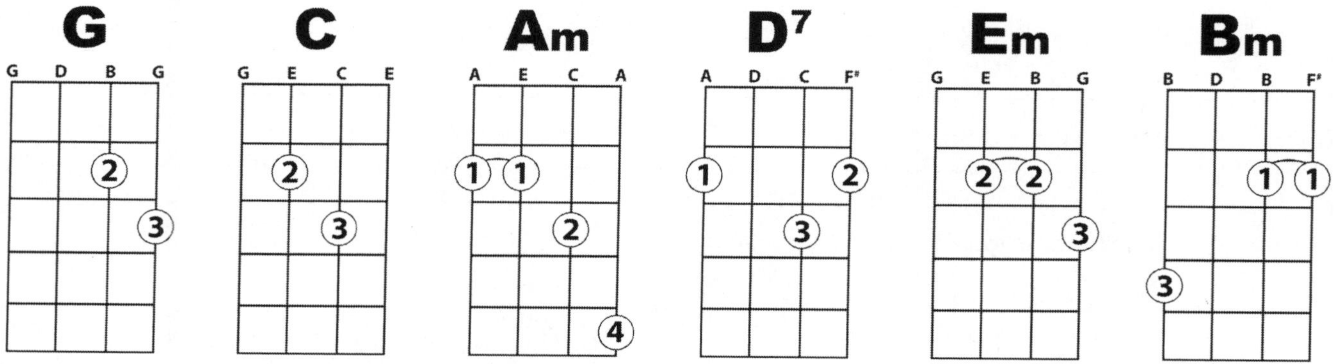

Rolling Down To Old Maui (page 1)

Basic Melody

Key of A Minor

This is another great old whaling song, in which the seafaring whalemen sing of how good things will be once the arctic trip is done and they are back in warm and beautiful Maui. Stan Rogers recorded a great version of this song, and it is still a favorite of Celtic and maritime singing sessions.

Words and Music Traditional

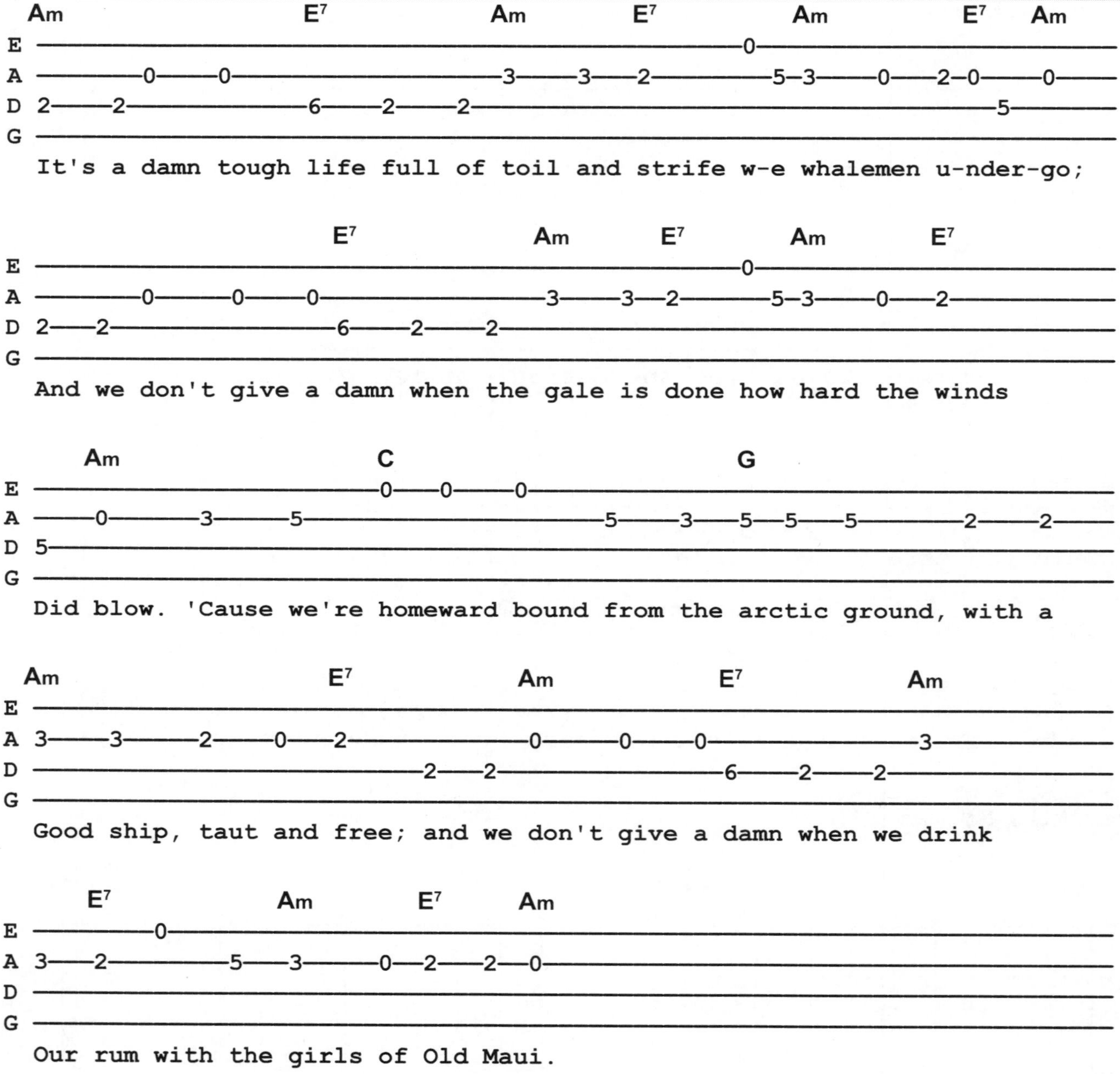

```
  Am                        E7                 Am          E7          Am          E7    Am
E ----------------------------------------------------------------0-----------------------------
A ----------0------0--------------------------3------3----2----------5--3------0----2--0------0----
D 2------2-----------------6------2------2----------------------------------------------5-----------
G ---------------------------------------------------------------------------------------------------
 It's a damn tough life full of toil and strife w-e whalemen u-nder-go;

                           E7                Am         E7          Am          E7
E ----------------------------------------------------------------0---------------------------
A ----------0-------0------0-------------------3------3----2---------5--3------0----2----------
D 2----2-------------------------6------2------2------------------------------------------------
G ---------------------------------------------------------------------------------------------
 And we don't give a damn when the gale is done how hard the winds

      Am                       C                          G
E -------------------------------0----0-----0----------------------------------------------
A ------0--------3------5--------------------------5-----3----5---5----5---------2-----2---
D 5-----------------------------------------------------------------------------------------
G -------------------------------------------------------------------------------------------
 Did blow. 'Cause we're homeward bound from the arctic ground, with a

  Am                        E7                 Am               E7                Am
E ---------------------------------------------------------------------------------------------
A 3------3-------2------0----2-----------------0-------0------0----------------------3---------
D ------------------------------------2----2--------------------------6------2------2-----------
G ---------------------------------------------------------------------------------------------
 Good ship, taut and free; and we don't give a damn when we drink

      E7                Am          E7         Am
E ----------0-------------------------------------------------------------------------------
A 3----2-----------5-----3------0----2----2----0--------------------------------------------
D --------------------------------------------------------------------------------------------
G --------------------------------------------------------------------------------------------
 Our rum with the girls of Old Maui.
```

Rolling Down To Old Maui
(page 2)

Basic Melody

Key of A Minor

CHORUS

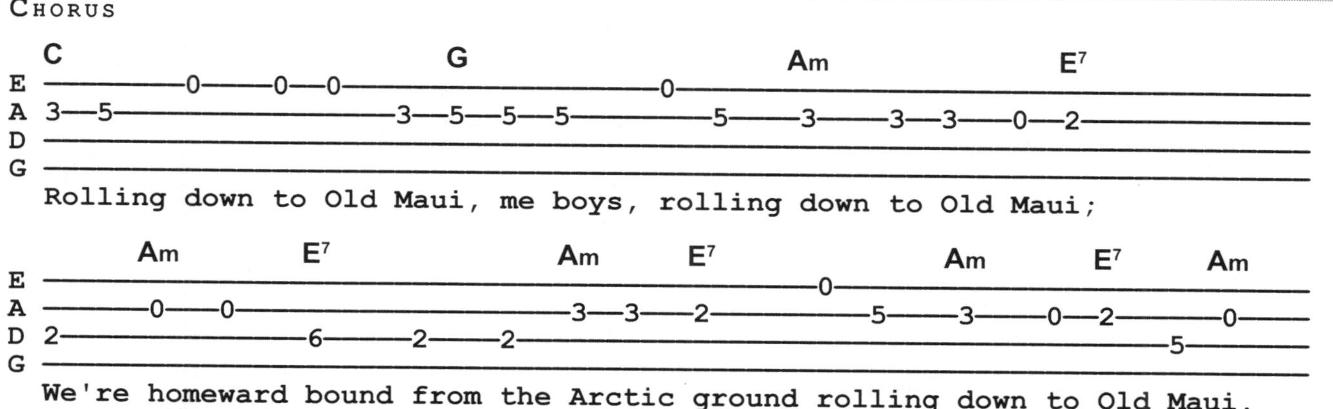

Chord Forms

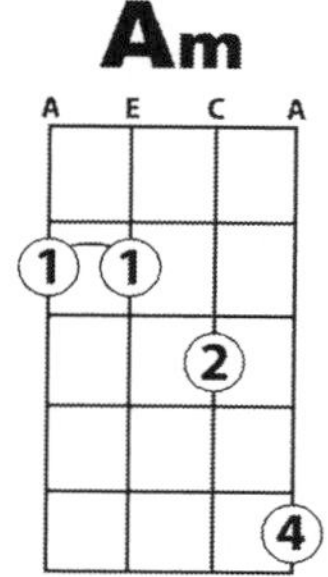

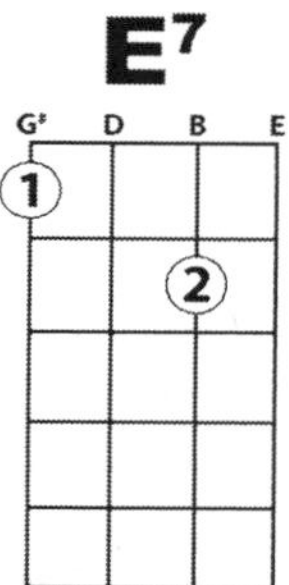

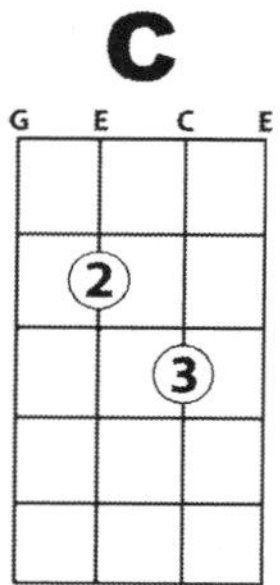

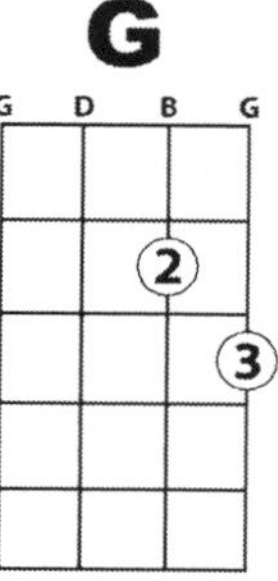

Additional Verses

Once more we sail with a northerly gale, towards our island home;
Our mainmast sprung, our whaling done, and we don't have far to roam.
Six hellish months have passed away on the cold Kamchatka Sea,
But now we're bound from the Arctic ground, rolling down to Old Maui.

Once more we sail with a northerly gale, through the ice and wind and rain;
Them coconut fronds, them tropical lands, we soon shall see again.
Our stu'n's'l booms is carried away, what care we for that sound?
A living gale is after us, thank God we're homeward bound.

How soft the breeze through the island trees, now the ice is far astern;
Them native maids, them tropical glades, are awaiting our return.
Even now their big brown eyes look out, hoping some fine day to see,
Our baggy sails runnin' 'fore the gales, rolling down to old Maui.

We'll heave the lead where old Diamond Head looms up on old Wahu;
Our masts and yards are sheathed with ice, and our decks are hid from view.
The horrid ice of the sea-caked isles that deck the Arctic Sea,
Are miles behind in the frozen wind, since we steered for Old Maui.

Rolling Down To Old Maui (continued - page 1)

Melody & Chords

Key of A Minor

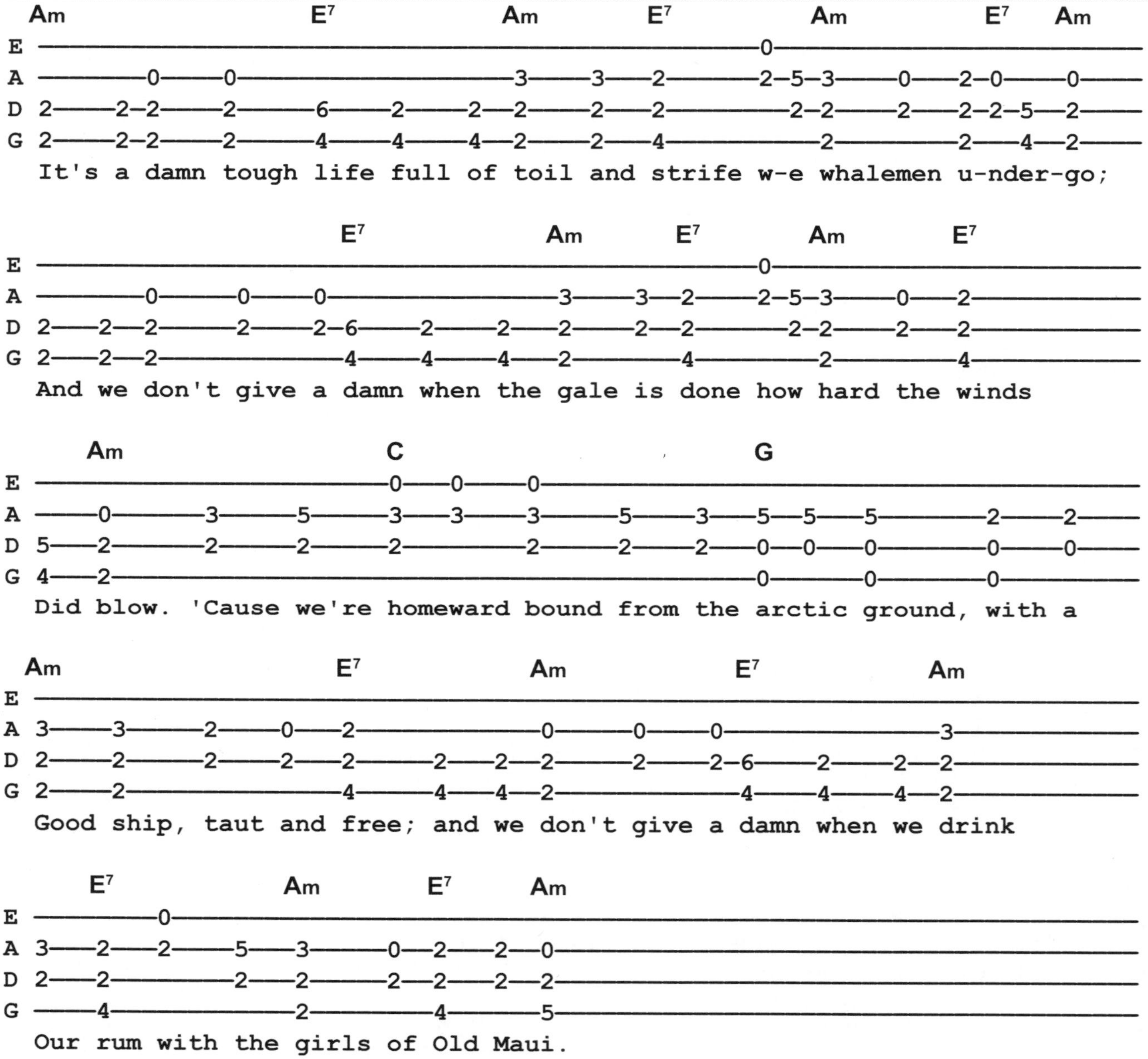

```
   Am                  E7            Am         E7           Am          E7   Am
E ----------------------------------------------------------0------------------------
A -------0------0-----------------------3-----3----2---------2-5-3-----0---2-0-----0---
D 2----2-2------2------6-----2-----2--2------2----2-------------2-2-----2---2-2-5--2---
G 2----2-2------2------4-----4-----4--2------2----4---------------2-----------2---4--2---
  It's a damn tough life full of toil and strife w-e whalemen u-nder-go;
```

```
                     E7            Am       E7        Am         E7
E ----------------------------------------------------0--------------------------
A -------0--------0-----0---------------3-----3--2-----2-5-3-----0---2-------------
D 2---2--2--------2-----2-6-----2----2---2-----2--2---------2-2-----2---2-----------
G 2---2--2----------------4-----4----4---2--------4-----------2---------4-----------
  And we don't give a damn when the gale is done how hard the winds
```

```
       Am                  C                            G
E ---------------------------0---0---0--------------------------------------------
A ----0------3------5------3---3----3------5-----3---5---5---5--------2----2-----
D 5---2------2------2------2--------2------2-----2---0---0---0--------0----0-----
G 4---2------------------------------------------------0-------0--------0--------
  Did blow. 'Cause we're homeward bound from the arctic ground, with a
```

```
   Am                 E7           Am              E7            Am
E --------------------------------------------------------------------------------
A 3----3------2----0---2-------------0------0-----0---------------3--------------
D 2----2------2----2---2-------2---2---2------2-----2-6------2-----2---2---------
G 2----2-----------------4-------4---4--2------------------4-----4-----4--2------
  Good ship, taut and free; and we don't give a damn when we drink
```

```
       E7            Am       E7      Am
E ----------0-----------------------------------------------------------------
A 3---2---2-----5----3------0---2---2---0-------------------------------------
D 2---2---------2----2------2---2---2---2-------------------------------------
G ----4--------------2----------4-------5-------------------------------------
  Our rum with the girls of Old Maui.
```

Rolling Down To Old Maui (continued - page 2)

Melody & Chords

Key of A Minor

CHORUS

```
  C                 G             Am          E7
E ------0--0--0--------------0------------------
A 3--5--3--3--3--3--5--5--5--2--5--3--3--3--0--2--
D 2--2--2-----2--2--0--0--0--0--0--2--2--2--2--2--
G 0-----------------0-----0--------2-----2-----4--
  Rolling down to Old Maui, me boys, rolling down to Old Maui;

     Am    E7       Am    E7       Am    E7    Am
E ---------------------------0--------------------
A ---0--0-----------3--3--2--2--5--3--0--2-----0--
D 2--2--2--6--2--2--2--2--2-----2--2--2--2--5--2--
G 4--2-----4--4--4--2-----4--------2-----4--4--2--
  We're homeward bound from the Arctic ground rolling down to Old Maui.
```

Chord Forms

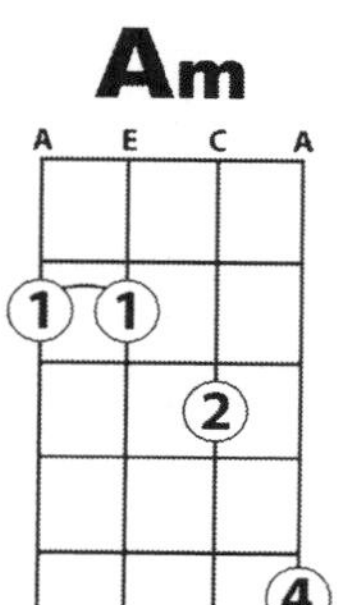

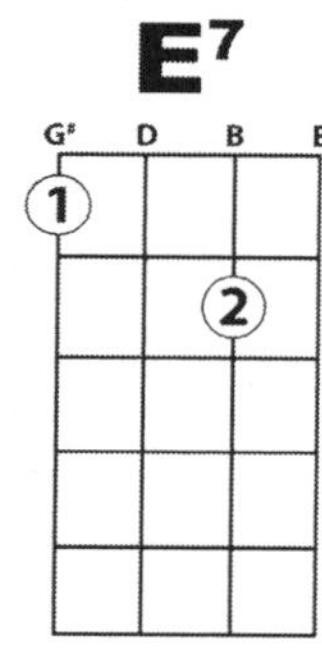

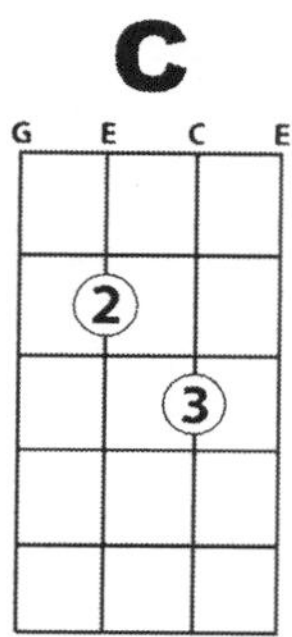

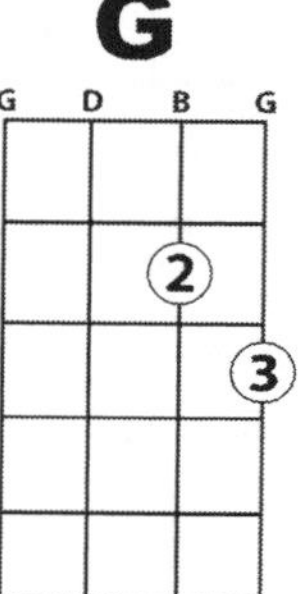

Rolling Down To Old Maui (continued - page 1)

Basic Melody

Key of E Minor (Low)

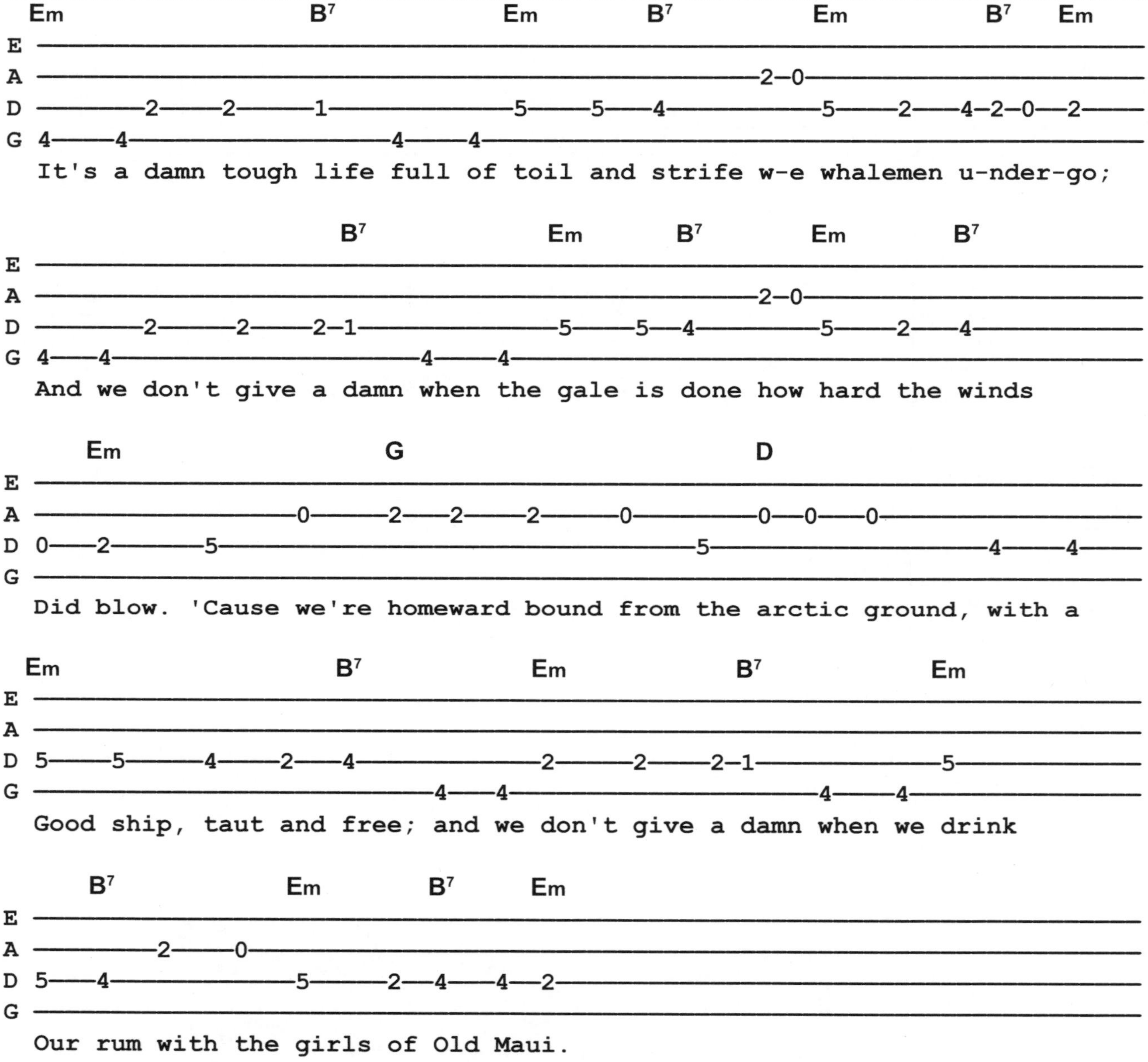

```
   Em                    B7           Em        B7          Em          B7    Em
E -----------------------------------------------------------------------------------
A --------------------------------------------------------2-0------------------------
D --------2-----2-----1------------5-----5----4-------------5-----2----4-2-0--2------
G 4----4---------------------4----4--------------------------------------------------
  It's a damn tough life full of toil and strife w-e whalemen u-nder-go;
```

```
                           B7            Em        B7          Em         B7
E -----------------------------------------------------------------------------------
A --------------------------------------------------------2-0------------------------
D --------2------2----2-1-------------5-----5---4------------5-----2----4------------
G 4---4--------------------------4-----4---------------------------------------------
  And we don't give a damn when the gale is done how hard the winds
```

```
     Em                  G                       D
E -----------------------------------------------------------------------------------
A ---------------------0------2----2----2-----0---------0---0---0--------------------
D 0---2-------5---------------------------------5--------------------------4----4----
G -----------------------------------------------------------------------------------
  Did blow. 'Cause we're homeward bound from the arctic ground, with a
```

```
  Em                   B7          Em           B7           Em
E -----------------------------------------------------------------------------------
A -----------------------------------------------------------------------------------
D 5----5------4----2---4-----------------2-----2----2-1------------5-----------------
G ---------------------------4----4-------------------------4----4-------------------
  Good ship, taut and free; and we don't give a damn when we drink
```

```
     B7             Em      B7     Em
E -----------------------------------------------------------------------------------
A -------2----0----------------------------------------------------------------------
D 5---4-------------5-----2---4----4--2----------------------------------------------
G -----------------------------------------------------------------------------------
  Our rum with the girls of Old Maui.
```

Rolling Down To Old Maui (continued - page 2)

Basic Melody

Key of E Minor (Low)

CHORUS

```
 G                              D                              Em                 B7
E ---------------------------------------------------------------------------------------------
A ---0-----2-----2--2-----------0---0---0------2---0-------------------------------------------
D 5-------------------------5------------------------------------5------5--5----2---4-----------
G ---------------------------------------------------------------------------------------------
  Rolling down to Old Maui, me boys, rolling down to Old Maui;

       Em          B7                      Em       B7                        Em         B7       Em
E ---------------------------------------------------------------------------------------------
A --------------------------------------------------------------2---0--------------------------
D --------2----2-----1------------------------5----5----4-------------------5------2---4----0--2----
G 4------------------------------4------4------------------------------------------------------
  We're homeward bound from the Arctic ground rolling down to Old Maui.
```

Chord Forms

Em

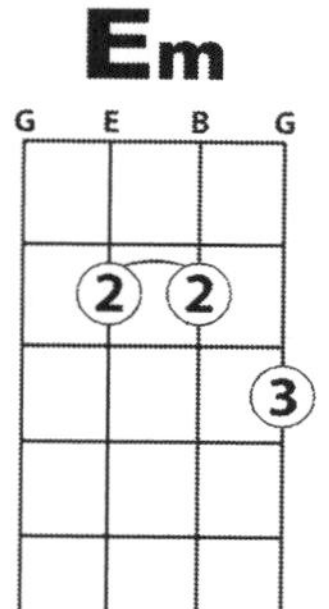

B7

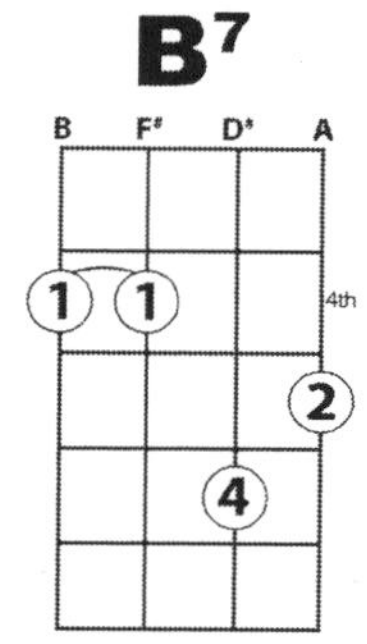

G

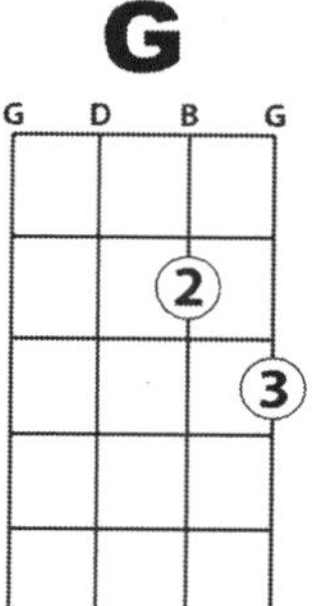

D

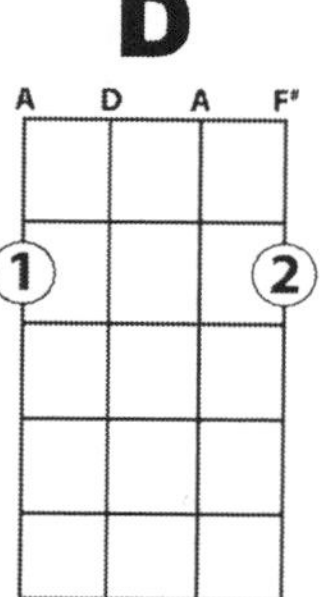

Rolling Down To Old Maui (continued - page 1)

Basic Melody

Key of E Minor (High)

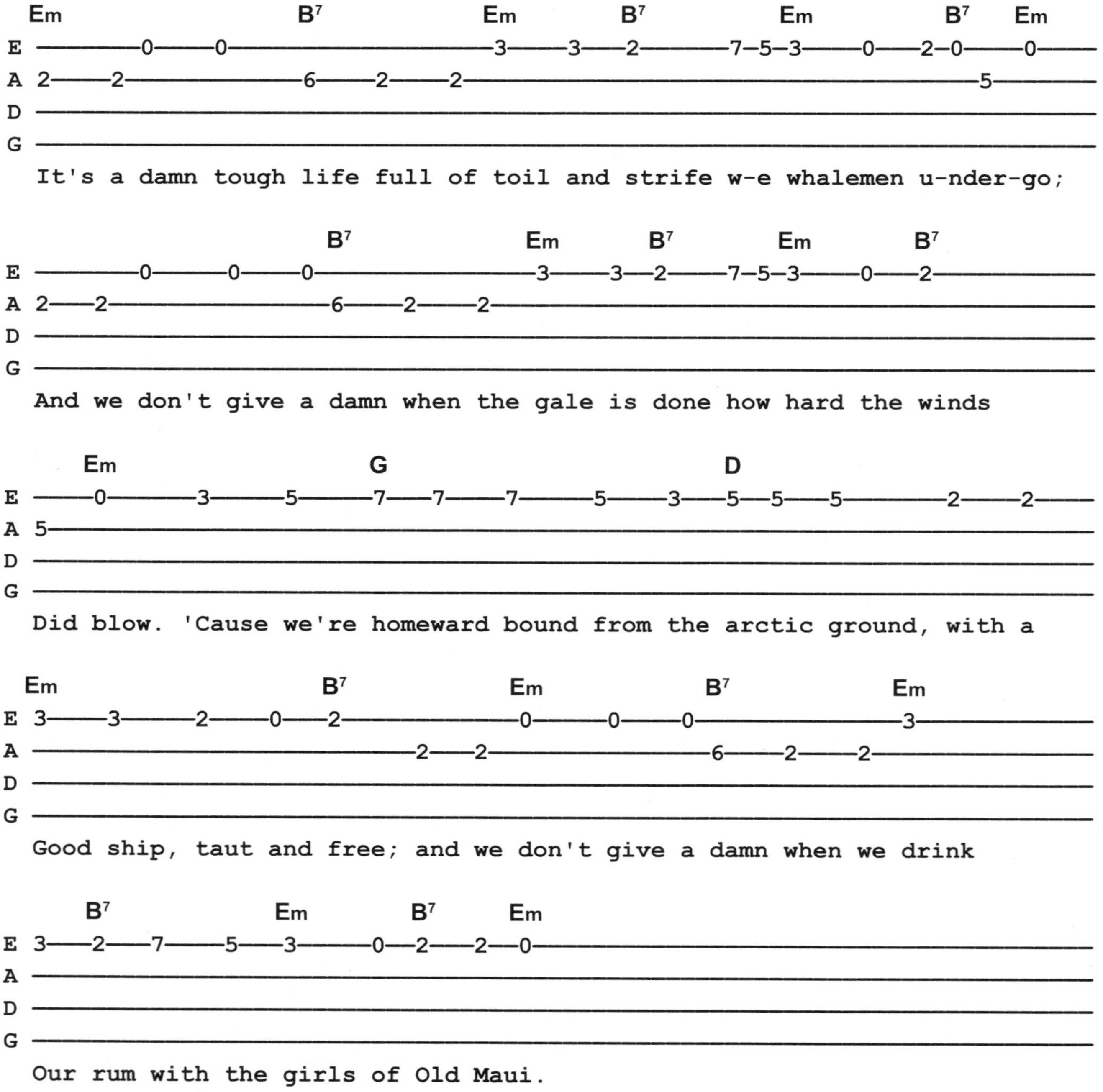

```
  Em                          B7                 Em          B7               Em              B7     Em
E ----------0-------0-------------------------3-------3----2-----------7--5--3------0----2--0-------0------
A 2------2----------------------6------2------2-------------------------------------------------5-----------
D ----------------------------------------------------------------------------------------------------------
G ----------------------------------------------------------------------------------------------------------
  It's a damn tough life full of toil and strife w-e whalemen u-nder-go;
```

```
                                B7                 Em          B7           Em            B7
E ----------0--------0------0-------------------------3------3---2------7--5--3-------0-----2---------------
A 2-----2------------------------6------2------2------------------------------------------------------------
D ----------------------------------------------------------------------------------------------------------
G ----------------------------------------------------------------------------------------------------------
  And we don't give a damn when the gale is done how hard the winds
```

```
      Em                        G                                      D
E ------0---------3-------5-------7-----7-------7-------5-------3-----5----5-----5-----------2------2-------
A 5---------------------------------------------------------------------------------------------------------
D ----------------------------------------------------------------------------------------------------------
G ----------------------------------------------------------------------------------------------------------
  Did blow. 'Cause we're homeward bound from the arctic ground, with a
```

```
  Em                           B7                Em                B7                Em
E 3------3-------2------0----2-----------------0-------0------0--------------------3------------------------
A ----------------------------------------2-----2-------------------6------2------2--------------------------
D ----------------------------------------------------------------------------------------------------------
G ----------------------------------------------------------------------------------------------------------
  Good ship, taut and free; and we don't give a damn when we drink
```

```
      B7                 Em         B7      Em
E 3----2----7-------5----3--------0----2-----2---0----------------------------------------------------------
A ----------------------------------------------------------------------------------------------------------
D ----------------------------------------------------------------------------------------------------------
G ----------------------------------------------------------------------------------------------------------
  Our rum with the girls of Old Maui.
```

Rolling Down To Old Maui (continued - page 2)

Basic Melody

Key of E Minor (High)

CHORUS

```
  G                          D                         Em                 B7
E 3—5———7———7—7———3—5—5—5————7—5———3————3—3———0—2——————————
A ——————————————————————————————————————————————————————————
D ——————————————————————————————————————————————————————————
G ——————————————————————————————————————————————————————————
  Rolling down to Old Maui, me boys, rolling down to Old Maui;
```

```
         Em      B7                   Em     B7                 Em      B7      Em
E ———————0———0————————————————————————3—3———2————7—5———3————0—2——————0————
A 2——————————————————6————2————2——————————————————————————————————5——————
D ————————————————————————————————————————————————————————————————————————
G ————————————————————————————————————————————————————————————————————————
  We're homeward bound from the Arctic ground rolling down to Old Maui.
```

Chord Forms

Em

G E B G

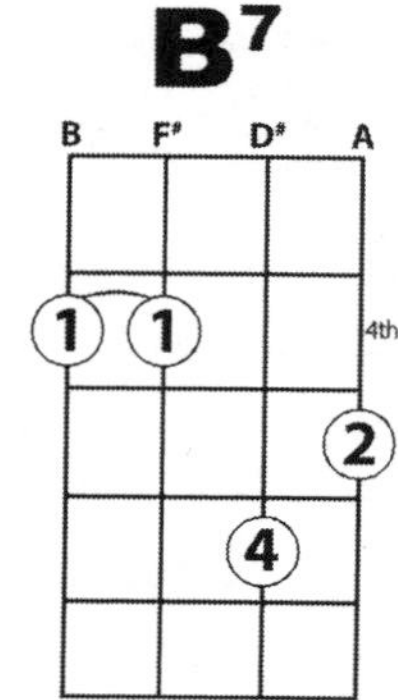

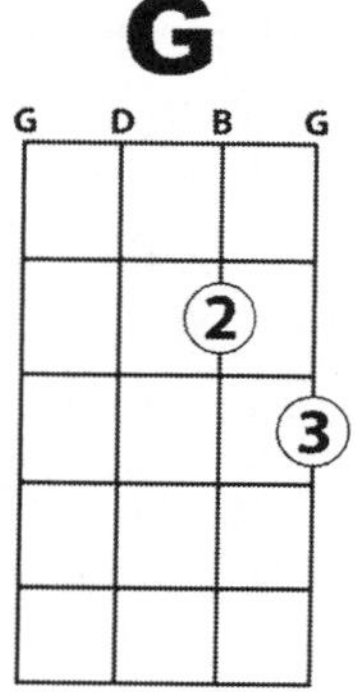

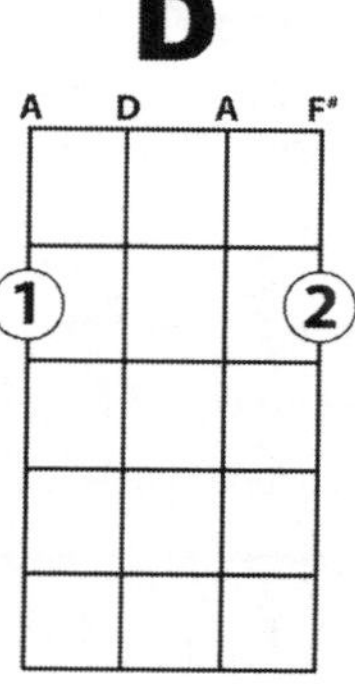

Rolling Down To Old Maui (continued - page 1)

Melody & Chords

Key of E Minor (High)

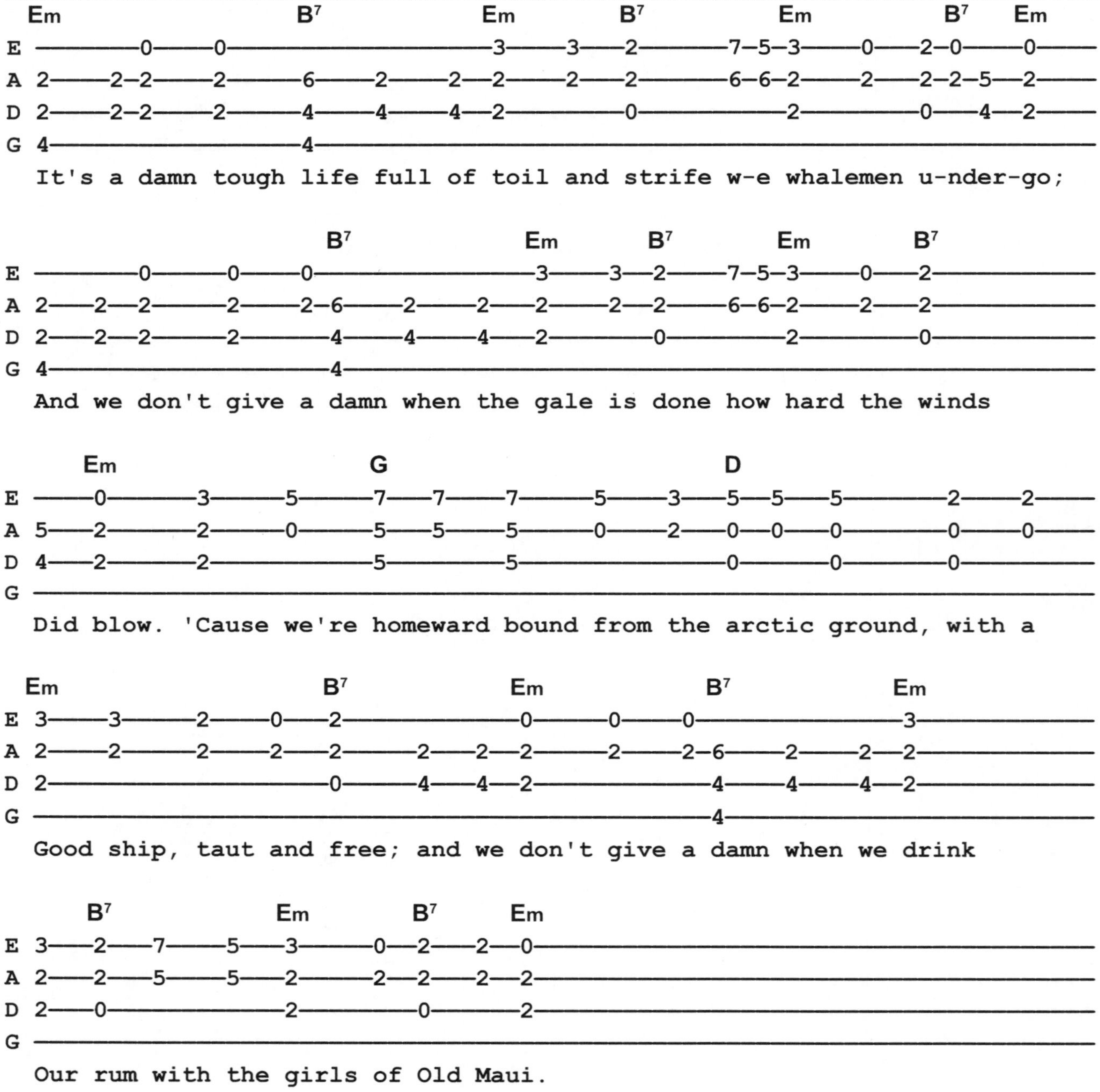

```
  Em                          B7              Em         B7          Em          B7    Em
E ----------0------0-------------------------3-----3----2--------7-5-3-----0----2-0-----0-----
A 2------2-2------2-------6------2------2----2-----2----2--------6-6-2-----2----2-2-5---2-----
D 2------2-2------2-------4------4------4----2----------0------------2----------0---4---2-----
G 4-----------------------4-------------------------------------------------------------------
  It's a damn tough life full of toil and strife w-e whalemen u-nder-go;
```

```
                              B7              Em         B7          Em         B7
E ----------0-------0------0-------------------3-----3----2------7-5-3-----0-----2-----------
A 2----2----2-------2------2-6------2-----2----2-----2----2------6-6-2-----2-----2-----------
D 2----2----2-------2--------4------4-----4----2----------0----------2-----------0-----------
G 4--------------------------4---------------------------------------------------------------
  And we don't give a damn when the gale is done how hard the winds
```

```
      Em                      G                         D
E -----0-------3------5------7----7-----7------5-----3---5----5----5--------2-----2------
A 5----2-------2------0------5----5-----5------0-----2---0----0----0--------0-----0------
D 4----2-------2-------------5----------5----------------0---------0--------0------------
G ---------------------------------------------------------------------------------------
  Did blow. 'Cause we're homeward bound from the arctic ground, with a
```

```
  Em                      B7              Em            B7              Em
E 3-----3------2-----0----2---------------0-------0-----0---------------3-------------
A 2-----2------2-----2----2-------2----2--2-------2-----2-6-----2----2--2-------------
D 2-----------------------0-------4----4--2---------------4-----4----4--2-------------
G ----------------------------------------------------------4-------------------------
  Good ship, taut and free; and we don't give a damn when we drink
```

```
     B7           Em        B7     Em
E 3---2---7----5---3------0---2---2---0-----------------------------------------------
A 2---2---5----5---2------2---2---2---2-----------------------------------------------
D 2---0------------2----------0-------2-----------------------------------------------
G ------------------------------------------------------------------------------------
  Our rum with the girls of Old Maui.
```

Rolling Down To Old Maui (continued - page 2)

Melody & Chords

Key of E Minor (High)

CHORUS

```
  G                                D                      Em              B7
E 3—5——7——7—7——3—5—5—5———7—5———3———3—3——0—2——————————
A 2—0——5——5—5——2—0—0—0———0—0———2———2—2——2—2——————————
D 0————5——————5——————0————0————0————0————0————0——————————
G ———————————————————————————————————————————————————
  Rolling down to Old Maui, me boys, rolling down to Old Maui;
```

```
          Em       B7                      Em      B7                   Em        B7       Em
E ————————0——0——————————————————————————3——3——2——————7—5———3———0—2————————0———
A 2————————2——2———6———2———2———2——2——2——————6—6———2———2—2——5—2———
D 4————————2——————4———4———4———2——————0——————————————0—————0——4—2———
G ———————————————————————————————————————————————————————————————
  We're homeward bound from the Arctic ground rolling down to Old Maui.
```

Chord Forms

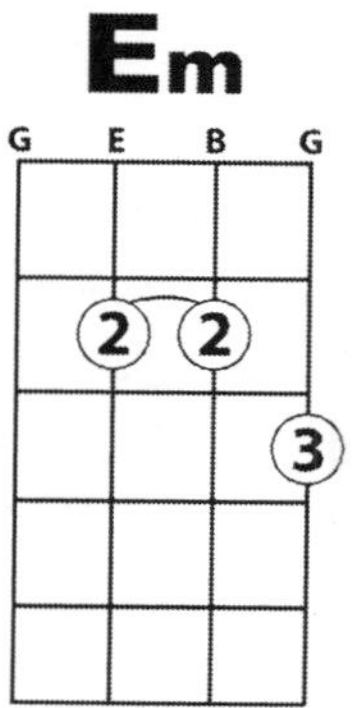

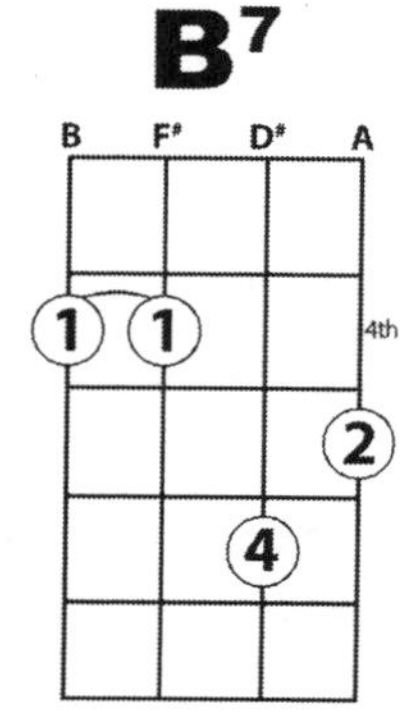

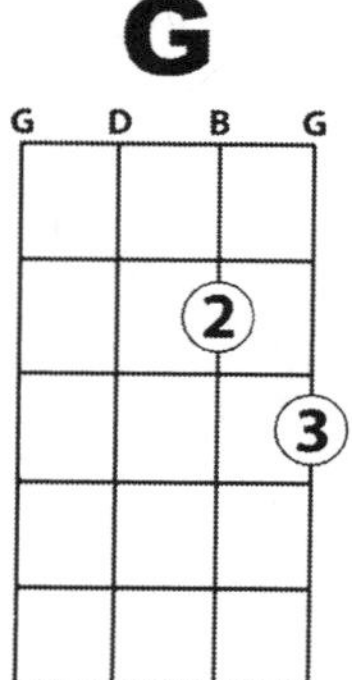

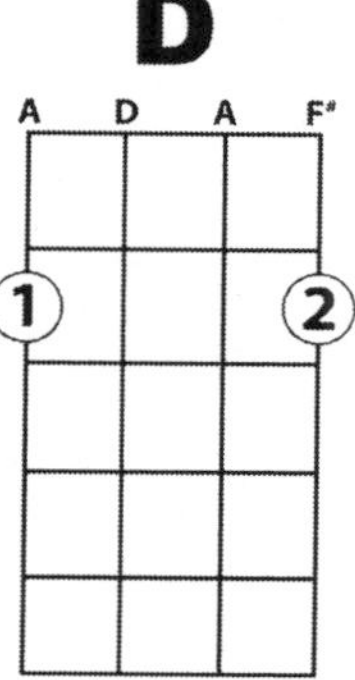

Rolling Home

Basic Melody

Key of C (Low)

This was one of the favorite of the homeward bound sea songs, thought to have been sung on both British and American ships. The words are based on a poem by Charles Mackay, which he wrote in the mid-1800's while aboard a ship. The destination mentioned in the chorus has been changed over the years: dear old England, dear old Ireland, Old New England, and even Hamburg in Germany.

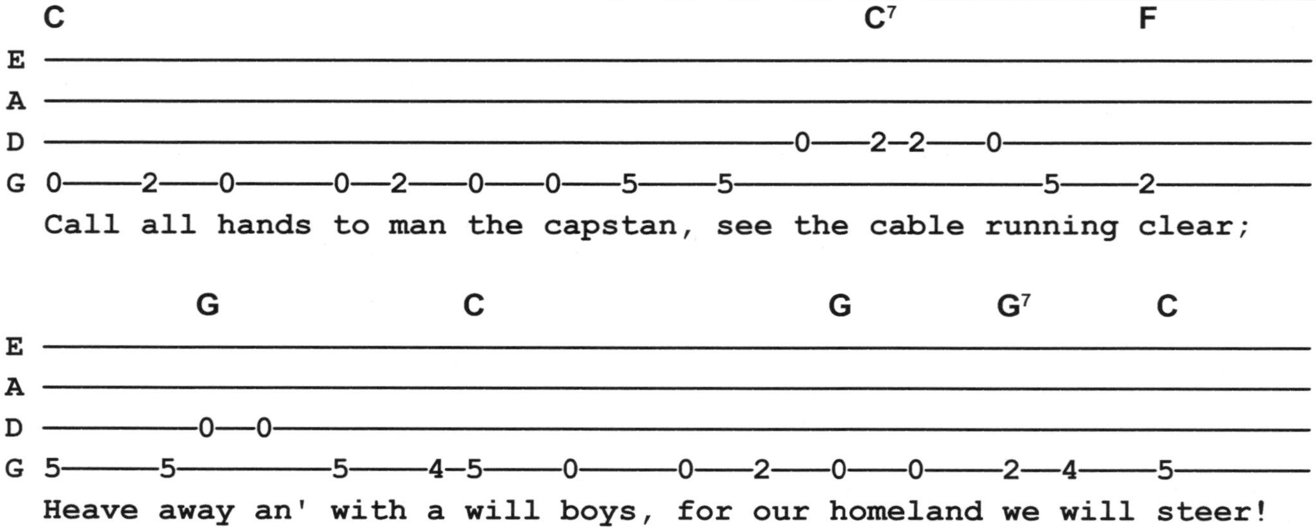

Words and Music

Traditional

```
  C                                              C7            F
E ------------------------------------------------------------------------
A ------------------------------------------------------------------------
D ---------------------------------------------0---2-2---0----------------
G 0----2---0-----0--2---0----0----5----5-------------------5-----2--------
  Call all hands to man the capstan, see the cable running clear;

         G           C                 G        G7       C
E ------------------------------------------------------------------------
A ------------------------------------------------------------------------
D --------0--0------------------------------------------------------------
G 5----5-------5----4-5----0-----0---2---0----0----2---4----5-------------
  Heave away an' with a will boys, for our homeland we will steer!
```

Chorus

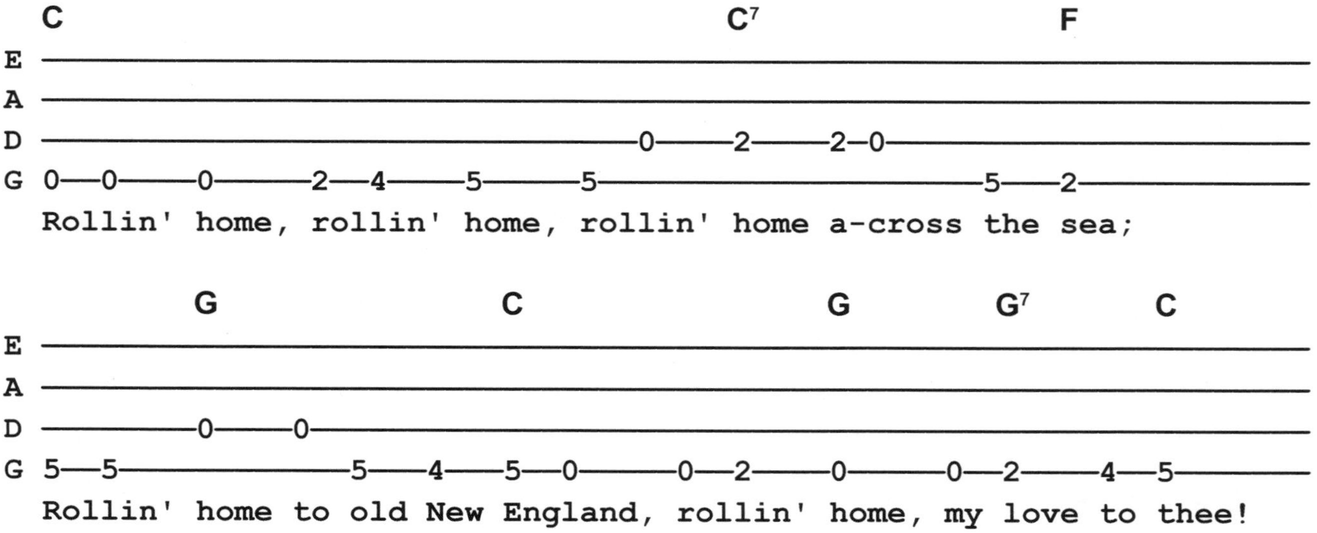

```
  C                                    C7                F
E ------------------------------------------------------------------------
A ------------------------------------------------------------------------
D -------------------------------0-----2-----2-0--------------------------
G 0--0-----0------2---4----5----5------------------------5----2-----------
  Rollin' home, rollin' home, rollin' home a-cross the sea;

         G             C               G        G7       C
E ------------------------------------------------------------------------
A ------------------------------------------------------------------------
D --------0-----0---------------------------------------------------------
G 5--5-----------5----4----5--0-----0--2-----0-----0--2-----4--5----------
  Rollin' home to old New England, rollin' home, my love to thee!
```

See Chord Forms and Additional Verses on Next Page

Rolling Home (continued)

Chord Forms and Additional Verses

Chord Forms

C

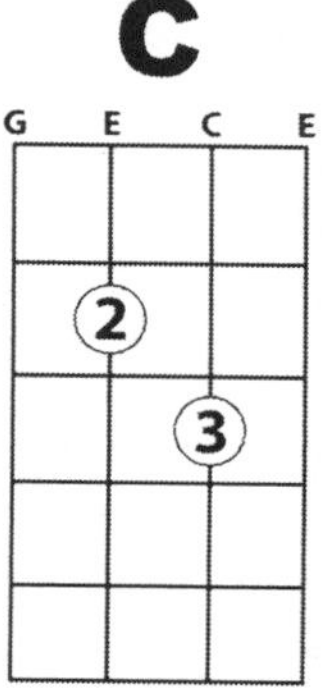

C7

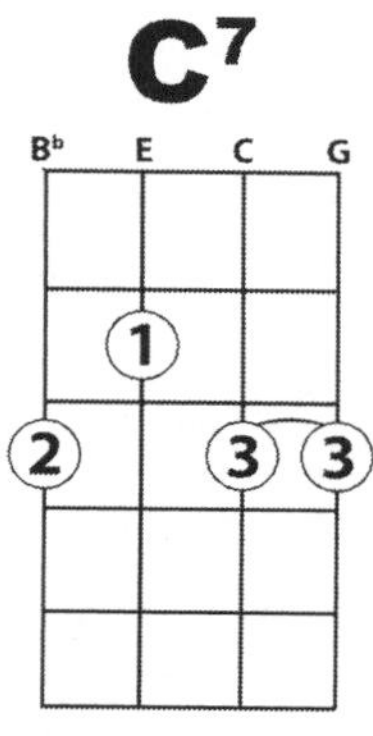

F

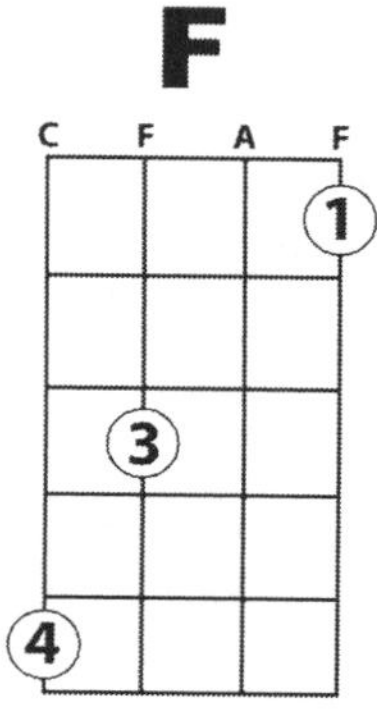

G

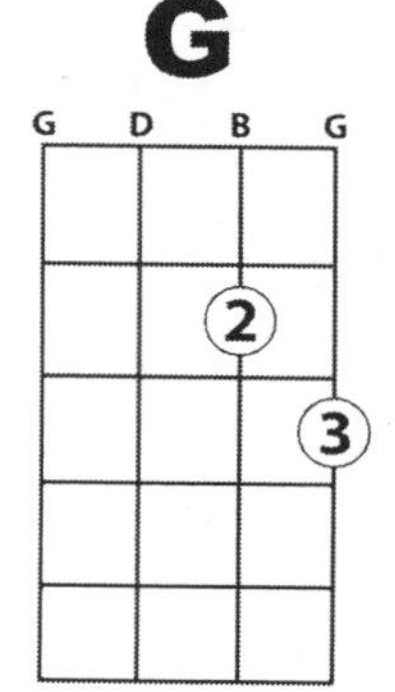

G7

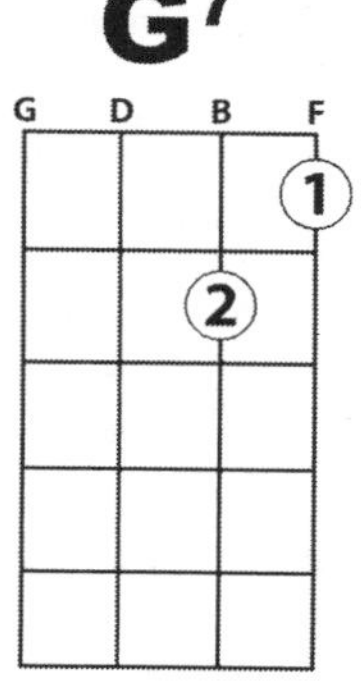

Additional Verses

Fare thee well, sweet Spanish ladies,
Fare thee well, and fond adieu;
Happy times we spent together,
Happy times we spent with you.

Round Cape Horn one frosty morning,
And our sails were filled with snow;
Clear your sheets and sway your halyards,
Swing her out and let her go.

Now the way we leave behind us,
Seems to know the way we go;
There's a hearty welcome waiting,
In that land to which we go.

Many thousand miles behind us,
Many thousand miles before;
Ancient ocean have to waft us,
To the well-remembered shore.

Cheer up Jack, bright smiles await you,
From the fairest of the fair;
And her loving eyes will greet you,
With kind welcomes everywhere.

Rolling Home (continued)

Basic Melody

Key of C (High)

```
   C                                                   C7              F
E -------------------------------------------------------0-0-------------------------
A -----0-------------0------------3----3----5--------------5--3----0-----------------
D 5----------5----5--------5---5-----------------------------------------------------
G -----------------------------------------------------------------------------------
  Call all hands to man the capstan, see the cable running clear;
```

```
          G              C                     G        G7       C
E -----------------------------------------------------------------------------------
A 3------3-5--5---3---2-3----------------0-----------------0---2----3----------------
D -----------------------------5------5---------5----5-------------------------------
G -----------------------------------------------------------------------------------
  Heave away an' with a will boys, for our homeland we will steer!
```

CHORUS

```
   C                                           C7                F
E ---------------------------------------------0------0------------------------------
A -----------------------0--2----3-----3--5--------------5-----3---0-----------------
D 5--5-----5-------------------------------------------------------------------------
G -----------------------------------------------------------------------------------
  Rollin' home, rollin' home, rollin' home a-cross the sea;
```

```
          G                C                   G        G7       C
E -----------------------------------------------------------------------------------
A 3--3-----5-----5--3---2---3-------------0----------------0----2--3-----------------
D -----------------------------5------5--------5------5-------------------------------
G -----------------------------------------------------------------------------------
  Rollin' home to old New England, rollin' home, my love to thee!
```

Chord Forms

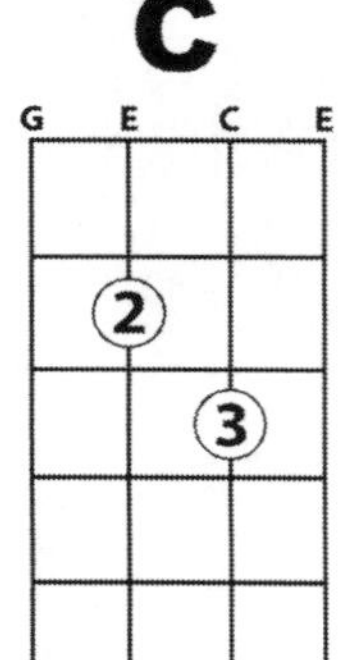

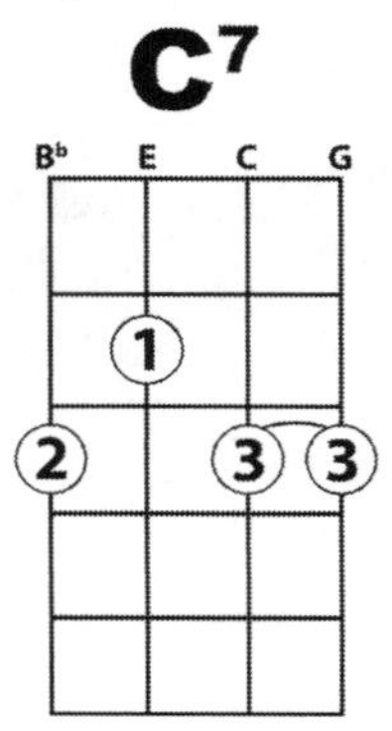

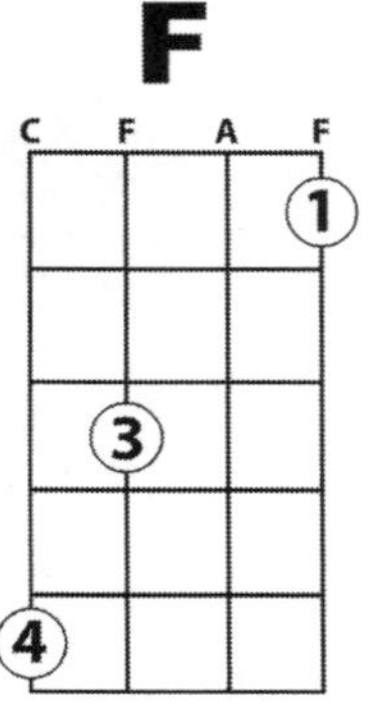

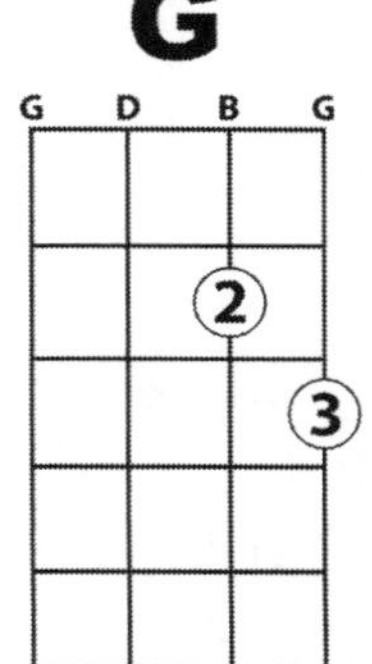

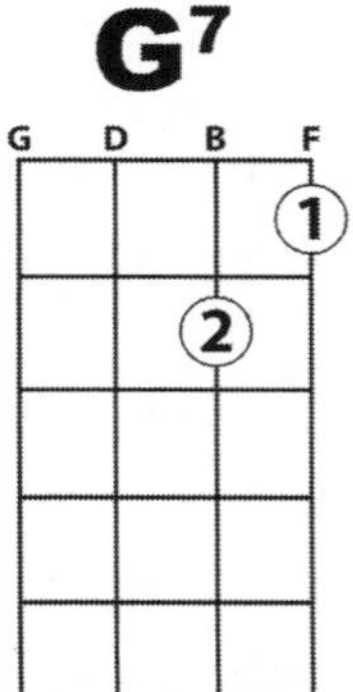

Rolling Home (continued)

Melody & Chords

Key of C (High)

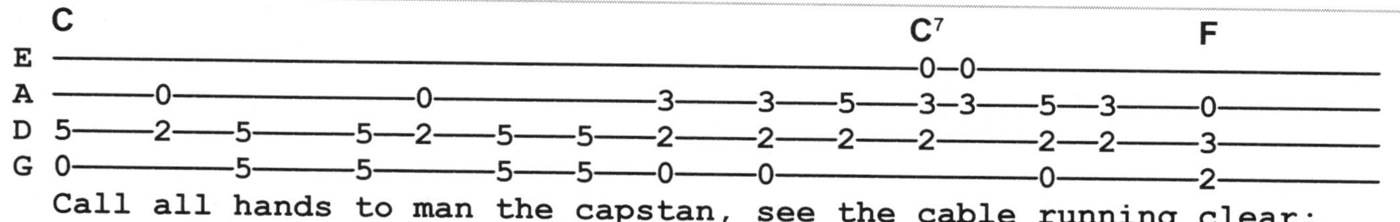

Call all hands to man the capstan, see the cable running clear;

```
        G              C                       G        G7      C
E ———————————————————————————————————————————————————————————————————
A 3———3-5—5——3———2-3————————————————0——————————————0—2———3———
D 3———3-0—0——0———0-2————5——————5—2——5——5———3—3———2———
G 2————0—————0————0————5——————5———————0——0———4—————0———
```

Heave away an' with a will boys, for our homeland we will steer!

Chorus

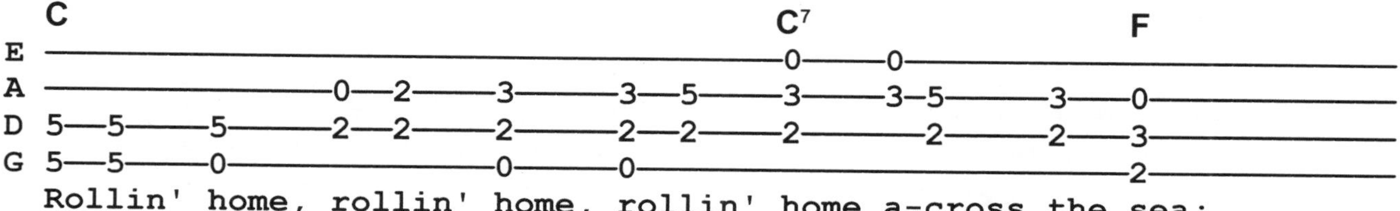

Rollin' home, rollin' home, rollin' home a-cross the sea;

```
       G              C                       G        G7      C
E ———————————————————————————————————————————————————————————————————
A 3—3———5———5—3——2——3———————————0———————————————0———2—3———
D 3—3———0———0—0——0——2—5—————5—2————5————5—3————3—2———
G 2—————0—————0—————0—5—————0——————0————0———————————0———
```

Rollin' home to old New England, rollin' home, my love to thee!

Chord Forms

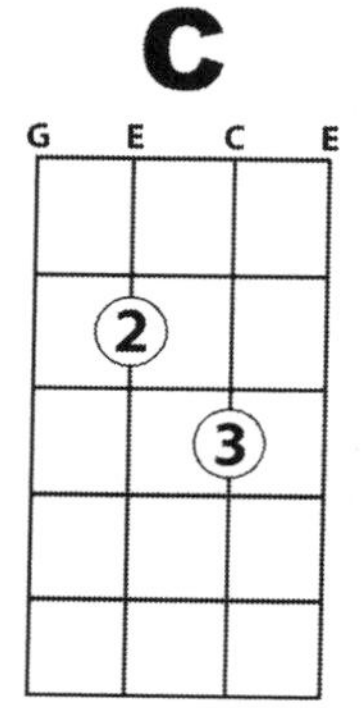

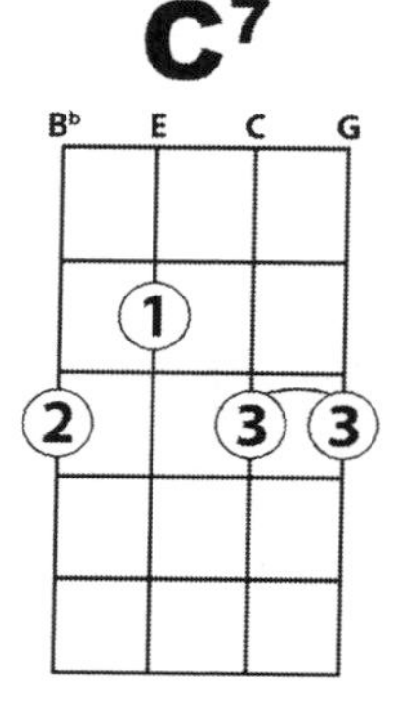

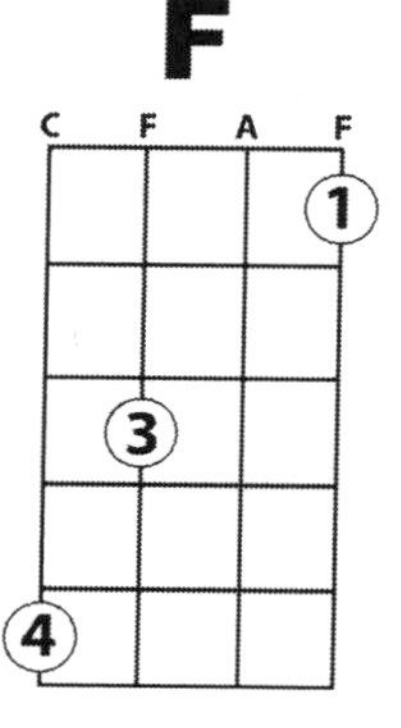

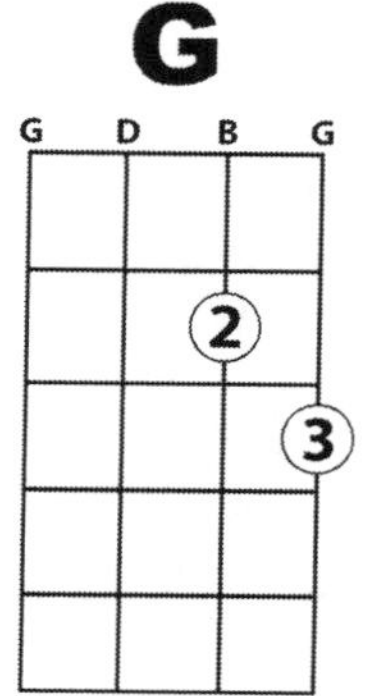

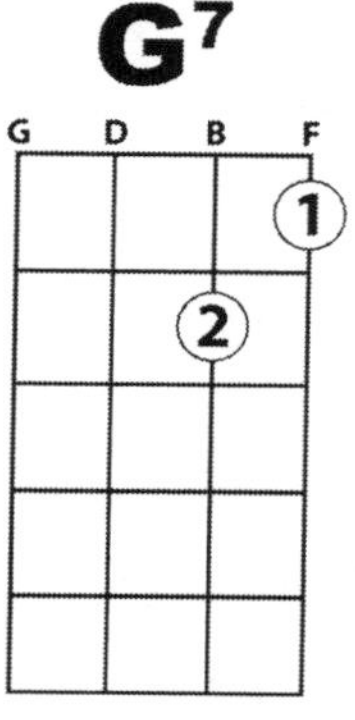

Rolling Home (continued)

Basic Melody

Key of G (Low)

```
  G                                                                        G7                       C
E ---------------------------------------------------------------------------------------------------------
A --------------------------------------------------------------------0------2--2------0--------------------
D 0-------2------0--------0---2-----0-----0-----5------5-----------------------------------5-------2-------
G ---------------------------------------------------------------------------------------------------------
  Call all hands to man the capstan, see the cable running clear;

              D                   G                          D            D7           G
E ---------------------------------------------------------------------------------------------------------
A -------------0---0-------------------------------------------------------------------------------------
D 5--------5-----------5------4--5------0--------0-----2-----0------0------2----4-----5--------------------
G ---------------------------------------------------------------------------------------------------------
  Heave away an' with a will boys, for our homeland we will steer!
```

Chorus

```
  G                                                   G7                          C
E ---------------------------------------------------------------------------------------------------------
A ---------------------------------------------------0-------2-------2--0----------------------------------
D 0--0-------0-------2---4-------5-------5--------------------------------------5-----2--------------------
G ---------------------------------------------------------------------------------------------------------
  Rollin' home, rollin' home, rollin' home a-cross the sea;

              D                     G                        D            D7           G
E ---------------------------------------------------------------------------------------------------------
A -------------0-------0---------------------------------------------------------------------------------
D 5--5-------------------------5----4-----5---0--------0---2--------0--------0---2------4---5--------------
G ---------------------------------------------------------------------------------------------------------
  Rollin' home to old New England, rollin' home, my love to thee!
```

Chord Forms

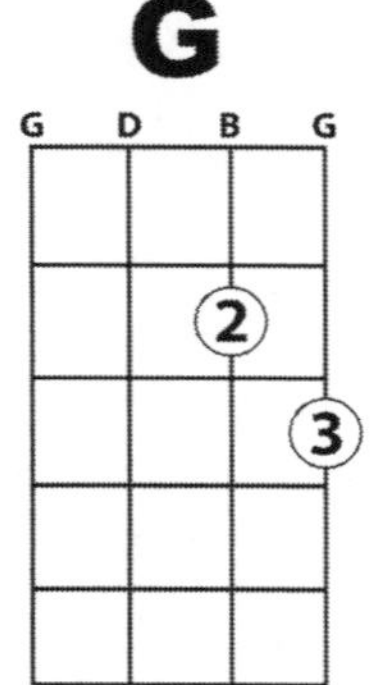

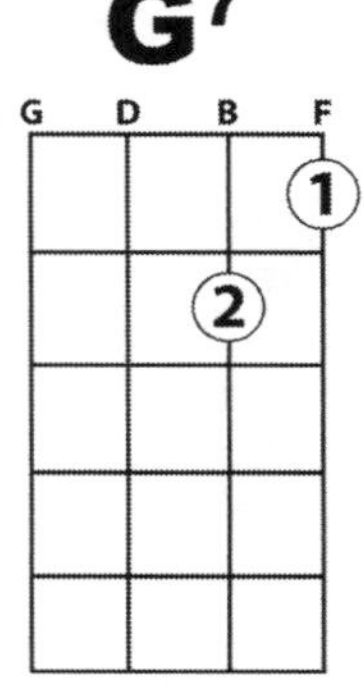

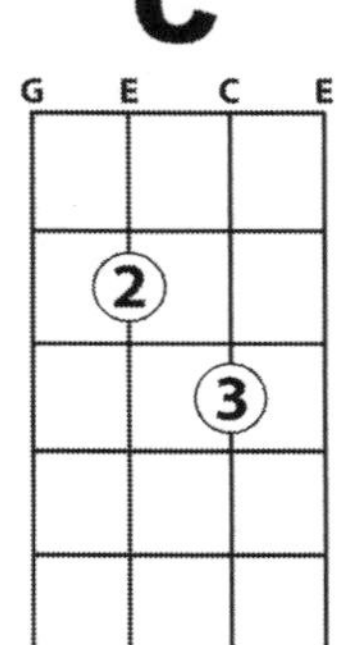

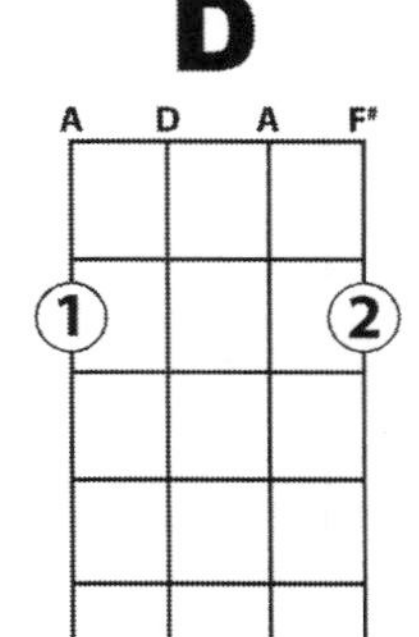

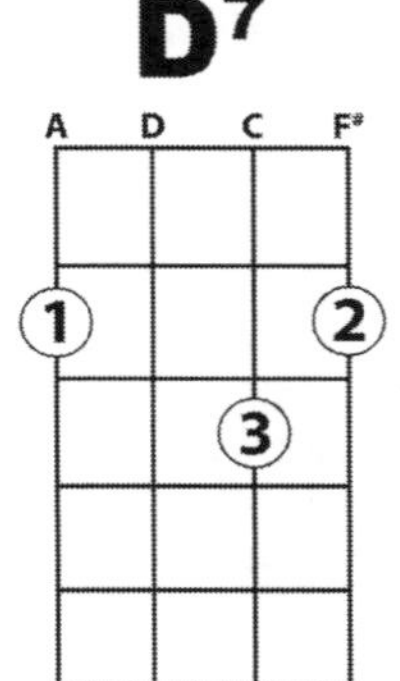

Rolling Home (continued)

Melody & Chords

Key of G (Low)

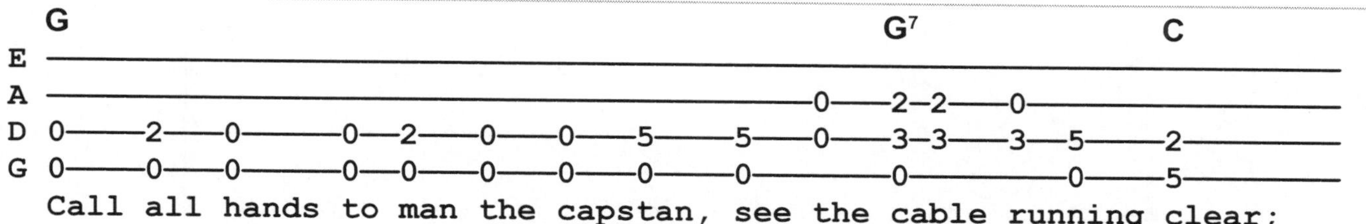


```
        D               G                    D        D7       G
E ─────────────────────────────────────────────────────────────────
A ────────0—0──────────────────────────────────────────────────────
D 5———5-0—0———5———4-5———0————0———2———0———0————2—4————5─────────────
G 5———5-2——————2———2-0———0————0———0———2———2————2—2————0─────────────
  Heave away an' with a will boys, for our homeland we will steer!
```

Chorus

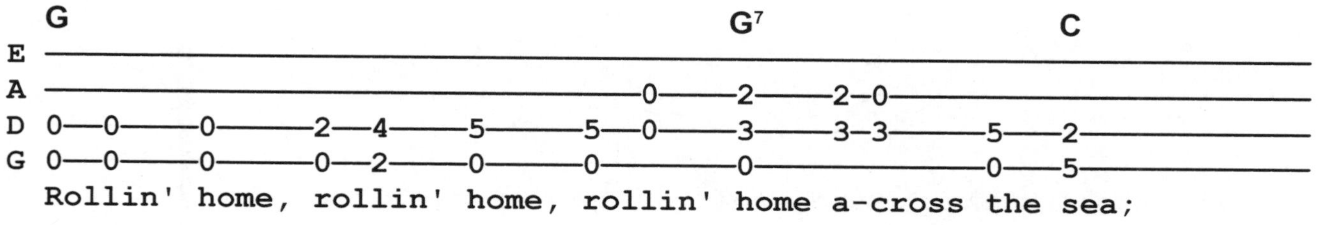


```
       D                  G                     D         D7       G
E ─────────────────────────────────────────────────────────────────────
A ─────────0———0───────────────────────────────────────────────────────
D 5—5——————0———0—5———4———5—0————0—2————0————0—2————4—5─────────────────
G 5—5——————2—————————2—2—0—0————0—0————2————2—2————2—0─────────────────
  Rollin' home to old New England, rollin' home, my love to thee!
```

Chord Forms

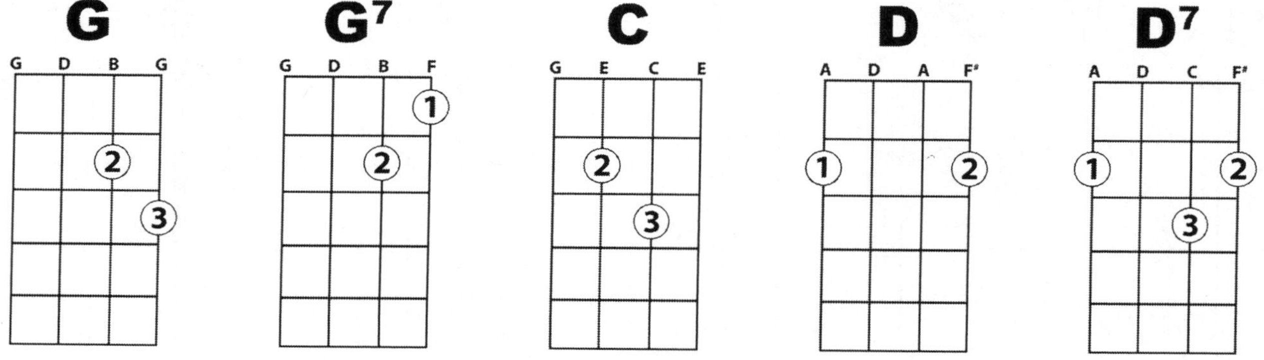

Rolling Home (continued)

Basic Melody

Key of G (High)

```
  G                                                 G7           C
E ----0-----------0---------3----3---5---7-7---5--3---0---------
A 5-------5----5-------5--5-------------------------------------
D --------------------------------------------------------------
G --------------------------------------------------------------
  Call all hands to man the capstan, see the cable running clear;

          D           G                   D       D7     G
E 3----3-5--5---3---2-3-----------0-------------0--2---3-------
A -----------------------5----5--------5---5--------------------
D --------------------------------------------------------------
G --------------------------------------------------------------
  Heave away an' with a will boys, for our homeland we will steer!
```

CHORUS

```
  G                                       G7                  C
E -------------0--2----3-----3--5----7-----7-5------3---0-------
A 5--5----5-----------------------------------------------------
D --------------------------------------------------------------
G --------------------------------------------------------------
  Rollin' home, rollin' home, rollin' home a-cross the sea;

          D             G                 D        D7     G
E 3--3----5----5--3---2---3---------0-------------0----2--3-----
A --------------------------5----5--------5----5----------------
D --------------------------------------------------------------
G --------------------------------------------------------------
  Rollin' home to old New England, rollin' home, my love to thee!
```

Chord Forms

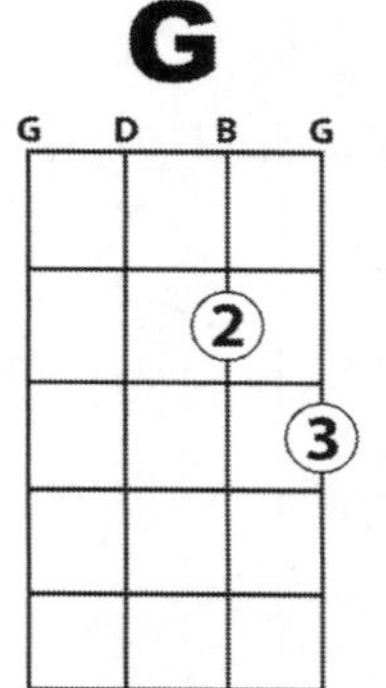

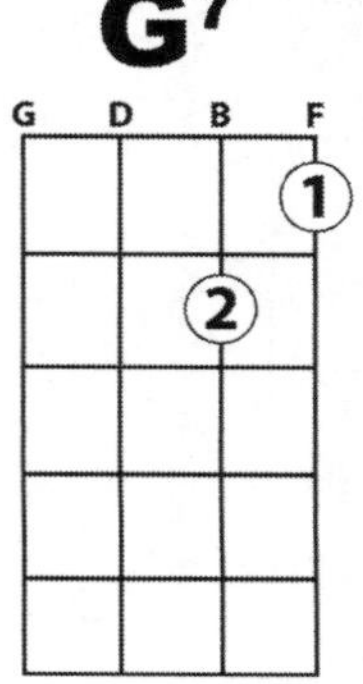

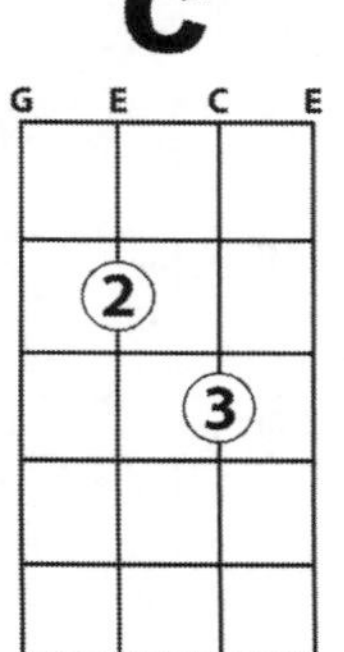

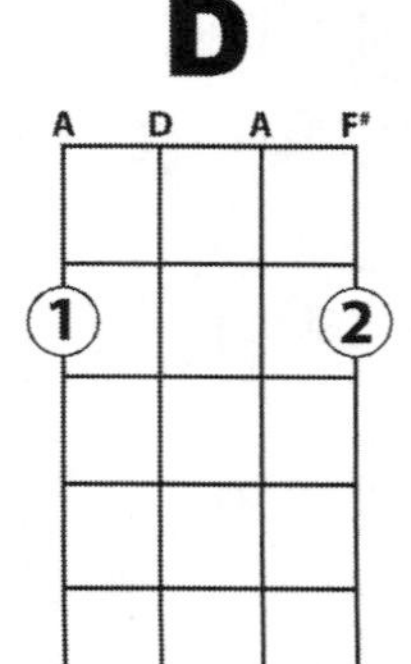

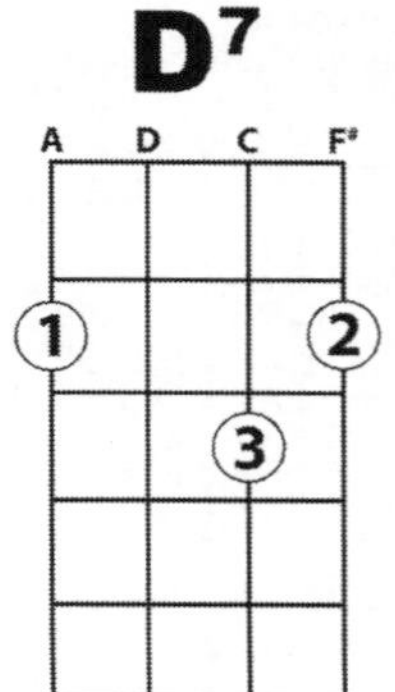

Rolling Home (continued)

Melody & Chords

Key of G (High)

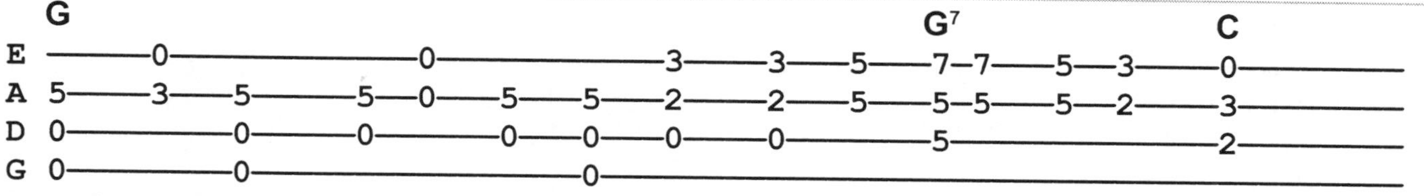

Call all hands to man the capstan, see the cable running clear;

```
        D            G                      D        D7      G
E 3————3-5—5——3———2-3———————————————0———————————0—2———3————
A 3————3-0—0——0———0-2————5——————5———3———5———5————0—0———2————
D 2————0——————0———0——————0——————0————————0———0————0—0———0————
G ———————————————————————0——————0————————2—————————————————
```

Heave away an' with a will boys, for our homeland we will steer!

Chorus

```
G                                  G7                  C
E ——————————————0—2———3————3—5————7————7–5——————3————0———————
A 5—5————5——————2—2———2————2—5————5————5–5——————2————3———————
D 0—0————0————————————0————0——————5——————————————————2———————
G 0——————0——————————————————————————————————————————————————————
```

Rollin' home, rollin' home, rollin' home a-cross the sea;

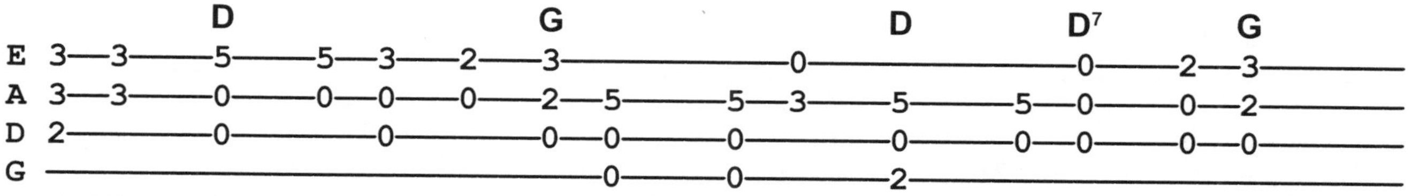

Rollin' home to old New England, rollin' home, my love to thee!

Chord Forms

G

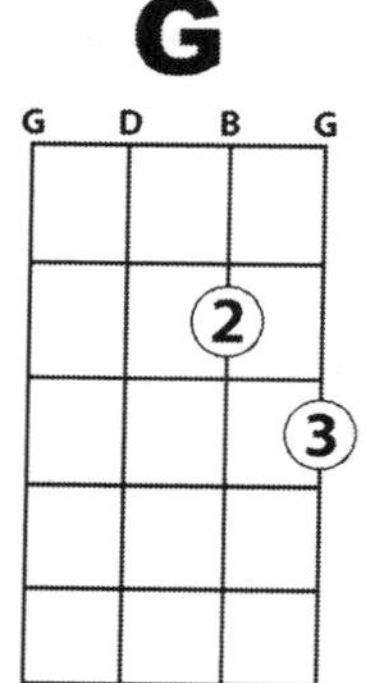

G7

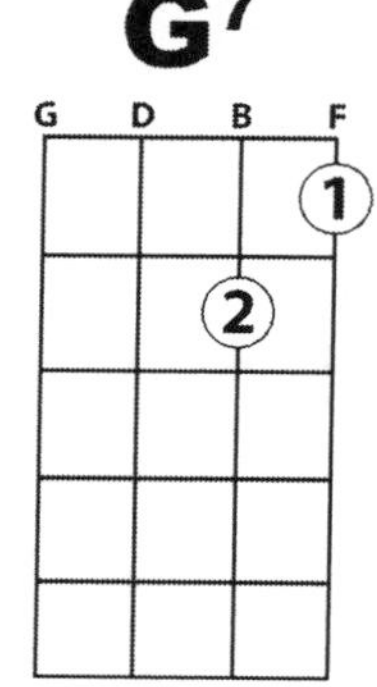

C

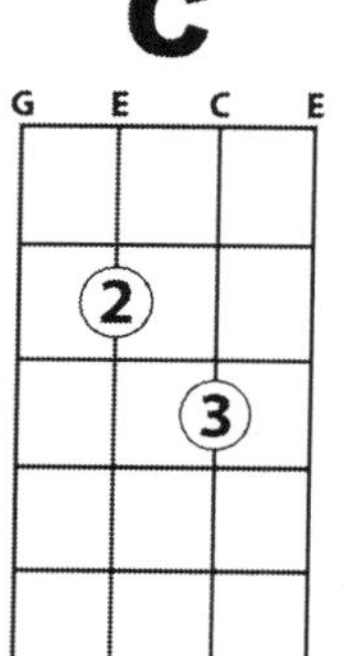

D

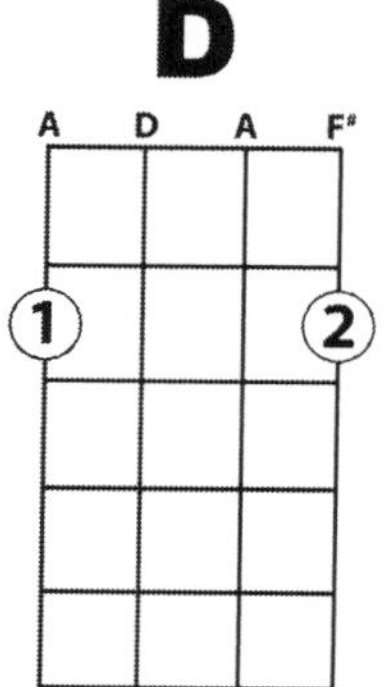

D7

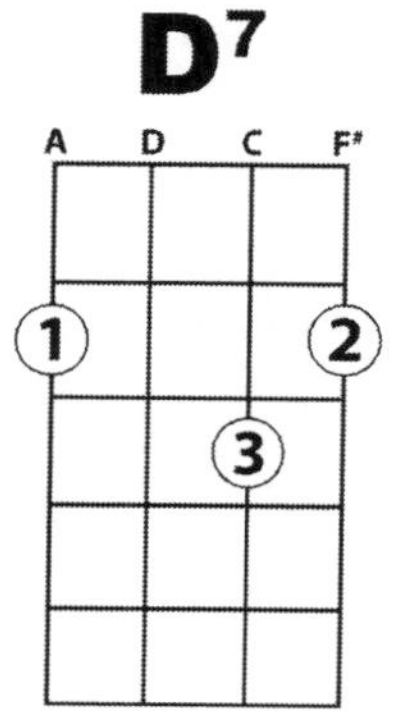

Roll the Old Chariot Along

Basic Melody

Key of A Minor (Low)

This is one of the best of the old sea shanties for bellowing out with your best shipmates whenever the occasion arises. Believed to have originated as an African-American spiritual, in the context of this song, the "chariot" was the flywheel used to turn the large pumps that removed water from a ship's bilge.

Words and Music

Traditional

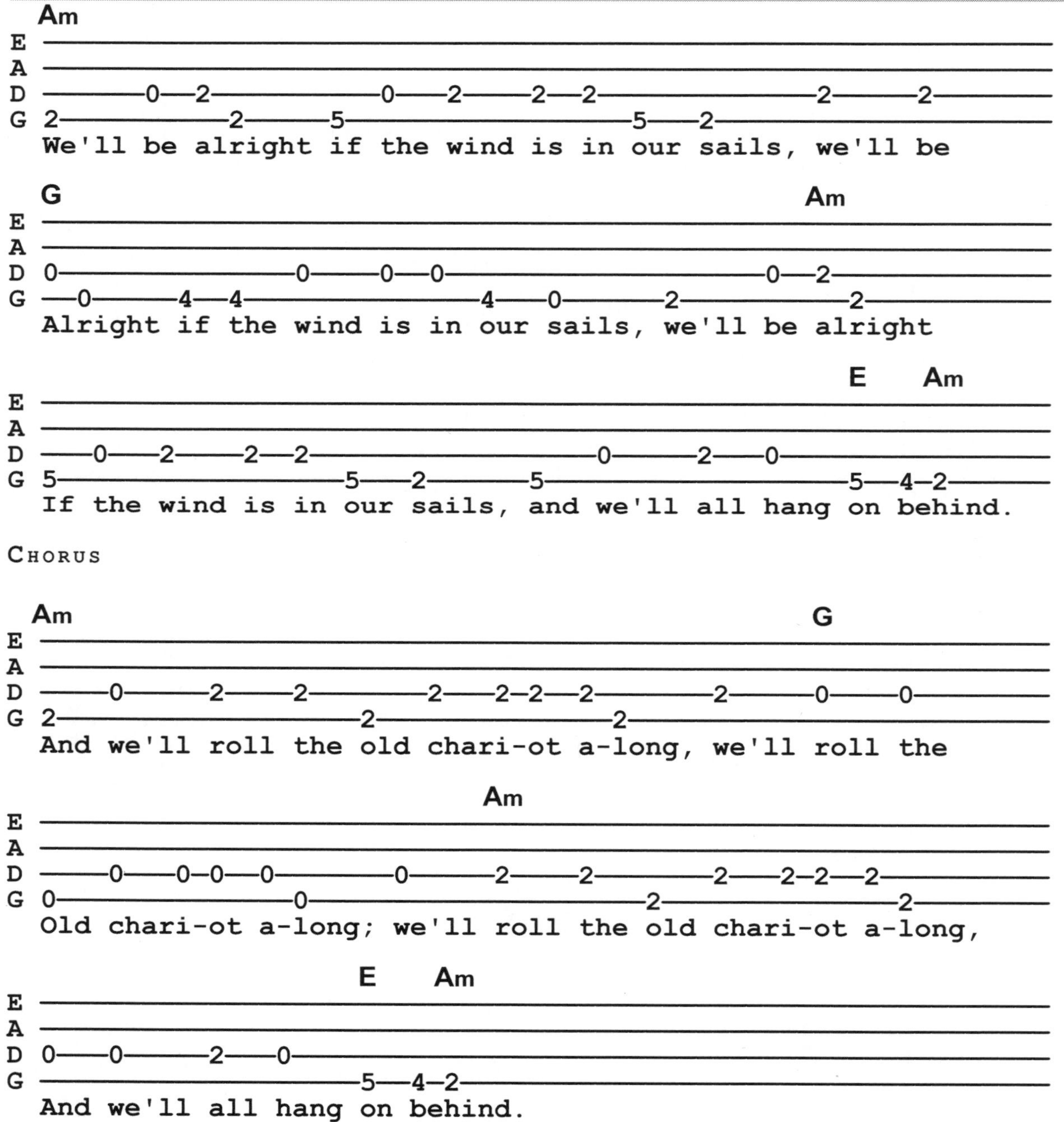

See Chord Forms and Additional Verses on Next Page

Roll the Old Chariot Along (continued)

Chord Forms

Am

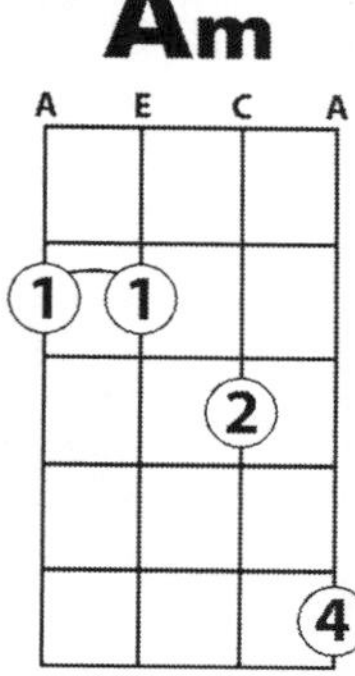

G

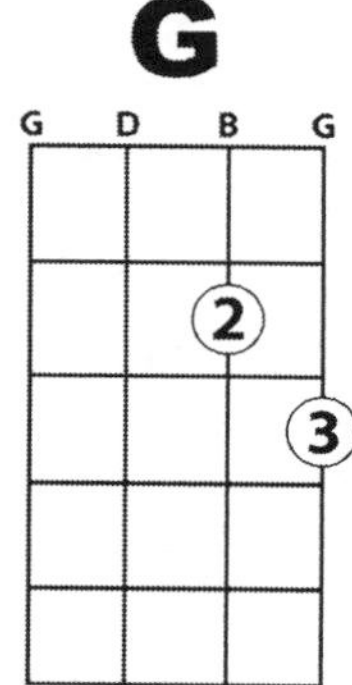

E

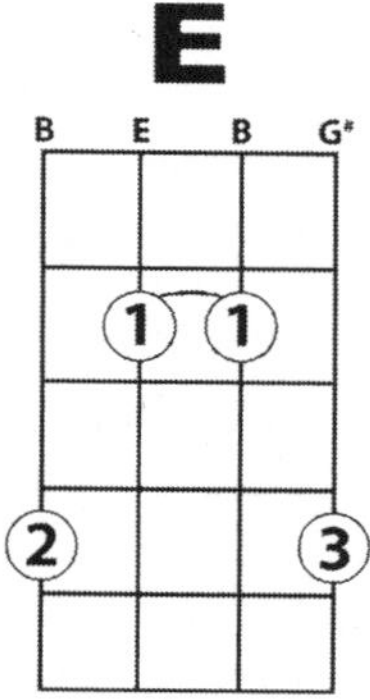

Additional Verses

We'll be alright if we make it 'round the horn,
We'll be alright if we make it 'round the horn;
We'll be alright if we make it 'round the horn,
And we'll all hang on behind.

A night's watch below wouldn't do us any harm,
A night's watch below wouldn't do us any harm;
A night's watch below wouldn't do us any harm,
And we'll all hang on behind.

Well a drop of Nelson's blood wouldn't do us any harm,
No a drop of Nelson's blood wouldn't do us any harm;
Well a drop of Nelson's blood wouldn't do us any harm,
And we'll all hang on behind.

One glass of rum wouldn't do us any harm,
One glass of rum wouldn't do us any harm;
One glass of rum wouldn't do us any harm,
And we'll all hang on behind.

Just one night ashore wouldn't do us any harm,
Just one night ashore wouldn't do us any harm;
Just one night ashore wouldn't do us any harm,
And we'll all hang on behind.

And a night with the girls wouldn't do us any harm,
Yes a night with the girls wouldn't do us any harm;
No a night with the girls wouldn't do us any harm,
And we'll all hang on behind.

Roll the Old Chariot Along (continued)

Basic Melody

Key of A Minor (High)

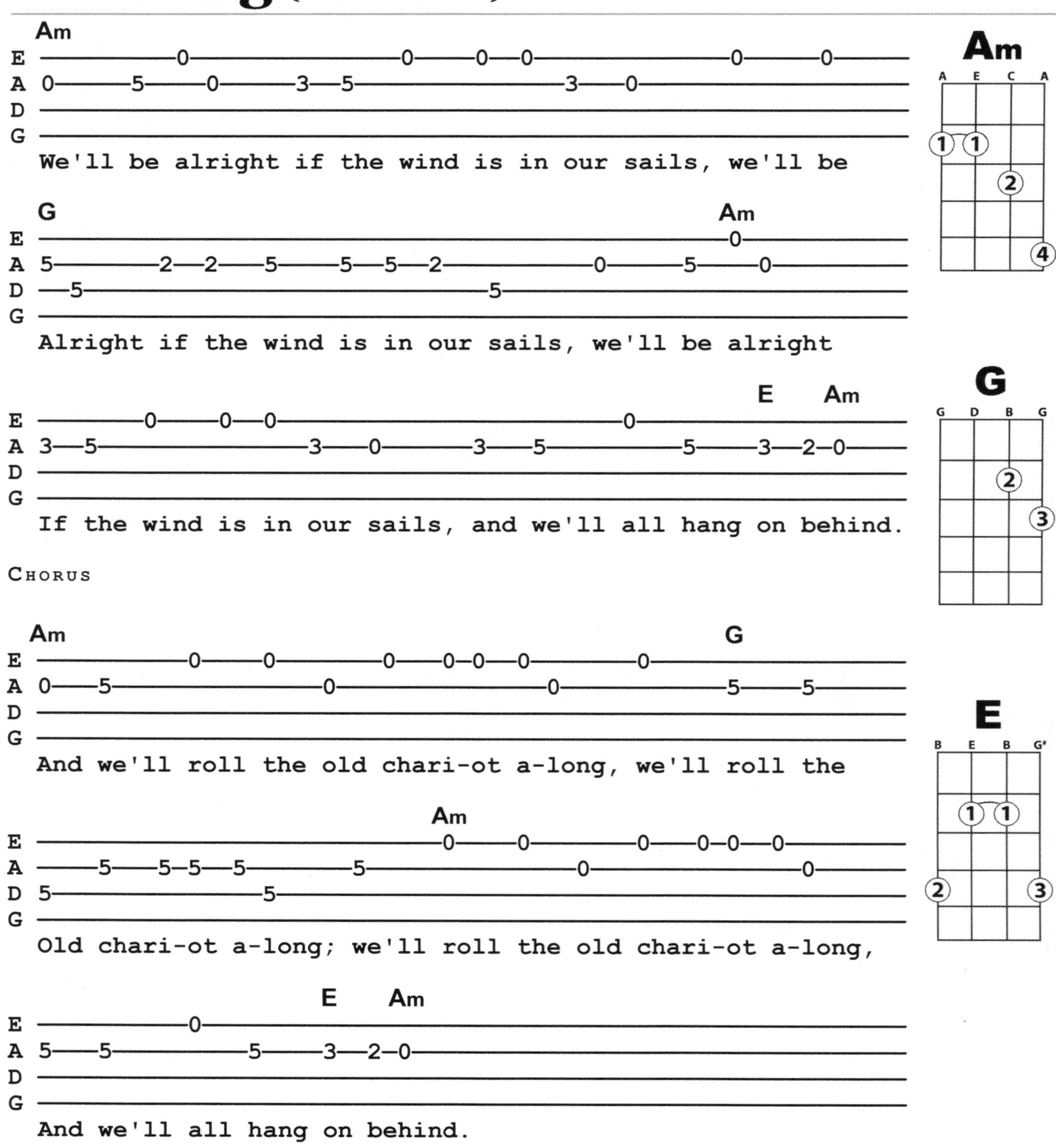

Roll the Old Chariot Along (continued)

Melody & Chords

Key of A Minor (High)

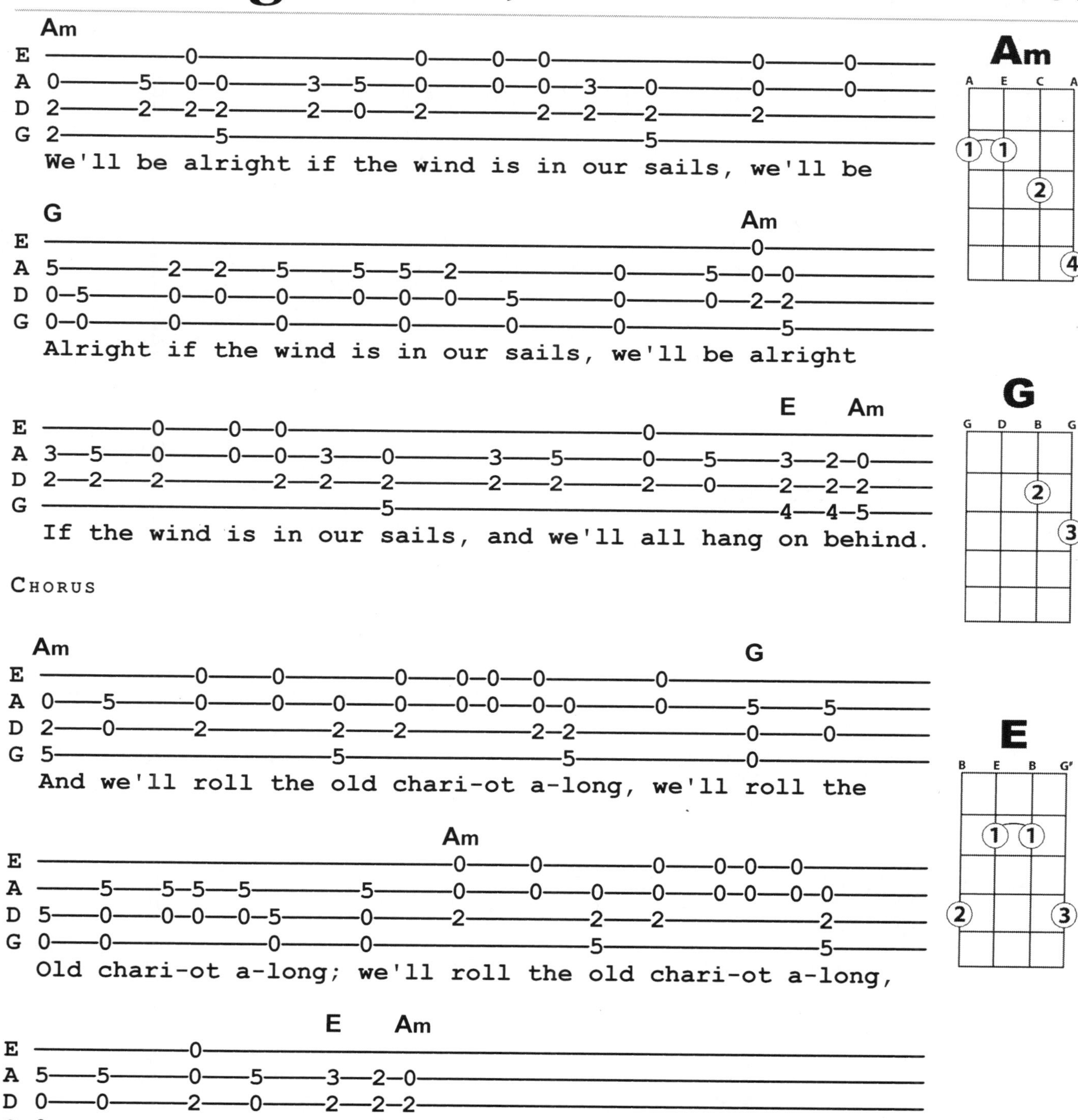

Roll the Old Chariot Along (continued)

Basic Melody

Key of E Minor (Low)

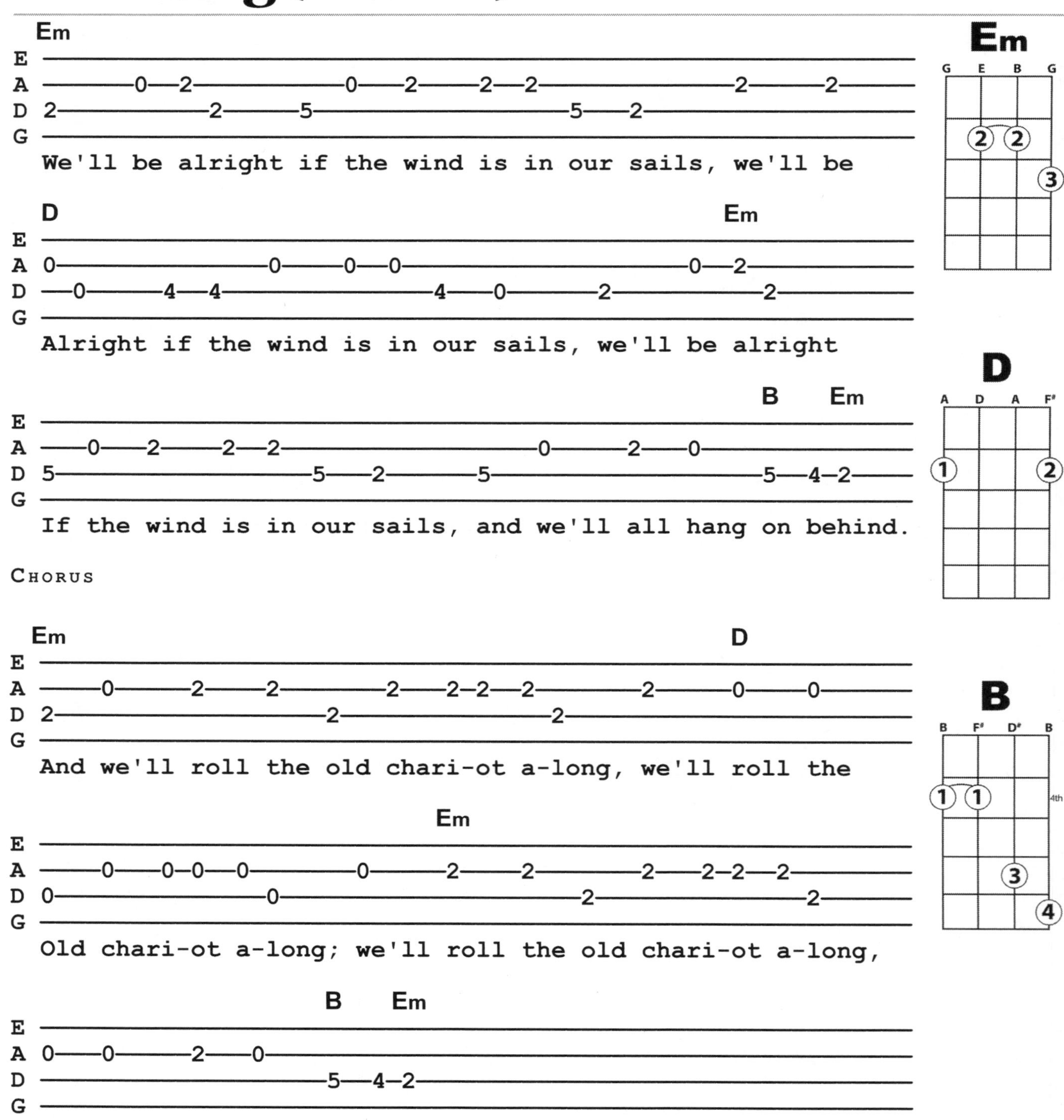

Roll the Old Chariot Along (continued)

Melody & Chords

Key of E Minor (Low)

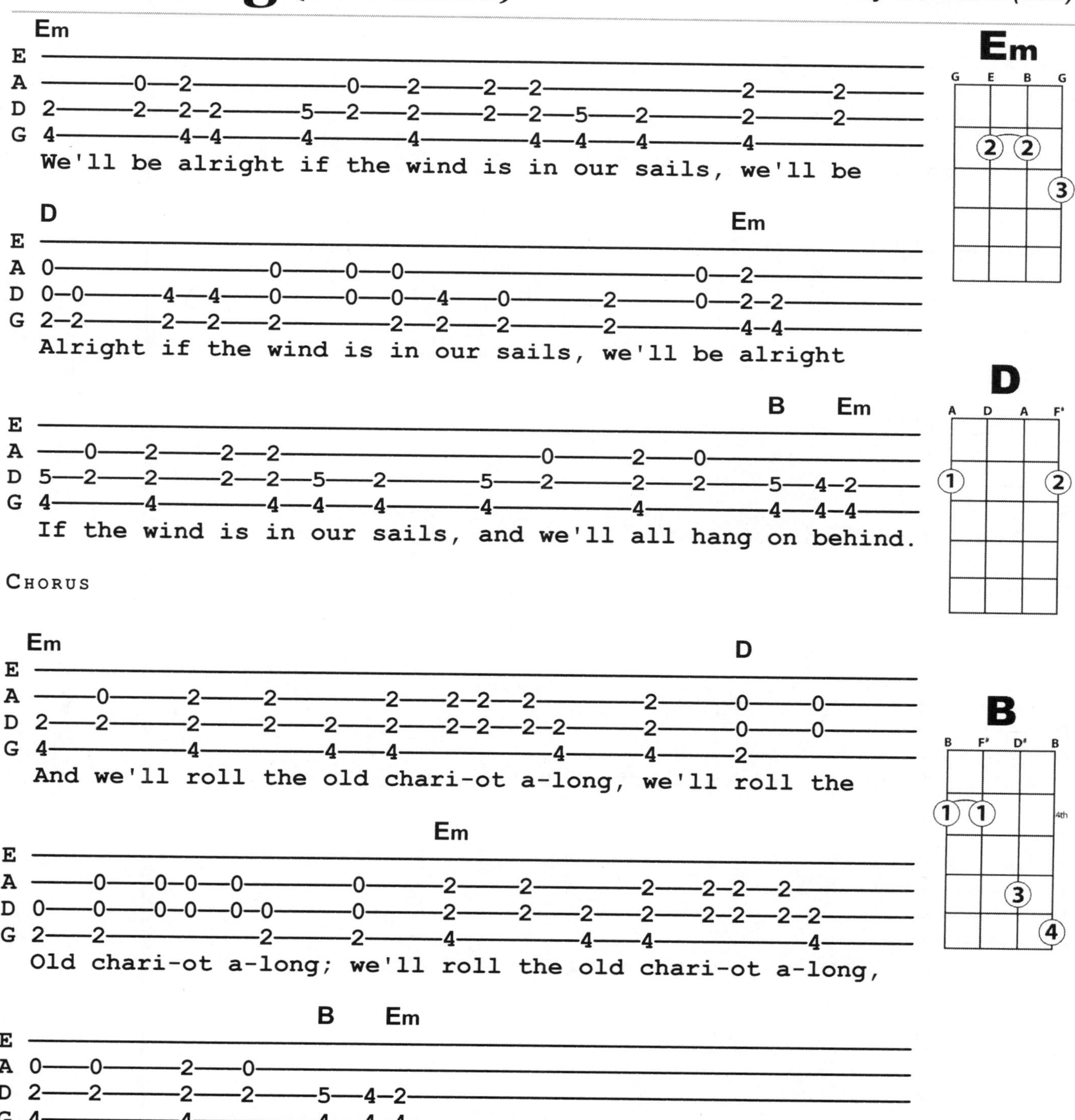

Roll the Old Chariot Along (continued)

Basic Melody

Key of E Minor (High)

```
  Em
E 0-----5--7--0-------3--5---7------7--7--3---0--------7-------7------
A --------------------------------------------------------------------
D --------------------------------------------------------------------
G --------------------------------------------------------------------
```

We'll be alright if the wind is in our sails, we'll be

```
  D                                                    Em
E 5--------2--2---5-----5--5--2-------------0-----5--7-0----------
A --5---------------------------------5---------------------------
D -----------------------------------------------------------------
G -----------------------------------------------------------------
```

Alright if the wind is in our sails, we'll be alright

```
                                                         B    Em
E 3--5---7-----7--7--3---0--------3---5------7---5-----3--2-0----
A ----------------------------------------------------------------
D ----------------------------------------------------------------
G ----------------------------------------------------------------
```

If the wind is in our sails, and we'll all hang on behind.

Chorus

```
  Em                                                   D
E 0---5------7-----7----0---7----7-7---7-0-------7------5-----5-----
A ------------------------------------------------------------------
D ------------------------------------------------------------------
G ------------------------------------------------------------------
```

And we'll roll the old chari-ot a-long, we'll roll the

```
                                  Em
E -----5---5-5--5---------5------7------7----0----7-----7-7---7-0-----
A 5-------------------5-----------------------------------------------
D ---------------------------------------------------------------------
G ---------------------------------------------------------------------
```

Old chari-ot a-long; we'll roll the old chari-ot a-long,

```
                          B    Em
E 5---5------7----5------3---2-0---------------------------------------
A ---------------------------------------------------------------------
D ---------------------------------------------------------------------
G ---------------------------------------------------------------------
```

And we'll all hang on behind.

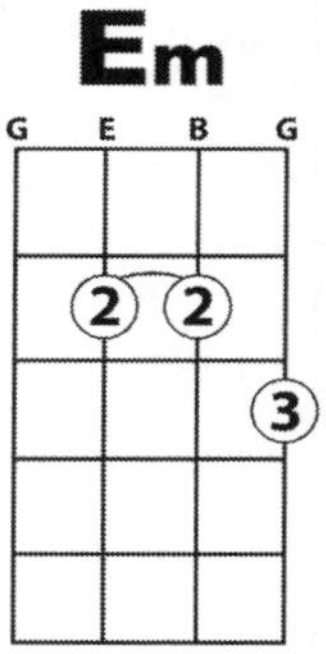
Em
G E B G
2 2
3

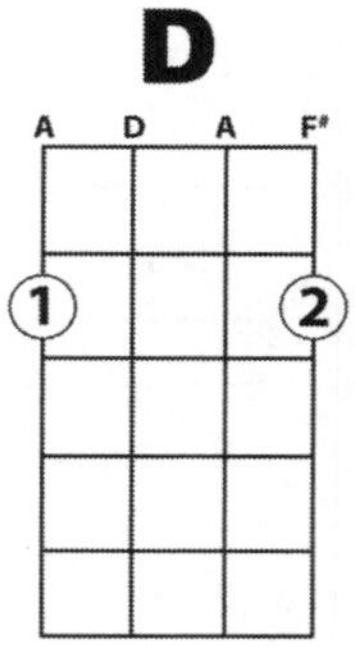
D
A D A F#
1 2

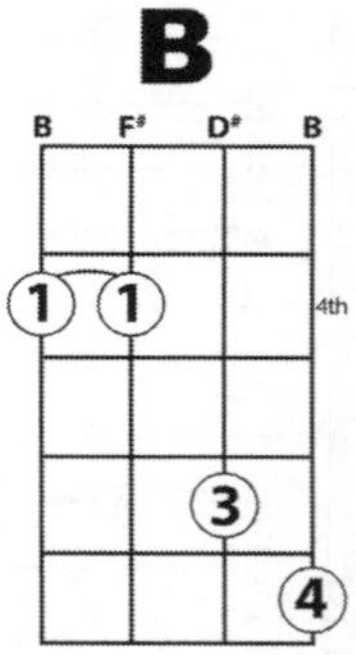
B
B F# D# B
1 1
4th
3
4

Roll the Old Chariot Along (continued)

Melody & Chords

Key of E Minor (High)

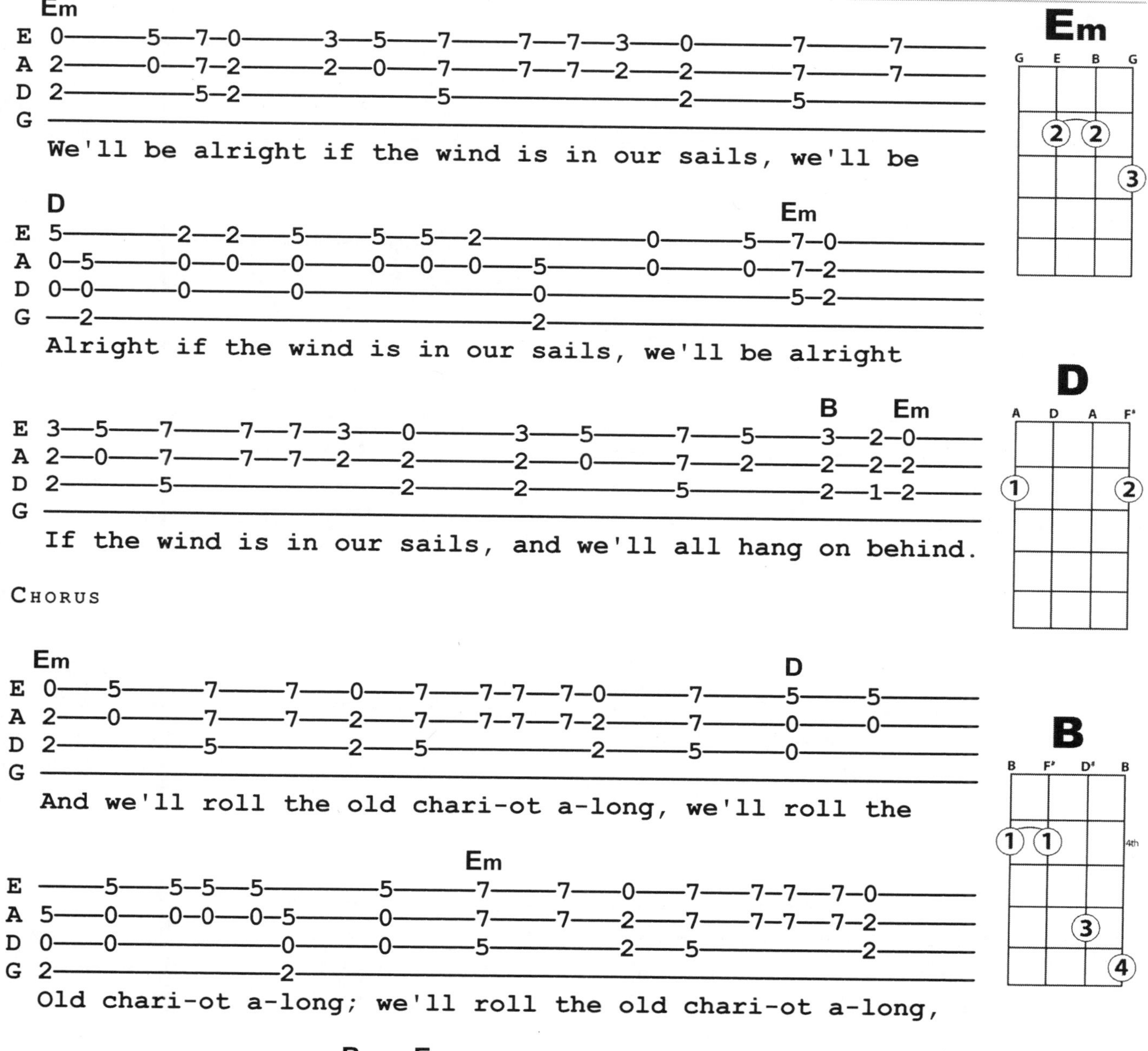

SEA SHANTY

Roll, Boys, Roll

Two Versions

Key of A Minor (Low)

Words and Music

Traditional

This is an old sea shanty that got some recent attention by being included on the sound track for the video game "Assassin's Creed." It is a minor-key variation of the "Sally Brown" shanty given a couple of pages ahead, and is very similar in theme and style.

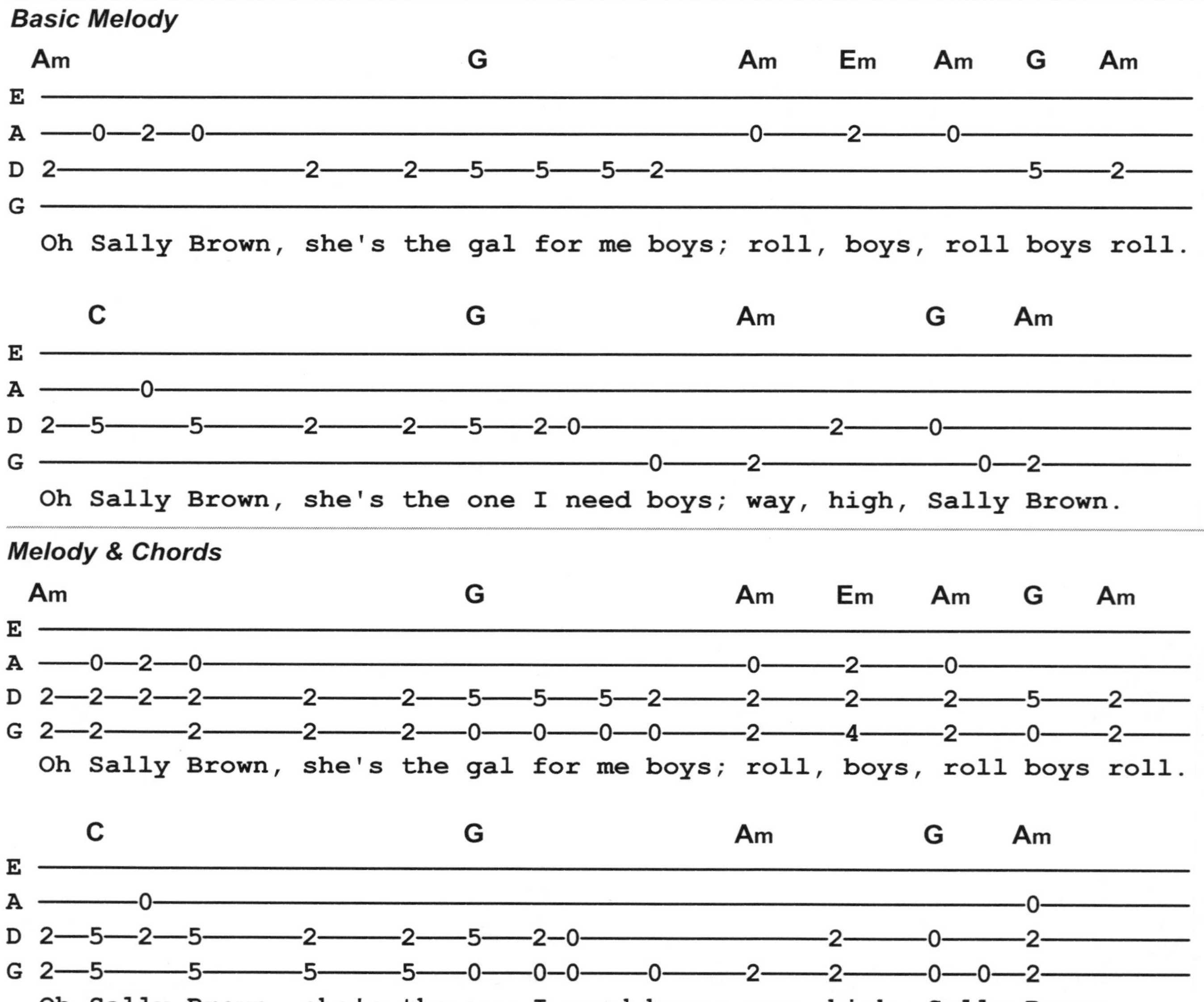

See Additional Verses on Next Page

Roll, Boys, Roll (continued)

Chord Forms

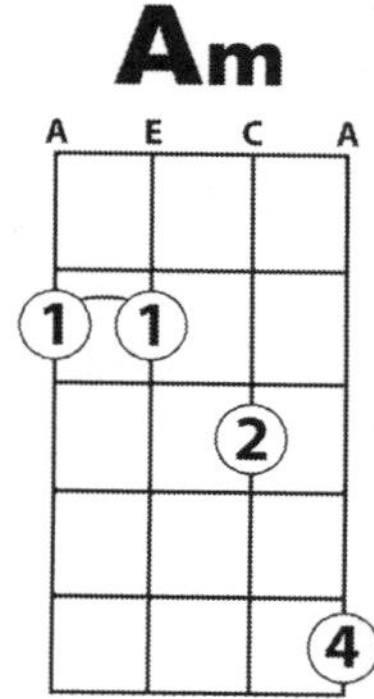

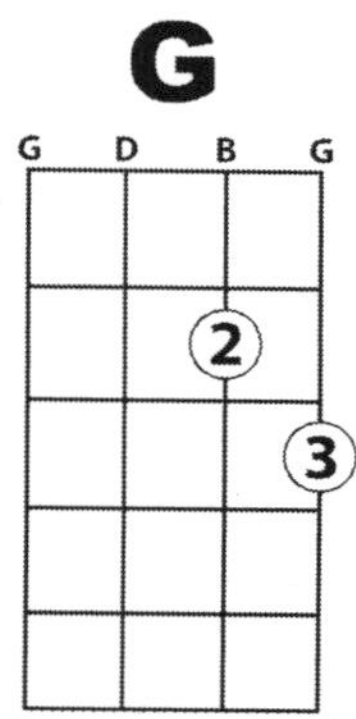

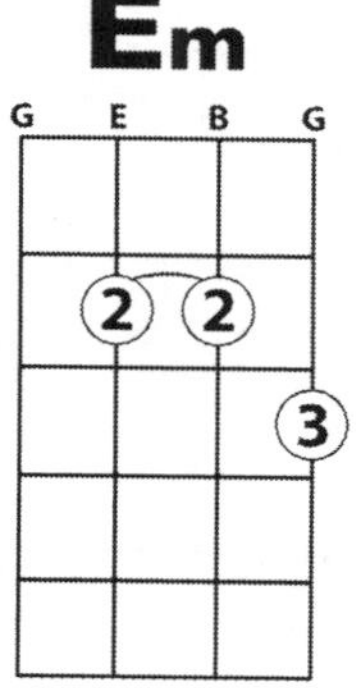

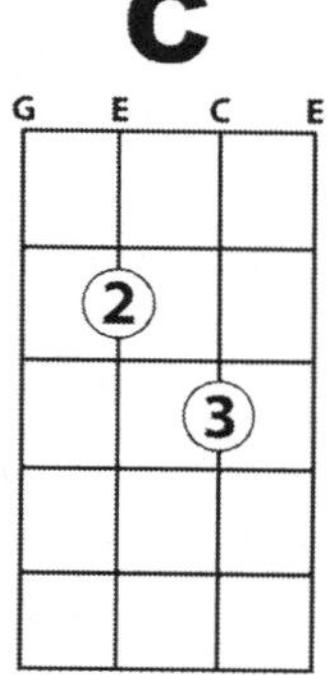

Additional Verses

It's down to Trinidad to see Sally Brown boys,
Roll boys, roll boys roll!
Down to Trinidad to see Sally Brown boys,
Way high, Miss Sally Brown.

She's lovely on the foreyard, an' she's lovely down below boys,
Roll Boys, roll boys roll!
She's lovely 'cause she loves me, that's all I want to know boys!
Way high, Miss Sally Brown.

Ol' Captain Baker, how do you store yer cargo?
Roll Boys, roll boys roll!
Some I stow for'ward, boys, an' some I stow aft'ward,
Way high, Miss Sally Brown.

Forty fathoms or more below boys,
Roll Boys, roll boys roll!
There's fourty fathoms or more below boys.
Way high, Miss Sally Brown.

Oh, way high ya, an' up she rises,
Roll Boys, roll boys roll!
Way high ya, and the blocks is different sizes,
Way high, Miss Sally Brown.

Oh, one more pull, don't ya hear the mate a-bawlin?
Roll Boys, roll boys roll!
Oh, one more pull, that's the end of all the hawlin',
Way high, Miss Sally Brown.

Roll, Boys, Roll (continued)

Two Versions

Key of A Minor (High)

Basic Melody

```
   Am                                 G                     Am      Em      Am     G      Am
E 0--5--7--5--------0-------0--3----3----3--0-----------5-------7-------5------3------0------
A -------------------------------------------------------------------------------------------
D -------------------------------------------------------------------------------------------
G -------------------------------------------------------------------------------------------
  Oh Sally Brown, she's the gal for me boys; roll, boys, roll boys roll.
```

```
      C                               G                     Am               G      Am
E 0--3--5--3--------0-------0--3---0----------------------------0-------------------------
A ---------------------------------------5-------------0--------------------5------0------
D -----------------------------------------------5--------------------------------5-------
G ----------------------------------------------------------------------------------------
  Oh Sally Brown, she's the one I need boys; way, high, Sally Brown.
```

Melody & Chords

```
   Am                                 G                     Am      Em      Am     G      Am
E 0--5--7--5--------0-------0--3----3----3--0-----------5-------7-------5------3------0------
A 0--3--5--3--------2-------2--2----2----2--2-----------3-------7-------3------2------0------
D 2--2-----2--------2----------0---------0--0-----------2-------5-------2------0------2------
G -------------------------------------------------------------------------------------------
  Oh Sally Brown, she's the gal for me boys; roll, boys, roll boys roll.
```

```
      C                               G                     Am               G      Am
E 0--3--5--3--------0-------0--3---0----------------------------0-------------------------
A 0--3--3--3--------3-------3--2---2-5-------------0------0---------------5------0--------
D 2--2-----2--------2----------0---------0----5-------2------2------------0--5--2--------
G ---------------------------------------0----0-------2-------------------0--0--2--------
  Oh Sally Brown, she's the one I need boys; way, high, Sally Brown.
```

Chord Forms

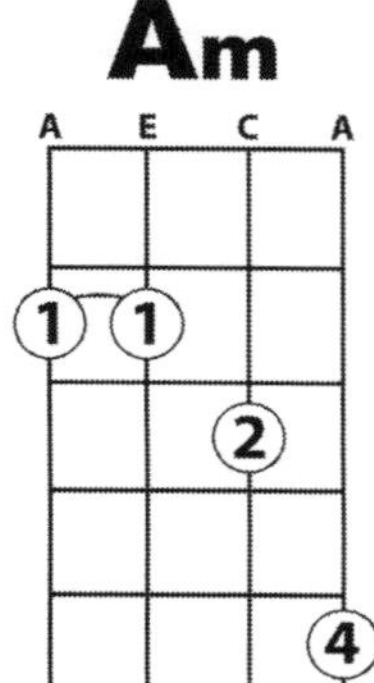

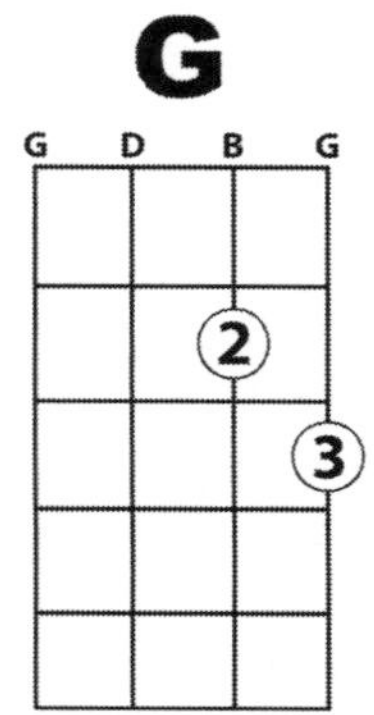

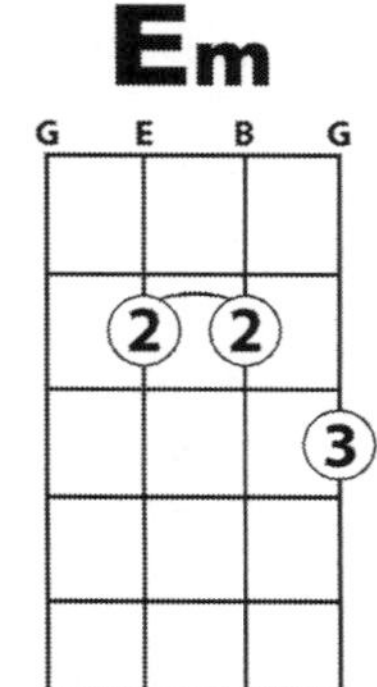

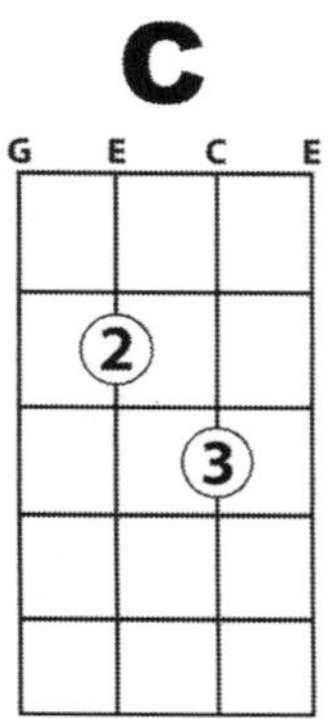

Roll, Boys, Roll (continued)

Two Versions

Key of E Minor

Basic Melody

```
  Em                             D                         Em    Bm    Em    D    Em
E ——0—2—0——————————————————————————————————————————————————0—————2—————0———————————————
A 2————————————————2—————2——5———5———5——2———————————————————————————————————5—————2—————
D ——————————————————————————————————————————————————————————————————————————————————————
G ——————————————————————————————————————————————————————————————————————————————————————
  Oh Sally Brown, she's the gal for me boys; roll, boys, roll boys roll.
```

```
     G                           D                         Em          D     Em
E ————————0—————————————————————————————————————————————————————————————————————————————
A 2—5—————5—————2—————2——5——2—0—————————————————————————————2—————0—————————————————————
D ——————————————————————————————————————0—————2————————————————————————0——2—————————————
G ——————————————————————————————————————————————————————————————————————————————————————
  Oh Sally Brown, she's the one I need boys; way, high, Sally Brown.
```

Melody & Chords

```
  Em                             D                         Em    Bm    Em    D    Em
E ——0—2—0——————————————————————————————————————————————————0—————2—————0———————————————
A 2—2—2—2——————————2—————2——5———5———5——2———————2———————————2—————2—————2—————5—————2———
D 2—2———2——————————2—————2——0———0———0——0———————2———————————4—————2—————0—————————————2———
G 0————————————————0————————2———————2——2———————————————————————————————————————————————0———
  Oh Sally Brown, she's the gal for me bo 1, boys, roll boys roll.
```

```
     G                           D                         Em          D     Em
E ————————0—————————————————————————————————————————————————————————————————————————————
A 2—5—2—5———————2—————2——5——2—0—————————————————————————————2—————0—————————————————————
D 2—0—————0—————0—————0——0——0—0—————0—————2—————————————————2—————0——0——2———————————————
G 0—0—————0—————0————————2——————2———2—————4—————————————————4—————2——2——4———————————————
  Oh Sally Brown, she's the one I need boys; way, high, Sally Brown.
```

Chord Forms

Em

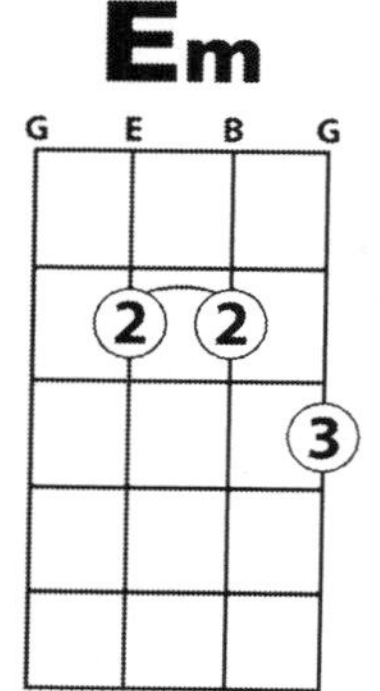

D

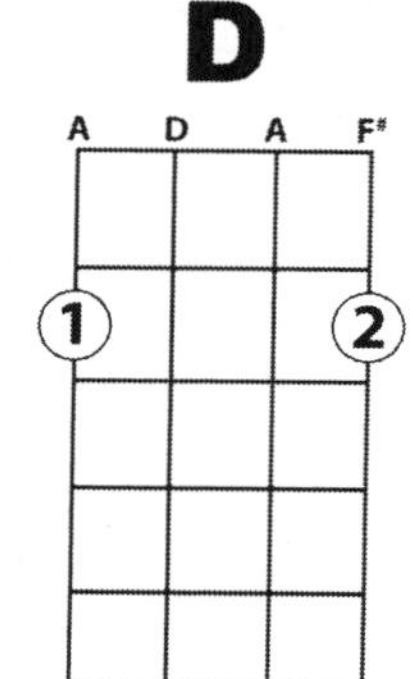

Bm

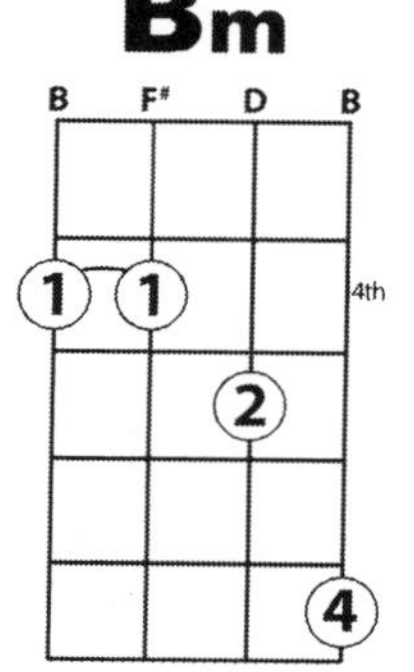

G

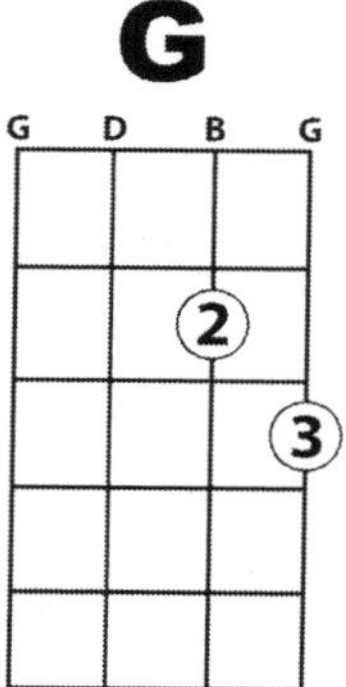

Sally Brown

Two Versions

Key of C

This is an old sea shanty extolling the virtues (mostly) of a lady named Sally Brown. It has a classic "call and response" shanty style, where the main singer would call out the first part of each line, and the rest of the singers would respond with the second part. Sally Brown is also the topic of the preceding shanty, "Roll, Boys, Roll", which has a similar structure but different melody and lyrics.

Words and Music Traditional

Basic Melody

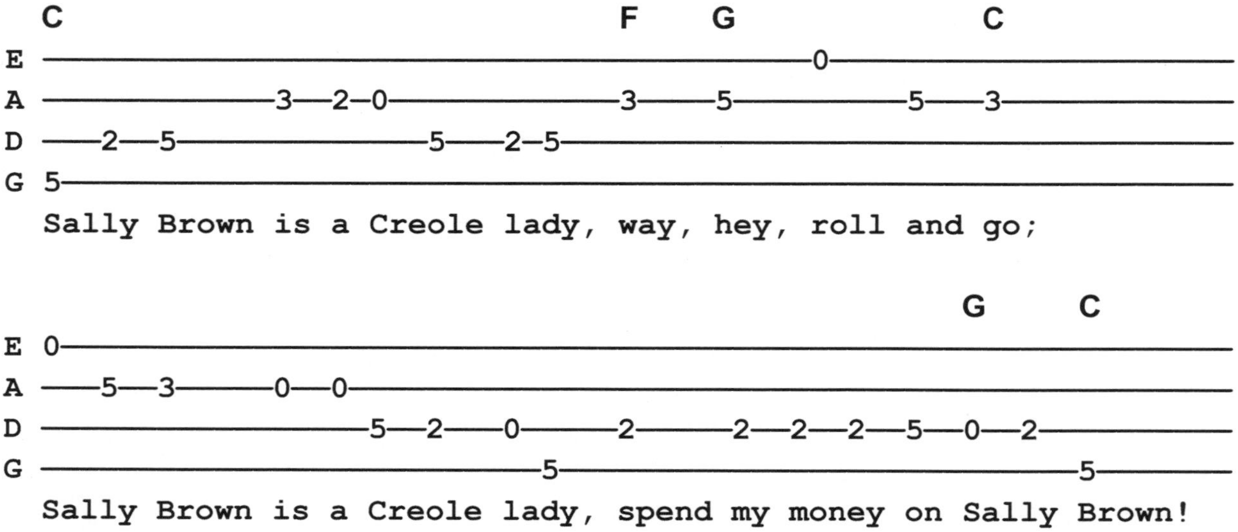

```
   C                                        F     G                  C
E ------------------------------------------------------0---------------------------
A ----------------3--2--0------------------3-----5----------5----3------------------
D ---2--5-----------------------5----2--5-------------------------------------------
G 5---------------------------------------------------------------------------------
  Sally Brown is a Creole lady, way, hey, roll and go;
```

```
                                                               G      C
E 0---------------------------------------------------------------------------------
A ---5--3-------0--0----------------------------------------------------------------
D ---------------------5--2----0------2------2--2--2--5--0--2-----------------------
G -----------------------------------5---------------------------5------------------
  Sally Brown is a Creole lady, spend my money on Sally Brown!
```

Melody & Chords

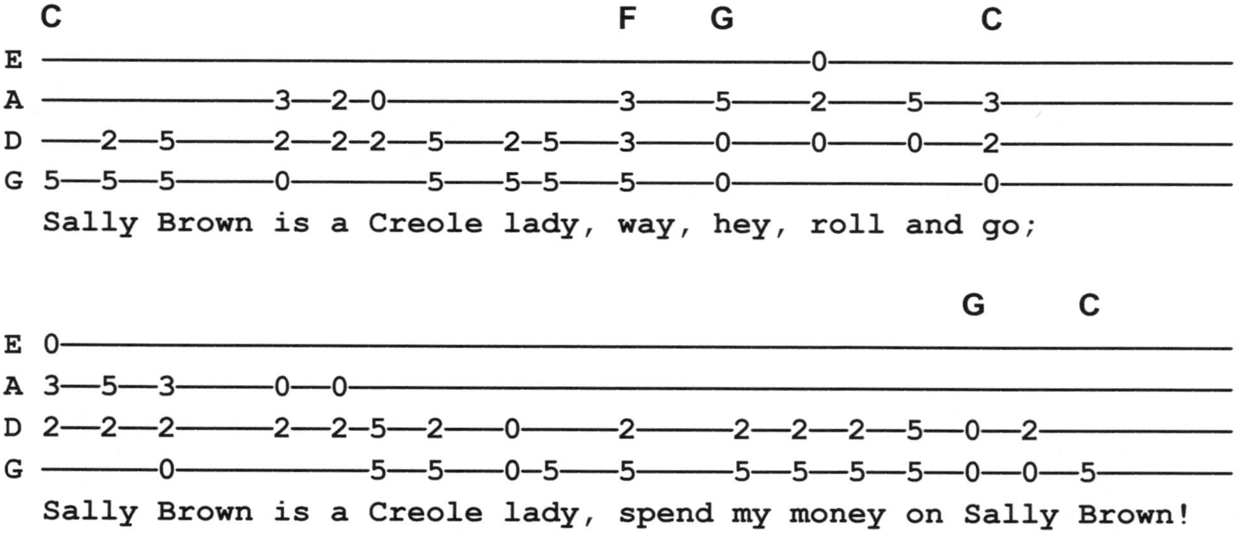

```
   C                                        F     G                  C
E ------------------------------------------------------0---------------------------
A ----------------3--2--0------------------3-----5-----2-----5----3-----------------
D ---2--5------2--2--2--5----2--5---------3-----0-----0-----0----2------------------
G 5--5--5------0-------------5----5--5----5-----0----------------0------------------
  Sally Brown is a Creole lady, way, hey, roll and go;
```

```
                                                               G      C
E 0---------------------------------------------------------------------------------
A 3--5--3-------0--0----------------------------------------------------------------
D 2--2--2------2--2--5--2----0------2------2--2--2--5--0--2-------------------------
G ------0--------------5--5----0--5--5------5--5--5--5--0--0--5---------------------
  Sally Brown is a Creole lady, spend my money on Sally Brown!
```

Sally Brown (continued)

Chord Forms

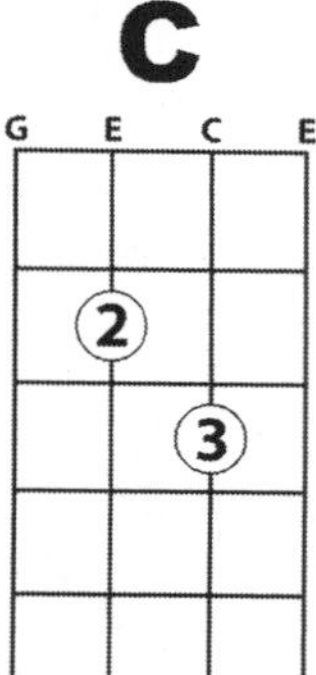

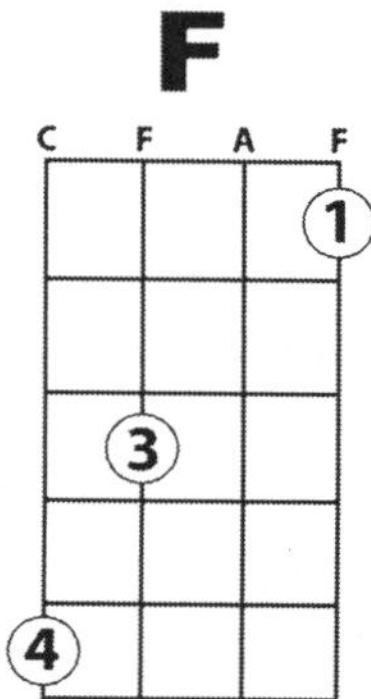

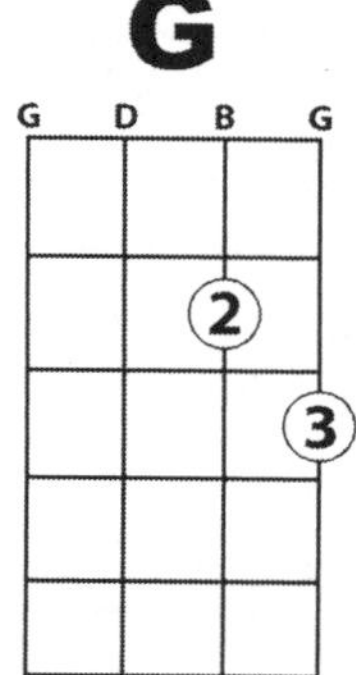

Additional Verses

Oh Sally Brown, of New York City,
Way, hey, roll and go;
Oh Sally Brown you're very pretty,
Spend my money on Sally Brown!

Sally's teeth are white and pearly,
Way, hey, roll and go;
Her eyes are blue, her hair is curly,
Spend my money on Sally Brown!

Oh Sally Brown is a Creole Lady,
Way, hey, roll and go;
She's the mother of a sweet little baby,
Spend my money on Sally Brown!

Seven long years I courted Sally,
Way, hey, roll and go;
Sweetest girl in all the valley,
Spend my money on Sally Brown!

Seven long years she wouldn't marry,
Way, hey, roll and go;
And I no longer cared to tarry,
Spend my money on Sally Brown!

Now my troubles are all over,
Way, hey, roll and go;
Sally's married to a dirty soldier,
Spend my money on Sally Brown!

Sally Brown (continued)

Two Versions

Key of G (Low)

Basic Melody

```
  G                                   C     D                 G
E ------------------------------------------------------------------------
A ------------------------------------------0-----2-----0-----------------
D ------0-----5--4--2--0-----0---5------------------------5---------------
G 0--4---------------------4----------------------------------------------
  Sally Brown is a Creole lady, way, hey, roll and go;
```

```
                                                        D     G
E ------------------------------------------------------------------------
A 2--0--------------------------------------------------------------------
D ------5-----2--2-0------------------------------------0-----------------
G --------------------4---2-0---4-----4--4--4-----2--4--0-----------------
  Sally Brown is a Creole lady, spend my money on Sally Brown!
```

Melody & Chords

```
  G                                   C     D                 G
E ------------------------------------------------------------------------
A ------------------------------------------0-----2-----0-----------------
D ------0-----5--4--2--0-----0---5----0-----0-----0---5-------------------
G 0--4--0-----0--2--2--0---4-0---5----2-----2---------0-------------------
  Sally Brown is a Creole lady, way, hey, roll and go;
```

```
                                                        D     G
E ------------------------------------------------------------------------
A 2--0--------------------------------------------------------------------
D 0--0--5-----2--2-0------------------------------------0--------5--------
G 0-----0-----0--0-0--4---2-0---4-----4--4--4--0--2--4--0-----------------
  Sally Brown is a Creole lady, spend my money on Sally Brown!
```

Chord Forms

G

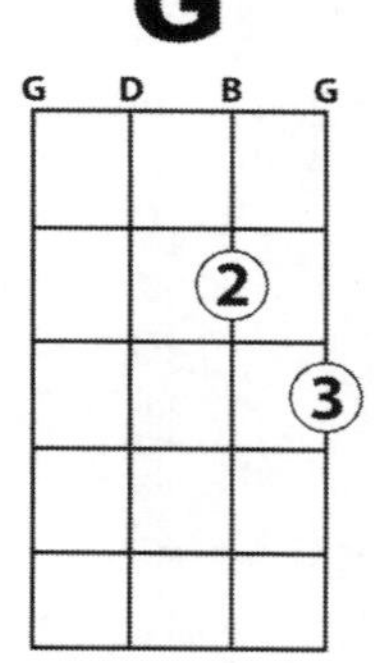

C

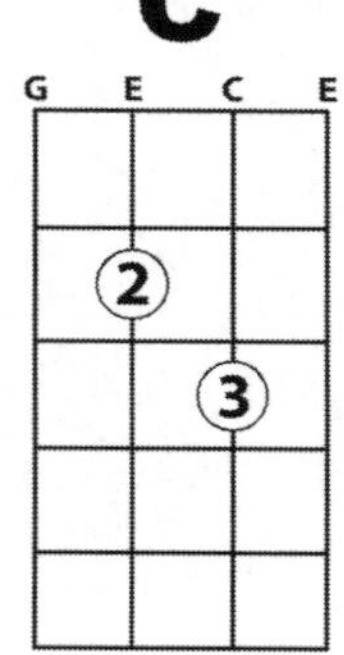

D

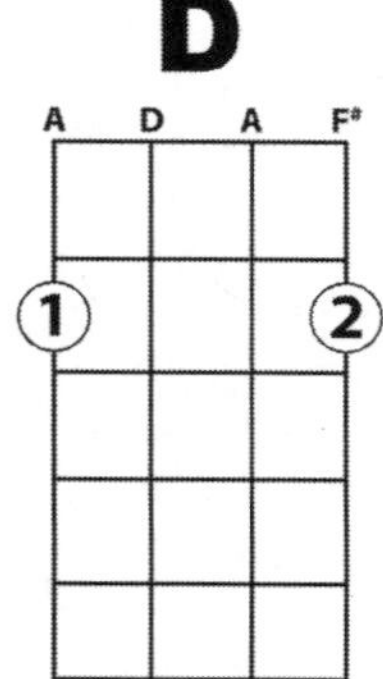

Sally Brown (continued)

Two Versions

Key of G (High)

Basic Melody

```
  G                                  C    D              G
E ────────────3──2─0─────────────────3────5────7────5────3────────
A ──2──5─────────────────5───2─5──────────────────────────────────
D 5───────────────────────────────────────────────────────────────
G ────────────────────────────────────────────────────────────────
  Sally Brown is a Creole lady, way, hey, roll and go;

                                                     D     G
E 7──5──3─────0──0────────────────────────────────────────────────
A ─────────────────5──2───0─────2──────2──2──2──5──0──2───────────
D ──────────────────────────5───────────────────────────5─────────
G ────────────────────────────────────────────────────────────────
  Sally Brown is a Creole lady, spend my money on Sally Brown!
```

Melody & Chords

```
  G                                  C    D              G
E ────────────3──2─0─────────────────3────5────7────5────3────────
A ──2──5──────2──2─2──5───2──5───────3────0────5────5────2────────
D 5──0──0──────────0──0───0──0───────2────0──────────────0────────
G 0─────0─────────────────0───────────────────────────────────────
  Sally Brown is a Creole lady, way, hey, roll and go;

                                                     D     G
E 7──5──3─────0──0────────────────────────────────────────────────
A 5──5──2─────2──2──5──2───0─────2─────2──2──2──5──0──2───────────
D 5─────0──────────0──0───0──5───0─────0──0──0──0──0──0──5────────
G ─────────────────0──────0──0───0─────────0─────0──2──2──0───────
  Sally Brown is a Creole lady, spend my money on Sally Brown!
```

Chord Forms

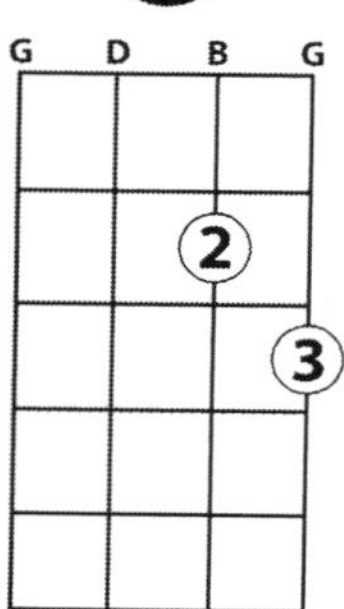

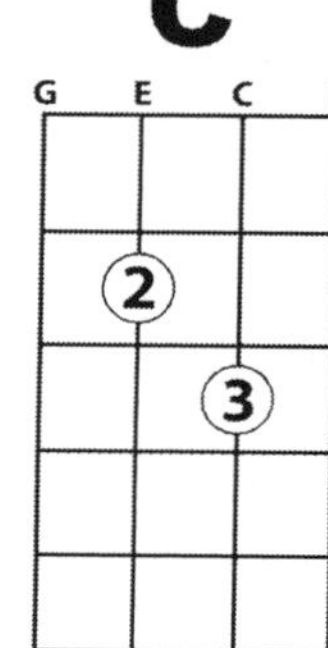

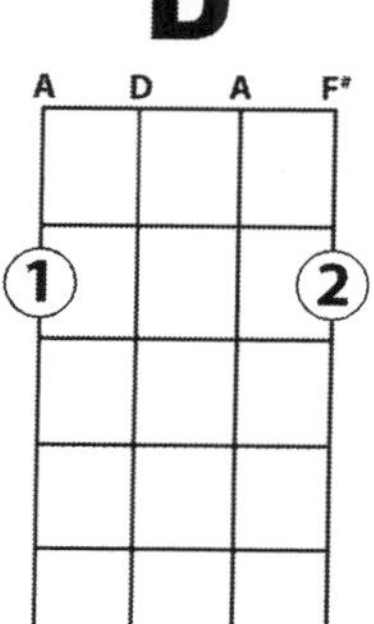

Shenandoah

Basic Melody

Key of C (Low)

Words and Music

Traditional

This is a traditional American folk song, which is actually believed to have began as a sailor's song sung aboard ship during long voyages. It is thought to have been written in the early 1800's, and may actually be an amalgamation of two separate songs.

```
  C                                    F     C                 F
E ---------------------------------------------------------------------------
A ------------------------------------0--------------3---2---0---------------
D -------------------------0-2------5-------5--------------------------------
G 0---5----5-5---------------------------------------------------------------
  Oh Shenandoah, I long to see you... a--a--way,
```

```
                      C            F                G            Am
E ---------------------------------------------------------------------------
A -----0---------------------------0---0---0---------------------------------
D 5--------5-----2-5-----5---------------------2-5-----2---0-----------------
G ------------------------------------------------------------5--------------
  You rolling river; oh Shenandoah, I long to see you;
```

```
  F    C                     Em                C          G    C
E ---------------------------------------------------------------------------
A ----------------------------0----------------------------------------------
D --0-2----------2-----------5-----------0----2---------0--------------------
G 5---------5------------------------5------------------5-------5------------
  A-a-way, I'm bound away, 'cross the wide Missouri.
```

Chord Forms

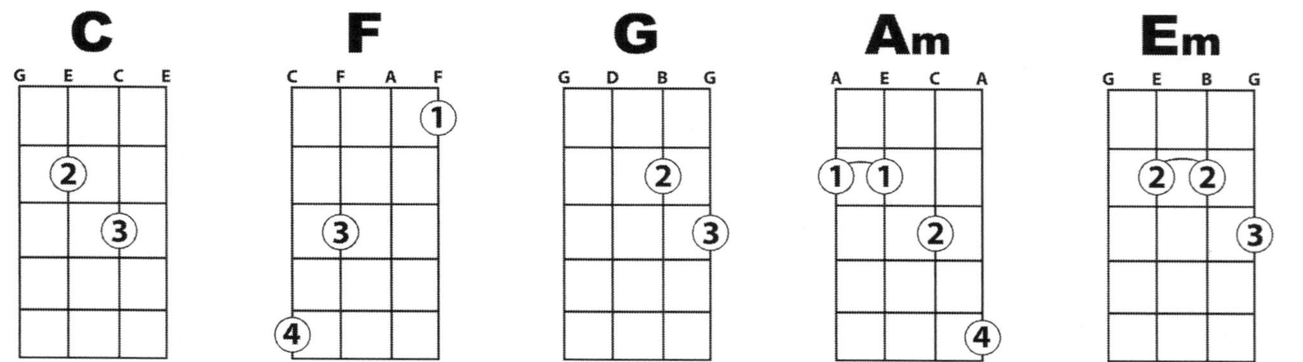

See Additional Verses on Next Page

Shenandoah (continued)

Melody & Chords

Key of C (Low)

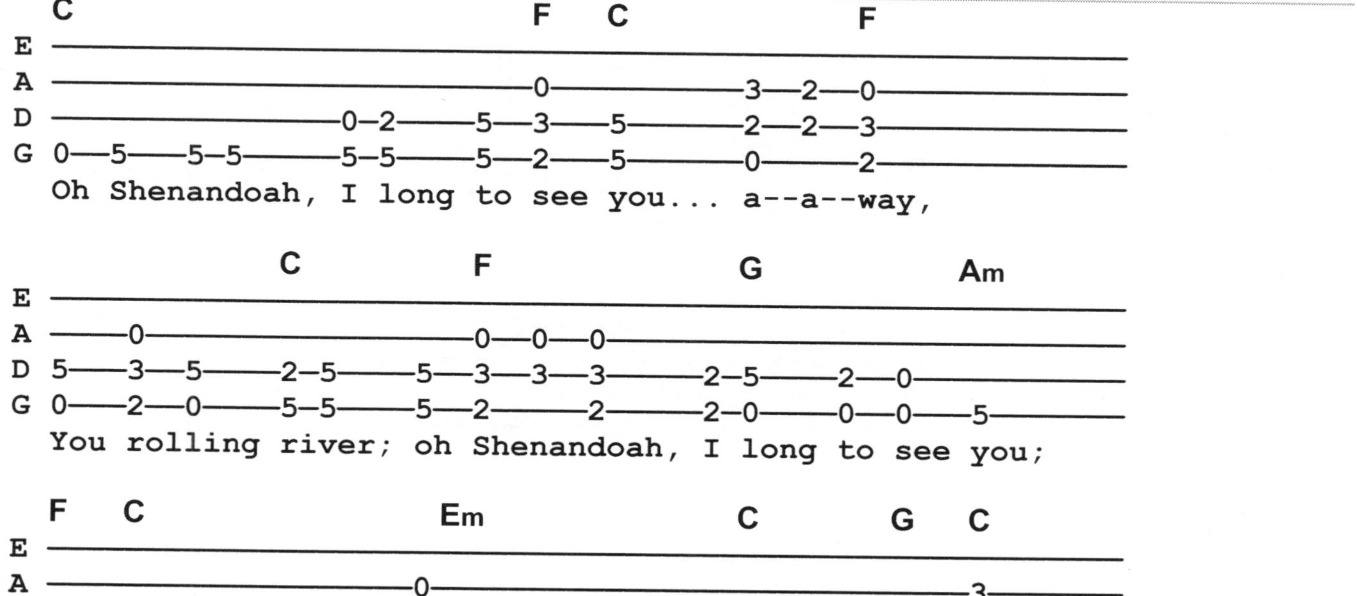


```
F    C                    Em                     C       G   C
E ----------------------------------------------------------------
A ------------------------0-------------------------------3-------
D --0-2------------2------2-5-------------0---2-------0---2-------
G 5-2-5-------5----5----------4----5------4---5----5--0---5-------
A-a-way, I'm bound away, 'cross the wide Missouri.
```

Additional Verses

Oh Shenandoah, I love your daughter,
Away, you rolling river.
For her I'd cross your roaming waters,
Away, I'm bound away, 'cross the wide Missouri.

'Tis seven years since last I've seen you,
Away, you rolling river.
'Tis seven years since last I've seen you,
Away, we're bound away, 'cross the wide Missouri.

Oh Shenandoah, I long to hear you,
Away, you rolling river.
Oh Shenandoah, I long to hear you,
Away, we're bound away, 'cross the wide Missouri.

Oh Shenandoah, I long to hear you,
Far away, you rolling river.
Oh Shenandoah, just to be near you,
Far away, far away, 'cross the wide Missouri

Shenandoah (continued)

Two Versions

Key of C (High)

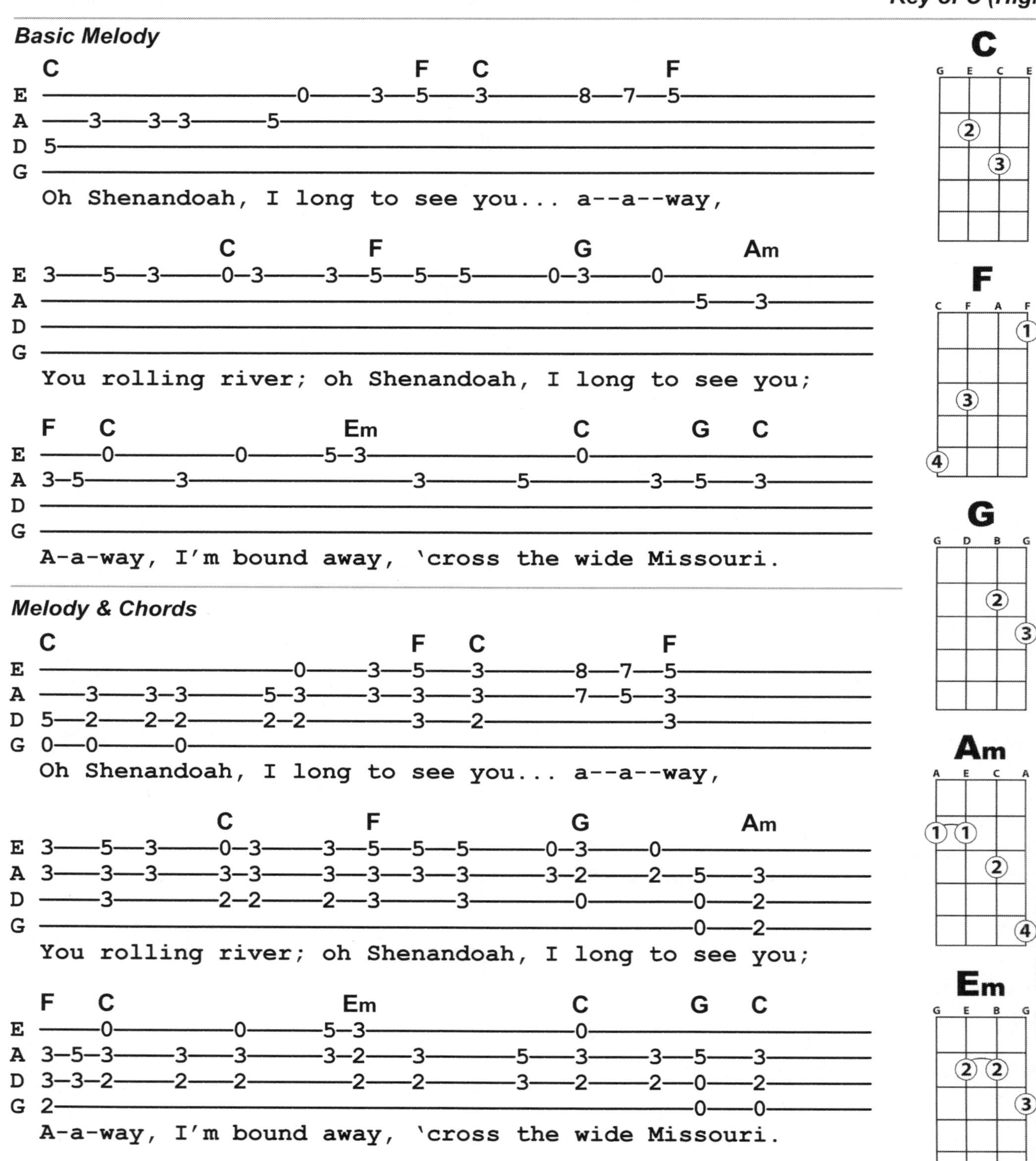

Shenandoah (continued)

Two Versions

Key of G

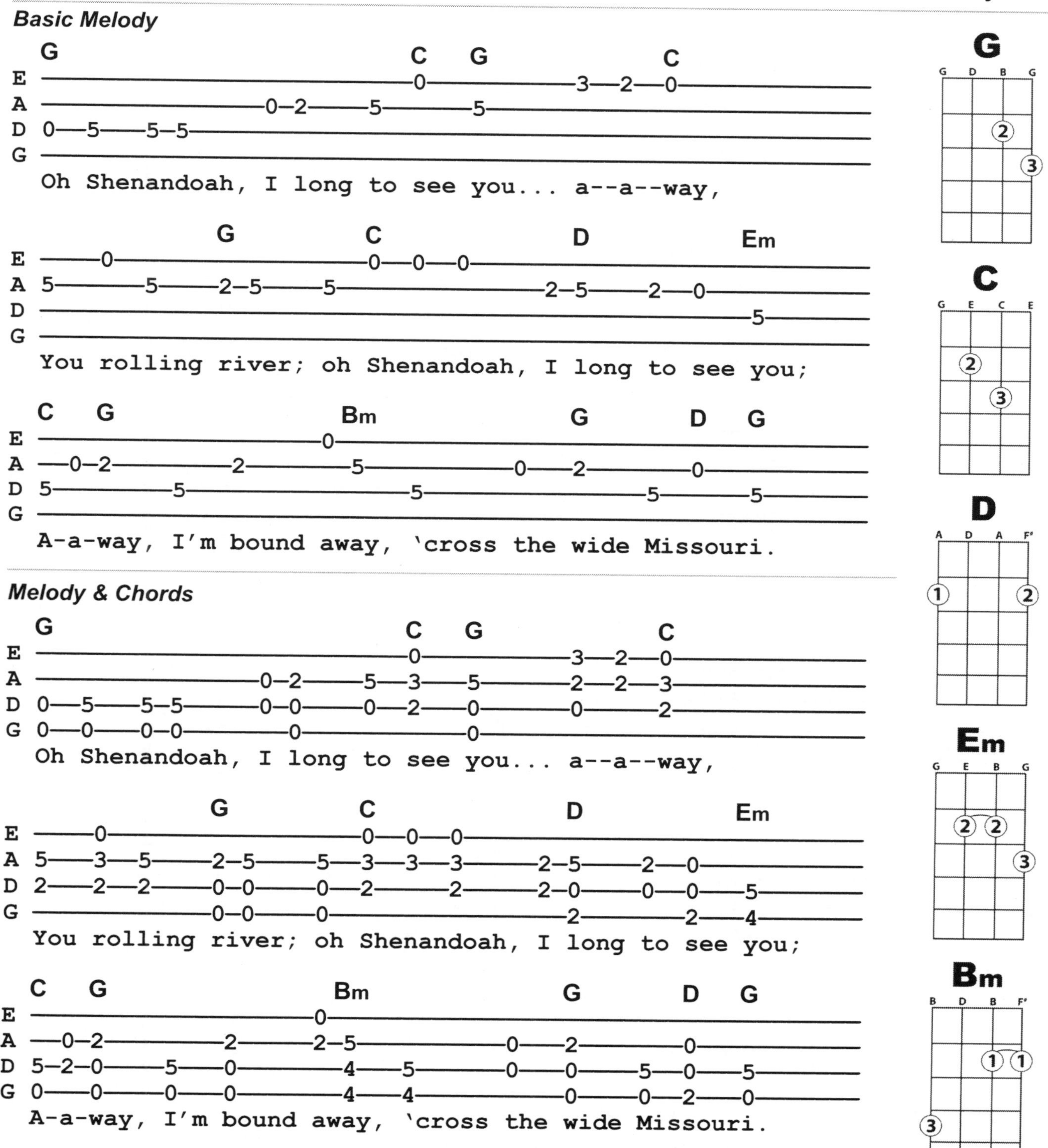

The Skye Boat Song

Basic Melody

Key of C (Low)

Words and Music

Traditional

This is another old Scottish song that deals with the story of Bonnie Prince Charlie and his ill-fated attempts to ascend the throne of Scotland. In particular this song tells of Charlie's flight by boat to the Isle of Skye after the defeat at Battle of Culloden Field in 1746.

CHORUS

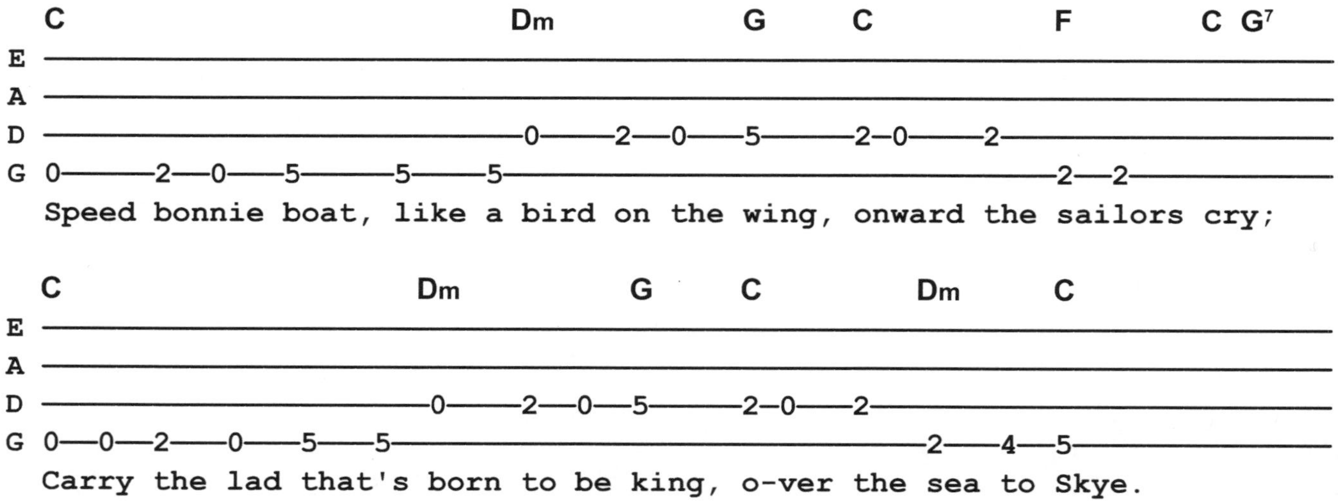

```
  C                                   Dm             G       C              F          C  G7
E ----------------------------------------------------------------------------------------------
A ----------------------------------------------------------------------------------------------
D -----------------------------------0------2---0----5--------2--0------2-----------------------
G 0--------2---0----5-------5-----5--------------------------------------------2---2------------
  Speed bonnie boat, like a bird on the wing, onward the sailors cry;
```

```
  C                              Dm              G       C          Dm        C
E ----------------------------------------------------------------------------------------------
A ----------------------------------------------------------------------------------------------
D -------------------------------0------2---0---5-------2--0----2-------------------------------
G 0---0---2-----0-----5----5---------------------------------------------2-----4---5------------
  Carry the lad that's born to be king, o-ver the sea to Skye.
```

VERSE

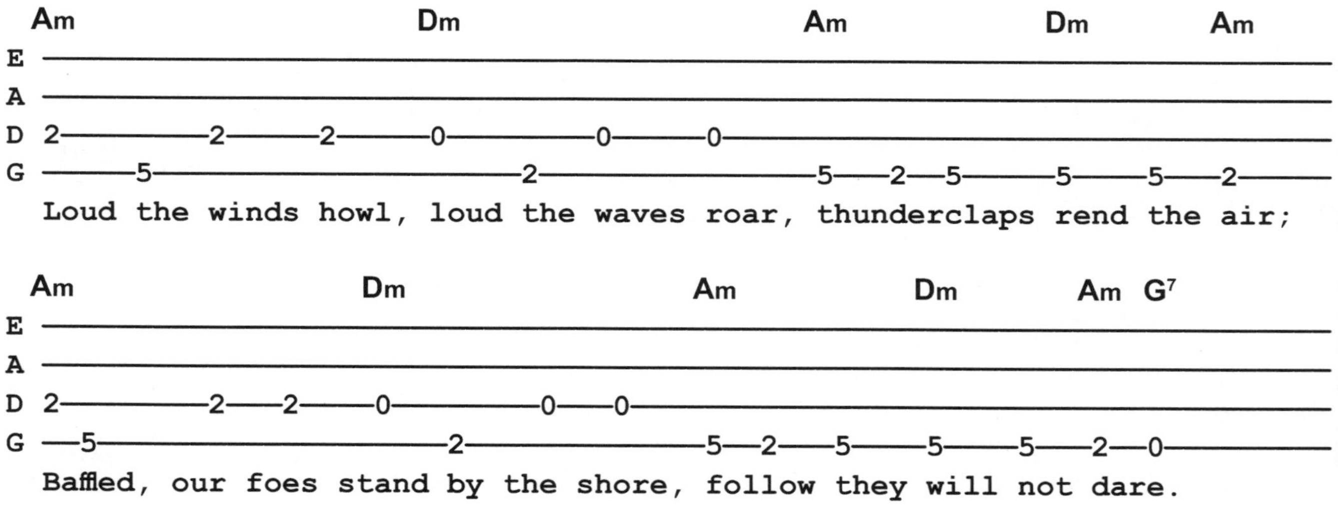

```
  Am                           Dm                           Am                 Dm          Am
E ----------------------------------------------------------------------------------------------
A ----------------------------------------------------------------------------------------------
D 2-----------2--------2--------0-----------0-------0-------------------------------------------
G -------5-------------------------------2-------------------------5----2---5-------5-----5---2--
  Loud the winds howl, loud the waves roar, thunderclaps rend the air;
```

```
  Am                       Dm                        Am                Dm            Am  G7
E ----------------------------------------------------------------------------------------------
A ----------------------------------------------------------------------------------------------
D 2-----------2----2------0-----------0----0----------------------------------------------------
G ---5--------------------------2--------------------5---2----5-----5-----5----2---0-------------
  Baffled, our foes stand by the shore, follow they will not dare.
```

See Chord Forms and Additional Verses on Next Page

The Skye Boat Song
(continued)

Chord Forms and Additional Verses

Chord Forms

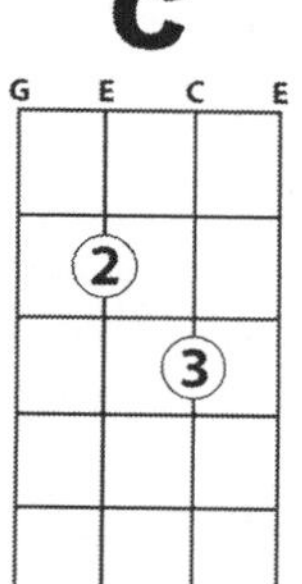

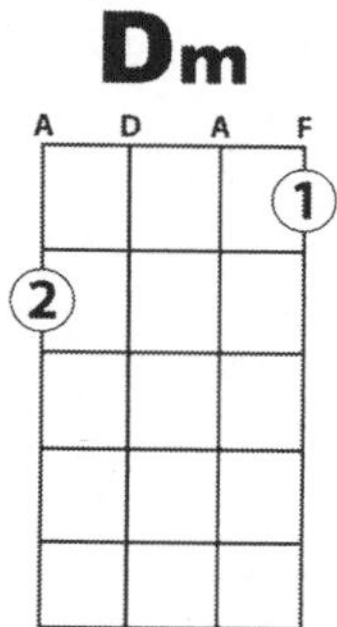

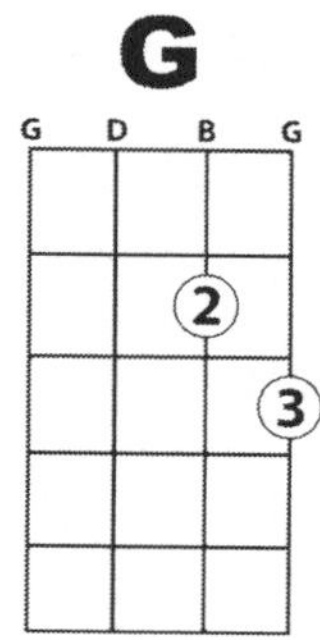

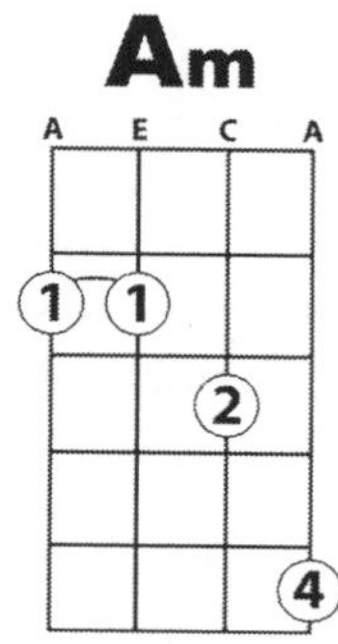

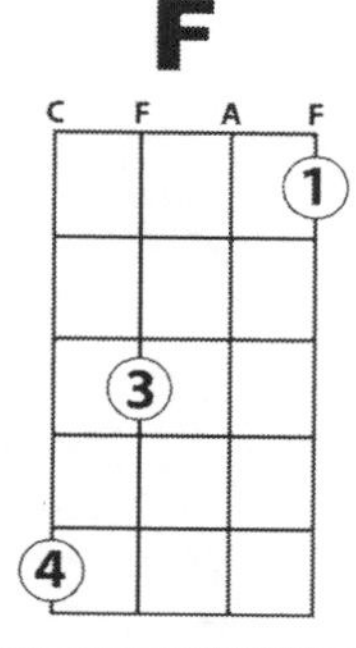

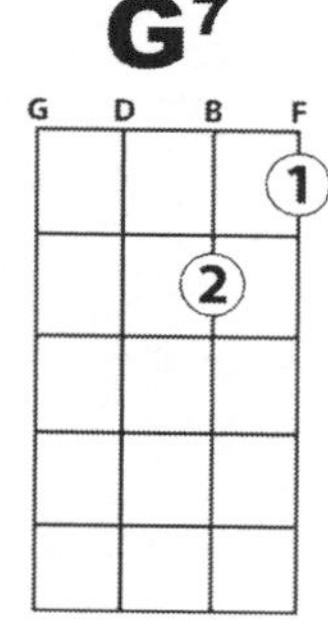

Additional Verses

Many's the lad, fought in that day,
Well the claymore did wield;
When the night came, silently lay,
Dead on Culloden's field.

Though the waves leap, soft shall ye sleep,
Ocean's a royal bed;
Rocked in the deep, flora will keep,
Watch by your weary head.

Burned are their homes, exile and death,
Scatter the loyal men;
Yet ere the sword cool in the sheath,
Charlie will come again.

Loch Coruisk, Isle of Skye painted in 1874 by Sidney Richard Percy.

The Skye Boat Song
(continued)

Basic Melody

Key of C (High)

CHORUS

```
  C                                Dm              G       C          F           C  G7
E ------------------------------------------0-------3-------0--------0--------------------
A ------0--------3-------3------3--5--------5------------------5----------0---0-----------
D 5--------5--------------------------------------------------------------------5---------
G ----------------------------------------------------------------------------------------
  Speed bonnie boat, like a bird on the wing, onward the sailors cry;
```

```
  C                          Dm             G       C       Dm       C
E -------------------------------------0-------3-------0-------0-------------------------
A -------0-------3----3---5------5--------------5----------0----2---3-------------------
D 5--5--------5-------------------------------------------------------------------------
G --------------------------------------------------------------------------------------
  Carry the lad that's born to be king, o-ver the sea to Skye.
```

VERSE

```
  Am                          Dm                          Am              Dm         Am
E 0---------0-------0-------------------------------------------------------------------
A ------3--------------------5------0------5------5------3----0---3------3------3----0--
D --------------------------------------------------------------------------------------
G --------------------------------------------------------------------------------------
  Loud the winds howl, loud the waves roar, thunderclaps rend the air;
```

```
  Am                   Dm                      Am              Dm           Am  G7
E 0--------0----0-----------------------------------------------------------------------
A --3------------------5-------0---5----5---------3---0----3------3-----3----0---------
D ---------------------------------------------------------------------------5----------
G --------------------------------------------------------------------------------------
  Baffled, our foes stand by the shore, follow they will not dare.
```

Chord Forms

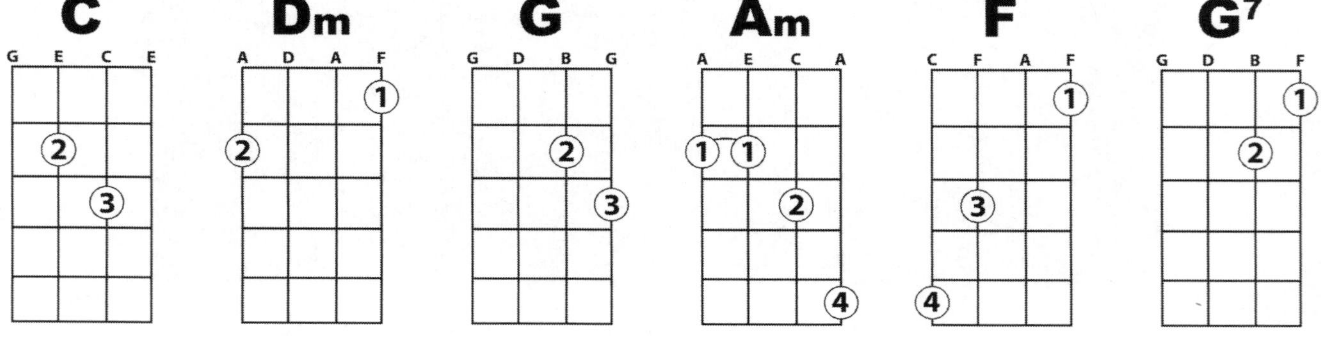

The Skye Boat Song
(continued)

Melody & Chords

Key of C (High)

CHORUS

```
  C                                       Dm                G        C             F         C  G7
E ———————————————————————————————————————————————0———————3———————0————————0——————————————————————
A —————————0————————3————————3———————3–5——————0———5————2———————3–5——————3——————0——0————————————————
D 5————————2———5————2————————2———————2–3———————————3————0———————2–2————————————————3——3——————5——5——
G 0———————————0————0————————0——————————2————————————————————————————————————————2——————————5——0——
  Speed bonnie boat, like a bird on the wing, onward the sailors cry;
```

```
  C                                Dm              G        C             Dm        C
E ————————————————————————————————————————0———————3————————0————————0—————————————————————————
A —————————0——————————3————3————5————————0———5————2————————3–5——————3———————0————2——3———————————
D 5——5———2————5————2————2————3—————————————3————0————————2–2——————————————0—————0——2———————————
G 5——5————————0————0———————————2———————————————————————————————————————2——————————0———————————
  Carry the lad that's born to be king, o-ver the sea to Skye.
```

VERSE

```
  Am                               Dm                          Am                 Dm          Am
E 0———————————0———————0———————————————————————————————————————————————————————————————————————————
A 0—————3—————0———————0———————5————————0————5————————5————————3————0———3————————3———————3————0——————
D 2—————2—————2———————2———————3————————3————3————————3————————2————2———2————————0———————0————2——————
G —————————————————————————————2————————————2————————2————————2————————2————————2————————————2——————
  Loud the winds howl, loud the waves roar, thunderclaps rend the air;
```

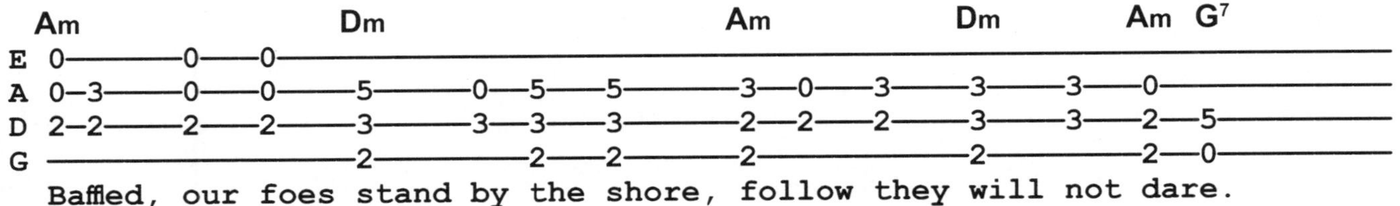

Chord Forms

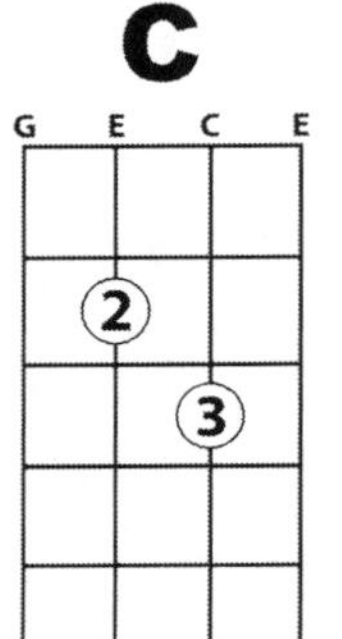

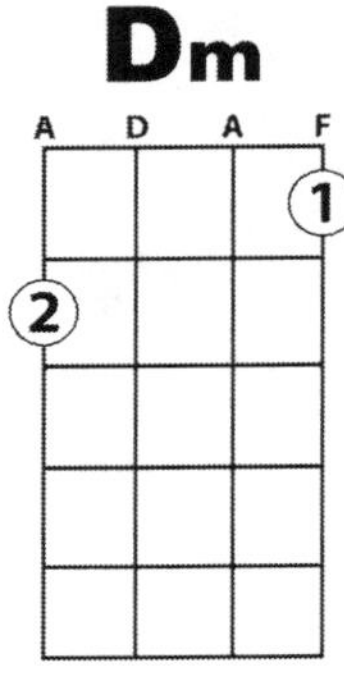

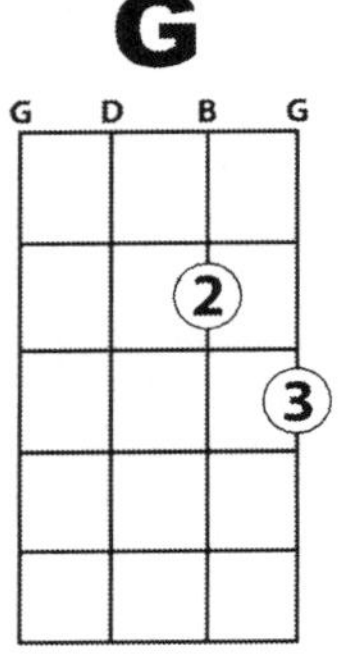

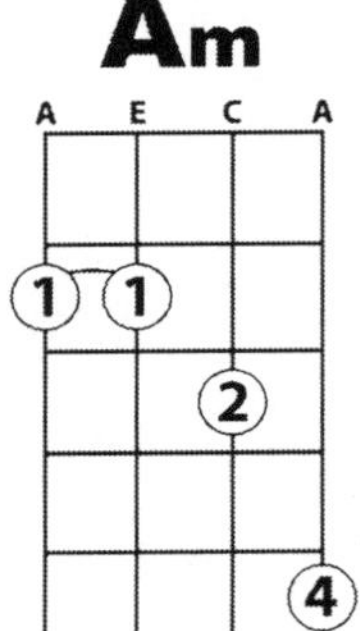

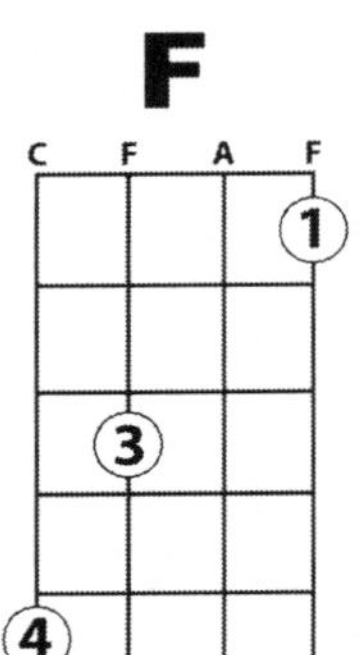

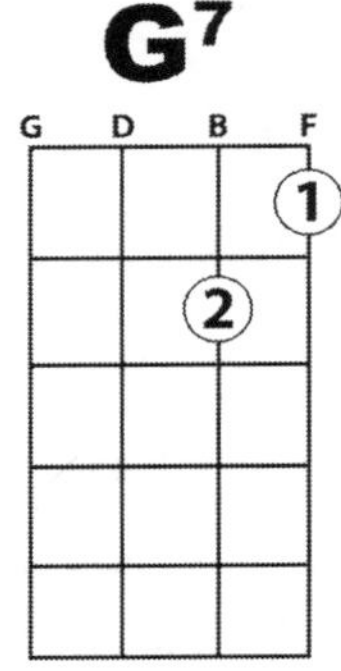

The Skye Boat Song
(continued)

Basic Melody

Key of G

CHORUS

```
  G                                        Am                 D         G                C            G D7
E ---------------------------------------------------------------------------------------------------------
A ----------------------------------------0-------2---0---5--------2--0-------2----------------------------
D 0---------2---0-----5--------5-----5--------------------------------------------------2----2------0------
G ---------------------------------------------------------------------------------------------------------
  Speed bonnie boat, like a bird on the wing, onward the sailors cry;

  G                              Am               D        G              Am         G
E ----------------------------------------------------------------------------------------------------
A -------------------------------0--------2---0---5--------2--0----2---------------------------------
D 0---0---2------0------5-----5--------------------------------------------2------4---5---------------
G ----------------------------------------------------------------------------------------------------
  Carry the lad that's born to be king, o-ver the sea to Skye.
```

VERSE

```
 Em                              Am                               Em                Am           Em
E ----------------------------------------------------------------------------------------------------
A 2-----------2--------2--------0-------------0--------0---------------------------------------------
D --------5-----------------------------2--------------------------5-----2----5--------5-------5----2--
G ----------------------------------------------------------------------------------------------------
  Loud the winds howl, loud the waves roar, thunderclaps rend the air;

 Em                       Am                              Em               Am            Em D7
E ----------------------------------------------------------------------------------------------------
A 2-----------2-----2-------0-----------0----0-------------------------------------------------------
D -----5--------------------------------2-----------------------5---2-----5------5------5----2---0----
G ----------------------------------------------------------------------------------------------------
  Baffled, our foes stand by the shore, follow they will not dare.
```

Chord Forms

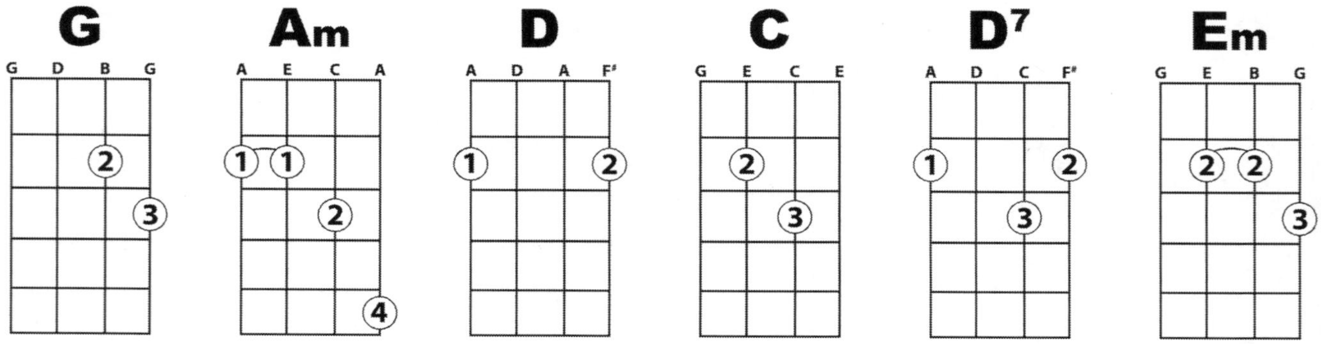

G (G D B G): 2, 3

Am (A E C A): 1, 1, 2, 4

D (A D A F#): 1, 2

C (G E C E): 2, 3

D7 (A D C F#): 1, 2, 3

Em (G E B G): 2, 2, 3

SCOTTISH BALLAD

The Skye Boat Song
(continued)

Melody & Chords

Key of G

CHORUS

```
  G                                     Am                 D        G                C          G  D7
E ------------------------------------------------------------------------------------------------------
A --------------------------------------0------2---0----5-------2-0-------2-----------------------------
D 0-------2---0----5-------5------5-2----------2---2----0-------0-0-------0-----2----2--------0---------
G 0-------0---0----0-------0------0-5-------------------2-------0---------0-----5----5--------0---------
  Speed bonnie boat, like a bird on the wing, onward the sailors cry;
```

```
  G                              Am            D        G            Am          G
E -------------------------------------------------------------------------------------------
A -------------------------------0------2---0---5--------2-0------2---------------------------
D 0--0--2----0----5----5---2-----------2---2---0--------0-0------0----2-----4--5-------------
G 0--0--0----0----0----0---5-----------------5---2------0---------------5-----5--0------------
  Carry the lad that's born to be king, o-ver the sea to Skye.
```

VERSE

```
  Em                           Am                          Em              Am           Em
E ---------------------------------------------------------------------------------------------
A 2--------2-------2-------0-----------0-------0------------------------------------------------
D 2-----5--2-------2-------2------2----2-------2-------5----2---5-------5-------5----2----------
G 4-----4----------4-------5------5------------5-------4----4---4-------2-------2----4----------
  Loud the winds howl, loud the waves roar, thunderclaps rend the air;
```

```
  Em                     Am                         Em            Am           Em  D7
E ------------------------------------------------------------------------------------------
A 2-------2---2-----0-----------0----0-------------------------------------------------------
D 2---5---2---2-----2-------2---2----2-------5---2----5------5------5----2---0---------------
G 4---4-------4-----5-------5--------5-------4---4----4------2------2----4---2---------------
  Baffled, our foes stand by the shore, follow they will not dare.
```

Chord Forms

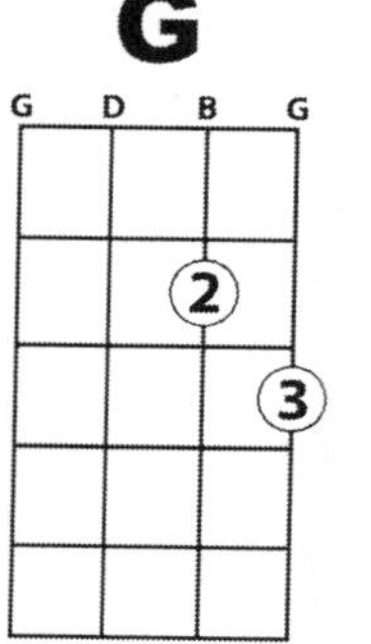

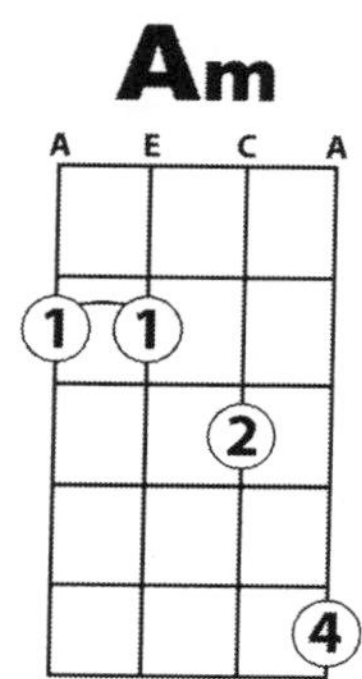

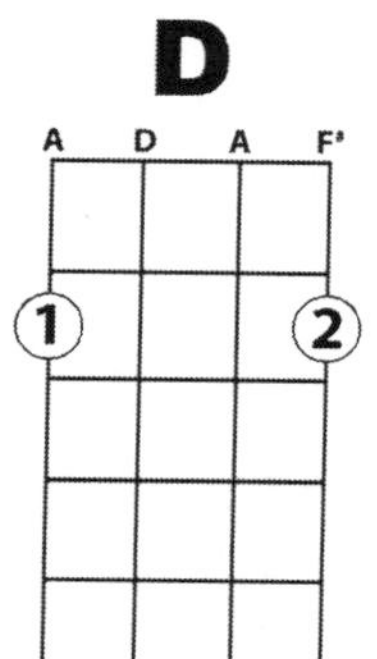

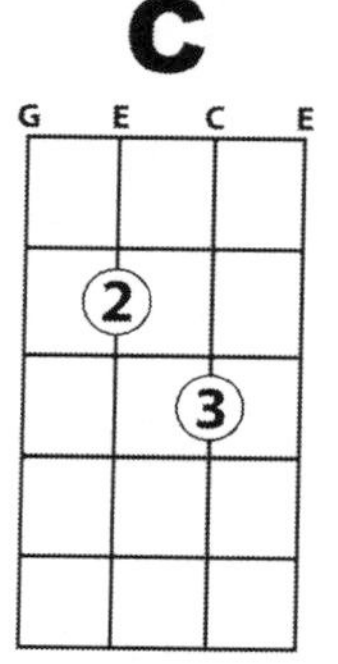

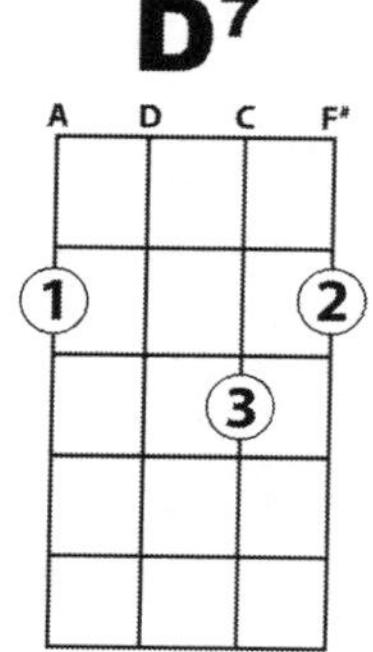

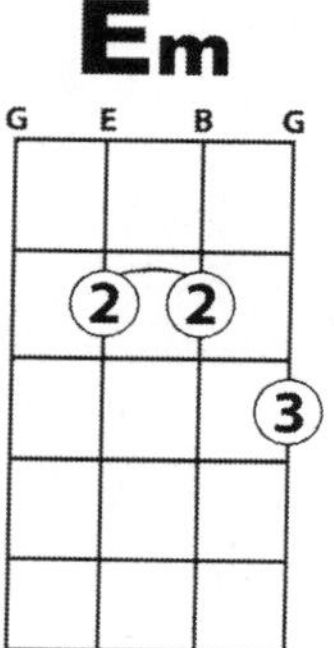

South Australia

Basic Melody

Key of C

Words and Music

Traditional

Part seafaring song and part drinking song, this great old traditional tune is perfect for belting out over a few pints in your favorite pub. Patrick Boyle has been performing this one for many years at sessions and Irish music parties in and around Dover, New Hampshire.

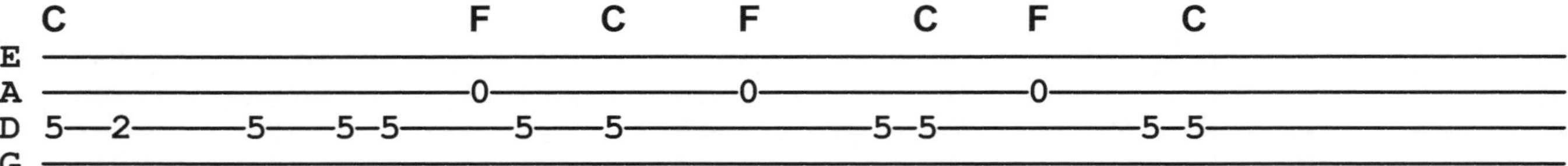

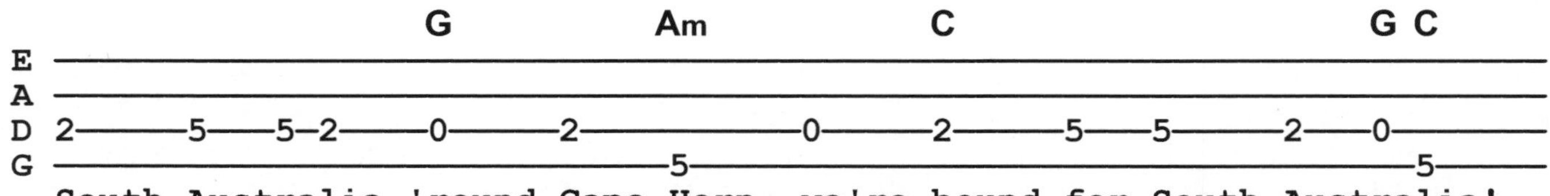

CHORUS

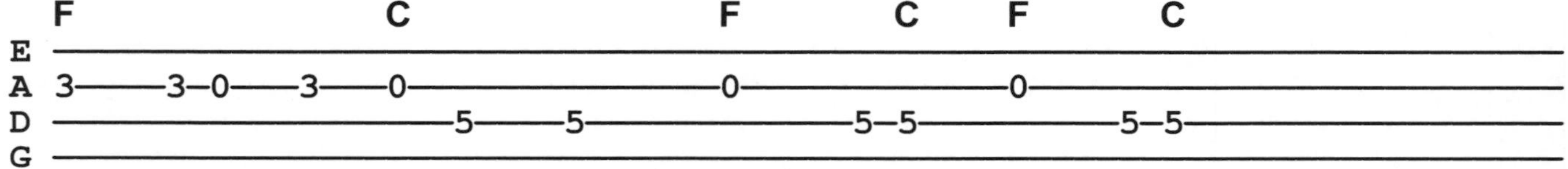

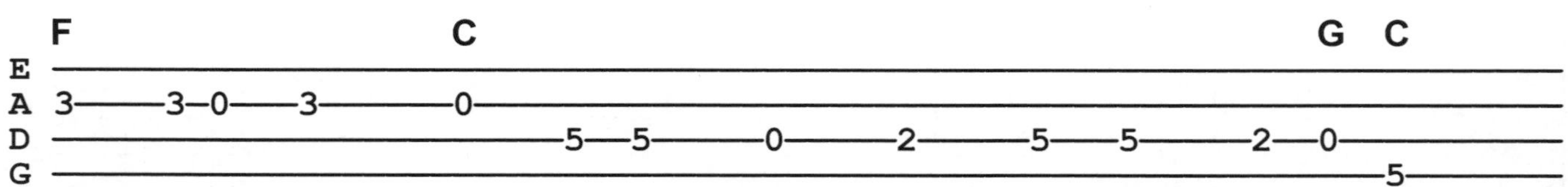

Chord Forms

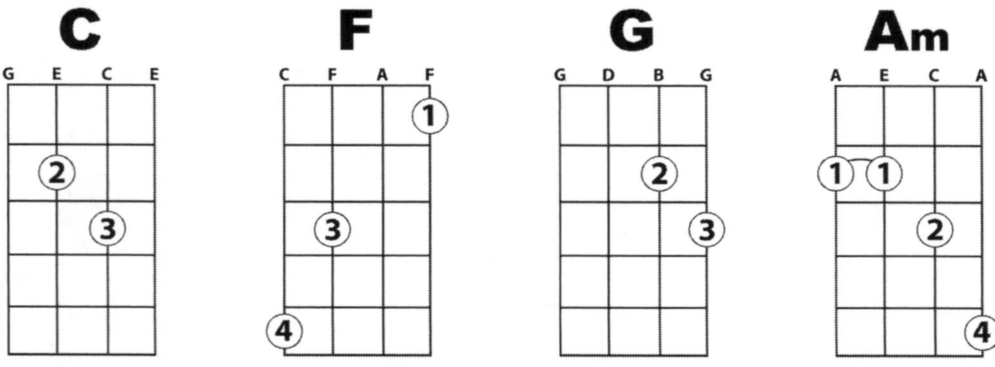

See Additional Verses on Next Page

South Australia (continued)

Melody & Chords

Key of C

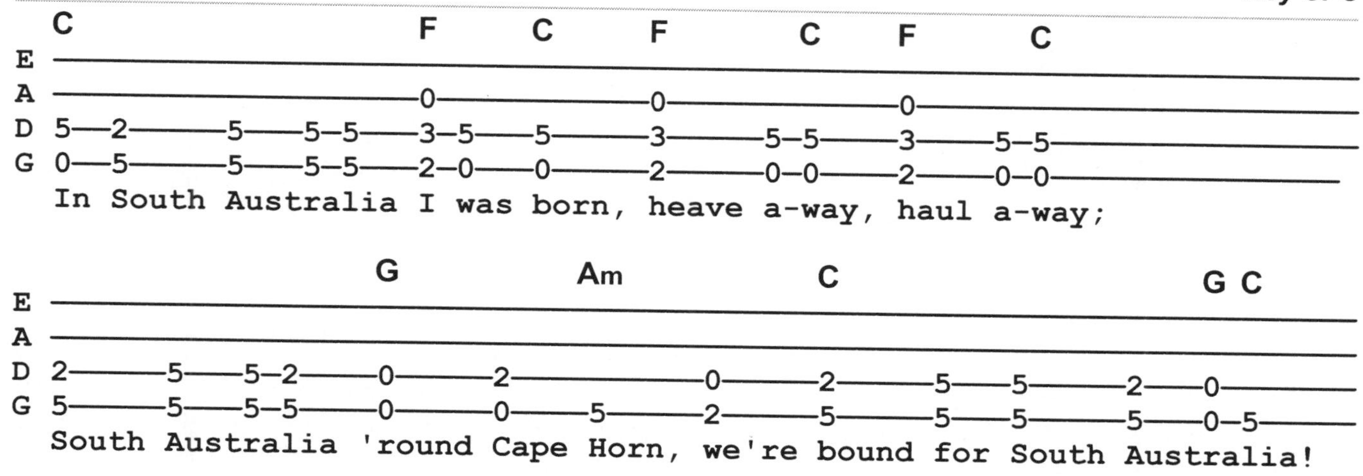

```
  C                  F     C     F       C    F     C
E ------------------------------------------------------------------
A ------------------0-----------0-------------0---------------------
D 5--2-----5---5-5---3-5---5-----3-----5-5-----3----5-5---------------
G 0--5-----5---5-5---2-0---0-----2-----0-0-----2----0-0---------------
  In South Australia I was born, heave a-way, haul a-way;
```

```
                  G         Am          C                  G C
E ------------------------------------------------------------------
A ------------------------------------------------------------------
D 2-----5---5-2---0-----2-----------0-----2----5---5-----2---0------
G 5-----5---5-5---0-----0-----5-----2-----5----5---5-----5---0-5----
  South Australia 'round Cape Horn, we're bound for South Australia!
```

Chorus

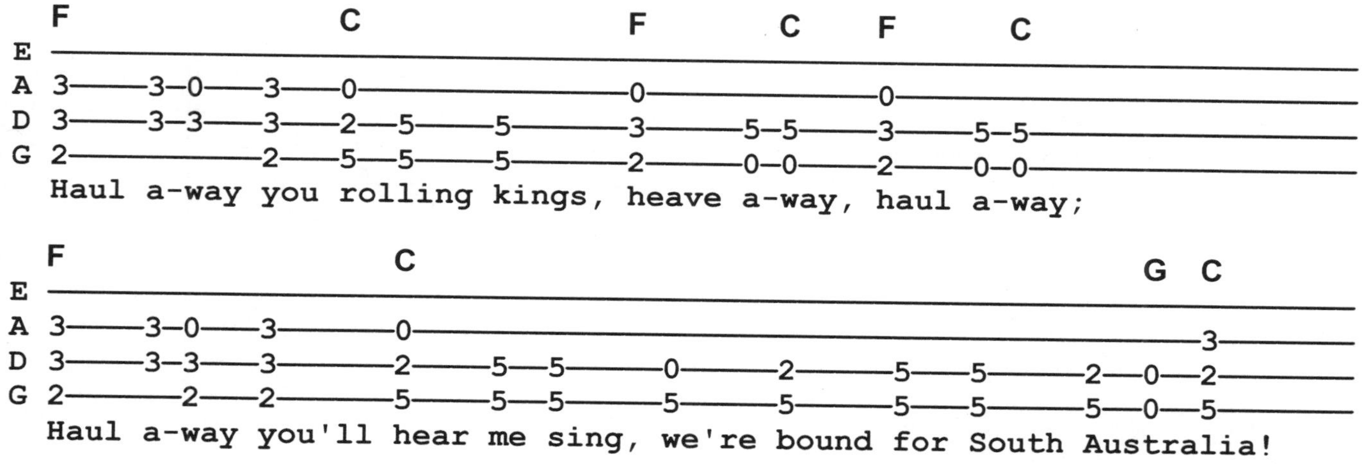

```
  F             C              F      C     F     C
E ------------------------------------------------------------------
A 3----3-0---3---0-------------0------------0-----------------------
D 3----3-3---3---2---5----5----3-----5-5----3----5-5----------------
G 2----------2---5---5----5----2-----0-0----2----0-0----------------
  Haul a-way you rolling kings, heave a-way, haul a-way;
```

```
  F                C                                    G  C
E ------------------------------------------------------------------
A 3----3-0---3-----0-----------------------------------------3------
D 3----3-3---3-----2----5--5----0----2----5---5----2--0--2---------
G 2-------2--2-----5----5--5----5----5----5---5----5--0--5---------
  Haul a-way you'll hear me sing, we're bound for South Australia!
```

Additional Verses

As I walked out one morning fair,
Heave away, haul away;
It's there I met Miss Nancy Blair,
We're bound for South Australia.

I shook her up, I shook her down,
Heave away, haul away;
I shook her 'round and 'round the town,
We're bound for South Australia.

There is just one thing grieves me mind,
Heave away, haul away;
To leave miss Nancy Blair behind,
We're bound for South Australia.

And as we wallop around Cape Horn,
Heave away, haul away;
You'll wish to Christ you'd never been born,
We're bound for South Australia.

South Australia (continued)

Basic Melody

Key of G (Low)

```
   G                          C       G       C          G      C        G
E ------------------------------------------------------------------------------------
A ------------------------------------------------------------------------------------
D 0----------0----0-0----2-0----0-------2-------0-0-----2-----0-0--------------------
G ---4--------------------------------------------------------------------------------
  In South Australia I was born, heave a-way, haul a-way;

                       D            Em            G                          D G
E ------------------------------------------------------------------------------------
A ------------------------------------------------------------------------------------
D --------0----0--------------------------------------------0----0-------------------
G 4--------------4-----2------4-----0-------2--------4-------------------4---2-0------
  South Australia 'round Cape Horn, we're bound for South Australia!
```

Chorus

```
  C                  G                  C         G      C        G
E ------------------------------------------------------------------------------------
A ------------------------------------------------------------------------------------
D 5----5-2----5----2--0------0--------2--------0-0-----2-----0-0---------------------
G ------------------------------------------------------------------------------------
  Haul a-way you rolling kings, heave a-way, haul a-way;

  C                       G                                               D   G
E ------------------------------------------------------------------------------------
A ------------------------------------------------------------------------------------
D 5----5-2----5---------2-----0--0-----------------------0----0-----------------------
G ----------------------------------------2------4-------------------4---2---0--------
  Haul a-way you'll hear me sing, we're bound for South Australia!
```

Chord Forms

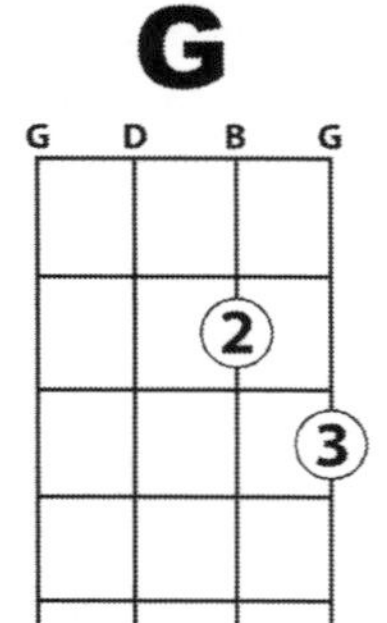

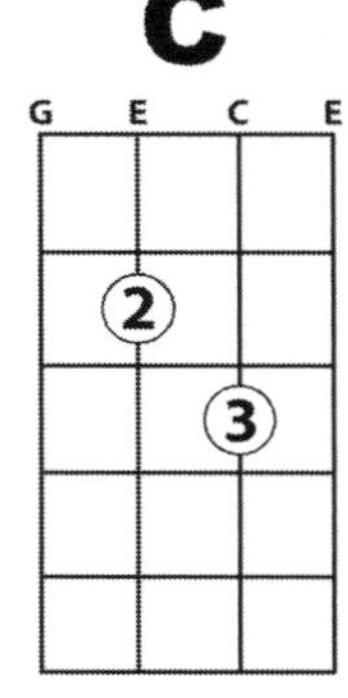

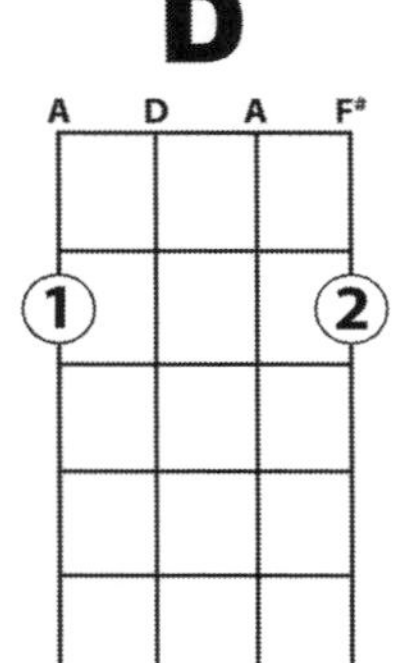

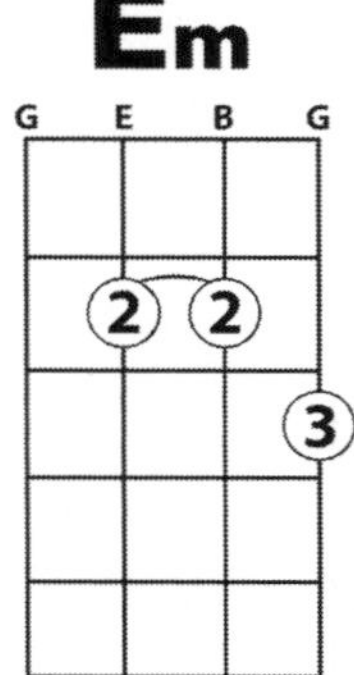

South Australia (continued)

Melody & Chords

Key of G (Low)

```
  G                    C     G     C        G    C      G
E ---------------------------------------------------------------------
A ---------------------------------------------------------------------
D 0--------0---0-0---2-0---0------2------0-0----2----0-0---------------
G 0-4------0---4-4---5-5---0------5------5-0----5----5-0---------------
  In South Australia I was born, heave a-way, haul a-way;
```

```
                  D          Em         G                    D G
E ---------------------------------------------------------------------
A ---------------------------------------------------------------------
D -------0---0-------0----------2----------0-----0---0-------------5---
G 4------0---0-4-----2----4-----0-----2----4-----0---0-------4---2-0---
  South Australia 'round Cape Horn, we're bound for South Australia!
```

CHORUS

```
  C               G              C        G    C      G
E ---------------------------------------------------------------------
A ---------------------------------------------------------------------
D 5----5-2---5---2-0-----0-------2------0-0----2-----0-0---------------
G 5----5-5---5---0-0-----0-------5------0-0----5-----5-0---------------
  Haul a-way you rolling kings, heave a-way, haul a-way;
```

```
  C                G                                        D  G
E ---------------------------------------------------------------------
A ---------------------------------------------------------------------
D 5----5-2---5-------2----0-0------------------0---0-----0--0--5-------
G 5----5-5---5-------0----0-0-----2------4-----0---0-----4--2--0-------
  Haul a-way you'll hear me sing, we're bound for South Australia!
```

Chord Forms

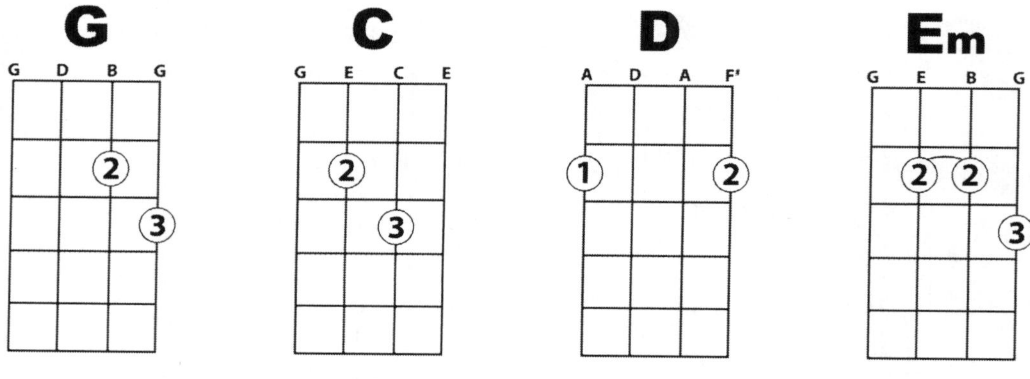

South Australia (continued)

Basic Melody

Key of G (High)

```
   G                                    C     G       C            G       C         G
E -------------------------------------0-------------0--------------------0--------------------------
A 5--2--------5----5-5-------5----5--------------------5-5--------------5-5----------
D --------------------------------------------------------------------------------------------------
G --------------------------------------------------------------------------------------------------
  In South Australia I was born, heave a-way, haul a-way;
```

```
                        D             Em              G                        D G
E --------------------------------------------------------------------------------------------------
A 2-------5----5-2------0-------2--------------0-------2--------5----5------2----0--------------
D -------------------------------------5-------------------------------------------------5------
G --------------------------------------------------------------------------------------------------
  South Australia 'round Cape Horn, we're bound for South Australia!
```

CHORUS

```
  C                   G                     C          G       C        G
E 3------3-0----3----0----------------------0----------------0------------------------------
A -------------------------5------5----------------5-5---------------5-5------------------
D --------------------------------------------------------------------------------------------
G --------------------------------------------------------------------------------------------
  Haul a-way you rolling kings, heave a-way, haul a-way;
```

```
  C                      G                                              D    G
E 3------3-0----3-------0-----------------------------------------------------------------
A ------------------------------5---5--------0--------2--------5----5------2---0-----------
D -------------------------------------------------------------------------------------5------
G -----------------------------------------------------------------------------------------
  Haul a-way you'll hear me sing, we're bound for South Australia!
```

Chord Forms

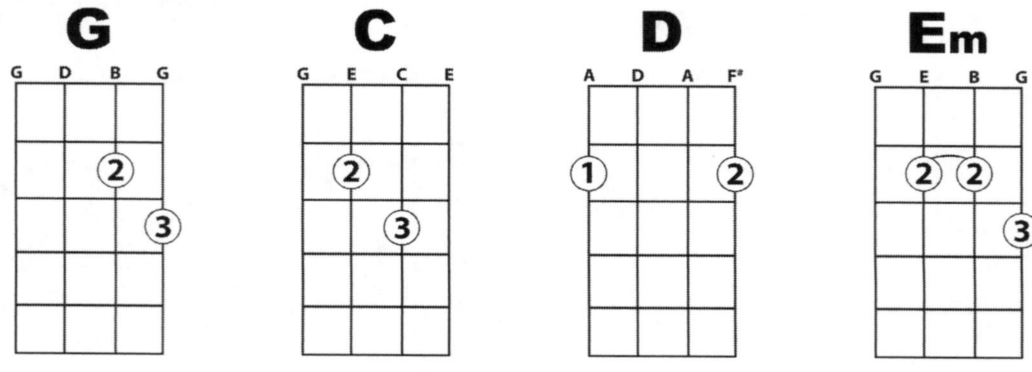

South Australia (continued)

Melody & Chords

Key of G (High)

```
  G                             C       G       C        G      C      G
E ------------------------------0---------------0-----------------0----------------------
A 5—2-------5----5—5----3—5-----5---------------3--------5—5------3------5—5-------------
D 0—0-------0----0—0----2—2-----0---------------2--------2—0------2------2—0-------------
G 0—0-------------0-------------0------------------------0---------------0---------------
  In South Australia I was born, heave a-way, haul a-way;
```

```
                         D         Em           G                            D G
E ---------------------------------------------------------------------------------------
A 2------5----5—2-------0-------2-------------0-------2-------5----5-------2----0--------
D 0------0----0—0-------0-------0------5------2-------0-------0----0-------0----0—5------
G 0-----------0---------2--------------4--------------0-------------0-----------2—0------
  South Australia 'round Cape Horn, we're bound for South Australia!
```

Chorus

```
  C               G                     C        G      C      G
E 3------3—0----3---0-------------------0-----------------0----------------------------
A 3------3—3----3---2—5--------5--------3--------5—5------3------5—5-------------------
D 2------2----------0—0--------0--------2--------2—0------2------2—0-------------------
G ------------------------------0-----------------0---------------0--------------------
  Haul a-way you rolling kings, heave a-way, haul a-way;
```

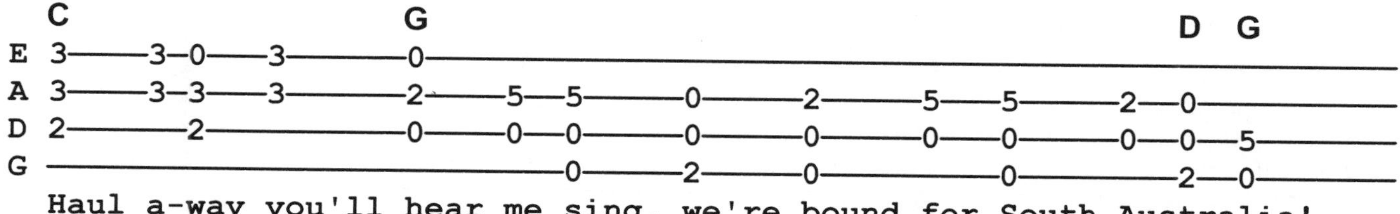

Chord Forms

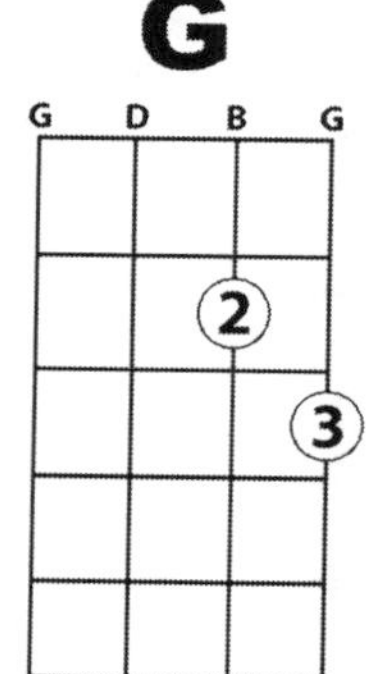

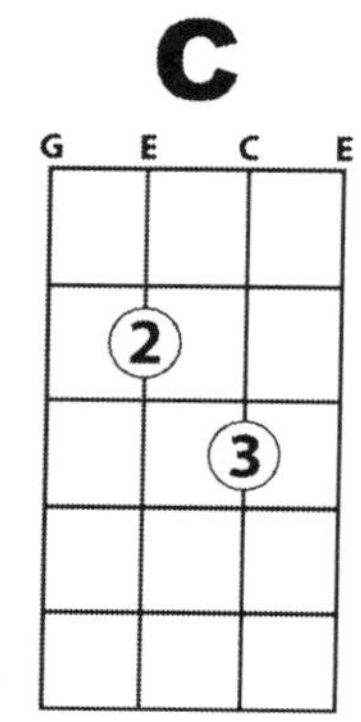

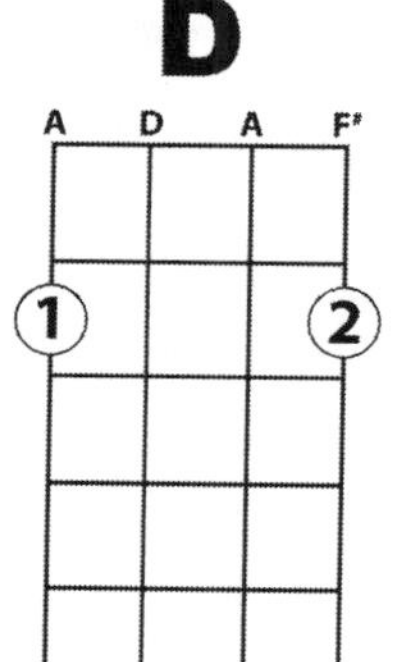

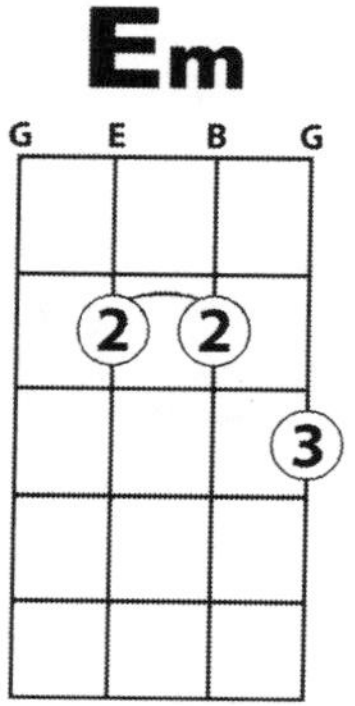

Spanish Ladies

Basic Melody

Key of A Minor

Words and Music

Traditional

This is another traditional British naval song, sung not just by the British but also the Irish, Scottish and other nationalities that sailed on their ships. The lyrics of the song roughly describe a voyage on a naval ship from Spain to the shore of England, off of Kent.

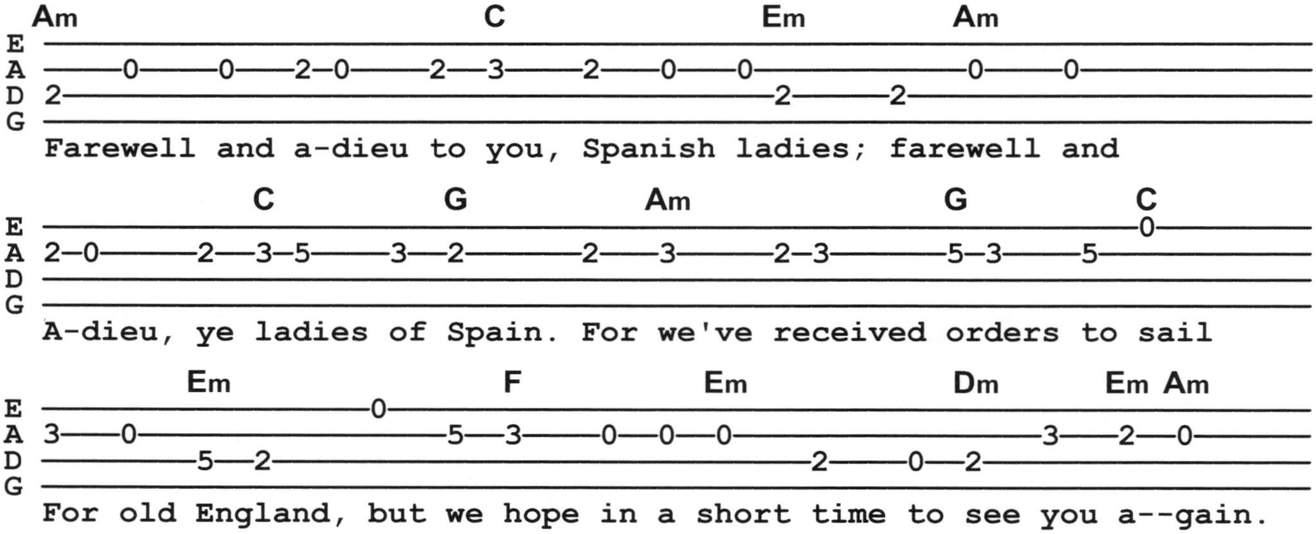

```
   Am                         C                Em         Am
E ----------------------------------------------------------------------------
A -----0-----0----2-0-----2---3-----2----0----0-----------0-----0-------------
D 2-------------------------------------------------2------2------------------
G ----------------------------------------------------------------------------
  Farewell and a-dieu to you, Spanish ladies; farewell and
```

```
             C           G           Am                   G         C
E ----------------------------------------------------------------0-----------
A 2-0-------2---3-5-----3---2-------2----3------2-3-------5-3-----5-----------
D ----------------------------------------------------------------------------
G ----------------------------------------------------------------------------
  A-dieu, ye ladies of Spain. For we've received orders to sail
```

```
          Em                   F          Em             Dm        Em  Am
E -----------------------0----------------------------------------------------
A 3---0-------------------5---3----0--0---0-----------------3----2---0--------
D ------------5---2--------------------------------2-----0--2-----------------
G ----------------------------------------------------------------------------
  For old England, but we hope in a short time to see you a--gain.
```

CHORUS

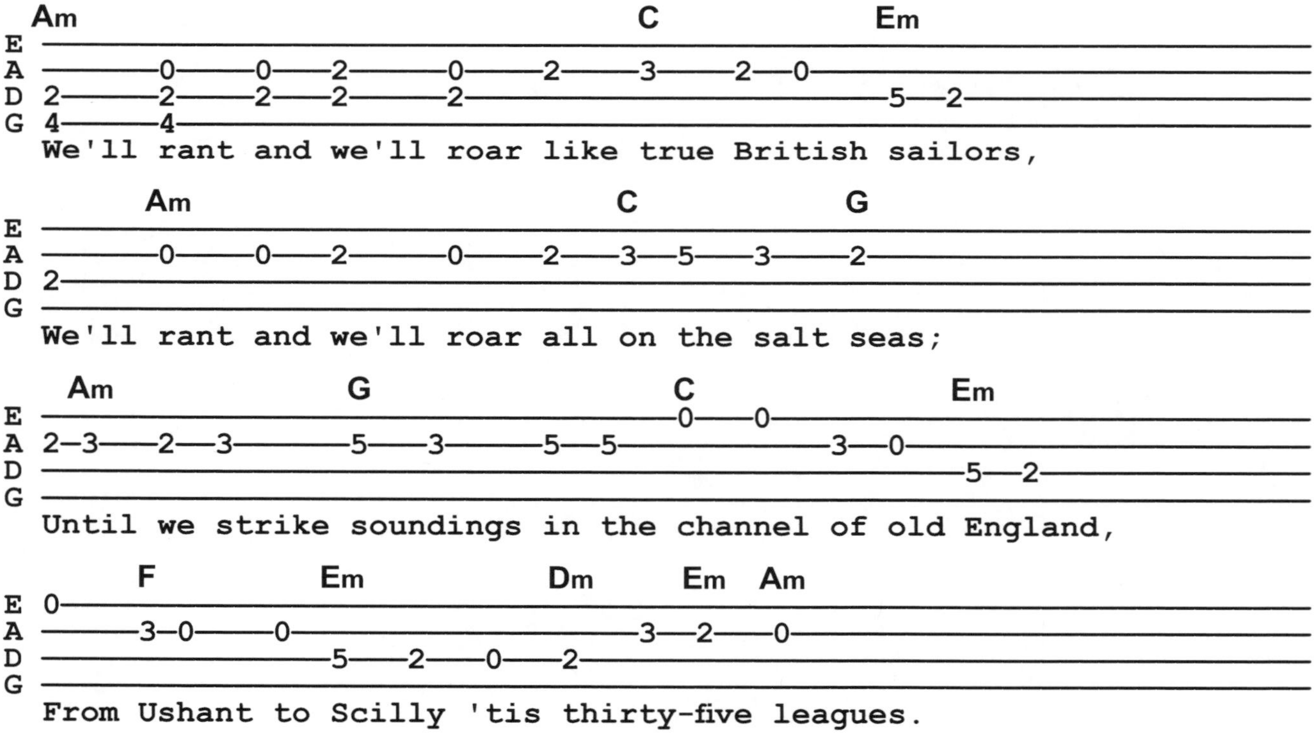

```
   Am                                   C            Em
E ----------------------------------------------------------------------------
A ------0------0-----2------0-----2-----3-----2---0---------------------------
D 2-----2------2-----2------2-----------------------------5---2---------------
G 4-----4---------------------------------------------------------------------
  We'll rant and we'll roar like true British sailors,
```

```
        Am                             C          G
E ----------------------------------------------------------------------------
A ------0------0----2------0-----2----3---5----3------2-----------------------
D 2---------------------------------------------------------------------------
G ----------------------------------------------------------------------------
  We'll rant and we'll roar all on the salt seas;
```

```
    Am            G                   C                 Em
E ------------------------------------0----0----------------------------------
A 2-3----2--3-----5----3-----5--5------------------3---0----------------------
D -----------------------------------------------------------5---2------------
G ----------------------------------------------------------------------------
  Until we strike soundings in the channel of old England,
```

```
        F          Em          Dm       Em  Am
E 0---------------------------------------------------------------------------
A ------3-0-----0------------------3---2---0----------------------------------
D ----------------5----2----0----2--------------------------------------------
G ----------------------------------------------------------------------------
  From Ushant to Scilly 'tis thirty-five leagues.
```

See Chord Forms and Additional Verses on Next Page

Spanish Ladies (continued)

Chord Forms and Additional Verses

Chord Forms

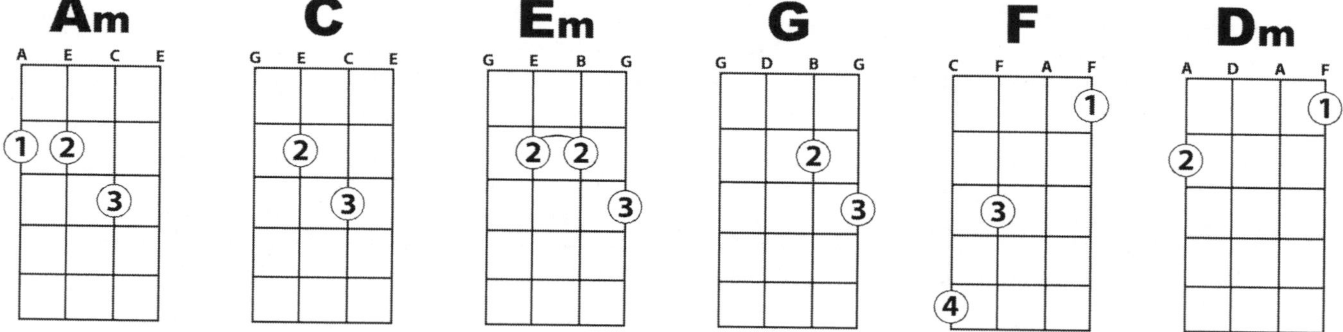

Additional Verses

We hove our ship to, with the wind at sou'west boys,
Then we hove our ship to, for to strike soundings clear;
'Twas forty-five fathoms with a white sandy bottom,
So we squared our main yard, and up the channel did make.

So the first land we made, it is called the Deadman,
Next Ram Head, off Plymouth, Start, Portland and Wight;
We sailed by Beachy, by Fairly and Dungeness,
And then bore away for the South Foreland light.

Then the signal was made for the grand fleet to anchor,
All in the Downs that night for to lie;
Let go your shank painter, let go your cat stopper,
Haul up your clewgarnets, let tack and sheets fly.

Now let every man drink off his full bumper,
And let every man drink off his full glass;
We'll drink and be jolly, and drown melancholy,
And here's to the health of each true-hearted lass!

Melody & Chords

Key of A Minor

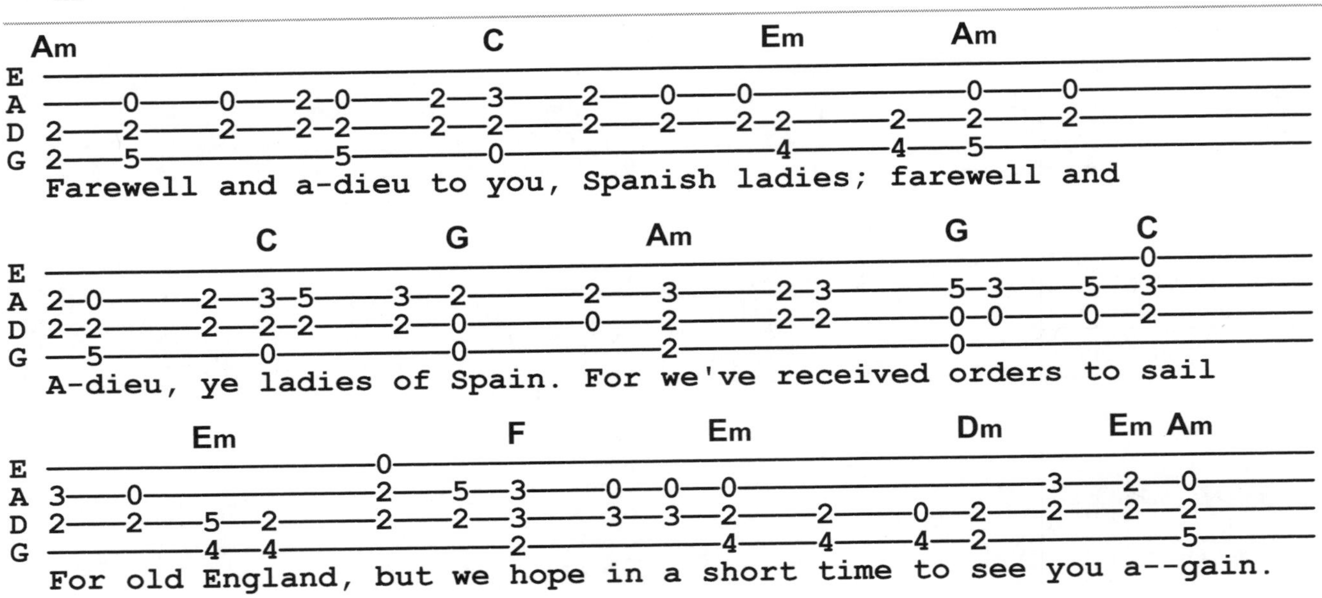

Spanish Ladies (continued)

```
  Am                           C                 Em          Am
E ---------------------------------------------------------------------
A -----0-----0----2-0-----2---3-----2----0----0-------------0----0-----
D 2----2-----2----2-2-----2---2-----2----2----2-2-----2-----2----2-----
G 2----5----------5-----------0---------------------4-----4-----5------
  Farewell and a-dieu to you, Spanish ladies; farewell and

             C        G          Am              G          C
E ------------------------------------------------------------0--------
A 2-0-------2--3-5-----3--2-------2---3-------2-3-------5-3------5--3--
D 2-2-------2--2-2-----2--0-------0---2-------2-2-------0-0------0--2--
G --5----------0----------0-----------2-----------------0--------------
  A-dieu, ye ladies of Spain. For we've received orders to sail

         Em               F          Em              Dm         Em Am
E ------------------0--------------------------------------------------
A 3---0-------------2---5---3-----0---0---0------------------3---2---0-
D 2---2---5---2-----2---2---3-----3---3---2-----2-----0---2--2---2---2-
G ------------4---4-----------2-----------4-----4-----4---2----------5-
  For old England, but we hope in a short time to see you a--gain.
```

Chorus

```
  Am                                C             Em
E ---------------------------------------------------------------
A -------0----0----2------0----2----3-----2--0-------------------
D 2------2----2----2------2----2----2-----2--2-----5---2---------
G 2------5----------------5---------0--------------4---4---------
  We'll rant and we'll roar like true British sailors,

       Am                         C           G
E ---------------------------------------------------------------
A -------0----0----2------0----2----3----5----3----2-------------
D 2------2----2----2------2----2----2----2----2----0-------------
G 4------5----------------5---------0--------------0-------------
  We'll rant and we'll roar all on the salt seas;

    Am              G                C                Em
E -------------------------------------0----0--------------------
A 2-3---2---3-------5----3------5--5---3----3----3---0-----------
D 0-2---2---2-------0----0------0--0---2---------2---2----5---2--
G 0-2---------------0----------------------------0--------4---4--
  Until we strike soundings in the channel of old England,

         F          Em          Dm       Em    Am
E 0--------------------------------------------------------------
A 2------3-0-----0-------------------3---2----0------------------
D 2------3-3-----3---5----2----0---2-3---2----2------------------
G -------5-----------4----4----4---2-2---4----2------------------
  From Ushant to Scilly 'tis thirty-five leagues.
```

See Chord Forms on Next Page

Spanish Ladies (continued)

Chord Forms (Key of A Minor)

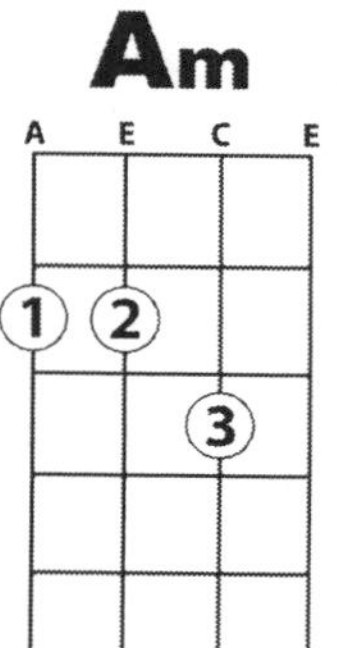

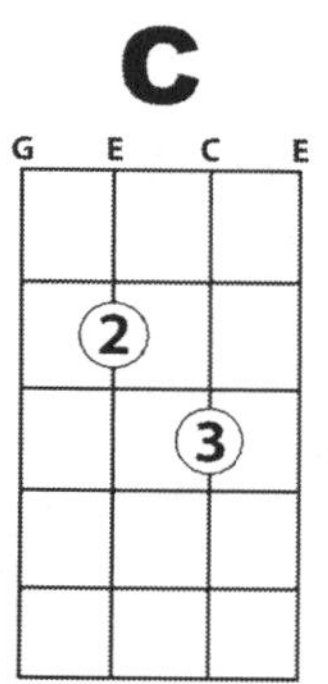

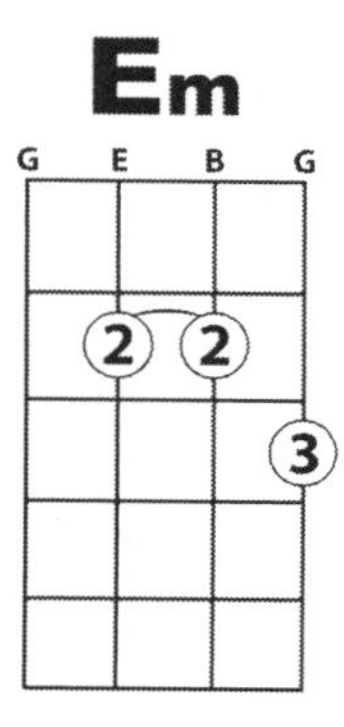

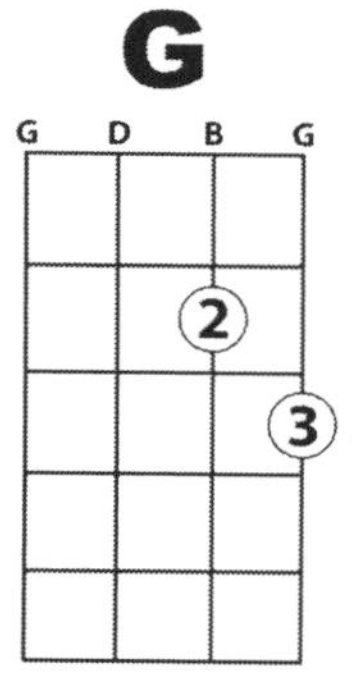

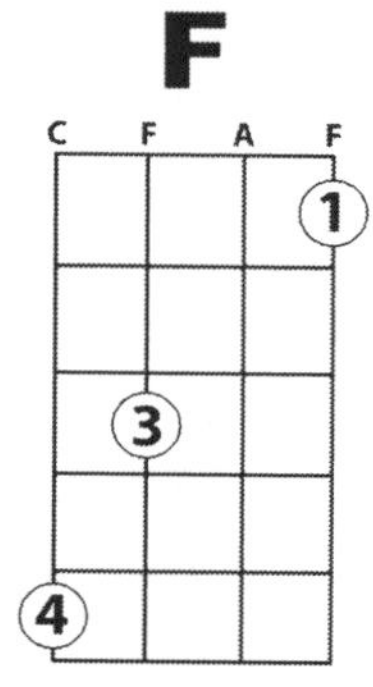

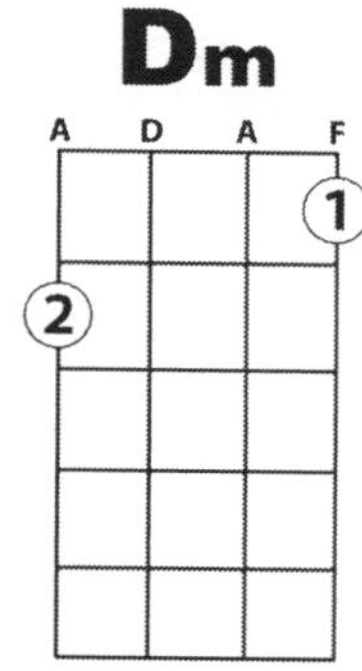

Chord Forms (Key of E Minor)

See Arrangements on Following Pages

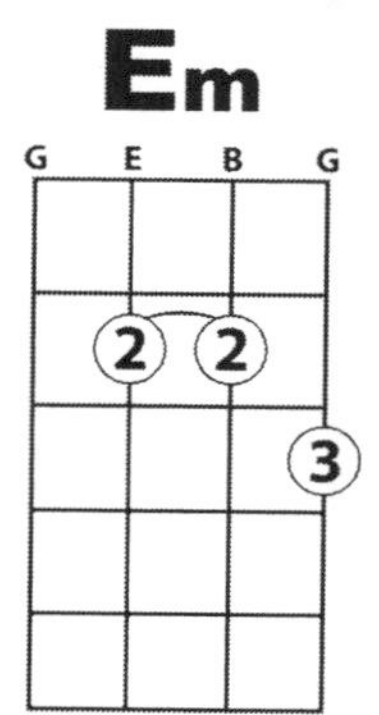

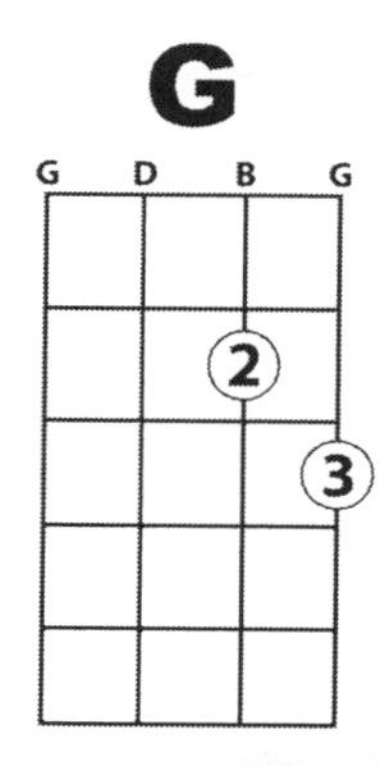

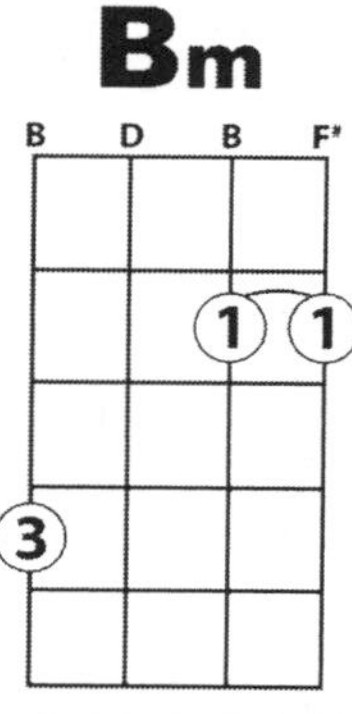

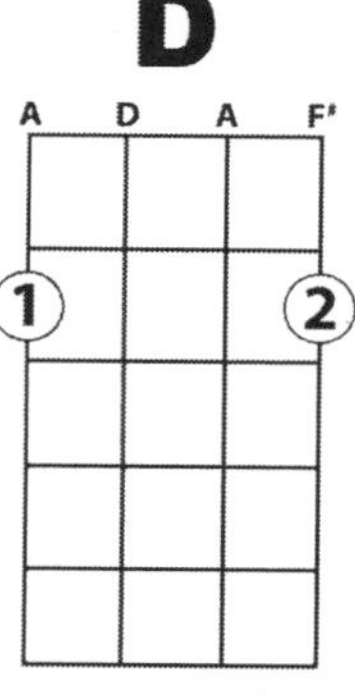

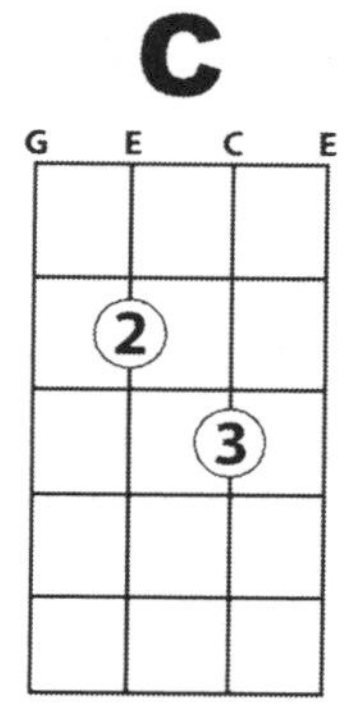

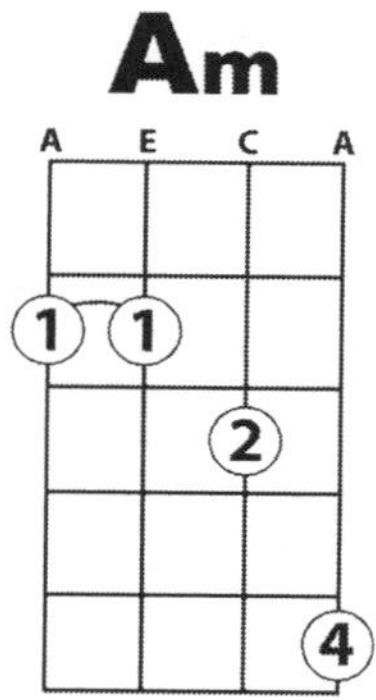

"The Clipper Ship Flying Cloud off the Needles, Isle of Wight
by James E. Buttersworth, 1859-60

Spanish Ladies (continued)

Basic Melody

Key of E Minor (Low)

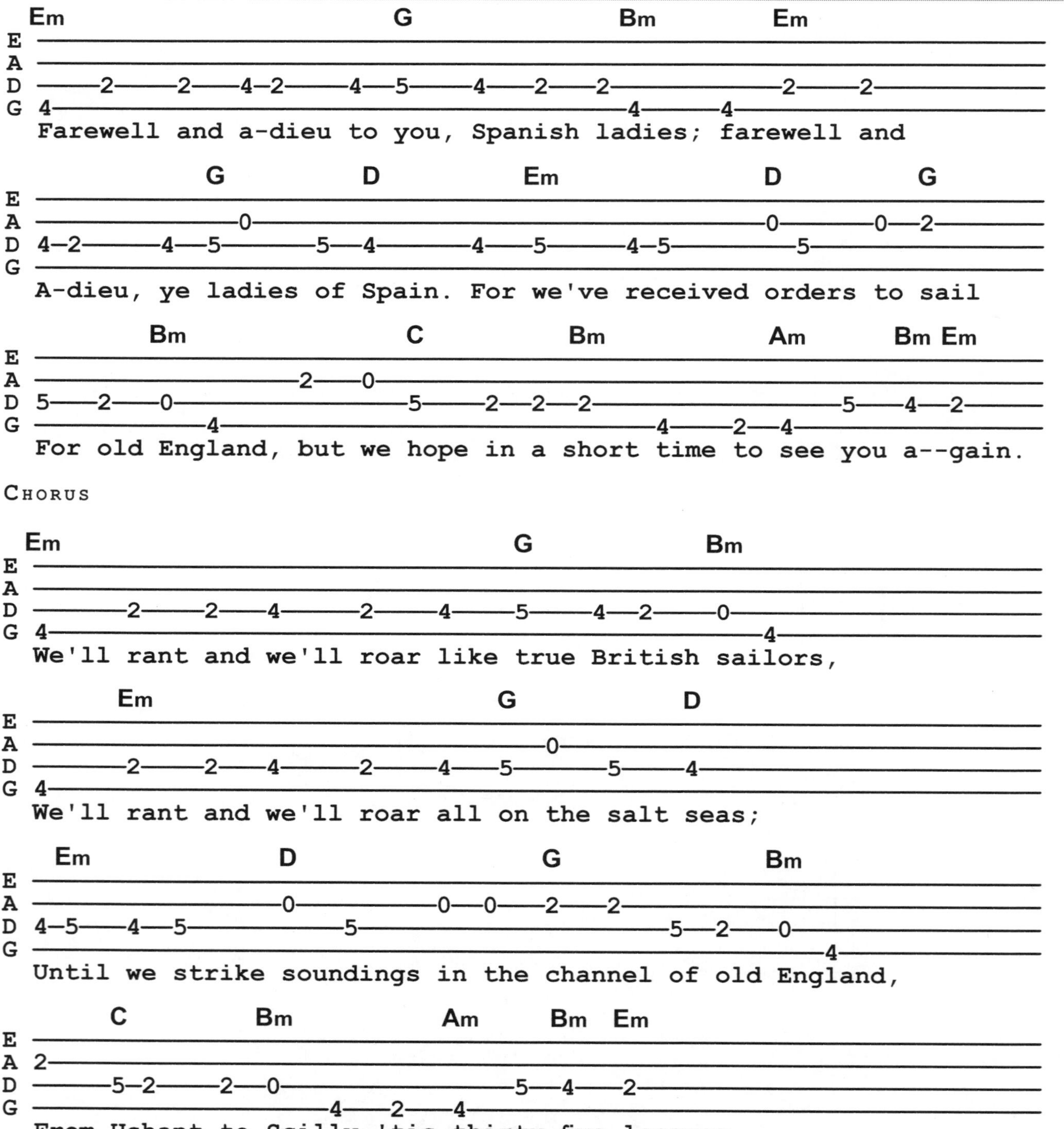

See Chord Forms on Previous Page

Spanish Ladies (continued)

Melody & Chords

Key of E Minor (Low)

See Chord Forms Two Pages Previous

Spanish Ladies (continued)

Basic Melody

Key of E Minor (High)

```
 Em                                      G                      Bm                Em
E ------0------0-----2--0------2---3------2-----0-----0------------------0------0-----------
A 2--------------------------------------------------------2-------2------------------------
D ------------------------------------------------------------------------------------------
G ------------------------------------------------------------------------------------------
  Farewell and a-dieu to you, Spanish ladies; farewell and
```

```
                  G            D               Em                      D          G
E 2--0-------2---3--5------3---2----------2----3--------2--3----------5--3-------5---7------
A ------------------------------------------------------------------------------------------
D ------------------------------------------------------------------------------------------
G ------------------------------------------------------------------------------------------
  A-dieu, ye ladies of Spain. For we've received orders to sail
```

```
               Bm                         C               Bm                   Am        Bm  Em
E 3-----0--------------------7-----5-----3------0----0----0-------------------------3----2----0------
A ----------------5----2-------------------------------------------2------0---2----------------------
D ---------------------------------------------------------------------------------------------------
G ---------------------------------------------------------------------------------------------------
  For old England, but we hope in a short time to see you a--gain.
```

Chorus

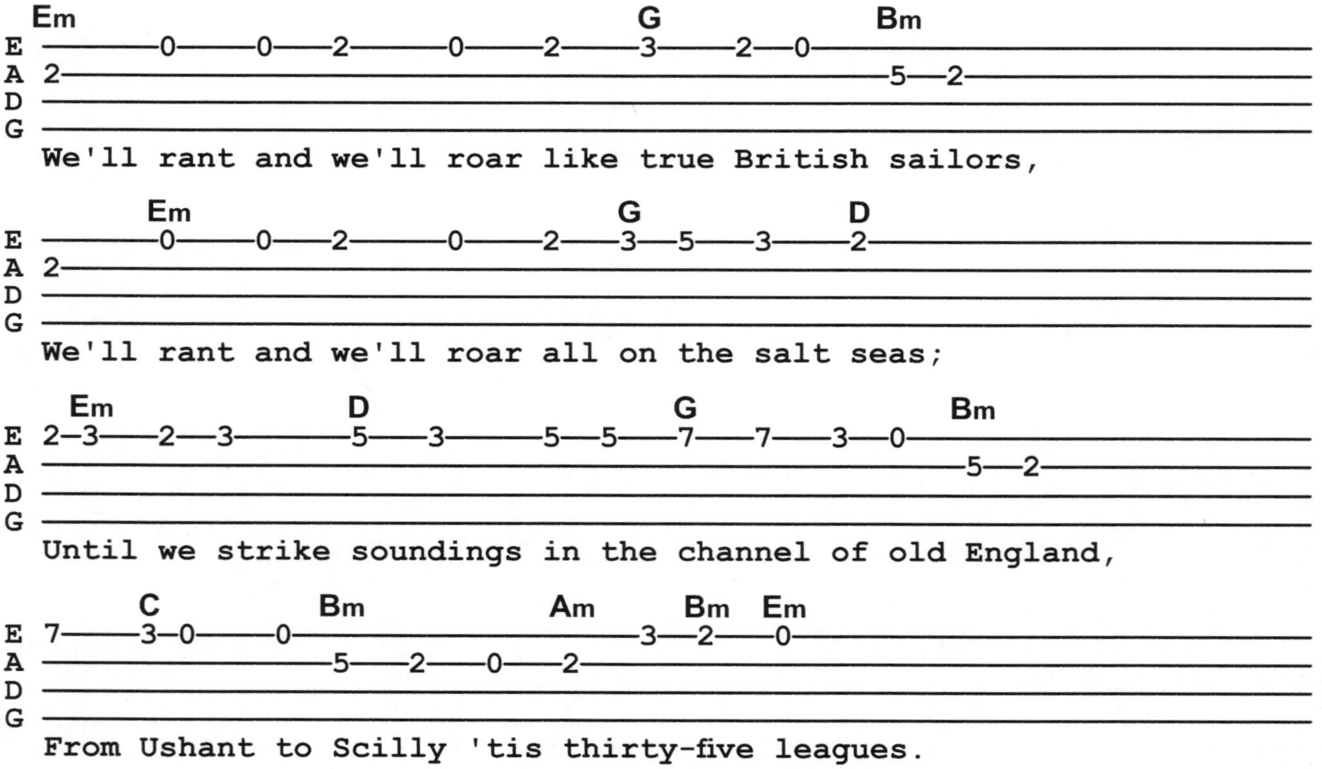

```
 Em                                               G                     Bm
E -------0------0----2--------0-------2-----3------2---0--------------------------------
A 2-------------------------------------------------------------5----2------------------
D --------------------------------------------------------------------------------------
G --------------------------------------------------------------------------------------
  We'll rant and we'll roar like true British sailors,
```

```
          Em                                    G               D
E -------0------0----2--------0-------2-----3----5------3-------2---------------------------
A 2-----------------------------------------------------------------------------------------
D -------------------------------------------------------------------------------------------
G -------------------------------------------------------------------------------------------
  We'll rant and we'll roar all on the salt seas;
```

```
   Em                   D                      G                            Bm
E 2--3-----2----3----------5------3--------5----5----7------7------3----0-----------------------
A ----------------------------------------------------------------------------5-----2-----------
D ----------------------------------------------------------------------------------------------
G ----------------------------------------------------------------------------------------------
  Until we strike soundings in the channel of old England,
```

```
        C           Bm            Am       Bm   Em
E 7-----3--0------0-------------------------3----2------0-----------------------------------
A -------------------5------2------0------2-------------------------------------------------
D ------------------------------------------------------------------------------------------
G ------------------------------------------------------------------------------------------
  From Ushant to Scilly 'tis thirty-five leagues.
```

See Chord Forms Three Pages Previous

Spanish Ladies (continued)

Basic Melody

Key of E Minor (High)

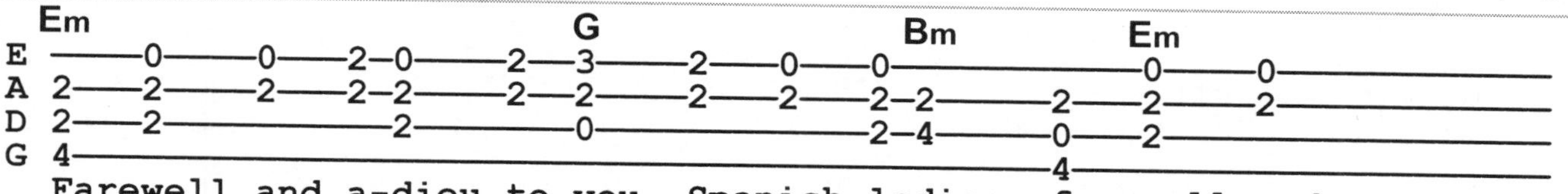

Farewell and a-dieu to you, Spanish ladies; farewell and

```
         G           D           Em             D       G
E 2-0---2-3-5---3-2---------2-3------2-3------5-3----5-7--
A 2-2---2-2-2---2-0---------0-2------2-2------0-0----0-5--
D --2-----0-------0---------0-2---------------0--------5--
G ---------------------------------------------------------
```

A-dieu, ye ladies of Spain. For we've received orders to sail

```
         Bm             C            Bm               Am       Bm Em
E 3--0-------------7--5--3----0--0--0------------------------3--2--0--
A 2--2--5--2-------5--5--3----3--3--2------2------0--2------3--2--2--
D -------4--0------4-----2----------4------4------4--2-----------2--
G ------------4------------------------------------------5-----------
```

For old England, but we hope in a short time to see you a--gain.

CHORUS

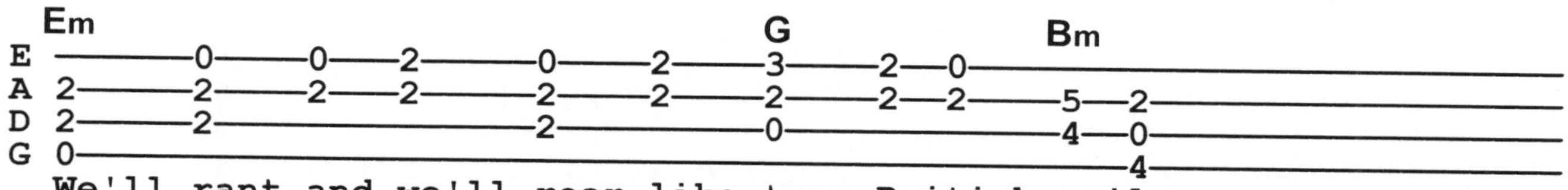

We'll rant and we'll roar like true British sailors,

```
        Em                          G           D
E ------0----0--2-----0---2---3--5---3---2---
A 2-----2----2--2-----2---2---2--0---0---0---
D 0-----2-------------2-------0----------0---
G 4------------------------------------------
```

We'll rant and we'll roar all on the salt seas;

```
   Em              D                    G                   Bm
E 2-3--2--3--------5--3-------5--5--7---7--3--0-----------------
A 0-2--2--2--------0--0-------0--0--5---5--2--2----5--2---------
D 0-2--------------0----------------5--------------4--0---------
G -------------------------------------------------------0------
```

Until we strike soundings in the channel of old England,

```
      C          Bm             Am      Bm  Em
E 7---3-0---0-------------------3---2---0---
A 5---3-3---3--5--2--0--2-------3---2---2---
D 4---2--------4--0--0--2-----------------2---
G --------------------4--5------------------
```

From Ushant to Scilly 'tis thirty-five leagues.

See Chord Forms Four Pages Previous

Three Score and Ten (page 1)

Basic Melody

Key of C (Low)

The words of this song were written as a poem by William Delf, in memory of the English fishermen who lost their lives in a gale in 1889. Later the words were set to music, and some of the verses changed, to create this great old folk song that has been recorded by a number of performers over the years, including The Dubliners.

Words by William Delf

Music Traditional

```
  C                                Em                F        C
E ------------------------------------------------------------------------
A ----------------------------------0-------------------------------------
D 5-2------2-2---0-2----5---5-----5-----------5-------------0-2-----------
G -----------------------------------------------------5------------------
  Methinks I see a host of craft spreading their sails a-lee,

     F              C                                                  G
E ------------------------------------------------------------------------
A ------------------------------------------------------------------------
D 5--5----3---3--3---3-----2-0-2-----------2--5------5---5---3--2-----0----
G ----------------------------------5--------------------------------------
  As down the Humber they d-o glide a-ll bound for the Northern Sea.

    C                                           Em        F         C
E ------------------------------------------------------------------------
A ------------------------------------------0-----------------------------
D 5-2-------2-2---0--2----5------5------5------5-----------0--2-----------
G ----------------------------------------------------5-------------------
  Methinks I see on each small craft a crew with hearts so brave,

                  F          G7             C      G7       C
E ------------------------------------------------------------------------
A ----------------0---------------2--2-----0------------------------------
D 5-5---5---5----------5-----5-------------------5--3---2--0--------------
G ------------------------------------------------------------5-----------
  Going out to earn their daily bread upon the restless wave.
```

Chord Forms

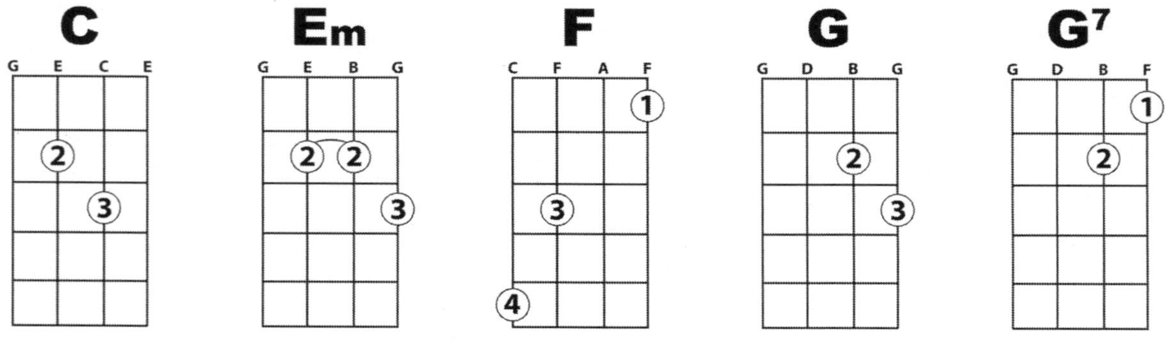

Three Score and Ten (page 2)

Basic Melody

Key of C (Low)

CHORUS

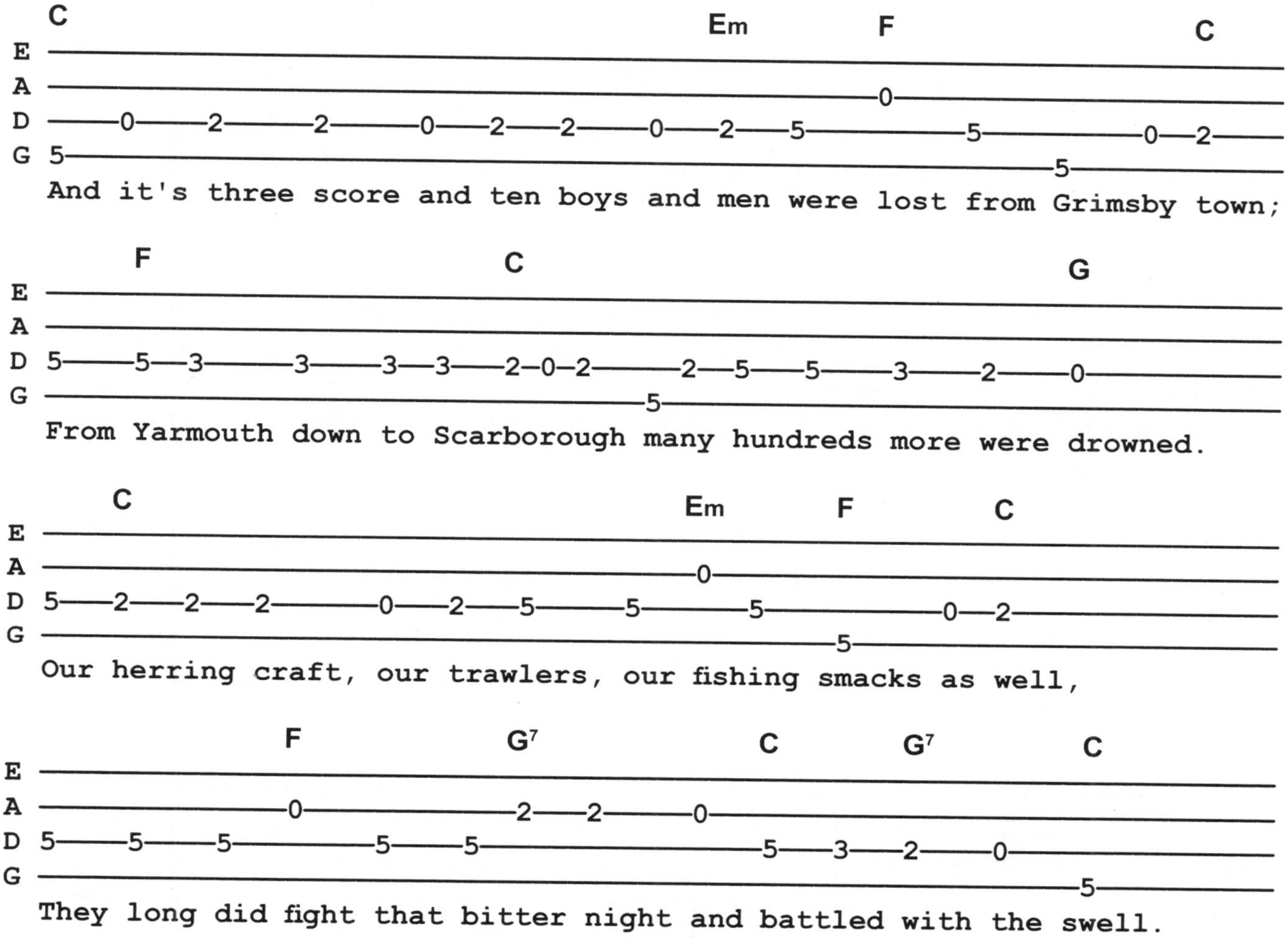

```
  C                                    Em       F                  C
E ------------------------------------------------------------------------
A -------------------------------------------------0----------------------
D ---0----2-----2-----0---2---2----0---2---5--------------5-----------0--2-
G 5-------------------------------------------------------------5---------
  And it's three score and ten boys and men were lost from Grimsby town;
```

```
      F                C                                G
E ------------------------------------------------------------------------
A ------------------------------------------------------------------------
D 5----5--3------3-----3--3---2-0-2------2--5---5----3-----2----0---------
G ----------------------------------5-------------------------------------
  From Yarmouth down to Scarborough many hundreds more were drowned.
```

```
     C                                 Em       F        C
E ------------------------------------------------------------------------
A ---------------------------------------0--------------------------------
D 5---2---2---2-------0---2---5-----5--------5----------0--2--------------
G -----------------------------------------------5------------------------
  Our herring craft, our trawlers, our fishing smacks as well,
```

```
                 F          G7          C      G7       C
E ------------------------------------------------------------------------
A ---------------0-----------2---2-----0----------------------------------
D 5----5----5-------5----5----------------5---3---2----0------------------
G ------------------------------------------------------------5-----------
  They long did fight that bitter night and battled with the swell.
```

Additional Verses

Me thinks I see them yet again,
As they leave this land behind;
Casting their nets into the sea,
The herring shoals to find.
Me thinks I see them yet again,
And all on board's a-right,
Their sails close-reefed, their decks all cleaned,
And their side-lights burning bright.

October's night brought such a sight,
'Twas never seen before,
There were masts and yards and broken spars,
Washed up upon the shore.
There was many a heart of sorrow,
There was many a heart so brave,
There was many a true and noble lad
To find a watery grave.

Three Score and Ten
(continued - page 1)

Melody & Chords

Key of C (Low)

```
   C                                  Em                 F        C
E ------------------------------------------------------------------------------
A ----------------------------------------0-------------------------------------
D 5-2--------2-2---0-2-----5---5------5-----2----5-----------------0-2----------
G 5-5--------5-5---5-5-----5---5------4-----4----4-------5---------2-5----------
  Methinks I see a host of craft spreading their sails a-lee,
```

```
      F                 C                                                 G
E ------------------------------------------------------------------------------
A ------------------------------------------------------------------------------
D 5--5----3----3--3----3------2-0-2--------2--5------5---5---3--2-------0-------
G 5--5----2----2--2----5------5-5-5-----5-5--5------5---5---5--5-------0-------
  As down the Humber they d-o glide a-ll bound for the Northern Sea.
```

```
     C                                     Em          F          C
E ------------------------------------------------------------------------------
A -----------------------------------------0------------------------------------
D 5-2--------2-2---0--2----5------5-----5-2------5------------------0--2--------
G 0-5--------5-5---5--5----5------5-----5-4------4-------5----------2--5--------
  Methinks I see on each small craft a crew with hearts so brave,
```

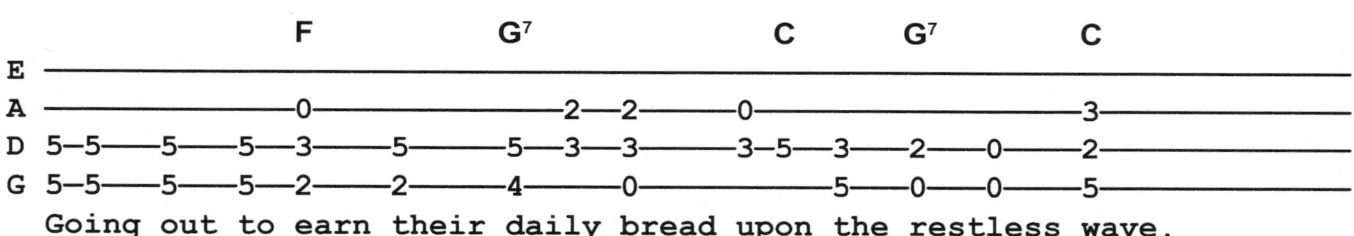

Chord Forms

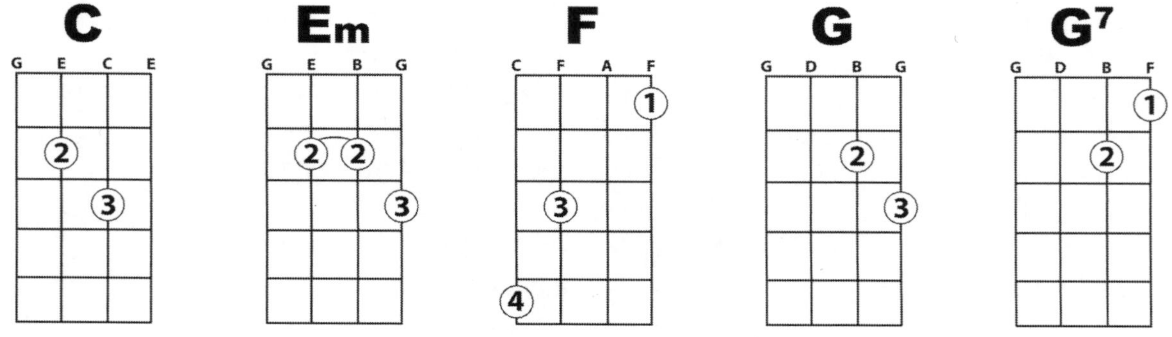

Three Score and Ten
(continued - page 2)

Melody & Chords

Key of C (Low)

CHORUS

```
   C                                      Em       F                 C
E ---------------------------------------------------------------------
A -------------------------------------------------0-------------------
D ---0----2----2----0---2---2----0---2---5----3----5-------------0--2--
G 5--0----5----5----0---5---5----0---4---4----2----2-----5-------2--5--
  And it's three score and ten boys and men were lost from Grimsby town;

       F                   C                              G
E ---------------------------------------------------------------------
A ---------------------------------------------------------------------
D 5----5--3-----3----3--3--2-0-2----2--5---5----3----2----0------------
G 5----5--2-----2----2--2--5-5-5----5-5--5---5----5----5----0----------
  From Yarmouth down to Scarborough many hundreds more were drowned.

      C                                  Em      F       C
E ---------------------------------------------------------------------
A -------------------------------------0-------------------------------
D 5---2----2---2------0----2----5-----5--2--5------------0--2----------
G 0---5----5---5------0----5----5-----5--4--4-----5------2--5----------
  Our herring craft, our trawlers, our fishing smacks as well,

                 F          G7             C        G7         C
E ---------------------------------------------------------------------
A ---------------0----------2---2-----0--------------------3-----------
D 5----5----5----3----5----5--3---3-----3----5----3---2----0---2-------
G 5----5----5----2----5----5--0---0---------5----5---4----4---5--------
  They long did fight that bitter night and battled with the swell.
```

Three Score and Ten
(continued - page 1)

Basic Melody

Key of C (High)

```
  C                                    Em                 F        C
E 3-0-------0-0-------0----3--3--------3-----5-----3-------------0---------
A --------------------5------------------------------------3------5--------
D -------------------------------------------------------------------------
G -------------------------------------------------------------------------
```

Methinks I see a host of craft spreading their sails a-lee,

```
     F                C                                                 G
E 3--3----1---1--1----1----0----0---------0--3------3---3--1--0----------
A ------------------------------5------3-------------------------------5--
D -------------------------------------------------------------------------
G -------------------------------------------------------------------------
```

As down the Humber they d-o glide a-ll bound for the Northern Sea.

```
   C                                        Em         F          C
E 3-0-------0-0--------0----3------3-------3-5-----3-------------0-------
A ------------------5-------------------------------------3-------5--------
D -------------------------------------------------------------------------
G -------------------------------------------------------------------------
```

Methinks I see on each small craft a crew with hearts so brave,

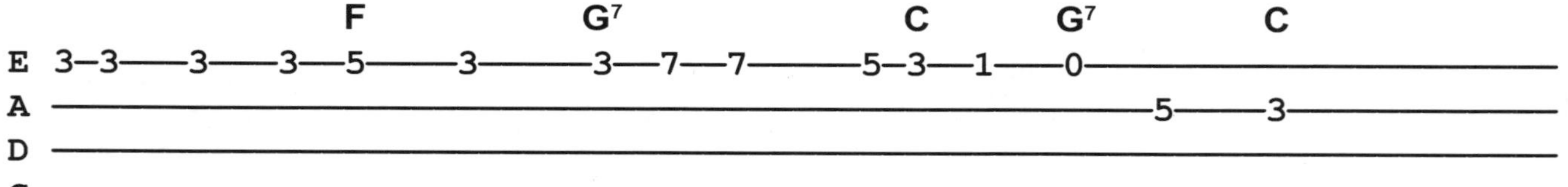

Going out to earn their daily bread upon the restless wave.

Chord Forms

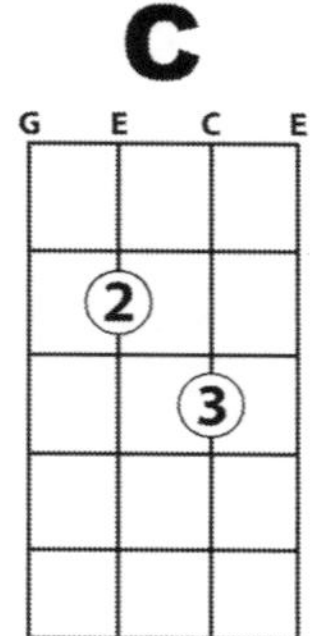

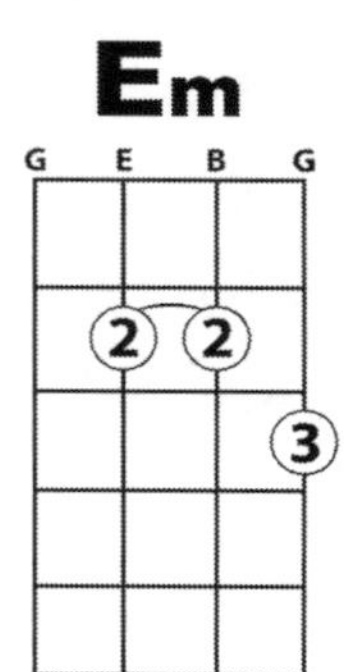

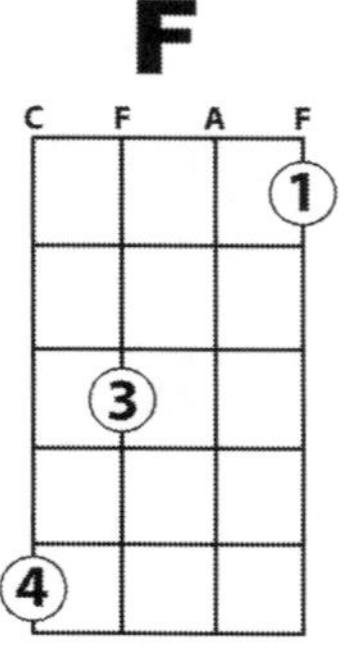

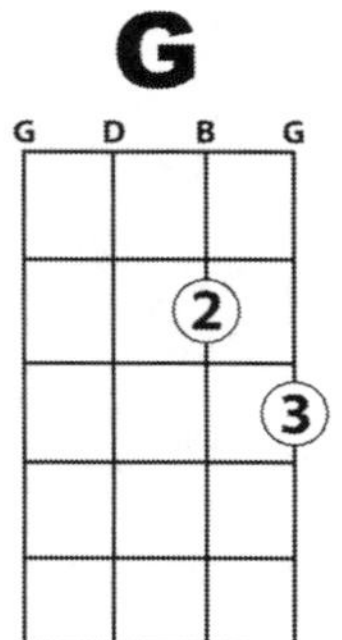

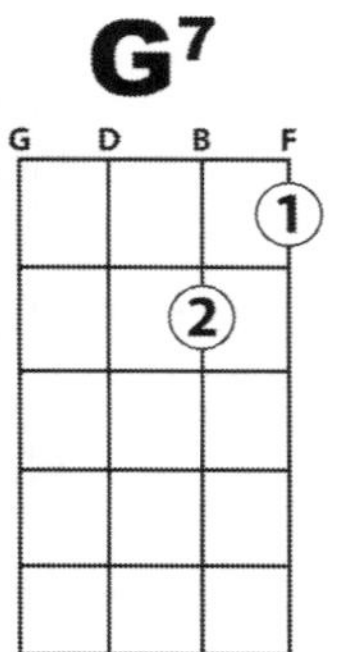

Three Score and Ten
(continued - page 2)

Basic Melody

Key of C (High)

CHORUS

```
  C                                               Em       F                  C
E ----------0------0-----------0----0---------0----3----5----3------------0---
A 3---5------------------5------------5-----------------------------3---5------
D -----------------------------------------------------------------------------
G -----------------------------------------------------------------------------
```
And it's three score and ten boys and men were lost from Grimsby town;

```
      F                C                                         G
E 3----3--1-----1----1--1--0----0------0--3---3----1----0--------------
A -------------------------------5-----3-------------------------5------
D ----------------------------------------------------------------------
G ----------------------------------------------------------------------
```
From Yarmouth down to Scarborough many hundreds more were drowned.

```
    C                                    Em      F        C
E 3---0---0---0-----------0---3-----3---5---3------------0-----
A ---------------------5------------------------3-----5---------
D --------------------------------------------------------------
G --------------------------------------------------------------
```
Our herring craft, our trawlers, our fishing smacks as well,

```
                  F            G7              C     G7           C
E 3----3----3---5----3----3---7----7-----5---3----1---0----------------
A ---------------------------------------------------------5----3-------
D ----------------------------------------------------------------------
G ----------------------------------------------------------------------
```
They long did fight that bitter night and battled with the swell.

Three Score and Ten
(continued - page 1)

Melody & Chords

Key of C (High)

```
   C                                     Em               F        C
E  3–0——————0–0——————0—————3—3—————3—————5—————3——————————————————0——————————
A  3–3——————3–3————5–3—————3—3—————2—————2—————2—————————3—————5–3——————————
D  2–2————————2————2–2———————2—————2—————————————————————3—————3–2——————————
G  ——————————————————————————————————————————————————————2———————————————————
   Methinks I see a host of craft spreading their sails a-lee,
```

```
      F                C                                                     G
E  3—3————1————1—1————1————0————0——————————0—3——————3————3————1—0————————————
A  3—0————0————0—0————3————3-5-3——————3-3—3——————3————3————3—3————————5——————
D  2—3—————————3——————2——————2-2——————2———2——————2———————————————————0——————
G  ——————————————————————————————————————————————————————————————————0——————
   As down the Humber they d-o glide a-ll bound for the Northern Sea.
```

```
     C                                        Em           F            C
E  3–0——————0–0——————0—————3——————3——————3–5——————3————————————————————0——————
A  2–3——————3–3————5———3———3——————3——————3–5——————2————3——————————5————3——————
D  0–2————————2————2———2——————————2———————————————2————3——————————3————2——————
G  ————————————————————————————————————————————————————2————————————————————————
   Methinks I see on each small craft a crew with hearts so brave,
```

```
                   F            G7                C        G7          C
E  3–3————3————3———5————3—————3————7————7————5–3————1—————0———————————————————
A  3–3————3————3———3————3—————2————5————5————5–3————3—————2—————5—————3———————
D  2——————2————————3——————————0—————————5————————2————————0—————3—————2———————
G  ———————————————————————————————————————————————————————————————————0———————
   Going out to earn their daily bread upon the restless wave.
```

Chord Forms

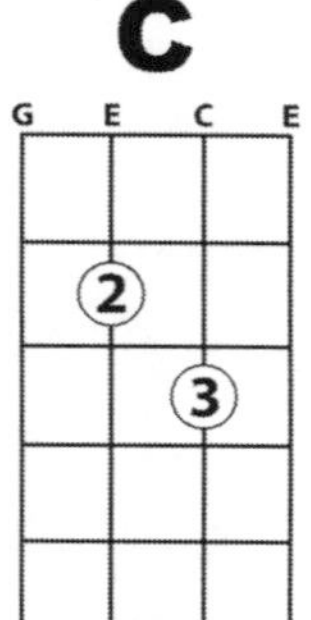

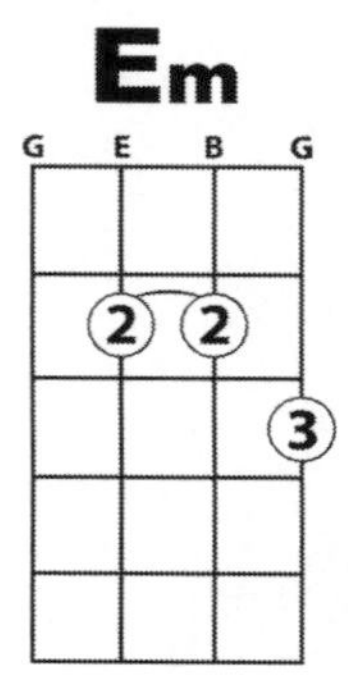

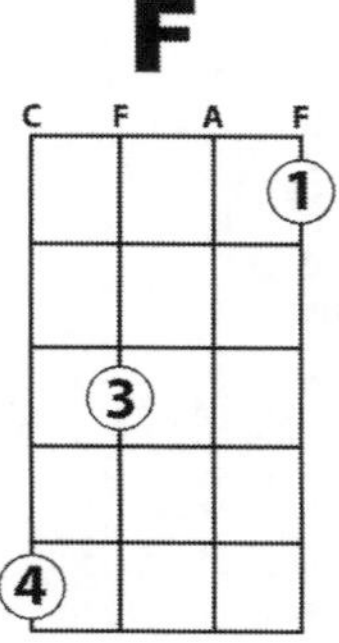

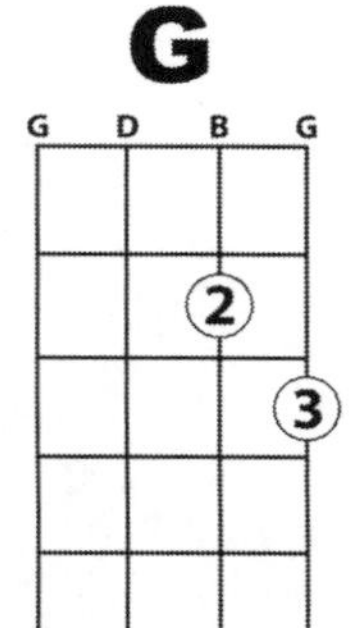

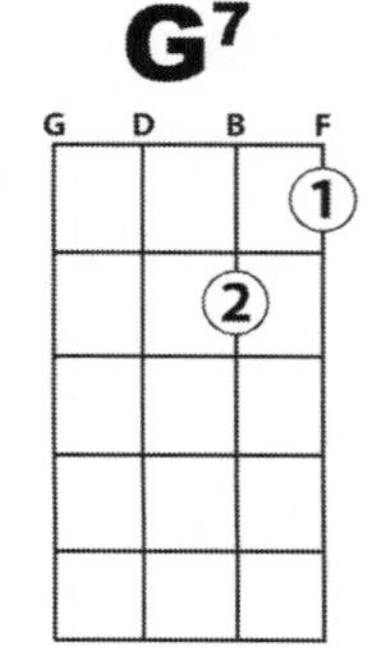

Three Score and Ten
(continued - page 2)

Melody & Chords

Key of C (High)

Chorus

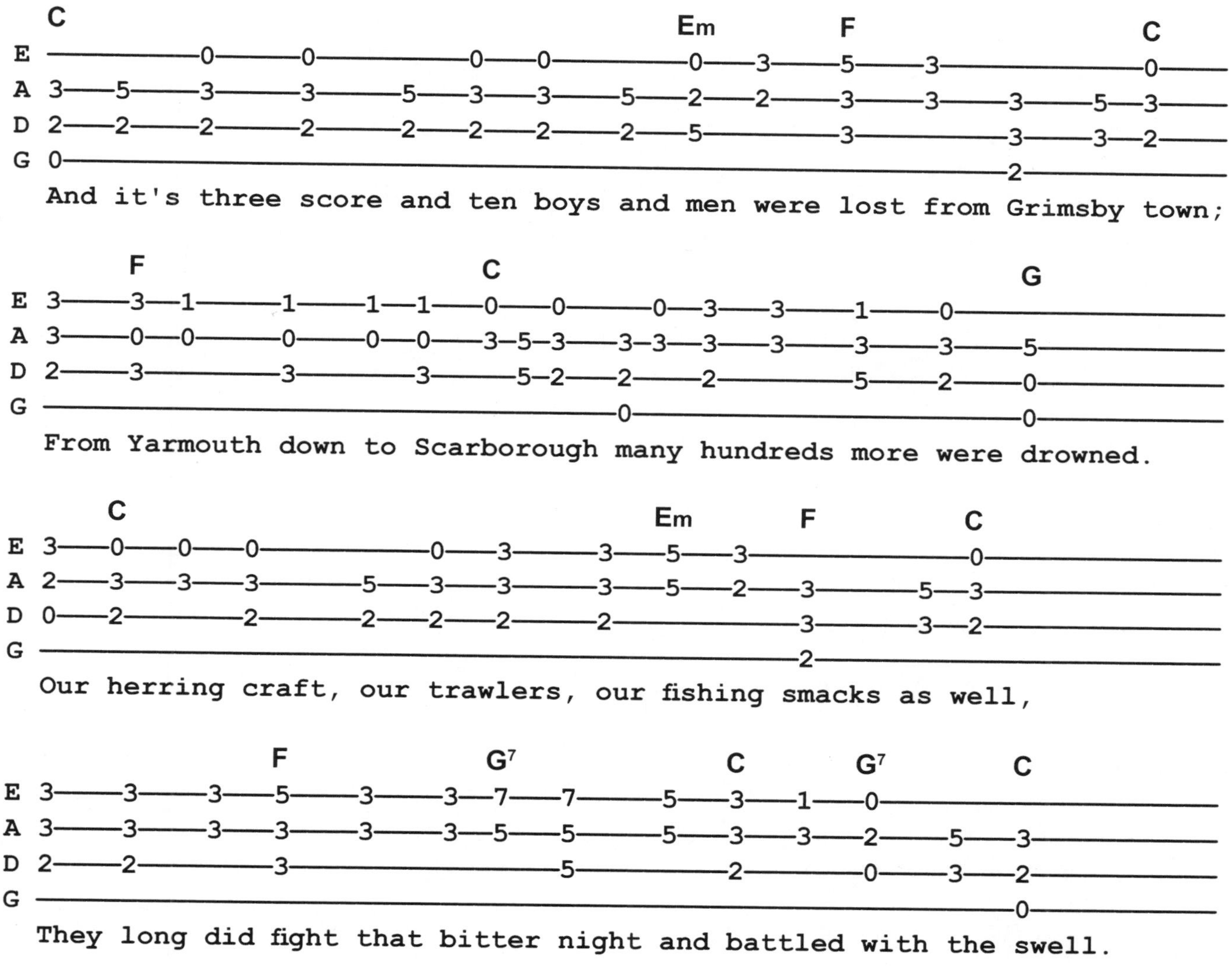

```
   C                                            Em       F                  C
E ----------0-----0---------0---0------------0---3----5---3-------------0----
A 3---5-----3-----3-----5---3---3------5-----2---2----3---3-----3---5---3----
D 2---2-----2-----2-----2---2---2------2-----5--------3---------3---3---2----
G 0-----------------------------------------------------------2--------------
  And it's three score and ten boys and men were lost from Grimsby town;
```

```
        F                C                                   G
E 3---3--1----1----1--1--0---0-----0--3---3----1----0-----------
A 3---0--0----0----0--0--3-5-3-----3-3--3---3----3----3----5----
D 2---3-------3--------3-----5-2---2------2---------5----2----0----
G --------------------------------0-------------------------0----
  From Yarmouth down to Scarborough many hundreds more were drowned.
```

```
       C                               Em      F          C
E 3---0---0---0----------0---3-----3---5---3---------------0-------
A 2---3---3---3------5---3---3-----3---5---2---3------5----3-------
D 0---2-------2------2---2---2-----2-----------3------3----2-------
G ---------------------------------------------2-------------------
  Our herring craft, our trawlers, our fishing smacks as well,
```

```
                 F            G7               C         G7          C
E 3----3----3----5----3----3--7---7-------5----3----1----0-----------------
A 3----3----3----3----3----3--5---5-------5----3----3----2-----5-----3-----
D 2----2---------3----------------5------------2---------0-----3-----2-----
G -------------------------------------------------------------------0-----
  They long did fight that bitter night and battled with the swell.
```

Three Score and Ten
(continued - page 1)

Basic Melody

Key of G

```
  G                                    Bm                  C        G
E ------------------------------------------0-----------------------------------
A 5-2------2-2---0-2---5---5---5---------------5------------0-2-----------------
D -----------------------------------------------------5------------------------
G ------------------------------------------------------------------------------
  Methinks I see a host of craft spreading their sails a-lee,
```

```
     C              G                                                  D
E ------------------------------------------------------------------------------
A 5--5----3----3---3----3----2-0-2-------2--5------5----5----3--2-----0---------
D -------------------------------------5----------------------------------------
G ------------------------------------------------------------------------------
  As down the Humber they d-o glide a-ll bound for the Northern Sea.
```

```
   G                                        Bm        C          G
E -----------------------------------------0------------------------------------
A 5-2------2-2---0---2----5-----5-----5-------5----------------0---2------------
D ----------------------------------------------------5-------------------------
G ------------------------------------------------------------------------------
  Methinks I see on each small craft a crew with hearts so brave,
```

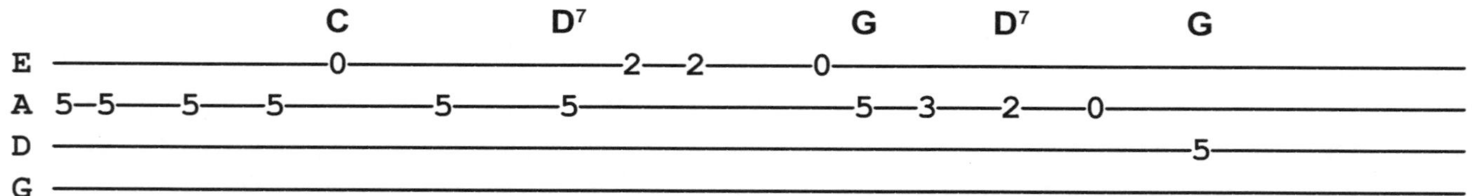

Chord Forms

G

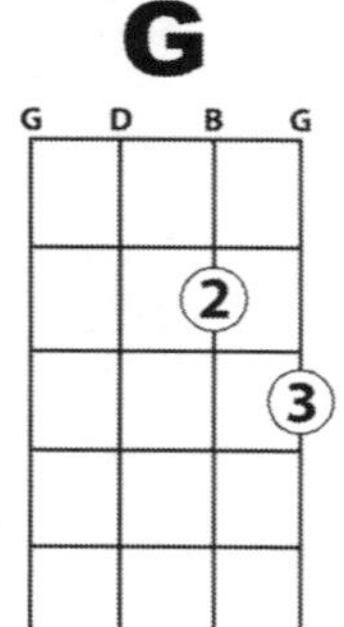

Bm

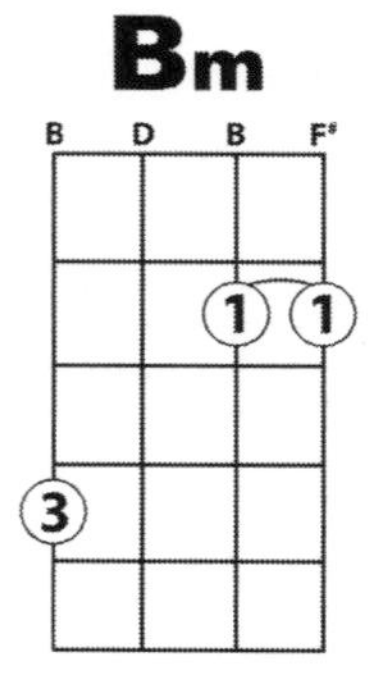

C

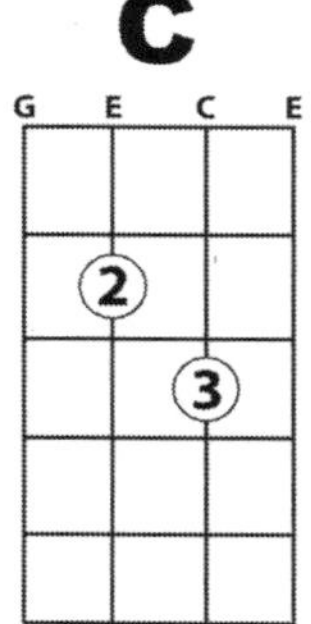

D

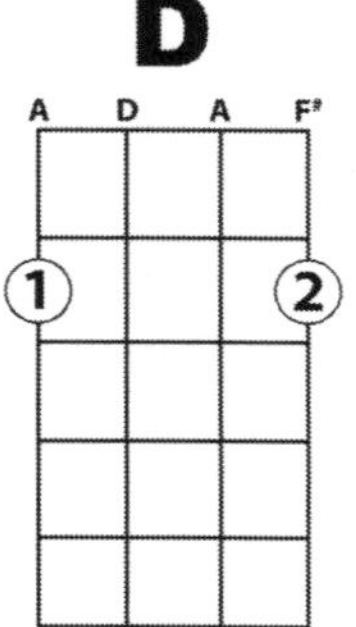

D7

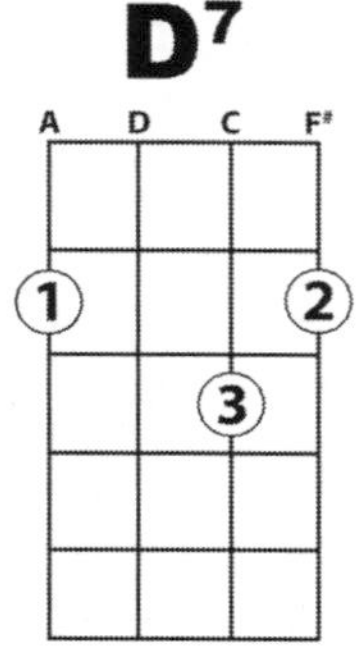

Three Score and Ten
(continued - page 2)

Basic Melody

Key of G

Chorus

```
   G                                                  Bm        C                     G
E ---------0------0----------0----0----------0---3----5----3-----------------0---
A 3---5-----------------5--------------5-----------------------------3----5------
D -------------------------------------------------------------------------------
G -------------------------------------------------------------------------------
  And it's three score and ten boys and men were lost from Grimsby town;
```

```
       C                      G                                            D
E 3----3--1-----1-----1--1----0----0-----0--3---3----1-----0-------------------
A --------------------------------5-----3---------------------------5----------
D ------------------------------------------------------------------------------
G ------------------------------------------------------------------------------
  From Yarmouth down to Scarborough many hundreds more were drowned.
```

```
      G                                       Bm        C        G
E 3---0---0---0-------------0---3-----3---5---3----------------0---------
A --------------------5---------------------------------3----5-----------
D -----------------------------------------------------------------------
G -----------------------------------------------------------------------
  Our herring craft, our trawlers, our fishing smacks as well,
```

```
                    C              D7               G       D7         G
E 3----3----3----5----3----3--7----7-----5----3----1---0----------------------
A ---------------------------------------------------------5----3-------------
D -----------------------------------------------------------------------------
G -----------------------------------------------------------------------------
  They long did fight that bitter night and battled with the swell.
```

Three Score and Ten
(continued - page 1)

Melody & Chords

Key of G

```
  G                                       Bm                C       G
E ------------------------------------------------0--------------------------
A 5-2--------2-2----0-2----5--5-----5-----2-----5-------------0-2-------------
D 0-0--------0-0----0-0----0--0-----4-----------4------5------0-0-------------
G 0-0--------0------0------0--------4------------------5------0-0-------------
  Methinks I see a host of craft spreading their sails a-lee,
```

```
     C               G                                                      D
E ----------------------------------------------------------------------------
A 5--5----3---3--3---3----2-0-2------2--5------5---5---3--2-------0----------
D 0--2----3---3--3---0----0-0-0----5-0--0------0---0---0--0-------0----------
G ---0--------0------0--------0----0----0--------------0--0-------2----------
  As down the Humber they d-o glide a-ll bound for the Northern Sea.
```

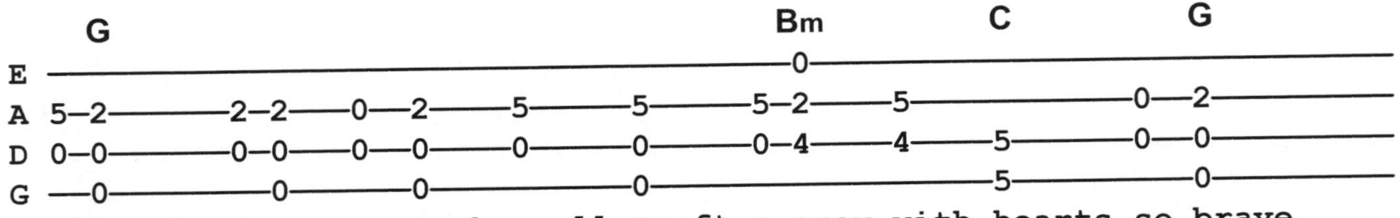

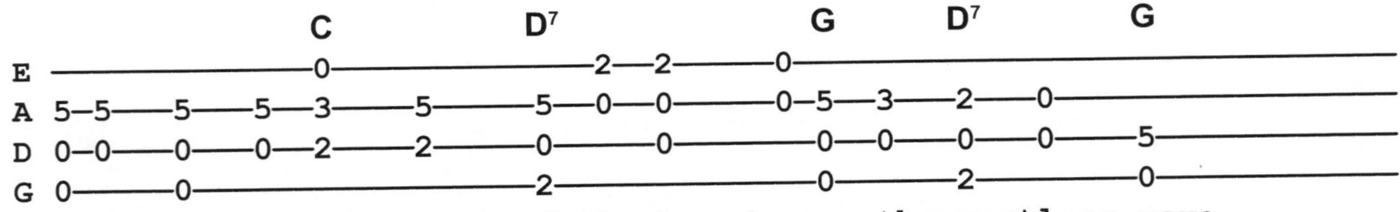

Chord Forms

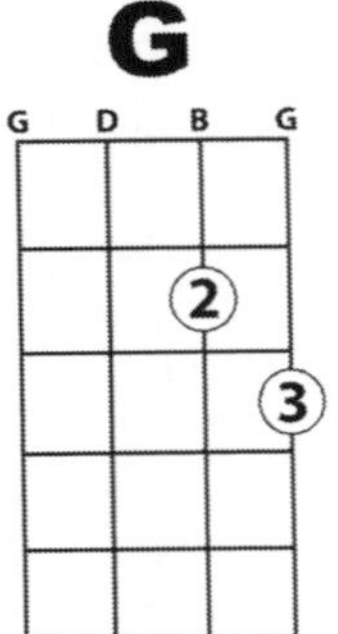

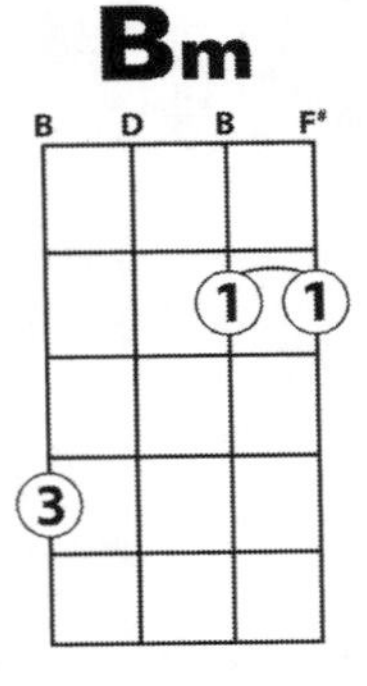

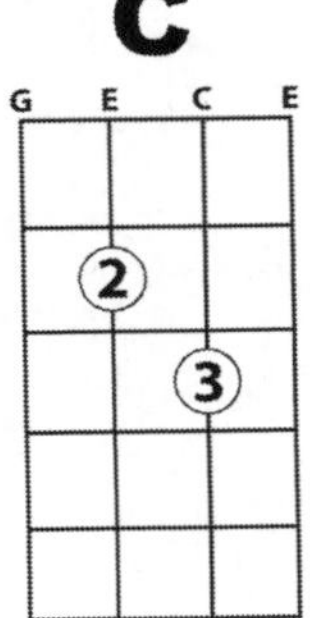

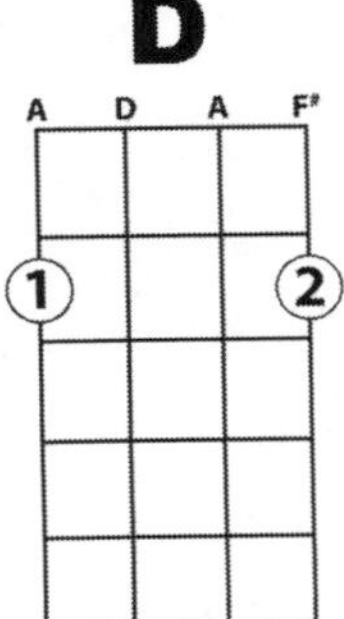

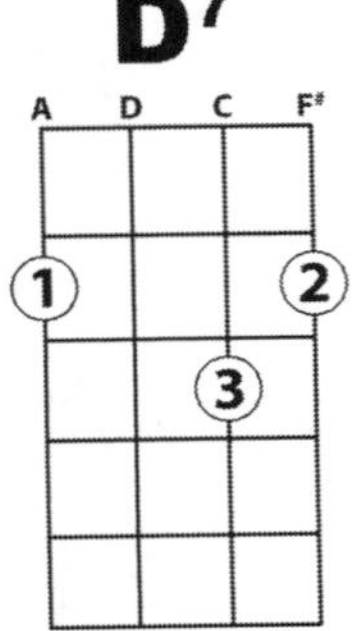

Three Score and Ten
(continued - page 2)

Melody & Chords

Key of G

CHORUS

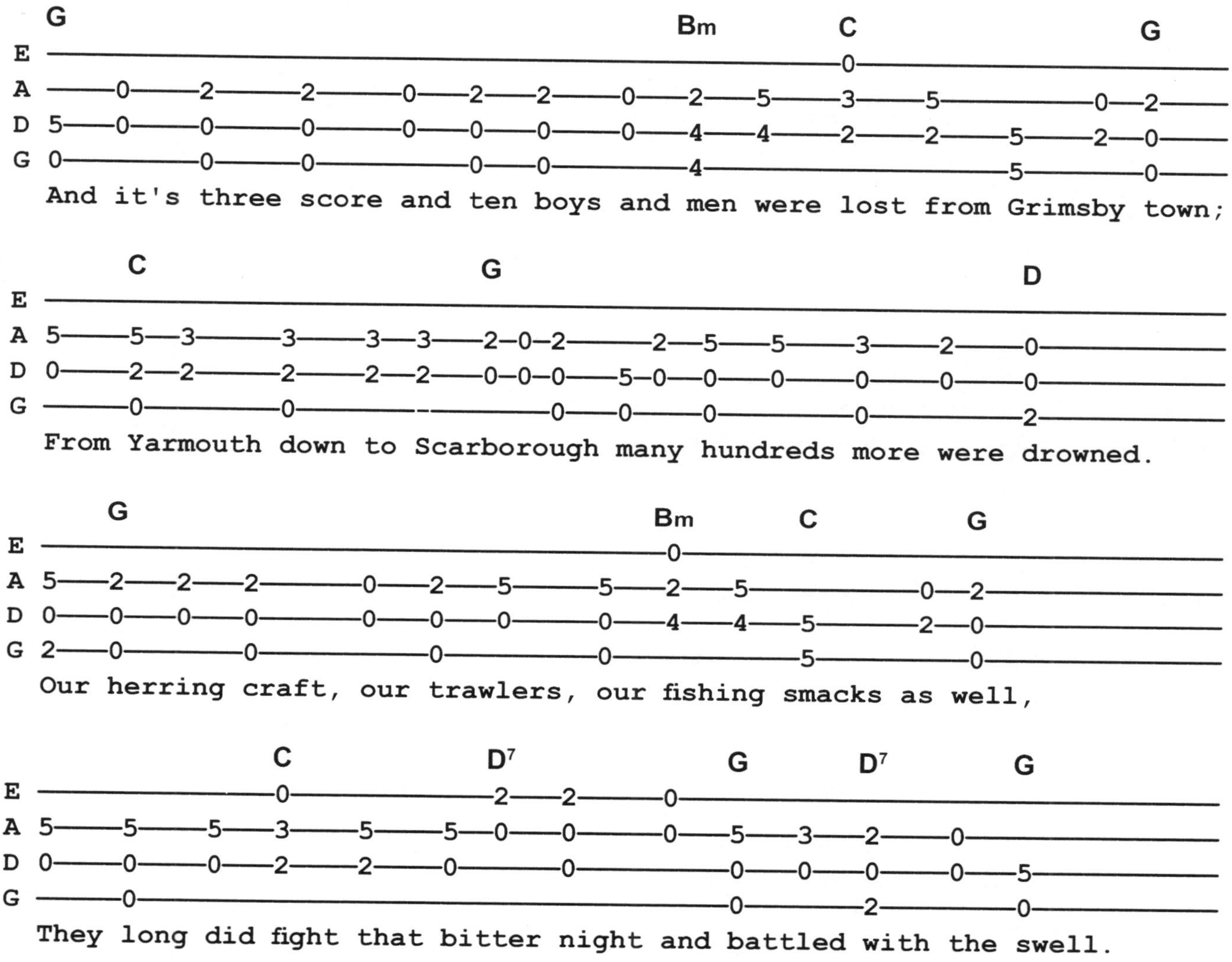

```
  G                                                  Bm        C                   G
E ---------------------------------------------------------------0---------------------------
A ----0----2-----2-----0----2----2----0----2----5----3----5------------0--2----
D 5---0----0-----0-----0----0----0----0----4----4----2----2-----5------2--0----
G 0--------0-----0----------0----0---------4---------------------5---------0----
  And it's three score and ten boys and men were lost from Grimsby town;
```

```
        C                      G                              D
E ------------------------------------------------------------------------------
A 5----5--3-----3----3--3---2-0-2-------2---5---5----3----2----0-----
D 0----2--2-----2----2--2---0-0-0----5-0---0---0----0----0----0-----
G -----0--------0-------------------0----0---0--------0--------2-----
  From Yarmouth down to Scarborough many hundreds more were drowned.
```

```
      G                                         Bm      C          G
E -------------------------------------------------0------------------------------
A 5---2---2---2-------0---2---5------5---2---5-----------0--2------
D 0---0---0---0-------0---0---0------0---4---4---5-------2--0------
G 2---0-------0-----------0----------0-----------5----------0------
  Our herring craft, our trawlers, our fishing smacks as well,
```

```
                 C            D7              G      D7        G
E ---------------0-------------2---2-----0-----------------------------------
A 5----5----5----3----5----5--0----0-----0---5---3---2-----0---------
D 0----0----0----2----2----0-------0---------0---0---0-----0---5-----
G -----0-------------------------------------0-------2---------0-----
  They long did fight that bitter night and battled with the swell.
```

SCOTTISH BALLAD

The Water Is Wide

Basic Melody

Key of C (Low)

Also known as "O Waly, Waly", this traditional folk song originated in the 1600's in Scotland. It is related to other folk pieces from the time period, some of which were based on true stories. Even in the 21st century it remains a beautiful, haunting lament for love lost.

Words and Music

Traditional

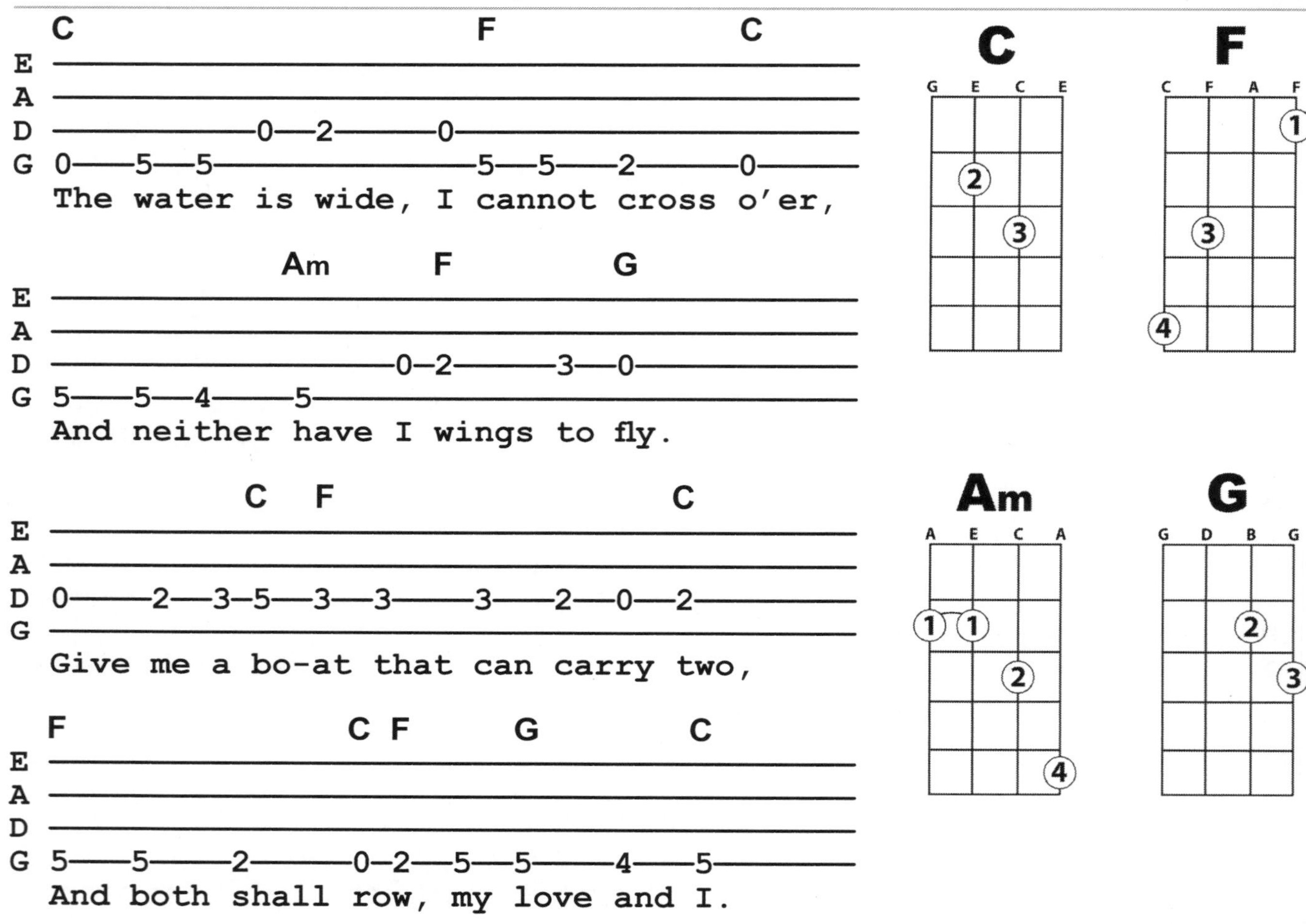

Additional Verses

There is a ship, and she sails the sea,
She's loaded deep as deep can be;
But not so deep as the love I'm in,
I know not if I'll sink or swim.

I leaned my back against an oak,
Thinking it was the strongest tree;
But first it bent and then it broke,
So did my love prove false to me.

Oh love be handsome and love be kind,
Gay as a jewel when first it's new;
But love grows old and waxes cold,
And fades away like the morning dew.

The Water Is Wide
(continued)

Two Versions

Key of C (High)

Basic Melody

```
  C                       F            C                     Am     F        G
E ------------0-----------------------------------------------------0------1-----
A ----3--3--5---------5-3--3--0------------3--3-2---3----5-----------------5--
D 5---------------------------------5-----------------------------------------
G -----------------------------------------------------------------------------
  The water is wide, I cannot cross o'er, and neither have I wings to fly.
```

```
         C  F             C    F             C F          G   C
E ----0--1-3--1-1---1--0---0---------------------------------------
A 5--------------------5--------3---3---0--------0--3--3---2---3---
D ----------------------------------------5-------------------------
G -------------------------------------------------------------------
  Give me a boat that can carry two, and both shall row, my love and I.
```

Melody and Chords

```
  C                       F            C                     Am     F        G
E ------------0-----------------------------------------------------0------1-----
A ----3--3--5--3------5-3--3--0------------3--3-2---3----5-0-------0--5--
D 5---2--2--2--2------2-3--3--3-----5------2--2-2---2----2-3-------3--0--
G 0---0--------0---------2-----2----5------0--0-----2-----------------0--
  The water is wide, I cannot cross o'er, and neither have I wings to fly.
```

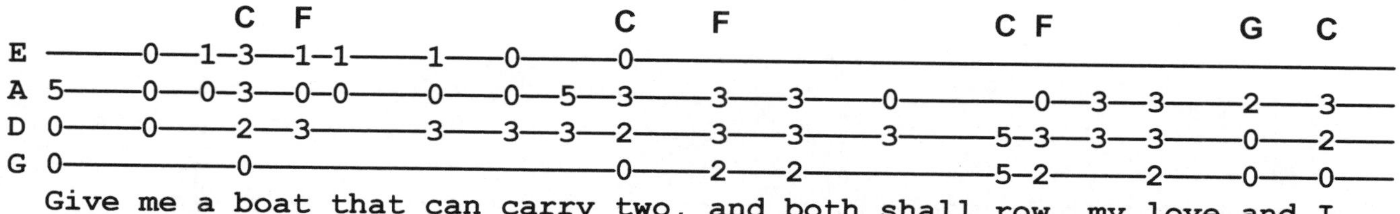

Chord Forms

C

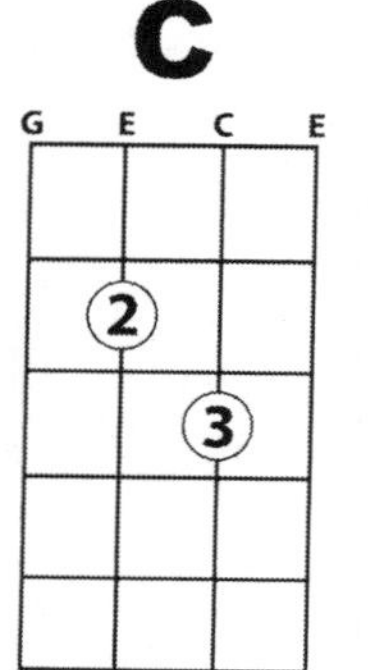

F

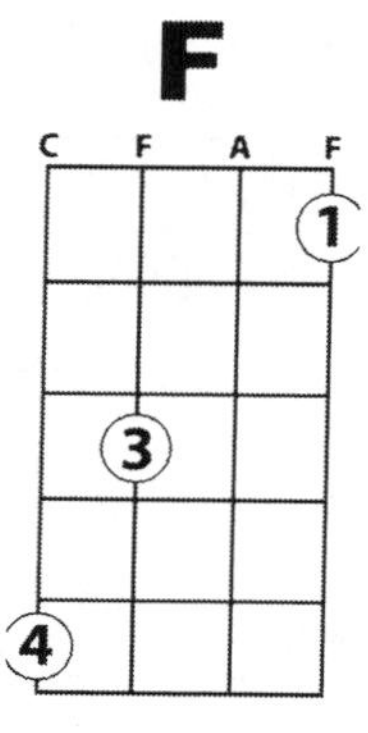

Am

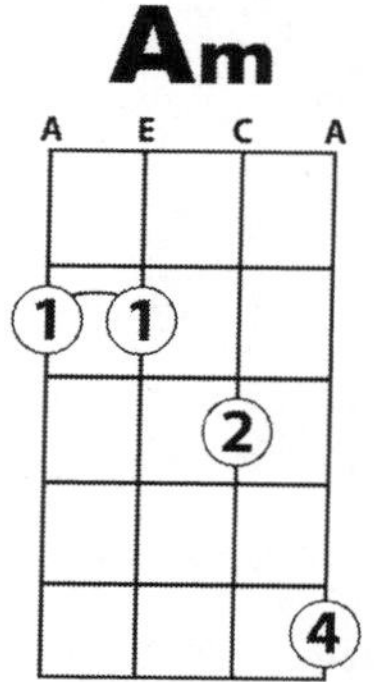

G

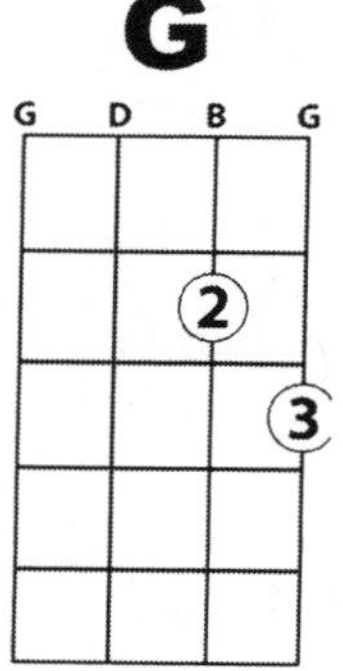

The Water Is Wide
(continued)

Two Versions

Key of G (Low)

Basic Melody

```
   G                          C                 G                      Em       C          D
E ---------------------------------------------------------------------------------------------
A --------------0--2-------0--------------------------------------------------0--2------3--0--
D 0---5---5--------------------5---5---2------0------5---5---4------5---------------------------
G ---------------------------------------------------------------------------------------------
  The water is wide, I cannot cross o'er, and neither have I wings to fly.
```

```
              G   C                       G      C                 G C               D    G
E ---------------------------------------------------------------------------------------------
A 0------2--3-5---3-3-----3----2---0---2-------------------------------------------------------
D ---------------------------------------------5-----5-------2--------0-2---5---5------4----5--
G ---------------------------------------------------------------------------------------------
  Give me a boat that can carry two, and both shall row, my love and I.
```

Melody and Chords

```
   G                          C                 G                      Em       C          D
E ---------------------------------------------------------------------------------------------
A --------------0--2-------0--------------------------------------------------0--2------3--0--
D 0---5---5--0--0-------0-5---5---2------0------5---5---4------5---------2--2----------2--0--
G 0---0---0-----0-----------5---5---5------0------0---0---2------4---------0---------------2--
  The water is wide, I cannot cross o'er, and neither have I wings to fly.
```

```
              G   C                       G      C                 G C               D    G
E ---------------------------------------------------------------------------------------------
A 0------2--3-5---3-3-----3----2---0---2-------------------------------------------------------
D 0------0--0-0---2-2-----2----2---2---0-------5-----5-------2--------0-2---5---5------4----5--
G 2------2----0-----0----------0-------0-------5-----5-------5--------0-5---5---5------2----0--
  Give me a boat that can carry two, and both shall row, my love and I.
```

Chord Forms

G (G D B G): ② on 2nd fret of B string (3rd string), ③ on 3rd fret of G (1st) string

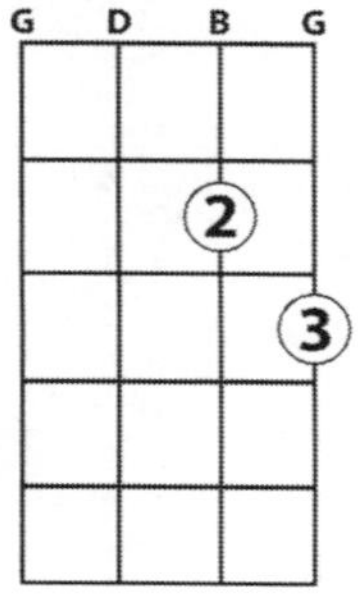

C (G E C E): ② on 2nd fret of D string, ③ on 3rd fret of A string

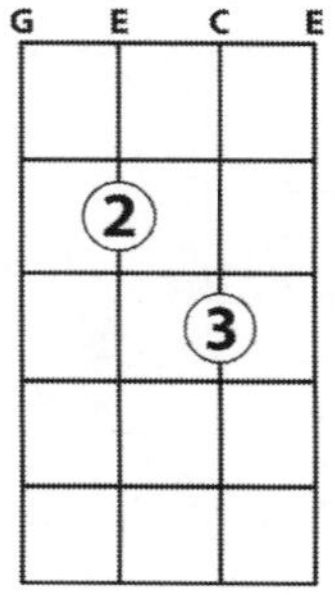

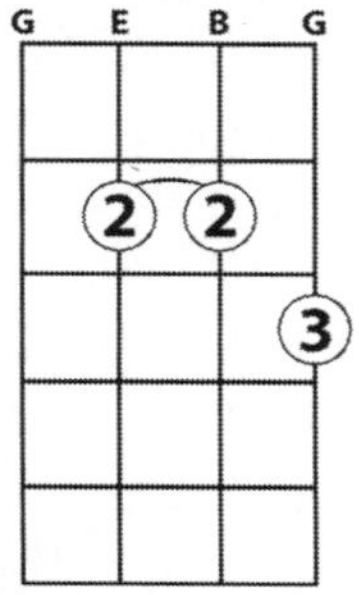

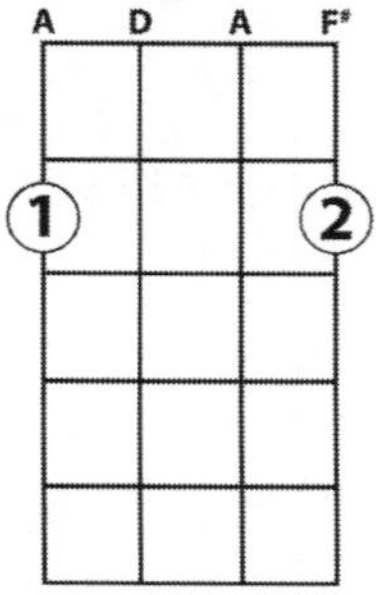

Em (G E B G): ② ② on 2nd fret of D and A strings (barred), ③ on 3rd fret of E string

D (A D A F#): ① on 2nd fret of G string, ② on 2nd fret of E string

SCOTTISH BALLAD

The Water Is Wide
(continued)

Two Versions

Key of G (High)

Basic Melody

```
 G                             C               G                                Em       C          D
E ——3—3—5—7———5-3—3——0———————————————3——3—2——3———5-7————8—5—
A 5———————————————————————————5————————————————————————————
D ———————————————————————————————————————————————————————————
G ———————————————————————————————————————————————————————————
 The water is wide, I cannot cross o'er, and neither have I wings to fly.
```

```
          G  C                        G    C                      G C            D   G
E 5———7—8-10-8-8———8——7—5—7———3——3———0—————————0—3—3———2——3——
A ———————————————————————————————————————————5———————————————
D ———————————————————————————————————————————————————————————
G ———————————————————————————————————————————————————————————
 Give me a boat that can carry two, and both shall row, my love and I.
```

Melody and Chords

```
 G                             C               G                                Em       C          D
E ——3—3—5—7———5-3—3——0———————————————3——3—2——3———5-7————8—5—
A 5—2—2—2—5———5-3—3——3———5———————————2——2—2——2———2-5————5—5—
D 0——0———0—5———5-2—2——2———0——————————0——0————2————5—————7—
G 0————————0———————————————0————————————————————0—————————————
 The water is wide, I cannot cross o'er, and neither have I wings to fly.
```

```
          G  C                        G    C                      G C            D   G
E 5———7—8-10-8-8———8——7—5—7———3——3———0—————————0—3—3———2——3——
A 5———5—5-10-7-7———7——7—5—5———3——3———3—————5-3—3—3———0——2——
D 7———7———9—5-5——————————5———2——2———2—————0-2—2—2———0——0——
G ———————————————————————————————————0—————————0———0———2——0——
 Give me a boat that can carry two, and both shall row, my love and I.
```

Chord Forms

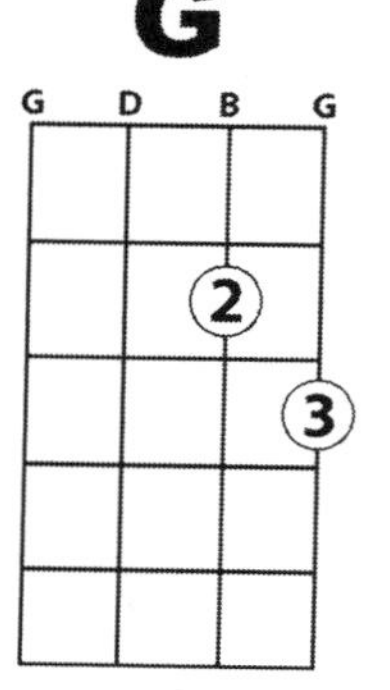

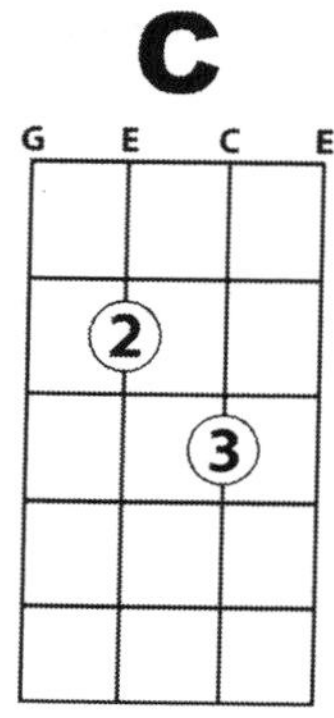

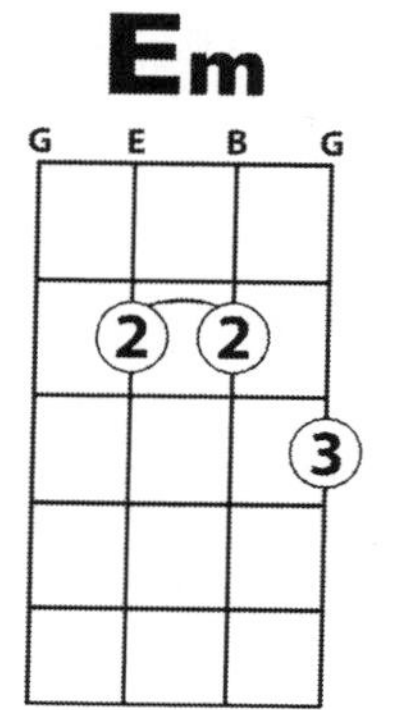

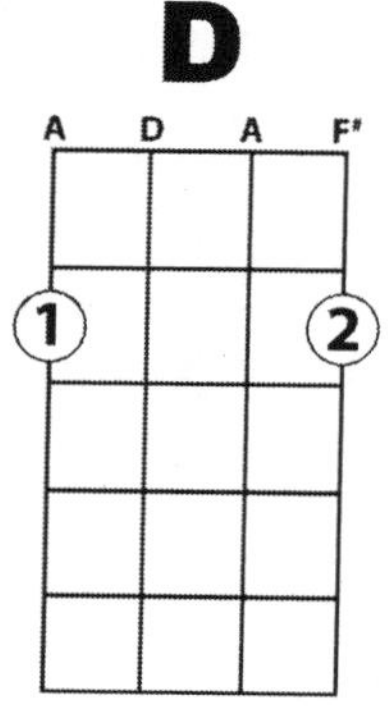

Playing Notes - This arrangement includes higher notes further up the high E string than most others in this book. This song is very beautiful when played in this higher key, and this arrangement can be used as an instrumental "solo" of sorts when playing/singing the low G arrangement.

The Wellerman

Basic Melody

Key of A Minor (Low)

Words and Music

Traditional

This old whaling song tells the fictional tale of a whaling ship fighting one of the great whales in the seas around New Zealand. The Wellermen were ships owned by the Weller Brothers of Australia that would carry supplies to whaling stations and ships. This song, as sung by Scottish mail carrier Nathan Evans, helped spark a renewed in interest in sea shanties in the early 2020's.

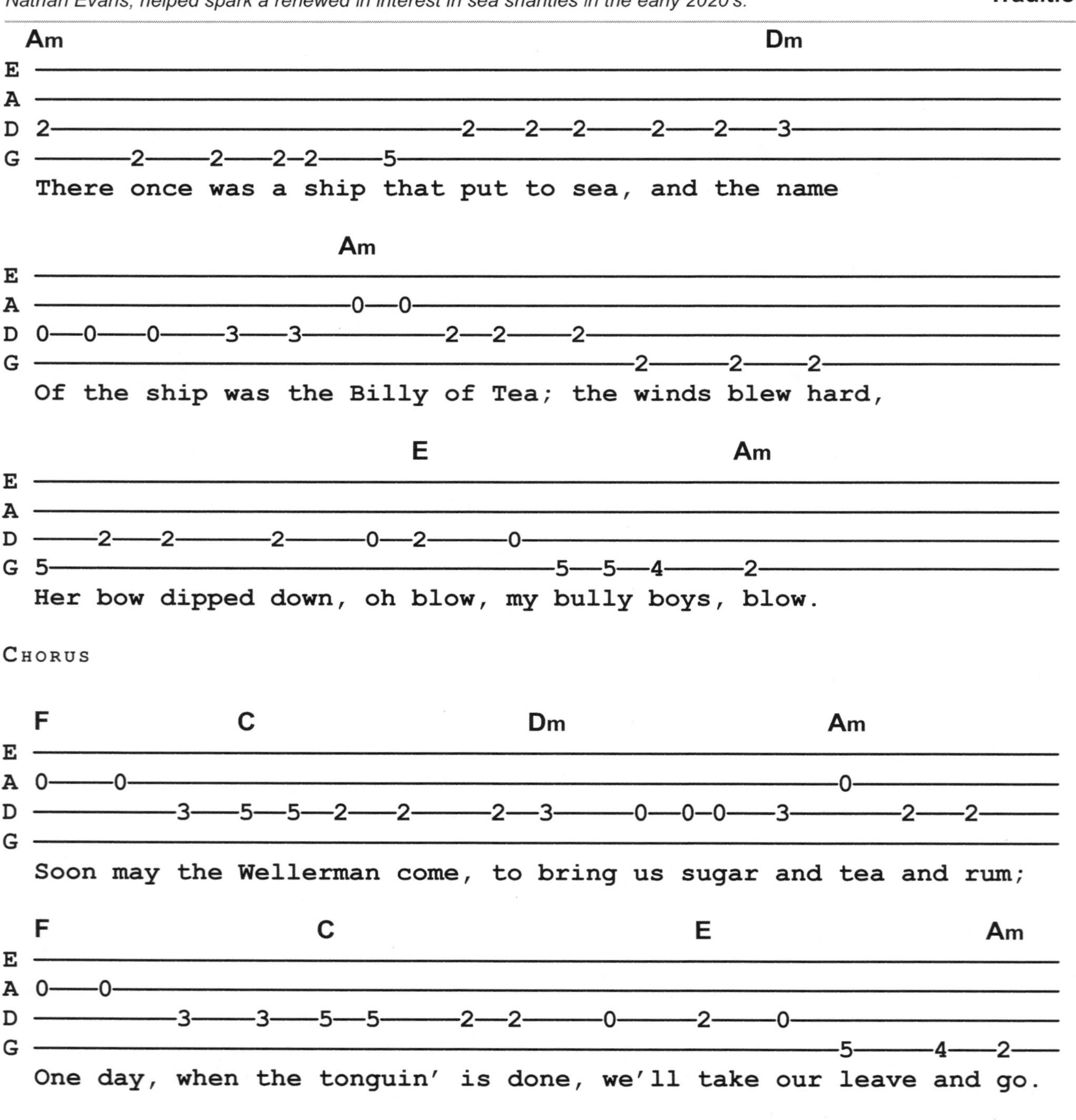

See Chord Forms and Additional Verses on Next Page

The Wellerman (continued)

Chord Forms and Additional Verses

Chord Forms

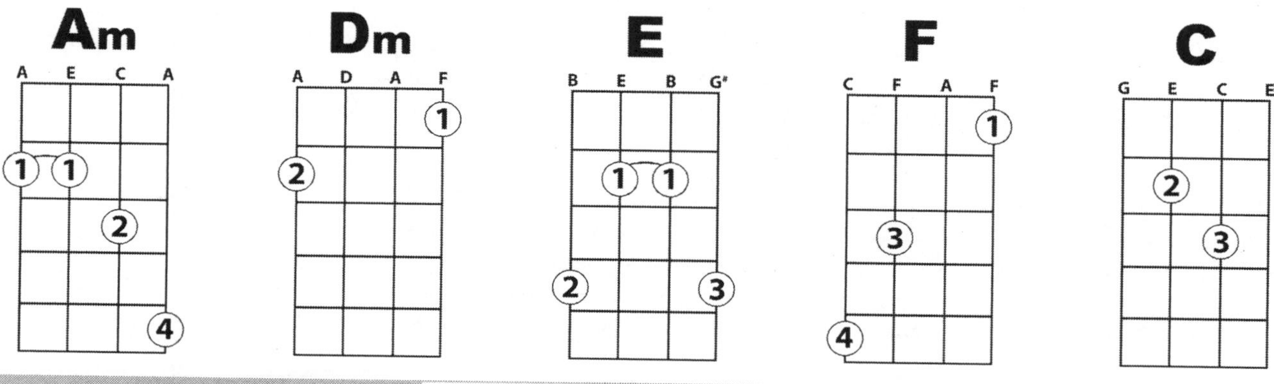

Additional Verses

She had not been two weeks from shore,
When down on her a right whale bore;
The captain called all hands and swore,
He'd take that whale in tow.

Before the boat had hit the water,
The whale's tail came up and caught her;
All hands to the side, harpooned and fought her,
When she dived down below.

No line was cut, no whale was freed,
The captain's mind was not of greed;
But he belonged to the whaleman's creed,
She took the ship in tow.

For forty days, or even more,
The line went slack, then tight once more;
All boats were lost (there were only four),
But still that whale did go.

As far as I've heard, the fight's still on,
The line's not cut and the whale's not gone;
The Wellerman makes his regular call,
To encourage the captain, crew, and all.

Melody & Chords

The Wellerman (continued)

Key of A Minor (Low)

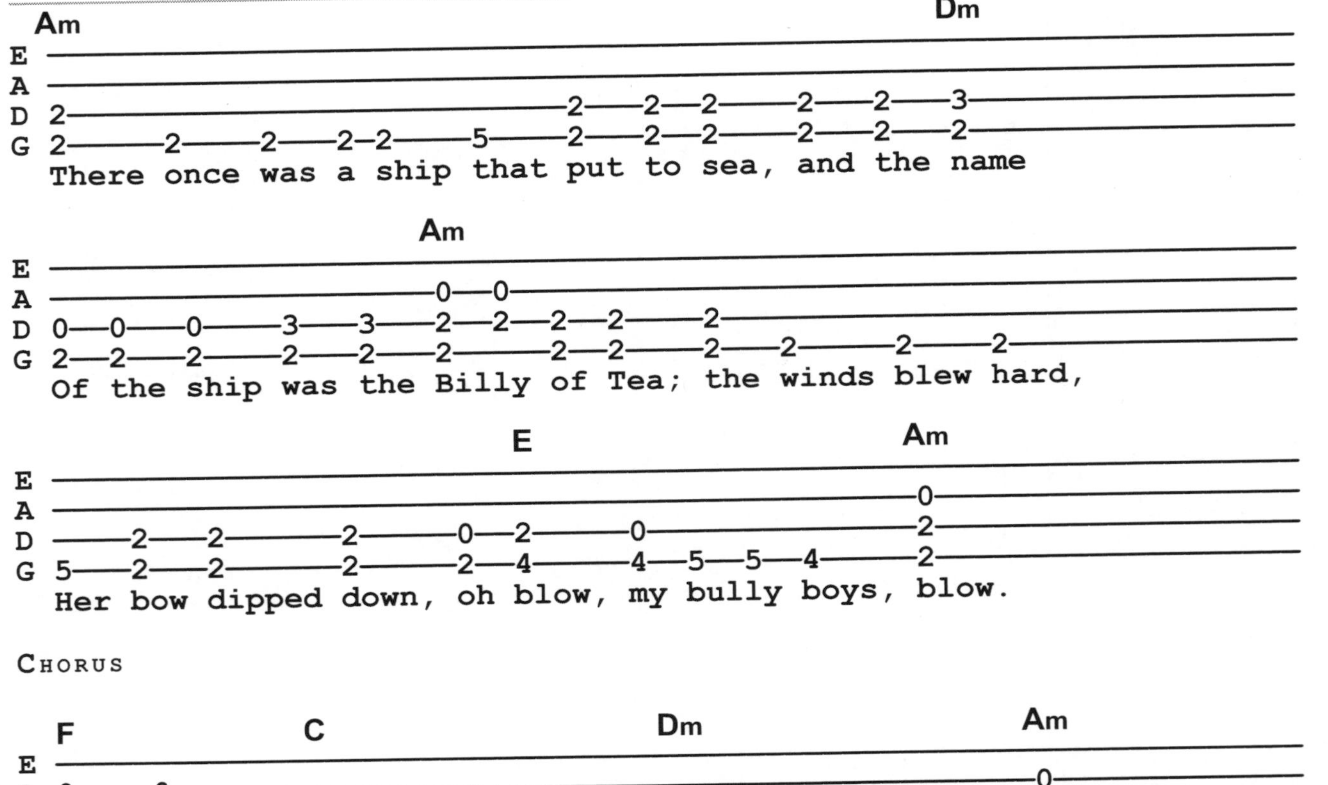

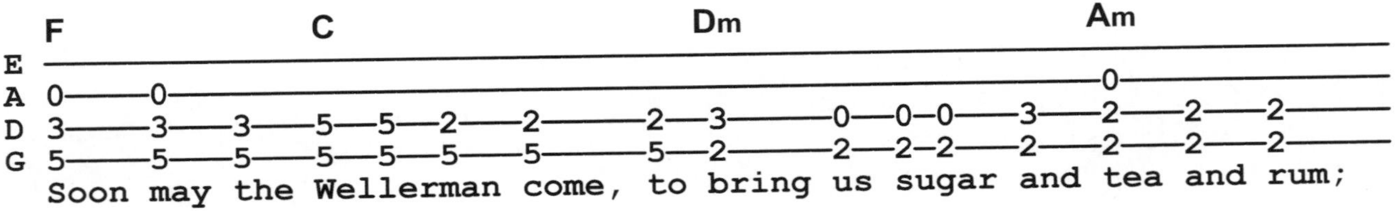


```
  F                 C                              E                       Am
E ---------------------------------------------------------------------------------
A 0--0------------------------------------------------------------------------0---
D 3--3----3----3----5--5------2--2------0-----2-----0---------------------------2---
G 5--5----5----5----5--5------5--5------0-----4-----4-----5-------4-----2---
  One day, when the tonguin' is done, we'll take our leave and go.
```

Chord Forms

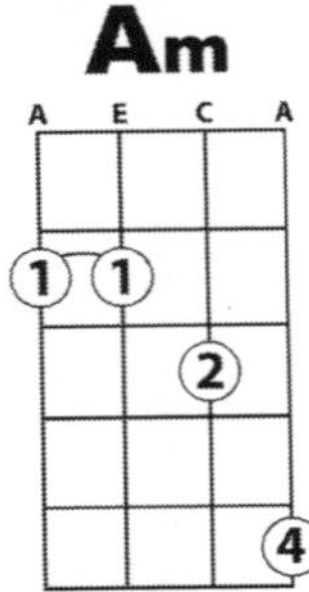

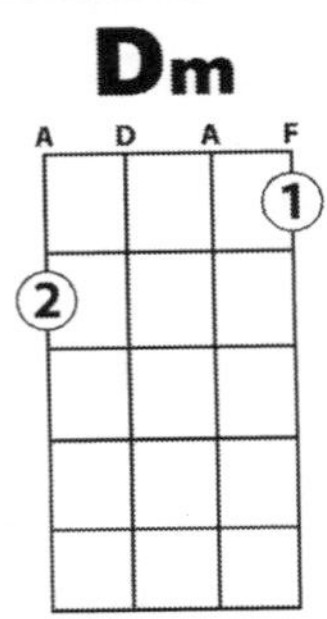

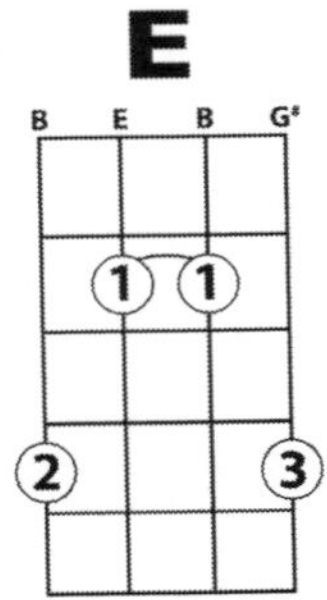

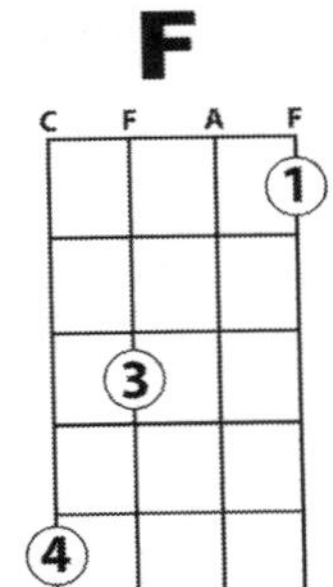

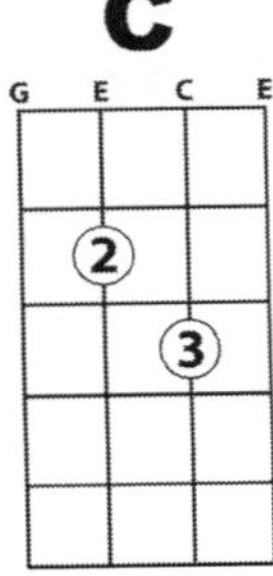

The Wellerman (continued)

Basic Melody

Key of A Minor (High)

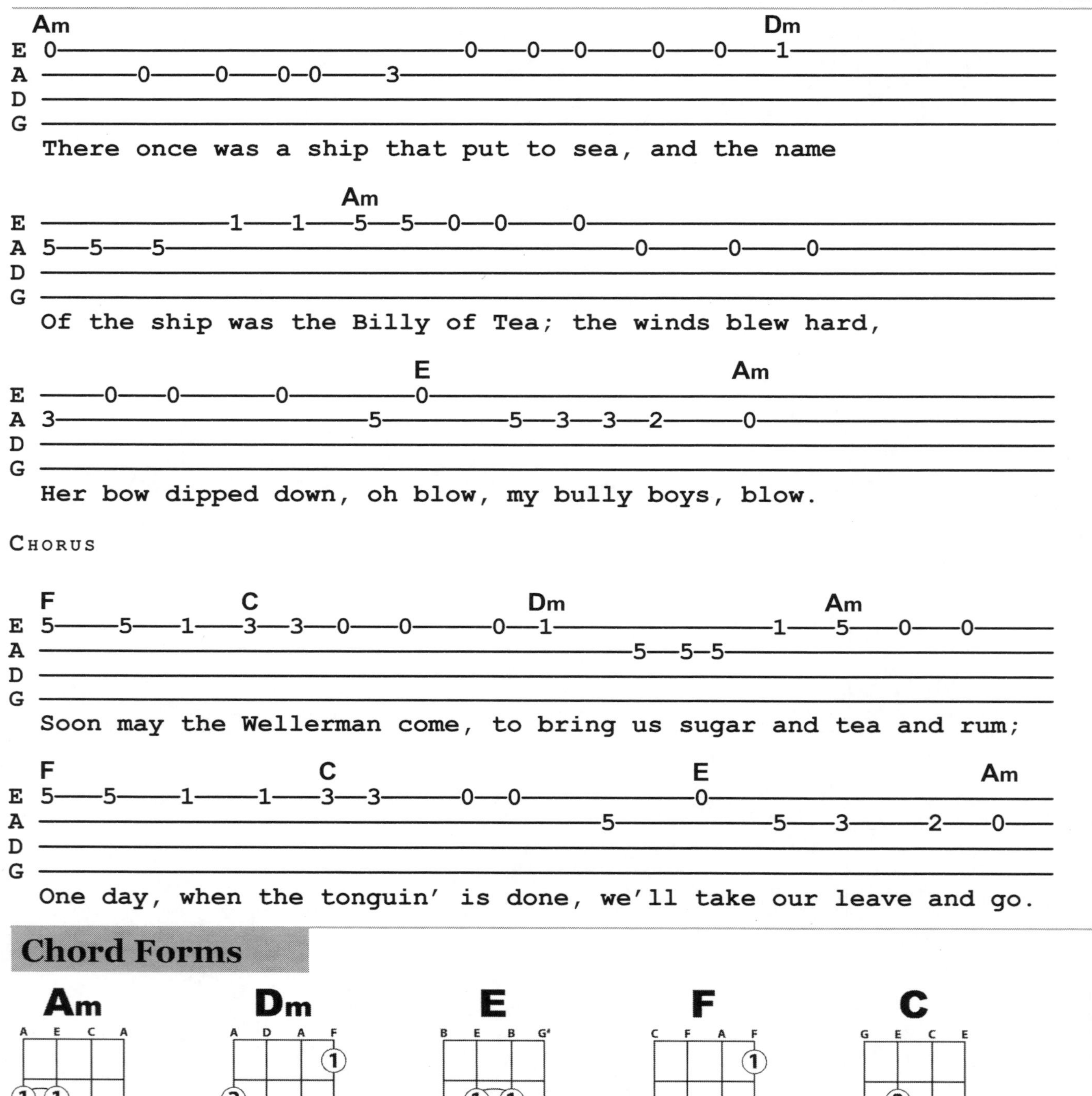

The Wellerman (continued)

Melody & Chords

Key of A Minor (High)

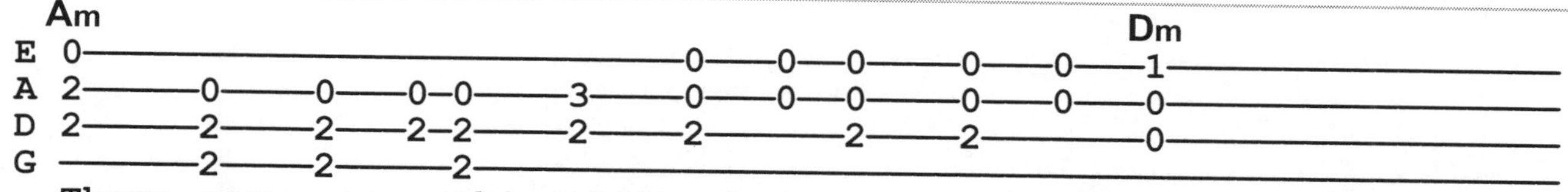

```
   Am                                          Dm
E |-0-----------------------0---0---0---0---0---1--|
A |-2---0---0---0---0---3---0---0---0---0---0---0--|
D |-2---2---2---2---2---2---2-------2---2-------0--|
G |-----2---2-------2------------------------------|
   There once was a ship that put to sea, and the name
```

```
                       Am
E |-------------1---1---5---5---0---0---0--------------|
A |-5---5---5---0---0---3---3---0---0---0---0---0---0--|
D |-3---3---3---0-------2-------2---2---2---2---2---2--|
G |---------2-------------------------------2-------2--|
   Of the ship was the Billy of Tea; the winds blew hard,
```

```
                       E                   Am
E |-----0---0---0-------0----------------------|
A |-3---0---0---0---5---2---5---3---3---2---0--|
D |-2---2-------2---2---2---2---2---2---2---2--|
G |-------------------------------------1---2--|
   Her bow dipped down, oh blow, my bully boys, blow.
```

CHORUS

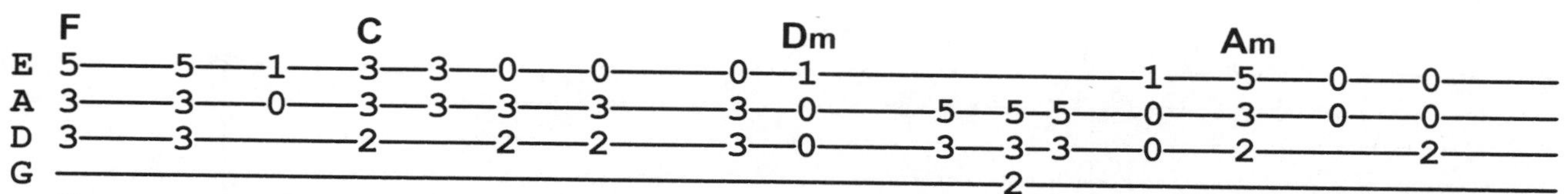

```
   F           C                   Dm                  Am
E |-5---5---1---3---3---0---0---0---1---------------1---5---0---0--|
A |-3---3---0---3---3---3---3---3---0---5---5---5---0---3---0---0--|
D |-3---3-------2-------2---2---3---0---3---3---3---0---2-------2--|
G |-----------------------------------------2----------------------|
   Soon may the Wellerman come, to bring us sugar and tea and rum;
```

```
   F               C                   E               Am
E |-5---5---1---1---3---3---0---0-------0------------------|
A |-3---3---0---0---3---3---3---3---5---2---5---3---2---0--|
D |-3---3-----------2-------2---2---2---2---2---2---2---2--|
G |-------------------------------------------------1---2--|
   One day, when the tonguin' is done, we'll take our leave and go.
```

Chord Forms

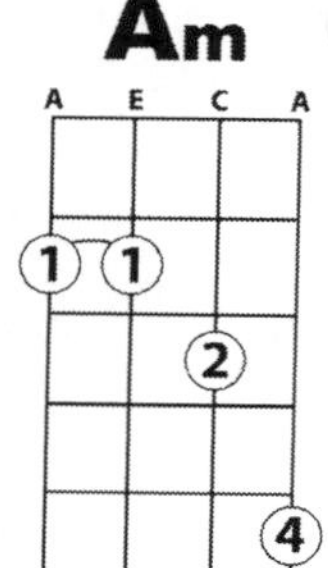

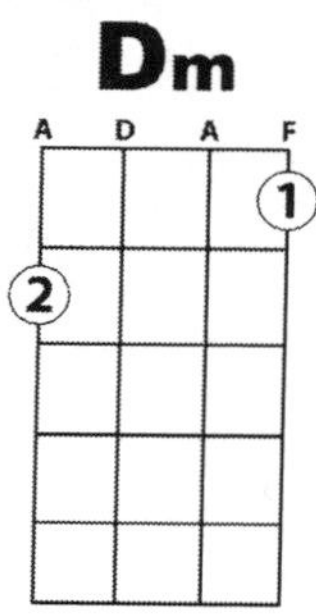

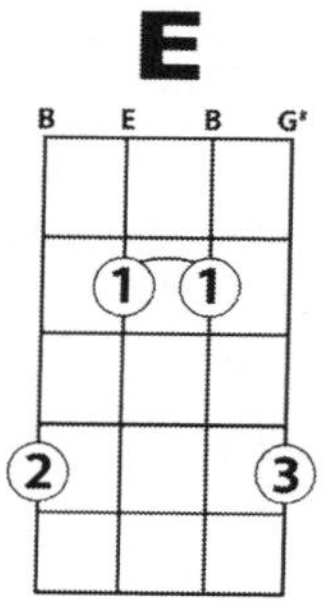

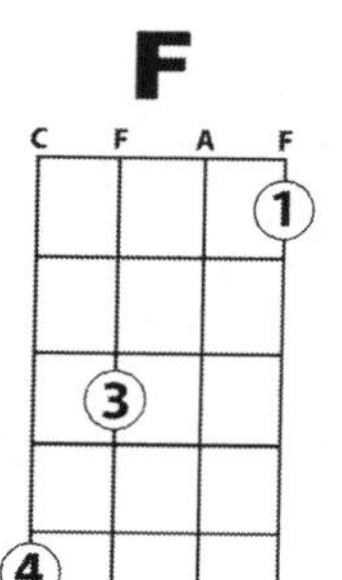

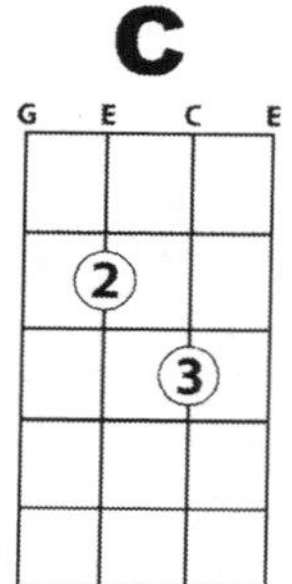

The Wellerman (continued)

Basic Melody

Key of E Minor

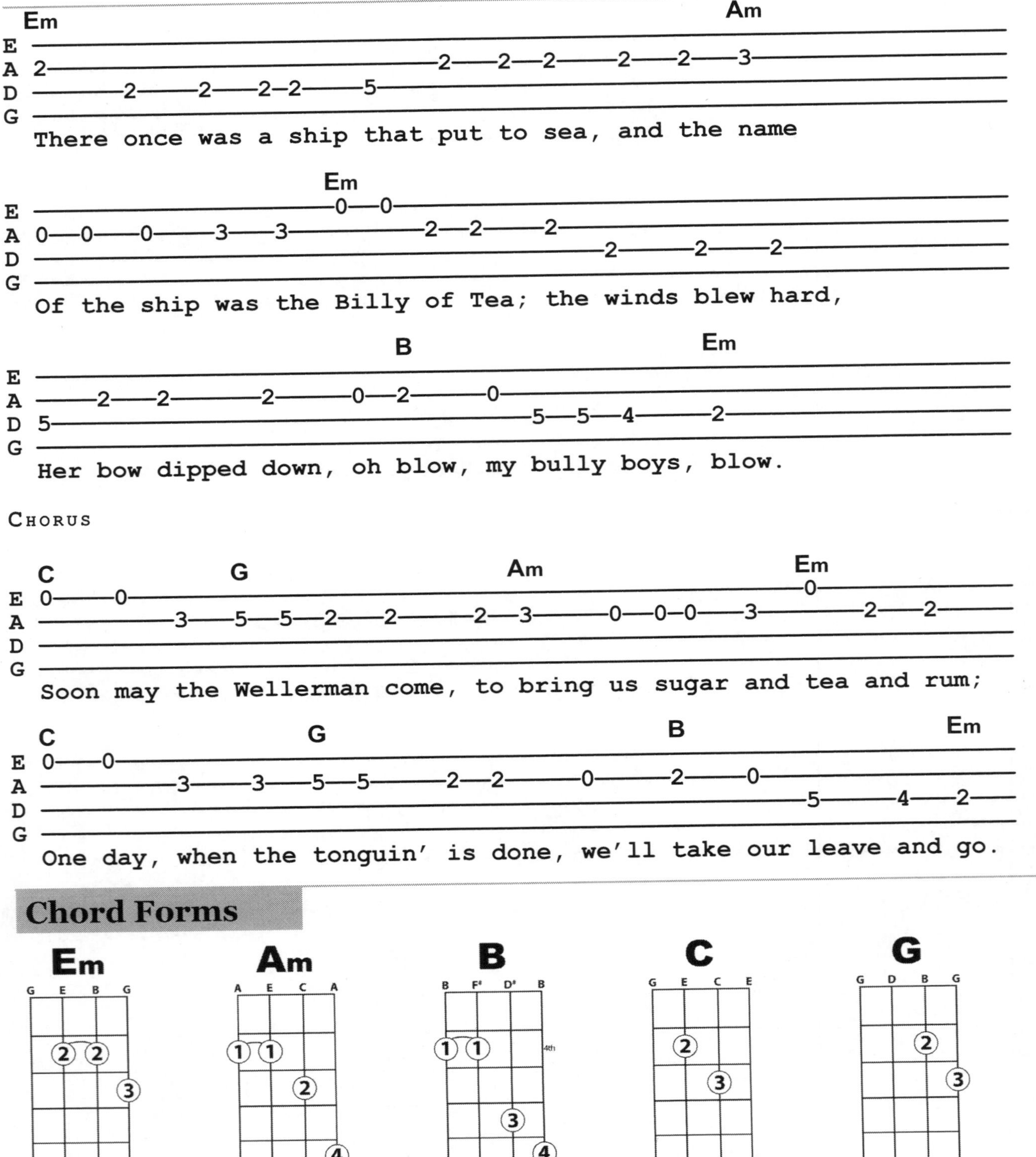

The Wellerman (continued)

Melody & Chords

Key of E Minor

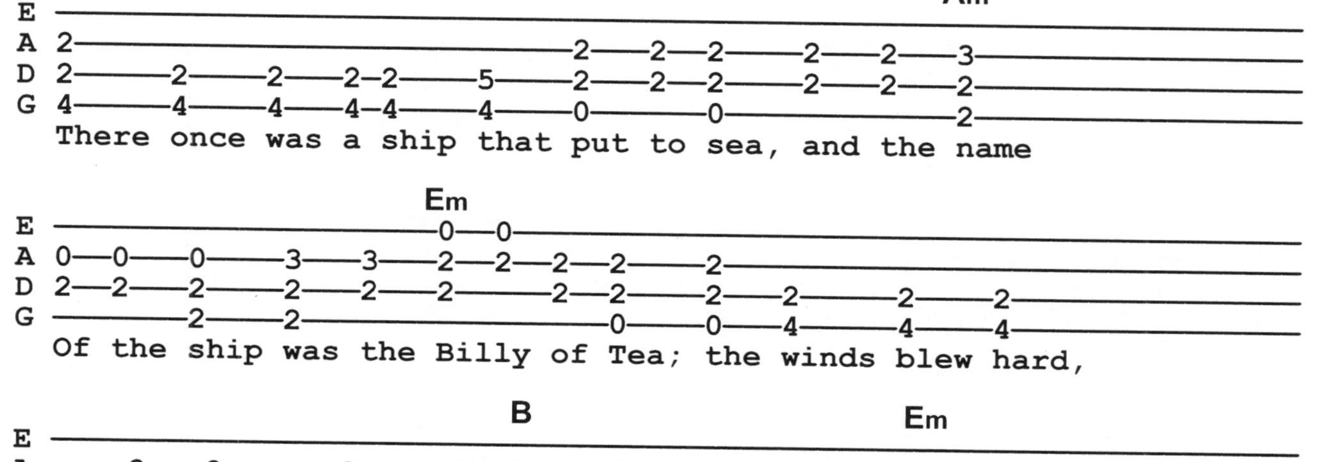


```
                         B                                Em
E ------------------------------------------------------------------
A ----2--2------2-----0--2-----0------------------------------------
D 5---2--2------2-----2--4-----4--5--5--4-----2---------------------
G 4---4---------0--------4--------4--4--4-----4---------------------
  Her bow dipped down, oh blow, my bully boys, blow.
```

Chorus

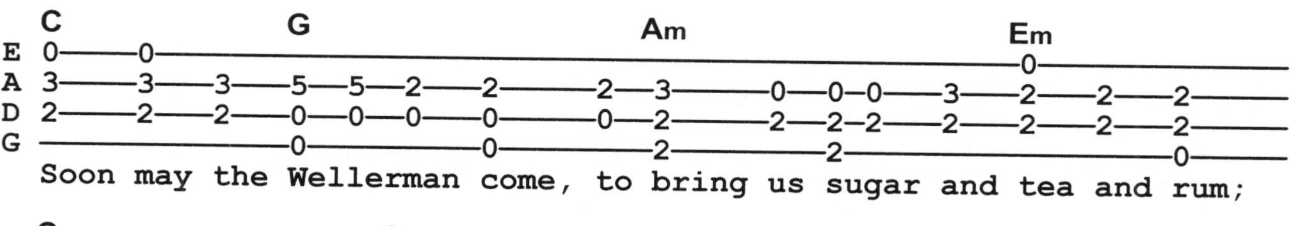


```
  C                  G                          B                  Em
E 0---0------------------------------------------------------------------
A 3---3----3----3----5--5------2--2-----0----2----0----------------------
D 2---2----2----2----0--0------0--0-----0----4----4----5------4---2------
G -------------------0------------0---------4---------4------4---4------
  One day, when the tonguin' is done, we'll take our leave and go.
```

Chord Forms

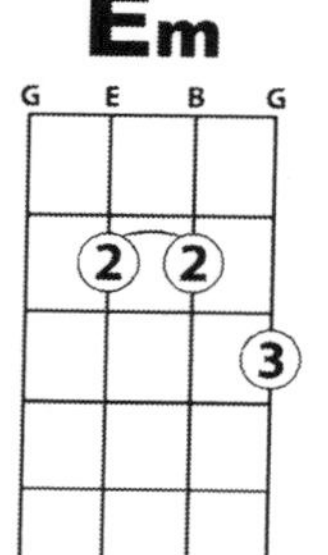

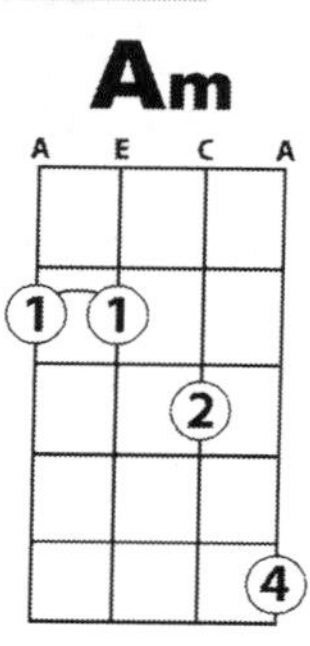

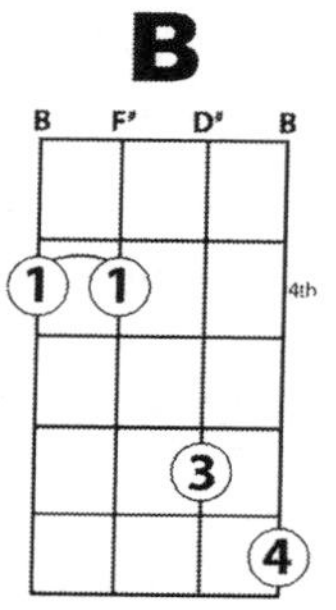

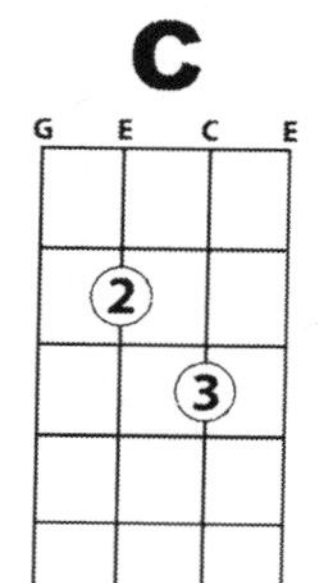

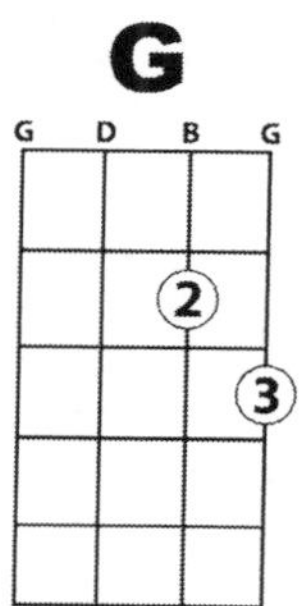

Westering Home

Basic Melody

Key of C (High)

This words to this song were written by Hugh Roberton and tell of the joys of returning back to Scotland after traveling abroad. It is believed by some to be a derivation of an older Gaelic song entitled "Trasna na dTonnta." The tune is a slightly modified version of an older traditional piece, "The Mucking o' Geordie's Byre."

Words by Hugh Roberton

Music Traditional

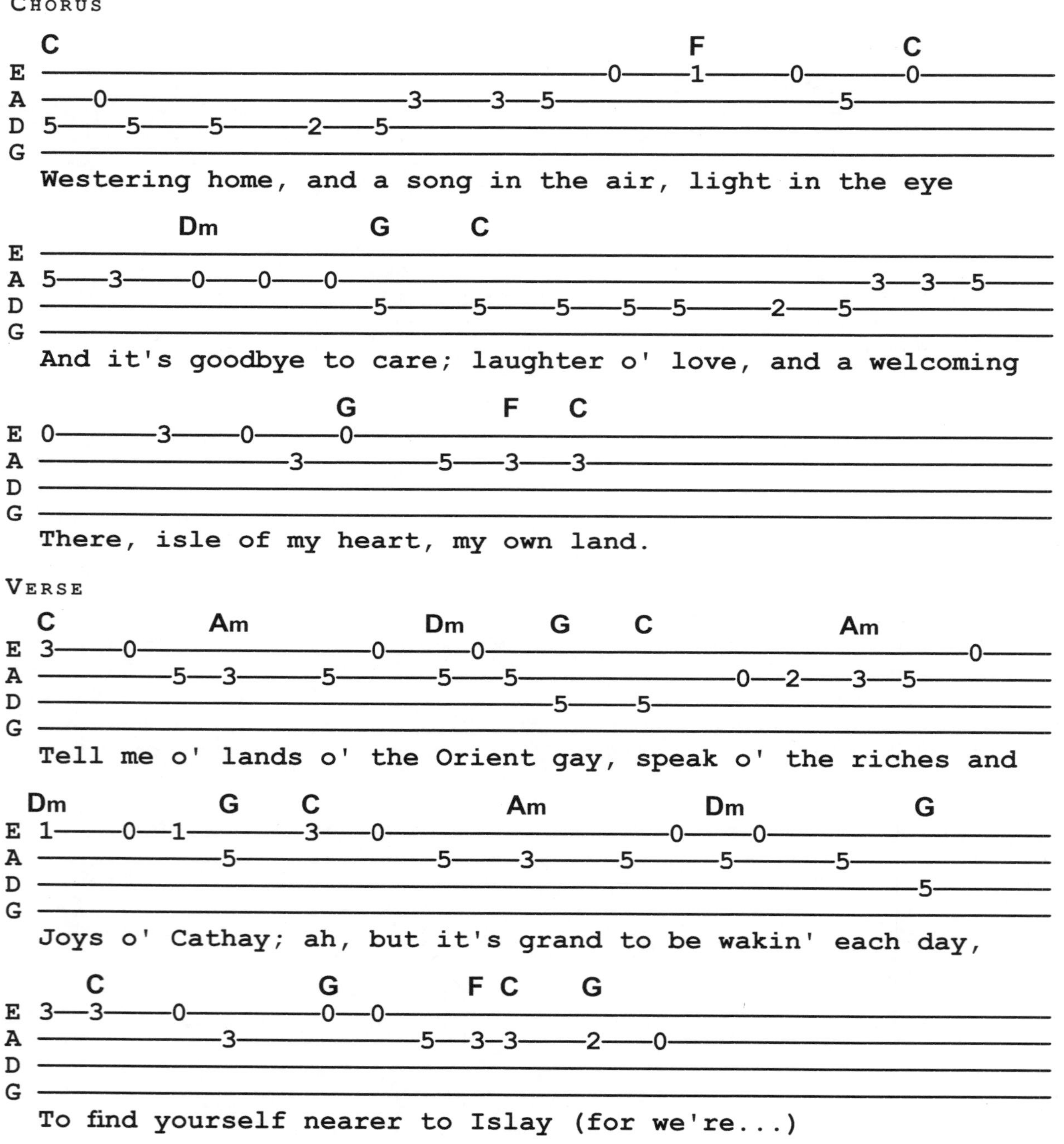

See Chord Forms and Additional Verses on Next Page

Westering Home (continued)

Chord Forms and Additional Verses

Chord Forms

C

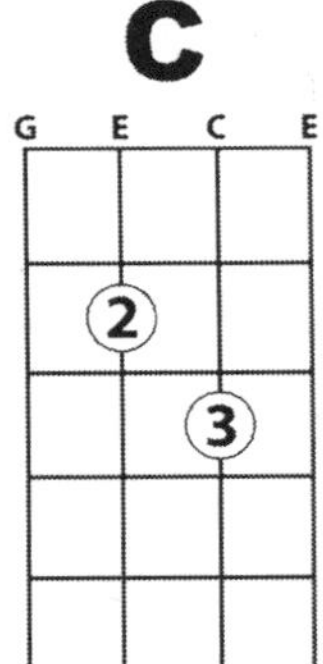

F

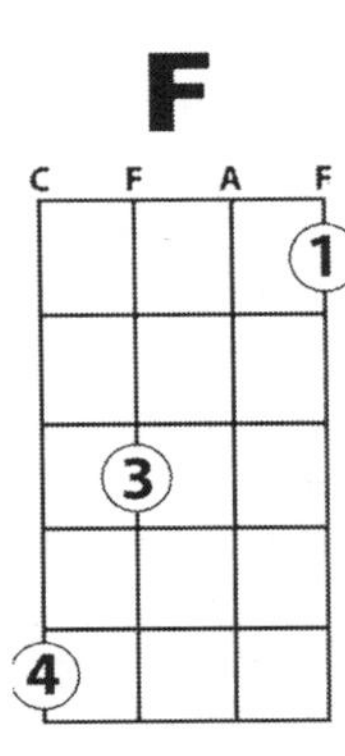

Dm

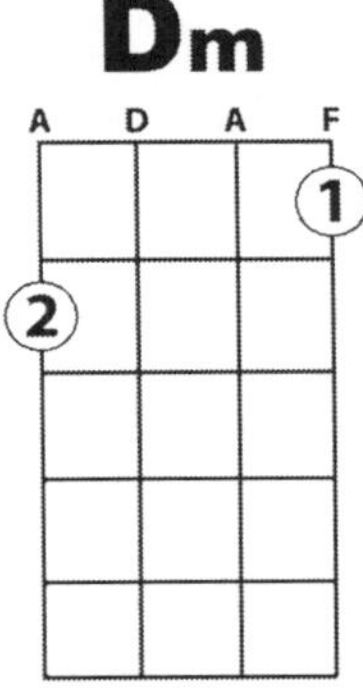

G

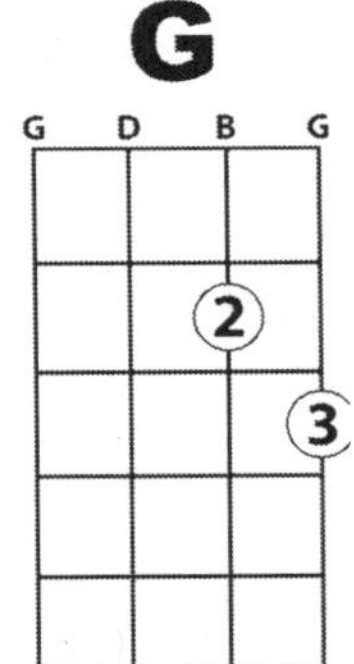

Am

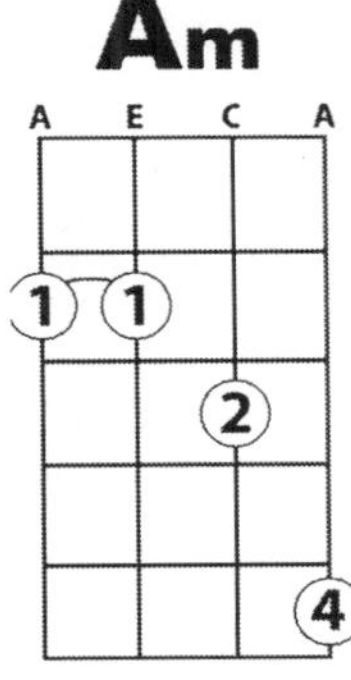

Additional Verses

Where are the folk like the folk o' the west?
Canty and couthy and kindly, the best.
There I would hie me and there I would rest,
At hame wi' my ain folk in Islay.

Now I'm at home and at home I do lay,
Dreaming of riches that come from Cathay;
I'll hop a good ship and be on my way,
And bring back my fortune to Islay.

Westering Home (continued)

Melody & Chords

Key of C (High)

CHORUS

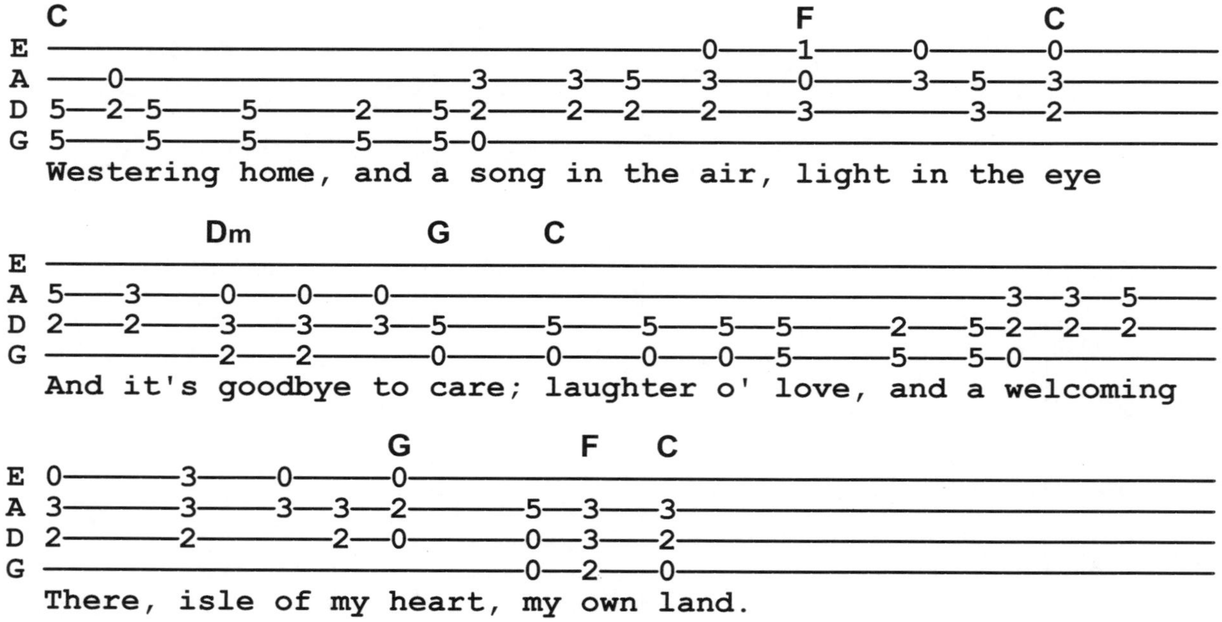

```
  C                                                                F               C
E ——————————————————————————————————————————————————————————————0———1———————0———————0——————————
A ——0——————————————————————————3—————3——5————3————————0———————3——5————3———————————
D 5——2–5—————5—————2———5–2—————2——2————2————3—————————3————2———————————
G 5—————5—————5—————5———5–0——————————————————————————————————————————————
  Westering home, and a song in the air, light in the eye

            Dm            G       C
E ————————————————————————————————————————————————————————————————————
A 5———3—————0———0———0———————————————————————————————3———3———5————
D 2———2—————3———3———3——5————5————5————5——5—————2———5–2——2——2————
G ——————————2———2———————0————0————0————0——5—————5———5–0——————————
  And it's goodbye to care; laughter o' love, and a welcoming

                        G            F    C
E 0—————3————0—————0——————————————————————————————————————
A 3—————3————3——3——2——————5——3————3————————————————————————
D 2—————2——————————2——0——————0——3————2————————————————————————
G ——————————————————————————0——2————0————————————————————————
  There, isle of my heart, my own land.
```

VERSE

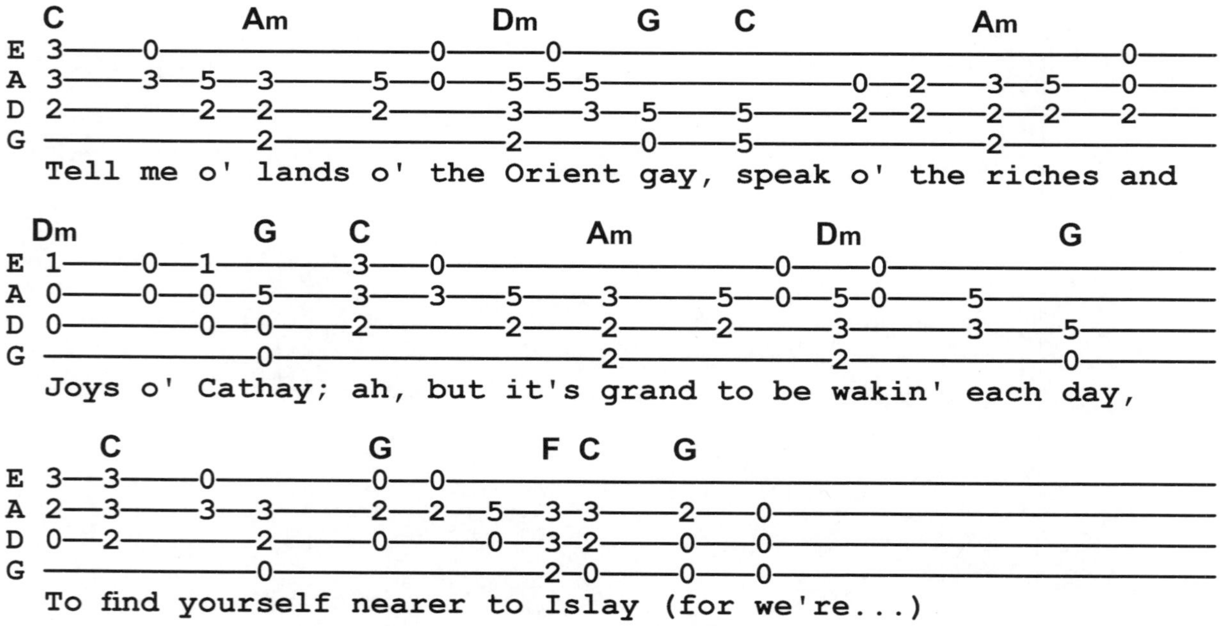

```
  C           Am                 Dm       G       C                  Am
E 3————0——————————————————0——————0——————————————————————————————————————0————
A 3————3——5——3————5——0————5–5–5—————————————————0——2————3——5————0————
D 2—————————2——2————2—————————3————3——5————5————2——2————2——2————2————
G ————————————2——————————————2—————————0————5—————————————2————————————
  Tell me o' lands o' the Orient gay, speak o' the riches and

 Dm         G    C              Am           Dm                G
E 1————0——1—————3————0——————————————————————0—————0——————————————————
A 0————0——0——5——3————3————5————3——————5——0——5–0—————5————————————
D 0————————0——0——2—————————2————2——————2———————3—————3————5————
G ——————————————0————————————————2———————————————2——————————0————
  Joys o' Cathay; ah, but it's grand to be wakin' each day,

      C                  G        F C     G
E 3——3—————0——————————0——0————————————————————————————————
A 2——3—————3——3————2——2——5——3——3————2————0————————————————
D 0——2—————————2————0————————0——3–2————0————0————————————————
G ——————————————0—————————————————2–0————0————0————————————————
  To find yourself nearer to Islay (for we're...)
```

See Chord Forms on Previous Page

Westering Home (continued)

Basic Melody

Key of C (Low)

CHORUS

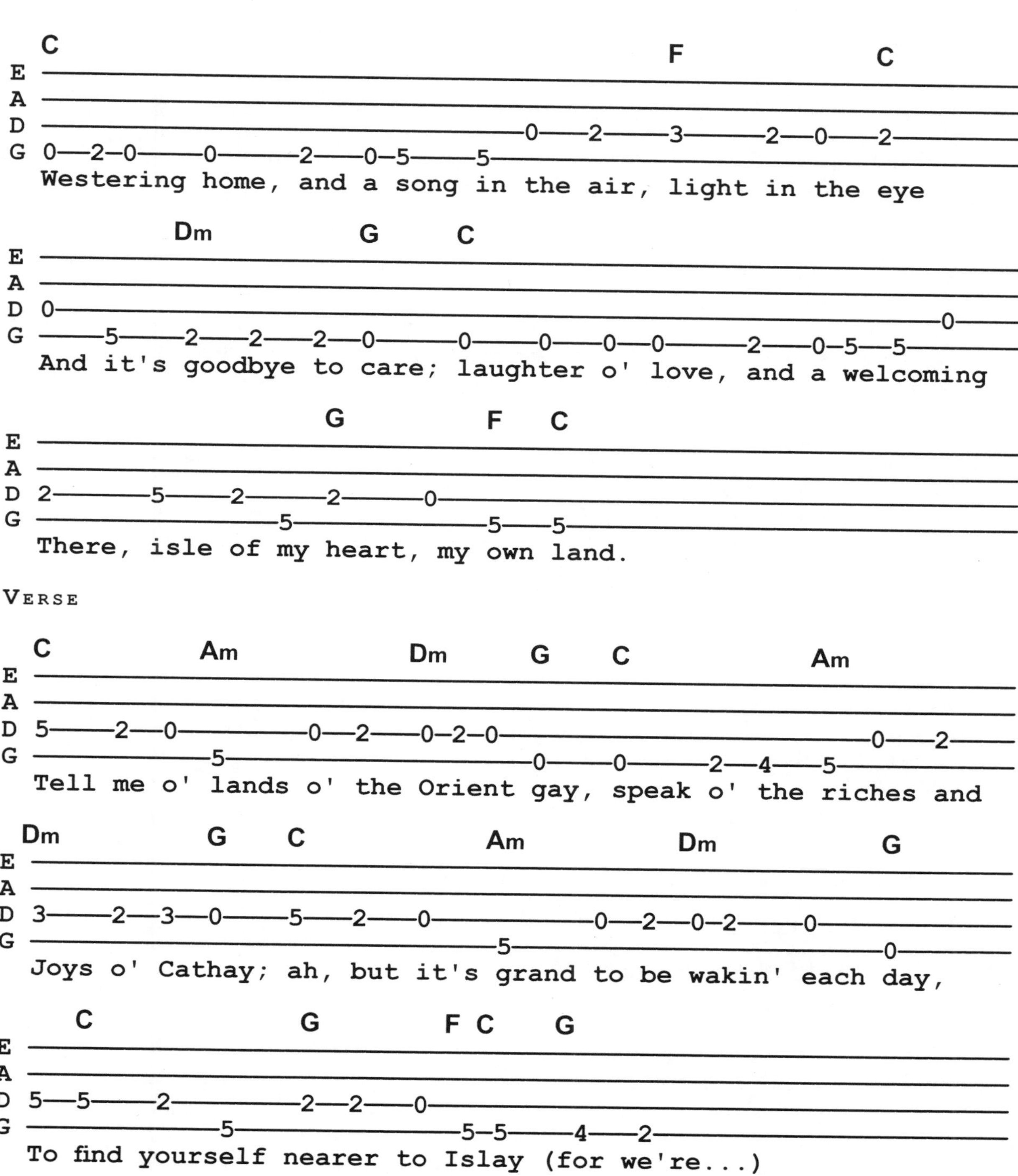

See Chord Forms Two Pages Previous

Westering Home (continued)

Basic Melody

Key of G

CHORUS

```
  G                                        C            G
E ------------------------------------------------------------
A ------------------------------0---2----3-----2---0---2------
D 0--2-0----0---------0-5----5--------------------------------
G -------------4----------------------------------------------
  Westering home, and a song in the air, light in the eye

          Am          D     G
E ------------------------------------------------------------
A 0--------------------------------------------------------0--
D ----5----2---2---2--0-----0----0---0--0-----------0-5--5----
G ----------------------------------------------4-------------
  And it's goodbye to care; laughter o' love, and a welcoming

                  D         C   G
E ------------------------------------------------------------
A 2------5----2-----2-----0-----------------------------------
D ---------------5-----------5---5----------------------------
G ------------------------------------------------------------
  There, isle of my heart, my own land.
```

VERSE

```
  G         Em          Am      D    G           Em
E ------------------------------------------------------------
A 5----2--0--------0--2---0-2-0--------------------0---2------
D -----------5--------------------0----0----2--4--5-----------
G ------------------------------------------------------------
  Tell me o' lands o' the Orient gay, speak o' the riches and

 Am         D    G          Em         Am           D
E ------------------------------------------------------------
A 3----2--3--0----5---2---0--------0--2--0-2----0-------------
D ---------------------------5-------------------------0------
G ------------------------------------------------------------
  Joys o' Cathay; ah, but it's grand to be wakin' each day,

    G         D       C G   D
E ------------------------------------------------------------
A 5--5--2-------2--2--0---------------------------------------
D -----------5----------5-5---4---2---------------------------
G ------------------------------------------------------------
  To find yourself nearer to Islay (for we're...)
```

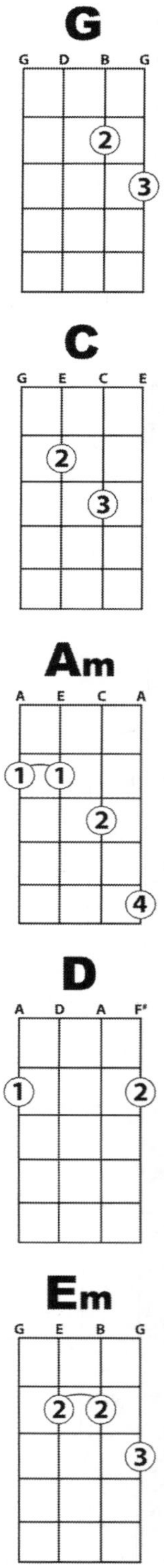

G (G D B G): 2, 3

C (G E C E): 2, 3

Am (A E C A): 1 1, 2, 4

D (A D A F#): 1, 2

Em (G E B G): 2 2, 3

Westering Home (continued)

Melody & Chords

Key of G

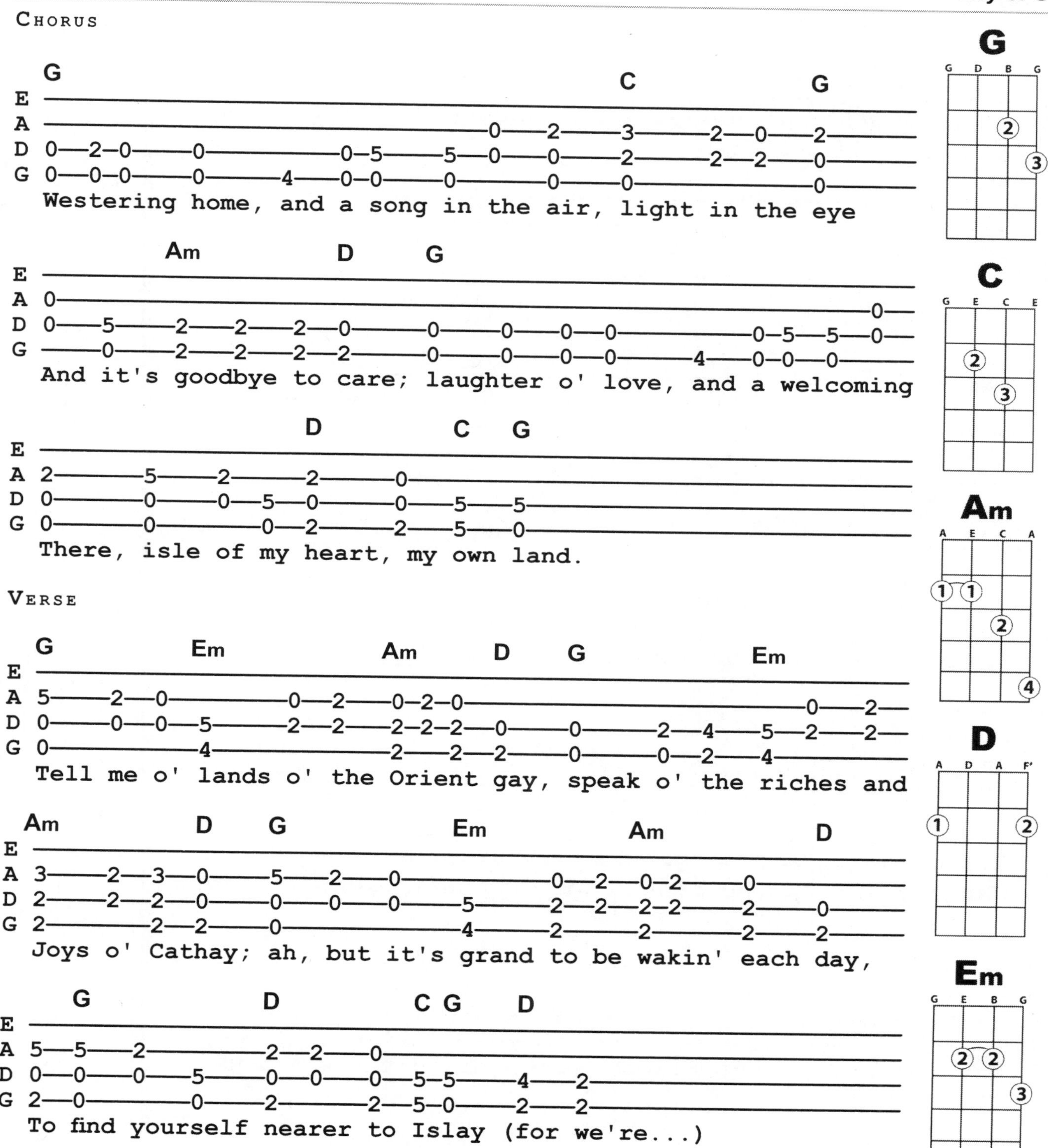

What Do We Do With A Drunken Sailor

Basic Melody

Key of A Minor (Low)

This is one of the quintessential sailing songs, or sea shanties, known throughout the English-speaking world. It asks the question of what the crew is to do with one of their inebriated fellows, and proposes some more or less humorous courses of action. Quite a few other verses have been penned over the years, some of them quite bawdy. We have only included a few of the tamer ones here.

Words and Music

Traditional

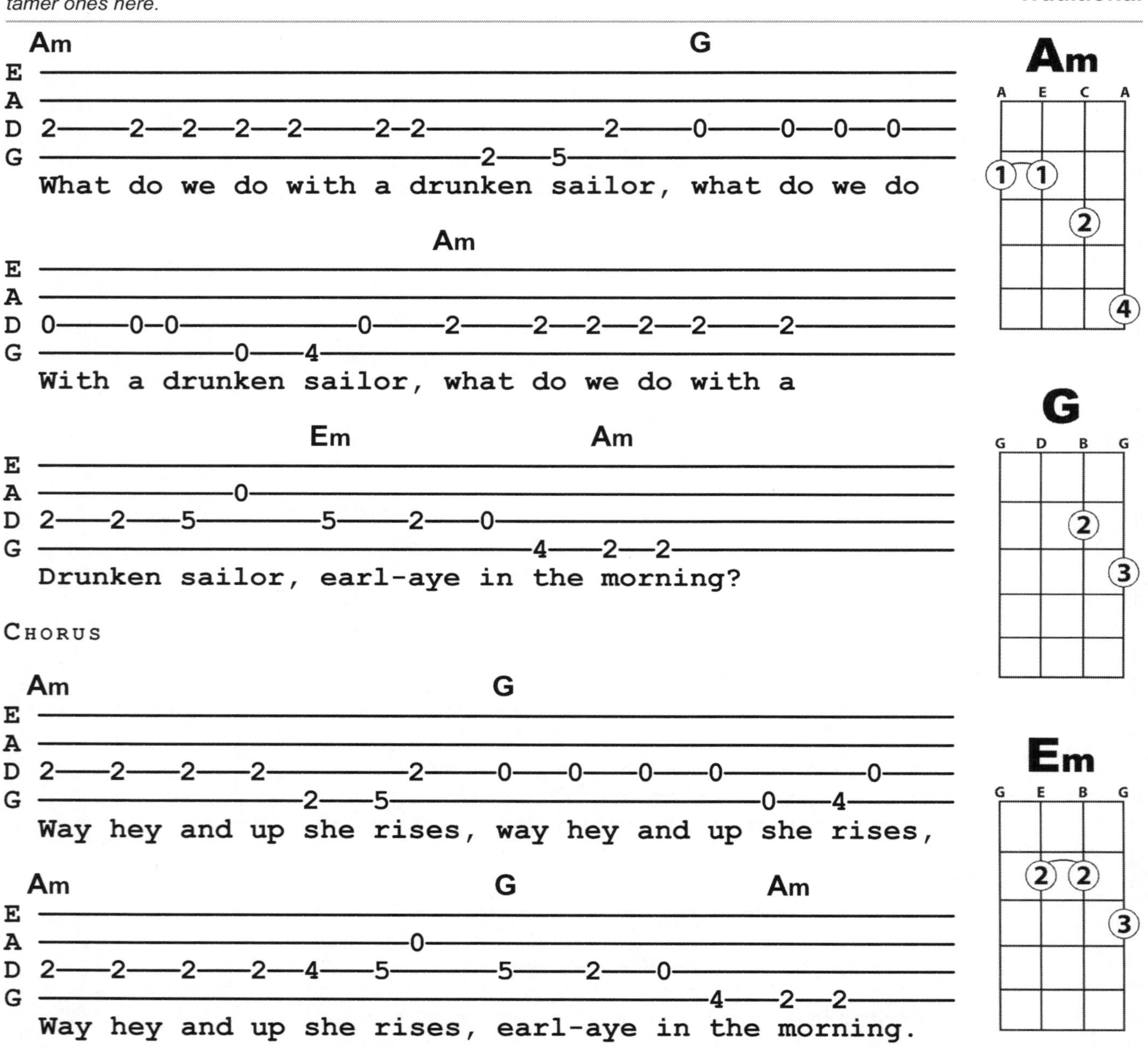

See Additional Verses on Next Page

What Do We Do With A Drunken Sailor (continued)

Melody & Chords

Key of A Minor (Low)

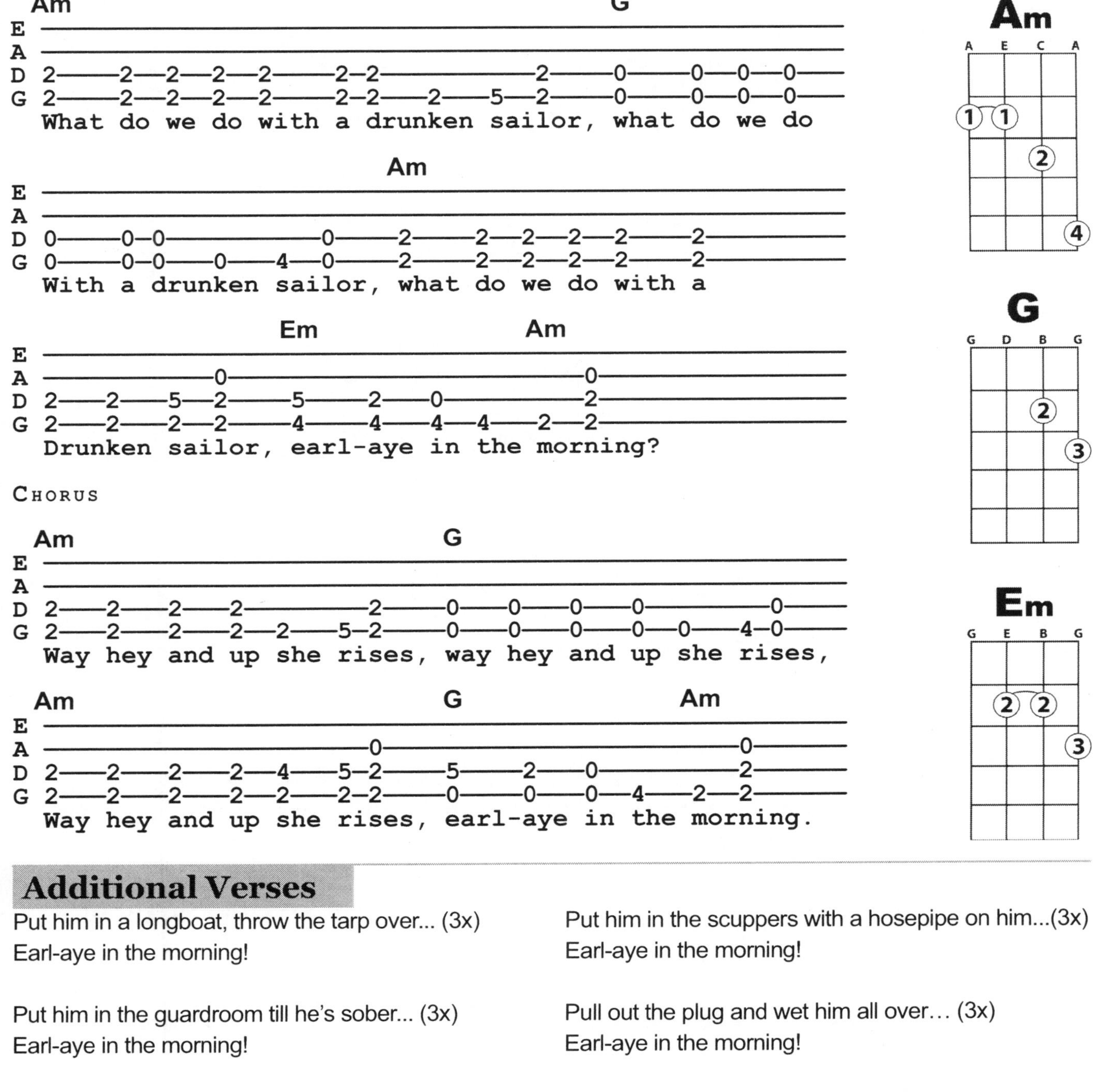

Additional Verses

Put him in a longboat, throw the tarp over... (3x)
Earl-aye in the morning!

Put him in the guardroom till he's sober... (3x)
Earl-aye in the morning!

Shave his belly with a rusty razor... (3x)
Earl-aye in the morning!

Put him in the scuppers with a hosepipe on him...(3x)
Earl-aye in the morning!

Pull out the plug and wet him all over… (3x)
Earl-aye in the morning!

Give 'im a hair of the dog that bit him… (3x)
Earl-aye in the morning!

What Do We Do With A Drunken Sailor (continued)

Basic Melody

Key of A Minor (High)

```
  Am                                           G
E 0----0---0---0---0-----0--0----------0-----------------------
A ---------------------------------0---3-------5-----5---5---5-
D -------------------------------------------------------------
G -------------------------------------------------------------
  What do we do with a drunken sailor, what do we do
```

```
                            Am
E ----------------------------0-----0---0---0---0-----0-------
A 5-----5--5---------2--5-------------------------------------
D -------------5----------------------------------------------
G ------------------------------------------------------------
  With a drunken sailor, what do we do with a
```

```
                    Em               Am
E 0----0----3--5----3-----0-----------------------------------
A -----------------------------5--2----0--0--------------------
D ------------------------------------------------------------
G ------------------------------------------------------------
  Drunken sailor, earl-aye in the morning?
```

CHORUS

```
  Am                          G
E 0----0----0----0--------0-----------------------------------
A -----------------0---3------5----5----5----5--------2--5----
D ------------------------------------------------5-----------
G ------------------------------------------------------------
  Way hey and up she rises, way hey and up she rises,
```

```
  Am                          G                   Am
E 0----0----0----0--2---3-5---3----0--------------------------
A ----------------------------------------5--2----0--0--------
D ------------------------------------------------------------
G ------------------------------------------------------------
  Way hey and up she rises, earl-aye in the morning.
```

Am (A E C A): 1 1 2 4

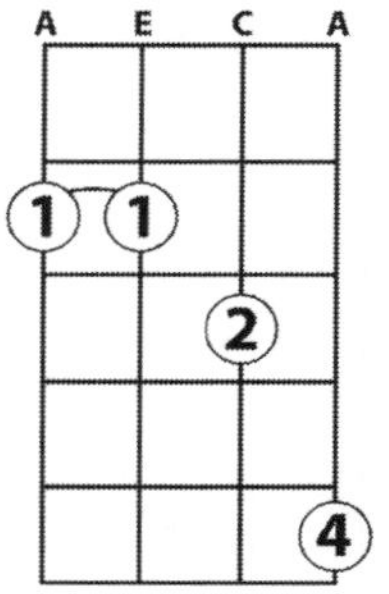

G (G D B G): 2 3

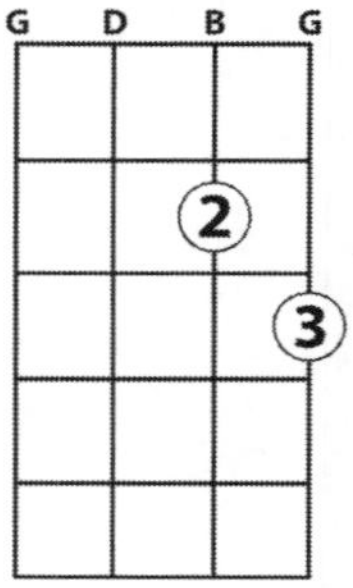

Em (G E B G): 2 2 3

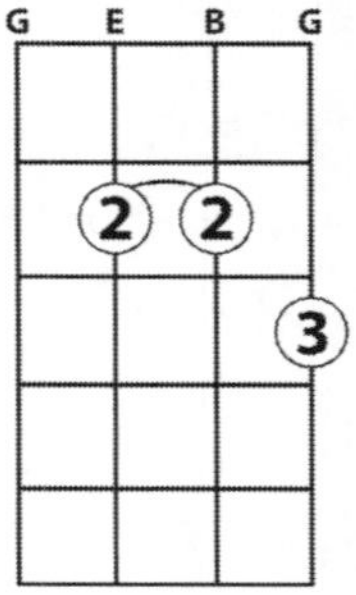

What Do We Do With A Drunken Sailor (continued)

Melody & Chords

Key of A Minor (High)

```
  Am                                              G
E 0----0--0--0--0----0-0-----------0-------------------------
A 0----0--0--0--0----0-0----0---3--0-----5-----5---5---5-----
D 2-----------2--------2----2---2--2-----0-----0---0---0-----
G --------------------------2---2---------0-------------0-----
  What do we do with a drunken sailor, what do we do

                              Am
E ----------------------------0----0--0--0--0----0-----------
A 5----5-5---------2--5-------0----0--0--0--0----0-----------
D 0----0-0----5----0--0-------2-----------2------------------
G ---------0----0-------0------------------------------------
  With a drunken sailor, what do we do with a

                     Em                 Am
E 0---0---3--5---3-----0-------------------------------------
A 0---0---0--0---2-----2----5--2---0--0----------------------
D 2-------2--2---2----------2--2---2--2----------------------
G --------------------------0------2--2----------------------
  Drunken sailor, earl-aye in the morning?
```

Chorus

```
  Am                          G
E 0---0---0---0-------0--------------------------------------
A 0---0---0---0--0----3-0----5---5---5---5--------2-5--------
D 2---2-------2--2----2-2----0---0---0---0---5----0-0--------
G ---------------2----2------0---0-------0---0----0----------
  Way hey and up she rises, way hey and up she rises,

  Am                          G                Am
E 0---0---0---0--2----3-5----3------0------------------------
A 0---0---0---0--0----0-0----2------2----5--2---0--0---------
D 2---2-------2-------2-2----0-----------0--0---2--2---------
G ---------------------------------------0------2--2---------
  Way hey and up she rises, earl-aye in the morning.
```

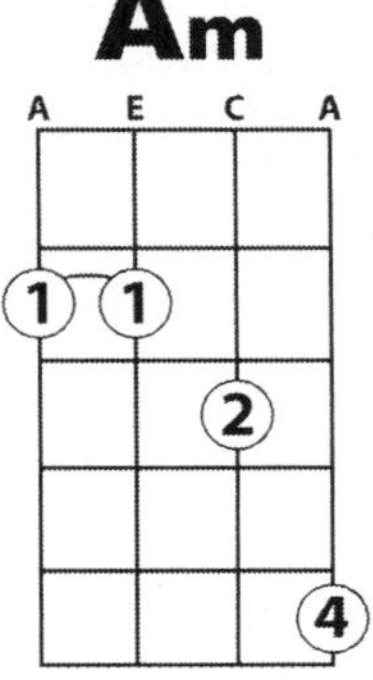

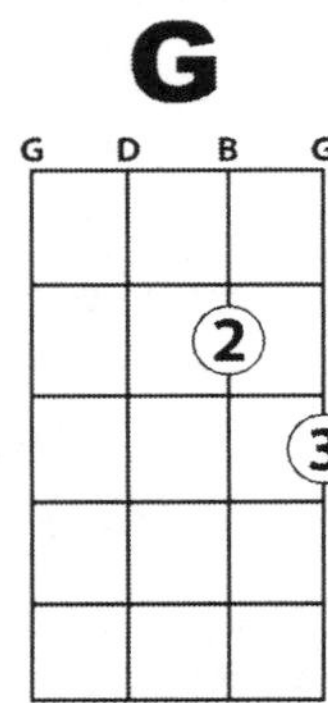

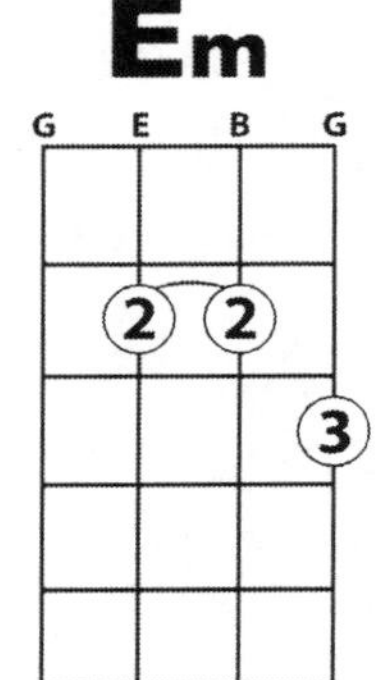

What Do We Do With A Drunken Sailor (continued)

Basic Melody

Key of E Minor

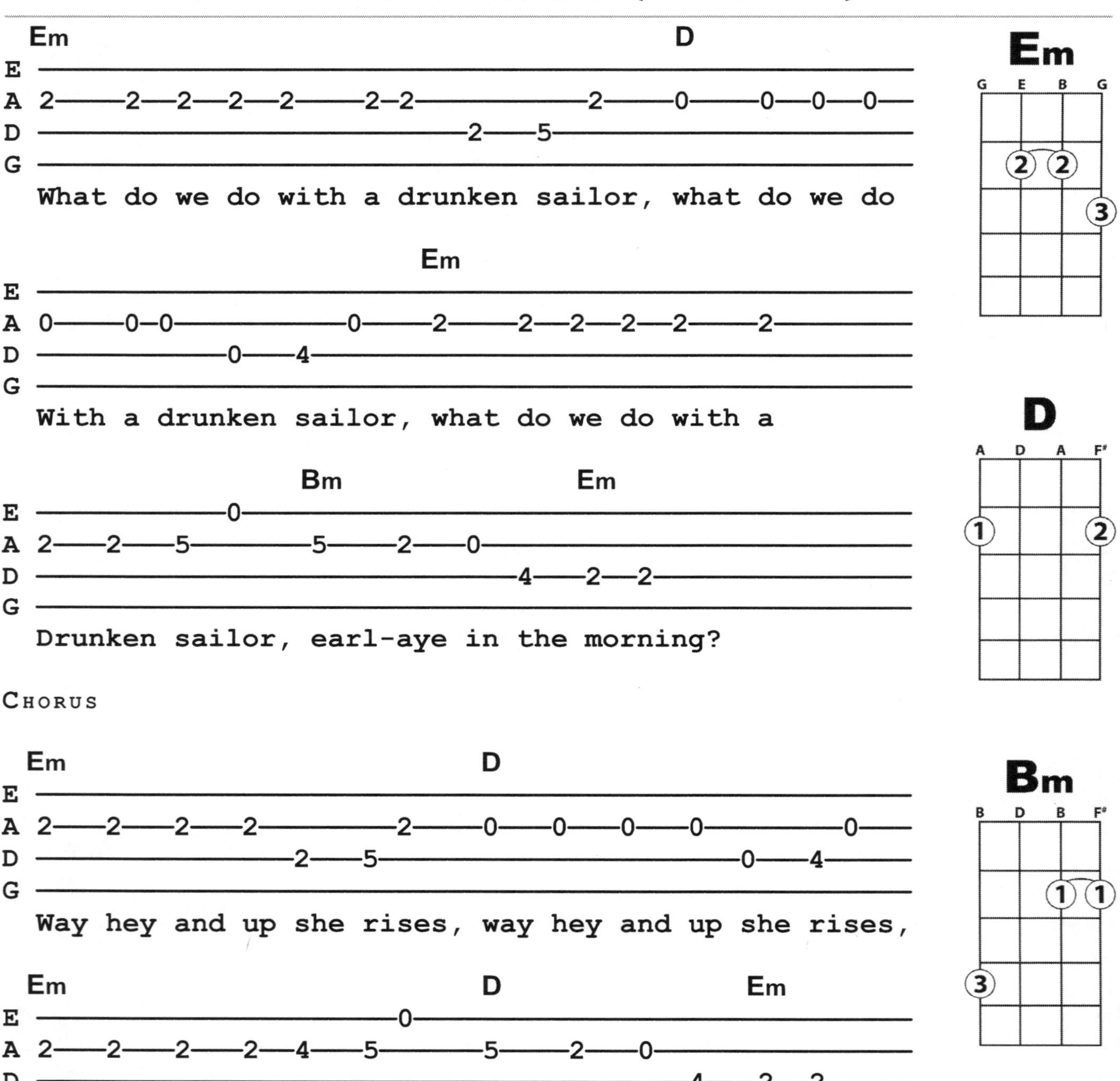

What Do We Do With A Drunken Sailor (continued)

Melody & Chords

Key of E Minor

```
 Em                                                  D
E ─────────────────────────────────────────────────────────────────
A 2────2──2──2──2─────2─2──────────────2──────0─────0──0──0──
D 2────2──2──2──2─────2─2─────2────5──2──────0─────0──0──0──
G 0─────────────0──────────────0────4────4───────2───────────2──
 What do we do with a drunken sailor, what do we do
```

```
                              Em
E ─────────────────────────────────────────────────────────────────
A 0────0─0────────────────0─────2─────2──2──2──2─────2─────
D 0────0─0─────0────4──4──────2─────2──2──2──2─────2─────
G ──────────2────2────2──2─────0────────────0──────────────
 With a drunken sailor, what do we do with a
```

```
                    Bm               Em
E ─────────────0─────────────────────────────────────────
A 2────2────5──2──────5──────2────0──────────────────────
D 2────2────2──2──────4──────4────4──4────2──2───────────
G 0─────────0─────────4───────────4──4────4──4───────────
 Drunken sailor, earl-aye in the morning?
```

Chorus

```
 Em                          D
E ─────────────────────────────────────────────────────────────────
A 2───2────2────2────────────2─────0─────0─────0─────0───────────0──
D 2───2────2────2────2────5──2─────0─────0─────0─────0────0────4──0──
G 0───0─────────0────4────4────────2─────2───────────2────2────2─────
 Way hey and up she rises, way hey and up she rises,
```

```
 Em                          D                  Em
E ───────────────────────0─────────────────────────────────────
A 2───2────2────2───4────5──2─────5─────2────0─────────────────
D 2───2────2────2───2────2──5─────0─────0────0───4────2──2─────
G 0───0─────────0─────────────────2──────────2───2────4──4─────
 Way hey and up she rises, earl-aye in the morning.
```

Em

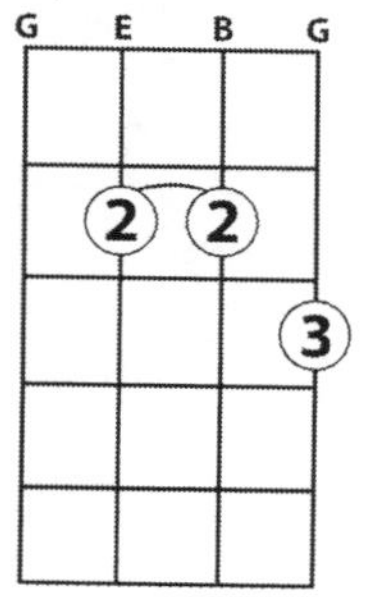

G E B G

(2) (2) (3)

D

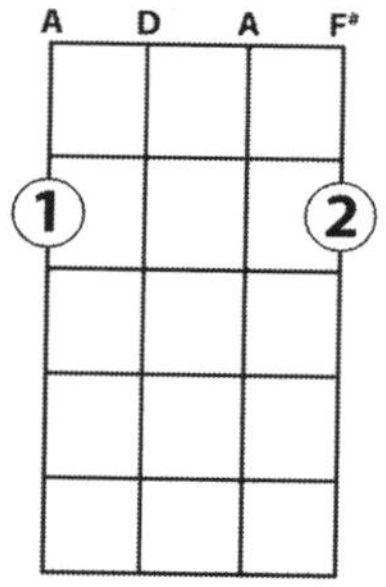

A D A F#

(1) (2)

Bm

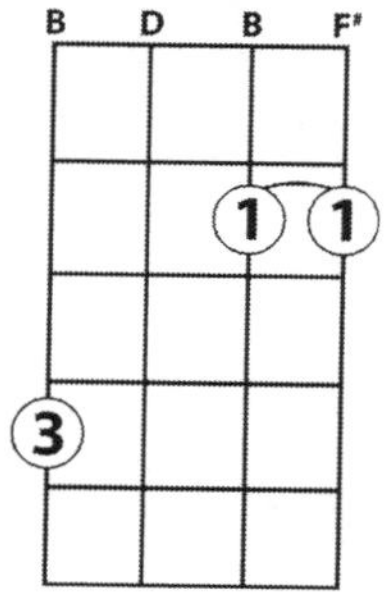

B D B F#

(1) (1) (3)

Whiskey Is the Life Of Man

Basic Melody

Key of C (Low)

This was another favorite shanty to be sung while on a sailing voyage. It is said that the sailors would especially sing this one when working within earshot of the captain's quarters, in the hopes of softening his heart into ordering up an extra round of grog for the men.

Words and Music

Traditional

Whiskey is the life of man! I'll drink whiskey when I can.

CHORUS

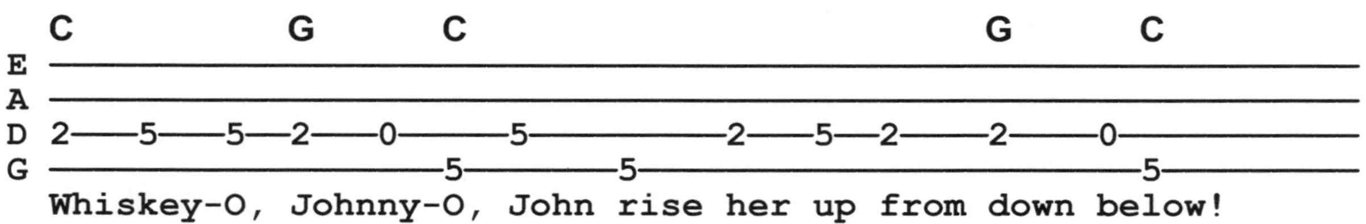

Whiskey-O, Johnny-O, John rise her up from down below!

```
   C                     F       C                  G         C
E ────────────────────────────────────────────────────────────────────
A ────────────3─────0───────────3──0──────────────────────────────────
D ───2────5──────────────3───5──────────5────2────5────2──────────────
G 5────────────────────────────────────────────────────────────5──────
```

Whiskey, whiskey, whiskey-O, up a-loft this yard must go.

```
   C                     G       C
E ────────────────────────────────────────────────────────────────────
A 3───────────────────────────────────────────────────────────────────
D ──────────2───5──2───2────0─────────────────────────────────────────
G ─────5──────────────────────5───────────────────────────────────────
```

John rise her up from down below.

Chord Forms

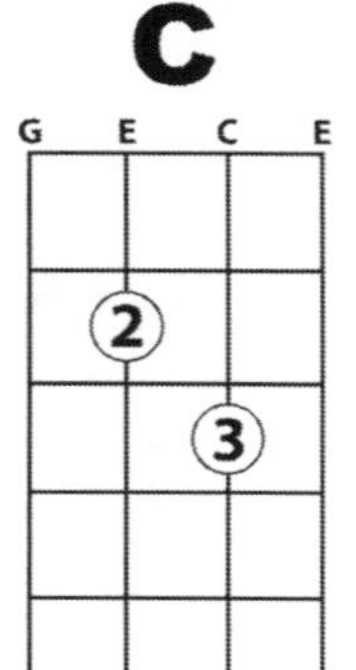

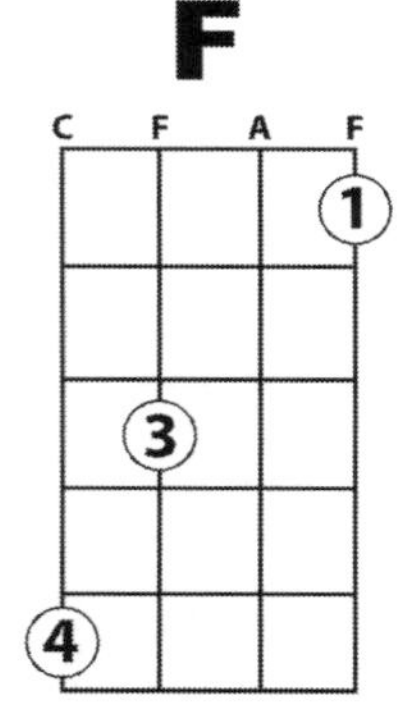

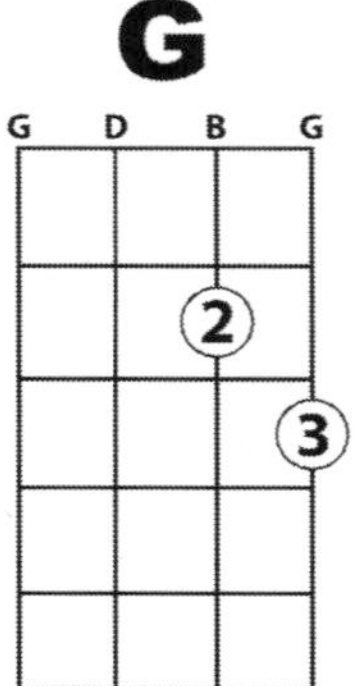

See Additional Verses on Next Page

SEA SHANTY

Whiskey Is the Life Of Man (continued)

Melody & Chords

Key of C (Low)

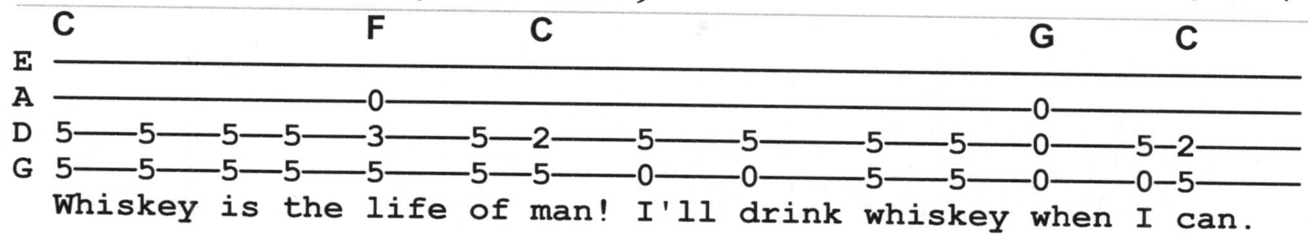

```
  C                        F            C                                       G          C
E ------------------------------------------------------------------------------------------------
A ------------------------0---------------------------------------------------0-------------------
D 5-----5-----5---5-----3-------5---2-------5--------5---------5----5------0-------5-2-----------
G 5-----5-----5---5-----5-------5---5-------0--------0---------5----5------0-------0-5-----------
  Whiskey is the life of man! I'll drink whiskey when I can.
```

Chorus

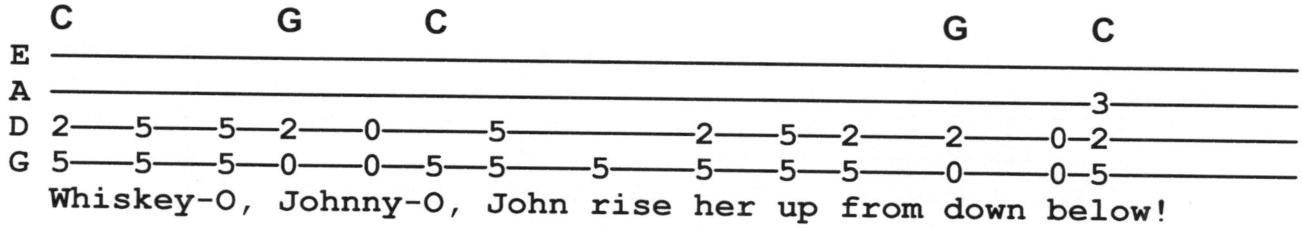

```
  C                G          C                                          G          C
E ------------------------------------------------------------------------------------------------
A ---------------------------------------------------------------------------------3--------------
D 2-----5-----5---2-----0----------5---------------2-----5---2-------2-------0-2--------------
G 5-----5-----5---0-----0---5----5--------5--------5-----5---5-------0-------0-5--------------
  Whiskey-O, Johnny-O, John rise her up from down below!
```

```
  C                          F           C                          G               C
E ------------------------------------------------------------------------------------------------
A ---------------------3-------0--------------3---0----------------------------------------------
D -------2-------5----2-------3-----3-----5---2---2-5-------2-------5-------2-------------------
G 5------5-------5----0-------5-----5-----5---0-------5-----5-------0-------0-------5-----------
  Whiskey, whiskey, whiskey-O, up a-loft this yard must go.
```

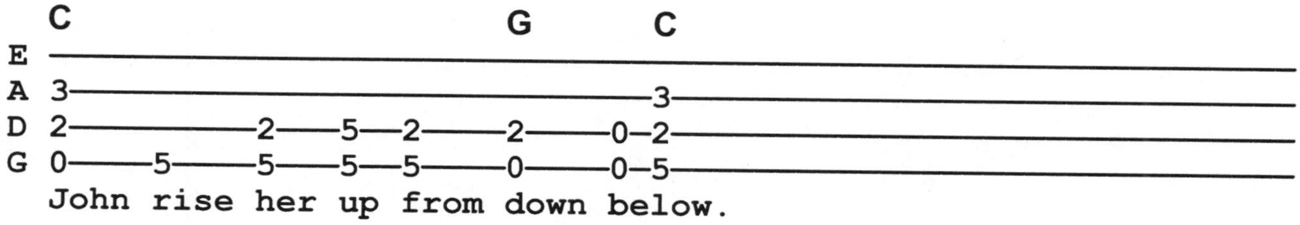

```
  C                              G           C
E ------------------------------------------------------------------------------------------------
A 3----------------------------------------3-----------------------------------------------------
D 2---------------2-----5----2------2------0-2---------------------------------------------------
G 0------5--------5-----5----5------0------0-5---------------------------------------------------
  John rise her up from down below.
```

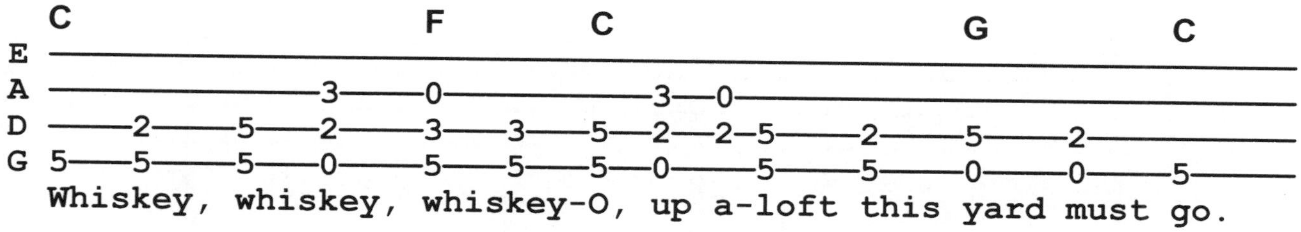

Additional Verses

Now whiskey made me pawn me clothes,
And whiskey gave me a broken nose.

Now whiskey is the life of man,
Whiskey from an old tin can.

I thought I heard the first mate say:
I treats me crew in a decent way.

I treat me crew in a decent way,
Give them whiskey twice a day.

O whiskey killed my poor old dad,
And whiskey drove my mother mad.

O whiskey hot and whiskey cold,
O whiskey new and whiskey old.

See Chord Forms on Previous Page

Whiskey Is the Life Of Man (continued)

Basic Melody

Key of C (High)

```
  C                 F        C                                       G       C
E 3---3---3---3-----5----3---0-----3-----3------3-----3---5------3---0-------
A ---------------------------------------------------------------------------
D ---------------------------------------------------------------------------
G ---------------------------------------------------------------------------
  Whiskey is the life of man! I'll drink whiskey when I can.
```

CHORUS

```
  C            G         C                                    G          C
E 0---3---3---0--------------3-----------0---3---0-----0-------------------
A -------------------5---3---------3--------------------------------5---3---
D ------------------------------------------------------------------------
G ------------------------------------------------------------------------
  Whiskey-O, Johnny-O, John rise her up from down below!
```

```
  C                      F         C                          G           C
E ----0-----3----8-------5----1----3---8---5---3------0-------3------0-------
A 3------------------------------------------------------------------------3-
D ---------------------------------------------------------------------------
G ---------------------------------------------------------------------------
  Whiskey, whiskey, whiskey-O, up a-loft this yard must go.
```

```
  C                           G           C
E 8-----------0----3----0-----0-------------------------------
A ------3-----------------------------5---3-------------------
D -------------------------------------------------------------
G -------------------------------------------------------------
  John rise her up from down below.
```

Chord Forms

C

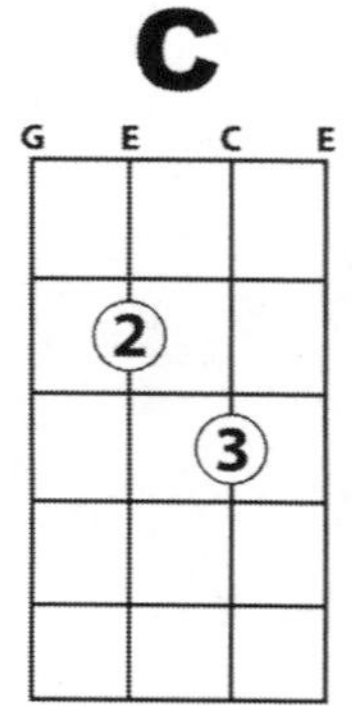

F

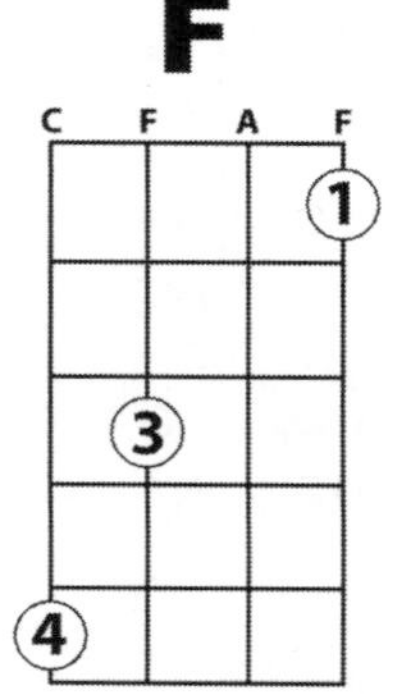

G

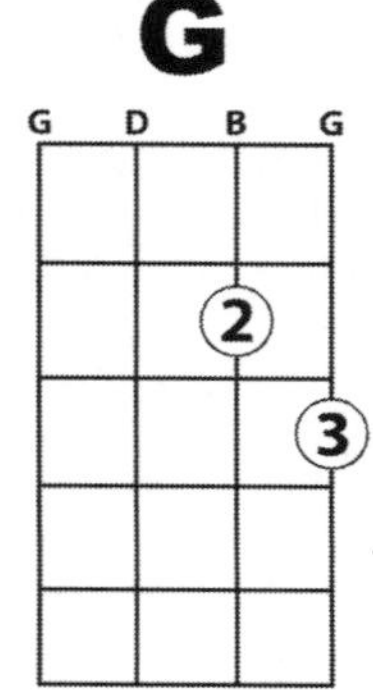

Whiskey Is the Life Of Man (continued)

Melody & Chords

Key of C (High)

```
   C                    F        C                                G      C
E 3——3——3—3——5———3—0———3————3————3———3——5———3–0———
A 3——3——3—3——3———3—3———3————3————3———3——5———2–3———
D 2—————2————3—————2———2—————————2——————5———0–2———
G ————————————————————————————————————————————————
  Whiskey is the life of man! I'll drink whiskey when I can.
```

Chorus

```
   C         G      C                                 G     C
E 0——3——3—0———————3————————0———3—0————0———————————
A 3——3——3—2———5—3—3————3———3———3—3————2————5–3—————
D 2—————2—0———0—2—2————2————————2—2————0————0–2—————
G ————————————————0————0———————————————————————0————
  Whiskey-O, Johnny-O, John rise her up from down below!
```

```
   C                      F         C                         G           C
E ———0————3———8————5———1———3——8——5–3———0————3————0—————
A 3——3————3———7————3———0———3——7——3–3———3————2————2————3——
D 2———————2———5————3———————2——5————2———2————0————0————2——
G 0———————————————————————————————————————————————————0——
  Whiskey, whiskey, whiskey-O, up a-loft this yard must go.
```

```
   C                              G      C
E 8——————————0——3——0————0——————————————
A 7————3—————3——3——3————2————5–3———————
D 5————2————————2——2————0————0–2———————
G ————-0————————————————————0–0————————
  John rise her up from down below.
```

Chord Forms

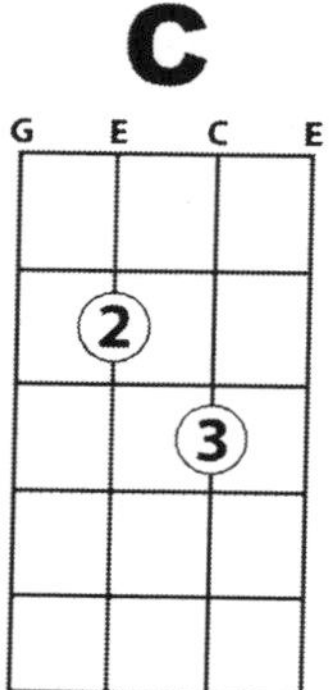

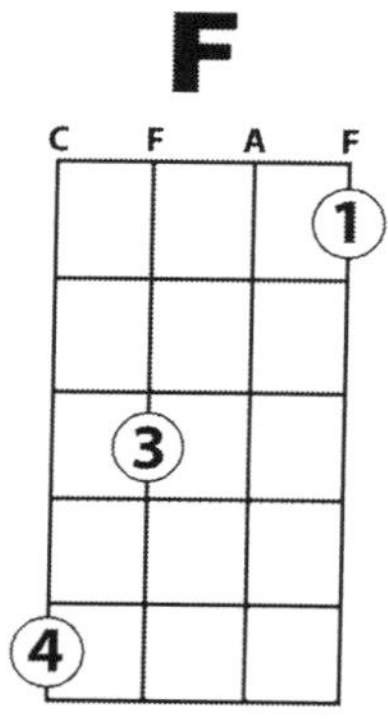

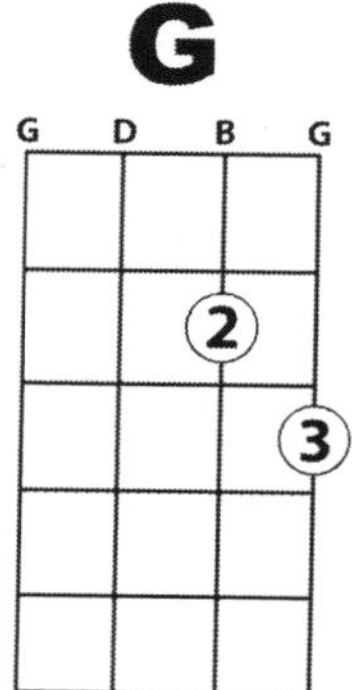

Whiskey Is the Life Of Man (continued)

Basic Melody

Key of G

```
  G                C      G                          D     G
E ----------------------0------------------------------------0----------------
A 5---5---5--5-------------5--2-----5-----5------5---5---------5--2-----------
D ----------------------------------------------------------------------------
G ----------------------------------------------------------------------------
  Whiskey is the life of man! I'll drink whiskey when I can.
```

CHORUS

```
  G           D      G                           D      G
E ----------------------------------------------------------------------------
A 2---5---5--2---0-------5-----------2---5--2----2-----0----------------------
D ------------------5---------5---------------------------5-------------------
G ----------------------------------------------------------------------------
  Whiskey-O, Johnny-O, John rise her up from down below!
```

```
  G                  C       G                 D          G
E ---------------3----0-----------3--0----------------------------------------
A ----2----5--------------3---5---------5----2----5----2----------------------
D 5------------------------------------------------------5--------------------
G ----------------------------------------------------------------------------
  Whiskey, whiskey, whiskey-O, up a-loft this yard must go.
```

```
  G                    D       G
E 3---------------------------------------------------------------------------
A -----------2---5--2----2----0-----------------------------------------------
D ----5-------------------------5---------------------------------------------
G ----------------------------------------------------------------------------
  John rise her up from down below.
```

Chord Forms

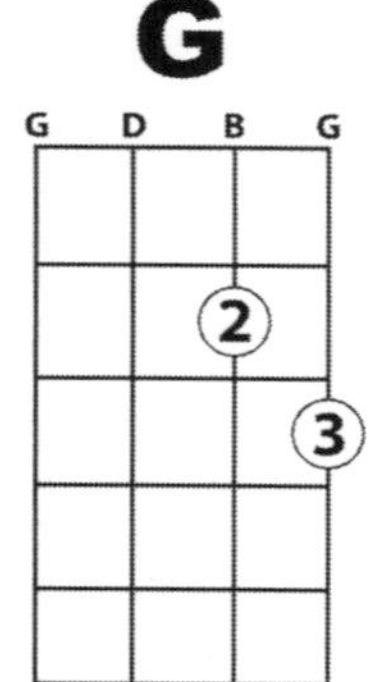

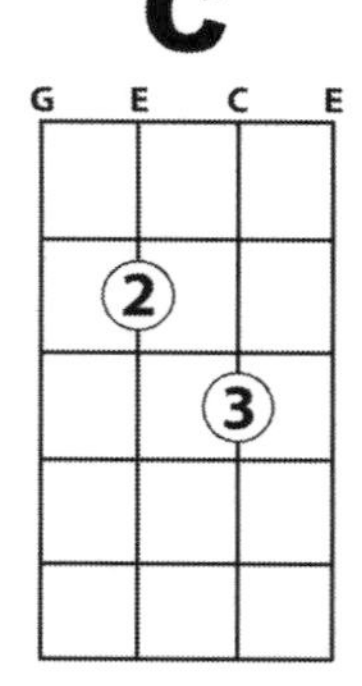

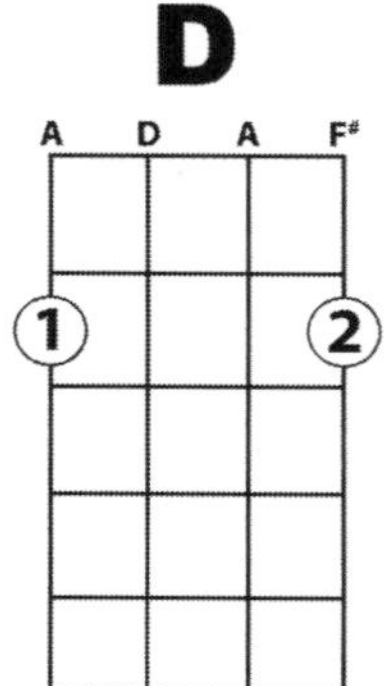

Whiskey Is the Life Of Man (continued)

Melody & Chords

Key of G

```
  G                    C          G                            D       G
E ---------------------0---------------------------------------0-----------------
A 5---5---5--5---3-----5--2-----5-----5------5---5---0------5-2------
D 0---0---0--0---2-----2--0-----0-----0------0---0---0------0-0------
G 0-------0---------------0-----0------------0--------------2-0------
  Whiskey is the life of man! I'll drink whiskey when I can.
```

CHORUS

```
  G           D       G                           D       G
E ----------------------------------------------------------------
A 2---5---5--2----0-------5-------------2---5--2-----2-----0-----------
D 0---0---0--0----0--5----0------5------0---0--0-----0-----0-5---------
G 0-------0--2-------0----0------0----------0--------2-------0---------
  Whiskey-O, Johnny-O, John rise her up from down below!
```

```
  G                       C        G                     D         G
E ----------------3-------0-------------3--0------------------------------
A -----2-----5----2-------3----3----5---2--2-5-----2-----5-----2----------
D 5----0-----0----0-------2----2----0---0------0---0-----0-----0-----5----
G 0----------0----------------------0----------0---------2-----2-----0----
  Whiskey, whiskey, whiskey-O, up a-loft this yard must go.
```

```
  G                       D      G
E 3-----------------------------------------------------------
A 2--------------2----5--2-----2-----0------------------------
D 0-------5------0----0--0-----0-----0-5----------------------
G --------0-----------0--0-----2-----0------------------------
  John rise her up from down below.
```

Chord Forms

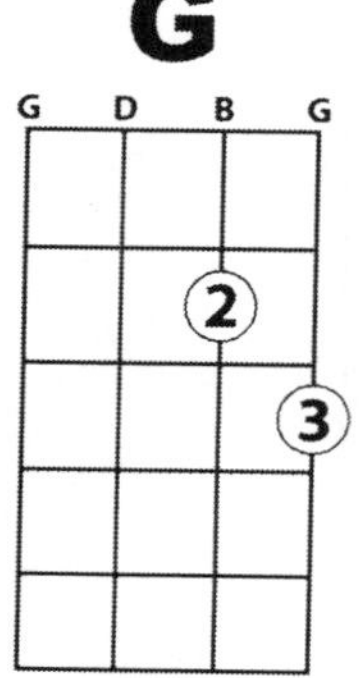

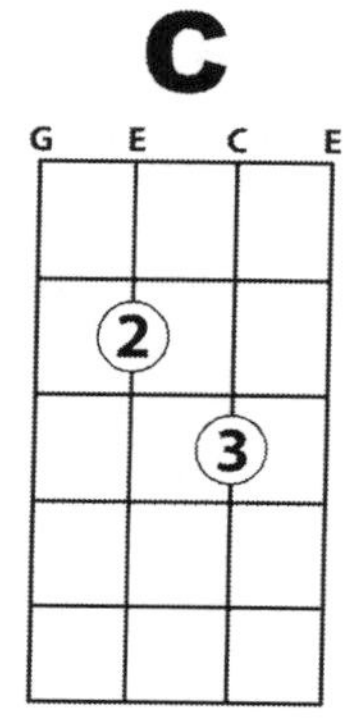

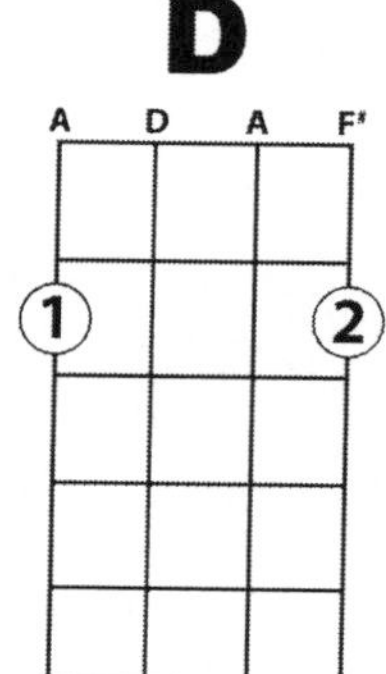

Yarmouth Town

Basic Melody

Key of C

Words and Music

Traditional

This bawdy old English seafaring song tells the tale of a certain pub in the town of Yarmouth, and specifically of the very popular daughter of the landlord there. A number of prominent performers have recorded versions of this, including Liam Clancy and Gaelic Storm.

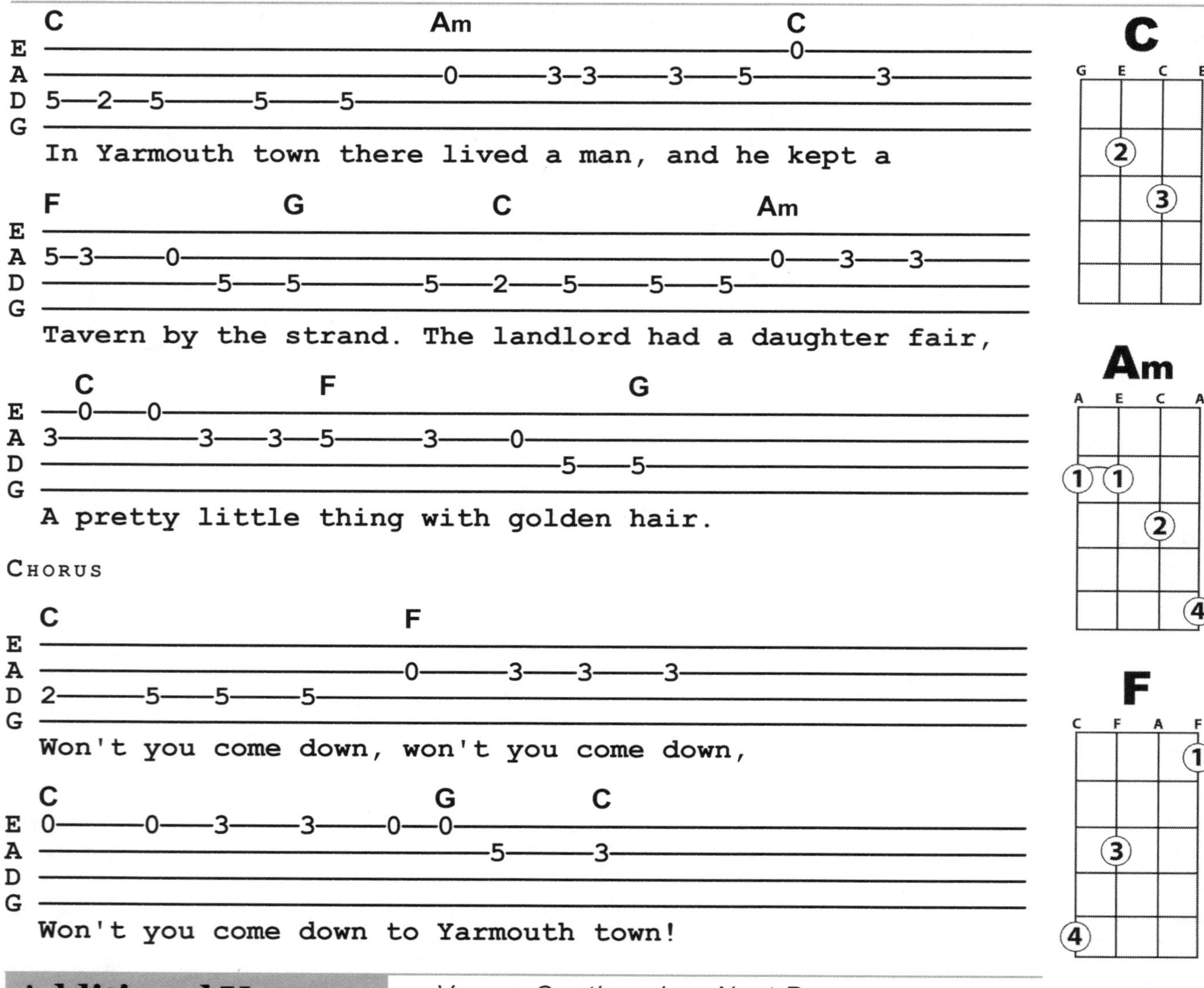

Additional Verses

Verses Continued on Next Page

Now to this tavern come a sailor-man,
He asked the daughter for her hand.
"Why should I marry you?" she said,
"I get all I want without being wed."

"But," she says, "If you want with me to linger,
I'll tie a bit of string all around my finger.
As you pass by, just pull on the string,
And I'll come down and I'll let you in."

Yarmouth Town (continued)

Melody & Chords

Key of C

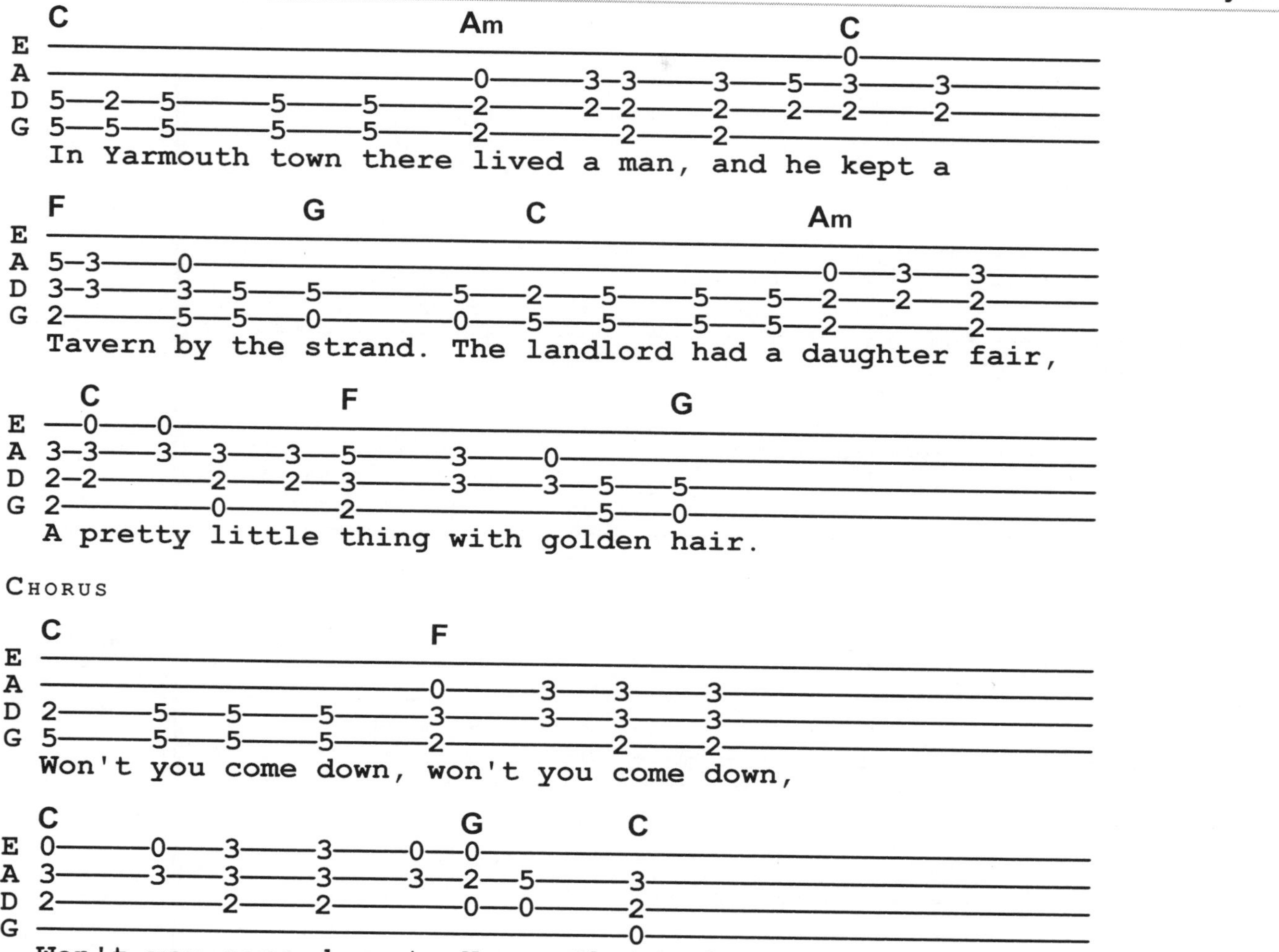

Additional Verses

Continued from Previous Page

At closing time the sailor-man,
He went to the tavern by the sand.
And then he went and he pulled on the string,
And she came down and she let him in.

Well, he's never seen such a sight before,
'Cause the string around the finger was all she wore.
And when he went and he pulled the old string
She pulled back the blanket and let Jack in.

So, the sailor stayed the whole night through.
And early in the morning went back to his crew,
Where then he told them all about that maiden fair,
The plump little thing with the golden hair.

And the story, that soon got around
And the very next night in Yarmouth Town
There was fifteen sailors pulling on the string
And she come down and she let them all in.

So all young men what ever to Yarmouth do go,
See a plump little girl with her hair hung low,
Well, all you got do is pull the old string,
And she'll come down and she'll let you all in.

See Chord Forms on Previous Page

Yarmouth Town (continued)

Basic Melody

Key of G

```
  G                                   Em                             G
E ---------------------------------------------------------------------------------------------
A --------------------------------------------------------------------------0---2--------------
D 0---------0---------0-------0---------2--------5--5-------5-------------------------5--------
G -----4---------------------------------------------------------------------------------------
  In Yarmouth town there lived a man, and he kept a
```

```
  C                    D                 G                       Em
E ---------------------------------------------------------------------------------------------
A 0--------------------------------------------------------------------------------------------
D ---5-------2---0-----0-----------0-------------0-------0-----0----2-----5-----5---------------
G -------------------------------------------4-------------------------------------------------
  Tavern by the strand. The landlord had a daughter fair,
```

```
     G                   C                          D
E ---------------------------------------------------------------------------------------------
A ---2----2--------------0---------------------------------------------------------------------
D 5-------------5----5---------------5-------2----0------0-------------------------------------
G ---------------------------------------------------------------------------------------------
  A pretty little thing with golden hair.
```

CHORUS

```
  G                                C
E ---------------------------------------------------------------------------------------------
A ---------------------------------------------------------------------------------------------
D ---------0-----0-------0---------2--------5-----5------5-------------------------------------
G 4--------------------------------------------------------------------------------------------
  Won't you come down, won't you come down,
```

```
  G                                  D            G
E ---------------------------------------------------------------------------------------------
A 2---------2-----5-------5------2---2----0----------------------------------------------------
D ---------------------------------------------------5-----------------------------------------
G ---------------------------------------------------------------------------------------------
  Won't you come down to Yarmouth town!
```

Chord Forms

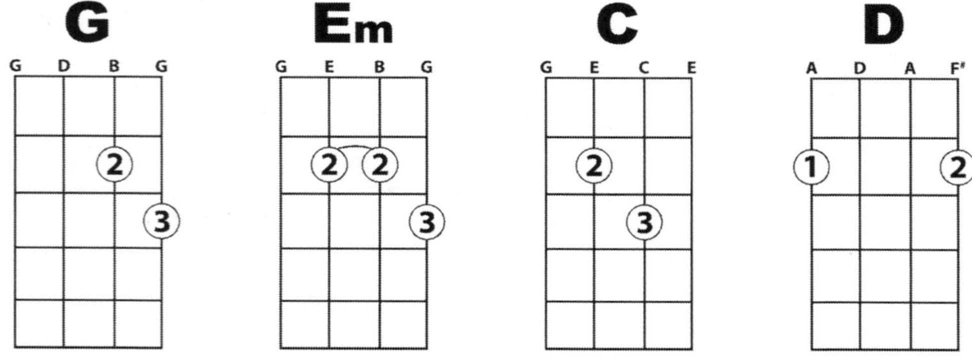

Yarmouth Town (continued)

Melody & Chords

Key of G

```
    G                         Em                    G
E ----------------------------------------------------------------
A ------------------------------------------------0--2------------
D 0-----0-----0-----0-----2-----5-5-----5---2--0-----5-----------
G 0--4--0-----0-----0-----4-----4-4-----4------0-----0-----------
  In Yarmouth town there lived a man, and he kept a

  C             D           G              Em
E ----------------------------------------------------------------
A 0---------------------------------------------------------------
D 2-5----2--0--0-------0-------0----0---0--2---5---5-------------
G 0-5----5--0--2-------2---4---0----0---0--4---4---4-------------
  Tavern by the strand. The landlord had a daughter fair,

    G              C                  D
E ----------------------------------------------------------------
A --2---2-----------0---------------------------------------------
D 5-0---0--5----5---2------5-----2--0----0------------------------
G 4-0------0----0---0------5-----5--0----2------------------------
  A pretty little thing with golden hair.
```

CHORUS

```
  G                    C
E ----------------------------------------------------------------
A ----------------------------------------------------------------
D -------0---0----0----2------5---5----5--------------------------
G 4------0---0----0----5------5---5----5--------------------------
  Won't you come down, won't you come down,

  G                       D        G
E ----------------------------------------------------------------
A 2------2---5----5----2--2--0------------------------------------
D 0------0---0----0----0--0--0------5-----------------------------
G 0----------0----0-------2---------0-----------------------------
  Won't you come down to Yarmouth town!
```

Chord Forms

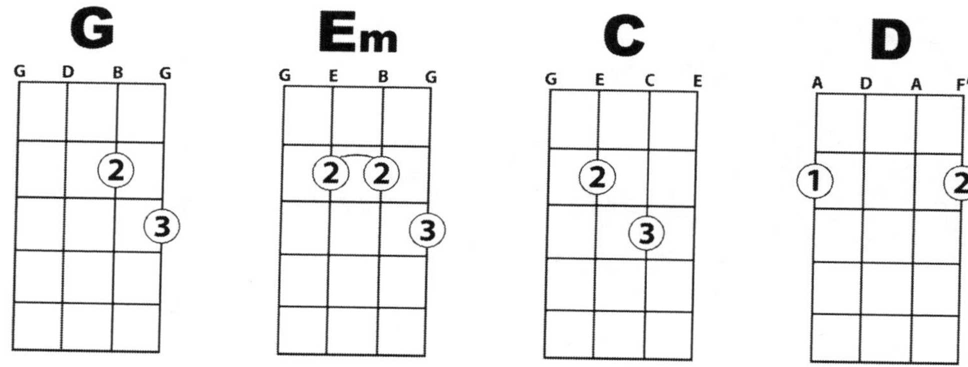

More Resources

www.CigarBoxGuitar.com - If you want to branch out from mandolin and try building your own cigar box guitar, there is a growing library of free cigar box guitar how-to and tablature available on this site. Just click the "How to Build Cigar Box Guitars" and "How to Play Cigar Box Guitars" links on the home page to get started. When you're ready to start playing, tablature selections include some more modern songs, with pieces by The Beatles, the Violent Femmes, Bob Dylan, Elvis, Willie Nelson, Johnny Cash and more, in addition to some of the traditional public domain songs contained in this songbook. Best of all, it's all free!

www.CigarBoxNation.com - Cigar Box Nation is the home base and nerve center of the worldwide homemade/handmade instruments movement. In addition to information about cigar box guitars, you can find a vast collection of photos, videos, forum posts and more related to canjos, washtub basses and all sorts of other handmade instruments.

Elsewhere on the Internet - If you are looking for more mandolin-family resources, well you're in luck - the Internet is full of them. From YouTube videos teaching you how to play songs, to websites dedicated to playing these instruments, there is more than enough free info out there to keep you strumming for years to come.

Educational Outreach

We have worked with many teachers all around the United States and internationally to help them get instrument building projects added to their school's curriculum. Building handmade instruments fits nicely into most STEAM (Science, Technology, Engineering, Arts & Math) programs!

We have created a number of kits and packages specifically for teachers, from basic one-string canjos (tin can banjos) through ukuleles and more advanced electric guitars. Teachers from grades 3 through 12 have used our kits and parts to teach everything from art and basic music theory and performance through advanced placement high school science courses studying the physics of electrical waves and sound.

If you know of a school or teacher that might be interested in this idea, let them know about us! We also work with summer camps, church groups, Boy Scout troops, community centers, senior centers, and folks wanting to host a local workshop.

E-mail us at **support@cbgitty.com** to get the ball rolling!

About the Author

Ben “Gitty” Baker founded C. B. Gitty Crafter Supply in the basement of his New Hampshire home in 2009, with a mission of providing affordable parts to homemade instrument builders.

Over time the company and product line has grown, now occupying 15,000 square feet of space in an old New Hampshire woolen mill. C. B. Gitty employs fifteen people, producing many unique parts, kits and instruments in-house as well as supplying hundreds of quality parts. They ship thousands of orders each month, all around the world, while also maintaining active help desk and community support, educational outreach, event and musician sponsorship and much more.

But most importantly, over the years the core mission has expanded: to spread the word that ANYONE, ANYWHERE can build their own instrument and make music on it.

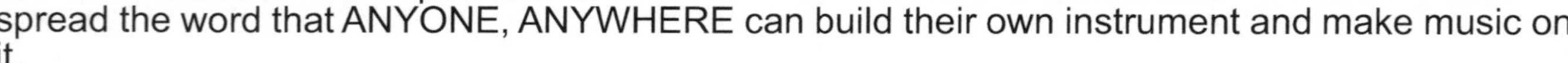

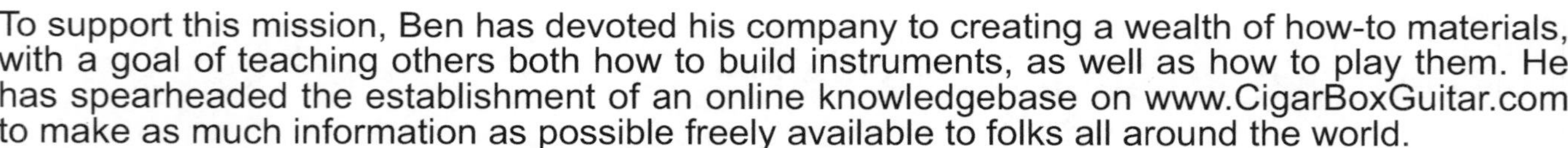

To support this mission, Ben has devoted his company to creating a wealth of how-to materials, with a goal of teaching others both how to build instruments, as well as how to play them. He has spearheaded the establishment of an online knowledgebase on www.CigarBoxGuitar.com to make as much information as possible freely available to folks all around the world.

Ben has also devoted uncounted hours of his own time to creating songbooks like the one you now hold, arranging hundreds of beloved traditional songs especially for three and four-string cigar box guitars and other handmade instruments.

Ben writes: “My motto is: Build What You Play, and Play What You Love. And also: If You’re Having Fun, You’re Doing It Right. In this amazing hobby, the only rules are the ones you set for yourself. Find an old cigar box, wine box, cookie tin, whatever... or build your own box out of scrap wood. Find a hardwood stick for the neck. Use old eye bolts from your granddad’s odds and ends drawer for tuners, and a couple of rusty bolts for a nut and a bridge. Maybe wrap some salvaged copper wire around the neck for frets, and twist it tight with pliers.

Get some old guitar strings, or baling twine, or screen door wire, or weed whacker line... and put it on there as strings. Twist them up into some semblance of a tuning, and give them a strum. Maybe it will sound horrible at first. That’s OK. Tweak and tinker until it makes YOUR sound, the sound only something you built with your own hands can make.

My mission is to spread the message that when it comes to making music, you don’t need some shiny factory-made guitar straight off the rack of some chain store. You can make your own, and it will mean far more to you than whatever soulless cookie-cutter guitar you might find out in the retail world.

Trust me. You can build your own. You can build what you play, and learn to play what you love. It is worth the effort!”